HAND OF HISTORY
BURDEN OF PSEUDO-HISTORY

Sub-title
TOUCHSTONE
OF
TRUTH

Tom O Connor

Dedicated to all who have contributed to the contents in one way or another and without whose sharing of their knowledge this book would not have happened.

Second Edition

Cover design, book formatting and layout by Noel Mulryan.

Front cover and title page photo of the Turoe Stone on Turoe hill, Co. Galway, Ireland

Photo Plates by Tom O Connor. Map designs by Tom O Connor and Kieran Jordan.

Map and photo scanning by Adrian Wan

First published in 2005 and revised in 2007 by Tom O Connor.

In the text cardinal points and other points of the compass are most often expressed by the use of the capital initial for each such as N for north or Northern, W for west or Western, and SSE for south-south-east. And so on.

Book Internet Web Sites by Trafford Publishing Co. and Tom O Connor provide further details, colour photos and new information, and will be updated from time to time.

The book's webpage: www.handofhistory.com
                        www.trafford.com/robots/04-1286.html

Order this book online at www.trafford.com
or email orders@trafford.com
Most Trafford titles are also available at major online book retailers.

Printed in the United States of America.

ISBN: 978-1-4120-3458-6 (sc)
ISBN: 978-1-4122-0283-1 (e)

 www.trafford.com

North America & international
toll-free: 1 888 232 4444 (USA & Canada)
phone: 250 383 6864 ♦ fax: 812 355 4082

TABLE OF CONTENTS

ACKNOWLEDGEMENTS

This work draws heavily on published works, on the extensive research and excavation of British Belgic oppida, Ptolemy of Alexandria's Irish Record, information preserved on Ordnance Survey maps, far-flung fieldwork among the material remains, dindshenchas texts, and on the memory bank of the farming community throughout the West of Ireland. The debt of gratitude owed to authors and experts in different fields and to countless country folk for their fund of pertinent information and local toponymy is immeasurable. Many distinguished academics were generous with their advice and support. Professors and authors Francis John Byrne, Etienne Rynne and Dáibhí Ó Cróinín kindly read the manuscript and gave enthusiastic encouragement. Their wise and valuable council corrected, shaped, toned, shortened and simplified the text. Their own published and unpublished works and articles were a constant check on the early material projected in this work. To select a few names for mention seems unjust to countless others who have made a unique contribution to this book but must remain nameless. A few are named in the text. Others are named in the bibliography and in the short popular version of this work published in 2003 under the title 'Turoe and Athenry – Ancient Capitals of Celtic Ireland' edited by Kieran Jordan. While proof-reading the present work, his keen editorial eye recognized the need for a short popular version and promptly brought it to publication. In the absence of so much cooperation from so many this material might have gone unrecorded and been lost forever. Without that imput from the store of local history, topographical features and almost lost toponymy this book would not have happened.

The initial inspiration came some sixty years ago from intriguing stories heard round winter firesides of remnants of an 'ancient 'city' cum royal site, ancient roads and the quarrels of grasping landlord and later family disputes over the manner of levelling the linear embankments across miles of countryside. Farmers pointed out widespread vestiges of these linear embankments. The communal memory told not only of their ancient Fir Belg construction but of their landlord destruction in land improvement schemes of the late 19th century. Specialized early British history and Irish legendary history reveals a surprising connection between these linear embankments and the defensive system surrounding Belgic oppida in SE Britain.

The excitement of discovering that at the centre of the linear earthen embankments pointed out by local farmers stood what the 1st/2nd century AD Ptolemy of Alexandria recorded as a Royal Capital and an extensive urban-like population centre in the West of Ireland prompted extensive research. Much of the groundwork had been done by generations of scholars and authors whose works, in books and learned articles, are represented here. The footwork was exhaustively extensive, but intensely exciting and hugely rewarding. Acknowledgement of the contribution of so many, and our debt to them, is given in the main body of the text, in footnotes, and in the bibliography. Apologies are herewith made to any authors from whose works information may have been culled without acknowledgement because they have either been lost or forgotten in countless notes and updates in manuscript form over several decades. It is hoped that this gathering together of information will prove to be a synthesis and provide a pathway through the maze that is Iron Age and Early Irish history and political geography.

Special thanks is owed to the following for permission to consult hard to find Manuscript material, books, journals, articles and to browse over and use their map materials.
The National Library, Dublin.
The University College Library, Galway.
Trinity College Library Board of Directors, Dublin.
Ordnance Survey Office, Dublin.
The Office of Public Works, Dublin.
National Monuments and Architectural Protection Division.
To all of these I am enormously indebted.

List of Map and Image Plates

Map of Europe (p. 11) showing Celtic expansion across Europe reproduced from 'The Celtic Way of Life'.

Figure 1 The British Isles plotted from Ptolemy's data from OS Map of Roman Britain.

Figure 2 Map of Ireland plotted from Ptolemy's data reproduced from Barry Raftery's 'Pagan Celtic Ireland'.

Figure 3 Commius' British Belgic oppida reproduced from Barry Cunliffe's 'The Regni'.

Figure 4 Verulamium Belgic oppidum reproduced from Keith Brannigan's 'The Catuvellauni'

Figure 6 Confiscation of Celtic lands reproduced from I. Andrews' 'Boudica Against Rome'.

Figure 7 maps and images reproduced from Simon James' 'The Celts'.

Figure 8 Maps reproduced from W.A. Hanna's 'Celtic Migratrions' (lower), M. Dillon & N. Chadwick's 'Celtic Realms' (top left), and Simon James' 'The Celts' (top right).

Figure 9 Location map of Belgic tribes forced south of the Rhine by Germanic tribes and of Belgica showing Germanic penetration of Belgic lands from Dutch Archives Holland.

Figure 10 Turoe Stone & pattern reproduced from Michaerl Ryan's 'Illustrated Archaeology'.

Figures 11, 12, 16, 18, 21, 23, 25, 27, 44 & 45 reproduced from OS maps, OS Office, Dublin

Figures 13, 14 and 16 insert maps reproduced from maps in Trinity College Library with permission of the Board of Trinity College, Dublin.

Figure 22 Carrowkeel reproduced with permission of the Office of Public Works, Dublin.

Figures 27, 39, 54 and 61 based on OS Road Maps, Discovery Series.

Figure 50 Map of Ireland and its counties. Map of Co. Galway, p. 172.

Figure 51 Series of outer ward linear embankment extensions drawn by Kieran Jordan.

Figure 53 based on OS Townland map reproduced from Norman Mongan's 'Manapia Quest'.

Figure 55 Map of Athenry reproduced from A. Healy's 'Athenry'. Inserts from OS maps.

Figure 62 Dun of Drumsna reproduced from Barry Raftery's 'Pagan Celtic Ireland'.

Figure 63 Medb's Tain Bo Cuailgne and Tain Bo Flidais routes according to Westropp.

Figure 64 Dun Guaire reproduced from John Hinde's 'Ireland Peoples and Places'.

Figure 66 Maps reproduced from Walsh & Bradley's 'History of Irish Church (top) and from Daithi O hOgain's 'The Celts' (lower).

Figure 67 Maps reproduced from F.J. Byrne's 'Irish Kings and High Kings'.

Pronunciation Glossary of selected Old Celtic Names and Words

Old Celtic personal and place names could be rendered phonetically. However, the difference between these and spellings encountered in other books, between Old Irish and modern English forms, is so great that one may not immediately be recognizable as the other. For instance, 'Cu Chulainn' is often spelt as Cuchulainn or Cu Chulaind, and in other ways. This book sticks to the Old Celtic versions, although in quotations taken from other authors, the latter's version is retained. The phonetic and other forms offered here are no more than a broad guide to pronunciation. The following list is not exhaustive.

Adomnan: a-dhov-nán
Airgialla: ar-yíala
Badb: baav
Bodb: bov
Brighid; Brigit: bri-yid; bríd
Cenel Conaill: ke-nèl go-nil
Cenel nEogain: ke-nèl nó-ghin
Ciarraige: kee-aree; kia-ree
Corcu Baiscind: kor-ku vash-kin
Corca Duibne: kor-ka ghí-ni
Crimthann: kri-fin
Cuailgne: cooley
Daghdha: da-ya
Daithi: da-hi
Dal Cais: dál gash
Dal Fiatach: dál vía-tach
Dindshenchas: din-hen-chas
Emain Macha: au-in mah-kha
Eochaid: ech-íd; o-kí; yo-hee
Eoganacht: ó-nacht
Erainn: er-en; ai-rin
Feidlimid: fèi-li-mee
Finndabara: finn-uura
Labraid: lau-ree
Laigin: la-yin; lain
Lebor Gabala: laur ga-wá-la
Loeguire; Laegaire: loi-ure; lee-re
Lug; Lugh: luu; looh
Lugaid: loo-ee; lú-í
Magh Sanb: maa sanv
Magh Seolgha: maa seola
Medb: mèv; meave
Morrigan; Mor-rioghain: mor-ree-ahn
Mumhan: mu-in; mo-on
Niall Noigiallach: níal noi-yial-ach
Osraige: os-ra-ye; os-a-ree
Sadb: saav
Sanb: sanv
Sidh: shee
Slí Mhór: shlee wore
Tadhg: taig
Temair: tau-ir; chau-ir
Tethbae: te-fa
Ughaine: oo-in-eh; oo-ahne
Ui Failge: ee al-ye; í fal-ye
Ui Maine: ee wa-ne
Umor: uvor; iuvor
Ulaid: ul-idh; ul-ee

PREFACE PREVIEW

This book presents a Celtic Royal complex, unprecedented in Ireland for its size and layout, but similar to Belgic Centres of Power, called oppida by Caesar, in SE England and on the Continent. It was centered on Turoe in Co. Galway, site of the famous Turoe Stone. No one has satisfactorily explained why this finest example of La Tene Celtic stone art in all of Europe was set on the summit of Turoe hill (*Cnoc Temhro*) in the wilds of the West of Ireland. Here its hitherto unrecognised Celtic Royal Sanctuary trappings at the centre of a vast Belgic-like oppidum defensive system of linear embankments and its surprising connection with the Celtic invasion of Ireland are unfolded. A whole series of sets of linear embankments expanded out from Turoe across Counties Galway, Clare, Mayo, Sligo, NW Roscommon and across the Shannon into Westmeath and Longford, and even further afield. Some of these are recorded in early *dindshenchas* (history of the famous places) material associated with the names of archaic kings and queens[1].

There are several early references to this Royal Capital. The most famous of these is by the renowned first/second century Greek geographer, Ptolemy of Alexandria, who recorded two capitals, and two only, in the Ireland of his day. One is accepted as representing Emain Macha near Armagh in the NE of Ireland. The second has never been definitively identified. Ptolemy located it approximately at the centre of Co. Galway, precisely where Turoe is today (2). He named it REGIA E TERA (*Regia e Te[mh]ra*) which is the genuine early Celtic/Old Irish name for 'The Capital at Turoe' (*Cnoc Temhro*). Turoe's expansive inner ward set of linear embankments enclosed an acropolis and a necropolis. Part of a sprawling urban-like complex along the western slopes of Turoe and Knocknadala (Hill of Assemblies/Parliament) has finally been placed under preservation order by The National Monuments Department. Knocknadala (early *Cnoc na nDál*) was rendered by Ptolemy as NAG-NA-TA[Λ] and named by him as "the most illustrious city in all Britannia and the most considerable in size, located in the western part of Ireland"[2]. The sole reference to a dense population anywhere in early Irish literature points directly to this very area[3].

The Turoe inner ward had all the hallmarks and definitive layout of a Celtic Royal Sanctuary, an assembly and ceremonial site with its illustrious coronation stone, a royal cemetery, an arena for the poets and literati (*Aber na bhFhille*) and an extensive acropolis, evidenced by their respective townland names. It had a vast defensive system, ever expanding over several centuries. Its Fearta necropolis held some 150 large burial mounds, some of which bore the names of early Irish kings. Several more early kings and their Celtic gods and goddesses are remembered in other place names and forts around this cluster of Celtic sanctuary sites further signifying a Celtic Royal Centre of Power. A very much more extensive Royal necropolis surrounding Athenry to the NW of Turoe is stated in archaic texts in the Book of Leinster to be the '*Releg na Rí lamh le Cruachain*' where the Royal Household of Turoe (*Rígrád Temhróit*) was interred, including Queen Medb and her father king Eochaid Ferach Mhor whose palace stood beside the Turoe Stone[4].

Two ancient roadways, the *Slí Mór* and *Slí Dála*, converged on Turoe and Knocknadala. The Rót na Rí, Royal Road of the Kings, ran straight from Turoe/Knocknadala to the renowned ancient seaport of *Ath Cliath Magh Rí* near Clarenbridge in Galway Bay. Legendary history states that "*Ath Cliath Magh Rí was the chief seaport of Ireland through which Ireland has most often been invaded*"[6]. A dindshenchas tale tells that "*the swift ships which sailed the high seas frequented Ath Cliath Magh Rí in Galway of the harbours.*"[7] It was there that a large segment of the Celtic invasion force landed before advancing on Turoe, the core of its primary settlement area, as recorded in the *dindshenchas* of *Cnoc na Dála*[5]. Several segments of Belgic tribes from Britain and the Continent, such as the Manapi, the Atrebates and the Canti (from Kent), are remembered in townland names within this vast Turoe oppidum complex.

Who were these Celts and where did they come from?

Large segments of the Northern Continental Belgae fled to southeast England from Roman and Germanic conquest in Caesar's time. In 27/26 BC as preparations for a massive Roman invasion of Britain proceeded some considerable way before being cancelled, Commius, king of Belgae in the Silchester, Winchester and Chichester/-Selsey regions of the south of England, led a folk-movement of his subjects to the Shannon estuary in the West of Ireland. There they are recorded by Ptolemy as the Ganngáni[2], the decendants of Gann which was the genuine Celtic name of Commius, the Romanised form of his name. His descendants expanded north into Connacht where Déla, Gann's grandson, landed his invasion force at the great seaport of *Ath Clee Magh Rí* in Galway Bay and advanced inland to set up court on the Hill of Dail (*Cnoc na nDála*, Knocknadala today) beside Turoe (*Cnoc Temhro*)[5]. There he established the famous Feis Temhro as recorded in Irish legendary history. From there his descendants, the ancient Fir Belg (Belgae, the Romanised form of their name) of Connacht pushed the aboriginal Cruthin, the men of Ulster, inexorably north-eastwards over the following centuries. The two Regia of Ptolemy's Irish record were the Capitals of these two warring provinces. The warfare involved is recorded in Ireland's oldest legendary history, the Ulidian Tales. This is further corroborated by vestiges of the great linear embankments thrown up by both parties as boundary fortificatious which scar the face of the Celtic Irish landscape to this day and tell of the ferocity of the long drawn-out warfare between the Fir Belg of Connacht and the men of Ulster.

These facts of history were suppressed by pseudo-historians of the Ui Neill warlords and the monastic federation of Armagh in favour of their own concocted glorification. As this Turoe oppidum was of major importance in the late Irish Iron Age, its identification and recovery calls for a total re-evaluation of the origins and history of Celtic Ireland.

Footnotes:

[1] *Dindshenchas of Magh Mucrama*.

[2] *'Claudii Ptolemaei Geographia'*, p.79 tI ed. Muller (paris 1883).

[3] *Dindshenchas of Maen Magh* (Magh Main).

[4] *Senchas na Releg, De Gabail an tSida, De Copur in da Muccida* in the Book of Leinster, 2468, line 32931-5; 290a 37234-7; and 155a 20348-50; also in Lebor na hUidre and elsewhere.

[5] Dindshenchas of *Cnoc na nDála* ,

[6] Edmund Hogan in *'Onomasticon Goedelicum'* under Ath Cliath Magh Rí, p. 56 ff

[7] Met. *Dindshenchas of Sliabh Bladhma* in Book of Leinster, 192 a.

CHAPTER I

ROMAN CONQUEST OF THE CELTS OF GAUL AND BRITAIN

THE COMING OF THE BELGIC CELTS TO IRELAND WITH THEIR UNIQUE DEFENSIVE SYSTEM

IRELAND DIVIDED BETWEEN ABORIGINAL CRUTHIN AND INVADING FIR BELG

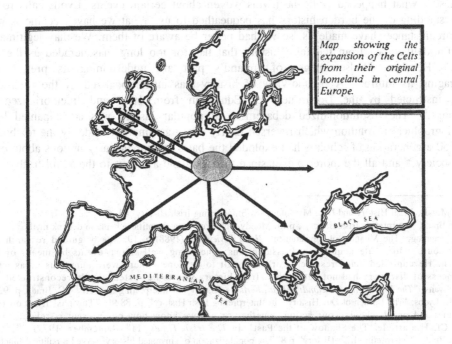

Map showing the expansion of the Celts from their original homeland in central Europe.

> **"The Master has laid open to us both past and present history, and even an anticipatory taste of the future as well."** (Epist. of Barnabas 2: 1 – 2)

HAND OF HISTORY - BURDEN OF PSEUDO-HISTORY

'History' is a stubborn, sanctimonious, sly, slippery serpent, notoriously so in Ireland. History does not lie. Not so Irish 'historians'! They personify Samuel Butler's dictum that "though God cannot alter the past, 'historians' can." Their 'histories' pulverized early Irish history. "Myth-making is an ancient Irish industry"[1] masking political propaganda. The hand of history weighs heavily on Ireland, the burden of pseudo-history infinitely more so.

Myth maims Ireland. Debunking it is paramount. To bring about 'a revolution in the aims, method and style of historical writing, concerned for a purer, more scholarly Irish history,' T.W. Moody[2] warned of two competing, but equally destructive, myths fatal to the writing of Irish history - the separatist sectarian myth of Ulster loyalism and the unitary nationalist myth of southern republicanism, both wielding manipulated history to advance conflicting agendas. "History is too important to be abandoned to those who prostitute it for political purposes."[3] Moody animated superb scholarship. Yet, major areas are totally ignored.

Evans' censure of Irish historians for "neglect of the physical environment within which our past has been lived"[4] pales against Lyons' rebuke: **"Given that the study of our history is on a far firmer professional base than ever, may we not assume that the processes of revision are in perfectly safe hands? Unfortunately, the case is much worse than Evans imagined. Not only have historians too often disregarded the physical evidence, they have not even fully explored the literary evidence to give us a rounded view of our society. The fact that historians are inarticulate about the different cultures which collide in this island is merely a symptom of a more profound ignorance exhibited in excelsis on the other side of the Irish Sea (in Ireland)."[6]**

Linked to our contemporary predicament is the fact that we can no longer distinguish the realities of what happened from the myths woven about certain events. Lyons calls for an "understanding of the burden history has bequeathed to us. What we have become is what past circumstances have made us, so we had better be aware of them. We may legitimately pray for deliverance from the false history that has for too long masqueraded as the real thing."[5] Hearken! "False images of Ireland's past are undermining its present and mortgaging its future."[6] A pseudo-view of history was institutionalized by the Irish Free State, instructed by the Department of Education from 1922 and 'memorialized' in textbooks.[7] "The institutionalized debasement of popular history was accompanied by a historiographical revolution which reversed nearly every assumption made by the textbooks. By 1960 a generation of scholars had exploded the basis for popular assumptions about early Irish society,"[7] and all the more so ever since then.[8] Ireland awakens to the awful truth.

---

[1] T. W. Moody, 'Irish History and Irish Mythology' in 'Interpreting Irish History' ed. C. Brady, p.71

[2] Ciaran Brady, 'Interpreting Irish History', p. 3. Moody embarked on a scientific scheme to debunk myth.

[3] Ronan Fanning, 'The Meaning of Revisionism', *'Irish Review'*, 4 (1988) p. 19. Moody guided research into unused sources to refute unquestioned assumptions concerning well-known events by means of new research. He conceded much research work had still to be done - there were numerous areas where the process of discovery had not yet started. Irish history was to be systematically reconstructed.

[4] Estyn Evans, *"The Personality of Ireland: habitat, heritage, history'* in 'Interpreting Irish Hist.' C. Brady, p. 92

[5] F. S. L. Lyons, 'The Burden of Our History', in 'Interpreting Irish History', p. 88-91. "The past lives on in us both for good or ill, shaping our action, whether or not we know how our present is related to our past." Cf. His article 'The Shadow of the Past', in *The Irish Times*, 11[th.] September, 1972.

[6] Ciaran Brady, "Interpreting Irish History" p 8. The popularization of 'invented history' served a political function

[7] Roy Foster in C. Brady, Op. Cit. p. 139. The 'Tara/Patrick Myth' epitomizes Irish pseudo-history which buried Iron Age history and proclaimed Tara as the seat of the 'High Kingship' of Ireland.

Awareness of the spurious nature of Irish 'history' grew from 1900 on. Accumulated findings of historians show Ireland's High Kingship did not exist before 800 AD.[9] The old history book was buried. A new one replaced it, minus vital facts on the making of Ireland. Unlike Continental and British counterparts, at a EURO-moment in time when awareness of Continental links is crucial, the Irish are robbed of knowledge of their Celtic roots. The coming of the Celts to Ireland and their expansion at the expense of the aboriginal people, underpinning the perennial split in Irish society, is either denied or stated in the vaguest terms. Some claim "there is no material evidence to uphold the theory of a mass invasion of Celtic people."[10] They look for wrong evidence (La Tene), of the wrong time (500BC) and place (Tara/Rathcroghan). None was found to support a Celtic invasion as Tara and Rathcroghan belonged to the aboriginal pre-Celtic people, the Cruthin, until early medieval times. There was no La Tene evidence and no major change at these sites between the Bronze and Iron Age in the archaeological data.

Dáibhi Ó Cróinín and Donnchadh Ó Corráin expose the fallacy of the anti-Celtic-invasion movement. Ó Cróinín had occaision to rue the fact that "there is nothing in Irish archaeology remotely comparable to the work of our English, French and German neighbours", but this sad situation is changing rapidly.[11] A case in point is the reconstruction of Belgic oppida in Britain and the Continent, but not in Ireland. A glaring example of such spurious interpretation is the claim that since no material evidence was found at Tara or Rathcroghan to uphold the theory of a Celtic invasion, no Celtic invasion took place. Ó Corráin claims that the coming of the Celtic language to Ireland is itself proof of a Celtic invasion, not one mass invasion, but a series of invasions which, over time, constitute a largescale invasion. The Celticization of Ireland could only have been possible by great numbers of Celtic-speaking families settling there. An army of warriors or a small cultural aristocracy could not have made it a Celtic-speaking land. It takes women with families to transfer a language, a folk movement involving entire families. Ó Corráin noted that the major source and strongest evidence in support of the arrival of the Celtic language is the Greek geographer Ptolemy of Alexandria's Irish record dating to c. AD 150. This is the first absolute proof that the Irish language and the Celts had arrived. The newfangled anti-Celtic-invasion theory is diametrically opposed by the presence of Belgic tribes on Ptolemy's 2nd century map of Ireland. His placement of the Iverni, Brigantes, Manapi, Osdiae and Gangani is corroborated by their physical presence in the early historic period. The trappings of their invasion and expansion around their primary settlement areas, noted in legendary history, survive but have never been archaeologically investigated as were those of their kinsmen in Britain and the Continent.

New history books eliminate the Belgae (Fir Belg) from the Irish population. They are now seen as a mythical people despite Ptolemy's record, early history and the fact that the majority of Irish people are descended either from these invaders or from the aboriginal pre-Celtic Cruthin. O Rahilly's analysis of Ptolemy's Irish record shows that it portrays an Ireland dominated by Celtic Belgae from the Continent and Britain. It corresponds largely to legendary history from that early period. It is substantiated archaeologically in Belgic settlement areas. The Belgae had a unique defence system. British archaeology has

---

[8] Francis J Byrne, Pref. 2nd Edition 'Irish Kings and High Kings': "There has been a veritable explosion of activity in all fields of early Irish History and archaeology." Yet, major areas are still neglected. John Waddell in 'The Prehistoric Archaeology of Ireland', "Irish prehistoric archaeology has made enormous progress...and, without doubt, new discoveries will continue to illuminate the prehistoric past", p. 6. This book does exactly that.

[9] Eoin MacNeill noted in 1904 that "the received frame-work of early Irish history was an invention of chroniclers working assiduosly for the glorification of their patrons".

[10] Carmel McCaffrey and Leo Eaton, 'Ancient Ireland', p. 53-56.

[11] D. Ó Cróinín, "Early Medieval Ireland 400 - 1200", p. 9-10; editor of "Prehistoric & Early Ireland" in the new Oxford History; Royal Irish Acadamey/Discovery Programme Reports, Dublin.

extensively researched the Belgic defensive system in England. Ptolemy's record portraying a Belgic dominated Ireland makes it imperative that the same is done for Ireland. Until it is, the Tara/Patrick Myth and the 'pious cause' of restoring the myth of a united Ireland will continue to reign supreme in the Irish psyche!

Unaware of its origins, young Ireland shows little interest in its history or archaeological heritage. So it destroys the latter on a scale no nation on earth would tolerate. Take away homes or lands, but not knowledge of ancestral origins or cultural heritage. "The need to accept one's culture as a structuring element of one's personality, in the initial stages of life, is a fact of universal experience whose importance cannot be over-estimated. It is on the basis of this essential relationship with one's origins that people acquire a sense of their nationality, and culture takes on a "national" configuration."[12] "Just as individuals cannot exist as complete persons without knowledge of their past, so human societies must have their self-knowledge to preserve their corporate identity and distinctive patterns of living. To supply this is one of the primary functions of the history of nations"[13]

Scholars accept that the political geography and older tribal capitals of Iron Age Ireland were superseded by new provincial capitals in the post-Patrician era. The sites of most archaic capitals are known, but not of the most illustrious of all, thanks to its deliberate suppression in favour of the 'Tara Myth' by the monumental medieval manipulation and carefully engineered structural subversion of the stream of Irish history. Despite the convergence of evidence, classical, literary, legendary, toponymic and archaeological, the Tara Myth was so mighty that for the past millennium Ireland has been blissfully unaware of the existence of the site of an Iron Age Belgic oppidum in Western Ireland which was the core of Ireland's heroic past. In Chapter 2 this Celtic Oppidum will be reconstructed.

Britain tears itself apart, fanned by fears of losing its identity and an exaggerated paranoia germinated by what is called the "Abolition of Britain"[14] as it rewrites its history to accede to the needs of a multiracial society. For good race relations it is deemed necessary that its national story be 're-imagined'. Ireland must rediscover its true identity in its archaic past before it can understand itself. While mankind rediscovers its ancient roots, Ireland's archaic origins are written off as 'myths' which 'do not belong to history'. Her chief prehistoric capitals belong to the 'lost worlds' of the past. Her illustrious Iron Age Capitals have been removed from the pages of history by a subtle sleight of hand. The chain of Irish history dangles in the air cut off from its ancient roots. It is replaced by the fraudulent Tara/Patrick Myth. Lament with Tolstoy all you who suffer from an exaggerated nostalgia for that myth: "'History' would be a wonderful thing were it only true."

THE IRISH RECORD OF PTOLEMY OF ALEXANDRIA

"The most detailed account of pre-Christian Ireland is that of Ptolemy, an Alexandrian-Greek geographer who based his account on a lost work of Marinus of Tyre (1st-2nd cent. mariner)."[15] His record lists 55 Irish tribal and place names indispensable for early Irish history and political geography. His 'map' of Ireland, "when drawn from the available figures, is surprisingly accurate."[16] Contrary to the Tara Myth Syndrome analysis of Ptolemy's Ireland, the Atlantic coast was **not** "less familiar to sailors nor less exactly surveyed." Ireland's renowned Iron Age Sea Port was Ath Cliath Magh Rí at Clarenbridge in Galway Bay. The most apt reference to any seaport in Irish records points unerringly to *"Ath Cliath Magh Rí: gur ab e an cuan so, aon chuan gabala na hEirionn mar do frioth a*

[12] Pope John Paul 11's Message for World Day of Peace, 1st. January, 2001, paragraph 6.
[13] T. W. Moody, 'Irish History and Irish Mythology', in 'Interpreting Irish History' ed C. Brady, p. 71.
[14] Bagehot in "The Economist", October 14 - 20, 2000; Peter Hitchens' 'Abolition of Britain.'
[15] Donnchadh O Corráin, 'Prehistoric & Early Christian Ireland', 'The Oxford History of Ireland', p. 3-5.
[16] Barry Raftery, 'Pagan Celtic Ireland', p. 205.

n-ar leabhraibh, oir is ann is mionca do hionnsuighe Eire riamh" ("Ath Cliath Magh Rí was **the Irish seaport** visited by sea-going vessels **through which Ireland was most often invaded"**).[17]

Archaic texts corroborate this claim of all ships calling at Ath Cliath Magh Rí.[18] When Ptolemy's river and place names on the Irish Atlantic coast are read rationally from left to right, rather than from back to front (clockwise), his West Coast record is the most accurate of all, with all names in correct positions. The erroneous upside-down reading is exposed by the placing of the Shannon mouth in Galway's *Dur/Dughiortach* River mouth in the Shannon estuary. Of the 11 'cities' (πολισ=acropolis) listed by Ptolemy, Nag-na-Tal (ΝΑΓ ΝΑ ΤΑΛ) is named as "*the most illustrious city with the most celebrated name in all Britannia and the most considerable in size, set in the West of Ireland.*"[19] Ath Cliath Magh Rí was **the** Iron Age port serving Ireland's "most illustrious city," Nag na Tal and Regia E Tera, which was the core of Ireland's "most considerable" oppidum. Ptolemy was the sole authority who left a geo-political record of the Capitals of Iron Age Ireland. His record is all the more precious for that.

In Ptolemy's record, 2 peoples, Υολυντιι (Ulaid) and Ιυερνι (Erainn/Fir Belg), and their 2 (2 only) Royal Capitals (REGIA), dominate the North and South of 2nd century Ireland. Neither was Tara. **Tara, pseudo-history's so-called 'Capital of Ireland from time immemorial', is conspicuous only by its absence from Ptolemy's record. Tara was unknown as a major Royal Capital to Ptolemy's informants for the reason that it was not such in his day.** He has one REGIA in NE Ireland approximately where Armagh is today. "The Ulster Capital of Emain Macha *(Isamnion:* Navan Fort, Armagh) is recorded as a city on Ptolemy's map"[20]

Ptolemy's 2nd Capital in Western Ireland has not been identified. His record in its present miniscule Greek form has 'regia e tera'. It should be emended to the original majuscule 'REGIA E TERA' (Royal Capital in 'Tera').[21] His 'REGIA E TERA' is as close as he possibly could get to rendering the Celtic 'Regia e Temhra' in majuscule Greek letters. He placed it 'at *Temhair*' ('e TE(mh)RA') at the centre of Co. Galway. The only *Temhair* in that part of Galway is *Cnoc Temhro*, Turoe hill today (*e Te[mh]ra* in the O-Irish gen. form). This place alone accommodates Ptolemy's (ΡΕΓΙΑ Ε ΤΕΡΑ) REGIA E TERA completely and precisely, as will be shown. His record is vital evidence for late Iron Age Ireland (Figure 1). It led to the rediscovery of Regia e Temhra and its 'most illustrious city' to be reconstructed here. The archaeological record corroborates the literary record in a most astounding manner.

It never dawned on Irish academics that **the political geography of Ptolemy's Ireland corresponds comprehensively to that of the Ulidian Tales, Ireland's oldest record. It is totally at odds with that projected by Irish pseudo history. Ptolemy is corroborated by the Ulidian Tales in projecting an Ireland dominated by 2 warring powers, Ulster and**

---

[17] Edmund Hogan 'Onomasticon Goedelicum'; He mistook it for Ath Cliath Duiblin.

[18] Book of Leinster, 192a, 'Blod MacCon "*Cechaing na luing lathar ngle o bun Gallm(h)e glanuaire, o Ath Cliath I nHerut uill*" refers to Ath Cliath Magh Rí in Galway Bay (Herut); Met. Dindsenchas of Sliabh Bladhma.

[19] 'Claudii Ptolemaei Geographia', ed. Muller, (Paris 1883), p. 79ff.

[20] F.J. Byrne, "Early Irish Society", in 'The Course of Irish History' by Moody and Martin, p.

[21] Error entered the text in the transition from majuscule to minuscule Greek letters which occurred well after Ptolemy's day. As O Rahilly noted, *Regia* is not a Latin word nor a Greek word. It is an early form of Celtic *Rigia*, Royal Capital. Similarly, the word *'E TERA'*, as used by Ptolemy, was not Latin or Greek but Celtic like other names in his Irish record. The transcriber of Ptolemey's *REGIA E TERA* into miniscule Greek lettering took the *'e tera'* to be the Greek word *etera•=* 'a different' regia, unaware that it was a royal Celtic place name. It was translated into Latin as *Altera Regia* = another Regia. Hence, editors have omitted 'etera' or 'altera' as of no significance. Ptolemy never used such vague terms. He was as precise as he could.

Connacht, the two provinces in which his 2 REGIA Capitals are located.[22] This is corroborated by the archaeological vestiges of Emain Macha in Ulster, of which Tara was a satellite, and the Connacht Iron Age Oppidum of Regia E Te[mh]ra to be reconstructed.

By 50 BC the south of Britain was dominated by Celtic Belgae. Caesar affirms this. Similar Belgic dominance at the expense of the indigenous Cruthin prevailed in the S of Ireland as a result of Caesar's Continental wars and the Roman invasion of Britain. When Ptolemy produced his record of Ireland the Érainn/Belgae had exerted their dominance over a considerable part of Ireland.[24] The Fir Belg were "known as Erainn ('Iverni')." Their name identifies them with the Belgae of the Continent and Britain. Irish tradition claims they were of the same stock as the Britons" O Rahilly wrote "No discussion of the history of pre-Christian Ireland could afford to ignore the history of the neighboring island. The Belgae occupied considerable parts of both countries. Earlier the Priteni (Cruthini) were dominant in Britain and Ireland." The pre-Celtic Cruthin (Pritini) were aboriginal inhabitants of Ireland and Britain before the Belgae colonized the S halves of both isles, pushing them N and hiving Cruthin communities off in isolated enclaves country-wide. Larger enclaves such as the Cruthintuatha Croghain of Roscommon and the Cruthin of Ulster tenaciously held on to their independence. Events which forced the Belgic exodus from the Continent to SE Britain led to their migration to Ireland. Later incursions compelled them to expand at the expense of the Cruthin.

Ireland's oldest history, the Ulidian Tales, tell of constant warfare between the aboriginal Cruthin and invading Belgae whose Capitals the Cruthin recognized to be, not in Tara in the East, but in Ól nÉgmacht centered on Turoe and Rath Cruacha of Galway in the Southwest as seen from their own Capital at Emain Macha in the Northeast. The history of this long drawn-out warfare is written across the face of the Celtic Irish landscape, speaking more eloquently than any written word. Decayed relics of ancient wars survive in vestiges of linear embankments, representing tribal frontiers which scar the face and soul of Ireland to this day.

In Chapter Two, 2 Belgic Centres of Power recorded by Ptolemy at the heartland of the Fir Belg settlement in W Ireland will be reconstructed. Methods used to suppress or manipulate their history and traditions for the glorification of Tara of Meath in the East and Croghan of Roscommon in the West from the 8th century will be exposed. Elaborately defended Belgic oppida and their histories in SE Britain have been reconstructed over the past 35 years.[23] Irish Belgic oppida await similar treatment. This neglected area and its ramifications for the history and political geography of early Ireland are dealt with extensively here.

---

[22] This calls for a reinstatement of Ptolemy as a unique 2nd-century classical authority on Irish Iron Age geopolitics and for a rational re-reading of his Irish record. It exposes the monumental hoax exploded by 20th century historians, yet embraced passionately by the Irish, of the so-called High Kingship of Ireland at Tara from time immemorial. It makes a radical rewriting of the history and political geography of Iron-Age Ireland, and its archaeological analysis, mandatory.
[23] F.T. O Rahilly, 'Early Irish History and Mythology', p. 40.

Figure 1:

THE BRITISH ISLES ACCORDING TO PTOLEMY
Sources dated approximately 100 A.D.

Anti-Roman chiefs of the Belgae of Britain and Belgic areas of the Continent, the
Atrebates, Morini, Cantiaci and Brigantes, led the Brigantes (Ui Bairrche) to the
SE of Ireland and the Gangani to the SW coast where they expanded north into
Connacht and set up Regia E Tera (Turoe), Nagnatal (Knocknadal) and Auteinri.

Figure 2 : Incorrect clockwise reading of Ptolemy's Irish data by many authorities.

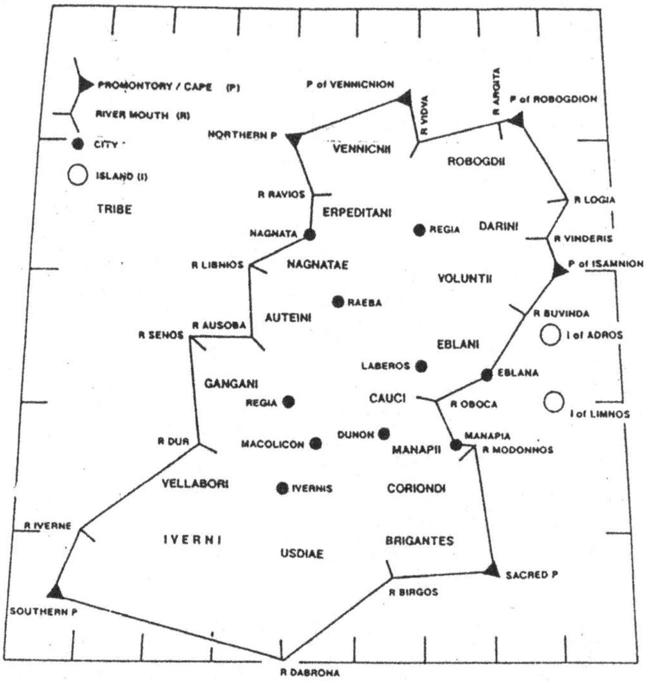

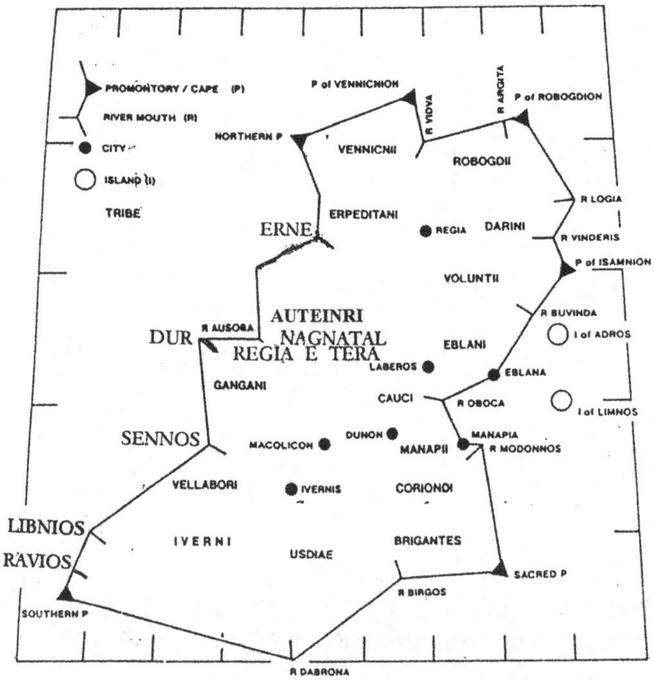

Correct left to right reading of Ptolemy of Alexandria's Irish Record.

The Fir Belg invasion is conspicuous in Irish records. History shows where the British Belgae came from and where they settled. Legendary history records settlements of the Fir Belg in Ireland. The Belgic occupation of Ireland by incursions from SE England due to the Roman invasion and conquest of the British Belgae is corroborated by archaeological sites and by Ptolemy's record (Figure 2). Pseudo history falsified this picture. It is vital to examine the evidence and names of Fir Belg leaders to determine the origin of the Fir Belg who came to Ireland, and their pre- and post-invasion story. Vital too is knowledge of the characteristic hallmarks of the Belgic oppidum. By recognizing the nature of the defence system they employed in their former habitat, which marked them off from their neighbors, one can identify the same defence strategy in their new habitat and pinpoint the core of their settlement areas in the S and W of Ireland. It will overturn **the monumental hoax of pseudo-history projecting Tara as the Capital of Ireland from time immemorial,** although devoid of all the trappings of a Belgic oppidum which could give it any right to be called the Capital of a Fir Belg dominated Ireland. Such aspects have so far received little attention from Irish academics.

WHO WERE THE FIR BELG? ORIGINS AND ORIGIN-LEGENDS

Irish pseudo-history effaced the distinctions of ethnic origin of the Irish people from the popular memory "by inventing for the Irish generally a common ancestor in the fictitious Mil of Spain. To provide the Irish with a common descent, pseudo-historians taught that the sons of Mil arrived in Ireland some 2000 years before their own time. Fortunately the authors of this elaborate attempt to obscure the origins of the Irish people did not succeed in obliterating all the evidence which told a different story. Their object was not so much to suppress popular traditions as to modify them so that they could be reconciled with the fiction of the 'Milesian' invasion."[24] From his study of "these popular traditions" and his analysis of Ptolemy's Geography of Ireland, O Rahilly concluded: **"That section of Ptolemy's Geography which treats of Ireland is by far the oldest documentary account of Ireland."[25] "The Ireland it describes is an Ireland dominated by the Erainn (Fir Belg)."[26]** Pseudo-history suppressed the fact that the Fir Belg dominated Ireland. Where are the typical Belgic Capitals, akin to the Belgic oppida and their unique defensive systems in Britain, to corroborate their dominance? They are as absent from Tara district as is Tara itself from Ptolemy's record. This question goes a-begging, ignored by Irish Archaeologists and historians alike. Here it is addressed head on.

The unique defence system enclosing Belgic oppida was called into being by the dire circumstances of the 1st century BC/AD Celtic Continent and Britain due to Roman invasion. Neither O Rahilly nor his contemporaries can be blamed for being unaware of the nature of the defence system of first century BC/AD Belgic oppida. It has been recognized in Britain and the Continent only in the last 35 years.[27] Had he become aware of Irish Belgic oppida he would have written a retraction of his highly influential thinking. His followers today are still unaware of vestiges of elaborately constructed Belgic oppida in the S and W of Ireland enclosed by peripheries of ancient woodland, lakes and bog land. Who says "Ireland is out on a limb with the rest of the Celtic world" in the matter of large defended oppida,[28] or that

---

[24] F. T. O Rahilly, 'Early Irish History and Mythology', p.15-16

[25] F. T. O Rahilly, 'Early Irish History and Mythology' p.1

[26] Ibid p.40

[27] W.G. Hoskins, *'The Making of the English Landscape'*, 13 f. cf Peter Salway: In 1976 Professor Hoskins, the great advocate of English landscape studies, wrote "a most significant retraction of some of his highly influential earlier thinking. "In many parts of England massive boundary banks survive. In Oxfordshire, boundaries of the Roman villa estate of Ditchley have been traced with considerable certainty, enclosing an area of about 875 acres. These consist of earthen banks thrown up about the middle of the 1st century AD (eve of Roman conquest), known as Grim's Dyke. A nearly complete periphery of ancient woodland can be traced around the villa estate."

[28] Richard Muir, 'Reading the Celtic Landscape'

"the monuments characteristic of the Iron Age in Britain and the Continent are unknown in Ireland."[29] The current opinion is that Ireland "could in no way be compared to the very advanced Belgic SE of England on the eve of the Roman conquest, the only fair comparison being the much more primitive NE of Britain, which "during the Iron Age, is relevant to the Irish scene."[30]

Ireland is out on a limb with the rest of Europe, not 'in the matter of large defended oppida', but in failing to recognize its own oppida. In Chapter 2 its Turoe/Knocknadala Belgic oppidum, one of the most expansive in Celtic Europe, at the core of which stands the illustrious Turoe Stone, will be reconstructed. 1st/2nd century AD Belgic Ireland was not only on a par with "the very advanced Belgic SE of England." It took up where the latter was cut off by Roman conquest. The "very advanced Belgic SE of England" and Continental backdrop had a profound bearing on contemporary Ireland. Its analysis will dispel medieval and modern myths regarding the Fir Belg in particular, Iron Age Ireland in general, and will counteract the negative attitudes of those who cannot accept the contemporary evidence of Ptolemy's record of *REGIA E TERA* (*Cnoc Temhro*/Turoe) as a Capital of the S half of Ireland and its urban-like *Nag-na-Ta[l]*, *"the most extensive city in all Britannia set in the West of Ireland."* As a prelude to examining the Belgic invasion and primary settlement areas, it is appropriate to look at their distant origins to dispel the many myths and fictions latched on to the name of the Fir Belg.

TRACING THE BELGAE AND THEIR MIGRATIONS - Continental Backdrop
Caesar recognized 3 divisions of Continental Celts; Galli (Gauls) occupying the territory from the Garonne to the Seine and Marne; Aquitani, between the Pyrenees and the Garonne; and Belgae, the most northerly, from the Marne and Seine to the Rhine. They differed from one another in language, customs and laws. Otherwise he always spoke of Gaul, and the Gauls in general, referring to all three.[31] The Celts did not all enter Gaul simultaneously or as a single nation. The latest arrivals were the Belgae. They began crossing the Rhine into NE Gaul in the 4th/3rd centuries BC, the Menapi being the last to complete the crossing in 54 BC.[32] The Belgae were closest in appearance to the Germans. They were Celtic in origin, in language, and in the names of their leaders. They were a federation of related Celtic tribes. Caesar found the Bellovaci and Menapi among his most formidable opponents. Their austere lifestyle preserved the virtues of heroic courage. Their unique type of fortification accounts for their rapid progress westwards. They had not many towns or fortified strongholds as other Celts. Those they had were unlike the typical hill-forts of Gaul. Belgic oppida were extensive, rectangular complexes sited in river valleys rather than on hilltops, depending on rivers, lakes and forests, to supplement formidable rampart defences with wide ditches and sloping outer faces.[33] Caesar lists 15 Belgic tribes that had crossed the Rhine into north Gaul. The Parisi made Paris their oppidum. The Bellovaci settled north of Paris. Their chieftains fled to SE England when their anti-Roman campaign collapsed. North of these were the Ambiani, Atrebates and Nervi of Nevers. Further east on the Maas were the Eburoni, a Briganten tribe. NW on the Belgium/Holland coast were the Morini, Marasi and Menapi. They disappeared off the Continental map and re-emerged in Ireland under Celtic forms of their name, Mac Morna & Morasi in Connacht, and Manach & Monaig (Fir Manach) of Fermanagh, Monaghan (Muineachán) and Munster.

[29] Anne Hamlin, 'Historic Monuments of Northern Ireland'
[30] T.G.E. Powell, 'The Celts' p.96.
[31] 'Commentaries' of Caesar, Book IV
[32] Nora Chadwick, 'The Celts' by p.55-56
[33] 'Berresford Ellis, The Celtic Empire' p.120-121.

By 300 BC the populous Belgae outgrew their homelands in the Celtic cradle in the upper Danube and led expeditions to Macedonia, Galatia, Greece and Rome,[34] sending out 300,000 men to win new lands. The leader of the 281 BC expedition was Bolgios. In 260 BC an army led by another Bolgios defeated Ptolemy Ceraunos, King of Macedonia. Part of Brennus' celebrated Belgic army went via Thessaly and burst past the Athenian army at the Battle of Thermopylae. Led by the Volcae Tectosages (Belgae) it fought through the Pass of Parnassos to loot the towns/sanctuaries of Greece, desecrating Delphi. The sack of Delphi passed into legend. The treasure of Delphi was taken to Toulouse by the Volcae.[35]

Excavation revealed traces of the passage of the Belgae through Bosnia Herzegovina and of their settlements in Yugo-Slavia.[36] Brennos' Belgic army "settled north of Macedonia between the Shar-Dagh (Mons Scordus; they were known as Scordisci) and the Danube on whose banks they founded Belgrade,"[37] (named after them). The Belgic Tectosages penetrated Bosnia and founded a kingdom stretching to Dobrudja in the Danube Delta. Their capitals had Celtic names, Ratia-ria, Durostorum-Silistria on the Danube and Noviodunum above its Delta. Its influence extended to Byzantium.[38] An extensive tribal territory of the Volcae-Tectosages (Belgae) existed from Thuringia, across Bohemia, Moravia, stretching across Slovakia to the Lower Danube and the Black Sea.[39] Those who survived in Moravia well into historic times were known as Wallacians (Valachove, an E European form of Volcae). The Cotini of Slovakia were remnants of the Volcae.[40] In the La Tene period the Volcae-Tectosages are found in France, the Balkans and as far east as Asia Minor. Caesar wrote that the Volcae-Tectosages were a very brave and by no means insignificant people. Ausonious claimed they called themselves Belgae. Belcae and Volcae are synonymous. Not only were there Volcae-Tectosages in the Galatian army which overran and settled Galatia (Turkey), they provided the leaders of that army in the expedition of 281 BC led by Bolgios.[41] Belgites was named after them.[42] There is evidence of the far-flung dominions of the Belgae stretching from the extremes of Eastern to Western Europe.[43/44]

From the 3rd century BC the Belgae crossed the Rhine from their original homelands in the Celtic cradle in the upper Danube on the E bank of the Rhine N of the river Main under Germanic pressure building up from N and E. They spread into N France, Belgium and Holland, establishing themselves along the lower Rhine valley. They set up independent states in a Belgic federation designed to protect them from Germanic invasion. The Rhine

---

[34] Pompeius Trogus, quoted by St Justin, 20 and 24.
[35] Henry Hubert, 'The Greatness and Decline of The Celts', p. 40, 108: "The gold of Toulouse was the gold of Delphi." The plunder brought ill omen to Brennos and Caepio, as it did to the Belgic Tectosages of Toulouse. Commemorative monuments and art works depicting the battle of Thermopylae, the sack of Delphi, the hurling of Celts from the heights of Parnassos and Brennos' suicide, were displayed at the temples of Apollo in Greece, in Italy, at Delos and in Rome, in the council-chamber of Athens, in works at Alexandria in Egypt, and at Naples.
[36] Patsch, in CV, ix, 1904, p.241. C.f. Henry Hubert, 'Greatness and Decline of the Celts', p. 42.
[37] Henri Hubert, 'The Greatness and decline of the Celts', p.42, 59.
[38] Jan Filip, 'Celtic Civilization and its Heritage', p.66. Belgic septs withdrew into Central European regions, esp. Czech Lands, from the 3rd to the 1st centuries BC. Celtic settlement became denser in the Pannonian-Slovac region. Celtic cemeteries survive in Slovakia on the left bank of the Danube and in Nitra district. "Central Bohemian (Czecho-Slovak) cemeteries, are attributed to the Volcae-Tectosages, as also all the finds in Moravia and Slovakia.
[39] Op. cit., p.72-73
[40] Op. cit., p.73
[41] St. Jerome noted that these Belgic Galatians to whom St. Paul wrote his Epistle spoke their native Celtic tongue, and he particularly compared their language to that of the Belgic Treviri who gave their name to Trier on the Rhine, with whose dialect he was familiar: C.f. Henri Hubert, 'The Greatness and decline of the Celts.' p. 67, 68.
[42] Pliny, iii, 148.
[43] Henry Hubert, Op. cit., 67. Archaeological remains preserve memories of the Belgae in the East. "The statuette at Naples of the suicide of Brennos, the statue of a Gaul in New York Museum, and similar works show the Gauls (Belgae) of the Danubian armies dressed in wide, flapping trousers.
[44] Op. cit. p. 67: There is a statuette in the British Museum of a Belgic woman wearing trousers, a garment that was never worn by any other Celtic tribe, but was peculiar to the Belgae who introduced it to the Western world.

became the new frontier. By the end of the 2nd century BC the Germanic Cimbri thundered from their strongholds NE of the Rhine through Celtic lands. They forced Belgic tribes to migrate W pushing others before them,[45] They caused great upheaval in the Celtic world, forcing tribes to migrate to SE England. These became the British Celts of Caesar's 'interior parts' who claimed they had been in the country 'from time immemorial'.

ROMAN INTERVENTION IN CELTIC AFFAIRS

"By 400 BC the Bituriges dominated the Celtic peoples. By the 2nd century BC the Celtic hegemony had passed to the Arverni, who among their subordinates included the once powerful Allobriges of the Rhone valley."[46] The celebrated Celtic Chief Louernius was King of the Arverni at the height of their power before being imprisoned by the Romans.[47] His son Bituitus was king in his father's absence. He was to suffer the same fate as his father, with repercussions which resonated all the way to Britain and Ireland.

Massalia (Marseilles) on the Mediteranean coast was a centre of the Greek commercial world. In 154 BC the Salyes attacked it. Rome, as a gesture of 'friendship', drove back the Salyes. In 125 BC they attacked again. Rome annexed Massalia. Its terms for military aid were the annexation of the entire Cisalpine area of Gaul, including Massalia. Massaliots, for whom the security of their trade and commerce meant everything, accepted the terms. Roman legions under Fulvius Flaccus drove the Salyes back, demanding their surrender. They took refuge with the Allobriges N of Massalia. The Allobriges refused to surrender them. Going from the Salyes to the Allobriges, a Roman army under Domitius Ahenobarbus set off up the Rhone in 122 BC to show that Rome's enmity was a thing to be feared. At Vindalum he was surprised by 20,000 Celtic warriors led by Bituitus, king of the powerful Arverni.[48] Ahenobarbus delayed battle until reinforced by Fabius Maximus' army. They routed the Celts. Fabius Maximus led a punitive expedition against the Allobriges destroying all before him. Ahenobarbus began a round of clenching treaties with Celtic tribes as far as the Helveti (Switzerland), Volcae Tectosages and Arecomici of Toulouse, allies of the Arverni, persuading them to accept Rome's 'forced friendship'. This led the Aedui to seek alliance with Rome. Rome made itself master of the whole area between the Alps and the Mediterannean. Gallia Narbonensis became a Roman 'Province', a name retained in modern 'Provence'. Rome had thus gained a foothold in the Celtic hinterland.

Bituitos escaped with Arvernian aristocrats, taking sanctuary among the Belgae, kinsmen of the Volcae, friends of the Arverni. After years in exile he sought peace with Rome. His fatal decision was to negotiate with the Senate in person, hoping to regain his throne. Rome imprisoned him in the Alban Hills SE of Rome. This prized hostage was manipulated to subjugate the Arverni. Determined to end Arvernian kingship, Rome apprehended all heirs to the throne. Ahenobarbus set up a monument at Nimes to celebrate this victory. After years in Roman custody, Bituitos' son, Congentiatos (Gann for short), was born. The Romans called him Commius.[49] He was held with his father to ensure he would not restore

[45] Henry Hubert, Op. cit. p.67 - 70

[46] Nora Chadwick, 'The Celts' p.58

[47] Sung by the bards, renowned for prodigality, Luernius used to drive his chariot through the countryside showering gold coins on his people. Poseidonius, quoted by Athenaeus (c200 AD) recorded an incident after a feast thrown by Luernius at which immense quantities of wine and food were freely served: A Celtic poet sung "magnifying Luernius' nobility, and lamenting his late arrival. Luernius was so elated he threw a bag of gold to the poet who sung an even more glorificatory song praising the very tracks of Luernius' chariot which gave gold and largesse to mankind." The largesse of legendary Luernius lapsed when he was imprisoned by the Romans.

[48] For offering sanctuary to Salyes chiefs, Rome swore the Allobriges would suffer the consequences, unaware of the bonds of clientship between them and the dominant Arverni which bound the Arverni to come to their aid.

[49] The name Congentiatos ('a born wardog'), like of his grandfather, Louernius (wolf god) was a typical Celtic name for a born fighter. Congentiatos was his *nom de guerre*. In intimate circles he was called 'Congenn' or 'Gann' for short. *"Nomen est omen"* to the Roman. Too long and ominous to their ears, they renamed him

the abolished Arvernian throne. He was given a classical education in Roman Rhetoric which exalted his nobility. On graduation he fled, like his father earlier, to the Belgic Federation of NW Europe. There he was later befriended by Julius Caesar who recognized his learning, political astuteness and leadership qualities. He would make him King of the Belgic Atrebates and Morini on the Continent and in England. He would use him to prepare for the Roman invasion of Britain. Commius turned against Caesar and took a leading part in the Pan-Celtic Revolt against him. Thus he became a *persona non grata* within the Roman Empire. He fled to SE England and later led his followers (the *Gangani*) to a new Celtic haven in W Ireland. Hence, the reason for alluding to these incidents in Southeastern Europe at some length.

A new menace bore down on Celtic and Roman worlds. The Cimbri from the Baltic shores opposite Scandinavia, a branch of the Celto-Scythians encountered there by Pytheas of Massalia in the 4th century BC, swooped on Celtic Europe from 113 BC.[50] The Volcae expelled them. The Scordisci forced them "to turn in their tracks. They ravaged the Raurisci"[51] on the Ruhr and joined forces with the Teutones. They forced the Helveti to vacate their settlements between the Rhine and upper Danube and move into Switzerland, pushing other Celts west. The Tigurini and Volcae Tectosages of Toulouse who called themselves Belgae joined them and rebelled against Roman occupantion.[52] Roman Consul Longinus separated the Tigurini, commanded by Divico, from their allies. Divico defeated the Romans near Agen. They lost their General, Longinus. Fifty years later Divico met Caesar in the lands of the Helveti among whom he took refuge after his massacre of the Romans,[53] underscoring the longevity of Celtic warriors.[54/55] "Rome was in turmoil - 3 Roman armies were defeated in 3 engagements. Panic reigned, the Celtic sack of Rome in 390 BC uppermost in the citizen's minds."[56] A 4th disaster followed leading to over-confidence and ultimate defeat for the Celts. It jolted Rome into building an army that would conquer the whole Celtic world, Ireland alone excepted. "Rome found a man equal to the task. He was Gaius Marius (157-86 BC), married to Julia, who was to become aunt to Julius Caesar. Marius was called from Africa to defend Rome against the Cimbri and their allies."[57][58]

The Teutones, stopped by the Belgae, left 6000 men behind in Belgica to guard their possessions. These formed the Aduatuci tribe and joined the Belgic federation. By 102 BC the Cimbri and Teutones were on the move again, finding no space to settle in Gaul. It was too full and completely assigned to existing proprietors. They advanced towards Italy. Marius forced them back and effected a skillful encirclement at Aix, with orders to spare no one. The butchery was so vast that for years the fields, saturated with blood, produced bumper crops."[59] 120,000 Cimbri were slaughtered. No one escaped.[60] The Germanic tribes, ancestors

'Commius'. This remained his official name until in old age he shed all Roman trappings. The dates of Bituitus' imprisonment and the birth of Commius (Congentiatus) are unknown. The battle of Vindalum took place in 120 BC. Bituitus was on the run for many years before opting to negotiate for peace with Rome. His imprisonment may have taken place in 110 BC or later. His son 'Commius' was born later still in his Alban prison.

[50] Henry Hubert, 'The Greatness and Decline of The Celts', p.99

[51] Jan Filip, 'Celtic Civilization and its Heritage', p.74-75

[52] Ordo Urbium Nobilium', xiii, 7-10. Belgae = Volcae. Cf. Pauly CCCLXVIII, iii, cols. 198-9

[53] P. Berresford Ellis, 'The Celtic Empire', p.122

[54] H. Hubert, 'The Greatness and Decline of the Celts', p. 107-108. The Volcae were forced to surrender the 200,000 pounds of gold from their temple treasures, the loot from their sack of Delphi, as tribute to the Romans

[55] Ibid p.108. Sent to Rome via Marseilles, the gold never arrived. Rome's general was defeated by the Celts.

[56] P. Berresford Ellis, 'The Celtic Empire', p.122-3.

[57] Ibid p.123.

[58] Ibid p.124: He moulded the conquering Roman armies of his nephew, Julius Caesar. "The legion, regular pay, standard weapons and battle-tactics were introduced by him. The army became a career for aspiring young men. Rome at last had a standing army, with terms of service and retirement pensions."

[59] Ibid p.124

[60] Ibid p.124-5

of Angles, Saxons, Franks and Frizians, were moving S in vast hordes occupying Celtic lands and driving Belgic tribes W of the Rhine. The Rhine had been the great Celtic waterway, its valleys dotted with innumerable Celtic place names, marking centuries of occupation. The Belgic Menapi held their lands longest E of the Rhine. They completed their crossing in 54 BC. With the Rhine as the new border, Celts in what is now Germany, Austria and Czechoslovakia became isolated from their kinsmen. Germanic tribes began crossing the Rhine, making deep inroads into Belgic tribal lands with Rome's connivance. Celtic "Gaul was doomed in a pincer movement."[61] Germanic tribes were penetrating from the North, Roman legions from the South. Instead of presenting a united front, Celtic tribes were throwing all their resources into a struggle for dominance and provincial power. When Caesar arrived on the scene he found the Aedui, Sequani and Arverni locked in just such a struggle. His diary of his conquest is a brilliant documentary of the political distribution and disunity of the various Celtic tribes in the latter stage of their independence. He explained his conquest of this brave and noble people, by his policy of 'divide and conquer'. "We watch the process at work among the Aedui in Caesar's account of the struggle between the former king of the Aedui, Divitiacus, and his successor and younger brother, Dumnorix."[62]

In 71 BC the Sequani quarreled with the Aedui whose Capital was Bibracte in central Gaul. They joined the Germanic Suebi under their chief Ariovistus. Taking advantage of the internal squabble, the Germans seized Celtic lands. Ariovistus defeated the Aedui in 61 BC. Celtic tribes were forced to pay tribute to him. In 60 BC the Aedui chief, Divitiacos, looked for a ally to drive back the Germans. Instead of appealing to the Celts, he went to Rome where he was allowed to address the Senate. As a guest of Cicero, Divitiacus strove to promote an alliance between Rome and the Aedui. Caesar was appointed Consul of Rome with Marcus Calpurnius Bibulus. He dismissed the alliance with Divitiacus on the ground that he had been promoted by Marcus Cicero, his enemy. He asked the senate to recognize Ariovistus as king and 'friend of the Roman people'. Thus approved of by Rome, Ariovistus proceeded to carve out a Germanic empire among the Celtic tribes of Gaul. Dumnorix, younger brother of Divitiacus, opposed his brother's pro-Roman attitude, when Caesar supported Ariovistus.[63]

In 58 BC Caesar emerged as Proconsul together with Pompey and Crassus, the First Triumvirate. Breaking with the Senate, they became virtual dictators of Rome, and divided their spheres of influence. Caesar took the governorship of Illyricum, Cisalpine Gaul and Gallia Narbonensis. Ultra ambitious, he wanted to achieve a military reputation greater than that of Pompey. New conquests would enhance his reputation. He eyed the mainly unchartered hinterland of the Celts. In 58 BC he was offered the excuse to intevene. Orgetorix died. The new king of the Helveti, pressured by advancing Germans from the north and aware of Rome's ambitions, decided on mass migration. The Boii joined the Taurisci for protection. Advancing Germanic tribes forced them onto the land of the Helveti, pressing the Helveti to migrate. The Helveti, with their Boii, Taurisci and Tigurini followers, planned to find new lands further west far from the Germans and Romans.

On the appointed day 400,000 Celts fired their towns and farmsteads to prevent them falling into the hands of the hated Germanic tribes, and began to move to the Pas de l'Ecluse. Divitiacos alerted Caesar. Delighted by this excuse to intervene, Caesar set off with 6 legions to confront them. By April 58 BC Caesar had reached the S end of Lake Geneva as the Helveti were assembling. He blocked them from turning south. To avoid the Romans

---

[61] Nora Chadwick, 'The Celts' p. 59

[62] Ibid p. 58

[63] Dumnorix's Queen was a daughter of Orgetorix, Swiss Helveti chieftain. Dumnorix entered into alliance with Orgetorix and Casticos, son of the Sequani chieftain, disillusioned by his father's alliance with Ariovistus, to unite the Celts to drive the Germans back across the Rhine and check the interference of Rome in the affairs of Gaul.

they turned NW into the territory of the Aedui. Whichever way they moved was an invitation for Caesar to attack. Divitiacos invited the Romans to 'protect' Aeduan territory from the migrating hordes. Caesar obliged. Finding the Romans entering their territory, the Aedui were split between their chieftain's pro-Roman policy and the pro-Celtic policy of his brother, Dumnorix. Caesar found them supporting the Helveti. The Aedui kept the Helveti informed of Caesar's movements and prevented corn supplies and other provisions from falling into his hands. His cavalry sent to cut off the Helvetan advance were misled by the Aedui. He wanted Dumnorix eliminated. The pro-Roman Divitiacos stood up for him, claiming his death would alienate Divitiacos among all Celtic peoples of Gaul. Hearing the Helveti were crossing the Saone, Caesar moved to intercept them. As he came upon them only the Tigurini were still crossing. They had previously decimated Longinus's army. Caesar cut them to pieces. He marched his 6 legions to Bibracte (Aeduan capital) which the Helveti would pass. The Helveti marched slowly into his trap. They fought desperately against Rome's legions. Of the 400,000 who began the exodus, only 100,000 survived Caesar's butchery. The remnant of the Boii were allowed to settle among the Aedui. The Helveti were forced back to their former homeland where they were promptly subjugated by Germanic tribes.[64]

Rome's ruthless efficiency impressed Celtic chieftains. Many arrived at the Aeduan capital to make 'friends' with Caesar and seek aid against Ariovistus and his Germanic hordes encroaching on their lands, using Divitiacos as spokesman. Precisely what Caesar desired! He could now claim to be champion and protector of Gaul. Despite the fact that the German King had been proclaimed 'friend of Rome' at Caesar's instigation, it was clear that Caesar set little store by such treaties. Ariovistus declined to meet Caesar.' Caesar ordered him to return E of the Rhine, release Celtic prisoners, cease military excursions into Celtic lands, and made it known that all Gaul was now under Roman protection. Ariovistus retorted that he had not interfered with the Romans or Rome's possessions and therefore they had no right to interfere with him. If Rome wanted to press the matter, Ariovistus, would fight. Germanic tribes crossed the Rhine to swell his army. They massed in the land of the Sequani, enemies of Rome. Many Sequani joined Ariovistus. Caesar marched to their capital, Vesonito (Besancon). They attacked his outposts. He pursued them across the Rhine. Men, women, and children were cut down mercilessly. Ariovistus's defeat was total. The German menace was broken. In N France, Belgium and Holland the confederation of Belgic Celts was dismayed with Divitiacus' naivete in calling Rome to his aid, ignoring his kinsmen. As Dumnorix foresaw, Caesar was bent on enslaving all of Celtic Gaul.[65]

THE BELGAE DEVISE A NEW DEFENSIVE SYTEM
The Belgic federation of Celtic tribes, hardened by years of border conflict, came into existence against encroachments by Germanic tribes. It learned valuable lessons from the failed military strategies of its Celtic cousins. It was not susceptible to Roman bribes and duplicity as were the latter. The Rhine provided no protection as Germanic incursions had shown. It saw hill forts turned into death traps by Caesar. New military strategies were necessary to outwit Rome's fighting force. It could not defeat highly trained disciplined Roman legions in set battle. New methods of guerrilla war were adopted by devising a radically new system of defences incorporating forests and marshes into a web of earthworks into which the Roman troops might be lured, unaware of lurking dangers. Belgic warriors would ambush unsuspecting Roman troops with guerrilla-type tactics in situations where the Roman war machine would not work. The Southern Belgae had no time to implement this new system

---

[64] The Helveti vanished as a distinct Celtic people, leaving only the name 'Helvetia', the native name for Switzerland, to mark their passing.
[65] P. Berresford Ellis, 'The Celtic Empire', p.127-133. Caesar was then raising new legions among their cousins in Cisalpine Gaul for a devastating campaign against the Belgae.

when Caesar invaded. The Northern Belgae on the Continental Lowlands were forced by the exegencies of their low-lying forest terrain to adopt something of this system from the beginning.

In 57 BC Caesar's 8 legions and Aeduan cavalry surprised the Belgae. The Aeduan king guided Caesar. A forced march brought them to the territory of the Remi, the most southerly of the Belgae. Reims was their capital. This caught them off guard. They surrendered without a fight. Taking hostages, Caesar moved swiftly to the River Aisne. The element of surprise was half the victory. The Suessiones, Bellovaci and Ambiani were slightly better prepared. After fierce fighting Caesar secured their submission. He marched to the River Somme to discover that the Nervi and Aduatuci awaited him on the opposite bank. Caesar admitted admiration for the awesome fighting spirit of the Nervi. They routed Caesar's cavalry and carried the attack to the far bank, swimming across in the dark and engaging the Romans in hand-to-hand fighting. On Caesar's right flank 2 legions were being over-run. He launched a counter-attack. His 8 legions broke the Celtic advance. They were in retreat by dawn. Roman archers poured a withering fire on those who swam back across the Somme. Of the 50,000 Celts who launched the attack, only 500 survived.

Celtic Gaul was being turned into a cemetery which Rome called 'peace' or 'civilization'. 'Divide and conquer' was Caesar's code of conduct. The Southern Belgae were crushed as clinically as were the Helveti the previous year with contemptuous impunity. Northern Belgic tribes, notably the Menapi then in the process of crossing the Rhine, held out due to their new defensive tactics which took Caesar by complete surprise. The Atrebates and Morini made tactical submission to gain time to complete this system. The major part of Gaul was under Roman control. The conquest of the Belgae was tenuous at best.

With the Belgic conquest incomplete, Caesar reported his success in Rome to claim the honours. He left his army in winter quarters to complete the task in his next campaign. The Armorican/Breton peninsula was still independent, something anathema to Caesar. In 56 BC Publius Crassus, sent by Caesar to seek alliances among Armoricans, arrived in Rome with disturbing news. He received token submission and assurances of friendship from Armorican tribes (as Caesar had from the Belgae) and sea-faring Veneti whose tribal capital at Vannes bears their name. No sooner had he set off, leaving officers of the VII Legion among them to act as emissaries, than the Veneti rose in defiance of Rome, taking these officers as prisoners. Caesar ordered a large fleet of galleys built at the mouth of the Loire, with rowers and pilots transported there immediately from Massalia. On arrival in Gaul Caesar found the Belgae up in arms and German tribes causing chaos by making further incursions across the Rhine. He dispatched 3 legions to crush the Belgic revolt, 3 more to tame the Germans. With his remaining 2 legions he set off to teach the Celtic Veneti the meaning of obedience to Rome. They were the maritime power of the day, a role Caesar wished to usurp for Rome. Their strongholds stood, inaccessible by land, on the headlands and isles of Quiberon Bay. They had a massive fleet of some 220 ships with which they traded along the coast of Gaul as far as Britain and Ireland, and south to the Mediterranean.[66]

The Veneti could be defeated only by the use a naval force sophisticated and large enough to overwhelm them at sea. Caesar gave command of his fleet of galleys to Decimus Junius Brutus, cousin of Marcus Brutus destined to become his assassin. He had to use extra-ordinary means to defeat the Venetic fleet in the treacherous Atlantic. Brutus equipped his

---

[66] The Italian sea-faring Venice state was founded by, and named after, the Veneti. Their opposition to Rome arose as much from rumour that Rome was about to invade Britain and destroy their marine dominance and their wealth, as from a reaction to foreign domination. Caesar described Venetic ships as powerful vessels with: "flat bottoms to enable them to sail in shallow coastal water. Their high prows and sterns protect them from violent storms, as do the strong hulls made of oak. Their sails are made of rawhide to withstand violent Atlantic winds."

fleet with scythes fastened to long poles to cut the rigging of Venetic ships. This tactic won the battle. With sails cut, Venetic vessels were easy prey to Roman boarding parties. Caesar watched the naval engagement from the headland. One by one Venetic vessels were overwhelmed. Those with sails intact were immobilized by a drop in the wind, while Caesar's oarsmen maneuvered as they pleased.[67] Caesar massacred the Veneti, executing their chiefs. Massive genocide! Those captured were sold into slavery. Many committed suicide rather than submit. Many sought sanctuary among the Belgae with whom they had close ties. Colonies of Veneti (Feini?) set up seafaring communities in Britain and Ireland.

Sabinus defeated the Morini who had ousted their pro-Roman chief. Their anti-Roman nobles fled to SW England where they established Moridunum adjoining the Dubunni. Insurrection by Belgic tribes was put down with ostentatious savagery, sending massive migrations to Britain which was swiftly becoming a refuge for displaced Continental Celts. Commius (Gann) was appointed King of the Continental and British Morini by Caesar.[68]

In 56 BC Germanic tribes crossed the Rhine. Caesar heard that anti-Roman Celtic chieftains loyal to Dumnorix were forming an alliance with them. He ordered the Usipetes and Tincteri to withdraw. They refused. He advanced against them. When their chiefs came to ask for a truce, Caesar arrested them. He attacked their peoples, in confusion with their chiefs captured, massacring hundreds of thousands of men, women and children as they fled. He boasted that of the 430,000 who came across the Rhine, only a few escaped. He crossed the Rhine while they were reeling from this massacre and spent 18 days wreaking vengeance, burning villages, taking hostages, and extracting forced submissions. When he recrossed the Rhine all Gaul was quiet. 'Peace'! Caesar was delighted. The subjugation of Gaul was complete, he thought. But at what a cost! Millions of lives lost! Genocide. Slavery.

Caesar returned to Gaul in Spring 56 BC. Divitiacos, his constant collaborator and negotiator in the conquest of Gaul, had vanished from the scene. How? Caesar is silent! Divitiacos was the antithesis of his brother Dumnorix, new king of the Aedui, implacable enemy of Rome. Divitiacos sold Celtic freedom to satiate Caesar's lust for conquest. Dumnorix was his antithesis, fiercely independent, a man of inflexible patriotism, entirely devoted to his native land and people. He would die rather than betray their trust.[69] "Dumnorix had succeeded to all the hereditary privileges of kingship (and engaged in) the cementing of wider Gaulish military and political alliances. All too soon he was inevitably assassinated by Caesar while resisting. The history of the two brothers is the epitome of the death-struggle of family and peoples under the ordeal of foreign invasion," Roman-style.[70]

COMMIUS: LEGEND CEASES; HISTORY BEGINS
Commius, a classically educated charismatic leader emerged on the Belgic stage. His sterling leadership qualities attracted Caesar's instant attention and respect. Having curbed Belgic Atrebaten resistance by expelling their anti-Roman chiefs, Caesar appointed Commius as their King. "Commius" he said "was a man both courageous and politic, a noble of great influence and learning." He used him as a negotiator to prepare for his invasion of Britain and as intermediary in treating with the Britons. For this service Caesar freed him from tribute and restored the rights of the Atrebates lost by their anti-Roman stance. Caesar made

---

[67] Tim Newark, 'Celtic Warriors', (1986). Explanation for such easy unexpected victory lies in that not only was Caesar's fleet built by Celts but manned by Celts. Caesar recognized not only the weaknesses of the Celts, but their strengths too, a tactician who exploited both. Much of Caesar's army was now made up of conquered Celts.
[68] The Morini (Mac Morna) vanished from the scene at the time of the Roman invasion. According to Irish tradition the Mac Morna (Morini) were part of the Fir Belg invasion of Connacht.
[69] Berresford-Ellis, 'The Celtic Empire' p.135
[70] Nora Chadwick, 'The Celts', p.58

him king over the Morini, a neighbouring Belgic state, when their anti-Roman rulers fled. Commius had an astute ability to be accepted as a leader of diverse Celtic tribes. He was acceptable to all, a pan-Celtic international, the first true European.

In 53 BC, the 6th year of Caesar's reign of terror, a pan-Celtic revolt erupted. Commius showed his true colours. He sided with his kinsmen against Caesar. He was elected one of the 4 supreme chiefs committed to take charge of the war. This shows his considerable influence down through Gaul where he was thus honoured by his kinsman, Vercingetorix, the Arvernian king and overall leader of the revolt. In the dramatic suppression of the revolt, Commius alone refused to submit, calling the Germans to his aid. When all failed he took refuge among them. He was the most wanted man in Europe. After miraculous escapes he slipped back through Belgic lands, inciting the Belgae to join him in a new exodus to Britain. There he reigned in peace for 20 years. On rumours of a Roman invasion, Commius handed over to Tincommius. His last recorded act before exiting the British scene and Roman records was rallying his sons to lead Belgic non-combatants to safe havens, the start of a Belgic invasion of Ireland. He led his Atrebates (Athreibh) and Morini thither. The Greek Geographer Ptolemy placed the Gangani (Commius/Gann's descendants) in the Shannon estuary where legend locates the Fir Belg invasion by Gann. This enclave evolved from a safe haven into a full-fledged invasion N into Connacht where Belgic tribes claimed descent from Gann/Commius well into historic times. Greek, Roman and Irish records fuse. Commius, son of the Arvernian king, Bituitus, had fled Rome on completing his classical education rather than remain a *persona non grata* under Rome's heel. Like his father, he sought political asylum among the Belgae with members of the Arvernian aristocracy outlawed in their Rome-ruled homeland.[71] When he became Caesar's enemy he cast off all Roman trappings, including Latin inscriptions on coins he minted in Britain. He renounced his Romanized name and reverted to his Celtic 'nom de guerre', Congentiatus, Gann for short. In Roman records he is 'Commius', his son is 'Tincommius'.

This practical affinity of names authorizes one to identify the Arvernian Commius with Commius, King of the Atrebates and Morini, and Gann who led the Belgic 'Gangani' (named after him) to W Ireland. It is corroborated by Ptolemy's Record, compelling one to accept that it was Commius and his son Tincommius, who disappeared from the British scene and Roman records in the face of Roman invasion, who finally emerged as leaders of the Irish Belgic invasion in their true Celtic colours as Gann and Sengann. The exit of Commius from Romano/British records, together with his son Dela, coincided with the exit of the Morini and some of the Atrebates. Legendary history names Gann and Sengann as leaders of the Fir Belg (Belgic) invasion of W Ireland precisely where Ptolemy's record located the Gangani. It locates the Morini (Mac Morna) and Atrebates (Aitreabh) in S Connacht into which the descendants of Gann and Sengann expanded. *Coiced Gann* and *Coiced Sengann* are names for early Connacht (*Ól nÉgmacht*) in manuscript materials. In the light of Commius/Gann' and Tincommius/Sengann's involvement in the Belgic migrations, the affinity of names can hardly have been mere coincidence. Commius' ancestors would have been proud of him. Should not his descendants too! <u>When legendary history is thus ever so subtly corroborated by Brito/Romano history, Ptolemy's geo-political record and the ominous contemporary Celto/Roman military menace in Britain, then legend ceases and history begins.</u>

---

[71] There is no absolute proof that the Commius, known to his friends as Gann, made King of the Continental Atrebates and Morini by Caesar, was Commius, the son of Arvernian King Bituitus, or the Commius who emerged as King of the British Atrebates, or the (Commius) Gann who led the Fir Belg to Ireland. Yet, the identification of the Irish Gann/Sengann with British Commius/Tincommius can hardly be labeled pure conjecture. Several factors support this identification, not least Celtic and Roman forms of their names.

Commius was over 60 years old. His son, Tincommius, and grandson, Verica, succeeded each other on their father's throne in SE Britain. Both disappeared mysteriously from the pages of Brito/Romano history. Under Celtic forms of their names, Sengann and Ferach, emerged in Irish legendary history as Fir Belg kings, succeeding their brother/uncle Dela, Fir Belg Overking in Irish legendary history, to reign at Knocknadala/Turoe (Ptolemy's REGIA e TE[*mh*]RA) of Galway in W Ireland. The Connacht Partrige claimed descent from Gann well into historic times.[72] Further insight into Commius' role, leader of the Belgic invasion of Britain and Ireland in the last century BC and its causes, demands an examination of Caesar's invasion of Britain and the consequences of the Celtic Continental revolt in which Commius was involved. It shows what an Iron Age invasion involved, be it Roman or Belgic, of Britain or Ireland, and the mobility and military preparedness of the Celts during Caesar's command of the mightiest military force on earth in 55/54 BC.

FIRST ROMAN INVASION OF CELTIC BRITAIN

Caesar's plan to invade Britain was formed in 57 BC while fighting the Celtic Belgae. Belgic clans fled to SE Britain, or were about to do so, rather than submit to him. He noted that the British Belgae migrated as conscious offshoots of continental tribes and retained the names of the Continental tribes from which they sprung. They introduced coinage to Britain modeled on that of Belgic Gaul.[73] They maintained lively contact with their mainland cousins, aiding them in the war against Caesar. This was his excuse for his invasion of Britain. Caesar distinguished the Britons of the maritime parts, who preserved a tradition that their ancestors had crossed from Belgium ('*ex Belgio*') from those of the interior, who had been there 'from time immemorial' (a few generations earlier).[74] The Belgae drove the aboriginal Priteni and early Celts north, as they later did in Ireland. Caesar noted that in living memory one Diviciacus, paramount chief of Gaul, held sway not only over Celtic tribes on the Continent, including the Belgic Suessiones, but also over Celtic tribes in Britain.[75] In 57 BC nobles of the Belgic Bellovaci who had urged an anti-Roman policy on their tribe fled to the Belgic area of Britain with their followers.[76] Belgic tribes, such as the Atrebates, settled in Britain, before and after Caesar's campaigns in 55/54 BC.

As King of the Continental Atrebates Commius could claim suzerainty over their kinsmen in Britain. Hence, Caesar chose him as negotiator in preparation for the planned invasion of Britain. Having completed his 'conquest' of Gaul and his massacre of the Germans on the Rhine by early August 55 BC, and having some months on hand before winter set in, Caesar, ever the ambitious man of action, looked across the sea towards Britain. He could wait no longer, keenly aware of the fact that he was due to give up his governorship of Gaul by March the following year. His conquest of Britain must be now or never! On 'expert' advice he chose 10,000 men for a 'reconnaissance in force'. With such an unusually large force to transport by sea, Caesar clearly had hoped this would be his conquest of Britain. It was his last chance for a full-scale invasion before his term of office ran out.[77]

80 transport vessels assembled at Portus Itius (Wissant) and 18 cavalry vessels at Ambletuse. Aware of such preparations, British tribes sent envoys to Caesar offering submission. Caesar sent Commius back with them to spread the news of the impending invasion and encourage submission to Rome. If they submitted, he would place Commius over them as he did over the continental Atrebates and Morini. Caesar's success depended on Commius to pave the

---

[72] Commius/Congann/Gann's role among the Belgae make this summary of the Roman conquest of Gaul, ranging from Italy to Ireland, a necessary foundation for the history of the Fir Belg of Ireland.
[73] A.L.F. Rivet, Town and Country in Roman Britain', p.45.
[74] Caesar, 'De Bello Gallico' v, 12
[75] Caesar, Op. cit. ii, 4.
[76] Caesar, Op. cit. ii, 14.
[77] Caesar's record is a justificatory excuse for failure, making it appear that it was meant to be a 'reconaissance'.

way for their submission. Neither the Britons nor, in the long run, Commius himself were to prove faithful.[78] It is noticeable that the Romans did not know of a suitable harbour in the SE of Britain. This lack of knowledge was to prove almost fatal to the Roman expedition.[79] Caesar dispatched Caius Volusenus to reconnoiter for a safe landing-place off the SE British coast and rendezvous with his fleet off the coast. It took him four days to find one. Caesar's fleet anchored beneath the white cliffs of South Foreland at dawn 25th August, 55 BC. Celtic warriors massed along the cliff-tops as far as the eye could see, placed on high alert by Commius. Cassivellaunus led their combined forces. Volusenus led to a landing place on the Kent coast, land of the Belgic Canti, split in septs under 4 kings, Cingetorix, Carnilios, Taximagulos and Segonax. Caesar discussed how best to secure the beachhead. Celtic war-chariots and cavalry followed the movement of the Roman fleet along the coastline, daring Caesar with dramatic war dances. When his cavalry failed to arrive, he ordered a landing by late afternoon at low tide. Ships ran aground 250 feet from shore. Heavily laden troops waded ashore through withering fire from Celtic bowmen and slingers, unencumbered at close range. Celtic cavalry horses pranced all over them. Expertly handled Celtic war chariots with scythes fitted to wheel hubs unnerved the Romans, encountering them for the first time, and mowed them down. Warriors raced chariots through the shallows, petrifying the invaders, and engaged them in hand to hand combat before darting back on the chariots and racing away. Romans were dismayed and disorganized by this unaccustomed manner of fighting. Caesar ordered into action all reserve troops on supply longboats of the galleys to race to the aid of those in trouble. Only thus did he save his legions from massacre. When his artillery turned their fire on the Celts, only then did they draw back, confused. By nightfall a beachhead had been secured and the Celts pushed back.

By dawn Canti chiefs, accompanied by Commius as their 'hostage', arrived at Caesar's camp to open negotiations. Commius warned them of the stratagems of the Romans and how easily Gaul had crumbled before them. He told Caesar he had been 'imprisoned' by Canti chieftains to prevent his warning him of their determination to fight on the beaches. Had he hoped to see a massacre of the Romans as they waded ashore, and see whether British Celts and their war-chariots could face Roman legions better than their continental kinsmen! Later events show that Commius would have gloried in Caesar's decisive defeat.

Caesar's cavalry vessels were destroyed by a storm which also smashed most of his beached infantry vessels. He dared not move without his cavalry. While engineers demolished the worst-damaged ships to repair those salvageable, he ordered the VII Legion to reap crops ready for harvesting and plunder supplies from nearby settlements. It was set upon by Celtic war-chariots lying in ambush. A dust-cloud swept up by the war-chariots alerted him to the danger. He ordered his whole army to the scene of action to save his legion. This drew from Caesar a glowing account of the methods of chariot warfare that terrorized and threw Roman ranks into confusion. "They show the mobility of cavalry and stability of infantry. By daily practice they become so accomplished that they gallop their chariot-teams down the steepest slopes without loss of control, check and swing round in split-second movement. They dart along the yoke-pole, leap into the midst of the fray, fighting on foot, then, quick as lightning, dart back on the chariot, ready to retreat when hard pressed by the enemy."

Nennius, brother of Cassivellaunus, King of the Catuvellauni, led the war-chariot force. Commius alerted all Celtic tribes to Caesar's imminent invasion. As Caesar retreated to his fortified camp, the Celts carried off large numbers of Roman prisoners. With great difficulty Caesar's much depleted army, without provisions, fled back to the Continent. From a military viewpoint the expedition was a disaster. Yet, Caesar had the opportunity to see for

---

[78] Peter Salway, 'Roman Britain', p. 27.
[79] Peter Salway, 'Roman Britain' p. 26.

himself just how expert the British Celts were at using their war-chariots, a new experience for him. He gained valuable, costly experience, but had seen nothing of the land.[80] As his war galley backed away from the British coast, Caesar was already planning a 'full-scale conquest' of Britain with a vastly larger force. First a major hurdle had to be crossed. He must persuade the Roman Senate to vote him a further 5 years of the governorship of Gaul. He convinced Rome that the conquest was all but a reality. To allow his governorship of Gaul to terminate at this crucial time would negate his 'success' so far, not only in Britain but on the Continent as well. The Senate voted him a further 5 years on the strength of his justificatory 'record'. During winter of 55/54 BC Caesar quartered his troops among the Belgae to check them, pacify them if necessary, and stand ready for the conquest of their kinsmen in Britain in the coming campaign season.[81] In March 54 BC on his return to Gaul he found 600 transport ships and 28 war-galleys ready for the invasion.

There was unrest in Gaul and Britain between pro- and anti-Roman factions at the prospect of the impending invasion. A close community of interests existed between Celts on both sides of the Channel. Caesar first dealt with unrest among the powerful Treviri on the Moselle whose tribal centre was Trier. They had never submitted to Rome. Two Treviri chieftains, Indutiomarus and Cingetorix, contended for leadership of the tribe. On discovering that Cingetorix was pro-Roman, Caesar provided him with military aid to overcome Induitomarus. Anger against Caesar was ready to spark a general uprising during his absence. He decided to pre-empt it by taking anti-Roman leaders to Britain. One was Dumnorix, Aeduan King, actively campaigning for pan-Celtic cooperation to shake off the shackles of Roman occupation. This won him popularity among Celtic tribes. He stood aghast at the sight of Celts fighting each other while Rome reaped the benefits. He forged diplomatic connections with anti-Roman elements among Celtic leaders. Should a general rising take place, Dumnorix was the obvious choice for leader. Under military escort, Dumnorix and other tribal chieftains whose loyalties were suspect were brought to Portus Itius, the port of embarkation. When they learned they were being taken to Britain, Dumnorix, their spokesman, declared that Caesar shuddered to spark a general uprising by assassinating them before their own people and planned to have them executed in Britain. Dumnorix refused to embark. The day before the fleet was due to sail, he and his followers eluded their Roman sentries, seized horses and rode off. Caesar halted the countdown to embarkation. He dispatched cavalry with orders to capture Dumnorix. They demanded his surrender. He refused. He and his band were overpowered and slain, proclaiming they were free men of a free nation.[82,83]

SECOND ROMAN INVASION OF BRITAIN

600 specially built ships and 200 more confiscated from the Celts transported Caesar's massive army to Britain. The landings were unopposed. "The enemy was nowhere to be seen." Captured prisoners informed Caesar that a large army had gathered to meet him on the beaches, but on observing the vast size of the Roman fleet, they retired inland. By evening of 7th July the Roman army had established a beachhead. Caesar ordered a night march to seek out the enemy forces. After a 12 mile march they sighted Celtic forces established in a strong position on the opposite bank of the Great Stour to defend the

---

[80] Caesar insisted it was meant to be no more than 'a military reconnaissance in force' in preparation for a full-scale invasion. One hard lesson learnt was that 10,000 chosen legionaries were grossly insufficient even for a mild reconnaissance. An apologetic note rings throughout Caesar's narrative of this fiasco.

[81] Caesar left orders with his 2nd in command, Labienus, to build adequate transport ships and war equipment, and raise an invasion force 3 times the size of that of his first expedition.

[82] Peter Berresford Ellis, 'The Celtic Empire', p. 154.

[83] Ibid p.155: Ellis noted, "even in the hostile eyes of Rome, Dumnorix was an extraordinary personality. Able Celtic leader, he was inflexible in his patriotism, an implacable foe of Rome's expansion in his country. His death served as a rallying point for all Celts who, within months, rose up in a 4-year war of liberation. In precipitating the Gaulish insurrection, the death of Dumnorix also cut short Caesar's plans for a full-scale conquest of Britain.

crossing in the land of the Canti. From high ground above, Celtic war-chariots raced down harrying the Romans as they attempted to cross the river. Withering fire from the Romans repulsed the Celts who were driven back by Caesar's cavalry. They retired to the woods where they had a fortified position of great natural strength, Caesar's first experience of the Belgic oppidum defence system. Some retreated into the nearby fortification surrounded by forest and other defensive features, inviting the Romans to follow. Others attacked the legion's passage through wooded areas. They set up an ambush, having the approaches to the fortress obstructed by felled trees. They harried the Roman advance along the route.

Caesar inspected the Belgic fortifications. Palisade-topped ramparts rose just 20 feet above the base of the wide deep defensive ditch dug around the earthen embankment. He ordered the VII Legion to storm the hill fort as bow-men and sling-men started a fusillade to keep the heads of Celtic defenders down while a pioneer corps piled up earth against the embankments in order to scale them. When complete, cohort after cohort poured over the rampart into the fortress only to find a deserted fort held by a handful of disappearing defenders. This ruse was of the essence of Belgic defensive tactics. Far from defeat, Canti chiefs and their main forces hid in woods along outer ward ramparts to engage Roman legions in guerilla warfare. Caesar forbade attempts at pursuit as his troops had already gone two nights without sleep. He realized that if the Celts were to ambush them, his troops were in no shape to repulse them. Besides, he was unacquainted with the situation in the surrounding countryside. That night disaster struck similar to that which had robbed Caesar of victory in his aborted campaign the previous summer. Next morning just as his cavalry made contact with the 'retreating' Belgae news arrived from his base camp on the Kent coast that the previous night's gale had devastated his fleet. The coastline was littered with wrecked vessels driven ashore by the freak storm. Anchors and cables had snapped. Heavy damage resulted from collisions and from the ships being thrown onto the shore.

Caesar withdrew to base camp. Ships not damaged were pulled ashore within the fortifications to prevent the Celts from exploiting this disaster. A swift war-galley was dispatched to Portus Itius with orders for Labienus to build replacement ships at once. There on the Kent coast the 48-year-old Caesar celebrated a wretched birthday on the 12th of the month of Quintilis, soon to be renamed in Caesar's honour as the month of Julius (July). It grew more somber when Labienus returned with devastating news from Rome that Caesar's only child, Julia, married to his rival Pompey, had died. More ominous still, her child, Caesar's grandson, had also died. "The joint heir of Caesar and Pompey might have prevented their civil war as each strove to make himself dictator of the Roman Empire. That year his mother, Aurelia, who played such a dominant role in his life, had also died."[84]

With these personal losses weighing on him, Caesar marched into the interior. The Belgae and Catuvellauni had erected the new defensive system. Its primary purpose was aimed at guerilla-type war where the Celts would feign retreat, draw the Romans into unfamiliar woodlands or marshy terrain where they might easily be separated from view of one another and their commanders, sink in quagmire under the weight of heavy encumbrances where they could no longer fight in tightly-knit formation. Caesar's military strategy was one of lightning-fast mobility to catch Celts off guard, unprepared, with no choice but to surrender or perish. The Belgic defensive strategy, adopted by the Catuvellauni, brought large tracts of forest and marshland within the fortifications into which the enemy was lured, ambushed, harried and delayed by every conceivable guerilla tactic. This shift of emphasis in strategic control of the region from smaller hill-forts to the extensive Belgic defence system of oppida settlements, such as at Quarry Wood, Loose, become evident.[85]

---

[84] Peter Berresford Ellis, 'The Celtic Empire', p.158
[85] Alec Detsicas, *'The Cantiaci'*, p. 2.

Caesar noted that the Celts of SE Britain unanimously agreed to confer the supreme command of operations against him upon Cassivellaunus, the Catuvellaunian chieftain. Cassivellaunus' objective was to keep his forces steadily in retreat before the Romans drawing them within target areas of his complicated system of fortifications where they would be at the mercy of his troops hiding in the woods, operating in small bands. This was of the essence of the defensive strategy. Caesar found in Cassivellaunus an astute military commander. His capital was the hillfort at Wheathampstead, just north of St. Albans.

THE EFFECTIVENESS OF THE BELGIC DEFENSIVE SYSTEM

Caesar's march inland was tortuous. He immediately felt the full force of the effectiveness of the tactical Belgic defence system, unlike anything the Roman army had experienced before. He had marched only a few miles when he found his troops engaged in running battles with the cavalry and war chariots of the Belgic tribes S of the Thames. It was obvious that the Belgic tactics were intended to slow the Roman march in the extreme without engaging in all-out set battle, and exasperate Caesar's tactic of lightning surprise. Time and again Celtic cavalry and war-chariots swooped on vanguard, rearguard, scouting and foraging parties and flanking detachments. Time and again Caesar called a halt to reorganize the attack only to find the Celts had vanished as quickly as they had come. Junior officers carried away by enthusiasm let their men pursue the Celts into the forests. When this happened it spelt disaster. Romans units were cut off by hidden marksmen lying in ambush and inevitably suffered heavy casualties.

After a grueling first day's march Caesar built a night camp for a much-needed rest. Cassivellaunus' troops burst from surrounding woods and attacked Roman fatigue parties, sentries and outposts, denying them sleep. Caesar claimed very heavy fighting ensued. He had to order two legions of his veterans at double strength to rescue outposts under threat. The rescue was a near disaster. Crack troops were cut off in fierce fighting. In his record Caesar praised Celtic tactics and bravery in their first day's success. When he tried to encircle them they withdrew following their new strategy. Among the night's numerous casualties was one of Caesar's ablest commanders, Quintus Laberius Durus. Celtic tradition claimed it was Cassivellaunus' brother, Nennius, leader of the attack on the illustrious VII Legion the previous year, whose heroic courage resulted in Durus' death. Caesar noted that "the day's success was dearly purchased by the death of Nennius himself, who fell in the last onset" that night. This was a heavy personal tragedy for Cassivellaunus who lost his beloved brother and ablest commander. British tradition tells that Nennius won Caesar's sword which became so lodged in his shield in a skirmish the previous year that Caesar could not extract it. Their sudden separation by the fury of the fray robbed Nennius of the glory of taking advantage of Caesar's dreadful dilemma and taking his head to boot. The Romans had never experienced such fierce fighting and such danger before.

Caesar painted a glowing picture of the strategy and tactics implemented by the Belgae and waxed lyrical on the effectiveness and sophisticated thinking behind the unique Belgic defensive system incorporating forests, marshes and rivers over a wide area. "In the whole of this kind of battle fought under the eyes of all in front of the camp, our men, on account of the weight of their arms (they could neither follow those who were giving war, nor dared to depart from their standards) were little suited for an enemy of this kind. The cavalry maneuvers were fought with great danger because the enemy would oft-times retreat even designedly, and, when they had drawn off our cavalry a little way from the legions would leap from their chariots and fight on foot in unequal combat. The enemy never fought in close order, but in small parties and at considerable distances, and had detachments placed about, which took the place of others, so that fresh troops continually succeeded those who were weary" (*De Bello Gallico*). The brilliant hit-and-run guerilla tactics employed by the

Celts took Caesar totally by surprise and took an enormous toll on his massive army. Thanks to the Belgic defensive strategy!

Commius operated behind the scenes. Cassivellaunus and his allies dealt with Caesar's vast army in a way none of the Celtic armies of Gaul had ever done. With no personal experience of Caesar's lightning, swift-foot strategy as he literally walked over the Celts on the Continent, Cassivellaunus was counseled by Commius, never to fall into the trap of engaging the Roman army in the close formation of set battles, but to employ the tactics he was now implementing so brilliantly of slowing down and constantly ambushing the Romans. The Continental Belgae, except for the Menapi, had not been given time to put this tactical defence system fully in place. Their British counterparts had time to prepare their defensive system and strategy. The past year had been spent preparing for war with the most formidable force on earth. British Celts showed themselves capable of taking on Caesar and the might of the Roman army.

Next day Cassivellaunus, despite personal loss, and loss of sleep to his warriors who spent the night harrying Caesar's camp, ordered his war-chariots to take up positions on the surrounding hills some distance from Caesar's camp, and in small parties to provoke his cavalry to combat, knowing that if they could eliminate his cavalry he would be in dire straits as in the previous year's campaign. Caesar forbade his troops to make any foolhardy move in answer to this provocation.[86] His vast army was running out of rations because the foraging parties had been unable to move far afield without being attacked. Besides, "the native population had removed themselves and their livestock out of the route of the Roman march. Caesar ordered Caius Trebonius to take command of the foraging parties and scour the countryside. It was just such a move that Cassivellaunus had been waiting for."[87] His warriors swooped on Caius' troops. Caius barely managed to withdraw to the protection of the main encampment with a considerable loss of life. Caesar launched a counter-attack on the pursuing Celts which turned their pursuit into a disorganized retreat. He drove the Celts headlong, "and slaying a great number of them, gave them no opportunity of rallying or of leaping down from their chariots." Cassivellaunus resumed his guerilla tactics, harrying the Romans' advance, wearing them down and cutting them off from base camp and supply lines. Observing that rich farm settlements were being foraged by Caesar's troops as his source of supply, Cassivellaunus ordered a scorched-earth policy. Farmers were to withdraw out of Caesar's route, set fire to their farmsteads and drive off their flocks and herds, destroying grain stores.[88] As they were still in the lands of the Belgic Canti, this order from Cassivellaunus proved unpopular and was the undoing of the combined resistance. Canti chieftains believed they were fighting a losing and destructive war. This was the reason why warriors from some of the tribes departed to their own tribal lands.

The Belgic Trinovantes, next on Caesar's route, had their own quarrels with Cassivellaunus which had temporarily been quelled for the sake of the combined resistance. When rumours of an imminent Roman invasion were in the air, Cassivellaunus had driven Imanuentios from the kingship of the Trinovantes, fearing his pro-Roman leanings. His son, Mandubratius, went to the Continent to appeal for Caesar's help to restore his usurped Trinovanten kingship. Nothing could have suited Caesar more. He had Mandubratius as his right-hand man as he set sail for Britain. He promised to place him on the Trinovanten throne. Caesar learned from him the name of his formidable opponent, Cassivellaunus. Chiefs of the Canti, Trinovantes, and other septs came to Caesar's camp to discuss terms to end the conflict to save their livestock and crops. What a relief for him! Through Mandubratius' mediation,

---

[86] Peter Berresford Ellis, 'The Celtic Empire' Ibid p.160

[87] Ibid p.160

[88] Ibid p.161

these gave Caesar valuable information. He learned the location of Cassivellaunus' stronghold, which, like strongholds of the Belgae S of the Thames, was strategically placed among woods and marshlands. Large numbers of men and cattle were assembled there. Caesar now had guides, desirous of personal gain, to direct him through the very complicated morass of the Belgic defensive system.

He crossed the Duro River (Medway) at Durobrivae (Rochester), and reached the Thames. Cassivellaunus with 4,000 war-chariots faced him on the N bank, ready to dispute the crossing. He destroyed the bridge at the original site of London, derived from the 'dun' of the god Lugh. This was a town and trading settlement of the Trinovantes. The River is fordable only at one point, at Brentford, a Celtic name cognate with Brigantia, at the confluence of the Brent and Thames. The place and river name indicates that it had belonged to the Brigantes before they were pushed north by the Trinovantes and Catuvellauni. Caesar noted "large native forces in battle order on the far bank which was defended by a line of pointed stakes; deserters in our custody revealed that more were set in the river bed," to disembowel his cavalry horses. The Romans removed these obstacles backed by fire from archers and bowmen which drove back the Celts. Under cover of fire the Roman cavalry crossed and secured the far bank. The legionaries followed, crossing with only their heads above water. This unexpected turn of events un-nerved the Celts who had hoped to have time to provoke Caesar's cavalry to combat before the main army attempted the crossing. They were driven back from their defensive positions. Caesar hoped to drive them headlong as he did when their lines broke in the land of the Canti. North of the Thames in the land of the Catuvellauni the intricate morass of inner and outer wards of the defensive system was in place to test Caesar's tightly organized military strategy in guerilla-type combat through woodlands and marshes. Guerilla warfare intensified as the Romans moved forward, hacking their way through thick woodlands, felled trees blocking the route, marshlands obstructed by a complicated system of close-set ramparts and transverse ramparts cutting off sections of the army from view of their commanders. Caesar had no over-all control of his army in these confines. His concern was that all sections of his army remain in close touch to support one another in difficulty. The route to Wheathamstead, Cassivellaunus' stronghold, took them along the Colne Valley past Denham and Watford. Caesar admitted Cassivellaunus' defensive system and guerilla tactics were so successful that his cavalry could not venture out of touch with the main army. Foraging parties could not be sent out. On all sides Cassivellaunos' warriors lay in ambush. Watchful defenders awaiting every chance infested the forests. Thirty-foot high earthen ramparts with deep fosse on the outer sides slowed down Caesar's progress to snail-pace. His troops could not sleep in their night camps with Cassivellaunus' warriors taking turns to attack his outposts and sentries.

It was mid-August before they had hacked their way through forests to gaze on the ramparts of the Catuvellaunian capital of the most powerful consortium of tribes in Britain. The inner ward at Wheathamstead enclosed 100 acres, too extensive to surround, as Cassivellaunus expected they would, since legions could be attacked and cut off at several points from outside or inside. His warriors were hidden in the outer wards to await developments. The Catuvellaunian ramparts were 30 feet high and over 100 feet wide, far more massive than Belgic ramparts. Caesar stormed it only to find the stronghold deserted. He raised the 'victory flag'. It had not dawned on him that by capturing the core of the Catuvellaunian oppidum he had not conquered the Celts. They were as free as ever. Their very complicated morass of extensive fortifications, natural and man-made, was intact. This was the enduring quality of this new defensive system. Had the Catuvellauni understood its full implications, as did the Belgae, from whom they learned it, they would have lured Caesar to their oppidum's inner ward where he hoped to trap the tribe with their stores of food and herds of cattle only to have his starving troops find it deserted and empty, his starving army trapped within. They would then have to run the gauntlet of fighting their way out without having gained anything. The Catuvellauni faltered fatally. They missed the supreme advantage this system offered. Instead, the hungry Roman army found vast provisions and livestock in the fortress where they should have been trapped and starved. While Cassivellaunus refused to submit the war was not won. There were a dozen similar strongholds throughout his territories. Caesar balked at having to reduce them one by one. Cassivelaunus was not 'on the run'. He had not been defeated. He asked the 4 Canti kings - Cingetorix, Carnilius, Taximagulus, and Segonax - to attack Caesar's camp on the coast. Cassivellaunus reasoned that this would force him back to the coast to find his ships destroyed, relieve pressure on Cassivellaunus, allowing him time to reorganise. The Canti Chieftains launched the attack. Atrius made a resolute defence. Cingetorix was captured.[89]

CAPITULATION BY THE BRITISH CELTS

The capture of supplies in the Catuvellaunian stronghold, Cassivellaunus' failure to have Caesar's fleet destroyed, and his failure to apprehend Caesar on his trip to or from the coast were factors which led other tribes to believe their efforts were in vain. A major factor in their withdrawal was that the Trinovantes, whose tribal territory bordered that of the Catuvelauni, received the pro-Roman Mandubratius as their king, as Caesar promised. Caesar was welcome in their territory. They provided food, men and logistic support. Caesar treated them honourably as Roman citizens. Seeing this, other chieftains decided surrender was the best way to preserve themselves and their territories. They withdrew and returned to their tribal lands. This was a severe blow to Cassivellaunus, who was unable to prevent the Romans from obtaining supplies.[90] Commius appeared at Caesar's camp! Where had he been at Caesar's landing? Caesar did not contact him to establish a basis for his invasion. Cassivelaunus used him as ambassador. This suggests that he and his people were allied to Cassivelaunus. Commius was a brilliant leader, not an unpopular pro-Roman king imposed by Caesar. He had ruled the British Atrebates for the past year and would rule them for the next 30 years. Caesar was relieved to be in a position to dictate his demands.[91] He did not chastise Commius. In late September Caesar and his much-depleted army returned to the Continent.[92] His was a pyrrhic victory. Britain retained independence for a further century. Cassivelaunus assumed his position of pre-eminence, taking advantage of the situation in Gaul to ignore the provisions of Caesar's treaty. No annual tribute was paid to Rome. No hostages were sent. Britain returned to being one of the most prosperous of the surviving independent Celtic countries."[93] The subsequent history of the Catuvellauni shows that Cassivelaunus was the real victor. Caesar's report to the Senate of his 'victory' may glow, but deliberately conceals consciousness of failure.[94]

IRELAND BECOMES A CELTIC HAVEN

The 30 years after Caesar's invasion saw the Belgic invasion of Ireland begin. Just as Britain became a safe haven for Continental refugees over the past 50 years, it was now Ireland's turn to fill this role due to the Roman invasion of Britain and rumours of more invasions. Much information can be gleaned from 1st century BC/AD British history and

---

[89] Ibid p.163 In a letter to his brother Marcus, Quintus Tullius Cicero tells that the attack sent Caesar racing back to base camp. He left his main force encamped at Wheathamstead. Caesar returned to Wheathamstead within days.

[90] 'De Bello Gallico':Caesar wrote with satisfaction: "So many losses received, his territories devastated, and distressed by the defections of the tribes, he sent ambassadors to me through Commius concerning surrender."

[91] Caesar, 'Bello Gallico' v.22: These were brief: "I demanded hostages, I fixed annual tribute payable by Britain into the Roman treasury, and I forbade Cassivelaunus to interfere with Mandubratius and the Trinovantes.

[92] 'The Celtic Empire' by Peter Berresford Ellis, p.164: What was gained after 3 traumatic months in Britain? Empty promises soon broken, and some hostages, the first of countless British Celts who, over the next 4 centuries, were to be sold into slavery by Rome, never to see their native land again."

[93] Ibid p.165

[94] There was public disappointment in Rome. Caesar's invasion was a financial fiasco. The Senate decreed no celebration for this 2nd campaign, unlike the previous year. The moral victory went to Casivelaunos' and the British Celts.

political geography which illumins that of Ireland and scans the evolving Celtic Irish landscape. Caesar's invasion opened Britain to the full light of history. Peter Salway drew together literary sources and the massive advances in archaeology of the last 50 years.[95] "When we compare our picture of the country Caesar found with the state of knowledge about Britain just before the Claudian invasion a century later, we must be struck by the difference that for the later period it is possible to construct a complete map of the tribes and people it with the names of a substantial number of rulers at whose policies we can make reasonable guesses. In Caesar's account few tribes are named. There are few identifiable personalities. By the Claudian invasion many individual tribes can be located and named and their relations with one another can be deduced." Caesar noted that Belgic tribes were established in SE England before his arrival. They brought over the names of parent tribes, rivers and tribal capitals in Gaul. From their parent tribes, some 15 in number, one can recognize settlements of the Belgae, the Atrebates and the earlier Catuvellauni. Smaller tribes under the sway of the Atrebates or Catuvellauni were lumped together under the generic name, 'Belgae', after the Claudian Conquest into one administrative region.

The Belgic defence system accounts for their rapid expansion. It locates their kingdoms and defines their limits. Belgic oppida were oval/rectangular, extensive, sited in river valleys, and depended on rivers, lakes, marshes and forests to supplement the defences. Reconstruction of the Belgic defence systems of Camulodunum, Verulamium[96] and Chichester/Selsey oppidum[97] in SE Britain were put on record over the last 35 years. This helps to clarify the emergence of the Belgae in Ireland and enables archaeology to locate their precise geographical locations and capitals. Information culled from the Romans enabled Ptolemy to draw up his substantially correct map of Britain for that period. It was being outdated by the time he wrote it early in the 2nd century AD because tribal centres were moved, boundaries altered for administrative and political purposes, and tribes divided or amalgamated by the Romans.[98] Such sources and those of Marinus, Agricola and other informants provided Ptolemy with his Irish account.

A source lacking in Ireland is the work on Celtic coinage resulting in the publication of maps showing the distribution of coins of different rulers, and the introduction to the Ordnance Survey 'Map of SE Britain in the Iron Age.' It projects a picture which is an approximation of the area of influence of various tribes, particularly the Belgae. Their coins expose the rise and fall of Belgic kings and tribes. Caesar noted that tribes of SE Britain were recent Belgic arrivals from the continent. The record of the movements of the peoples which created this situation in Britain depends on the interpretation of the coin evidence. Between 60 and 50 BC a new wave of coinage, Gallo-Belgic E, flooded into Britain, concentrating in Essex, Thames valley, and Sussex. "In Kent and Essex the aristocratic influx was accompanied by a folk movement, introducing specialized cremation rites and a new style of fine wheel-turned pottery.[99]

"Much more precise is the information about the changing scene which can emerge from the study of the successive names on coins and of the adoption of particular coin types by individual tribes. When we find persons appearing in Roman literary sources whose names are recorded on British coins we know for certain that British archaeology is at last

---

[95] Peter Salway, 'Roman Britain', p.40.
[96] Keith Branigan, 'The Catuvellauni', p.7-22
[97] Barry Cunliffe, 'The Regni', p.16-26
[98] Peter Salway, 'Roman Britain', p.40
[99] Barry Cunliffe, 'The Regni', p.13. "So extensive is the distribution that it points to intrusive elements rather than just trade - the archaeological manifestation of Caesar's remark that the chiefs of the Bellovaci took refuge in Britain from his advance into their territory in 57 BC.

emerging from the prehistoric world.[100] This exposes the manoeuvres of the Belgae at a time when they were in the full floodlight of history. The coinage shows that the Canti, ruled by 4 kings in 4 separate kingdoms under Belgic influence in Caesar's day, later fell under the control of the Catuvellauni when their rulers fled. West of the Weald was the kingdom of the Atrebates ruled by Commius from 54 BC to 25 BC occupying W Sussex, W Surrey, Hampshire, Berkshire, and NE Wiltshire, centered on Silchester/Selsey and linked to the Atrebatic kingdom of NW Gaul ruled by Commius until he fled to England after the great Celtic insurrection of 52 BC. "The connections of the British Atrebates with the Gallic tribe are emphasized by the fact that it is here (in SE Britain) that Commius is found striking coins after his flight from Gaul."[101]

In the thinly populated, forested lands of the Weald, SW Kent, E Sussex, and E Surrey, a group of small tribes, the Regni, came into existence with the Claudian invasion after the Atrebates departed. They used hillforts which were anathema to the Atrebates. During and after Caesar's time the chief centre of power at Chichester, (*Regno* in the Antonine Itinerary; *Navimago Regentium* in the Ravenna Cosmography - from Latin '*Regnum*', old Celtic *Regia*: Capital), was ruled by Commius. Negotiations, which led to the establishment of the Regni as a separate kingdom under Cogidubnus, took place at the beginning of the Claudian invasion a century later. It played an important role in the conquest of Britain. SE Britain's most powerful tribal group was the Catuvellauni whose expansive territories lay N of the Thames. "They had originally been centered on Hertfordshire, but between the invasions they expanded to dominate Cambridgeshire, Northamptonshire, Bedfordshire, Buckinghamshire, Oxfordshire, Middlesex and NE Surrey."[102] They annexed lands of the Belgic Trinovantes in Essex, which they swore to Caesar not to do, and spread into Belgic lands south of Thames. Their expansion was partly due to the arrival of displaced Celts from the Continent which boosted their population and armies. It set off a Belgic Atrebaten and Morini influx into the West and South of Ireland, creating a springboard for the Fir Belg expansion and domination of Iron Age Ireland.

Catuvelaunian coins suddenly appeared in Kent as the Catuvellauni overran the N of the Atrebatic kingdom and part of Kent, driving segments of the Atrebati and Canti off the SE coast of Britain to the W of Ireland where they left their tribal name on the Galway townland toponymy. Catuvelaunian ascendancy is detected among the Dubunni in W Oxfordshire, Gloucestershire, N Somerset, Avon, Hereford, Worcester and Warwickshire. The Dubunni developed the Belgic defensive system. North of the Catuvellauni and under their influence lay the Coritani, inhabiting Leciestershire, Nottinghamshire, Linconshire and S Yorkshire. Their coinage was struck by 2 rulers simultaneously, and at one time by 3. The Iceni lay E of the Coritani in Norfolk and Suffolk while the anti-Roman Belgic Parisi of Humbershire to the NE of the Coritani were insignificant in the extent of their territory but determined to retain their independence.

Central England was occupied by the Brigantes, largest of the old Celtic kingdoms determined to preserve their independence.[103] They settled in Britain and Ireland earlier than other Belgic tribes. In Leinster in SE Ireland they were known as the Ui Bairrche and recorded as Brigantes in Ptolemy's record. The Durotriges of Dorset lay W of the Atrebates and had many hill-forts. They offered stubborn resistance to Rome.[104] The Dumnoni

---

[100] Peter Salway, 'Roman Britain', p.41

[101] Peter Salway, 'Roman Britain' p.43

[102] Ibid p.43

[103] Ibid p. 43 Their Continental parent tribe hailed from Bregenz in Switzerland whence they spread to France (Burgondiones - Germano-Frankish form of their name) and N Gaul to join the Belgic federation.

[104] The Durotrigen Capital was Maiden Castle near Dorchester, erected in the 1st century BC with triple ramparts enclosing an area two-thirds of a mile long by a third of a mile wide, its ramparts rising 100 feet high.

occupied the Devon/Cornwall peninsula. This was the layout of the Belgic SE of England at the time of Caesar. An examination of the political history of this part of Britain from Caesar's day to the Claudian conquest a century later provides a historic back drop to the legendary history of Ireland at that time. "The literary evidence for the political history of Belgic SE Britain in this period consists of tantalizingly brief references by a number of authors, some contemporary, others considerably later but drawing on earlier sources. The coin evidence fills in this picture with further names of rulers otherwise unattested, and confirms some of those already known from literature.[105] How long Cassivellaunus continued to rule the Catuvellauni (no more is heard of him after Caesar's departure), Mandubracius the Trinovantes, or the 4 Kings their lands in Kent, is not recorded. Changes were taking place which enormously impinged on the Belgic invasion of Ireland.

An event of importance for which there is evidence was that in 52 BC Commius turned against Caesar. He led large forces to join the united forces of his kinsman, Vercingetorix, in the great insurrection which changed the course of European history. Coins struck by him and his sons among the British Atrebates confirm he was their king as late as 25 BC and that his son Tincommius held the throne subsequently down to the end of the century when his coins are displaced by those of his brother Eppillus. Although Commius led a popular folk movement of Atrebates, Morini, Morsaci and related tribes from the Continental coastal areas to the SE of Britain, his kingdom there began to diminish after his departure from the scene due to his leading a new folk movement. He set up a Belgic enclave around the mouth of the Shannon in W Ireland which became known, and was recorded by Ptolemy, as the Gangani, descendants of Gann, the short form of his full Celtic name. After this his former extensive British kingdom was rapidly whittled away by the Catuvellaunian over-kingship. Meanwhile, his sons took over from one another in surprisingly swift succession as kings in SE England as each in turn apparently re-emerged as kings of the expanding Belgic (Fir Belg) settlements of W Ireland.

After his role in the Pan-Celtic insurrection, Commius escaped from the Romans determined to capture him at any cost and make his death a spectacularly painful object lesson for the whole Celtic world. In the 9 years from 34 BC there were no less than 3 separate occasions in which full-scale preparations for a Roman invasion of Britain had proceeded some considerable way before being cancelled. Commius topped Rome's hit list. He was in dire danger in the event of invasion. He had gone to extraordinary lengths on the Continent to avoid the same fate as Vercingetorix to be made a public spectacle of. He was determined not to be caught. Commius was highly involved in relocating displaced Celtic tribes from the Continental Belgic Federation where Rome endeavoured to overwhelm the remaining Belgic tribes who put up fierce resistance. This resulted in serious overcrowding of his Belgic kingdom in SE England. This problem and the increasing pressure from the Catuvellauni, as much as the threatened Roman invasion, forced Commius to seek out a peaceful enclave in those intensely troubled times.[106]

---

[105] Peter Salway, 'Roman Britain' p.46
[106] It was surely then Commius, under his short O. Celtic name Gann (Genn), led the Belgic invasion to the mouth of the Shannon in Ireland. This weakening of his British Atrebatic kingdom left them easy prey to the expansionist policy of the Catuvellauni. Commius, and later, his son Tincommius, continued to rule his British subjects. The decline of the Belgae of Britain and the Fir Belg invasion of Ireland went hand in hand. This must be seen against the background of Catuvellaunian expansion in, and Roman conquest of, the South of Britain. Archaeological reconstruction of Belgic oppida in Ireland reflects these circumstances and authenticates its legendary history.

DECLINE of the BELGAE vis-as-vis CATUVELLAUNIAN and ROMAN Conquest

Complicated political events occurred during Caesar's campaigns. In his list of Celtic tribes the name of the Catuvellauni is absent, although it was against their kingdom that he marched in 54 BC. The name 'Catuvellauni' had not yet come into existence. Peter Salway, noting that Celts N of the Thames "were probably not all Belgic," says tribes, such as the Catuvellauni, were "formed out of elements related to the Belgae that had come at an earlier stage in the influx of Iron Age Continental people"[107] from South Belgica. The late last century BC and early 1st century AD saw the expanded Catuvellaunian over-kingdom annexing the Trinovanten kingdom and much of the Atrebatic and Canti kingdoms, thus giving it a substantial Belgic admixture.

British Celts agreed the joint resistance to Caesar be led by Cassivellaunus. He is not referred to as king by Caesar, nor said to lead any specific tribe. The names Belinos, Cassivellaunus, and Cunobelinus (Shakespeare's Cymbeline) and the tribal name itself, are cognate with that of the god Belenos. Catu Velauni = the tribes of the god Belenos; Cassi Velaunus = servant of Belenus; Cuno Belinus = hound of Belenos. Cunobelinus moved his Capital to Camulodunum, fort of the god Camulos, a Trinovanten god. Cassivellaunus' oppidum of "great natural strength and excellently fortified"[108] has not been identified. Parliament Hill Fields (Cnoc Na Dal) in N London may be the site, cognate with the Capital of the Belgic oppidum in W Ireland recorded by Ptolemy as Nagnata[l], to be reconstructed in Chapter 2. At the time of Caesar's 2nd British campaign Cassivellaunus drove out the Trinovanten king and claimed over-kingship of his territory. Legendary history relates that Lud, brother of Cassivellaunus, rebuilt the Trinovanten port and renamed it Lud Dun - Lud's fortress, which is how London got its name. Lud usurped the Trinovanten throne until Caesar restored it to its rightful ruler who had fled to him for help. There is no London in Caesar's record. It was renamed Lud after Caesar's day.

Brannigan analyzed the political geography of the area N of the Thames in 54 BC and the nature of the politics emerging there after Caesar. South of the Thames Caesar lists 4 kings (in Kent) whereas by Augustus' time (20 years later) there was but one. Here Caesar names 5 tribes in addition to the unnamed tribe one must assume Cassivellaunus led continually warring with the Trinovantes (whom Caesar describes as 'the strongest in the area') before Caesar's intervention. None of the 5 tribes mentioned by Caesar ever reappear on the stage of history due to Catuvellaunian expansion. "Taking all scraps of information into account, Caesar gives a brief but valuable glimpse into the process of early state formation in SE Britain, as small tribal units engage in warfare in order to assert themselves and extend their territory."[109] In 55/54 BC this power struggle was being won by Cassivellaunus. Following Commius' departure, the Atrebaten over-kingdom was decimated by the expanding Catuvellaunian over-kingdom.[110]

---

[107] Peter Salway, 'Roman Britain' p.12.

[108] Caesar in 'De Bello Gallico V, 2.

[109] Keith Branigan, 'The Catuvellauni', p.3-4

[110] This is a valuable insight into a parallel process of state formation taking place in Ireland. It is evident from Irish legendary history and the implications of the rapidly expanding Belgic oppida in Western Ireland. Following Commius and Tincommius to Ireland where they are remembered under the Celtic form of their names as Gann and Sengann, a similar process was taking place. Small named tribal units were submerged by the general name of the expanding Fir Belg federation. Before looking at this or following up the expansion of the Catuvellaunian overkingship under Cunobelinus, it is appropriate to follow the chronological order of Roman conquest and trace the fate of Commius in his role in the Pan-Celtic revolt on the continent, then back to Britain, and finally to Ireland.

PAN-CELTIC INSURRECTION AND HOLOCAUST

Returning from a failed campaign in Britain in 54 BC Caesar summoned a council of pro-Roman Celtic chieftains. Harvest in Gaul that summer had been disastrous, adding fuel to the fires of discontent throughout Gaul. Hence, Caesar informed the chieftains that he was quartering his troops over a wide area for winter so as not to put too big a burden on any particular tribe. Many scattered tribes were obliged to provide food for Caesar's enormous army of 80,000 men billeted over a 200-mile radius. Caesar himself set aside his custom of spending the winter in Rome. He remained at full alert at Amiens at the centre of the circle of his troops, having been warned of the seething discontent of the continental Celts.

Belgic Alliance and Instigation to Insurrection: Spirit of Celtic Europe Set on Fire:
Indutiomarus, king of the Treveri, whom Caesar expelled by enabling his pro-Roman brother, Cingetorix, to become chief, was instigator of the immediate unrest. Celtic tribes stung into action by the assassination of Dumnorix led by Indutiomarus, rose against Caesar. Indutiomarus had to dispel the belief that the Romans were invincible. He made an alliance with Ambiorix and Catavolus, joint chieftains of the Eburones and convinced them that if but one Roman legion were wiped out the whole of Gaul would rise up. Roman legions were billeted far apart due to the famine. Starving Celts were forced to feed the enemy that crushed them. During that bitter winter of 54 BC Ambiorix welded together an alliance of Belgic tribes, comprising the Eburones, Menapi, Nervi and Atuatuci, allied to local German tribes. He launched an attack on the 9,000 Roman troops under Sabinus and Cotta, Caesar's beloved Generals, at Tongres. When he appeared before the Roman camp with an overwhelming Celtic force, the Romans fled towards Namur, 50 miles away. Ambiorix's forces ambushed them. The Roman army was wiped out. News of the annihilation set the spirit of Celtic Gaul on fire. It rose up in arms - a mortifying shock to Caesar. The prestige of Roman arms was humiliated. The Nervi, Senones and tribes on the Meuse and Somme revolted. Quintus Cicero's XIV Legion was surrounded by 60,000 warriors led by Ambiorix. Cicero sent a message to Caesar who ordered 3 Legions to relieve Cicero. Indutiomarus overthrew his pro-Roman brother Cingetorix and marched against Labienus' army, preventing it from relieving Cicero's army which was saved from annihilation only by the arrival of Caesar's Legions. To his horror, Caesar found two of every three of Cicero's garrison gravely wounded. Gaul was ablaze. Celtic tribes united against Rome, thanks to Caesar's savagery! His hour had come to drink the gall of Celtic wrath to the dregs.

In 54/53 BC, Indutiomarus built a united Celtic army. His stronghold at Trier was a hive of activity, the centre of Gaulish resistance to Rome. In the depth of winter a council of war was held to which chieftains of all Celtic tribes were invited. Caesar identified Indutiomarus as instigator of the insurrection. He offered an irresistible reward for the capture of Indutiomarus. A Gaulish traitor ambushed Indutiomarus and claimed his reward - a massive body blow to the Celtic resistance movement. Ambiorix wreaked revenge on Roman Legions. Realizing how strong resistance was, Caesar raised 2 fresh legions and borrowed a third from Pompey. In summer of 53 BC he marched four new legions into the lands of the Nervi and conducted a ruthless campaign, burning villages, seizing livestock, destroying crops, slaughtering men, women and children and selling those captured into slavery. The Belgae fled across the Channel in large numbers. The countryside was depopulated. The dead were left to bury the dead. Burnt out ruins marked the passage of Rome,[111] creating a cemetery desert called 'Peace'.

Caesar called a council of chieftains at Amiens. Less than a handful of pro-Roman chiefs attended, those rejected by their own tribes in full-fledged revolt against Rome. Caesar conducted lightning campaigns on the Nervi, Senones and Carnutes, forcing them to sue for

---

[111] Peter Berresford Ellis, 'The Celtic Empire', p. 168

peace. He took Ambiorix's liquidation of his favourite commanders, Sabinus and Cotta, and their legions, heinously to heart. This affront could be effaced only by the liquidation of Ambiorix who now persuaded Germanic tribes to rise up. Caesar's armies were under constant siege by Ambiorix throughout the winter. Only drastic action could halt the spread of revolt. Caesar devastated German lands, annihilating young and old alike. He tried to separate the Manapi from Ambiorix's forces. They defied him and retreated into the morass of their Belgic oppida in inaccessible forest marshlands in the Maas/Schelde deltas, ready to ambush, dare Caesar enter. Mindful of the mauling meeted out to his legions in the British Belgic oppida, he dared not risk his legions in forest marshlands of the Menapi oppida. He skirted the fringes of Menapian territory burning villages and taking cattle and hostages as a warning that he would treat them as enemies should they allow Ambiorix into their territory or join his army.

Leaving Cicero's XIV Legion to hold his position at Tongres, he hunted down Ambiorix. Failing in this he vented his wrath on the Belgic Treviri among whom Ambiorix had set up his headquarters. Cicero's camp was attacked by the Germans. By the time the Romans succeeded in repelling the attack they had suffered enormous casualties. Caesar was livid. He ordered a manhunt for Ambiorix and called for extermination of his Eburoni tribe. Dreading to send his troops into the forested Belgic oppida of the Eburoni, Caesar called surrounding Germanic tribes to conquer the lands of this rebellious tribe who had stirred up the insurrection. He encouraged them to maul and murder, plunder and pester, cattle-raid and devastate Eburonian lands with his aid and protection. His legions manned the periphery to mop up those fleeing in terror. He determined to exterminate the Belgic Brigantes in revenge for their annihilation of his commanders, Sabinus and Cotta, and their legions. Germanic hordes, enemies of the Belgae, from both banks of the Rhine, lusting for loot and lands, rushed into this free-for-all with Caesar's blessing. The Eburoni were ruthlessly ravaged in all-out genocide.[112]

Despite hordes hunting him with an irresistible prize on his head, Ambiorix was never captured. He escaped, elusive as Commius. He disappeared from the pages of Continental history. Caesar vented his frustrations in the massacre of men, women and children of Ambiorix's terrorized Eburoni, Senones and Carnuti and in the savage slaughter of the latter's king, Acco, as a typical Roman warning to Celtic chieftains who preached rebellion against Rome. The smell of death wafted on the Continental air. At the onset of insurrection Ambiorix sent women and children to safe havens. More fled in terror of the coming genocide.[113] Finally Ambiorix led fleeing Eburoni, Senoni, Treviri and Carnuti into exile. The Eburoni re-emerged in Britain and S Ireland under their Celtic name, Ui Bairrche. Celtic Gaul settled to an uneasy death-like quiet at the end of 53 BC. Caesar, sated by his savage slaughter, thought the threat to Roman rule had been snuffed out. Belgic tribes devastated by endless war, unable to stomach Caesar's brand of 'Roman Civilization', were pulling up their roots and heading across the sea in search of safe havens. Caesar, pleased as hell with his ethnic cleansing, wintered in Rome in style, discussing the political organization of Britain over goblets of prime Mediterranean wine.[114]

---

[112] S.A. Handford, (ed.) 'Caesar - The Conquest of Gaul', 1984, p.177. All their buildings in every village were set on fire; all across the country cattle were driven off in vast cattle-raids; crops and wheat were harvested (it was autumn) and consumed by the raiding hordes of horses and men. Gloating in the genocidal mayhem, Caesar cried out: "Even had any inhabitants escaped by hiding they were certainly doomed to die of starvation."

[113] The Eburoni (Ui Bairrche) established themselves in SE Ireland, as they already had done in England, and expanded westwards across southern Ireland from this time. Slaighne led the Eburoni to Ireland! Legend tells that the Galioin (Continental Ui Bairrche) were led to SE Ireland by Slaighne. He gave his name to the River Slaney in Wexford. Ptolemy and history record the presence of the Briganten Ui Bairrche there.

[114] Peter Berresford Ellis, 'The Celtic Empire', p.169

PAN-CELTIC INSURRECTION: SWAN SONG OF CELTIC EUROPE

Caesar's massacres introduced a new element into Celtic politics, an appreciation of pan-Celtic co-operation. All Celtic tribes were in alliance for the first time ever, outraged by the slaughter of the innocents. The strongly pro-Roman Aedui who brought Rome to intervene in Gaul were now solidly anti-Roman. As Caesar wined and dined the winter away in Rome celebrating his 'conquests', Celtic chiefs were planning a universal pan-Celtic uprising. "A system of signals had been arranged. The spark was to be the uprising of the Carnutes." The signal was given. The Carnutes slaughtered Roman officials in revenge for the execution of their chieftain, Acco. The spirit of revolt spread across the country."[115] Celtic Europe was aflame as never before!

The most formidable Celtic leader to take on the might of Rome, Vercingetorix ('Highking who faced the foe'[116]), king of the Arverni, took his stand. He was chosen overall leader of the pan-Celtic federation. During winter 53 BC "he built up a united army, requesting each tribe to supply arms and men.[117] In a snow-covered continent when the Carnutes gave the signal for the uprising, word was flashed to Caesar who marched night and day without sleep up the valleys of the Rhone and Saone outstripping Vercingetorix and surrounding Avaricum, Capital of the Bituriges. "Vercingetorix ordered a scorched earth policy. The Romans must be prevented from gaining supplies or provisions. All tribes were to fall back before Caesar, not only to wear him out but so that no contact with the legions in battle formation should occur before Vercingetorix was ready." The Bituriges burnt 20 of their towns in a single day. Neighbouring tribes followed suit. From end to end of Celtic Europe "the horizon at night was a ring of blazing fires as Gauls sought to deprive the Romans of supplies. Vercingetorix had thousands of young Gauls, on light war-horses, harrying the Roman' supply lines and communications."[118]

Caesar swore to annihilate Vercingetorix and smash his stronghold at Gergovia. He began his ascent from the bank of the Allier with 6 full-strength legions. Vercingetorix was confident his hill-fort was impregnable, despite the numerous hill-forts that became sitting ducks for Caesar. Positioning his army in such a strategic situation at Gergovia that any attack would put the enemy at a serious disadvantage, he resolved it would not suffer the fate of Avaricum or other death-trap hillforts before it. "Caesar's assault troops captured 2 heights outside the city. Vercingetorix's counter-attack successfully drove them back. The brilliant strategist followed up the attack as Caesar's army was in full flight, leaving 46 officers and 700 men dead. A fierce rearguard action by the X Legion prevented Caesar's army from annihilation. Caesar's record of invincibility was smashed. For the first time, Rome's most formidable General was beaten in battle by a Celt."[119] The stunning news re-echoed across Europe. Tribes forced to submit and pledge provisions burnt supplies intended for the Romans. Caesar's army in headlong retreat "withdrew north in an attempt to link up with Labienus" in the Seine valley. Labienus was beset with his own problems. As the uprising began he decided to pacify the Belgic Paris region. Hearing of Caesar's defeat, he

115 Ibid p.169
116 Ibid p.169
117 Ibid p.169: Vercingetorix devised a general plan of campaign to prevent Caesar from returning to Gaul and thereby cut him off from his legions in winter quarters among the Belgae. Vercingetorix recognized Caesar as a formidable military strategist. He wanted to prevent him from exercising control."
118 Ibid p.170: The Bituriges refused to evacuate Avaricum and shut themselves in. Caesar stormed it and slaughtered all but 800 of the 4,000 inhabitants. These were sold into slavery. He confiscated their food supplies. The massacre and enslavement underscored Vercingetorix's strict orders, convincing the Celts of the need to consent to a universal sacrifice. They burnt their farmsteads, villages and townships before the advance of Caesar's legions.
119 Ibid p.171

returned to his defended position at Agendicum to await developments.[120] Caesar's forces linked up with Labienus due to Vercingetorix's tactical error. Ceasar felt confident to march his united force against Vercingetorix who was observing the Roman army from high positions. His strategy was to ambush the strung-out legions. The encounter took place in the Vingeanne valley. As the Celtic cavalry attacked the marching legions, they rapidly formed square battle formations, a tactical situation Vercingetorix warned his men to avoid. After brisk fighting the Celts withdrew. Caesar ordered his cavalry to chase them before they had a chance to reform. It was Vercingetorix's turn to flee, Caesar hot on his heels.[121] He withdraw into the stronghold of the Mandubi at Alesia (Alise Ste-Reine). He prepared for a siege. Alesia stood atop a plateau with precipitous slopes, impregnable to every form of assault barring a blockade, protected by the Ose and Oserain rivers.[122] Caesar surrounded Alseia, determined on total surrender or death to all – just what Vercingetorix wanted to avoid! This severely burdened the town.

50,000 Celtic warriors at Alesia were surrounded by over 100,000 Roman legionaries and huge numbers of Germanic mercenaries. Caesar swore this would be Celtic Europe's swan song. Its death-knell rang out. He took enormous precautions - more than ever before. His legions dug trenches and erected palisade siege-works in a vast circuit around the entire hill-top town with look-out posts at various strategic points from which to observe enemy activity. Vercingetorix sent out daily and nightly sallies to delay construction and destroy what had been erected each night. Caesar's engineers laboured inexorably to strengthen his position. Two lines of earthworks encircled Alesia, consisting of ramparts and ditches with hidden traps and pointed stakes. This enormous engineering feat is still visible - the inner line to keep Vercingetorix pinned inside, the outer line to repel expected reinforcements. The grave of Celtic Gaul was dug.

COMMIUS' ROLE IN THE INSURRECTION IN GAUL

Alarmed by this ominous development, Vercingetorix sent a band of cavalry, in a daring dawn dash, crashing through Roman lines back to their tribes to raise reinforcements and issue a clarion call to all tribes to attack Caesar's positions.[123] Commius heard the call. He and his son-in-law, Vercassivellaunus, led vast forces to the relief of their tribesman, Vercingetorix. Commius finally wore his true colours. He was no friend of Caesar! Was he not son of Bituitos, grandson of the great Luernios, kings of the Arverni long before Celticus and his son, Vercingetorix, became their chiefs! Were it not for his father's imprisonment by Rome, Commius would now be on the Arvernian throne.[124] Because of his leadership qualities, and links to Vercingetorix, Commius was made one of the 4 chiefs to whom the principal charge of the war was committed. 100,000 warriors on foot and 10,000 cavalry converged on Alesia. Attacked from outside and inside, Caesar repositioned his troops as the first wave swept upon his legions. The Celts constructed ladders to scale Caesar's siege-works.

---

[120] He was cut off from base by Camulogenus who held a strong position south of the Seine, ordering part of his army into a similar position on the N side. Caught between the two, Labienus feigned to march north fooling Camulogenus into sending part of his forces to aid those N of the Seine. In a surprise manoeuver Labienus swung round, recrossed the Seine and cut through Camulogenus' positions, killing Camulogenus in the process.

[121] Caesar's policy was to pursue an enemy headlong to avail of disarray and instill fear and confusion.

[122] Due to overcrowding, Vercingetorix ordered his men to camp outside the walls and fortify their positions. Aware of the Roman reputation for butchering women, children and elderly noncombatants, Vercingetorix ordered all noncombatants to leave Alesia, and any Mandubian menfolk who choose not to fight. It was too late. They were turned back into the camp by Caesar who then appeared on the scene.

[123] Ibid p.172

[124] Caesar considered Commius pro-Roman. He had made him king of the Belgic Atrebates and Morini, a unique honour for a Celtic chieftain. As Caesar's 'agent' in his 1st campaign in Britain, he was 'rewarded' with the kingship of the British Atrebates which he held for 30 years. Commius' contingent of British Celts was swollen by their Continental kinsmen as they passed through the lands of the Continental Belgae on their way to Alesia.

Day 2: Vercassivellaunus led the Celtic attack. Caesar ordered Mark Anthony and Caius Trebonius to be ready to move cohorts to whatever point Celtic pressure looked like breaching Roman lines. He ordered into action heavy artillery weapons, the *'catapulta'* and *'balista'* which cut down huge numbers of Celts taken by surprise by such sophisticated long-range weapons. Commius' reinforcements, weary from marching night and day, were sucked right into this stark struggle.[125] The siege of Alesia was still not raised.

Day 3, Vercassivellaunus' 60,000 warriors launched an all-out attack on the N of the Roman siege-works coinciding with a determined thrust from Vercingetorix from within. Caesar sent 6 cohorts under Labienus to reinforce the legions holding the N sector at Mont Rea. So doggedly did the Celts strive to breach this line that Caesar was forced to order more reinforcements under Brutus and Caius Fabius. The fate of Celtic Gaul swung back and forth. One moment the Romans seemed to be winning. Then the Celts had the upperhand. Caesar took the remaining reserves into action. Against such odds, the Celtic attack wavered, then finally broke. Caesar ordered German mercenaries to hew down the Celts as they struggled to disengage. Cavalry chased Celtic foot soldiers, capturing them by thousands. The relief army was defeated. Celts were slain indiscriminately as Vercingetorix watched helplessly from the heights of Alesia.

Vercingetorix called a council of chieftains. He went to war to liberate Gaul. He failed. His people faced prospects of starvation, slavery and death. Women and children would be butchered. He made a stark choice, taking the consequences for his failure on himself - Kill him and send his head to Caesar, or, send him to Caesar alive. They did neither. They asked for terms of surrender. Caesar demanded unconditional surrender. They accepted. Seated in splendour amid devastation at the foot of Alesia, Caesar accepted their surrender. The chieftains bowed before him. Vercingetorix was taken in chains to Rome.[126]

Acco's successor, Guturatus, joined the Bituriges and Bellovaci in a combined force under Commius. Commius was made overall leader of the federated Belgic Atrebates, Morini, Carnutes, Bituriges, Bellovachi and Eburoni. He ambushed Caesar's legions with consummate skill, allowing them no respite or sleep to their considerable annoyance.[127] He entered Germany and led Germans in a series of raids against the Romans. He was one of the 4 chiefs Rome wanted executed for the rebellion. Labienus, Caesar's 2nd in Command, ordered that if he could not be captured, an agent should be sent to assassinate him in view of the enormous problems he was causing and the spirit of revolt he was fomenting. He was **the** major threat to Roman control of Gaul. "Labienus sent Volusenus in the guise of an envoy, with instructions to have Commius murdered. Volusenus met Commius but failed in his mission. Commius swore he would never again hold direct intercourse with a Roman (a

---

[125] Commius stood aghast seeing how his fellow Celts once again allowed themselves to become sitting ducks for Roman legions within a hill-fort they considered a strong vantage point. He was shocked at seeing reinforcements of simple farmers unused to battle brought face to face with professional Roman legions who moved in precise formation following an overriding plan and who through a regimen of strategic long-practiced maneuvers entrapped and cut down the untrained Celts. Commius had to make the best of a most unfavourable situation!

[126] Ibid p.174: Vercingetorix was imprisoned in Tullanium under the Capitol and beheaded during the celebration of Caesar's official triumph in 46 BC. His head appeared on the silver *'denarius'* in 40 BC. "Caesar stamped his military lesson on the Gaulish psyche to ensure Gaul would never rise again." He wasted Carnutan lands, burnt farmsteads and villages, butchering men, women and children, taking countless prisoners into slavery.

[127] The spark of resistance still glowed in some of Vercingetorix's tribe who attempted to hold out in their hill-fort of Uxellodunum in the SW of the Arvernian lands. It took Caesar a considerable time to reduce it, having to mine tunnels through rock under its fortifications to cut off the water supply and thus force the determined garrison to surrender

pledge kept until his death). He continued the war and had the satisfaction of wounding the treacherous Volusenus, in single combat,"[128]

FURTHER BELGIC EMIGRATION IN THE WAKE OF COMMIUS

As Celtic Gaul expired under Rome's heel, Britain was free despite Caesar's failed attempts to conquer it. Commius slipped back across the Rhine, informing the Belgic Eburoni, Manapi, Atrebates, Morini, Bituriges and Bellovachi he could no longer stand Caesar's savage brand of 'civilization' and would no longer be their king in Gaul. Many Belgae followed him to his British kingdom in the last Celtic folk movement to Britain. "The migration is confirmed by archaeological evidence."[129] In 50 BC Commius "narrowly eluded the Roman army and sailed to Britain"[130] rather than endure savage 'Roman Civilization' which turned Celtic Gaul into a hell, rather than allow a single free anti-Roman nationalist reside within its borders.

There was a consistent motive underlying Rome's quest for conquest which lay behind her attitude to the world. Wells[131] focused attention on critical passages in Roman literature at Caesar's time which expose this attitude.[132] Livy had Jupiter declare: "Announce to the Romans that the gods desire that my city, Rome, shall be Capital of all countries of the world. To that end they shall cultivate the arts of war and transmit their knowledge to their descendants so that no power on earth shall resist the military might of Rome."[133] Virgil hammered this home in words put in the mouth of Rome's founder: "Forget not, Roman, your special genius is to rule all peoples, to impose the ways of peace, to spare the defeated, and crush those proud men who will not submit."[134] Rome had absolute right on its side.[135] Caesar was the epitome of this doctrine. "Render unto Caesar". Tribes likely to succumb were considered fair game. Any means likely to achieve his purpose were justified. Caesar skillfully utilized the tactic which Tacitus coined as 'divide and conquer'. This was a cornerstone of the Roman system of controlling peoples or destroying them as Caesar did with the Celts. He had it coming to him. He had crossed the Rubicon with his armies. He fell to "the unkindest cut of all"[136] (Figure 5).

To avoid Rome's revenge for their part in the failed insurrection of Alesia, many of his Belgic Marasaci, Manapi, Atrebatic and Morini subjects followed Commius outside the current limits of Rome's control. His British kingdom was greatly expanded. Its main stronghold is recorded by Ptolemy as *Kaleva* (Celtic *Calleva* - O.Irish *Coillibh:* forest) which became Silchester.

---

[128] Hirtius, continuator of Caesar's 'De Bello Gallico'. 'Phases of Irish History' by E. MacNeill,p.169-70. Commius was a *'persona-non-grata'* on the Continent, a man 'on the run'. The huge price on his head made him the top target among Germanic peoples, hordes of whom had served as Caesar's mercenaries at Alesia who would gladly claim the reward offered for his head. He must depart! But where could he go?

[129] Peter Berresford Ellis, "The Celtic Empire - The 1st Millennium of Celtic History" p. 192.

[130] ''The Regni' by Barry Cunliffe, p.14

[131] Wells, 'German Policy', 3 f. as quoted by P. Salway in 'Roman Britain' p.66

[132] Virgil's 'Aeneid', i. 278 f. Virgil puts words into the mouth of the supreme Roman god Jupiter: "I set upon the Romans bounds neither of space nor time; I have bestowed upon them empire without limit."

[133] Livy, I. xvi. 7.

[134] Virgil, op cit. vi. 851 f. 134134 S.A. Handford, (ed.) 'Caesar - The Conquest of Gaul'.p.127-128; 164-177.

[135] Roman Britain', Peter Salway, p. 66: "This doctrine explains why Romans treated minor kingdoms in their power as they wished, or why it was permissible to exterminate whole tribes who proved intractable. Complete ruthlessness was a justifiable means to further the divine mission, whether applied to barbarians outside the limits of Roman rule or to rebellious non-Roman communities within it." This explains why Agricola was glorified as 'ideal' Governor of Britain for annihilating the Ordovices of Wales.

[136] Shakespeare, 'Julius Caesar'.

This exodus of large segments of the Belgae decimated their ancestral tribes, leaving their territory easy prey to Germanic tribes. Manapian refusal to submit to Rome brought her wrath upon the tribe. It was caught in a pincer movement. Rome, having failed to subjugate the Manapi, conspired with the Germans to penetrate their lands. Germanic septs made deep inroads into lands of the Eburoni, Manapi, Morini and Atrebates and Marasci.

Under pressure, the Manapi moved along the Rhine's right-bank before crossing. In 56 BC "the Usipetes and Tenctheri marched on the Manapi who had lands on both banks of the Rhine. Terrified by the sudden arrival of the multitudinous horde, the Manapi abandoned their dwellings on the German side and set outposts along the Gallic bank to prevent the invaders from crossing. The Germans tried every ruse; but without boats, and prevented by Manapian patrols from crossing by stealth, they pretended to return home. The marched slowly away for 3 days, then turned back, covering the distance in 1 night. Their cavalry swooped on the Manapi who, informed that the enemy had departed, recrossed the Rhine to their villages. The Germans massacred them, seized their boats and crossed before the Manapi on the Gallic side knew what was afoot. They took possession of all their farmhouses and lived on their possessions throughout the winter."[137] Thereafter there was a permanent Germanic presence on the W bank of the Rhine with Rome's blessing.[138]

The Manapi crossed the Rhine into the N lands of the Eburones, Atrebates, Morini and Marasci, pushing them S into the Meuse Delta. Within a century most of the Manapi, Morini, Marasaci, Attrebates and Cannan Fatads had faded from the Continental map in N France, Belgium and Holland, their place taken by incoming Germanic Friesians, Batavi, Cheruski, Tungri, Franks and Saxons. Descendants of Belgic tribes left behind, Aduatuci, Eburones and Manapi, although overrun by Germanic tribes still retain memories of their identity. The Aduatuci, overrun by the Tungri, became the Aduatuci Tongrorum, later Tungri, leaving their name on Dutch Tongeren. The Manapi, Marasaci, Morini and Fotads (Cannan Fatads) septs resurfaced in Britain and Ireland together with the Atrebates. Commius, wielding enormous influence, directed this folk-movement. These immigrants boosted the extent of his British 'Atrebatic' and Belgic over-kingdom in SE Britain (Figure 3) and Ireland.

---

[137] Caesar, 'De Bello Gallico'

[138] The Manapi were the last Belgic tribe to cross the Rhine westward when Germanic tribes overran their lands with Rome's blessing. They filled the vacuum left by other Belgae who migrated to Britain. They held back the Germanic onslaught until many decided to bid farewell to the ever-growing pressure from Germans and Romans.

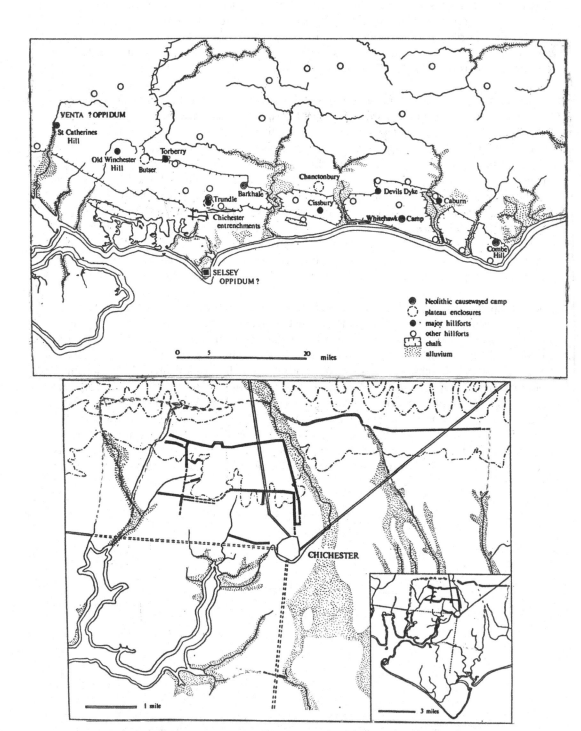

Figure.3: **Belgic Atrebaten oppida ruled by Commius and sons in England: 1.**
Calleva (Silchester), 2. Venta (Winchester; top map), 3. Chichester/Fishbourne
with a 2 mile long inner ward (lower). Selsey was the latter's sea port. Calleva
was overrun by the Catuvellauni. From B. Cunliffe's 'The Regni', p. 8 & 22.

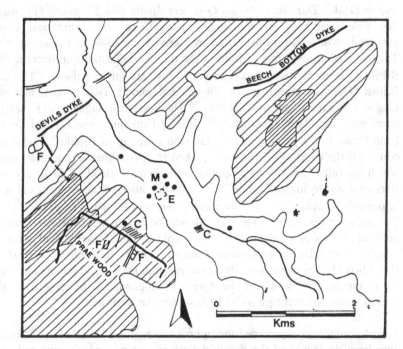

KEY

M – Coin Moulds
E – Enclosure
C – Cemetery
F – Farmstead

Figure 4: A schematic plan of the Devil's Dyke, Beech Bottom and Prae Wood Dykes around the oppidum of Verulamium (St. Albans, north of London; top, from Keith Branigan's 'The Catuvellauni', p. 17). A section cut across the linear embankment of Thickthorn Dyke, Dorset (lower).

"The development of the coinage represents these events."[139] British Q coins, dated to the time-bracket of 40-20 BC, are associated with the historical Commius who fled while Caesar was in Gaul.[140] Derivative British Q staters divide into 2 classes: (1) single-faced coins with the triple-tailed-horse on the reverse, (2) those with same design supplemented by a patterned obverse. From the latter are derived the coins in Britain on which Commius and Tincommius' names appear, reinforcing the view that the introduction of Gallo/Belgic F & British Q is to be connected with Commius' arrival in Britain.[141] The distribution of these British Q coins concentrates on Sussex and middle Thames area into which the Atrebatic kingdom expanded under Commius. "The sequence suggests (1) that the Gallo-Belgic F coins were introduced soon after 50 BC by Commius, and (2) that the Commius who fled from Caesar's troops is the Commius who turns up in Britain,"[142] who struck the British Q coins. "If the coins of Commius are taken to approximate to the extent of the kingdom over which he ruled, his territory spread from Beachy Head to Salisbury Avon and from the Berkshire downs to the Channel Coast, the territory of the Atrebates at its most extensive. It is possible to distinguish 3 constituent groups on the basis of pottery typology"[143] It reflects Commius' tribal groups who settled within this area. Politico-economic boundaries and political centres of power can be recognized in the archaeological record. As the Atrebatic kingdom expanded under Commius many changes took place. Farmsteads multiplied and flourished. Towns began to form, mirroring the increase in population after the exodus from the continent. The wealth of the Atrebatic kingdom can be gauged by the number of coin hoards found and recorded as of 1970 within the territory.

The old order was superceded throughout the region controlled by Commius. Hill-forts were abandoned in favour of the Belgic defensive system[144] which appeared in the territory ruled by Commius. The catalyst precipitating change was Commius. Cunliffe noted: "There developed in their (hill-forts) stead large urban centres or *'oppida'* which served as the site of the tribal mint and king's court. The Belgae "created urban settlements which were in fact towns, such as St. Albans (Verulamium), Silchester (Calleva), Winchester (Venta) and Colchester (Camulodunum)"[145] (Figure 4). The Atrebates possessed 3 such oppida: Silchester (*Caleva*), Winchester (*Venta*) and one in Chichester-Selsey region (under Roman **Chichester'**). Silchester fell to the Catuvellauni. The Chichester-Selsey oppidum remained the focus of Atrebatic power to the end, defended by "a series of banks and ditches running for miles across the country side."[146] Belgic oppida were sprawling urban population centres or towns. One should not be incredulous at Ptolemy's record of such an urban centre in Ireland. Rather one should be amazed if Belgic Ireland were devoid of an urban population centre.

---

[139] At about this time a new type, Gallo-Belgic F, is found in the S (of England; B. Cunliffe)."

[140] Frontinus, 'Stratagems', 2, xiii, II. Harding noted: "The final wave of Gallo-Belgic numismatic influence to reach Britain is represented only in the Whaddon Chase hoard and at Portland in Dorset. But the effect which Gallo-Belgic F coins had upon the insular series is clearly demonstrated by the adoption on British Q coins of the triple-tailed-horse motive which characterized the continental proto-types.

[141] D.W. Harding, 'The Iron Age in Lowland Britain", p.208

[142] Barry Cunliffe, 'The Regni', p.14:This cannot be proven emphatically, but the assumption is a reasonable one. Nor can it be proven that the Congentiatos (Congen/Gann/Commius), son of Bituitus, grandson of Luernius, was the Commius whom Caesar made king of Continental and British Atrebates, who turned against Caesar and reverted to his original Celtic name Gann when he went to aid Vercingatorix and later led his people to the Shannon estuary in Ireland where Ptolemy placed the Gangani. This seems eminently reasonable and not without foundation.

[143] Op. cit. p.14

[144] Commius had seen how even the most impregnable hill-fort had made Celts sitting ducks at Caesar's mercy and how the new Belgic defensive system had turned professional Roman legions into sitting ducks to be ambushed at will by the Celts. Widespread change in the defensive system was called for following Caesar's conquest of Gaul.

[145] Anne Ross, 'The Everyday Life of the Pagan Celts.', p32 and 'Pagan Celtic Britain'. 1974.

[146] Cunliffe, Ibid p.16-17:"chiefdoms represented by the forts were replaced by a different style of government."

In Commius' kingdom the intention was "to strengthen the landward approaches to Selsey peninsula and Chichester harbour, using earthworks where the land was open and relying on the densely wooded river valleys to guard the flanks. The earthworks ran from the stream flowing into Bosham harbour, across the gravel coastal plain to Lavant River and entered the sea at Pagham harbour. An additional earthwork extended the line E to Aldingbourne Rife, a south-flowing stream. The area of land thus protected was considerable, but later modifications tended to focus defensive strength on the Fishbourne-Chichester region. The urban nucleus lay here by the close of the pre-Roman period."[147] By the time Rome came to know the full story of the atrocities perpetrated by Caesar it was too late.[148] Mass migrations of Belgic tribes to England and Ireland reached a peak. All Gaul was in turmoil. After Caesar's death there followed a spell of civil war and confusion which ended in 27 BC when Octavianus, cousin and adopted son of Caesar, was proclaimed Emperor Caesar Augustus.[149] For the safety of his fleet along the Flevo Meer, Drusus subjugated surrounding tribes including the Friesians who supplied troops and mariners for the Romans. Menapian mariners were forced to retreat westwards.

In the 20 years after Caesar's assassination, Commius' British kingdom grew in size and wealth. In the nine years from 34 BC there were 3 occasions, 34, 27 and 26 BC, when preparations for a full-scale invasion of Britain proceeded some way before being cancelled.[150] It came to a head in 34 BC when Octavian set out to invade Britain but turned aside to put down insurrection in Dalmatia. In 27 BC he set out again to invade Britain but got entangled in Gaul. He embarked on a 3rd invasion in 26 BC but again it was delayed because of insurrection in Spain. News of each impending invasion affected Commius. He had sworn never to speak to a Roman again. Now Rome was coming to turn Caesar's failure into conquest. Commius headed Rome's hit list, a huge price on his head. He had developed the Belgic defence system ready to take on Roman legions. Yet, aware that his presence among the Atrebates would attract Rome's wrath, he would leave for their sake. Commius was not about to offer Rome the glory of capturing him. Not that he was afraid to die! His life was bravery embodied, ready to risk all for his people. Nor would he be of service to Rome again. His disappearance from Romano/British history and appearance in Irish legendary history suggests that it was then he set up a haven in Western Ireland to which women, children and elderly non-combatants from SE England could be evacuated in the event of invasion to ensure Rome could not use them as a bargaining chip for surrender or slavery.

Political events in Celtic areas of the Continent and Britain from Caesar's death to the Claudian invasion impacted the puzzling maneuvers of Commius' descendants and the Belgic invasion of Ireland. The Catuvellauni overran Atrebaten and Canti lands. In Irish tradition Gann and Sengann (Celtic forms of Romaized 'Commius' and 'Tincommius') led the Belgic invasion of Ireland. It would be too great a coincidence were Gann and son Sengann other than Commius and son Tincommius. This is corroborated by the unique fact that 2 further 'sons' of Commius, Eppillus and Verica, reigned in succession after Tincommius before suddenly disappearing mysteriously, while 2 descendents of Gann bearing Irish forms of these names, Eochaill (Celtic 'p' to Irish 'ch') and Ferach, succeeded Sengann as Fir Belg

---

[147] 'The Regni' by Barry Cunliffe, p.16-17. C.f. Stephens, C.E. 1951, Boon G.C. 1969, Bradley,R. 1971

[148] For 20 years after Caesar's invasions in 55/54 BC no follow-up action was taken by Romans, beset by their own problems. Caesar had no further desire to tangle with British Celts after his two disastrous encounters.

[149] The new Emperor tried to push the border of the Empire N to the River Elbe. The leader of this war was Drusus, adopted son of the Emperor. He made a treaty with the Batavi (of Holland) by which they became allies of Rome, supplying troops for its armies. In return the Batavi were free of taxes. When Drusus sailed the Rhine to Utrecht he straightened the course of the Vecht River and stationed a Roman fleet, Fectio, at its entrance.

[150] Peter Salway, 'Roman Britain', p.48. e.g. Virgil, Georgics, i.30; Horace, Odes,Lxxxv.29-30: "Roman poets persistently spoke of the conquest of Britain as imminent or even accomplished."

kings in the West of Ireland. Rath Ferach Mhor (Verica's fort) stood beside the illustrious Turoe stone in Galway in Ireland until razed within living memory.

The Belgic tribes ruled by Commius, the Atrebates (*Aitrebh*) and Morini *(Mac Morna)*, were the same tribes led by Gann, Sengann, Dela, Eochail Airimh (of the Atrebates) and Ferach (Verica) to W Ireland where they set up their Belgic oppida.[151] Coill Aithreibh (Atrebaten Forest: Killarriv) formed a forest periphery of Dela's Turoe/Knocknadala oppidum. The Mac Morna (Morini) were the fighting men of the Fir Belg of Connacht posted along the W and N periphery of the oppidum. Equally significant are the river names in Commius' British and Continental kingdoms corresponding to the river names of Ireland's W coast. The Shannon is akin to the Seine. The Moen, Lavant (Lefa), Dur, Adur (Abha Dur), Arun, Ern (Aeran), Ouse and Rother on the SE British Atrebatic and Kent coast correspond to the Main, Leamhan, Dur (Deur), Oss Abha (Ausoba), Aran (Ern), Roe and Rother along Ireland's W coast. These parallel the Rhine tributaries of the Main (Men), Lippe (Levan), Dur and Ruher (Ruhr) in the lands of the Atrebates, Morini and Manapi before and after their Rhine crossing. There were Erin (Ern), Lippe (Liffe) and Men rivers in Irish Menapian lands just as in those of the Continental Menapi; the River Liffy (Lippe) in Dublin and the River Ern and its lakes along which the Fir Manach (Manapi) lived in the NW of Ireland, corroborating Caesar's claim that the Belgae retained the names of the peoples and rivers from which they came.[152] Galway's O-Irish name, *Gailimh (Caillibh,* forest*)*, is akin to that of the Atrebaten capital of Calleva in S Britain and Calles (Calleva forest) on the Belgic coast inhabited by the same tribes. The Forest of Bere near Chichester corresponds to the ancient forest of *Óc mBéthra* (Bera) along the Galway coast and the forest in the Belgic area of the Rhine. Many such examples exist. The Morini of Pas-de-Calais Belgic coastal region ruled by Commius, neighbours of the Atrebates are deemed by Hubert[153] and others as cognate with the Clanna Morna (Mac Morna) whose lands marched with those of the Atrebates in W Ireland.

Having set up a Fir Belg base in Ireland, Commius and his sons did not abandon it after the danger of the Roman invasion of Britain in 34 BC had passed. They expanded and streamlined its defence after the manner of the Atrebatic capital in Britain. The archaeological evidence is emphatic. The two further occasions when serious rumours of invasion were widespread in 27 and 26 BC sent a flood of emigrants fleeing from Commius' British kingdom to his Irish haven, and steeled his determination to strengthen the defences of his Irish oppidum. Plans had advanced so far in 26 BC that Emperor Augustus had proposed terms for a treaty with the Britons before embarking on an invasion. The Britons refused the terms, guaranteeing a largescale savage invasion was inevitable. If Britain fell, would Ireland be spared? Commius took no chances. A Belgic defensive system was erected around his Irish stronghold. His son Dela set up on Knocknadala (Hill of Parliament) in Galway in W Ireland. Around this and the adjoining Turoe hill he erected linear embankments. Having established his Irish oppidum Commius considered his life work accomplished. He was too old to do more. His had been a dynamic life for his beloved people. Tincommius succeeded his father by 20 BC based on British numismatic evidence.

A Salassi revolt in the Alps and trouble in the Pyrenees diverted Augustus' attention from Britain. "There is a hint of diplomatic activity when he visited Gaul in 16 BC. At this time Tincommius struck coins of a distinctly Romanized type. Good relations were establishhed with Tincommius."[154] "With the advent of inscribed coinage and the proximity of the literate

[151] The presence of the Atrebates is attested by numerous instances of 'aithrebh' and its short form 'atti' in compound place-names scattered profusely throughout the W of Ireland.
[152] Caesar, 'De Bello Galico', v, 12.
[153] Henry Hubert, 'The Rise of The Celts', p.228
[154] Peter Salway, 'Roman Britain', p.52

Roman world, the broad outlines of Atrebatic politics can be reconstructed." Commius' last coins were struck in 20 BC. "Tincommius ruled the territory of his father and maintained his inherited anti-Roman position until 16 BC when he abandoned the old coin design and introduced a Romanised version based on a type issued by Augustus between 15 and 12 BC."[155] By 15 BC Cassivellaunus' kingdom passed into the hands of Tasciovanus. His coinage is widespread there, in neighbouring kingdoms, and in Trinovanten lands concurrently with those of their ruler, Addedomarus, proof of their coming under the control of his overlordship. Addedomarus' coins dried up while those of Tasciovanus prospered. His father, Cassivellaunus, had expelled the Trinovanten king and annexed his territory, but was ousted by Caesar who installed Mandubratius, son of the expelled king. Tasciovanus was succeeded by the most famous king in popular folk memory, Cunobelinus.

Coins of Dumnovellaunus, son of Mandubratius who was installed as king by Caesar,[156] appeared in Trinovanten lands in Essex after he supplanted Addedomarus. As the Trinovanten kingdom fell again to the Catuvellauni under Cunobelinus, Dumnovellaunus and followers fled S to Kent. His new coinage appeared there E of the Medway where he was prominent around the turn of BC/AD. His Essex and Kent coins are of two distinct series. Coins of his Essex series have been found in Kent while none of his Kent issues have been found in Essex - going some way to corroborate the fact of his expulsion from his Trinovanten throne by Cunobelinus before being expelled by him from Britain with Tincommius. Dumnovellaunus' coinage dried up simultaneously with that of Tincommius as Cunobelinus overran their lands. Dumno and Tincommius fled to Rome for help. Cunobelinus' coins are sufficiently common in North Kent to suggest that he seized control of that part of Kent east of Medway and installed his son, Adminius, while his brother, Epaticus, was given control of the northern part of Tincommius' Atrebaten kingdom.[157] To seek aid against the Catuvellauni and impress his 'pro-Roman leaning', Tincommius replaced his coin design with one based on that issued by Emperor Augustus in 15-12 BC. In his biographical account of his reign, *Res Gestae,* Augustus noted that 2 exiled British kings, Tincommius and Dumnovellaunus, sought his aid to be restored to their thrones usurped by the Catuvellauni.[158] None was given. Both exited the British scene. "In 14 AD a monument set up at a temple to Augustus in Ancyra (Galatia, Turkey) records the names of two British kings who came to him as suppliants."[159] Peter Salway suggests that the imperial reception of the 2 British kings coincided with Augustus' disastrous attempt to bring the Germans under Roman rule.[160] The conquest of Britain, including aid to Tincommius and Dumno despite their pro-Roman stance had no place in the plan. After Augustus' death in 14 AD this was treated by Tiberius as a sacred trust.[161]

Eppillus replaced Tincommius with his pro-Roman tactic of using the title *'rex'* (king) on his coins. The Catuvellaunian overkingship expanded into his shrinking kingdom. It annexed the central Atrebaten capital, Calleva, where Tincommios and Eppillus struck their coins. Numismatic evidence reflecting Tincommius' switch from an anti- to a pro-Roman stance

[155] Op. cit. p.52
[156] Peter Berresford Ellis, Op. cit. p. 192.
[157] Keith Branigan, 'The Catuvellauni'p 9; Allen in *Britannia, 1976, vii, 96-100;* Frere 1978, 61; Webster 1980, 67: Adminius and Epaticus brought about the destruction of Cunobelinus' expansive kingdom by Rome's legions.
[158] Peter Salway, 'Roman Britain', p. 47; *Res Gestae xxxii.*
[159] Peter Berresford Ellis, 'The Celtic Empire' p. 106, 194; *Res Gestae, xxxii*
[160] Rome made Varus Governor of Germany. A German Cherusken leader, Arminius, set out to liberate Germany. In 9 AD Varus led 3 Roman legions through Teutoburger Forest. He was attacked by Arminius. Heavy rain turned pathways into treacherous quagmires. Light-armed Germans raced swift-foot as heavy-laden Romans were easy prey on the soggy, slippery ground. The Roman army was wiped out. Varus and his officers committed suicide. Rome's will to expand against the Germans wilted. Augustus' policy was reversed. Unlimited expansion was replaced by a decision to consolidate the empire within the boundaries as they existed after that defeat.
[161] Peter Salway, 'Roman Britain', p.52

marks his desperation to obtain Roman aid against the Catuvellauni. "Under Tasciovanus the Catuvellauni consolidated their position north and south of the Thames, driving the distribution of Tincommius' coins well back within the area occupied by the British Q coins, which marked the extent of the kingdom of Commius around 50-20BC."[162] Tincommius' about-face to a pro-Roman stance was eclipsed by the Catuvellaunian adoption of a pro-Roman stance too. "In the Catuvellaunian heartland, the move from Wheathamstead to Verulamium must have taken place about this time shortly after the coins of Tasciovanus acquire a Romanizing aspect. They are also found bearing the mint-mark 'VER', providing further confirmation of the change of tribal capital. Early in the 1st century AD under Cunobelinus, the Catuvellaunian capital was moved again, this time to the coast at Camulodunum (Colchester, the Belgic Trinovanten Capital) in response to the need for a major port on the E coast to handle the increased volume of foreign trade. A policy of territorial expansion was pursued by Tasciovanus, whose coins appear in increased numbers beyond the Ouse, in the upper Thames basin and S of the Thames."[163]

After Tasciovanus' died in AD 5, "Catuvellaunian aggression was directed more particularly under Cunobelinus towards the Atrebates." London grew to prominence as a seaport. The move of the Catuvellaunian capital from Wheathampstead under Tasciovanus, and the further move to Camulodunum under Cunobelinus mark stages in the expansion of the Catuvellaunian overkingship N of the Thames, just as the retreat of the Atrebaten capital from Caleva (Silchester) S to Venta (Winchester) and S again to Chichester mark the extension of its over-kingship into Belgic areas S of the Thames. It resulted in the defection of 2 kings, Tincommius and Dumnovellaunus, to Rome seeking aid to regain lost lands. Failing in this, bereft of all hope for their British kingdoms, Tincommius and Dumno led their followers to Ireland. The Dumnann of Connacht's Belgic oppidum may be Dumno's followers. Tincommius succeeding Commius, expanded his kingdom N along Connacht's coast with Dumnann aid.[164] Epillus and Iovar ruled Tincommius and Dumno's British kingdoms. Epillus issued coins at Calleva, styling himself *'REX'* in Roman lettering emphasizing his pro-Roman stance, hoping Rome might notice. Ousted from Calleva, he left his kingdom to his brother, Verica. Territories annexed by Cunobelinus were ruled by client kings allied to the Catuvellauni, indicated by the coins of Epaticcus, across the Middle Thames, and of Andoco in the SE Midlands"[165]

A close relationship between Commius' kingdom in SE England and the Fir Belg kingdoms in W Ireland is seen in the elusive manoeuvres of Epillus, Commius' grandson, puzzling commentators. Epillus, who succeeded Tincommius as king of the Atrebates for a time, suddenly became prominent in Kent in AD 1 in tandem with its king, Iuvar/Umhor, his son or brother as British authors reckon. Iuvar was one of 4 kings of the Canti tribes. In this elusive manoeuvre, Epillus is espied in the act of organizing a wave of emigration to Ireland in face of all-out Catuvellaunian aggression? Soon thereafter he, Iuvar and 2 other Canti kings disappeared from the Romano/British scene and records,[166] never to return. In Irish legendary history in the time of Eochail (O. Celtic 'Epill') Airemh (Aithrebh=of the Atrebates) a certain Umhor (Iuvor) and his sons, the Mac Umhoir, became involved in the Connacht Fir Belg expansion. In Caesar's day 4 kings of the Canti tribes ruled concurrently. Only one remained as Cunobelinus over-ran their territories. The Canti were in manners and customs akin to the other Belgic tribes.[167] Rath Iuvor (Ivor/Umhor) is on the Connacht Mayo

[162] D.W. Harding, *'The Iron Age in Lowland Britain'*, p. 214.
[163] Ibid, p. 214
[164] The Partrige in SW Mayo and NW Galway claimed direct descent from Sengann (Tincommius) into historic times. Cf.Paul Walsh, in 'Journal of the Galway Archaeol. & Hist. Society', Vol.xix, Nos 1 & 2, 1940, p. 12
[165] D.W. Harding, 'The Iron Age in Lowland Britain', p.214 - 215
[166] Peter Salway, 'Roman Britain', p.56
[167] D.W. Harding, 'The Iron Age in Lowland Britain', p. 224.

coast. Mod mac Umhor, Aengus Mac Umhor and other sons of Umhor had their stongforts along this coast. The Mac Umhoir may have been descendants of this Iuvor (Umhor). Commius' (Gann's) descendants, led by Dela, were involved in the more extensive Belgic invasion of Connacht.

In early manuscript material Queen Medb's kingdom, Ól nÉgmacht, is also called *Coiced Gann* and *Coiced Sengann,* the province of Gann and Sengann. Galway/Mayo townlands known as Ganty (*Na gCanti*), Rath Morissy (*Morasci, Marasaci*) and buffer states of Mac Umhoire, Manapi (*Managh*), Dumnoni and Morini (*Mac Morna*) stood along the W and NW flanks of Dela's Connacht oppidum, as did the Partrige who claimed descent from Sengann well into historic times.[168] These kingdoms grew as their British counterparts declined. Epillus was succeeded by Verica, his brother, among the Atrebates. Iuvar (Umhor), was brother/son of Epillus and father of the leaders of the extended Fir Belg invasion led by Oengus Mac Umhor (Iuvor). The Mac Umhoir were descendants of Genann (Gann).[169] The N extension of the Fir Belg invasion of Ireland occurred when Epillus (Eochail) became Overking of the Fir Belg a generation before Queen Medb's time. Eochail Athrebh and Eochaid Dala are discerned apart by their cognomens. In Irish tradition Eochaid Dala, greatgrandson of Dela, was accepted by Medb as king of Connacht on condition that she would be his Queen. Epillus organized an exodus of Belgic peoples to Ireland which materialized in the invasion of the people of Iovar (Umhor) under Oengus mac Umhor, 'grandson' of Gann (Commius). This extended the invasions led by Gann and Dela in W Ireland, consolidating the Fir Belg expansion further N into Connacht. This much is implicit in Irish tradition, despite the original story being distorted in favour of the Tara Myth.

Verica succeeded Epillus as king of the British Atrebatic kingdom. In 42 AD Verica fled to Rome to solicit the Emperor's support against the Catuvellauni. Ferach (Verica) Mhor, alias Eochaid Fedlech, 'ideal king' of the Irish Fir Belg, was brother of Eochaidh (Epillus) Athrebh (Airemh) in Irish tradition. As they vanished from the BritoRoman records and geo-political scene, these SE British kings, Commius (Gann), Tincommius (Sengann), Epillus (Eochaill Athrebh of the Atrebates), Iuvar (Umhor), and Verica (Ferach), were involved in a folk-movement of Belgic tribes to W Ireland. The sheer coincidence of the affinity of these names descended from Commius (Gann) in their Romano/British (Latin) and O-Irish forms and contexts is far too great to be rejected as conjecture. The similarity is so evident that the burden of proof to the contrary lies with those who would discard any equation between the family of the British Commius and that of the Irish Gann.

---

[168] Paul Walsh, in 'Journal of the Galway Archae. & Histor. Society', Vol xix, No. 1 & 2, 1940, p. 12
[169] Gen. Tracts 88.

Figure 5: Commius became one of Caesar's most bitter and worrisome enemies and devoted more time than anyone else to bring his gruesome career to an end.

British Celts, ordered off land they once farmed, faced starvation and had nothing to loose by rebellion

Courtesy Ian Andrews in 'Boudica Against Rome', p. 19-20

Chariots and arms were all confiscated including the decorated weapons of the aristocrats.

Figure 6: Retired and pensioned Roman soldiers tricked British Celts into selling their farms. Those who refused to sell were ordered off their lands (top), had their homes ripped apart and their daughters raped. They were forced to serve as slaves or die of starvation, adding insult to injury. Nobles and peasants alike were forced to hand over their arms, including decorated weapons and chariots (bottom). Anger boiled over. Such people had little to loose by rebellion.

Chaos ensued in the Belgic states S of the Thames due to incessant Catuvellaunian expansion.[170] As the Roman invasion loomed, a quarrel broke out at the court of Cunobelinus between his pro- and anti-Roman sons. Adminius, the younger son, successor of Dumnovellaunus whom he expelled from Kent, led the pro-Roman faction, swayed by the Empire's wealth and power, believing it in their best interests to side with Rome. Caratacus and Togodumnus, the elder sons, led the anti-Roman party. Adminius posed such a threat that by 40 AD Cunobelinus banished him from Britain. "He went to Emperor Gaius Caligula then campaigning against the Germans at Mainz. He broke off his campaign and marched his legions to the coast opposite Britain."[171] Mad Caligula ordered them to slash the waves, claiming great victory, and gather seashells as spoils of war. Adminius was joined by Verica (Bericus, in Cassius Dio's record). "Verica fled to the Emperor to solicit support"[172] to restore his kingdom. He received none.

Numerous gold and silver coin hoards found buried in the territory of the Belgic Atrebates are a poignant reminder of the turbulent times. They contained late issues of Verica, indicating they were deposited towards the middle of the 1st century AD, in the troubled years of AD 40-43 when the aggressiveness of the sons of Cunobelinus, the flight of Adminius and Verica to the Emperor and the Roman invasion caused considerable upheaval and unrest. "Matters came to a head in AD 40 when rumours reached Britain of a threatened Roman invasion. The situation occasioned considerable internal conflict between pro- and anti-Roman tribes. To make matters worse, Cunobelinus, the Catuvellaunian king died. He was replaced by his 2 sons, Togodumnus and Caratacus, who embarked on an all-out expansionist policy"[173] against the Atrebates. The skies over the Belgic tribes of SE England caved in. There was no place for Verica in Britain.[174] *Finem respice!* Ireland welcomed him with open arms.

By 25 AD a Catuvellaunian ruler, Epaticus, Cunobelinus' brother, was minting coins from the old Atrebaten capital of Calleva. Catuvellaunian coins later dominate the area as far S as the River Kennet. Epaticus conspired with the Romans in preparing the ground for their conquest of Britain. Claudius' set out to conquer Britain 'to end hostile Belgic supremacy in SE England and stem Belgic support to their kinsmen on the Continent' which still endangered stability there. As a reward for facilitating the conquest, Epaticus was given support to bring Winchester (Venta) Belgic oppidum and the N of the old Atrebaten kingdom under his control. The Belgic population of SE England shrunk dramatically. A Belgic folk-movement to Ireland took place.[175] "Britons threatened vengeance because the Senate refused to extradite certain deserters who had landed in Gaul during Cagilua's reign." Ellis noted "this can only be a reference to Adminius and Bericus (Verica)." The arrival of these royal fugitives provided Rome with the diplomatic excuse for the long delayed invasion.

CLAUDIAN INVASION OF BRITAIN: Fall of Celtic Britain/Rise of Celtic Ireland
Claudius ordered the invasion of Britain in 43 AD. Aulus Plautius was commander of 4 legions and several auxiliary regiments, including Batavi and Cannan Fated. The invasion force was 50,000 men. There is no firsthand account of this invasion. The main landing place was at the fortified site of Rutupiae (Rootoupiaci in Ptolemy), Richborough.

---

[170] The only safe haven for pressurized Belgae in the menacingly trying times from AD 1 to the Claudian invasion was Ireland where sections of their peoples had already taken refuge under Gann, Sengann and Dela.
[171] Peter Berresford Ellis, 'The Celtic Empire', 195
[172] 'The Regni' by Barry Cunliffe, p.18.
[173] Barry Cunliffe, 'The Regni', p.17-18
[174] Barry Cunliffe, 'The Regni', p.16. Substantial areas of Atrebatic territory were lost during Verica's reign.
[175] Gaius Suetonius, the source for the Claudian invasion, gave that as the reason for the invasion. British Belgic loss was Irish Fir Belg gain. Fir Belg gain was decidedly at the expense of the pre-Celtic Cruthin tribes of Ireland.

Simultaneous landings occurred at Dubris (Dover) and Lemane (Lympne) to confuse and outflank the British Celts. All landings were unopposed. The Belgae welcomed the Romans. When they reached the Medway, Caratacus was encamped on the opposite bank, thinking the Romans could not cross without the bridge he had destroyed. That night Plautius sent the Batavi, trained to swim in full armor, across. Instead of attacking Caratacus' men they wounded all his chariot horses. Celtic cavalrymen were unable to save themselves.

Vespasian, future Emperor, crossed further down river to outflank the Celts. Caratacus retired across the Thames. The Batavi swam across fully armed. The legions found bridge-crossings and mowed down the Celts from all sides. The Romans suffered casualties when they pursued Caratacus' army into Lea Marshes W of Tilbury. There Caratacus' brother, Togodumnus, was slain. Caratacus withdrew into his fortified Camulodunum. The legions surrounded its massive fortifications and laid siege. As agreed, with victory in sight, the Emperor was summoned. He sailed from Ostia to Massalia, then went by land to the coast opposite Britain and sailed across. With Claudius in command the assault began. Caratacus' forces took their stand outside the fortifications. Consternation at the sight of Claudius' elephant detachment turned the tide of battle against the Celts. Claudius entered Camulodunum in triumph. While receiving submission of local chieftains, he offered to make Caratacus a client king under Roman suzerainty. "But Caratacus fled west stirring up Celtic tribes against Rome. Camulodunum was made capital of the new Roman province. Legions were dispatched to Verulamium (St Albans) near Wheathamstead and a fortress built there."[176] A bridge was built over the Thames. Soon the town of Londinium (London) flourished. It was better sited than Camulodunum (Colchester).

Rome reinstated Adminius as a client king over the Catuvellauni, under Roman suzerainty, to replace his brothers Caratacus and Togodumnus. Epaticus, Cunobelinus' brother, provided food, logistics, safe passage and vital information which facilitated the invasion. He was not only confirmed in his position but rewarded with the wherewithal to extend his Catuvellaunian dominion over almost the entire Belgic territory S of the Thames from his base at Calleva. Roman collaboration with Epaticus led to the alienation of Verica who fled in despair, disappearing without trace from Roman records. The Romans had betrayed his trust. All hope was gone for his Atrebaten kingdom. His fate thereafter is unrecorded. He never appears again on the British scene. Rome put Cogidumnus in his place. Where did he go? The only plausible answer is that he joined his kinsmen in Ireland. There are a number of pointers in this direction. First, the buried coin hoards containing the late coins of Verica were buried at the time of his flight. That they were never recovered by him indicates that he fled in haste and never returned to recover his many buried coin hoards. He went elsewhere. Where could he have gone if not to Ireland which had become the Belgic overkingdom, the only safe haven for the Belgae unless they were prepared to face the twin ruins of Catuvellaunian and Roman conquest.

Secondly and significantly, the archaeology of the crucial years between the threat of Roman invasion by Gaius and its actuation under Claudius 3 years later, offers a very suggestive impression of the final political fall-out. Between the rivers Moen and Ouse, at the heart of the remnant of the Belgic Atrebatic kingdom on the SE coast, there is no trace of any defensive activity to meet the imminent Roman invasion or to defend itself against Catuvellaunian aggression. This is in conspicuous contrast to the feverish activity all around it. "West of the Moen and east of the Ouse there are indisputable signs of redefence. At Cadburn the ditch was redug and the rampart heightened. The same happened at Danebury, while at Boscombe Down West a new defensive enclosure was constructed, and at Bury Hill

---

[176] Peter Berresford Ellis, Op. Cit. p. 199-200.

near Andover the hill-fort was given multivalate defences."[177] How does one interpret these contrasting phenomena? Is it not the clearest sign that the dejected Verica fled Britain and went to join his kinsmen in W Ireland where he emerged as the Irish Fir Belg Overking, as told in Irish legendary history.

Barry Cunliffe offers as his interpretation that "the inescapable conclusion must be that, west of the Moen or Itchen, Verica's territories realigned themselves with their anti-Roman neighbours, the Dubunni and Durotriges, while the small block of Downland east of the Ouse joined the anti-Roman tribes of Kent. Thus, all that was left was a much shrunken area centered on the capital. Surrounded by enemies and with the old king gone, the future must have looked decidedly uncertain."[178] 'With the old king gone'! 'Where? A more plausible interpretation is that Verica and his people did not prepare to defend themselves against Roman or Catuvellaunian invasion but decided to pull out en masse and head for Ireland! Small segments of the Belgae and other tribes left behind realigned under pro-Roman Cogidumnus and his Regni.

More significant still, the 'shrunken kingdom' centered on Chichester/Selsey oppidum was given an entirely new name, 'Regni'! What is its significance? Had the old king remained with the Emperor he would have returned with him at the time of the conquest to be restored to his throne. Had he died, one of his descendants would have succeeded him. There is no further mention of Verica or his descendants in Roman records. Instead, the numerous coin hoards buried in an emergency in troubled times were never recovered. That no new defensive measures were taken indicates that the Irish option was so tempting that the remnant of his British kingdom hardly seemed worth defending in a worsening situation. Disgusted by Rome's support of his enemy, Epaticus, Verica took the Irish option. Had he remained he would have been exterminated. Along the W and NW outer wards of the Turoe/Knocknadala oppidum in the west of Ireland, at whose centre stood Rath Ferach Mhor (Verica/Ferach's fort), there are clear traces in river and place names of the Atrebates, Canti (*na gCanti* townlands) and Dumnann. Did these not come to Ireland together with Verica and Dumnovellaunus then? If not then, when?

Epaticus later turned against Rome due to personal grievances. Hence he lost the territories he had earlier conquered. These reverted to Atrebaten control. The remnant of the Atrebaten kingdom latterly ruled by Verica from a capital in the Chichester-Selsey region (Roman Noviomagus), was reconstituted under a new client king, a pro-Roman Atrebaten, Cogidumnus, with no connection to Verica's family, under Roman suzerainty, as the kingdom of the Regni. Although Cogidumnus was Atrebaten and his capital the Chichester/Selsey capital of Verica's former Atrebaten kingdom, the loss of domination by the Atrebates over formerly subject peoples due to decimation by emigration would explain the reason for the new name, Regni, of the erstwhile Belgic Atrebaten kingdom. Had Verica died his people were unlikely to change the name. The new name indicates a newly constituted people filling the void left by Verica's people. The kingdom of the Regni was the creation of the Claudian administration as a separate entity from the newly liberated Atrebatan kingdom further north. The new N Atrebaten kingdom emerged under Roman administration following the Claudian invasion, well north of the coast on former Atrebatic lands previously overrun by the Catuvellaunian, and, significantly, not from the 'shrunken Atrebaten kingdom' of Verica. Other Belgic lands too were freed from Catuvellaunian control through Roman intervention after the conquest. Verica's Atrebaten kingdom vanished. Cogidumnus, who facilitated the Claudian conquest of the Catuvellauni, proclaimed his pro-Roman stance and renamed himself Tiberius Claudius Cogidumnus, kowtowing to the Emperor. He was

---

[177] Barry Cunliffe, 'The Regni', p. 19.
[178] Op. cit, p. 19

rewarded with the Roman title *'rex et legatus Augusti'* and the wherewithal to live a luxurious lifestyle at his pompous royal villa at Fishbourne.

Verica refused to sink to this level of servile deference. He exited the British scene on the eve of the Roman conquest after ruling the Atrebatic kingdom for 40 years. He re-emerged in Ireland as Ferach Mhor (Celtic form of Verica), *alias* Eochaid Ferach (Fedlech), often confused with his brother Eochaid Aireamh - in British records Epillus (*Eochail*) and Verica (*Ferach*) were brothers. Irish tradition tells that Eochaid Fedlech (Ferach Mor) set himself up on Cnoc Temhro as Rí Temhro, overking of the Erainn (Fir Belg tribes). The archaeological site known as Rath Ferach Mhor on Turoe Hill in Galway in the W of Ireland, in front of which stood the celebrated Turoe ceremonial stone, was excavated out of existence in 1938. Was this not the throne of Verica, king of the Atrebates of SE Britain, who, together with his kingdom, disappeared 'without trace' off Roman records and off the mid-first century AD geo-political map of Britain? The original Atrebaten over-kingdom was divided into 3 Roman administrative districts, Regni, Belgae and Atrebates.

Ferach Mhor is "ideal king of the Fir Belg" in Irish tradition. Legendary history tells that he set up his daughter, Medb, as Queen of Connacht at Rath Cruacha. Irish pseudo-history deliberately substituted this Rath Cruacha of Galway with Rath Croghan of Roscommon. In Chapter Two it will be shown that Cnoc Temhro and Rath Cruacha were at the core of a Belgic oppidum at the centre of Co. Galway, surrounded by one of the most extensive Belgic defensive systems ever constructed, stretching well into neighbouring counties. Ferach Mhor made strategic alliances with the Belgae of Munster and Cruthin of Ulster by marrying off his daughters to their princes. Fir Belg kingdoms consolidated in an Over-kingship under Ferach at Cnoc Temhro (Ptolemy's *Regia E Tera* in Galway), building their defensive system against the day Rome might turn her greedy eyes on Ireland.

Claudius returned to Rome. Plautius completed the conquest. He sent Vespasian and Sabinus through Sussex and Hampshire. The future Emperor captured 20 fortresses and the Isle of Wight (Vectis). Further west overlooking the Frome River was one of Britain's most imposing hill-forts, Maiden Castle (*Maigh dun*), the mile-long hillfort of the Durotriges. It had sevenfold ramparts rising 100 feet high to awe any enemy. The Durotriges assembled there. High on the ramparts they watched Vespasian assess the situation. This was a setting in which Romans revelled in defeating Continental Celts. The W entrance was too formidable. Vespasian led his legions to the less formidable East gate. His artillery opened fire. The defenders, unused to *ballista* which shot arrows over amazingly long ranges, and *catapultae* which threw large stones considerable distances, were mown down in the first barrage. As they withdrew in consternation at the capacity of Roman weapons, "houses outside the E gate were set on fire by legionaries who, under cover of smoke and a barrage of arrows climbed each rampart rather than force entrance through the gates. By nightfall Britain's strongest hill-fort had fallen."[179] The remnants were rounded up in 70 AD in Dorchester (*Duro ceastor* military township).

The fugitive Caratacus, spurred on by the Druids of Anglesey who fled with him from Camulodunum, stirred up the fighting in the West of Britain.[180] Vespasian's II Augusta Legion reached Isca Silurum supporting Caratacus, on the river Isca in SE Wales and

---

[179] Peter Berresford Ellis, 'The Celtic Empire' p. 201: The Romans made a savage massacre of men, women and children. Archaeologists have uncovered "evidence of merciless killing, shown in the way a woman was buried, her arms pinioned behind her, her skull smashed by death-dealing blows. The pall of death overhung the silenced landscape. News of the butchery sent shivers up the spine of Britain, electrifying all Celtic tribes

180 Graham Webster, 'Rome Against Caratacus', p. 20: With their help Caratacus established himself as leader of the Welsh tribes and roused them against Rome. He carried out attacks deep into Roman-held territory to link with the anti-Roman Durotriges and Dubunni. Tacitus telescopes the events of several years into a few short sentences.

brought it forcibly to heel. It was renamed Caerleon (legion town) from the legion based there. This forced Caratacus to move to the central Welsh Mountains where he established himself in a strong political and military position with forward posts across the English border. His name is preserved in several military posts such as Caradoc (*Caer Caradoc,* Caratacus' fortress) in Herefordshire. "He had the support of the Ordovices, Deceangli, Demetae, Cornovi and Silures."[181] The Legions reached Chester (Deva on the Dee, Celtic *Dur Diu)* in NE Wales, and Lincoln by 47 AD.

In Autumn Governor Scapula, arrived. He went with troops to bring Caratacus to bay. On Scapula's arrival Caratacus went on the offensive. Scapula counter-attacked with a punitive raid on the Deceangli (Clwyd) in N Wales whence he believed Carataus was conducting his offensive. A series of uprisings began among tribes across SE Britain whom the Romans considered 'pacified'. They ordered the forced disarmament of Celtic tribes, searching homesteads until no weapons remained. This annoyed the natives. When war chariots were confiscated, furious nobles rose in revolt. The Iceni of E Anglia rose first. Their king, Prasutagus, was angered by this affront to his integrity, having sworn fidelity to Claudius.[182] He rued his submission to the Emperor. The Dobunni and Silures then revolted. Scapula set up a military garrison at Glevum (Gloucester) to keep the situation under control. The largest tribe in Britain, the Brigantes, stretching across Britain from the Mersey to Humber, rose in support of their fellow Celts. The Romans were forced into a truce with the Briganten Queen, Cartimandua.

Scapula's ex-soldiers at Camulodunum were given the lands of farmers forced off their home-steads. Some falsely accused farmers of being troublemakers to confiscate their lands, adding insult to injury. Such farmers were left to starve. Callous cruelty bred hatred of the Romans (Figure 6). "The ferocity of the inhabitants was intensified by their belief in Caratacus' prowess, whose victories made him pre-eminent among British chieftains," wrote Tacitus. Roman Legions converged on him. An all-out battle was inevitable. Near the English/Welsh border he met the Romans and roared: "Fellow warriors, remember your heroic ancestors who chased Caesar from Britain."[183] The Roman battlecry was "All things give way before valour." The Celts were pushed back "having neither breastplates nor helmets, unable to maintain the conflict." Rome won this 50 AD battle. Celtic tribes melted into the woods handing Scapula an empty victory. Caratacus fled to the Brigantes to continue the struggle. Queen Cartimandua, balancing a betrayal of the law of Celtic hospitality against her truce with Rome which impinged on the peace of her people, she handed him over to the Romans to grace Claudius' triumph. "Scapula died from an illness intensified by sheer exhaustion and failure."[184]

In 54 AD Nero became Emperor. His tutor, the 'philosopher' Seneca, sought ways to be wealthier by pouring money into the Provinces to obtain high interest. He loaned money to the Iceni and Trinovantes for this purpose. Claudius rewarded Cogidumnus with money gifts. They thought Seneca's money were gifts too. Little did they realize that his loans were to be repaid with exorbitant interest, by force if need be. Nero decided to conquer all Britain. The money to bankroll the war would be raised from conquered Celts. Nero sent Catus Decianus as Procurator to raise this money by heavy taxes. For having been recommended for this task by Seneca, he was to call in Seneca's loans with huge interest. Behaving like a bandit, he became the most hated Roman. In AD 58 Suetonius Paulinus,

---

[181] Peter Berresford Ellis, Op. Cit. p. 202.

[182] Peter Berresford Ellis, Op. Cit. p.202.

[183] The Romans were awed at the spirit which animated Celtic warriors and by the lack of defence. Fighting was fierce. When he was handed to the Romans, what a shock it was for Caratacus! What a coded message to the Romans! It saved Cartimandua and her people from savage Roman treatment until Rome broke its treaty in 74 AD.

[184] Graham Webster, 'The Cornovi,' p. 27.

new governor of Britain, led his legions to Wales. Catus behaved as he pleased. "The Iceni king was Prasutagus, his wife Boudicea. They had two daughters. Seeing difficult times ahead as he died in AD 59, he left half his kingdom to Nero, hoping his wife and daughters could keep the other half. Catus declared the whole kingdom belonged to Nero and the money-gifts given by Claudius to the Iceni were loans that had to be repaid with interest at once. He set about enforcing orders. His robber-like officials with ex-soldier out for plunder pounced on the Iceni. Estates of the nobles were seized. They were treated like slaves. The poor lost what little they had. Queen Boudicea resisted. They flogged her. Her daughters were barbarously assaulted."[185] The real Barbarians had arrived in Britain!

Suetonius stormed the Druid's headquarters in Anglesey on the N Welsh coast.[186] "The druids were slain, their sacred altars smashed."[187] Celtic religion suffered its most devastating blow. Celtic gods were furious. Rebellion broke out all across Britain. With Suetonius 250 miles away, a furious horde burst from the Iceni forests seeking revenge. At their head was the multi-colour-tuniced, fiery-eyed Boudicea, gold-broach-fastened cloak over her shoulder, a gold torc round her neck and flowing red hair falling to her hips. Chosen by the Iceni, Trinovantes and Catuvellauni as leader of the rebellion,[188] she had nothing to lose, many wrongs to right (Figure 7). Cassius Dio claims she marshaled 120,000 warriors. Her eloquent battle oration fanned their frenzied fury: "Day of retribution has dawned! Fear not the barbarous Romans hiding behind helmet, breastplate and stone palisade, trembling in fear. Show them they are but hares and foxes trying to lord it over wolves and dogs. Dream the forbidden dream. Freedom! End of depravity, injustice and slavery! Victory or death this day of days." In unison they roared "Boudicea!" (Old Celtic for victory – Queen Victoria was thus named after her).

The mob surged forth burning Roman settlements through Trinovanten lands. Their numbers multiplied as they descended on the Roman Capital, Camulodunum. Thunderous uproar sent shivers through Roman residents who appealed for Catus' help. He sent just 200 men. Camulodunum seized up in panic. Rumour spread that the statue of Victory had fallen, its back to the enemy as if in flight. Roman author Tacitus described the horrific scene: "Delirious women chanted the destruction at hand, outlandish yells reverberated through the senate; the theatre re-echoed with blood-curling shrieks; at the mouth of the Thames a ghost settlement was in ruins. The sea was blood-red, shapes like human corpses left by the tide littered the beaches..."

Boudicea's massed warriors crashed through the defences. Terrified colonists took refuge in the temple, paralyzed by fear. Peeping behind the portals they saw the town on fire. The Celts gave no thought to plunder as they set shops with imported luxury goods on fire. "Imagine the thoughts of a veteran soldier who, knowing how he had ill-treated the natives, saw them charging down the ridge to the temple, with flames and smoke of the town as a backdrop. He could expect no mercy. Neither could any defender. For 2 days the colonists held off the mob. Then the natives broke in. They slew soldiers, colonists, women and

---

[185] Ian Andrews, 'Boudicea Against Rome', p. 22 - 23.

[186] Graham Webster, 'The Cornovi,' p. 33: "The Romans had come to appreciate the widespread influence of the Druids. This priestly hierarchy fled from their sacred groves near Camulodunum and took refuge in remote Anglesey (NW Wales). These priests with their connections to the British ruling houses fostered anti-Roman feelings. Resistance to Roman rule in Britain could only be crushed by the destruction of the Druids and their religious centre. The Druids called for all-out rebellion. Anglesey became the main target of the Roman thrust to the NW."

[187] Ian Andrews, Op. Cit. p. 23.

[188] Roman historian Tacitus in his 'History' and Dio Cassius' letters.

children; no one was left alive. Claudius' temple was pulled down and the statue of the Emperor smashed to smithereens."[189]

Petilius Cerealis, Commander of IXth Legion heard the startling news at Lincoln (Lindum). With legionaries and cavalry he headed S for Camulodunum. In guerilla attacks, the Celts cut his forces to shreds. Only Cerealis and his cavalry escaped, leaving thousands of legionaries dead. Queen Boudicea's marshalling art was tested in restraining her forces' premature jubilation. Nothing stood between them and the unwalled new towns of Lundinium (London), Verulamium (St Albans) and small Roman posts in SE England.

In London Catus Decianus shivered in his boots. Without evacuating women or children, he deserted his post, and, with a few wealthy friends, boarded a ship and fled to the Continent. Robbed of the glory of the conquest of the Druid's headquarters, Suetonius Paulinus sent orders to the IInd Legion in London to come out to meet his cavalry at a pre-arranged point. When he reached the place, the IInd Legion was not there.[190] He raced ahead with his cavalry to London despite the danger from rebel bands. He reached London without mishap. The situation was appalling. Catus had fled, leaving the Romans without food or logistics. There was no hope of holding the town against Boudicea's forces. If London fell, the Roman link with the Continent would be cut with no way to bring reinforcements and food supplies directly to the scene of action. Suetonius abandoned London although the people begged him not to go. Ablebodied men were allowed to join him; with Boudicea's rebels closing in he did not have time or men to organize a general evacuation. The elderly, women and children were left to their fate. Some escaped S to the pro-Roman Regni. Suetonius sped back to his marching legions, rejoining them in the Midlands.

Success went to the heads of Boudicea's rebels who felt they had achieved all they set out to do: the Capital of Camulodunum was freed, the hated temple of the spirit of Claudius destroyed, and Catus Decianus with his brood of vampires driven from Britain. They had wiped out the IXth Legion. London, "which had housed the hated procurator, full of traitors and money-lenders who came to swindle people"[191] lay open before them. Boudicea had difficulty controlling her forces drawn from various warring tribes. Hence the rebelion was to change course. The Roman-held towns of London and Verulamium were attacked by her forces, burned to the ground and their inhabitants slaughtered. Tacitus described the horrifying scenes as "gallows, fire and cross", which suggests the Celts tortured the colonists in typical Roman style. Within a few weeks the 3 largest towns in Britain were destroyed and 70,000 people killed. "This was the worst disaster to have befallen a civil population in the Roman Empire for a very long time."[192] The Romans were furious. They demonized Boudicea. Archaeology revealed subterranean layers of ash from Roman villas set alight in Colchester, St Albans and London, confirming the fury of her back-lash. What else could one expect from a Queen who had witnessed the wanton way her people had been treated, who herself had been scourged almost unconscious and her daughters gang-raped in her presence by barbarous Romans! As M. Mackie noted, her violent rebellion came only after extreme provocation. "She had trusted the Romans." It was only after their debauched behaviour "that she turned against them – as you would." [193]

---

[189] Ian Andrews, 'Boudicea Against Rome', p. 25.

[190] The II Legion's General was away from his post. It was left under Poenius Postumus who disobeyed the order to march, because he felt he should suppress local tribes rising in rebellion. Suetonius had no idea how large the rebel force was. Should he wait for the XIVth and XXth Legions from Wales to catch up with him or press on?

[191] Ian Andrews, 'Boudica Against Rome', p. 28: They failed to apprehend Suetonius as he raced to London, failed to trap him when there, and stop him as he retreated to rejoin his legions.

[192] Op. Cit. p. 29.

[193] Mary Mackie, author of 'The People of the Horse' (The Iceni – *Echni*). - Reuters

Photo insets of Queen Boudicea and her daughters (left and right) from 'The Celts' by Simon James.

Boudicea, Queen of the British Iceni, led the mighty rebellion against the Romans after she and her daughters were humiliated and brutally abused by barbarian Roman magistrates.

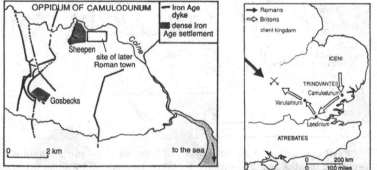

Figure 7: The political geography of the Belgic tribes of Britain at the time of the Claudian invasion (top map). The sprawling Trinovanten oppidum of Camulodunum (Colchester) taken over by Cunobelinus, King of the Catuvellauni (lower left). Map of the course of the Boudicea-led revolt of British Celts against the Romans (lower right).

Boudicea and contemporary Celtic Queens, Cartimandua and Medb, achieved considerable political status and often wielded more power than their husbands. Boudicea and Cartimandua played central roles in the drama of the Roman annexation of Britain.

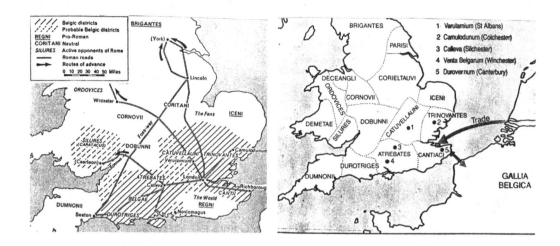

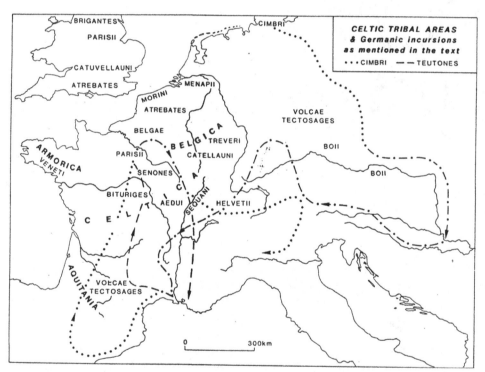

Figure 8: Belgic tribes caught in a pincer movement between Germanic incursions from the NE, (lower map from 'Celtic Migrations' by W.A. Hanna), and Roman invasion from the SE fled to SE England. They kept up a lively trade with Belgic Gaul from the main Atrebaten Chichester port (Noviomagus; top right, from 'Celtic Realms' by M. Dillon & N. Chadwick) in Commius' time. But as he and his people were forced to move to Ireland because of Catuvellaunian expansion and Roman invasion, trade with the Continent was transferred to the Catuvellaunian controlled ports of Camulodunum (Colchester) and London (top right: from 'The Celts' by Simon James).

Suetonius with 10,000 legionaries marched on Queen Boudicea's army which far outnumbered the Roman army. Celtic warriors were so sure of victory that they brought along entire families to share their glory. This slowed their freedom of movement. After the commanders of both armies had delivered battle orations, Suetonius gave the signal for battle. The Celts raced forward in a wild yelling charge towards the legionaries lined up in disciplined ordered blocks. The Romans balanced their javelins and at 30 yards range hurled them at the Celts whose shields went up to protect them. Spears stuck deep in the shields and, impossible to pull out, rendered these useless. Pushed forward by yelling comrades, the Celts threw away their now useless shields. Thus exposed to the second volley of javelins at shorter deadly range, transfixed Celts dropped like flies becoming a huge obstacle to their comrades behind. Celtic hordes pressed on stumbling over the dying. Yells mingled with the cling-clang of iron. Heavy spear thrusts occasionally penetrated the wall of Roman armor. Celts were dispatched by drilled Roman swordthrusts or brought down by deadly blows of Roman-shield bosses and trampled to death. In the din of battle only the disciplined close-set blocks of Romans showed signs of order. Suetonius saw his legions gain the upper hand. At the right moment they burst forward in wedge formation accompanied by victorious shouts. Swift darting swords forced the Celts back. Charging cavalry swept round them, pinning them together with extended lances. Boudicea's forces panicked, broke ranks and retreated. Hemmed in by their wagons and families to view 'certain victory', these became deadly obstacles. Cries of alarm! Galloping horses! Screaming Celts cornered and cut to pieces by Romans drunk with the glory of success, killing everything in sight, men, women, children and baggage animals. Shrieks of women! Roars of men! Horror of horrors! Massacre most foul. "Heaps of dead" (Tacitus' words). 80,000 corpses piled high. Earth soaked in blood! Utter shame! Woe! 'Sure Victory Day' turned into inglorious Dooms-Day for Celtic Britain by day's downfall.

"Fierce fiery warriors fought upon the clouds which drizzled blood upon the Capitol,
  The noise of battle hurtled in the air. Horses did neigh and dying men did groan.
  And ghosts did shriek and squeal about the streets."[194] That day the very sky did moan.

His loss of only 400 men gave Suetonius grim satisfaction. Calm under strain at the crucial moment won the Battle for Britain. Surrounded by fleeing Celts, Boudicea poisoned herself.[195] Cherished by feminists, an enigma to historians, Boudicea "has been turned into a meta-historical icon."[196] She disappeared from the records in the Dark Ages but was resurrected by the 16th century Queen Elizabeth 1. Keen to promote the concept of a noble warrior queen, she plucked her from historical obscurity.[197] Had Boudicea avoided open battle and adopted Commius' guerilla tactics, what a different Britain might have emerged. Iceni aristocrats and followers fled Britain from certain Roman revenge. This impinged on the early history of Britain and Ireland. Iceni buffer states on the fringes of the Fir Belg oppidum in W Ireland date presumably from this defeat. Iceni placenames such as Cloon Iceni, Dun Iceni, Sli Iceni, Kilconiceni (corruption of *Coill Clann Iceni)* and Coill Eceni (both Iceni forests) in the Fir Belg oppidum in Galway in W Ireland, adjoining the gCanti (the Canti from Kent), pinpoint their final destination. Vestiges of an ancient route there known as Sli Iceni corresponds to the ancient Icenifeld Way they left behind in England.

Despite this defeat, the rebellion was not over. All tribes refused to surrender for fear of Roman revenge. Suetonius received an extra 6,000 legionaries and 2 cavalry regiments of 1,000 men from Rome in that woeful Winter. Famine stalked the countryside as no crops or

---

[194] Shahespeare, 'Julius Caesar'. His wife Calpurnia's nightmare warned him to 'Beware the ides of March."
[195] Dio Cassius noted that Celtic Britain deeply mourned its charismatic Queen.
[196] Boudicea as described by folklorist Dr Juliette Wood.
[197] Dr Juliette Wood.

corn had been sown due to the rebellion. Multitudes died of starvation. Rome sent Classicianus as procurator to replace Catus Decianus. He made an alarming discovery: The harsh ultra force used by Suetonius to quell the rebellion was ruining Britain - if it continued there would be no people to tax. Classicianus confronted Suetonius, urging the people to hold out until a new governor came. Classicianus told Nero "There is no hope of ending the fighting until a governor is sent out."[198] Suetonius was recalled. Publius Petronius Turpilianus, sent to replace him, ended the war. After 2 years he returned to Rome to be awarded with a triumphal procession. Traders had fled. Wealth was destroyed by the rebellion and its suppression. Most Britons found it impossible to pay taxes. The greed of money lender Seneca and procurator Catus Decianus had been the main cause of the rebellion. Sea trade with Britain was reduced to a tricle. Hence Tacitus truthfully noted that Irish seaports were better known than those of Britain. Nero sent Trebillius Maximus as new governor in 63 AD. In his 6 years of governorship he restored peace across Britain. Too late! Britain was a corpse. Countless Celts were dead or had fled - to Ireland.

Nero was assassinated in the rebellion of 68 AD. Vaspasian, general in Britain during the Claudian invasion, became Emperor. He appointed Petilius Cerealis governor of Britain. He set out to conquer the Brigantes whose main Capital was York (Celtic *Ebaricum*). In 68 AD the Briganten Queen, Cartimandua, divorced her husband Venutius in favour of Vellocatus, her charioteer. Venutius and his anti-Roman faction overthrew her. Because of her truce with Rome, the new governor sent the legions N to restore her to her throne. Venutius escaped and later raised another insurrection against her. Again she appealed to the Romans. Again they sent the army to rescue her. By this time anti-Roman Venutius had become so popular with the Brigantes that the Romans could do no more than rescue Cartimandua and leave the Brigantes in the hands of Venutius. It was not until 74 AD that Venutius and the Brigantes were finally conquered by Rome. Briganten aristocrats and their followers fled from Ebaricum to their Ui Bairrche kinsmen in the SE of Ireland. This resulted in a westward expansion of the Irish Briganten kingdom across S Ireland from Tulach Ui mBairrche (Ballyragget, Co. Kilkenny) through the golden vale of Tipperary into E Limerick impinging on the expanding Fir Belg kingdoms of West Munster.

The Continental Batavi and Fotad Cannine (Cannan Fatad) were being treated as enslaved peoples. The Batavian leader Julius Civilis assembled the Batavi in a sacred grove for a religious meal to declare rebellion against Rome. In summer of 69 AD the Fotad Cannine launched the revolt by capturing a Roman camp. The Batavi, Manapi and Friesians joined them. German tribes E of the Rhine crossed to support them too. Roman camps on the Rhine were destroyed. Julius Civilis took over the whole lower Rhine as far as Castra Vetera. Vaspasian sent his vast army against him, forcing him to flee N of the Rhine pressuring the Fotad Cannine. Rome made peace with the Batavi. But the Fotad Cannine (Votadini to the Romans) who launched the revolt feared Rome's revenge. Their chiefs fled to SE Scotland.[199] Manapi septs N of the Rhine had moved W to the Dutch coastal strip in the lands of the Fotad Cannine (Cannane Fates). Between 50 and 12 BC these Fotads had come with the Batavi from beyond the Wezer River having quarreled with the Chatti. With Rome's sanction they overran Manapian and Morini lands. The Batavi settled between the Rhine and Waal in Holland, giving their name to the "Isle of the Batavi." The Fotad Canine settled W of them. Due to this pressure the Capital of the Morini, Castel Morinorum (Kasel today) changed hands and became Castel Manapiorum[200] (Figures 8 and 9). The Fotad Cannine who overran the W flank of the Manapi were now in danger of being overrun by

---

[198] Ian Andrews, 'Boudicea against Rome' p. 36.
[199] 'Oude Geschiedenis' translated from the Dutch by Ferdinand Vergeer;
[200] 'Oude Geschiedenis' translated from the Dutch by Ferdinand Vergeer; p. 22-27; 'Map Den Nederlanden in Den Romeinschen Tijd', Nederlands Archives.

the Friesians. The Fotads, Celticized by the Manapi whom they had earlier overrun on the Dutch coast, welcomed this Manapian incursion to withstand the Friesian pressure.

Manapian mariners held tenaciously to their ports up the Dutch coastline, surrendered by the Morini and Marasci. Lugdunum (Lyden) at the mouth of the Old Rhine was dedicated to the god Lug. Templum Nehellinia (ngEthelinn), a shrine at the Rhine/Meuse Delta river mouth, was dedicated to the sea goddess Ethelinn/Chethelenn.[201] The Morini and Marasci manned these ports before being pushed S by the Manapi, Cannine Fates and Friesians.[202] The Manapianized Fotads (evidenced by the form of the name, Mannau Gododin (*Mannagh-ngFhotad*) and Manapi disappeared off the Continental map fearing retaliation by Emperor Vespasian and mounting pressure from Germanic tribes. They re-emerged as the Mannau Goddodin (Mannagh 'ngFhotadin', a federated Fotad/Manapian kingdom) inland from a Manapian seaport in SE Scotland. Later, the MannauGoddodin joined Lughaid mac Con's invasion of W Ireland through Ath Clee Magh Rí (Clarenbridge, Co. Galway) where colonies of Manapian mariners established themselves in the Bally-na-Mannagh (Manapian) townlands on the headland facing Tawin island at Ath Cliath (Clee) Magh Rí. Manapian and Fotad buffer states stretching inland towards Loughrea through the Colla Mann (Magh Cola Manapian buffer states) manning the S flank of Lughaid Mac Con's stronghold. The Fotads (Votadini) of Magh Fot manned the N of Lughaid's kingdom.[203]

It is not surprising then to find sites of Lug, Cethelenn, Ethelinn, Manannan, Lir and other Manapi, Marasci, Morini and Fotad deities in their primary settlement areas in W Ireland. Dun Cethelenn (Dunkellin, dedicated to the sea goddess Cethelenn) stands on the tongue of land between the Dunkellin and Clarin rivermouths at the Ath Clee Magh Rí Iron Age seaport in Galway Bay. Cethelenn's temple stood at ngChethelennia/nEthelennia on the Dutch coast. She was guardian sea-goddess of sailors. Her daughter Ethlinn was consort of Fir Belg god Cian. She gave birth to Lug, god of arts and crafts, of Lugdunum (Lyden) of Holland and Lug[h] Bhru of Turoe and Athenry in Ireland. Lug was fostered by Manannan, Manapi sea-god whose Otherworld Abode was under the waters of Lough Corrib. The god Lir, father of Manannan, had his Otherworld abode under the waters of Loughrea Lake (*Lind Lir* in *Dindsenchas of Loch Riach*) in Galway at the head of a string of Manapian townlands. Lug Bru (Otherworld Abode of Lugh) and Sidh nEthelinn (Ethelinn; St. Ellens is a corruption of Sidh nEthelinn) are near Athenry some miles inland. These underline the enduring ethno-religious beliefs of the Belgae. The Manapi established settlements in many parts of Ireland, apart from the Wicklow coastal colony recorded on Ptolemy's map. The Belgic invasion of Ireland at the expense of the indigenous Cruthin must be seen against this background. Spearheaded from Turoe and Athenry, the Fir Belg expanded at their expense in centuries-long warfare between Ulster and Connacht recorded in Irish tradition. Just as

---

[201] Op Cit., translated by F. Vergeer, p. 22-27: Celtic seamen made votive offerings for safe passage before venturing out to sea or in thankfulness for safe return. It stood on the isle of North Bevesland (Colinsplat) off the Walgeren island coast near the Dutch town of Domburg. Walgeren stretched further west but was submerged by rising sea levels in the 4th century AD. In the 17th century it was visible when sea levels fell abnormally low. Foundations and votive stones were visible under water or were washed up on Domburg beach. In 1970/1971 archaeologists found 100 temple altar stones at Colinsplat on which were engraved the effigy of the goddess Nehelennia holding a basket of fruit, the sign of fertility and prosperity. Some bore the effigy of a ship's helm, showing one of her traits was the protection of seafarers.

[202] The Romans cut Fossa Corbulonis canal from Lugdunum (Lyden) at the silted-up mouth of the Old Rhine to Templum Nehellinia at the mouth of the new Rhine to avoid rough seas before reaching this point. Many of Rome's seamen were Celts and felt the need to offer sacrifice there before or after sea voyages.

[203] The so-called 'Fotad High Kings' never set foot in Tara. Magh Fot in Galway on the Turoe and Athenry oppida boundary was their sole settlement area in Ireland until driven south by Cormac Mac Art. They were later led into Munster by Corc (Gorgin) who served as overking of those vassal allies for a time before employing them in his conquest of Cashel of Munster where they survived into historic times as the Munster Uaithni.

"with Caesar's (*De Bello Gallico*) *Commentaries* prehistory begins decisively to give way to history"[204] so too, the above background begins to bring Ireland into the spotlight of history.

One may now go directly to Chapter Two. Those interested in differences between the Belgae and Catuvellauni and their defence systems will find the following pages relevant.

CHARACTERISTIC DIFFERENCES BETWEEN BELGAE AND CATUVELLAUNI

What lay behind the aggressive chauvinism of the Catuvellauni that led to the Belgic folk movement to Ireland? Cunobelinos was given the title *'Rex Britannia'*, 'King of Britain', by Rome, the only Celtic chief to enjoy this distinction. He tried to make it a reality at the expense of the Belgae. He expelled their rulers and brought their lands within his overkingship. Catuvellaunian aggressiveness went deeper. With their tradition of staunch chauvinism towards other Belgic tribes, the question arises as to what extent the Catuvellauni were Belgic in their immigrant phase. Cunobelinos' Catuvellauni overkingdom had a stong Belgic admixture, but what of the original 'Catuvelauni'? It is thought that the tribes north of the Thames, including the Catuvellauni, "were formed out of elements related to the Belgae that had come in at an earlier stage in the influx of Iron Age Continental people"[205] for whom the new Belgic defensive system was a foreign import. One must return to Caesar's weighty authority[206] and the archaeological remains on the ground..

The name Catuvellauni contains the plural *'catu'*, a group of tribes. Caesar did not refer to it. He spoke of Cassivellaunus' kingdom without naming it. "The inland region (*pars interior*) is inhabited by people proud of their native ancestry, by contrast with the maritime regions (*maritima pars*) occupied by tribes who migrated from Belgic Gaul." The archaeological evidence corroborates this. Clearly from the coins of Tasciovanos and Cunobelinos (Cassivellaunus' son and grandson) the Catuvellauni expanded over the Thames to make inroads into Atrebaten lands. The distribution of the earlier coins of the 'Catuvellauni' spread throughout SE England with no regard for the Thames boundary, showing they were masters of the entire region until the Belgae came and pushed them N of Thames. This was the situation when Caesar invaded. "But with Caesar's withdrawal, we see the aggressive independence of the Catuvlauni reasserting itself in the distribution of British LA coins (equated with Cassivellaunus). The same indignant patriotism was being registered by Cunobelinus in choosing the ear of corn emblem for his coins by contrast with the vine-leaf, symbol of continental Mediterranean wine adopted by the pro-Roman Verica, S of Thames."[207] Due to the increment of Continental Celts entering their territory, the dominant Cautvellauni expanded across the Thames south into the Belgic 'maritime' states.

BELGIC AND CATUVELLAUNIAN DEFENSIVE SYSTEMS

As a prelude to the central theme of Chapter 2, it is well to examine the Belgic and Catuvellaunian defensive systems. The Catuvellauni version is similar to, yet different from, the system of the Belgae S of the Thames in Commius' kingdom at Calleva and Chichester/Selsey complex, those in the lands of the Belgic Dubunni and in W Ireland.[208] The Catuvellauni adopted the Belgic system, like so much else that was essentially Belgic, from the Belgic Trinovantes. Before Commius' day a clear distinction could be traced between the Catuvellauni and Belgic tribes, reflected in the unique type of defence fortifcations employed by each.[209] They unified their systems into a unique, yet not identical,

---

[204] Peter Salway, 'Roman Britain', p. vi.

[205] Peter Salway, 'Roman Britain', p. 12

[206] Caesar, 'De Bello Gallico', 5, 11-14.

[207] D.W. Harding, Ibid, p.223-4

[208] Due to its resounding success in Caesar's advance against the Catuvellauni in 54 BC, Commius' military engineers wed any effective defensive features the Catuvellaunian system had over their own to the Belgic system.

[209] D.W. Harding, 'The Iron Age in Lowland Britain', p. 225.

system under Commius and the direction of Cassivellaunus. Sadly, there is not a fuller account of the Belgic defence system from Caesar. There are hints from his passage through their lands that the Belgae were using a similar type of defence system. Archaeological remains of the unique Belgic dyke defence systems in Britain and Ireland make the similarity, as well as the contrast, obvious.

Hawkes[210] claimed the distribution of Fecamp-type earthworks, common in the S of Belgic Gaul but limited in Britain to a few sites, is concentrated in the area S of the Thames occupied by the Belgae, who in the teeth of Roman and Germanic invasion, developed this system into the full-fledged defensive system. It was put in place by Commius in the area he ruled in SE England. Harding claims the Belgic defence system was modelled on the Catuvellaunian system. In comparing the Belgic Fecamp-type earthworks with the Catuvellaunian defensive system he wrote: "The Catuvellaunian method of defence, by contrast, was a network of low-lying dykes embracing a wide area incorporating natural features as part of its defensive system, as at Camulodunum."[211] This is a perfect description of the Belgic defence system on the Continent, in Britain and in Ireland. Camulodunum was the capital of the Belgic Trinovantes before it came under Catuvellaunian control. Hence, its defence system cannot be described as typically Catuvellaunian. Its unique type of defensive earthwork is Belgic, not Catuvellaunian. Harding refuted prehistorians who had taken the wealth of the Lexden tumulus, and its situation in the tribal capital of Camulodunun (of the Trinovantes until Cunobelinus subjugated it) as a clue to its equation with the tomb of Cunobelinus himself. "Attractive though this notion may have been, we must surely now recognize that the Lexden tumulus was erected several decades before the death of Cunobelinus around AD 40. If an equation with any historical figure is possible, Peacock's[212] suggestion of Addedomaros of the Trinovantes is the more plausible."[213] Nothing indicates that the Camulodunum system was erected by the Catuvellauni. It was strengthened by Cunobelinus, but had been erected by the Belgic Trinovantes. It is the classic Belgic defensive system.

Harding's examples of similar defensive earthworks, North Oxfordshire's Grim's Ditch and Bagendon in Dubunni territory, are, he claims, adoptions of the Catuvellaunian type of earth-work for these rather than allowing for a Belgic origin. "The form of the earthwork itself at Bagendon, not a hillfort in the earlier Iron Age manner, but a system of extensive dykes, was surely derived from the essentially Catuvellaunian form of oppidum-like Wheathampstead and Camulodunum".[214] He disagrees with those who have taken the Dubunni system, due to its similarity to that of the Belgae, as a measure of the Belgic origin of the Dubunni. The Dubunni were closely allied to the Atrebatic kingdom of Commius until Tincommius dropped his anti-Roman stance to seek Roman aid. The Dobunni rejected his pro-Roman policies and promoted a new commercial alliance with the Catuvellauni whilst preserving their Belgic defences. Celtic tribes switched allegiance when the party to which they allied lost out to another power which was in the ascendance. There were rifts between Atrebaten pro- and anti-Roman parties. The main sea trade was no longer through the Atrebaten port of Hengitsbury Head but through the new Catuvellaunian capital of Camulodunum. The Dubunni wished to avail of opportunities for foreign trade which alliance with the Catuvellauni would bring, as well as avoiding annexation by the latter. The Dobunni

[210] C.F.C. Hawkes, 'New thoughts on the Belgae', 'Antiquity', 42, 6-16
[211] D.W. Harding, Op. cit.., p.225
[212] Peacock, 'Roman amphorae in pre-Roman Britain', (1971) p.178-9.
[213] D.W. Harding, Op. Cit. p.123-4.
[214] Op. cit., p.222

were a "Belgic power" from their coinage.[215] Nothing indicates the Dubunni defence system (Grim's Ditch/Bagendon) was not of Belgic origin as was their coinage.

"The alliance against Caesar was scarcely sufficient to repair the underlying enmity between the Catuvellauni and Belgic tribes. Even during Caesar's campaigns of 55 and 54 BC there was a strong element of dissent which was liable to erupt into open conflict between the Catuvellauni and Trinovantes. The fundamental antipathy between the Catuvellauni and Belgae did not prevent the former from adopting higher material standards of living comparable to that of the Belgae."[216] They adopted the higher military defensive system from the Belgae, rather than vice versa! The Catuvellauni were not its originators.

Harding concluded: "Until they were driven inland by invading Belgic tribes at the end of the 2nd cent. BC the native population - who subsequently appear as the historical Catuvellauni - occupied a much wider territory which embraced much of the SE of England, territory which under Tasciovanus and Cunobelinus they attempted in some measure to recover. The Catuvellauni were descended from Continental immigrants, not from Belgic Gaul, but from the early La Tene culture of the Marne several centuries earlier. Their adoption of Belgic pottery, (higher living standards, the Belgic defensive system) and the innovating (Belgic) burial rite, need excite little surprise, since, for all their chauvinism, the Catuvellauni were not ultimately native" in the sense of 'from time immemorial'. They adopted the ways of the Belgae, rather than vice versa! If the Catuvellauni controlled the SE of Britain before the coming of the Belgae, then where were the archaeological remains of their 'Catuvellaunian type' of defence system S of the Thames? Only with the coming of the Belgae did this new defence system appear at Calleva, Chichester and Selsey, in the Belgic kingdoms S of the Thames, Bagendon and Grim's Ditch in the lands of the Dubunni, Camulodunum, capital of the Belgic Trinovantes, and at Wheathamstead N of the Thames, the capital of Cassivellaunus. There was not a trace of this unique defence system of extensive dykes S of the Thames until the Belgae erected it. The old hill-forts were slighted by the Belgae in favour of their own unique system. In the final analysis, the Catuvellaunian system adopted from the Belgae had much in common with the latter. Rampart dimensions distinguish them apart. The overall width of the Catuvellaunian version was approximately 120ft by 30ft high whilst that of the Belgae was a mere 60 ft wide by 20 ft high. Their tactical plan was similar. Hence, it will be called the Belgic defensive system here.

In addition to the Belgic dyke defence "the Belgae, not seldom regarded forests and swamps as the best protection...The same is true in Britain."[217] Filip lists a whole series of Celtic oppida extending in a belt from Czech Lands to Bayreuth in Bavaria and to the Main River in Germany (cradle of the Belgae) which have features akin to the later Belgic defensive system. They were extensive, utilized natural topographical defensive features such as forests, rivers and marshlands, and had inner and outer wards.[217] Filip gives examples of central European oppida with these features of the Belgic defensive system in common[218]

---

[215] E.M. Clifford, 'Bagendon: A Belgic Oppidum" (1961): Harding noted that "The coins of the Dubunni were based upon the distinctive Atrebatic staters which depicted a 3-tailed horse on the reverse, and in consequence it has been argued that the Dubunni were themselves an offshoot of S Belgic invaders, infiltrating into Worchestershire around 30-20 BC. That the overlords of the Dubunni were Belgic is corroborated by the strongly Belgic aspect of their culture as witnessed by Mrs Clifford's excavations at Bagendun.".

[216] Jan Filip, 'Celtic Civilization and its Heritage', 125.

[217] Instead of the later Belgic earthen rampart defence system these were surrounded by the 'Gallic wall' (*murus gallicus*) described by Caesar or the even older Halstatt method of vertical timbers let into the ground.

[218] Op. cit., p.126: Manching, oppidum of the Vindelici on the upper Danube in Bavaria, had fortifications over 7 miles long and 12 miles wide, enclosing an area of some 380 hectares. It had inner and outer wards. In 15 BC it was taken by the Romans and its Celtic name subsequently forgotten. At Kelheim on the N bank of the Danube, some 30 km northeast of Manching, the oppidum Alkimoennis recorded by Ptolemy was still larger, ... occupying

such as Hradiste nad Savisti near Zbraslav.[219] In the war with Rome, the Belgae realized the ineffectiveness of the conventional forms of earthwork, the 'box rampart' (*murus Gallicus*) surrounding a hill-fort, against the artillery and aparatus of the Roman army. They reassessed their entire defensive strategy. They undercut the box rampart of the Remi at Bibrax, showing its ineffectiveness even in intertribal warfare! The Belgae reacted to the introduction of the Roman siege-engine and improvised a response to render it obsolete. This is demonstrated by their development of the new earthwork with broad ditch and steep-sloping outer-face dump rampart.[220] This strategy was most effective. Caesar failed to capture a Fecamp-style capital of the Suessioni at Noviodunum in 57 BC despite the fact that it was garrisoned by a small force.[221] He attributed this to the breadth of the ditch and height of the rampart. Wheeler's sections across Fecamp defences and allied earthworks reveal that the waterlogged ditch was too broad to be spanned by timbers. Hence siege engines must be man-handed into the ditch before advancing to the rampart. The dump-rampart can not be set on fire or undermined, unlike the box rampart. The lack of a vertical face to the rampart rendered the siege-towers, with their protected inner stairway for scaling walls, obsolete.

The Belgae slighted early Iron Age hill-forts in S Britain and established fortified strongholds of linear dykes in low-lying positions. "The loss of a commanding hilltop situation is compensated for by the choice of a natural promontory formed by the course of a river, as in the case of Dyke Hills camp at Dorchester-on-Thames."[222] In their continental Lowlands, the Belgae had realized the advantages of incorporating additional defence features such as rivers, forest, marsh lands and lakes into a defensive network, since it provided opportunity for both ambush and escape in terrain unfamiliar to the enemy. The Rhine estuary provided unique opportunities in such natural defences where high ground was in scarce supply. The Morini and Menapi played hide and seek with the Romans with such tactics. Caesar admitted such tactics were employed against him with outstanding success by the British Belgae in his disastrous British campaign in 54 BC. After landing on the Kent coast, the VIIth Legion engaged the Belgae who withdrew into the forests where they had their stronghold well fortified by nature and man-made defences.[223] This is first class contemporary evidence, all too succinct, of the unique Belgic defensive system.

The British Belgae refined their defence system. Caesar recorded the guerilla tactics employed by them and their methods to defend the entrances to their strongholds. A narrow passageway led through forest where defenders hid. They felled trees to obstruct the enemy's advance, ideal for guerilla fighting. It represented a sea change in military defensive tactics They engaged the Romans in small bands in confined areas, instead of confronting them in pitched battle. Caesar noted that the enemy never fought in close order, but separated in small parties.[224] Such tactics annoyed Caesar. It lowered the legions' morale,

---

about 600 hectares, protected by earthen ramparts and rivers. Heidegraben in Wurttemberg "constitutes a whole system of fortifications defending an area of 1400 hectares and having a circumference of about 30 km."
[219] Op. cit., p.127 *'propter latitudinem fossae murique altitudinem paucis defendentibus expugnare non potuit'*: Ptolemy's 'Tarodunon' near Freiburg, reminiscent of similar 'Tara's', 'Taruenna's', 'Turo's' and 'Turoit's' all the way to Ireland, has a rampart and 12 meter wide ditch surrounding an outer ward of 200 hectares. Donnersberg was one of the largest strongholds in Germany. Its outer-ward fortifications were extended as the tribal boundaries expanded. Czech Celtic oppida were well protected from the north from which direction the greatest threat was expected. Hradiste nad Savisti near Zbraslav is 'one of the most imposing systems of Celtic fortifications in central Europe. With the hill of Sance (Schanzen) to which it is joined by means of earthworks thrown across the valley, it occupies 170 hectares (425 acres), of which the actual inner ward takes up about 27 hectares. The entire area is ringed by a rampart and ditch some 9 km in length, still standing 6 meters high and 25 meters wide at the base.
[220] D.W. Harding, 'The Iron Age in lowland Britain.' p.73
[221] Wheeler and Richardson, 'Hillforts of Northern France, p. 12 (1957)
[222] D.W. Harding, Op. cit., p.74
[223] Caesar, 'De Bello Gallico', 5. 9: *locum nacti egregie et natura et opere munitum'*.
[224] Op. cit., 5, 16: *'numquam conferti sed rari magnisque intervallis proeliarenter'*

causing considerable losses. The Belgic defence system with parallel lines of ramparts and close-set transverse ramparts was devised to disorient and break up the disciplined order of Roman legions and their battle formations, hiding army divisions from one another. Such guerilla tactics were employed with success in harassing Roman foraging parties and luring legionary cavalry away from their infantry support by feigned retreat.

Cassivellaunus had similar defence structures in place N of the Thames. Yet, when Caesar marched on his headquarters north of the Thames,[225] Cassivellaunus showed that the earlier hill-fort culture still flowed in his veins. From Caesar's account, the high embankments of the Catuvellaunian inner ward, unlike those of the Belgae noted by Caesar S of the Thames, were clearly erected to be defended in the manner of the old hill-forts. Instead of leaving his hillfort headquarters at Wheathampstead deserted, he made the fatal error of keeping his food supplies and cattle there. This unforgivable blunder dismayed the Belgic tribes into deserting his leadership. Until that fiasco Cassivellaunus had Caesar's legions at his mercy, leading them on a merry dance of death. Until this fateful moment Caesar admits that Cassivellaunus' guerilla tactics were so successful that his cavalry could no longer venture out of touch with the main force of troops and foraging parties could no longer be sent out. This final error demonstrated the Catuvellaunian dependence on the old hill-fort system rather than on the Belgic guerrilla defensive system which had been manifestly so effective. They failed to exploit its most vital aspects and fullest potential. When Caesar's legions cut their way through outer defences, they gazed in amazement at the massive ramparts of Cassivellaunus' hill-fort. Therein ensconced were Cassivellaunus' cattle and food supplies. Caesar gave his men a feast to remember on the finest herds of cattle and best continental wine from Cassivellaunos' cellars to celebrate their victory. Disaster!

The Belgic centre described by Caesar was "defended by forest and marsh, incorporating natural and manmade barriers. This is what the Britons call an *oppidum*."[226] At Camulodunum "3 sets of linear ditches, Grym's Dyke, Triple Dyke (3 parallel dykes) and the Lexden Dyke, running from the Roman river to the Colne, form a defensive barrier across the neck of a peninsula, encompassed by river and forest, an area 3 miles across.[227] The Belgic system evolved as the Belgae grew more experienced in its defence possibilities. Harding noted the growing sophistication in streamlining the system. "This kind of fortification is developed into more extensive systems of dyke, stream, marsh and forest in the period between Caesar's invasion and the conquest, well illustrated by the complexity of earthworks at Colchester, Cunobelinus' adopted capital of Camulodunum."[228] It was the Belgic Trinovanten capital. The conquest restored its Trinovanten rule under Roman administration. Further from the area of primary Belgic settlement were similar strongholds. The primary criterion of a Belgic presence is found at Bagendon and Grim's Ditch in which the Belgae had formed the kingdom of the Dobunni. Oxfordshire's Grim's Ditch is the most extensive of these strongholds, dating to the final decades before the Conquest. Its earthworks are of relatively small proportions in classic Belgic style, although the territory embraced by their intermittent sections covers an area of 22 sq miles. That such a site could not be garrisoned in the same manner as an Iron Age hill-fort is self-evident. With forest and marsh providing additional hazards for the enemy and cover for the defenders, small

[225] D.W. Harding, 'The Iron Age in Lowland Britain", p.74
[226] Caesar, 'De Bello Gallico', 5, 21:'*silvis paludibusque munitum'...egregie natura atque opera munitum'*
..oppidum autem Britanni vocant, cum silvas impeditas vallo atque fossa munierunt.' Caesar's *'vallo atque fossa'* refers to the bank and ditch strengthened by natural barriers. The inner ramparts were never meant for defensive purposes like the hill-forts were. The defences were in the outer wards with their 'natural and man-made barriers'.
[227] D.W. Harding, Op. cit. p. 74: It would require a massive army to hold it against a coordinated attack from several directions. Yet, when its defenders used the Belgic system of guerilla tactics which had such a demoralizing effect upon Caesar's troops, such a stronghold would present a formidable target to capture and subdue."
[228] D.W. Harding, Op. cit. p.74.

bands of guerillas could ambush an invading force, inflicting severe losses, before withdrawing. Chariots were used to mount swift attacks upon the enemy's flank or rear.

From Caesar's records and modern reconstructs of the system the Catuvellauni depended on massive embankments (120 ft wide) around the inner ward of their hill-fort at Wheathampstead. Those of a typical Belgic oppidum are of relatively small proportions (60 ft. wide) never intended to defend the inner ward in the manner of a hill fort. Belgic inner-ward embankments simply delineate the limits of the Oppidum Core, Meeting Place, Sanctuary and Burial Grounds. They compensated for lack of Catuvellaunian massive ramparts by utilizing simpler Fecamp *glacis* ramparts, creating a more ingeniously complex system. "The *glacis* technique commended itself for simplicity and speed of construction in times of unexpected unrest. The use of dump-ramparts in association with a broad shallow ditch was tactical. Less pretentious in design, it nonetheless presented a formidable obstacle to assault.[229] Belgic military genius exploited it, taking advantage of many topographical features. It gained its ultimate sophistication in Ireland. Floodgates were placed on streams at strategic points to flood areas of lowland to enhance the defensive strategy.

Another ingenious reinforcement of the Belgic defensive system was the planting of thorn hedges along the outer face of the bank such as at Thickthorn Banks. This "affords some evidence for a practice which must surely have been quite common in the Iron Age for defensive earthworks."[230] Thickthorn Banks, Thorn Dyke in SE England and Clyskeagh in Ireland testify to the use of this tactic. Evidence on remnants of dykes of the Belgic oppidum in Western Ireland underscore the use of the poisonous purple-flowered hawthorn for defence purposes. Another tactic was the use of pointed stakes, as Harding noted: "Outside the main dyke at Callow Hill, Model Farm, Ditchley, and Blenheim Park, excavation has revealed lengths of palisade trench, which supported an additional barrier of stakes designed to impede a chariot or cavalry charge."[231] Use of pointed stakes planted in bogs in Ireland will be noted in Chapter Two. Cassivellaunus employed a similar technique to impede Caesar's crossing of the Thames by driving sharpened stakes into the riverbed concealed under water to impale man and beast.[232] *"The forest fortress, with its hidden troops and unexpected obstructions, afforded greater protection than did the earlier hill-forts situated as they frequently were in exposed positions from which there was no escape if the stronghold fell. Specific habitation sites are difficult to identify on account of the vast area available for settlement. At Camulodunum and Bagendon, material remains, including coin evidence, are sufficient to indicate that they were major tribal capitals, whose chieftains exercised considerable political sway over the surrounding regions."*[233]

Similar Belgic-type fortresses in Ireland point to the presence of the Belgae there, as is corroborated by legendary history and by Ptolemy's record. The reconstruction of a massive oppidum in Connacht will go some way to dispel the notion that western Ireland was a backwater devoid of any political importance. Belgic innovations to its defence system and choice of low-lying positions incorporating topographical features, rivers, streams, bogs, lakes, marshes, and forests, into a vast defensive network of dykes, continued to be streamlined in Ireland where Rome did not interrupt its growth. Classic examples are found in the Turoe and Athenry oppida in Western Ireland. One is amazed time and again by the consummate skill, consistency of plan and purpose, and insight into the defensive possibilities of the local terrain of Belgic engineers who laid out these extensive earthworks. They

[229] D.W. Harding, 'The Iron Age in Lowland Britain', p. 65.
[230] Op. cit., p. 84
[231] Op. cit., p. 74-5
[232] Caesar, 'De Bello Gallico' , 5, 18.
[233] D.W. Harding, Op. cit., p. 75

stretch mile on mile across a vast expanse of the Connacht landscape, pivoting around their core at the centre of Co. Galway and expanding out into neighbouring counties. In Chapter 2 these will be reconstructed and examined in detail. Attention will first be focused on Belgic settlements in Ireland in general. It will then zoom in on the oppidum complex forming a free, independent, Belgic enclave in Western Ireland. Nowhere else can one find a concentrated build-up of Belgic tribes corresponding to their earlier presence on the Continent and in SE England than in those districts centered around the Turoe/Knocknadala and Athenry/Magh Muc Dhruim oppida in the West of Ireland.

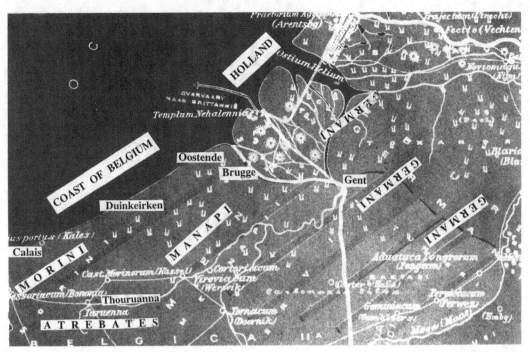

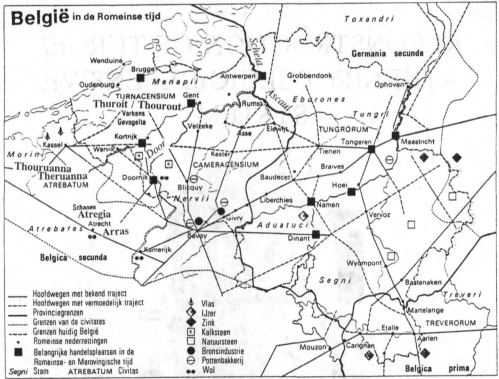

Figure 9: With Caesar's connivance, Germanic Friesians, Batavi, Cherusci, Chatti and Tungri pushed the Belgic Morini, Marasci, Atrebates and Manapi SW of the Rhine and made deep inroads into Belgic lands there (top map), forcing many, caught between Roman and Germanic forces, to migrate. The Manapi, the last to cross the Rhine, pushed the Morini and Atrebates SW, causing the Atrebates to lose their pre-Roman capital, Thourout, and establish new capitals, Thouruanna (Romanised) and Atrecht, SW of Gent and Doornik. The Morini lost their old capital, Casel Morinorum at Kassel, which thereafter became the Manapi capital, Casel Manapiorum (lower map).

CHAPTER 2

PRIMARY
SETTLEMENT AREAS
OF
THE BELGAE IN IRELAND

FIR BELG CENTRES OF POWER

RECONSTRUCTION OF TUROE/
ATHENRY BELGIC DEFENSIVE
SYSTEM

READING THE IRISH IRON AGE LANDSCAPE

Caesar's savage war-lording campaigns and Roman conquests rang Celtic Europe's death-knell and set off Belgic folk-moverments seeking new homelands in Ireland. Having examined Belgic oppida on the Continent and in Britain, it is time to take stock of the Belgic presence in Ireland in areas where the Belgae established their primary settlements. Dubhaltach Mac Fir Bhisigh, the last of the hereditary historians, listed the Belgic tribes of Ireland, 47 in number, supplementing his list with 2 archaic poems on the Fir Belg. In each instance their territorial location is given.[234] These were large communities (*tuatha*), each ruled by a petty king. Eoin MacNeill filled in these Belgic *tuatha* on a blank map of Ireland and found "that they practically filled the map."[235] Ptolemy's early 2nd century record projects an Iron Age Ireland dominated by Fir Belg (Belgic) tribes[236] which corroborates Fir Belg origin-legends.

BRIGANTES: UI BAIRRCHE AND OSSRAIGE: EARLIEST FIR BELG TRIBES

The Brigantes were established in Britain and Ireland before other Belgic tribes. Known as Ui Bairrche, they were led by Slaine to Inber Slaine (Slaney) in SE Ireland.[237] Ptolemy located them there. Descended from the Continental Brigantes, they joined the Belgic Federation and were known as Eburoni. 'Ui Bairrche' is cognate with the Romanized names 'Brigantes' and 'Eburoni' as 'Fir Belg' is cognate with 'Belgae'. Ptolemy's *Birgos* geographically corresponds to the Barrow. *Barrekos,* the god to whom the Barrow River was dedicated is the *Barreki* of the Carlisle *Marti Barreki* dedication in British Briganten lands. Ptolemy's record is corroborated by the historic presence of the Ui Bairrche in SE Ireland, preserved in the name of Bargy (Ui Bairrche Tire) in Wexford and Slievemargy (Sliabh mBairrche Tire) in Laois, Carlow and Kilkenny.[238] The Brigantes shared a common border with the Cruthin whom they pushed N as their kinsmen did in Britain. They in turn were pushed N by the later Laigin. Mael Mura tells how the Cruthin, fighting on behalf of the Laigin King, Crimthann Sciathbel, crushed them in the barony of Fort in Carlow and possessed their lands.[239] The Brigantes were called Galioin because they came from Gaul.[240] Slaine's people were the original Leinstermen. His burial place, Dumha Slaine, is identified as Dinn Rig on the Barrow at Leighlinbridge in Carlow. Labraidh Loingsech (the mariner) led the Brigantes from Gaul to Ireland and captured Dinn Rig. This is the origin-legend, handed down among themselves, of how they first arrived in Ireland. Slaine led the Gailioin. The Ossraige gave their name to Ossory. Their tradition shows they too were Brigantes from the Continental Belgic Federation who traced their pedigree back to Loegaire Bern Buadhach. It is carried back through 10 generations to Connla, son of Bresal Brecc (Barech; Celtic form of 'Brigantes'), son of Labraidh Loingsech, son of Ugaine Mór, the ancestor of the Brigantes who came from Gaul to Ireland.[241] The Ossraige possessed the Nore district and Magh Airgead-Rois spanning Ossory from Durrow to Three Castles. The Ui Bairrche name is perpetuated in Ballyragget (Tulach Ua mBairrche), Co. Kilkenny. The Ui Bairrche maic Niad Coirb descended from Nia Corb, son of Buan, son of Loegaire Bern

[234] Mac Fir Bhisigh's 'Book of Genealogies'. Older version of same list in Edinburgh MS in Revue Celt xx, 335
[235] Eoin Mac Neill, 'Celtic Ireland', p. 4-5.
[236] T.F.O Rahilly, ''Early Irish History and Mythology', p.80.
[237] Ibid, p. 99.
[238] Ibid, p. 36; R 122 b 1-9; LL 314 A; Lec. fo. 88 b 1; O Donovan on Mac Firbis, Lr. na gCeart 222n.
[239] Leabor Laign (Book of Leinster) 15 a 22-30.
[240] Galioin contingents in Queen Medb's service in Connacht left their mark in placenames and formed buffer-states protecting her conquests in Connacht. In Leinter they are reckoned as the original Leinstermen.
[241] Legendary history records Ugaine as an early 'Rí Temhro', Over-king of the Brigantes spread across S Ireland to Galway where cult sites of their goddess, Brigantia (*Brigde,* Brigit), survived in the Belgic pantheon. Their kings reigned as 'Rí Temhro' (Turoe of Galway) before the arrival of the later Belgae. Ugaine's Gaulish Queen, Cessair, was interred in Cairn Cessair, the Cairn tumulus on the summit of Cruach Magh Seoghla in Galway. Lec 36; 585; Lg 119; Fir 104 telling that Ugaine gave Magh Seoghla to his son Eocha and other Galway kingdoms to other sons would seem to corroborate this legendary history.

Buadach. Their stronghold was Rath Beathaigh on the Nore. St. Columbanus descended from them. Having spread W across Ireland they were pushed back E by Fir Belg invasions from the SW and West of Ireland.

THE MANAPI (MONAIG or FIR MANAGH) EXPANSION IN IRELAND

Following Caesar's genocide of the Celtic Veneti, chief sea-traders of Western Europe, Manapian mariners took over the lucrative sea trade. The Irish Sea was named Muir Meann (Manapian Sea) after them. Their settlements surrounded the seaports serving the 2 great Capitals of Iron Age Ireland. Emain Macha's seaports were Newry at the head of Carlingford Loch and Downpatrick in Strangford Loch in Ulster. The Turoe/Knocknadala/-Athenry seaport was Ath Clee Magh Rí in Galway Bay. In both areas the Manapi left their names on numerous townlands. A Manapi sept from the Lower Rhine settled around Arklow in Wicklow are recorded by Ptolemy. They extended inland to the Barrow and Dind Rig near Leighlinbridge.[242] Those expelled with the Ui Bairrche by the invading Laighin settled at Benna Boirce (Bairrche: Mourne Mts.) between Emain Macha's seaports of Newry and Downpatrick. They settled on the N flank of the Ui Bairrche, mirroring their Continental geographic proximity. With the Brigantes, they were driven N and are next found on the N Dublin coast around Lusk. They later formed the Colla Menn (Manapi defenders) Fermanagh/Monaghan buffer states on Connacht's frontier.

FIR BELG INVASIONS ON THE SOUTH AND WEST COASTS OF IRELAND

The Corcu Loigde of Cork claimed descent from Lugaid Loigde, an ancestor of the Munster Fir Belg akin to the Manapian maritime federation serving Irish ports. Corcu Loigde appellations carry 'mon' 'mend' connotations indicating Manapian origin. Moncha (O. Irish 'Monapia) was the Queen of Eoghan Mór of Munster.[243] Queen Ai-Mend, daughter of a Corcu Loigde king, was consort of Corc, founder of Cashel. Corc's mother was 'Bolga Manand Bretnach', a Manapi princess from SE Scotland. Corc's Eoghanacht descendants were at least half Manapian. Manapian septs were called 'Monaig'.[244] They gave Munster its original name, Mon/Man/Momhan/Mumhan, the Manapian province. Pressing inland to Cashel, the Corcu Loigde were still in the process of expanding NE at the expense of the Ossraige in the 5th/6th century. "From the time of Daire and Dergthene (ancestors of these Munster Fir Belg) to that of Ailill Olomm, Munster was ruled by the Corcu Loigde" and later by the Eoganachta.[245] The Corcu Loigde claimed to be Christian long before St Patrick's day. The Fir Belg Muscraige settled in Cork and Tipperary, the Corcu Duibne in SW Kerry and Corcu Baiscinn in W Clare.

Traces of the Belgic defensive system survive in Southern Ireland. Belgic tribes who invaded from the SW pushed back the earlier Brigantes beyond their 1st century linear embankment boundary running from the Ballyhoura Mts to the Nagles and down to Cork harbour. Slowly the Brigantes were pushed E beyond the River Suir and Knockmaeldown Mts. After the assassination of Crimthann Mac Fidaig, the Brigantes suddenly burst across the Suir and re-established themselves in their former territories as far W as Pallas Green, the Ballyhoura Hills and across the Blackwater to the Nagles Mts bounded by the Claidh Doo defensive dyke. The Corcu Loigde stood S and E of the Blackwater from Cappoquin to Fermoy and west along the Blackwater. Later with Corc and the Desi they began the process of pushing the Briganten Ossraige beyond a new boundary barrier from Youghal to Cappoquin to the E of Knockmealdown, Galtee and Silvermines Mts to Slieve Bloom Mts known as the 'Rian Bó Padraig'. O Riordain noted that the "Claidhe Dubh in E Cork is unimpressive, in places

---

[242] T. F. O Rahilly, Op. Cit., p. 24.
[243] T. F. O Rahilly, 'Early Irish History and Mythology', p 31.
[244] Ibid, p. 31-33: Monaig as representatives of the Manapi. Compare 'Monaic Ulaid' and Fir Manach.
[245] T. F. O Rahilly, Op. Cit., 189; Misc. Celt. Soc.6; Ir. Texts 1, 21; Fianaigecht 34 a; Eriu 111, 140 ll.

hardly distinguishable from a field fence." This is true of similar earthworks across the country due to natural defacement and human activity through the ages. The Black Pig's Dyke was reduced by cutting away of the greater part of the rampart to fill the fosse and the retention of only the outer lip embankment as a field fence.[246] The Manapian Mennraige and Corcu Loigde were settled in SW Cork well into historic times. Vestiges of the defence system of the early Belgic capitals of Munster beg for reconstruction before it is too late.

ANCIENT CAPITALS OF THE GANGANI ALONG THE WEST OF IRELAND

Congentiatus (Gann or Congenn for short, Commius in Roman records), King of the Atrebates and other Continental Belgic tribes, a chosen leader of the great Pan-Celtic revolt against Caesar which made him the most wanted man on Rome's hit list, fled to SE Britain and for 20 years ruled over the Belgic tribes there until 26 B.C. On persistent rumours of an imminent Roman invasion of Britain, he handed over power to his son Tincommius (in Roman records, Sengann in Celtic) and disappeared from the RomanoBritish geopolitical scene and Roman records. He led women, children and noncombatants to the West of Ireland out of harm's way. Irish legend tells that Gann and Sengann led a Fir Belg invasion which "landed in Clare (and Limerick) at the Shannon mouth,"[247] precisely where Ptolemy located the Gangani (Gann's followers), the one source corroborating the other. Belgic tribes from SE England, the Atrebates, Morini, Mac Umhoir, Domnann and related septs led by Gann's family in the late last century BC invaded along the West Coast of Ireland, establishing their primary settlements there in a northward expansion. One is amazed at the amount of surviving evidence regarding this creeping invasion and expansion, despite all pseudo historic efforts to subvert or manipulate it.

Gann's original settlement area extended from Kerry Head to Spanish Point and inland to Clarecastle at the inner estuary of Fergus river in Co. Clare. It is archaeologically engraved in traces of the Belgic defensive system, the 'Claidh Roo' ('Cleeroo'; 'Cladh' is O-Irish for Dyke, 'Roo' is a fossed dyke[248]) running from Cahercarbery beachhead cliff fort on Kerry Head on the N coast of Kerry (OS map, No. 13) ESE parallel to Ballyheige Bay shoreline, and thence NNE across Cashen River. Vestiges survived E of Maulin Hill, 8 miles from Kerry Head. In 1756 C. Smith[249] claimed that having passed the Cashen River (past Listowel) it crossed Knockanure into Limerick, and swung N to the Shannon, a distance of over 20 miles, cutting off a tract of land bounded by the coastal stretch of the NW Kerry Shannon estuary. A Tooraree (Temhair a' Rí) power centre in Gangani lands stands in NW Limerick near the Shannon mouth. In 1877 there still existed vestiges of extensive outer ward embankments running from the Blackwater River N through the Ballyhoura Mt. gap to Ardpatrick Tower and N to the Shannon. A line of pillar-stones from Lough Gur to Ludden Hill is a defaced section of this earthwork. The Limerick section is named 'Boher-liagan' on the Down Survey.[250] Legends of the 'Black Pig' indicate this section was a defensive dyke erected from material thrown up from the cutting of an outer ditch. 'Leaba na muice' and 'Black Pig's bed', on its route[251] corroborate this ancient tradition.

Gann expanded his kingdom to this Maigue/Knockainey district, a major centre of Iron Age Munster steeped in Fir Belg history long before Cashel became part of Munster. An editorial note to *Cath Magh Mucrama* states that "Oilill Olumm, ancestor of the Eoganacht branch of the Fir Belg, had his palace at '*Brugh righ*', Bruree on the Maigue." "Be it noted that Cashel, the seat of the Munster kings in Christian times, stands outside ancient

---

[246] W.F.De Vismes Kane has several references to such activity in his 'The Black Pig's Dyke'
[247] Henry Hubert, 'The Rise of The Celts', p.229
[248] T. F. O Rahilly, Op. Cit, p. 7 footnote 1, 'roe' like 'doe' (variants of roo and doo) mean a fossed embankment.
[249] C Smith, 'State of the Co of Kerry', p.219, 1756. T.J.Westropp,'Ancient forts of Ireland', p.139
[250] 'Down Survey'.
[251] R.S.A.I., Vol. xxxi., p.375.

Munster."[252] The Maigue district held the Otherworld abode, sanctuary and sacred yew tree of the god of music, Fer I, which belonged to the Ui Bairrche before being taken by the Eoganacht. The Eoganacht dynasty's mythological traditions centered on the sacred site of Knockainy (Cnoc Aine) and the area to the S and E of it.[253] The ram-headed serpent war god Segomon appears in the Eoganacht pedigree. He is represented on monuments at Paris and Rheims in Belgic lands on the Seine, indicating an Eoganacht connection with the latter. The name of Shannon River (*Senna/Sionna*) is cognate with the Seine. The sun goddess Aine is represented as consort of Manannan Mac Lir, Menapian sea god, compounding the earlier Menapian connection. She is said to have mythologically mothered Oilill Olomm's son, Eoghan Mór, from whom the Eoganacht are named.

Mac Neill and local lore, claimed the Fir Belg had a "capital of ancient Munster of the older tradition, 'Temhair Erann'."[254] O Rahilly judged "his premises unsound, his examination of the question superficial, his conclusions based on misconceptions,"[255] crimes O Rahilly himself was guilty of. Recently the archaeological complex around Friarstown Hill, 7 km. S of Limerick city, was shown to be Temhair Luachra (Tara Hill locally) near Knockainey, referred to in Mesca Uladh[256] as the N Munster Temhair visited by Queen Medb. Another archaic capital was Tory Hill (Temhair Rí) near Croom in Limerick, site of Druim nAsail named in Dindsenchas Druim nAsail, after Asal Mac Umhoir, the Fir Belg leader. The Mac Umhoir were descendants of Gann. Further east another outer ward defence system survived, facing the Briganten defence line, running N along the Suir River to the W of Cashel where it swung NW past Pallas Green along the Slievefelim foothills to the Shannon. Gann expanded his kingdom into the Golden Vale. This vast expansion in a short time span underpins a huge influx of Gann's followers from the Continent and SE England for whom he won new homelands. He had now secured the ritual landscape where his descendants, Eoghan Mór and early Munster kings, would reign.

DEATH OF THE GREAT HERO, GANN (COMMIUS), AFTER A GLORIOUS CAREER

After a heroic life, Gann (Commius) was laid to rest in *Ferta na Rí* in the shadow of the Sídh ar Femen (Femhin, Fremann), the cairn on Slievenamon SE of Cashel, burial ground of early Munster kings[257] and residence of Bodb,[258] Overking of the Fir Belg gods. His descendant, Eochaid Aireamh (of the Atrebates – *Aithrébh*, allegedly a brother of, but doubtless no other than, Eochaid Ferach Mhór, Queen Medb's father, who went from Fremen to Turoe to become Rí Temhro), had a fortress in Femen.[259]

North of the outer Shannon Estuary a comparable stretch of SW Clare extending N to Spanish Point and E to Clarecastle at the inner estuary of the Fergus River was similarly secured to form the northern segment of Gann's settlement area. This northwards-creeping invasion led by Gann's sons, Dela, Epillus (Eochall), Verica (Ferach Mhór), in alliance with Umhor and Dumno, extended the conquest up through Clare into Co. Galway. It expanded

[252] E. MacNeill, 'Phases of Irish History', p. 127

[253] F.J. Byrne, 'Irish Kings and High Kings', p.182: The grandson of Brian Boru, Toirrdelbach of the Dal Cais, cut down the yew tree at Emly (Imlech Ibair, site of the sacred yew tree), symbolizing the Dal Cais destruction of the Eoganacht power in Munster. Byrne related how this conquest is conveyed mythologically. Fer I was the son of the yew god Eogabul. His daughter, the goddess Aine, was ravished by Ailill Aulomm at the Otherworld Sidh of Cnoc Aine (Knockainy in Limerick). Fer I is the apple of discord by which the Otherworld took revenge on Ailill when his sons disputed the possession of Fer I and the sacred yew tree of the kingship of Munster with his fosterson, Lugaid Mac Con, when Mac Con tried to usurp the kingship.

[254] E. MacNeill, 'Saorstat Eireann Official Handbook', p. 42; 'St. Patrick', p. 108.

[255] T.F. O Rahilly, 'Early Irish History and Mythology.' p.183

[256] Eamon P. Kelly and Tom Condit, 'Limerick's Tara in 'Archaeology Ireland', Summer 1998, p.18

[257] Rawl. B. 502; Corpus Geneal. Hiber. Ed O Brien, 147b 45-52; Laud 610, 73b.

[258] F. J. Byrne, 'Irish Kings and High Kings' p166.

[259] Rawl B 502; Corpus Geneal. Hiber. Ed O Brien, 136a 22; Rev. Celtique, 20, 42; Eriu 8, 155-60; 12, 137-96.

from the Dealagh (Dela) and Inagh Rivers in Liscannor Bay to Aille River in Doolin Bay and inland to Ennistimon, Lisdoonvarna and Kilfenora. Buffering this N of the inner Shannon estuary, bounded by the Fergus estuary and Ennis, extending E to Slieve Bernagh and N to the foothills of the Sliabh Aughta in NE Clare are traces of the Belgic defensive system focused on the Magh Adhair coronation site founded by Adhar mac Umhoir. Earthen ramparts ran for several miles in the vicinity of Tradree. As with many archaeological sites, these were falsely attributed to Danes or Normans, but to country folk they were the *Dúncladh* of the Fir Belg. 'The Wars of Turlough' tells how Sir Thomas de Clare in 1277 repaired "a broad-based high-crested fossed rampart running from Abhann na Garna (through Sixmilebridge) towards the sea" (tidal part of Shannon) in Tradree along the W foothills of Slieve Bernagh. The Corra Chaitlin Dyke ran W past Bunratty and swung N through Newmarket-on-Fergus to Latoon along the E side of the Fergus, past Crusheen and Ballinruan, and swung E along the Slieve Aughta foothills to Scarriff. They swung S again via Bodyke to the Ahaclare River back to Abhann na Garna, circumscribing Magh Adhair.[260]

DELA WENT TO DAIL (CNOC NA DÁL) & ESTABLISHED THE FEIS TEMHRO

Legend corroborated by dindshenchas material, tells that Dela, great-grandson of Gann, led his invasion through Ath Cliath Magh Rí in Galway Bay. He made Turoe/Knocknadala his power base (Ptolemy's Regia e Te[mh]ra: *REGIA E TERA,* Capital at Turoe and NAG na TAΓ: Knocknadala). His Mac Umhoir cousins secured the Burren, the Aran Islands, and Aidhne (Crích Connli) in SW Galway.[261] **"To judge from Mac Liac's list of places they occupied, the Fir Belg were particularly numerous to the East and South of Galway Bay,"[262] where they had a powerful presence. The sons of Umhor are classed as Fir Belg in an ancient poem quoted by Mac Firbis[263] and in the 'Dindsenchas of Loch Ainninn'.** '*Tuath Mac Umoir*' settlements stretched from Dál Cais to SW Galway and up along Lough Corrib where '*Tuath Conchobairni ocus Mac Umoir*' was located (from Conchuirn mac Umhoir who erected his beachhead fort on the Aran Islands). Fir Belg leaders named are Bir at Rinn Burren, Irgus at Dun Irgus at Cinn mBairne, Laragh at Árd Laragh, Cing at Rath Aille (Bellafa) of Fídh Chinga, named after him. With the Fir Domnann (accompanying Verica and Iuvor/Umhoir) who invaded through Irrus Domnann (Erris on the Mayo coast) to which they gave their name, the Mac Umhoir led the invasion up along the N Connacht coast to Dún Umhoir (Iuvor) on Achill Island N of Clew Bay and Dún Mod Mac Umhoir at Modlind in Belmullet. This is corroborated by Mac Liac in the 'Dindsenchas' of Carn Conaill'[264] where he refers to all 17 settlement named after the leaders of the Fir Belg invasion; 9 are in Galway, 4 in Mayo, and 3 in Clare then part of Connacht.

Gann was great-grandfather of Dela. The *Lebor Gabála*[265] illogically named Dela as father of all 5 leaders of the invasion to correspond to the alleged 5 provinces, and suppress Dela's Turoe/Knocknadala associations to glorify Tara. Dela's own invasion is not counted. The 'Dinnsenchas of Medraige' (Maree, Co. Galway, a more genuine source than the fabulous *Lebor Gabala* version) gives Dela as son of Genann, son of Sengann. Its significant short genealogy of Dela's grandson identifies Turoe of Galway as the Fir Belg Capital: "Fermhor (Ferach Mhor) son of Eremon (Ercmon or Erc), son of Dela, son of Genann." Fermhór is

[260] Westropp, 'Ancient Forts of Ireland., p.139. Sean P.O Riordain, 'Antiquities of Irish Countryside' p. 64.

[261] Fir. 54 (Mac Firbhisigh's 'Book of Genealogies' p.54); EIHM 146;

[262] T. F. O Rahilly, Op. Cit. p. 146.

[263] 'General Tracts' 82

[264] 'Metrical Dindsenchas' iii, 440. Compare the prose version, RC xv, 478, Book of Ballymote, Book of Lecan.

[265] Eriu, viii, 56: Confusion reigns regarding Dela, 'father' of the 5 leaders of the invasion. The pseudo-historic *Lebor Gabála* made him the son of Umor. Redactors confused the record further. Like Gann and Sengann, they made Dela a Fomorian leader with a fictitious descent from Loth mac Artuat. Others made Gann the son of Sengann, thinking the latter was a compound of 'Sean' and 'Gann' = the 'elder Gann', 'father of Gann'. Sengann was son of Gann (Commius) and grandfather of Dela.

variously called Eochaid Ferach Mhór or Eochaid Fedlech, "ced ríg do shuidh ar thus i Temhróid de Fhearaibh Bolc", "Rí Temhro' (King of Turoe), 'Ideal King of the Fir Belg', and father of Queen Medb. The Turoe Stone stood in front of his royal residence, Rath Ferach Mhór, on Turoe Hill. The origin-legend states that Dela's (Dindsenchas of Medraige makes him son of Genann and leader of the Fir Belg invasion) 2,000 Fir Belg warriors landed at Ath Cliath Mag Rí in Galway Bay, captured 'Temhair', and "Dela went to Dáil (*Cnoc na Dála*, Knocknadala in Galway) and established the 'Oenach' (*'Feis Temhro'*) beside it." Even the fictitious Lebor Gabala accepted this tradition that Dela was the first to establish the Feis Temhro, but alleged it was at Tara. Adjoining Knocknadala is Turoe (*Cnoc Temhro*), a prominent height. This was the origin of Feis Temhro. The text is couched in O-Irish: "*Adnagar Delach ar Dáil. Roghni Oenach Dind re thaibh*" = 'Dela went to the Hill of Dail and established the Feis Temhro beside it)'[266] Turoe and Tara have the same O. Irish name, 'Temhair', (gen. '*Temhro*' as in 'Rí Temhro/Cnoc Temhro (Turoe); dat. 'Temhra' as in 'i Temhra). Turoe was the *Temhair* of Dela. Turoe traditions were suppressed when pseudo-history and pseudo-Dindsenchas came to be written from the 8th to the 11th centuries. By then the Cruthin were confined to the NE corner of Ulster. The tradition of a Temhair captured by the Fir Belg was transferred to the Temhair (Tara).

8th/9th century pseudo historians began to subvert these facts of history. "Foras Feasa ar Éirinn" by Séathrún Céitinn, "Lebor Mór nGenealach" by Dubhaltach Mac Fir Bhisigh and "Ogygia" by Ruaidhraidh Ua Flaithbhertaig showcase this in listing the earliest divisions (*Coiced* or *Rann*) of Ireland: Coiced Ulaid (al. C. Conchobair; Ulster) was taken by Ruaidhraidh, an Ulster Cruthin king.[267] Coiced Laighin (al. C. nGaileoin; Leinster) was taken by Slaighne, leader of the Brigantes.[268]

Coiced Gainn(d) extended from Belach Conglais (Cork) to Commar na dtrí-nuisci (Waterford)[269] "ó laimh le muir go Luimnech (Limerick).[270] It is also recorded as Rann Regaind, Coiced Cu Rui (Conroi) Mac Daire, Coiced Conganchnes and Coiced Eochu Mac Luchta. O Rahilly named Conganchnes as ultimately a double of Conroi. Both have an affinity with Gann's original nom-de-guerre, Congentiatus.

Coiced Sengainn, said to extend from Belach Conglais (Cork) to Limerick (*Iarmumha*, W Munster), a separate division from Gann's despite being his primary settlement area. Some say Coiced Eochu Mac Luchta was *Deasmumha* (S Munster) from "Commar na dtri-nuisci go Belach Conglais laim le muir." Others say it extended to Limerick, while others say it was S Connacht extending from Limerick to Rath Fidech (near Athenry). This latter territory is also said to belong to Clann Dedad (Deaghadh), the warrior clan of Curoi with their capital at Temhair Erand (T. Luachra Dedad) just S of Limerick city. Clann Dedad are called Síl Conaire, Curoi's people whose territory extended "from Ath na Bóroimhe to Leim na Con, from Easgar Riada (in Galway) to Luimneach, the land of the Seantuatha Fear mBolg."[271] In '*Cath Ruis na Rí*' Eochu is king of all Munster (excluding Cashel and E Munster) with his capital in Temhair Luachra, which in '*Mesca Ulad*' is Conroi's capital visited by Queen Medb.[272] O Rahilly showed how pseudo historians invented the theory that Munster consisted of 2 Provinces, that of Curoi and that of Eochu Mac Luchta (that of Gann and Sengann by extension). "The artificiality of this explanation is so obvious that no time

---

[266] 'Dindsenchas of Medraige'
[267] Bb 4a; 17a, Lec 23; 553. In *Lebor Gabala* Gann and Genann are brothers.
[268] Lec. 553.
[269] Lec 58; 553; Fir 54, Lg 34.
[270] Ll. 8; K. 121; Bb 17a; Lec 23
[271] Lu 51b, 41b; Lu., Tbf. 215; Hk 398; Ai 87 a; Ll 264 b; K 140 a; Sa 33 b 2. cf. Clann Dedad in Onomasticon Goedelicum.
[272] Md xxxiv; K 121a; K121b; Met. Dind.iii, 338; Rev. Celtique viii, 48; EIMH p.177.

need be wasted on refuting it. The official pseudo historical theory was that there was a hexarchy in ancient Ireland, namely, 5 Provincial Kings (2 of them from Munster) together with the High King of Tara."[273]

Coiced Genann (al. C. Ól nÉchmacht, C. Connacht, C. Cruachna) extended from Limerick to Esruaid (Ballyshannon). It excluded the NE of present-day Connacht which was still an integral part of archaic Ulster. It is also called Coiced Gainn, Coiced Sengainn, Coiced Sreing Mac Sengann and Coiced Medba. Early Belgic Overkings apparently reigned over the entire Fir Belg territories of Munster and Connacht.

Séathrún Céitinn and others listed the earliest Fir Belg Kings. First was Slaigne. After him Gann reigned, then Sengann, then Fiachu mac Starn. Fiachu was succeeded by Rindail son of Genann, son of Sengann, and he by Foidhbhgann son of Sengann. Foidhbhgain was succeeded by Eochaid Ferach son of Erc (Ercmon), son on Rindail. This genealogy of Gann equates that of the Dindsenchas of Medraige. Eochaid mac Erc is Eochaid Ferach (Férmhór/ Fedlech), father of Queen Medb. In Romano/British records Verica (Ferach) is given as 'son' of Commius. Based on obits, British authors say Verica cannot have been son, but rather great-great-grandson (macu) of Commius, as in this genealogy. After Foidhbhgann's death, Eochaid Ferach went N from Fremand ('tar Fremaind adthuaidh'), where Gann died, to take the Overkingship of Temhroit ('Rí Temhróit', Turoe). Eochaid Ferach was the first and only king to have a royal residence on Turoe Hill of the Fir Belg (*'ced ríg do suid ar tus i Temhróid de Fhearaibh Bolc'*).[274] Turoe accommodates this archaic claim. Tara was never the seat of Fir Belg Kings. Pseudo-history transferred this tradition from Turoe to Tara. Several alleged royal residences stand on Tara. None was ever named after Ferach. Nor was Tara ever known as Temhróit de Fhearaibh Bolc. Only Cruthin kings of Ulster and Scotland reigned at Tara until 637 AD, despite the fraudulent claims of pseudo-history which reinvented Eochaid Ferech as High King of Tara. Rath Ferach Mhór, in front of which stood the Turoe Stone, was the only residence on Turoe hill. It was named after the "Ideal King' of the Fir Belg, Eochaid Ferach Mhór, alias Eochaid Fedlech mac Erc, father of Queen Medb, the first and last king to set up his royal residence on Cnoc Temhro, as legendary history proclaims. Dela and his son Míl of Rath Mhíl had their royal residence on Knocknadala as archaic origin-legends and Dindshenchas of Meadraige proudly proclaim.

EXTENT AND DIVISION OF ÓL nÉCHMACHT: ARCHAIC CONNACHT

Eochaid (Ferach Mhór) divided Coiced Ól nÉchmacht (archaic Connacht) into 3 parts (ranna: divisions) among the Fir Belg tribes. He gave Fidech, son of Fech, of the Fir Craibhe from Fidech (Rath Fidech in N Aidhne, S of Athenry)[275] to Limerick. He gave Eochaid Allat the territory from Galway River to Dubh and Dróbhais (Drowes) Rivers, the W districts of Galway, Mayo and Sligo N to Ballyshannon, the territory of the Fir Domnann with its capital at Dún Eochaid Allat. He gave the middle kingdom from Fidech (Fidachi Regia in N Aidhne, S of Athenry) to Temhair Brogha Niad and E across the Shannon River at Athlone, namely, Sen Magh Sainbh and Tir Tuatha Taoídhen (the old districts of the Fir Taoídhe and the people around Sliabh Fuirri in E Galway to Tinni Mac Cónrach. Séathrún

---

[273] EIHM p.175; RC xiii, 36; "Tochmarc Etaine', ib, 118.

[274] Alwyn & Brinley Rees, 'Celtic Heritage – Ancient Tradition in Ireland', p. 162; LG, IV, 179.

[275] Fidich (Dún Fidech, Fidig, Fidachi Regia) SW of Athenry where Eoghan Mór of Munster set up his residence around which he settled the Oige Beatra/Ogaibh Bethra from Crích Ealla (now Duhallow in Co. Cork) when the Manapi had spread inland from their marine base around Ath Cliath Magh Rí towards Loughrea, turning their settlements in ancient Magh Colla along the Sli Mhannin (Mannin/Manapi Road) W of Loughrea into a power base threatening to overthrow the royal Fir Belg line descended from Gann and Dela, as they did when Ingcel Caech led 5,000 of them and their Conmaicne kinsmen against Conaire Mór in Temhair when he was Fir Belg Overking. Because of this growing threat, Cormac Mac Art later led a large contingent of the Manapi fighting men (Collaibh Oga) against Ulster at the Battle of Crinna and settled them along its border as the Airghialla; Laud 610; ZCP viii 312f; Ml 20; Ca 302; Ai 84 b: Lec 164 Fy Tp; RC xvii, 7; Ml 20; Hc 568 a.

Céitinn and others[276] recorded Temhair Brogha Niad in this middle division of Ól nÉchmacht. Late Leinster pseudo historians tried to claim it for Leinster. The ensuing confusion is evident in 'Onomasticon Goedelicum' which suggests it might be Tara of Meath, or Tara Tld. in Durrow (Offaly) or Tara Hill near Gorey in Co. Wexford. It was the Temhair of Ól nÉchmacht (archaic Connacht).

Tinni Mac Cónrach, a Domnann king wooing Eochaid's daughter, Medb, sought her father's favour. At Eochaid's request, he erected the 'fossa' earthworks enclosing Rath Cruacha of Athenry in record time with his Domnann tribe. For this feat, Eochaid Ferach made Tinni king of this middle kingdom of Ól nÉchmacht. When Tinni quarreled with other leaders, notably with Medb's chief suitor, Fidech Mac Feic of the Fir Craibhe whom Tinni slew out of jealousy, Eochaid expelled him and gave the throne of Ól nÉchmacht to his own daughter, Medb.[277] He replaced the slain Fidech with Eochu Rond as king of the Fir Craíbhe division. Tinni, from Caher Tinni near Loughrea, continued to visit Medb. However, it was Ailill Mac Mágach, whom Medb made guardian of Loughrea's sacred lake where she had a royal crannog, who won Medb's heart and became her consort. Ailill and Medb, Regents of Ól nÉchmacht, made Ailill's brother, Ceat Mac Mágach, hero of Main Magh, the next king of the Fir Craíbhe division of Ól nÉchmacht ("ó Eascar Riada go Luimnech, ó Ath Cliath Magh Rí go Boroimhe agus go Leim Con .i. an tír for a rabadar Seantuatha Fir mBelg").[278] They made the young Sanb Mac Ceat Mac Mágach king of the middle kingdom, which became known as Magh Sanb.

Contention arose over the lands of Fir Mallon E of Lough Ree and the Shannon which the Ulster King Conor mac Nessa had given to Queen Medb in a peace agreement to end the wars between the Fir Ól nÉchmacht and Ulster. After Conor's death, his sons fought to recover this territory, placing it under Glaisni mac Conor mac Nessa, king of Rathcroghan of Roscommon. Many early tales tell of the Fir Ól nÉchmacht marauding from Fir Mallon against Ulster. Glaisni, defending Rathcroghan just then being assailed by Medb's forces, insisted Medb's forces be expelled from Fir Mallon E of the Shannon. Medb, determined to defend Fir Mallon lands, placed them under Sanb as part of Magh Sanb.[279] She sent Domnann warriors under Artech Uchtlethan against Glaisni at Rathcroghan. She mustered the 3 divisions of Ól nÉchmacht led by Ceat Mac Mágach, Eochaid Beg Mac Eochaid Rond, Tinni and her son Maine with bands of her 3,000 Gaileoin mercenaries, to aid Sanb against Glaisni E of the Shannon in a pincer movement. Ainninn Mac Umhoir's stronghold in Westmeath supported Sanb. "From Ainninn mac Umhoir, Loch Ainninn (Ennel) gets its name (Dindshenchas of Loch Ainninn)."[280] The Dún of Drumsna at the upper Shannon shallows was erected to protect Glaisni's kingdom in NE Connacht. A massacre ensued, as told by Togail Bruidne Da Chóca. Medb's forces E of the Shannon were annihilated. Only her 5 leaders escaped. A great hosting of Ulstermen and Cruthin kinsmen from Scotland attacked the Domnann then preparing to invade Rathcroghan. Medb sent the same 5 leaders to aid the Domnann who had advanced to Artech (named after Artech Uchtlethan: Frenchpark, Co Roscommon). As told in Cath Artig, Medb's forces again suffered a frightful massacre. Conall Cearnach slew Ceat Mac Mágach. Medb replaced him with Eochaid Beg Mac Eochaid Rond as "Rí Fir Craíbe .i. Rí an tres Condacht".[281] The Fir Belg were driven back to the River Suck (Roscommon/Galway border) and held at bay there for centuries before finally conquering the Cruthintuatha of Rathcroghan. The fact that the NE of Connacht known as Cruthintuatha Chroghain, with its capital at Rathcroghan of

---

[276] K 121 b I, 137 a (Séathrún Céitinn), Of 269, 273, 282 (Ogygia), Lec 190, 585; Rc xxi, 152;

[277] 'Cath Boinde'; Eriu ii, 178.

[278] Hz 30, H, 4, 13, TCD.

[279] Ac. 42.

[280] LL, 6 a 22-24.

[281] BDC; RC xxi, 158.

Roscommon, was then, like Tara, an integral part of Ulster, was suppressed by pseudo historians who alleged that Medb reigned at Rathcroghan as Queen of Connacht. Their "official doctrine" was so sophisticated that it is held as gospel truth to this day.

Medb blamed Sanb for these fiascos and promptly made her son Maine king of what remained of the middle kingdom, from Rath Fidech in NW Aidne to Temhair Broga Niad ("west of and bordering Magh Senchenoil in E Galway. In it was Temhair Broga Niad"). Main Magh, the plain around Turoe/Knocknadala, is named after Maine, son of Queen Medb. Maine's palace was Cloghar Ui Mhain in the urban sector on the W fringe of Knocknadala. Medb's daughter, Fionndhabhair, was consort of Fraech mac Fidaig, king of Ól nÉchmacht. A later king, Conall of Clochar Chonail Cruachna (Clamperpark, Athenry), was king of Turoe.[282] Sanb retained the other subject tribes in NE Galway and S Roscommon but submitted to Glaisni. Creagh (Críoch = boundary) townland on the E bank of the Suck River in Ballinasloe (Béal Atha na Sluaigh – as spelt out by the name) proclaims this new boundary between Ulster and Connacht. The adjoining Cleagh Mór, Cleagh Garve, Cleagh Roo and Rooaun townlands proclaim the defensive embankments on this border line. Ballinasloe on this Suck border and on the Sli Mhór became the great market gateway where food and livestock were traded between Ulster and Connacht, luxury items (fluffy goose-down feathers destined for export from Ath Cliath Magh Rí for cushions and beds) for wealthy Romans and their armies in Britain and throughout the Roman Empire, and, not least, the trade in highly venerated horses by the Fir Belg and Cruthin alike. The swift steeds of the Mac Mórna and Mac Umhoir Fir Belg were renowned far and wide. "Studs of the steeds of the Fianna" were protected in forests on the Galway side of the Suck boundary, such as at 'Coill Eichan le Garaidh' (Mac Morna) and 'Ros na nEachraidh' (*Each* and *Eic* = horse).

Ulster availed of the Connacht Fir Belg weakened state and carried out numerous hit and run raids on the Rígrad Temhróit and Fir Belg Capitals in Connacht and Munster. They slew 2 Rí Temhro, Feredach Finn Fachtnach and Fiachu Finndola, grandfather and father of Tuathal Techtmhar. Ellim mac Conrach, the Dal nAraidi Cruthin king of Ulster, slew Fiachu and became Rí Temhro in his stead. He was allegedly associated with 3 other kings, Foirbre mac Fine of the Corcu Loigde, Eochaid Ánchenn of the Domnann, and Sanb mac Ceat mac Mágach. If Mael Mura's poem where this is related is not spurious and anachronistic, Sanb became a traitor in the hope of becoming the king of Ól nÉchmacht. Tuathal went overseas, allegedly to Agricola, the Roman Governor, then campaigning against the Cruthin (Picts) in Scotland, to seek his aid, but in vain. Aided instead by friendly British Celtic kings and faithful Fir Belg kings in Ireland, Tuathal returned and defeated Ellim,[283] was restored to his rightful throne as Rí Temhro, and held the Feis Temhro to celebrate his victory. But this is running too far ahead!

Three separate invasions (Fir Dumnann, Galioin and Fir Belg) are lumped together by *'Lebor Gabála'* (Book of Conquests) as one Fir Belg invasion.[284] The leaders are given as the 5 sons of Dela: Slaine, Gann, Sengann, Genann and Rudraige. Each took a different part of Ireland. This artificial lumping together was a attempt to explain how the chimerical 'Five Provinces' originated, a muddling of O-Irish *Coiced*.[285] It confused the leaders of the tribes and their relationship to each other. All are alleged to be sons of Dela despite racial diversity. This convention suggested itself to the *Lebor Gabála* compilers because Dela was said to be the first to establish the *Feis Temhro*. This was deemed to be the prerogative of

---

[282] Dindshenchas of Cnoc na Dála: *"Conall Cruachna, robo rí ar tuathaibh Temhrach"*
[283] LL 51, a-b; Lec. Fo. 8, b2; By Mael Mura's time Rí Temhro = King of Tara = Rí Erainn.
[284] T.F. O Rahilly 'Early Irish History and Mythology' p.99-100
[285] Francis John Byrne, 'Irish Kings and High Kings', new edition, Additional notes to p. 46-7 and 58-9.

the Leader when *Lebor Gabála* was written. Feis Temhro was claimed by pseudo-history to have been held at Tara of Meath rather than Turoe of Galway, Dela's Temhair.

Historical Connacht septs, such as the Partrige who gave their name to the Partry Mountains in Mayo and areas on both shores of Loch Corrib and Mask, claimed descent from Sengann and Genann. Rudraige, one of the alleged 5 leaders of the Fir Belg invasion, was not Fir Belg but overking of the Cruthin.[286] They were the original pre-Celtic inhabitants of Britain and Ireland and gave their name to the British Isles, Ireland and Britain, in the original form, Pritanic Isles. The Belgae pushed the Cruthin N to Ulster where they were known as the *Ulaid*. Fergus mac Roigh, king of Ulster in the Ulidian Tales, was grandson of Rudraige and contemporary of Queen Medb of Connacht. Rudraige was not one of the leaders of the Fir Belg or of the Cruthin invasion since the latter had given their name to the British Isles by the 6th century BC as recorded by Greek sailors. Of the invasion leaders, Slainge, Gann, Sengann, Genann and Dela were Fir Belg. Gann and Sengann were no other than Commius, leader of the Continental and British Belgae, and his son Tincommius. They led the Fir Belg invasion of W Ireland. Close kinship existed for centuries between the Fir Belg of Munster and Dela's Fir Ól nÉchmacht (archaic Connacht) despite the strident efforts by medieval pseudo historians to suppress this fact in favour of their own brand of propaganda. This close kinship was sealed regularly by royal marriage alliances and recorded in legendary history, as will be seen anon. The Galioin (Ui Bairrche/Ptolemy's Brigantes) came from the Continental Belgic Federation. Segments of the Canti and Dumnoni (followers of King Dumno Bhellaunus who vanished from Romano/British records) came with Ferach. The enmity between the Fir Belg invaders and aboriginal Cruthin, lasted for centuries.[287] [288] [289]

Medieval pseudo-history manipulated Fir Belg origin-legends as part of a carefully engineered structural transformation of Iron Age tradition in a campaign of denigration to bolster the Tara Myth. The pseudo historic version of the Mac Umhoir invasion, made the Fir Belg go first to a High King of Ireland at Tara, but were then transferred to Connacht in the reign of Queen Medb under the weight of strong surviving tradition which recognized that it was in Connacht they had their strongest presence and held out longest.[290] There was then no High King of Ireland at Tara. The Mac Umhoir went to Cnoc Temhro (Turoe) of Galway, not to Tara. Their strongholds were buffer states along the W defence frontier of the Turoe/Knocknadala Belgic oppidum circumscribing Ól nÉchmacht. The Mac Umhoir descended from Iuvor/Umhor, a Canti King descended from Gann. The compilers of *Lebor Gabála*,[291] following a fashion flourishing in Europe in the 10th/12th centuries, adopted the convention of linking all invaders with SE Europe ('the Greeks of Scythia,'[292] 'the Fir Belg came from Greece'). This device facilitated the invention of a Biblical ancestry for the Irish, the glory of monastic pseudo-historians. The Irish were led to believe they have Scythian,

[286] The Cruthin (*Cruthnigh,* Q-Celtic form of *Pritani*; Welsh *Prydyn*), the original Ulaid, were kinsmen of the Scottish Cruthin whom the Romans called *Picts* (Latin *'pictus'* denoting the pigment of their tattooed bodies).
[287] O Rahilly equated these invaders with the Gaels whom he claimed to be a distinct people from the Belgae: "The Southern Goidels pushed inland until they made Cashel their headquarters, as late as the beginning of the 5th century." The conquest of Cashel was a 4th/5th century expansion by Corc (Gorgin), founder of Cashel, setting out from Connacht with vassal tribes.
[288] EIHM p.141: *Lebor Gabala* pseudo-version of events, which studiously suppressed the Fir Belg, claimed the joint occupation of Ireland by the Fir Belg, Gailion and Domnann lasted 37 years. It was allegedly terminated by the Tuatha De Danann who are said to have defeated the Fir Belg with great slaughter. O Rahilly dismissed this as one of the many fictions of *Lebor Gabála*: "Inasmuch as the Tuatha De Danann were supernatural beings, we may dismiss their 'invasion' of Ireland as fictitious."
[289] Ibid p.141: O Rahilly upheld the allegation of a Fir Belg defeat posited by the fabulous *Lebor Gabála*.
[290] T. F. O Rahilly, Op. cit., p.146.
[291] According to the fictitious *'Lebor Gabála'*, Fergus Lethderg left Ireland for Britain with a his son, Britan, from whom Britain and the Britons are named: "These are the ancestors of all the Britons." No Englishman would fall for this Irish hoax.
[292] LL 6 a 13.

Semitic, Egyptian or Greek blood in their veins while being unaware that their Fir Belg ancestors hailed from the Belgic lands of the lower Rhine, N France, Belgium and Holland. This genre of pseudo-history can be seen for what it is and points to fictitious content. An example in the Dindsenchas of Slí Dála alleges that the 5 great roads of ancient Ireland converged on Tara. One is warned against such false claims by the fictitious opening lines: "Dala and Cannan came with their wives out of Scythia." T.F. O Rahilly[293] compounded this travesty of the truth by claiming the Fir Belg were led into Ireland from Britain by Lughaid Mac Con. The Belgae were known as Fir Belg/Erainn and spread rapidly throughout Ireland.[294] Ptolemy's 2nd century record projects an Iron Age Ireland dominated by Fir Belg septs. It corroborates Fir Belg origin-legends. While ancient Ulster was dominated by the pre-Celtic Cruthin, the Fir Belg/Erainn people were especially associated with the South and West, more generally with Munster and South Leinster, more specifically with the South of ancient Connacht. They spearheaded the Belgic thrust northwards against the aboriginal Cruthin.

O Rahilly's surprise at the site of Cath Magh Mucrama exposes his misreading of the Fir Belg invasion and the geo-politics of Iron Age Ireland: "Why the battle in which Lughaid Mac Con won the kingship of Ireland was located at Magh Mucrama (Athenry), it is impossible to say." This shows his confusion concerning the implications of the matter of Irish history which he attempted to elucidate. By the time he realized Tara was part of ancient Ulster and a minor seat of its kings well into historic times, it was to late to undo his errors.[295] These chapters will clarify why this battle and the assassination of Art took place where they did. When it is understood that this battle was fought near his Royal Capital (Regia e Te[mh]ra) which Ptolemy recorded in the West of Ireland where Art was assassinated defending his Fir Belg oppidum against the invasion of Lughaid Mac Con, it will be clear that O Rahilly's questioning of the site of the battle demands a far more academic assessment than that which he offered it.[296] O Rahilly fabricated a Laiginian invasion of Connacht which obsessed him based on his misreading of the Fir Domnann invasion as a Leinster invasion. "The landing place of the Domnann is given as Irrus Domnann, Inver Mor, Broad Haven in Erris," Co. Mayo[297],[298] "Clare is very rich in stone forts, the remains of 400 of which are known. Most are in the Burren district of Clare; they are akin to the great duns of the Aran Islands, and were evidently built by the same people."[299] Dun Belg and Caher Belg (named after the Fir Belg) overlook the Burren coast. Many of these great forts in Clare, Galway and Mayo, are named after the leaders of the Fir

---

[293] T.F.O Rahilly, 'Early Irish History and Mythology.' p. 77-79.

[294] T.F.O Rahilly, ''Early Irish History and Mythology', p.80.

[295] T.F. O Rahilly, 'Early Irish History and Mythology.' p. 485 (Additional notes)

[296] EIHM p.75-84; p.100: O Rahilly related how Lughaid Mac Con, defeated by Eoghan at Cenn Abrat in Munster, fled to Scotland. He led a huge army to Ath Cliath Magh Rí in Galway Bay in W Ireland. At Mag Muccrama of Athenry he usurped the Fir Belg over-kingship by assassinating Art, son of Conn, alleged High King of Ireland. O Rahilly called this an amalgam of 2 distinct traditions. (1) A legend of how Lughaid Mac Con, leading and typifying the Fir Belg of Munster was defeated by the Southern Gaels, and (2) a tradition which told, how in the 3rd century BC Lughaid, again typifying the Fir Belg/Erainn, invaded Ireland. He created this absurdity from 2 distinct events centuries apart: (1) A 3rd century BC coming of the Fir Belg, and (2) A 4th century AD invasion of Lughaid Mac Con with an army of Britons at Ath Cliath Magh Rí, the assassination of King Art and Lughaid's usurpation of the title *Rí Temhro*, Fir Belg Overking, centuries after the Fir Belg invasion. By Lughaid's time the Fir Belg were long established in Ireland.

[297] Ibid p.99 O Rahilly claimed a one-time dominance of Connacht by the Domnann. They were part of the Fir Belg Federation. He inferred, under the sway of pseudo-history, that the Fir Belg were defeated by the Domnann and driven to the outer isles where they took refuge. The stone fort of Dun Aengus on the Aran islands off Galway Bay is attributed to the allegedly fleeing Fir Belg. Visitors are led to believe that this is a suicidal last-stand outpost of the defeated Fir Belg, unaware of the existence of hundreds of similar massive forts along the West Coast mainland.

[298] Ibid p.96: "The Domnann suffered the same fate they had meted out to the Fir Belg a few centuries earlier."

[299] "Wakeman's Handbook of Irish Antiquities' , 3 ed., by J. Cooke, 175

Belg invasion. Clare's Magh Adhair coronation site is named after Adhar mac Umhoir, Dún Oengus on the Aran Islands after Oengus mac Umhoir and Dún Conchuirn after his brother. Conchuirn mac Umhor, ancestor of the Conchurini of Loch Corrib area, built Dún Conchuirn beachhead fort on the Aran Islands. He settled on the E shore of Loch Corrib where the Conchurini manned that flank of the expanding Fir Belg oppidum. Míl, Dela's son, set up his beachhead fort at Murvoch Mhil at Aran Mor's harbour. His mainland beachhead, Murvoch Mhíl, is near Oranmore. He then erected his royal residence, Rath Mhíl (Rathville), on the summit of Knocknadala when he succeeded his father, Dela. Dún Iuvor, named after Iuvor/Umhor, leader of the Fir Belg Mac Umhoir, is on the Mayo coast. Dún Mód Mac Umhoir is nearby. All proclaim their founders as conquering invaders, not defeated run-aways. "There is no reason to question the accuracy of the tradition which attributes their erection to the Fir Bolg."[300]

These massive 14 ft wide stone fortresses, among the finest of their kind anywhere, are not the work of a defeated people. They are the beachhead forts of the Fir Belg invasion of W Ireland. Similar Belgic fortifications on the SE coast of England, such as Bindon Hill beachhead fort, were a strategic part of their conquest of SE Britain and served the secondary purpose of controlling Lulworth Cove. The Aran forts and those studding Galway Bay's Iron Age seaport area of Ath Cliath Magh Rí and the Clare and Mayo coastline had the secondary purpose of controlling sea traffic there. They were a strategic part of the Fir Belg invasion, defence and domination of Iron Age Ireland. The Fir Belg tribes who much later became buffer states along Ulster's border, such as the Ciannachta, Luigni/Luaighni and Airgialla are assigned a Connacht origin. Ui Neill dynasts who spread to Donegal and Tyrone were offshoots of Connacht's Fir Belg royal line who hived off from the original stem in the 5th century. O Riordain described the expansion of the Connacht Fir Belg: "The general historical setting in Ireland fits the general picture deduced from the archaeological evidence. The ancient province of Ulster extended over much of the North of Ireland. Then the Connacht power expanded. It encroached on the NW of Ulster leading to the formation of the kingdom of Ailech whose capital was the multivallate hill-fort at Ailech in Donegal. Central Ulster became Airghialla. The Ulaid, having lost Emain Macha, survived E of the Bann with a capital at Downpatrick. Connacht dynasties had taken over much of the midlands."[301] The Connacht power remained firmly ensconced within Connacht as is underlined by the significant name they conferred on the territories they conquered E of the Shannon in central Ulster, the Airghialla (*'Oir Ghialla'*, Eastern Subjects - in relation to Turoe). "All this chain of events is the direct sequel of the rivalry between Connacht and Ulster which forms the basis of the *Táin Bó Cuailgne* and the Ulster cycle. In relation to Tara they were Northern, not Eastern subjects. The name Airghialla is based on the fact that the conquering power at the time when the name came into use was still regarded as the Western power. Its home was Connacht"[302] "The sagas support this general picture. The *Táin* reflects a conflict between Connacht's forces and Ulster."[303]

Vestiges of different alignments of frontier fortifications known as the 'Great Wall of Ulster'/'Black Pig's Dyke' and the Belgic Oppidum defence embankments in Connacht to be reconstructed here, are the monumental memorials of that supreme struggle for the domination of Iron Age Ireland written across the Irish landscape. They speak more eloquently than any words ever could. The words of Eugene O Curry, Professor of Irish History and Archaeology (1854–1862), regarding these monuments are as poignant today as when first uttered: "What marvelous manuscripts if we could only read them." The reading

---

[300] T. F. O Rahilly, "Early Irish History and Mythology." p. 146.

[301] Prof. S.P. O Riordain, 'Antiquities of the Irish Countryside', p. 24, revised by Ruaidhri de Valera

[302] E. MacNeill, 'Phases of Irish History', p. 125-6.

[303] Professor S.P. O Riordain, op. cit. p. 25.

of these manuscripts, indeed, the reading of the Iron Age Irish Celtic landscape, and its implications for Irish history, is the substance of this book. For a correct reinterpretation of the late Iron Age Irish geo-political landscape the reconstruction of these defensive earthworks is crucial. It corroborates saga tradition and Ptolemy's record. "The extent to which the formation of Iron Age Ireland is due to a considerable influx of people can be assessed on 2 grounds. First, the implantation of the Irish language. Second, because the eventual dominance of the ringfort tradition and its culture over all Ireland it seems that its bearers were the major Celtic conquerors of the land."[304]

An intimate association between ringforts and the Belgic defence system will become obvious, showing the Fir Belg were the bearers of this Celtic culture to Ireland. From Mac Liac's list of the primary settlement areas of the Fir Belg leaders, it is clear that the Fir Belg tribes were particularly numerous to the E and S of Galway Bay. There one should expect to find traces of Belgic oppida and defence systems. There, indeed, they are! The Belgic defensive system of linear embankments in Connacht is the most widespread and better known to older inhabitants than those in any other part of the country with the exception of vestiges of the Black Pig's Dyke. Before reconstructing its defensive system, it is apt to take a closer look at the Turoe/Knocknadala archaeological sites and immediate surroundings, the *Regia e Tera* and *Nagnata* of Ptolemy's record at the heart of the oppidum complex.

REGIA E TERA: ROYAL CAPITAL at TUROE and KNOCKNADALA ASSEMBLY PLACE

In his Irish record, Ptolemy of Alexandria, placed *'REGIA E TERA*, (Regia e Te[mh]ra, Royal Capital in Temhair), approximately at the centre of Co. Galway where Turoe hill (*Cnoc Temhro*) stands. His 2nd 'Regia' is in NE Ireland. It is believed to be the Capital of ancient Ulster, Emain Macha, in Armagh. Ireland's oldest legendary history recounts constant warfare between Ulster and Connacht. Its record is archaeologically written across the face of Ireland. The Cruthin of Ulster erected a defense rampart from Donegal on the NW to Dublin on the E coast as they were driven NE[305] to defend themselves from the ever-expanding Fir Belg power from its Connacht stronghold. It is known as the 'Black Pig's Dyke' (*Claidh na Muice Duibhe*). Vestiges, not only of this better-known Black Pig's Dyke, but of earlier and later defensive lines of fortification, survive as living testimony. What is less known is that the Connacht Fir Belg power had its own defensive earthworks, known as 'Dun Cladh', 'Muc Cladh', 'Muc Dhruim' (Magic Boar's Back), double ditches or mootes (*móta*), numerous segments of which survive as important living testimony to a lost history, lost Capitals, and lost people.

This Chapter will reconstruct Ireland's most imposing oppidum focused on Turoe, corroborated by Ptolemy's record, Ireland's earliest stratum of legendary history and archaeological findings. It will recreate the massive complex of the Belgic defensive system surrounding Turoe of Galway as it extends out into neighbouring counties and the adjoining Athenry oppidum, **the** Rath Cruacha of legendary history, as it was enveloped by the Turoe oppidum. This is a revolutionary reconstruction of Iron Age Irish history and political geography. This is a technical chapter. Those who endure this chase of the 'Magic Wild Boar' through page after page of townland names, along the route of this expanding oppidum will be rewarded with a unique insight into the making of Ireland. It paints a picture of the past enshrined in the close affinity between placenames, linear dykes, ring-forts and peoples. Thrill to the 'discovery' of Ptolemy's "most extensive acropolis in all

---

[304] S. P. O Riordain, op. cit. p. 25-6.

[305] **In this technical chapter the cardinal points and other points of the compass are expressed by the use of the capital initial for each such as N for north, W for west, and SSE for south-south-east.**

Britannia,"[306] one of the most massive oppida in the Celtic world. Those who cannot endure such a feat may go straight to Chapter 3.

The saga of the Belgic invasion led by Dela and the sons of Umhor is one of the few full accounts of the setting up of a Celtic oppidum on record. It is corroborated by Ptolemy's record and archaeological remains. The Mac Umhoir occupied territories in Galway, Clare, Mayo and Limerick, 17 in all.[307] Mac Liac's dindsenchas text tells that Dela, the Leader, went to the 'Hill of Dáil': "*Adnagar Delach ar Dáil,*" '*Cnoc na Dáil*' (Knocknadala) in prose versions, and *Cnoc na nDál* in 'Fiannaigheachta' texts, the Hill of Parliament/Great Assembly, the one hill with this unique name in Ireland. It was the seat of the Overkingdom. Pseudo-Dindsenchas hijacked Cnoc na Dála for Croghan of Roscommon as part of the Rathcroghan Myth concocted from the 8th century for its glorification. Dela established the *Oenach* (*Feis Temhro* on *Cnoc Temhro*/Turoe) adjoining his residence: "*Roighni Oenach Dind re thaibh.*" "(Celtic) cults were ancestor-worship, their feasts commemorations, the sanctuaries fair-grounds. The tribes assembled at the political and religious centre where the tombs of its ancestors stood, on Celtic feastdays (Samhain - November 1st, Oimelc/Imbolc - February 1st, and Beltaine - May 1st, the beginning of Summer, the fire-fest of the god Bel. Lugnassadh, the marriage of the god Lugh (August 1st), was celebrated at Carmen in Leinster"[308] and at Turoe and Athenry's Lugh Brugh. Feis Carmen of the Leinster kings was at the tumulus of Slaigne, leader of the Ui Bairrech. "These feasts were fairs, political/judicial assemblies and games, which were of religious origin (horse races at Emain Macha and of women at Carmen). Similar fests were held in Gaul (at all Celtic sanctuaries)."[309]

Guiraud listed several Continental Lugdunum where the feast of Lug was celebrated yearly on August 1st: "the Lugdunum from which Lyons derives its name, the Lugdunum which is Leiden in the Rhine delta, Laon Aisne of the Remi, Lugdunum of the Segusiavi and of the Cenomanni, Loudon (Lugh dun) at Sarthe, Lugdunum of the Voconci at Mont-Lahuc (Lugh Brugh), Drome, to mention a few."[310] It was celebrated with religious ceremonies, fairs (Oenach/Feis), races, and literary/poetic contests. Eochaidh Felech (Ferach Mhór), the father of Queen Medb, was the first and last king to have his royal residence on Cnoc Temhro[311] at Rath Ferach Mhór. He installed Lugh as the tutelary deity of Cnoc Temhro as tradition attests. Pseudo-history interpolated this as Tara of Meath. Clery's hill on Turoe beside Rath Ferach Mhór was known as *Lugh Bhru* (Otherworld Abode of Lugh), Ireland's Lugdunum close to Fearta Bre Nea. There was no Lugh Bhru/Lugdunum on Tara.

ACROPOLIS OF KNOCK-NA-DÁL AND THE NAG-NA-TA[L] OF PTOLEMY'S RECORD:
Ptolemy designated Knocknadala (Irish '*Cnoc na Dál*', Greek ΝΑΓΝΑΤΑΛ as the Acropolis. This is corroborated by its several urban-like sectors, including the Cetni-/Clogharevaun sectors. An affinity exists between Turoe/Knocknadala oppidum and the oppidum of '*Hradiste nad Savisti*' near Stradonice in Czech lands, a "most imposing system of Celtic fortifications in Central Europe"[312] occupied by the Volcae (Belgae). With '*Sance*' across a valley, it occupies 170 hectares. The defended area is ringed in by a rampart and

[306] Ptolemy, 'Geographica Hepigesis', Irish section.
[307] Dindsenchas of Carn Conaill, Met. D. iii, 440, 442, 444; Genealogical Tracts, 82, 115, 117f, 121; RC xv 478
[308] Henri Hubert, 'Greatness and Decline of the Celts", p. 240-1; P.W.Joyce,'Social History of Ancient Ireland',
   ii, p.436 & 441; 'Metrical Dindsenchas', iii, 57; Loth, 'L'Omphalos chez les Celtes', p.192.
[309] Hubert, Op. cit. p.242-3: Coligny Calendar has 2 seasons, Samonos (*Samhradh*),and Giamonos (*Giamhradh*).
[310] M. Guiraud, 'Les Assemblees provinciales" and Erneste Carette, 'Les Assemblees provincie de la Gaule'.
[311] This meant that only one royal residence stood on Cnoc Temhro. There is no trace of another on Turoe. There are several royal residences on Tara. Tara was then, and for centuries thereafter, firmly in the hands of the Cruthin of Ulster, enemies of the Fir Belg. The Cnoc Temhro on which King Eochaidh resided was Turoe of Galway.
[312] Jan Filip, 'Celtic Civilization and its Heritage' (Prague 1977), p. 129.

ditch, 6 meters high, 25 meters wide, 9 km in length, a mini version of the larger inner ward of the Turoe/Knocknadala oppidum. Hradiste and Sance form one fortified unit, with defence earthworks along the heights and thrown across the valley. 100 meters down the slope is the outer ward, *'Adamkovo Myto'*. Turoe/Knocknadala hills were similarly welded into one unit by dykes thrown across the valley separating them and along their slopes. At the foot of the slopes 100 yards lower another rampart paralleled the latter. These formed the inner ward of the Turoe/Knocknadala complex. With its urban and royal sectors it formed Ptolemy's *Acropolis* of Nag Na Ta[l]. Hradiste's densely populated area descended in steps to *'U Altanu'* above Ultava River, known as *'Akropol'*, the urban area. The densely populated W flank of Knocknadala descending to the Dunkellin River, known as Cetni, Carrowkeel on OS maps, had numerous traces of extensive occupation before being mostly obliterated in land reclamation. A 40-acre sector of this semi-urban area remains partly intact with traces of ringforts, houses and 'streets'. Local tradition claims that Cetni, Clogharevaun and adjoining areas in Kiltulla, Greyford, Killarriv, Knockatogher and Raford formed a sprawling ancient 'city'. The late John (Maneen) Cavanagh insisted until his dying day that he was taught in school that the Knocknadala/Cetni/Turoe complex was a Capital of ancient Ireland. A new generation of pupils scoffed at the idea that the overgrown area opposite their school could have been a Capital of Ireland: "Our schoolbooks say Tara was the Capital of Ireland from time immemorial? Surely history books don't lie!" Ironically, just then Irish historians began to question that claim of the history books and to call Tara's bluff. The chorus swelled to a crescendo as the 20th century wore on.

NECROPOLIS OF TUROE: TOMBS OF FEARTA, LUGH BRUGH, CRUACHU CHOOLAINN AND CRUACHAN NA hÚAIGHEANNA

Knocknadala's urban sector was the Acropolis. Turoe, Ptolemy's REGIA E TERA, with its Fearta, Lugh Brugh, Cruachu Choolainn and Cruachan na hÚaigheanna cemetries, was the Necropolis. 'Fert' (pl. 'Fearta') is O-Irish for the tumulus of an aristocrat. 'Fearta' (Fearta Claonta, Sloping Necropolis) on Turoe's NW scarp, Fearta Bre Nea, Cruachu Choolainn on its on NE scarp and Lugh Brugh to its S scarp, were Turoe's Royal Cemeteries. The last barrow burial mound on Turoe's N brow, known as Cruachan Airt, said to be the burial mound of King Art, son of Conn, and father of Cormac Mac Airt, was bulldozed into oblivion in 1994. There is a Cruach na hÚaigheanna and Cruacha Dhearg cemetery in the Benmor/Bellayarhag E flank of Turoe. There is a Cruachan na hÚaigheanna (*úaigh -e*, pl. – *eanna* = grave) on Carrowkeel (*Ceathramha Cill* al. *Ceall* = Cemetery Quarter) hill, the W extension of Knocknadala hill, linked by a trackway to the Cetni urban-like complex now under Preservation Order. The original Carrowkeel was reserved to the cemetery area in the south, where as the northern part of the townland had its own unique name, namely, Cetni. These and other archaic burial grounds within the Turope/Knocknadala inner ward highlight its former dense population. The archaeological report of the excavation of Turoe's Rath Feerwore (Ferach Mhór) at the W apex of Turoe by H.T. Knox in 1915 concluded with a remark: "Fearta, 'Graves', is a suggestive name. The next townland, Knocknadala, suggests 'Cnoc na Dála', Hill of Assembly, connected with these important tombs."[313] Local lore claims 150 burial mounds stood out on Turoe slopes before the famine but less than 50 at the turn of the 20th century. Starving peasants dug out the mounds seeking valuable grave goods to pay their passage to America. As a boy, Patrick Keane of Fearta saw burial mounds being dug near his home. One find was a miniature Turoe Stone replete with La Tene art work. Other finds were stone heads of three-faced gods and the skeleton of a huge dog with bronze collar and long chain, sold to a Jew. Martin Scarry and Joe Ruane found this (c.1930) in the Cruachu Choolan mound at Coolan Hill SE of Fearta. Local lore recalls an ancient blacksmith's forge on Coolan Hill, evoking the tale of the hound of Coolan slain by Cuchulann.

---

[313] H.T.Knox, in the journal of 'Galway Archaeological and Historical Society', p.193.

On a stepped hillock known as Clery's hill near the original site of the Turoe Stone are 'sunken graves' that have sagged visibly in living memory. The late Mrs. Smith of Ballyknock, and others like her blessed with a prodigious memory of 'lost' local place-names, recalled its older name as Loobroe (*Lugh Brugh*: Otherworld Abode of the god Lugh). King Eochaid Ferach Mhór is credited in legendary history with installing Lugh as the tutelary deity of Cnoc Temhro. Loobroe at Boyhill SE of Athenry is part of the ancient cemetery of *'Releg na Rí'*. The sunken graves and bones exposed by the hoofs of cattle hugging the W rim of this scarped hill peacefully enjoying the view of Connamara Mountains and Croagh Patrick some 50/60 miles to the W and NW, corroborate local lore that this is an ancient cemetery. It is said to have an entrance in its W frontage. Its position in relation to the former stone circle, the original site of Turoe Stone, Rath Ferach Mhór and Fearta, warrants careful archaeological examination. Cruachan Shíle on the E of Turoe was dedicated to the goddess Shíle, a fertility goddess. The Feis Temhro coronation ceremony was a 'marriage' of the new king and territorial goddess. Local farmers early last century were intrigued by large round holes forming a massive circle on Turoe's summit - the postholes of a massive temple? They were ploughed out as was Fearta's last saucer-barrow (referred to in the 1915 excavation report) on the N slope of Turoe in the 1940's.

CEREMONIAL AVENUE TO THE SANCTUARY: SLÍ COOLAN: ANCIENT ASSOCIATIONS
From the Slí Dála, on which the road along the W of Turoe is built, Slí Coolan ran E from the SW end of Fearta across Turoe's N slope to its NE end in Galboley skirting Coolan Hill, and along the EW stretch of Taillye road, zigzagging along the outer embankments to join a branch of the Slí Mhór which forms the Ben More/Brackloonbeg boundary. This became known as Sarsfield's Road after the passage of Sarsfield's army retreating to Limerick from the Battle of Aughrim. The Brackloon Beg/Ben More and Caraun Mor/Cross boundary was built on this branch of the Slí Mhór, whose main route ran from the summit of Knocknadala ENE along the Esker running on to Bellafa. A branch of the Slí Coolan ran SE through Bellayarha North to Crucha Dhearhag (Knockayearag/Vrooa-dhearag: variations of Bhru Dha Dherg). The main Slí Coolan Avenue circumvalated Turoe Hill.

'Togail Bruidne Da Derg' (Destruction of Da Derga's hostel) tells of the death of Conaire Mór Mac Éterscél, Fir Belg Overking (Rí Temhro, King of Tara in this pseudo-version). Conaire expelled the sons of Donn Desa from Ireland for their wrongdoing. They met Ingcel Caech, son of a British Manapi king, and went on a marauding expedition with him. Conaire was returning from Thomand (S portion of ancient Connacht) after settling a dispute between his serfs. The sons of Donn Desa and Ingcel Caech came ashore at *Tragh Fuirbthi* (Fuirbthen or Furbach) in Galway Bay. Ingcel Caech led a band of 5,000 Conmaicne and marched to Temhair (Tara in pseudo-history). As Conaire entered Slí Coolan which circled Temhair he saw the plain around Temhair overrun by invaders. He swung his chariot S from Slí Coolan to pass the night in the hostel of Da Derga which welcomed him. Ingcel Caech ordered the marauders to attack Da Derga's hostel as Conaire was being entertained there. They set it on fire and beheaded Conaire. Two pertinent points should be noted. This Leinster pseudo version was shaped in the 11th century from earlier versions. It was imbued with Leinster's 'official doctrine' of the Tara Myth. There was no High King of Ireland at Tara in Conaire's day. It remained in the hands of the Ulstermen until the 7th. century. The topography of the original tale has a West-of-Ireland setting which fits the Furbach/-Temhair/Slí Choolan/Cruach Dha Dherg context described above. The Tara Syndrome pseudo historians alleged Furbach, site of the marauder's embarkation, was on the E coast near Tara, ignoring Fuirbthi, Furbo (*Na Fuirbacha*) W of Barna on the N shore of Galway Bay in the territory of the Conmaicne led by Ingcel Caech.[314] The Connacht context is

---

[314] The tribal god of the Conmaicne, Lughaid Conmac, son of Oirbsiu Mór (al. Manannan Mór, after whom Loch Oirbsen, al. Loch Corrib, was named), shows that they were of Manapian stock. The gutteral 'ch' of 'Loch' in

preserved in Conaire's travels through Thomand, part of ancient Connacht, and in the landing place of Ingcel Caech. This saga was plundered from its original context to bolster Leinster's version of the Tara Myth.[315]

SLÍ MHÓR (ESCIR RIADA) AND SLÍ DÁLA: IRELAND'S ANCIENT ROAD SYSTEM CONVERGING ON TUROE/KNOCKNADALA: CONFOUNDING THE TARA MYTH

"The Celts were the great road-builders of N Europe. The ancient roads of Britain, ascribed to the Romans, had been laid by the Celts long before the coming of the Romans. Scholars, in the light of new archaeological finds, are only now discovering this. Celtic roads were mentioned by Strabo, Caesar and Diodorus Siculus. It is obvious, looking at Caesar's account of his Gallic campaigns, that he was moving his legions rapidly through Gaul because there was an excellent system of roadways in existence. When Caesar crossed to Britain, it becomes obvious to the careful historian that there had to be a well-laid system of roads in existence."[316] Several Roman words relating to road transport were borrowed from Celtic into Latin such as *carruca* and *carrus* from which 'car' derives in Anglo-related languages. 'Road' is a borrowing from the O. Celtic *'rót'* as in *Rót na Rí*. The 1985 discovery of a road, dated 150 BC, preserved under a Co. Longford blanket bog caused great excitement. Yet, the bulldozing into oblivion of long stretches of Ireland's famous ancient highways, the Slí (Slighe) Mhór (Escir Riada) and Slí Dála, over the past 50 years has not raised the slightest whimper of protest, thanks to the still all-powerful Tara Myth Syndrome which ignores all but itself. Who cares?

Pseudo history alleged that the 5 great roads of ancient Ireland converged on Tara. Antiquarians in the 19th century were called on to reconstruct these. Petrie marked them on his "restored map of Tara." They are not recorded on the OS maps brcause no trace of them could be found. Petrie's statement that "very indistinct traces now remain, though their ancient names as well as those other features at Tara are unfortunately forgotten" – "not a good basis on which to build a reconstruction of the system of the 5 great roads radiating from Tara. From actual evidence, all one can now say is that a track, possibly ancient, leads from near the N end of the 'Banqueting Hall' towards Rath Grainne where it bifurcates - one branch leading north-westwards, the other southwards along the foot of the upper slope of the W side of the hill" noted S.P. O Riordain, Professor of Archaeology.[317] The latter may be the Slí nAssail which ran W from Tara to Rathcroghan of Roscommon, the Cruthin capital of NE Connacht. The Connacht Fir Belg commandeered Slí nAssail and realigned it to accommodate their own plans when they overran the Midlands under Conn, Art and Cormac Mac Airt. Slí Midh-luachra ran N from Tara to Emain Macha, the Cruthin Capital of Ulster. The celebrated chief highways of ancient Ireland, the Slí Mhór (Escir Riada) and Slí Dála, never went anywhere near Tara except in pseudo-history (Figures 14, 15, 16, 17). They explode the vindictive Tara Myth. The *Temhair* on which they converged was not Tara but Turoe of Galway, *Cnoc Temhro*. Vestiges survive where they converge on or depart from the Turoe/Knocknadala inner ward and along their ancient routes.

The Slí Dála stretched across southeast Galway, Tipperary, Offaly, Laois and Kilkenny to Carlow. It branched off from the Slí Mhór on Knocknadala and ran south to Loughrea. It swung east above the lake and ran to the great ringforts of Masonbrook where it skirted the Silburyhill-like Hill of Doon. It crossed the Shannon near Portumna on its way to Roscrea

---

Loch Corrib is joined to Oirbsiu, forming 'Corrib'. Manapian settlements along Connemara coastal area are indicated by the 'Man' prefix in placenames such as Mannin Bay near Clifden and the Ballynamannagh townlands.
[315] T.F. O Rahilly,Op. Cit. p. 116-130.
[316] Peter Berresford Ellis, 'The Celtic Empire', p. 14
[317] Sean P. O Riordain, 'Tara', p.24: Others had no scruples anchoring not only the "other features at Tara' with ludicrous results, but the 5 great roads too. These were plundered by the highbrow highway hoaxers, the pseudo-historians, from the traditions of the Fir Belg of Connacht, like the Lia Fáil and so much else.

from where it ran along the Slieve Bloom foothills to Borris-in-Ossory where it is known as Ballaghmore. Bealach Gabran was its earlier name there.[318] It crossed Ely O Carroll and Upper Ossory which was formerly part of Laois. Bealach-Mór-Ossory and Boher Árd are also known as Slí Dála. It ran on east to Ballyroan just north of Abbeyleix where it branched off to the capitals of the Ui Bairrche at Ballyragget (Tulach Ui mBairrche in Kilkenny), to their ancient capital of Dinn Righ on the Barrow near Leighlinbridge in Carlow, the Dunon of Ptolemy's record, and to Nass (Nás na Rí) in Co. Kildare. Other ancient roads cross it or branch off at different points. Legendary history tells that the renowned Slí Dála ran from Temhair na Rí (interpreted by pseudo-history as Tara) to Roscrea and Borris-in-Ossory[319] and that it was founded by Dela, the leader of the Fir Belg invasion, who settled on Knocknadala in central Galway. He and his Cnoc na Dála, on which Slí Dála converges, gave it its name. The same legendary history relates that Roscrea, its original southern destination, got its name from Crea, the Munster Princess who became Dela's consort.[298] Rare indeed the Romeo who so literally cut a royal road straight to the heart of his lady! Dela did. Slí Dála proudly proclaims so to this day!

Farmers point out short stretches of the Slí Dála. A rare few like Joe Cooney, Joe Dunne, Joe Ruan, Ml. Casserly and James Scully passed on its ancient names and its route to its terminus.[320] The road from the SW of Knocknadala along Turoe's W boundary to its SW corner was built on the Slí Dála. Its round banks were leveled 60 years ago. Sections with banks intact survive just S of Turoe at Tonnawausa fort in Lackafinna and in field across the road from Loughrea's Rugby field where one of the best intact stretches survives. A long section survives between Loughrea and the Hill of Dún near Masonbrook. Like the Slí Mhór, it ran in a straight line for miles on end, so unlike present-day roads. Wider than many, it is 21 ft. wide at all points where it survives, excluding its earthen banks. The stretch from Knocknadala to Loughrea was still in use until the early 20th century when bridges were washed away. A route bifurcated from Slí Dála at Loughrea and ran S through Clare. Joe Cooney and Joe Dunne recalled hearing it called 'Slí Temhair Luachra'. Its Munster terminus may have been the Fir Belg Capital, Temhar Luachra (Tara hill) at Friarstown, 5 miles S of Limerick city.

The *Slí Mhór* ran along stretches of the Escir Riada ridge from Ath Cliath Cualainn on the S Dublin/Wicklow coast to Ath Cliath Magh Rí in Galway Bay, well clear of Tara. It entered Connacht at Shannonbridge and ran NW to Ballinasloe. It ran W to Kilconnell and swung SW through Bellafa to Knocknadala and Turoe. It met the *Slí Dála* and *Rót na Rí* at the summit of Knocknadala. From there it swung NNW through Raford to Knockatogher. It swung W along the Carnakelly road (or parallel to it) to Athenry. It bifurcated at Athenry. Its main branch swung SW and converged with *Rót na Rí* on the Iron Age Seaport of Ath Cliath Magh Rí near Clarenbridge on the S Galway coast. A branch, the Boher Mór, ran W towards Galway city and along the coast into Connamara, Con(maic)namara, a Manapian road. Long and short sections of the Sli Mhór to Ath Cliath Magh Rí (near Clarenbridge) survive between the massive Caherdrine fort (near Clarenbridge) and Athenry and between Athenry and Knocknadala while others are traceable on the OS Map. Extant vestiges of the Slí Mhór Escir Riada highway are 27 ft. wide, excluding its banks. New Housing, road makers and gravel miners bulldoze long stretches of these renowned ancient roads into oblivion. Does anyone care?[321]

---

[318] 'History of Queen's County', Vol 1, p. 61 O Hanlon, O Leary, Lawlor. Swayed by pseudo-history and Dr. Petrie, they claimed it ran to Tara, but knew no vestige of it running on to Tara. Cf. Book of Leinster, p. 196.

[319] Edmund Hogan, 'Onomasticon Goedelicum' c.f. 'Slige Dala' p. 613.

[320] Sli Dála is also known as Ballaghmore Muigh Dála, Sean Bealach Mór, Bealach Gabran, Bealach-Mór-Ossory & Slí Mór Dála.

[321] The National Roads Authority is routeing the N6 motorway through the ancient cemetery of Cruachan na hUaigheanna, overlooking Cetni urban-like complex under Preservation Order, and right across Knocknadala hill

Rót na Rí (Royal Road of the Kings: celebrated in the Dindshenchas of Loch Riach, *Magh Fót co fir ar Rót na Rí)*[322] ran as a ceremonial avenue from the summit of Turoe near the original site of the Turoe Stone down the N slope of Turoe to Fearta and then W along the SW edge of Fearta (marked by granite standing stones) and Abernavilla. It ran up to the summit of Knocknadala and straight to Clarenbridge's *Áth Clee Magh Rí* seaport through Moyode (*Magh Fót*), crossing the Athenry/Craughwell road near Pollnabanny Bridge and along the road past Caherbulligin junction to Stradbally's ancient seaports. A branch bifurcated at Caherbulligin junction, rounding the east side of Coldwood Lake to the Ballinillaun road and then ran W on the esker ridge on the N side of the river to the ancient docks at the mouth of Ballynamannagh River and the massive Dunbulcaun Fort marine entreport. Another bifurcated S to Rahashan lake (Dúr Loch) on the Dúghiortach (Dúr) River and ran W above its N shoreline. Vestiges of other local ancient routes such as Slí Iceni and Slí Mhannin (Manapi road) survive. The *Slí Mhór, Slí Dála, Rót na Rí, Slí Cualann* and *Slí Temhair Luachra,* familiar to Queen Medb, converged on Knocknadala/Turoe long before the Tara Myth Syndrome hijacked them. These ancient roads, archaeological sites and traditions in this ritual landscape must be preserved for future generations and for the sake of the thunderous challenge they roar at the fraudulent claims craftily contrived by Tara and Rathcroghan pseudo-historians!

SANCTUARY: CEREMONIAL SITE: RATH FERACH MHÓR: TUROE STONE SETTING

The archaeological report of the excavation of Rath Ferach Mhór at the western apex of Turoe by H.T. Knox in 1915 looked no further afield than the confines of the rath itself. It ended with a summary reference to the names of adjoining townlands, Fearta and Knocknadala, and a remark on a remaining defaced ring-barrow mound in Fearta townland. Knox wrote, "One hundred and fifty yards NW of this rath in the Tld. of Fearta is a small regular *dumha*, much ruined. It was opened many years ago and human remains were found."[323] Local tradition could have told him how numerous burial mounds there suffered the same fate within living memory. The excavation of Rath Ferach Mhór in front of which the Turoe stone formerly stood, "suggested an open ceremonial site round the stone dating to the last century BC." The Turoe stone was the centre of a 'ceremonial coronation site'.

The area around Rath Ferach Mhór had a circle of standing stones. Knox was aware of the presence of large stones on Turoe "The ring is studded at intervals with conglomerate drift blocks. The alignment stones are of the same material." The phenomenon of a ring of standing stones encircling an ancient cemetery, such as at Newgrange, dates from the megalithic tomb builders. The tombs of Turoe and Fearta appear to belong to the Iron Age and be contemporary with the Turoe Stone as suggested by two which bore the names of Iron Age kings, Cruachan Airt and Cruach Conari (Chon Rí?). Grave goods and human remains from cist burials at Rath Ferach Mhór date to the first century BC/AD.[302] Patrick Keane's grandfather pointed out to his grandsons the positions of the standing stones of the stone circle on the NW brow of Turoe. Like the Turoe Stone, some were of granite, others of limestone or conglomerates. The outer stone at the W tip of the alignment recorded by Knox was part of the great encirclement. A similar large stone formerly stood very close to

---

along a section of the esker running towards Bellafa on the route of the Slí Mhór. Conned and blinded by the Tara and Rathcroghan Myths, C O'Lochlainn ("Roadways in Ancient Ireland"), Peter O'Keeffe ("Ireland's Principal Roads 123AD – 1608"; The National Roads Authority 2001) and Hermann Geissel ("Slí Mhór: A Road on the Long Ridge"), converged on the wrong terminus, Tara, or lost their way in 'reconstructing' these ancient highways. From Knocknadala to Clarenbridge, Hermann Geissel took the 'shortest route', "absolutely bewildered" by the archaic historical geopolitical reality that might have guided him along the right path. When he stumbled on fragments of *Rót na Rí* and *Bealach na Fert* he promptly renamed them the Slí Mhór, totally missing the several genuine segments of the Slí Mhór both in the field and on the OS maps which he might have found had he followed its correct route through Athenry, a huge mis-step in an otherwise excellent work.

[322] Dindshenchas of Loch Riach: *Magh Fót co fir ar Rót na Rí*. Line 62-63.

[323] H.T. Knox, 'The Turoe Stone and the Rath of Feerwore, Co. Galway, in GAHS, P. 192-3.

this forming a narrow door-like ceremonial entrance. Just inside this entrance stood the Turoe Stone some 10 yards or so in front of this entrance to the now demolished Rath Ferach Mhór within the W part of the stone encirclement. A granite stone stands in the fir grove near the NW summit of Turoe.[324] Knox's excavation revealed that the Rath was finally used as a burial place and remained undisturbed thereafter. Two cists were found, one at the rampart centre indicating cremation, the other containing a large collection of animal bones, ox, pig, and bird, the remains of a Royal funeral feast. Whose funeral feast?

Knox claimed the presence of the Turoe Stone at the entrance to Rath Ferach Mhór showed the rath had been occupied by **a very important person**. Who? It is not by sheer coincidence that the most illustrious, richly ornamented Iron Age ceremonial stone in all Europe, carved in exquisitely stylized La Tene Celtic art form, stood in Turoe's sanctuary. "Certain standing stones were invested with a sacred character shown by their presence on ancient ceremonial sites such as the inauguration place at Magh Adhair in Clare. Certain highly ornamented stones of Iron Age date as at Turoe in Galway, were undoubtedly cult objects."[325] Clare O Kelly, the Newgrange Archaeologist, noted that had Bru na Boinne (megalithic mounds at Newgrange) not been salvaged from the lost worlds of the past, and had Irish Archaeology not become obsessed with that megalithic complex which pseudo-history alleged to be the royal cemetery of the kings of Tara, it is the Turoe Stone which would have become the focus of its attention.[326] Had Irish Archaeology become aware of the significance of what it missed in its excavations of Turoe's Rath Ferach Mhór, the stone circle in that sanctuary, the Iron Age cemeteries, and the inner and outer wards of the Belgic defensive system, its attention would have swung decidedly in Turoe's favour. It is not to late to make amends, despite all burial mounds (except Lugh Bhru) and some of the Belgic ramparts which survived when the excavations took place, having since been leveled.

TUROE STONE: THE LIA FÁIL: STONE OF DESTINY: FEIS TEMHRO

Mac Liac's *dindshenchas* poem[327] on Carn Conaill tells that the Fir Belg Leader, Dela, established the *Oenach (Feis Temhro*, Inauguration Festival) at a site next to his palace on Knocknadala: "*Roghni Oenach Dind re thaibh.*" Adjoining Knocknadala is Turoe hill with its illustrious Coronation Stone originally sited in front of Rath Ferach Mhór near the Royal Cemetery of Fearta. *Feis Temhro* was celebrated at this Inauguration Site. Names of all monuments on Tara are utterly misleading. Professors O Riordain and Anthony Weir noted that they were applied by the sheer guesswork of 19th/20th century fanciful antiquarians called on to identify those monuments, the names and purpose of which were long forgotten.[328] They played with names applied by medieval manipulators more interested in suppressing the truth of what was there 8 or 10 centuries earlier and replaced it with traditions plundered from the Turoe Fir Belg oppidum. Their 'learned identifications' were based on the Tara Myth and on names from topographical pseudo-tracts surreptitiously slipped in among otherwise genuine *dindsenchas* texts. Contradictions underline their conjectures. "Plaques erected by the Office of Public Works on the Tara monuments follow the 'identifications' made by Macalister and differ from the Ordnance Map in many instances. Macalister differs from Petrie's conclusions. Maps published by Macalister have

---

[324] As with Newgrange where only 12 of a total of 34 standing stones remain, most of Turoe's stones were carted off. The Turoe Stone was drawn away on a clod-crusher pulled by a team of horses and set up in the front lawn of Turoe House at the E side of Turoe before the excavations began. Patrick Lyons, a herd with Mr. Dolphin, Turoe's Landlord, was on hand in 1915 to point out to Knox the original setting of the Turoe Stone.

[325] S.P. O Riordain, 'Antiquities of the Irish Countryside', p. 144.

[326] Clare O Kelly, 'Illustrated Guide to Newgrange.'

[327] Met. D. iii, 440 in Book of Ballymote. Compare prose version, RC. xv, 478, and Book of Lecan version.

[328] O Riordain, 'Tara-the monuments on the Hill', p.8-9; A. Weir, 'Early Ireland - a field guide', p.196

several (critical) changes between the one of 1919 and that of 1931."[329] Myth-makers mayhem! (Figure 10).

It is implicit in Ireland's oldest origin-legends that the *Lia Fáil* Stone of Destiny is of Fir Belg origin. D*indsenchas* texts state that the Lia Fail stood on Cnoc Temhro, or *'i Temhra'* (pseudo-history's Tara of Meath). Pseudo-history continues to claim that the *Lia Fáil* stands on Tara hill. A plaque at Tara proclaims that the stone erected to mark the graves of those killed in the 1798 skirmish is the famous *Lia Fáil*. If this imposter indeed were the *Lia Fáil* it would surely never have been used as a gravestone. Until 637 Tara belonged to the Cruthin of Ulster, the aboriginal pre-Celtic people whose own art style differed totally from the highly stylized La Tene Celtic art style of the Turoe stone, a form of art common in Celtic areas of Britain, Ireland and the Continent. Conaire, Conn, Art and Cormac Mac Art, alleged by pseudo-history to have been crowned as High Kings at the *Lia Fáil* which roared its acceptance of them, never set foot on Tara. They were Fir Belg Overkings in W Ireland. There were no High Kings of Ireland then. The Fir Belg never resided at Tara. Turoe was their principal royal primary settlement area. It is there one should expect to find their *Lia Fáil*. There it stands. It was easy for pseudo-historians to transfer the traditions of Turoe to Tara since both have the same O-Irish name. This they did with the *Lia Fáil* Stone of Destiny just as they did with the *Slí Dála* and the Slí Mhór (*Escir Riada*). The Turoe Stone may have been commissioned by the early Briganten King, Ugain Mór. Pre-17th century writers, aware that there was no *Lia Fáil* Stone at Tara of Meath in their time, guessed it had been taken to Scone in Scotland. To hide Tara's embarrassment, a gravestone in the most ill-chosen position for a coronation stone, right inside 'Teach Cormaic', the equally bogus Royal Residence of Cormac Mac Airt, is now claimed to be the illustrious *Lia Fáil*. It stands beside an even more ill-appropriate statue of St Patrick (a vain attempt to bolster the Tara/Patrick Myth). As described by S. P. O Riordain, this so-called *Lia Fáil* inauguration stone is "an upright granite stone marked with a cross, the letters R.I.P. and initials - for it marks the grave of those killed in the battle of Tara in 1798. The stone over the 1798 grave is now taken to be the *Lia Fáil*."[330] Professor F. J. Byrne endorsed J. Carey's reference to O Broin's article on the real *Lia Fáil (1990),* claiming that it had 'disappeared' from Tara and concluding that "the phallic standing stone (now at Tara of Meath) was not the *Lia Fáil*."[331] Where then is the *Lia Fáil*, the Stone of Destiny? Oh Where?

Pre-17th centurty authors wrote of the *'Lia Fáil'* "that **used to be**" at Tara, implying that it was no longer there at time of writing. It was **not** there in the 16th century when Keating wrote his Irish History.[332] He noted 'rumours' of its transfer to Scotland. Scotland's Stone of Scone was taken by King Edward I in the 14th century to Westminster where, for centuries it has served as the inauguration stone of British Kings and Queens. As with other fancifully named Tara monuments, the stone pointed out as the Stone of Destiny is no more the famed *Lia Fáil* than the illset statue of St. Patrick beside it is a symbol of the alleged conversion of the High King and people of Ireland. This spurious stone setting is the standing memorial par excellence to the great Tara/Patrick Myth. The literary 'transportation' of the *Lia Fáil* from Turoe to Tara is just as fabulous as the fiction concocted by the founder of the Worldwide Church of God claiming it to be the Biblical Jacob's pillow. Iron Age Ireland celebrated the 'Feis Temhro' on Cnoc Temhro (Turoe) for the inaugural coronation of each new 'Rí Temhro' (Fir Belg Overking). The highly ornate Turoe Stone is the fabled *Lia Fáil* of ancient Ireland; the coronation stone of the Fir Belg overkings. It is a permanent

[329] Sean P. O Riordain, "Tara, The Monuments on the Hill ." 1982, p. 7.
[330] Sean P. O Riordain, "Tara, The Monuments on the Hill ." 1982, p. 10.
[331] Byrne, Op Cit. Addit. Note p. 63; Carey in *Eriu,*1 (1999) p. 165-8; O Broin 'Celtica' xxi (1990) 'Lia Fáil'
[332] Keating's 'History of Ireland'; H. 5, 32, T.C.D.

monument of the chief Royal Capital of the Fir Belg tribes who dominated Iron Age Ireland. It stood in front of Rath Ferach Mhór on Turoe.[333] (Figure 10).

"A large number of pillar-stones (are) believed to be of ritual significance. Some mark sacred spots. The most impressive of these is the Turoe Stone, divided into four panels decorated in "Waldalgesheim Style". It can be paralleled to the 4-sided stone at Pfalzfeld in the Rhineland"[334] supporting the idea that it had cult significance. "The Celts are identifiable above all by their art. They created what has been called the first true art-style found north of the Mediterranean areas. Professor Etienne Rynne left one of the finest descriptions of Celtic art, as found on the Turoe Stone. "It is curvilinear rather than rectilinear, asymmetrical yet balanced, sometimes geometric yet not rigidly so, abstract yet sometimes semi-representational, over-indulgent yet controlled, barbaric yet sophisticated, ever willing to absorb new motifs and ideas yet never willing merely to copy them. There is a tendency to geometricize what is zoomorphic, and to zoomorphize what is geometric: bosses and swirling curves often give the impression of a human or animal face peering out of the ornament. One can seldom be certain whether the artist has deliberately transformed the face into the design or vice versa. There is an air of mystery about it all, and it is clear that the Classical ideal of almost photographic life-like reproduction was anathema to the Celt. The overall design or pattern was of primary importance. The Celt decorated a surface, that is, ornamented what was already present so as to make it more pleasing. Celtic art, though not always merely decorative, is seldom descriptive – it is truly an art for Art's sake."[335]

The Turoe Stone is covered with continuous abstract curvilinear La Tene art with flowing design carved in relief, set off by a band of Greek-key decoration surrounding its foot, resembling the 'Naval Stone' of Delphi with its Greek-key design. The Continental Belgae, the Volcae Tectosages, plundered the sacred shrine at Delphi in Greece. On Turoe hill stands Celtic Europe's finest example of La Tene relief engraving on stone. From its conspicuous place in early records, the *Lia Fáil* was unique, not some inconspicuous stone like the impostor hugging Tara hill. The La Tene art of the Turoe Stone and of the bronze horsebit from nearby Atymon, links the area artistically to the Continental Celtic Kultur-provinz, cradle of the Belgae, La Tene artists par excellence. Tradition has it that there was a multiple echo from the original site of the Turoe Stone, the *Lia Fáil*, before the great burial mounds and defensive ramparts were leveled. Then it vanished. Imagine the 'roar' of the *Lia Fáil*, the thunderous 'roar of approval' as a rightful new king was proclaimed, and the echo in full reverberation.

RATH NA bhFHILLE: POET'S PALACE: *ABER NA bhFHILLE*: POET'S ARENA

Celtic Royal Assembly sites had special arenas for Poets and Bards. The Turoe/Knocknadala complex had two sites, one on the NE slopes of Knocknadala called Rath na bhFhille, Poet's Palace, and another on the NW slopes of Turoe, between Fearta and Knocknadala, called Aber na bhFhille (wrongly recorded as Aberanville on OS Maps), Poet's Arena, where poetic and literary feats were contested. While ploughing Aber na bhFhille townland, Patrick Keane of Fearta found archaic coins. Poets and bards held high position in Celtic society and were associated with the druids who included tribal chieftains like Divitiacos, Dumnorix and Conn Cedchathach, among their number. They were "a highly trained professional group who were the repositories of Celtic history and poetry under the

---

[333] Ferach Mhór was the official royal name of Eochu Ferach or Fedlech, ideal king of the Fir Belg, father of Queen Medb. There is good reason to believe that he was Verica (Roman equivalent of O. Irish 'Ferach'), King of the British Atrebates then being overrun by the aggressive Catuvellauni? His brother Epillus (Eochaill, early Celtic 'p' became later 'q'/'ch'), from whom he took over the Atrebaten kingship, was perhaps the Eochail Airemh (Eochaid Aithreabh) of the Atrebates who allegedly reigned in Ireland as in England prior to Ferach Mhór.

[334] Professor Etienne Rynne, 'Lecture Notes" 1b, Archaeology Dept., University College, Galway, p12.

[335] Professor Etienne Rynne, 'The Capuchin Annual', 36, (1969), p. 202.

patronage of the kings. The tradition was strictly oral, the bards having to commit to memory a vast store of knowledge and be word-perfect in their recitations."[336] Classical authors lauded the refinement and elegance of their use of language and appreciation of linguistic subtlety. Marcus P Cato (234-149 BC) wrote of the awe-inspiring sophistication of Celtic rhetoric. The oratory and eloquence of Celtic poets impressed the historian Poseidonius (135-50 BC, quoted by Athenaeus). He recorded an incident at a feast of King Louernios, Commius' (Gann's) grandfather, where a poet was richly rewarded with bags of gold. Poets played a privileged part in the Celtic assemblies (Dail). Celtic Capitals of Gaul and Britain provide numerous examples of the layout of Celtic Assembly places. The Turoe/Knocknadala complex is a classic example of a Royal Capital and Assembly place.

ARCHAEOLOGICAL SITES ON THE SUMMIT OF KNOCKNADALA
Five ringforts strung out along the summit of Knocknadala are recorded on the OS map as being, not in Knocknadala, but in Clashaganny, Carrowreagh and Carrowkeel.[337] The S section of Carrowkeel and Clashaganny (*Claisha gainimh*=trenches in sandy land) on which these stood is known locally as Slieve Knocknadala (K. summit). Clashaganny is restricted to the lower area on its N flank between Killarriv/Raford bog and Knocknadala. The Raford River's bank was raised behind floodgates to flood lowlying areas. Two adjoining ringforts stood at the E end of Knocknadala's summit. The largest, marked 'Children's Burial Site' was bulldozed into the ground 30 years ago.

TUROE/KNOCKNADALA OPPIDUM AND BELGIC DEFENSIVE SYSTEM
Little is published on linear embankments in Connacht while Ulster's Black Pig's Dyke has been well documented. Others are noted in Munster and Leinster. Yet, to people in Connacht, particularly in Galway, linear embankments, known as double ditches, mootes, *'dun chladh'*, *'muc chladh'* or *'muc dhruim'*, are a well-known feature of the landscape. They are familiar with these over short distances. Nobody has linked these up from one area to another, apart from Martin Finnerty's in respect of those surrounding Athenry in his *'Punan Arsa'*. In Roscommon the pair of Mucklaghs (muc chladh) at Rath Croghan and the Dún of Drumsna on the loop of the Shannon have been noted by Michael Herrity and Barry Raftery. Having examined various functional zones of this Fir Belg oppidum's focal point, and the characteristic hallmarks of a typical Belgic oppidum with its unique defensive system, corroborated by classical, literary, legendary and archaeological evidence, it is now opportune to reconstruct the vast network of the Belgic defensive system surrounding it. This Chapter addresses the issue of an elaborate series of linear earthworks extending out from this oppidum core at the centre of Galway across the Connacht landscape. It will reconstruct the linear embankments surrounding Turoe and Knocknadala (7 miles E of Athenry, 5 miles N of Loughrea) and those surrounding Athenry. A field survey of the area, local knowledge of existing vestiges of embankments, the memories of the older generation of leveled embankments going back to the end of the 19th century, legendary history and evidence from Ordnance Survey (OS) maps, have been used in this reconstruction.

A series of linear embankments facilitates the delineation of the focus and extent of the Turoe/Knocknadala oppidum. Various circumvallations of defensive dykes mark out an inner ward, outer ward, and several extensions of the latter, in typical Belgic fashion. The enclosing ramparts, which define the inner ward, will now be reconstructed. The adjoining hills of Turoe, representing the Necropolis, coronation site and ceremonial sanctuary, and of Knocknadala, representing the Acropolis and Assembly grounds, have their own inner

---

[336] Peter Berresford Ellis, 'The Celtic Empire', p.18.
[337] The arbitrary fixing of boundaries confused the site of Knocknadala. The local people rejected the OS Map's erratic entries: "How can this hill be called 'Clashaganny' while the lower ground is called a hill (Slieve Chnoic na Dála)?" they asked.

wards. They are welded into one joint inner ward by embankments thrown across the hollow and stream separating them. These create one oppidum core.

RECONSTRUCTION OF TUROE INNER WARD:
A set of linear embankments encircled the entire hill of Turoe bounded by streams along its N and S flanks. It ran EW along its N and S slopes stretching from Gortcam/Benmore (Claidh Draighin) in the E to Tooloobaunbeg/Tooloobauntemple in the W, as shown on the OS map (Figure 11). A clockwise direction will be followed in tracing these and other sets. Vestiges of these embankments are marked on the 1894 OS 25" map and 1933 OS 6" map, Sheet No. 97. They were lowered and narrowed in various ways. Generally only the smaller outer-lip rampart has been retained as a field fence. Near the SE[338] of Turoe a tree-covered 5 to 7 ft high, and 8 to 10 ft. wide embankment forms the S boundary of the fields on the righthand (W) side of the laneway to Turoe House (Turoe Pet Farm) 200 yards out towards the main road. It was cut down in size and dressed up as a demesne enclosure fronting the grounds of Turoe House, as was the custom among the landed gentry. The best preserved section was leveled recently. This embankment runs W just inside the righthand (N) side of the road along the S foot of Turoe hill - a vestige of one of the set of embankments forming Turoe's inner ward. Transverse ramparts knit the linear embankments into one set.

There are many instances of roads built on top of, in the fosse, or alongside linear embankments. They were used as right-of-ways through the ages. Frank Corcoran recalls hearing his grandfather recount how this section of embankment was 12 feet high and 12 feet wide on top in his young days. It was cut down almost to ground level to fill the fosse for the making of the road to its W end. The set of ramparts ran on W through Ballykeeran and Tooloobauntemple, then swung NNW to the Tooloobaun road. A long stretch of partly leveled rampart survives along that segment but is not marked on the OS map. Old OS maps show sections of rampart built up on the banks of the streams from Carramore and Ooshigh (Poll na nDoosigh, dyke bog) bogs which skirt the N and S foot of Turoe. Other surviving vestiges are shown on the OS 6" map, Sheet 97, forming the Fearta/Abernavilla boundary and running along Galboley's boundary with Sraheendoo (marshland dyke), Brackloonbeg and Turoe. The road through the S tip of Galboley on its boundary with Benmore runs along the fosse of the embankment which survives on both sides of the road. These inner ward embankments skirted the fort of Taillye and the cone-shaped fort at Patrick's Well SE of Bullaun. Cnoc Temhro was the original name of the entire hill right to its western extremity on the W boundary of Ballykeeren (Figures 12 and 13).

RECONSTRUCTION OF KNOCKNADALA INNER WARD
A set of embankments encircled the summit of the adjoining Knocknadala Hill (incorrectly entered on the OS map as the S half of Clashaganny), enclosing a line of 5 ringforts on its summit. Clashaganny road was laid along the fosse of the main rampart. Its outer-lip rampart survives along most of the N side of this road. The road along the E foot of Knocknadala hill through Carrowreagh and Galboley on the edge of Pump Bog is built on a rampart, accounting for its height above ground level. Vestiges of the linear embankments enclosing Knocknadala survive as shown on OS map. The original inner ward (Figures 18 and 19) was expanded W and NW to enclose a growing sprawling urban centre across Carrowkeel, Clogharevaun and Kiltulla South and North (Figure 21). This significant extension to the original Knocknadala inner ward corresponds to a similar WSW extension of Turoe inner ward to partly include an extension of the urban-like complex on its SW perimiter through Tooloobauntemple, Caherhenryhoe, and the Carrowbaun/Dunsandle

---

[338] **In this technical chapter the cardinal points and other points of the compass will be expressed by the use of the capital initial for each such as N for north, W for west, and SSE for south-south-east.**

boundary area. This appears to be the beginning of urbanization in Ireland, corresponding to that in SE Britain.[339]

A 40-acre site of the sprawling urban complex survives in the Carrowkeel segment of the Knocknadala inner ward. Cetni (Cotini) is its local name. The National Monuments and Historic Properties placed a Preservation Order on Cetni and listed it as a National Monument in the Sites and Monuments Register. It is recorded as a Complex of earthworks in Carrowkeel.[340] It is all that remains of the mostly reclaimed sprawling urban-like nucleated settlement, prior to the Preservation Order, which covered a much wider area. Eoin MacNeill's 'Saint Patrick' refers to a large population centre, Campus Cetni in South Connacht, visited by Patrick.[341] The 7th cent. pseudo-historian, Tirechan claimed this referred to Magh gCedne in N Connacht. It has never been identified. The renowned 2nd century Greek geographer, Ptolemy of Alexandria, recorded a population centre as "*the most extensive and illustrious acropolis (urban population centre) in all Britannia situated in the West of Ireland.*" He named it ΝΑΓΝΑΤΑΛ in Greek letters. This translates to Cnoc na Tal (Dal), Knocknadala today, the inner ward of which Cetni/Carrowkeel/Clogharevaun are a part. Corroborating Ptolemy's astounding record, several segments on the W, NW and SW of the Turoe/Knocknadala complex, including Cetni, were regarded as part of a town or urban centre. Local tradition pointed out surface ruins of numerous houses along narrow 'streets', a whole complex of earthworks including close-set ringforts, raised sites and a Celtic field system before the area was reclaimed. The section under Preservation Order (Figure 22) shows what the more extensive acropolis area was like.

The frequency with which *Dindshenchas* texts refer to sites within the Turoe/Knocknadala/-Athenry oppidum complex, corroborated by archaeological evidence, classical literature and oral history, deserves thorough investigation. A significant corroboration of Ptolemy's record and legendary history preserved in the Dindsenchas of Maen Magh refers to its dense population: "*O Maen na treibh tuillte co rein na fairrgi*" ("From densely populated Maen Magh to the sea" in Galway Bay). Maen Magh is the ancient Galway plain which has the Turoe/Knocknadala site at its core. No other area of ancient Ireland was accredited with a dense population. "Official" current Irish thinking that Iron Age Ireland had no urban centres is in direct conflict with this startling evidence and with the material remains of Belgic towns in SE England. The Belgae had towns in SE Britain and on the Continent (early Paris and Trier for example). Their oppida were in fact large urban centres.[342] Ann Ross cited a number of Belgic towns when she noted that the Belgae "created urban settlements which were in fact towns."[343] This calls for a total re-evaluation of the Turoe/Knocknadala oppidum trappings before it is too late.

Knocknadala's expanded inner ward stretched W from the road along its east foot across Cetni, Clogharevaun and the Bookeen Road into Kiltulla South and North and the E half of Greyford through which the urban settlement sprawled. It was bounded on the N flank by Clogharevaun/Raford River (*'An Dúghiortach'*, the *'Dúr'* River of Ptolemy's record). Banks of this river in Raford were built up as embankments to flood extensive low-lying areas behind the floodgates. Leveled embankments along the NW slope of Killarriv are still remembered as the "Curraghs". Killarriv (Coill Athreibh) bog is known as *Poll na Chládh* (dyke bog) (Figure 20). Raford is an anglicization of *Rath na bhFhille Droichead* (Fort of the Poet's Palace) which stands beside Raford bridge, and gave Raford its original name.

---

[339] Cf. Peter Salway, 'Roman Britain', p. 92; 112-114.

[340] Carrowkeel Tld., Parish of Kiltulla, Co. Galway: O.S. 6" Sheet 97 entered in the Register of National Monuments in accordance with subsection 2 of Section 5 of the National Monuments Act, 1987.

[341] Eoin MacNeill, 'St. Patrick', under population centres visited by the saint.

[342] Barry Cunliffe, 'The Regni', p. 16.

[343] Anne Ross, 'The Everyday Life of the Pagan Celts', p. 32.

Figure 10: The lavishly ornate carved granite monolith at the core of the Turoe/ Knocknadala oppidum on Turoe hill, Co. Galway, is regarded as the most magnificent example of Celtic virtuosity in La Tène art on a standing stone in all of Celtic Europe. The famous Turoe stone shows exceptional skill in stone-working by an Irish Iron Age La Tène craftsman. The expanded decorative ornamentation covering the surface of the stone shows that although the motifs of the pattern have a continuous rhythm, the overall design is planned care-fully to have four 'sides'. The cruciform pattern is shown above the stone. It is believed to have been used as a ceremonial coronation stone.

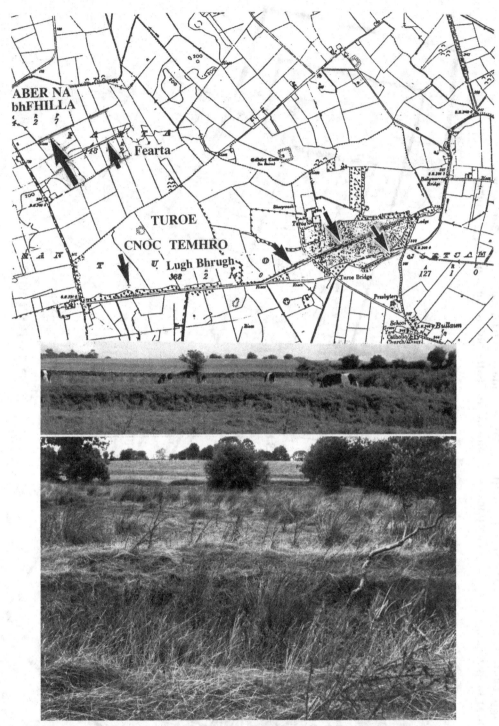

Figure 11: Arrows on OS map point to vestiges of inner ward embankments at Ptolemy's 2nd century Regia e Te(mh)ra (Cnoc Temhro = Turoe) along the north (top) and south slopes (lower) of the oppidum's ceremonial coronation/ inauguration site. Photo inserts show what they look like on the ground today.

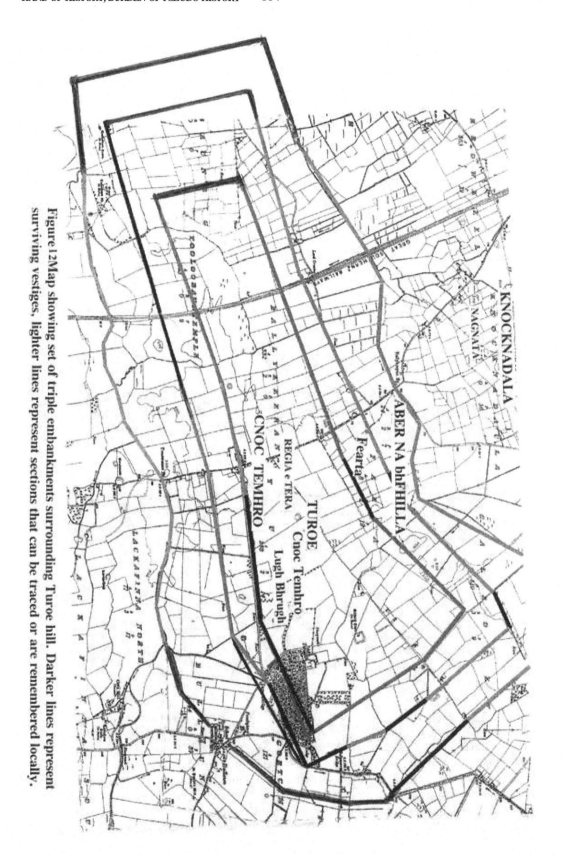

Figure12Map showing set of triple embankments surrounding Turoe hill. Darker lines represent surviving vestiges, lighter lines represent sections that can be traced or are remembered locally.

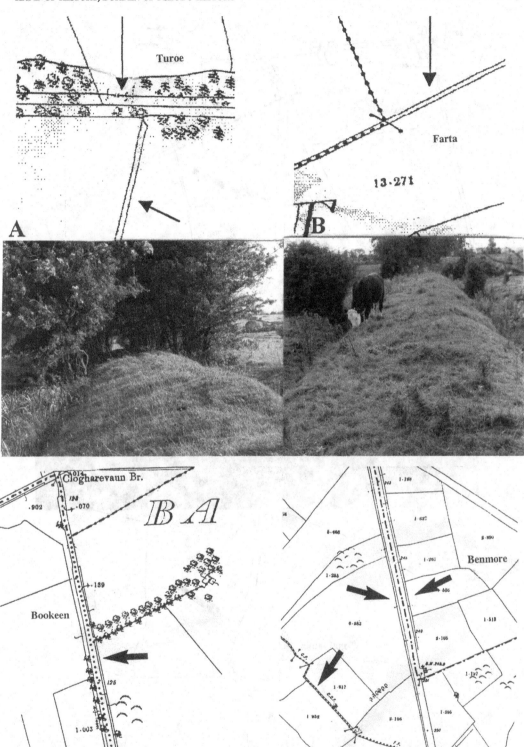

Figure 13: Methods used to depict embankments of the Turoe/Knocknadala inner ward on 1892 O.S. 25" map: (A top) a triple line for linear embankment, a double line for transverse embankment on the south flank and (B top) double line for a cut-down embankment on the north flank (with insert photo examples). Lower maps show four lines where the full width of the linear embankments were preserved, but lowered to fill in the fosse for the laying of the Bookeen Road (along the west flank) and the Benmore Road (along the east flank of the oppidum inner ward).

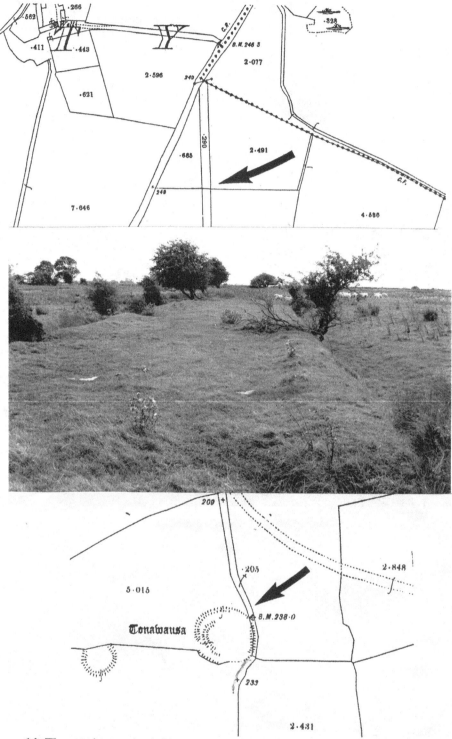

Figure 14: The ancient raised *Slighe Dala* road left Turoe, climbed Lackafinna hill and skirted Tonawausa fort as shown on 1894 OS map (lower). Its passage through Ballygasty (photo insert) near Loughrea is shown on the map (top).

Figure 15: Intact 2ft high, 21ft wide (exclusive of rounded banks) section of the ancient Slighe Dala highway). It ran in a straight line from Knocknadala to Ballygasty (top), Caheronnaun and the east side of Loughrea above the lake (cathedral spire showing at top right hand side of the ancient road). From Loughrea it headed ESE across the Shannon near Pertumna and on to Roscrea (middle).

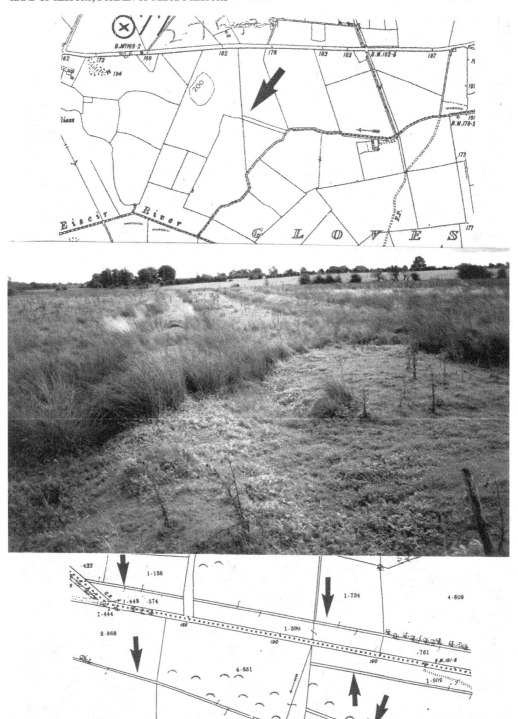

Figure 16 Embankments along the road dividing Carnakelly North and South, as shown on the 1894 OS map (lower). This section of road is built directly on the Escir Riada/Slighe Mór road. A section of the Escir Riada road (photo insert) through Gloves (*Na gChlaidhbhe*), Esker, as shown on 1933 OS map (top).

Figure.17: Section of the ancient 27ft. wide Escir Riada (Slighe Mór) across marshy land in Gloves Tld., north of Esker Monastery near Athenry, Co. Galway (2 lower photos). A long section of the Escir Riada from Athenry through Tonroe to the great Caheradrine fort near Clarenbridge (top). Adjoining farms replaced the ancient road banks with stone walls.

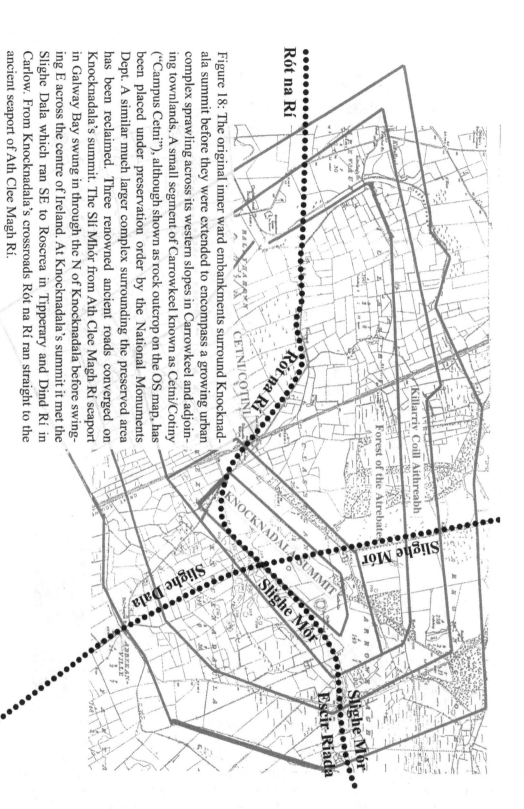

Figure 18: The original inner ward embankments surround Knocknadala summit before they were extended to encompass a growing urban
complex sprawling across its western slopes in Carrowkeel and adjoining townlands. A small segment of Carrowkeel known as Cetni/Cotiny
("Campus Cetni"), although shown as rock outcrop on the OS map, has
been placed under preservation order by the National Monuments
Dept. A similar much larger complex surrounding the preserved area
has been reclaimed. Three renowned ancient roads converged on
Knocknadala's summit. The Slí Mhór from Ath Clee Magh Rí seaport
in Galway Bay swung in through the N of Knocknadala before swinging E across the centre of Ireland. At Knocknadala's summit it met the
Slighe Dala which ran SE to Roscrea in Tipperary and Dind Rí in
Carlow. From Knocknadala's crossroads Rót na Rí ran straight to the
ancient seaport of Ath Clee Magh Rí.

Figure 19 Despoilt, partly cut-away, inner-ward embankments along the N, S and SE slopes of Knocknadala (Hill of Parliament/Assembly) in Co. Galway, the stronghold of Dela, the great Fir Belg leader. These inner ward embankments delineate the ceremonial site where the Great Assembly and Óenach were held in conjunction with the Feis Temhro (read Turoe in Galway).

Figure. 20: Remnant of a linear dyke through Kilarriv bog, known as *Poll a' Chladh* **(Dyke Bog) on the N flank of Knocknadala (top). A silhouette side-view of the same embankment (centre). A vestige of a linear embankment through Dunsandle wood on the W flank of Turoe (lower) connected to a banked-up stream prepared with flood-gates and with radiating cuttings (clais) to flood a wide area in times of danger.**

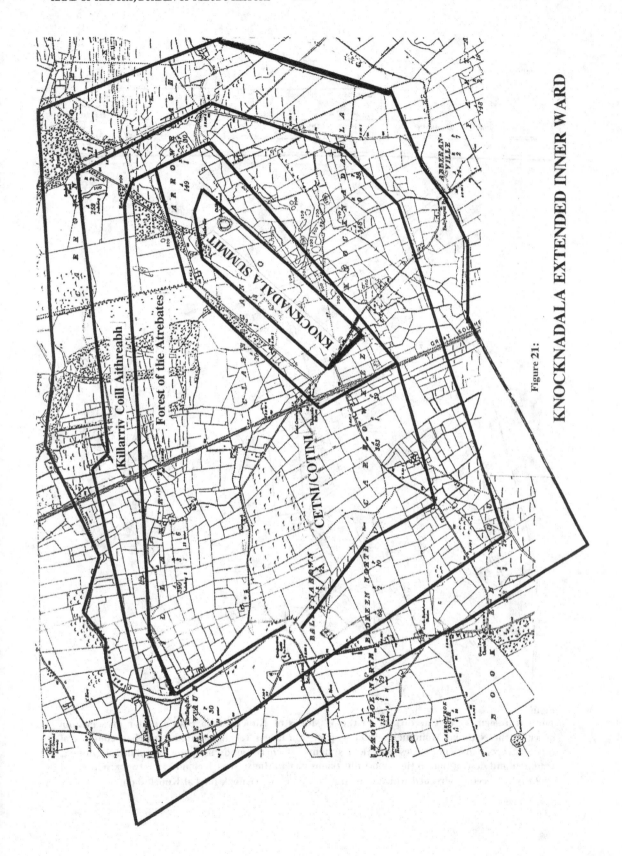

Figure 21:

KNOCKNADALA EXTENDED INNER WARD

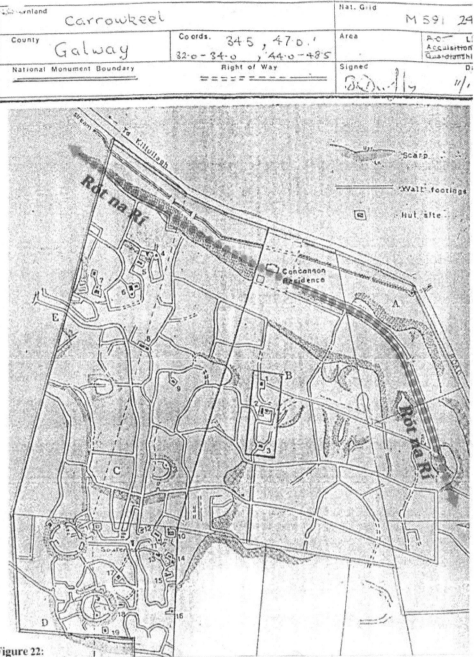

Figure 22:
The Cetni segment of Carrowkeel on the W slopes of Knocknadala placed under preservation order by the National Monuments Dept. is part of a larger reclaimed area, an urban complex of forts, 'streets', ancient houses and field systems. It corresponds in name, geopolitical context, tradition and description to the "most illustrious city in the west of Ireland" (πολισ επισεμοσ) of Ptolemy's 2nd century record which named it ΝΑΓΝΑΤΑΛ (Knock-na-Tal/Knocknadal).

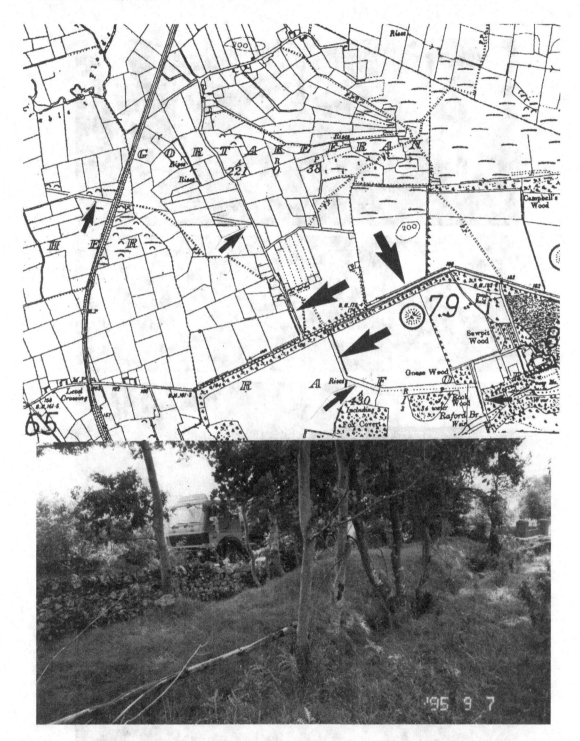

Figure 23 Thick arrows point to linear and transverse embankments of the outer ward of Turoe/Knocknadala oppidum along Raford road (photo insert) shown on the 1933 OS map, known locally as *Rooans* referring to the set of embankments. Smaller arrows show sections of the Escir Riada/Slighe Mór roadway which converged on Turoe and zigzagged as it entered through the ramparts.

Figure 24: Roads were built on leveled linear embankments (right-of-ways) and their filled-in fosse. Outer-lip ramparts (*rooans*) were retained as road banks, seen here on the Coraneena/Gortadeegan (Dyke Field) Road, Kilconnell (top), Raford Road (centre) and Lackalea (*Leac a' Chlaidh*) Road, Loughrea (lower).

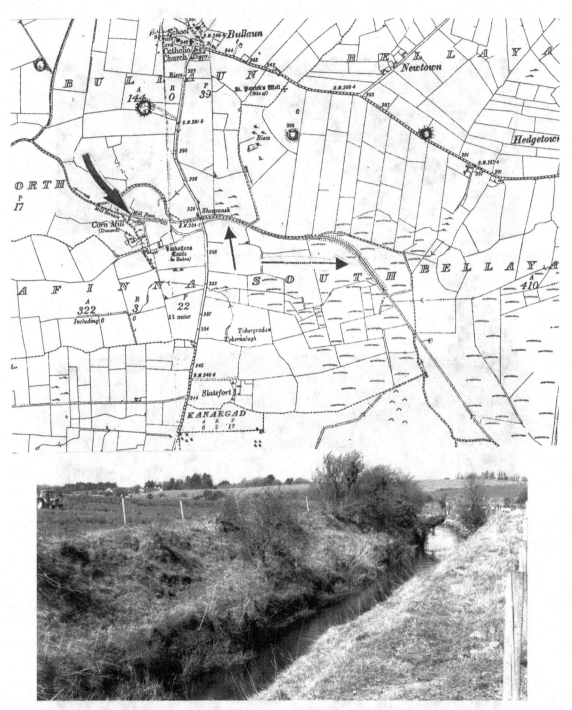

Figure 25 A stream from Poll na nDhoosigh and Bellayarhag to Turoe boundary has raised banks (photo inset) in classic Belgic style to create an artifical defence lake in the wetlands where the linear embankments swung W around the SE corner of Turoe, as shown on the 1933 OS map. Tradition tells that King Cormac Mac Art cut the mill race near Turoe Boundary for a cornmill.

Figure 26: These high man-made banks of Abha na nDhoosigh (= Embankment River, top) along the E of Lackafinna are a classic example of the sophisticated Belgic defensive system. Floodgates on the river could inundate large areas to enhance this defence line of the Turoe/Knocknadala oppidum. They also served a romantic secondary purpose of powering the nearby millrace for Cormac Mac Art's corn mill to save his beloved mistress the drudgery of grinding corn for his royal household by hand quern, as told in legendary history. Cuttings (claish) outside the banks to extend the area of flooding (middle).

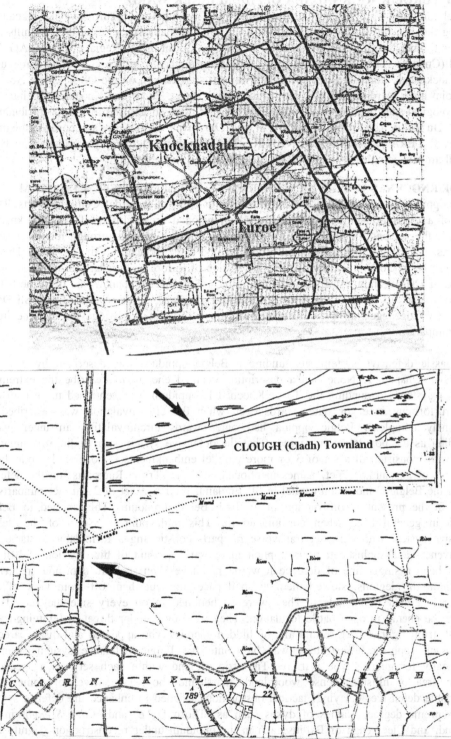

Figure   Position of 2 sets of linear embankments surrounding Turoe/Knocknadala oppidum core (top). Each set of 3 parallel embankments is represented by a single line. Section of the 7 mile long, 60ft wide, embankment from Greyford, Kiltulla, to Roudfield, Monivea, up left side of the 1894 OS map (lower), became known as the *New Line* when prepared for a Loughrea/Monivea railway line, a project never completed. Turoe and Athenry oppida marched together along this embankment. Inset of a similar 20 meter wide embankment through Clough (*Cladh* = Dyke) townland neat Tiaquin.

JOINT TUROE/KNOCKNADALA OPPIDUM INNER WARD

Parallel ramparts were thrown across the hollow (*srah*) between Turoe and Knocknadala. Linking their enclosing embankments on their E and W flanks they fused the two hills into one joint inner ward, the core of the 'REGIA E TE(mh)RA' (Regia e Tera)/NAG NA TA[L] (Cnoc na Dal) oppidum. Ptolemy placed it at the centre of Co Galway, where Turoe and Knocknadala stand. Vestiges of linking ramparts are shown on the OS 6" Sheet No. 97. This joint inner ward welded two multi-functionary zones, Turoe and Knocknadala, into one archaeological site, one formidable oppidum nucleus, wedged into the fork of two tributaries of the Dunkellin river (*An Dughiortach:* the *Dur* river of Ptolemy's record). Ptolemy's REGIA E TERA *[Te(mh)ra]* and NAG-NA-TAL [Cnoc na Dal] apply comprehensively to the full archaic complex.

TUROE/KNOCKNADALA OPPIDUM ENTRANCES AND BELGIC DEFENCE SYSTEM

Belgic oppidum entrances were not as formidable as those of the older Celtic hill forts. They were of a different nature, zigzagging through wooded areas. In the Turoe/Knocknadala oppidum the ancient Slí Mhór, Slí Dála, Rót na Rí roads passed through the inner ward ramparts. They zigzagged up wooded gradients and can be traced on the OS map. The Slí Mhór ran N on the E boundary of the S protrusion of Raford and zigzagged up the slope of the NE of Clashaganny. It zigzagged out through the wooded embankments from the S foot of Knocknadala to the esker of Killescragh (Coill Escragh). The entrance of the 'Slí Dála' on the SW zigzagged through a wooded area from Tonawausa Bridge through the inner ward ramparts.

The classic defensive system surrounding a Belgic oppidum was described by different authors in Chapter 1. None had a description detailed enough to describe the extremely complex system surrounding the Turoe/Knocnadala oppidum nor mentioned more than one rampart forming inner or outer wards even when the circumvalation was described as 'extremely complex'. Belgic oppida had outer wards circumvalating an inner ward, extending as the population increased. That the defensive system surrounding the inner or outer ward consisted of a set of 3 or more parallel embankments is not found explicitly in the work of any author. Yet, names mentioned, such as 'Triple Ramparts' on the defence line of the Belgic Trinovanten capital in SE England, refer to a set of 3 parallel ramparts as found in the present reconstruction of an Irish Belgic oppidum. This applied to Belgic oppida in general even when not alluded to. This multi-rampart aspect of the Belgic defensive system with close-set transverse ramparts constituting a formidable obstacle, its effectiveness and sophistication, is implicit in Caesar's account of his invasion of Britain. Had it been a single line of defence it would not have been such an enormous recurring obstacle to his legions, slowed them to snail pace, nor cut them off from view of one another and their commanders. They were so hemmed in on every side they could not engage the enemy in open battle formation. They were ever under threat of lightning-speed ambush from right, left, fore and aft, by hidden enemies who appeared and disappeared at will. Such sophisticated strategy was built into the Belgic defensive system designed specifically for guerilla-type warfare. The strip of land within each set was a specially-chosen area of hillside, dense wood-land, marshland, bog, lake, river or some other formidable defensive, delaying, tactical obstruction designed to enhance the defence system to a supreme degree. Names of dykes such as 'Thorn Dyke' and '*Cllee Sceagh*' in SE England, and Cleesceagh or Ballinsceagh in the oppidum under reconstruction, signify that the military engineers who oversaw the erection of these formidable barricades deliberately planted a dense covering of thornbush along their outer face and within the enclosed strip of land where no other obstruction existed to make them obnoxiously difficult to penetrate. This was its essence and raison d'etre.

RECONSTRUCTION OF TUROE/KNOCKNADALA OUTER WARD

An new outer ward circumvallation of the Turoe/Knocknadala oppidum core set was constructed on the outer side of the two tributaries of the Dunkellin River hugging the north and south flanks of the Turoe/Knocknadala inner ward. Working clockwise from the southeast corner, the reconstruction of this set starts from Oosigh Bog (*Poll na nDoosigh;* Dyke Bog) in Bellayarha and Lackafinna South, a mile southeast of Turoe. It runs west-southwest to Caherhenryhoe. Banks of the stream forming the east and northeast boundary of Lackafinna South were built up into linear embankments. They are among the finest surviving examples of the classic Belgic defensive ramparts (Figures 25 and 26). Floodgates were fitted to turn the wetlands into a defensive lake when danger loomed. They later served a more romantic secondary usage when Cormac Mac Art cut a millrace between the southeast of Turoe and Lackafinna Castle and built a water-mill to save his beloved mistress from the drudgery of grinding corn by handspun quern. Local farmers used numerous hand querns from the site of the more recent water mill for various purposes. Another water mill was erected beside Rath na bhFille (Palace of the Poets) near Raford Bridge. Similar water-mills operated in the Belgic oppida in SE England such as at Atrebaten Silchester, visited by Cormac mac Art.[344]

From NW Lackalea (Dyke Hill) the set of embankments ran through Ballybaun and Cahernamuck to Caherhenryhoe. A line of bullaun stones ran from Bullaun near Turoe across Lackafinna, Lisnagalhagh ('*galagh*' standing stone) and Ballybaun to Caherhenryhoe marking an ancient road skirting a string of ringforts and urban-like segments. Tonnawausa (*An tShonnagh Mhasa*, broad hill dyke) fort and eloquent placenames corroborate the former presence of the embankments, spelling out their ancient character where they have been obliterated. *Sonnagh* is the name of several places along the defence lines just as along the ancient Black Pig's Dyke boundary of Ulster. Vestiges of an ancient road from Turoe through Caherhenryhoe, Dunsandle, Lislondoon and Cahercormick ran through the S of Moyode (*Magh Fot*) and converged on *Rót na Rí* which ran straight from Knocknadala. The Slí Iceni and Slí Mhannin ran through the lands of the Iceni and Manapi buffer states. Cahernamuck (*Caher na muc*) refers to the magic boar. Defensive dykes were dubbed mythical boar's backs (*muc dhruime*). Their erection was referred to as the chase of the magic boar that mythologically dug up the dyke. Race with the boar, chase with the hounds.

CAHERHENRYHOE'S URBAN-LIKE ROYAL COMPLEX: HOME OF THE KINGS

In Caherhenryhoe the set of embankments swung NNW round the slopes of its cone shaped peak. The Caherhenryhoe (Caher na Rí Uabha, Royal Cemetery of the King's Palace)/- Carrowbaun area was a prehistoric royal cemetery complex, as the names proclaim, focused on the cone-shaped summit of Caherhenryhoe. It was the focus of a settlement complex of several 'cahers' (stone forts), along its summit. The late Pat Curley, Ml. Moran, Martin Quinn and the Ryans, to mention a few, recalled old people in their young days pointing out a Caher Tuthail (fort of Tuthal, grandfather of Conn Ced-chathach) and a Caherquinn (Fort of Conn) in this complex of stone forts with large souterrains. A Turoe-Stone-like granite stone beside the Tooloobauntemple cemetery mound across the stream from Caherhenryhoe marks Tuathal's tumulus, *Tuthal Ubhan,* from which the Tooloobaun is named. His fort, Caher Tuathal, stood in Caherhenryhoe. Caher Mac Con is in nearby Kilconierin, the site of the palace of Lughaid Mac Con who assassinated King Art, son of Con Cedchathach, and usurped his throne as Rí Temhro. He was aided by the Fotads whom he settled in adjacent Moyode (*Magh Fotad*), named after them. There were 2 Caher Cormaic. One was a massive despoilt stonefort in the SE of Dunsandle. The other was an earthen ringfort in the townland of Caher Cormick 3 townlands W of here in the ancient territory of Achall where Cormac

---

[344] Peter Salway, 'Roman Britain', p. 632.

Mac Art, the grandson of Conn Cedchathac, is said in legendary history to have retired after being blinded in one eye.

What is striking about the names of these forts is that they correspond to the names of some of the best known *'Rí Temhro'* Kings. Pseudo-history interpreted this to mean High Kings of Ireland reigning at Tara of Meath. Their names are rightly connected to Connacht's Turoe, not Tara of Meath. Add to this list the nearby forts of other early Kings of Connacht, Tinni (Queen Medb's paramour) and Maine, Queen Medb's son. They gave their names to two royal palaces in this plain named after Maine (Magh Main), Cahertinny and Clogherevaun (Cloghar Ui Mhain = Maine's palace). Cloghernaighy, the palace of the 4th/5th century King Na Thi or nDhathi) stood in Toorclogher [Clogher = royal palace] near Tober Naighey some 3 miles WSW near Seefinn. Later chapters will show that the true **Home of the Kings** was right here at the centre of Co. Galway. This sector of the Knocknadala/Turoe Belgic oppidum featured as a royal segment of Ptolemy's sprawling 'city' of Nagnatal (ΝΑΓΝΑΤΑΛ: *Cnoc na Dal*).

Local tradition described the unique character of Caherhenryhoe's cone-shaped hill disemboweled in gravel mining operations over many years. In the early 20th century a 14-ft high standing stone on the summit of Caherhenryhoe fell over. The army re-erected it. It was surrounded by a circle of granite standing stones, at least one of which was a 'bullaun'. Some cairn tumuli stood a little way back from this megalithic setting. These collapsed as gravel mining undercut each in turn. Ned Ryan pointed out the standing stone, broken in two, at the bottom of the sandpit, and a bullaun and granite stones pushed to the nearby walls. A similar 'bullaun' setting stood on the site of Bullaun Church.

On this S flank, the field grid was dictated by the linear embankment alignment. From Caherhenryhoe the hitherto WSW field-grid alignment followed that of the embankments as they swung NNW through Dunsandle to Lisnadrisha and along the Cahernalee (*Caher na Chlaidh*, Dyke fort)/Carrowroe boundary. From Carrowroe (Ceathramha Roo; Rampart quarter, 'Roo' is O-Irish for embankment) it crossed the Dunkellin River. This river is marked on the OS map as *An Dughiortach* in the new OS Discovery Series Map No 46, a form of its ancient name, 'Dur' or 'Deur' (pronounced Jour). *Dur, Dour* and *Duro* were Celtic names for rivers in Belgic areas of the Continent and SE Britain. They correspond to Welsh, Breton and Cornish forms *Dwfr, Dovr,* and *Dour*. The Belgae referred to the Rhine as the 'Dur'. Dornik and other towns on the lower Rhine retain this memory'. A number of 'Duro' rivers, such as Duro Brivae, were recorded in Britain by Ptolemy. Dover (Romanised *Duvris)* in SE England is the plural form *Dubhra*. Ptolemy recorded the river *Dur* on the W coast of Ireland because of its association with Turoe and Knocknadala. The mouth of the *Dur* on Ptolemy's record appears where the Shannon mouth is whilst *Senos* (the Shannon) appears where the Dunkellin (Dughiortach) is in Galway Bay, showing that Ptolemy's list of names along the W coast of Ireland has been erroneously read clock-wise from bottom to top rather than in the correct order from top to bottom. In his list of placenames the *Dur* is placed beside 'Regia E Tera' (REGIA E TERA) and 'Nagnatal' (NAG-NA-TAL), correctly anchoring the true position of all three. The *'Dur Fluvium'* of Ptolemy's record and this *Dughiortach* are one and the same. Rahashan Lake, 8 miles W along this river, was known as Dur Loch until the early 20th century.

Ten foot wide stone walls along Kiltulla South's boundaries with Greyford (*Rath Chlaidh*) and Clogharevaun replaced earthen embankments. Transverse ramparts linking these were also of stone and scar the surface of this townland. Sachell is a local name of part of this townland. The ancient name of the Tld., Clogharevaun (*Clochar Ui Mhain* = Maine's Family Palace), is significant. The Dindshenchas of Maen (Main) Mhaigh (*Magh Maine*; Plain of Maine) recounts how this plain around Loughrea was named after Maine, the son of

Queen Medb, who succeeded his mother as King of nÓl nÉgmacht. Similar scraps of legendary history show that Connacht's royal Capital stood at the centre of Co. Galway, not some 60 miles NE at Croghan of Roscommon in Queen Medb's time. None of the vestiges of 5 stone forts which studded this townland, not even that constructed from enormous stones bulldozed into the ground 30 years ago, are marked on the OS map. One was Cloghar Ui Mhain which gave its name to the Tld., another was Caheroki (*Caher Eochaidh?*). All were stripped of most of their stone work to build the medieval Norman Clogharevaun Castle to quarter 500 Mac Sweeney Galloglass mercenary troops, horses and apparatus. The Clochar (royal palace) stood on the site on which the castle was built, overlooking Cetni. Tradition claims that the whole townland north to Kiltulla cemetery area was regarded as a continuation of the urban nucleus of Cotny (Campus Cetni in Carrowkeel) across the river, linked by an esker road. When Landlords vied for projects during the famine years, Dunsandle and Kiltulla Houses conspired to have a proposed railway line from Monivea to Loughrea pass close-by to serve both. Before the idea was aborted due to the 1845-7 famine preliminary clearings were made and obstacles razed in a rush to provide the best route through the Clogharevaun/Kiltulla urban segment.

ANCIENT MONASTIC SITE: DOMHNACH SHACHELL

Part of Clogharevaun is known as Sachell. There was a Gallowglass family of that name but it did not give its name to this area. Among 'obstructions' destroyed in clearing for the proposed railway line were Downahachell (*Domhnach Shachell*) and Kelhachell (*Cell Shachell*). 'Domhnach' denotes an early basilica, 'Cell' a monastic cloister or cemetery. The name Sachell would denote the founder. The sole monastic founder of that name was the pre-Patrician Bishop, Sachellus, who led missionaries from Gaul to Ireland in the train of Palladius who was commissioned by Pope Celestin in 431 to organize the Irish Church. Sachellus set up his monastic community basilica beside the Turoe/Knocknadala royal palace. His missionary work espoused the dynasty of King Eochy Moyvane (*Eochu Muigh Mhain*), great ancestor of Connacht's Kings. Eochaidh's epithet proclaims he resided in this plain of Magh Mhain, perhaps here at Caher Eochaid in this urban complex.

The *'Leiden Glossary'*, a 12th century document based on 6th century Gaulish accounts, tells of a migration of religious 'learned men' from France to Ireland during the invasion of Germanic tribes at the beginning of the 5th century: "All the learned men on this side of the sea (Continent) took flight, and in Ireland, brought about a very great increase of learning to the inhabitants of that region."[345] Christianity was foremost in this body of learning introduced into Ireland. Patrick's mention of the presence of '*rhetorici*' is a direct reference to these scholarly fugitives.[346] The *domnach* churches were served by these '*rhetorici dominicati*' (Churchmen). Their churches were erected in places designated 'magh', areas of concentrated population in the early 5th century, especially centres of royal power. Mac Neill's 'Saint Patrick' refers to a large population centre, Campus Cetni in South Connacht.[347] Ptolemy recorded the most extensive population centre, ΝΑΓΝΑΤΑΛ which translates to Cnoc na Tal (Dal), Knocknadala today, the inner ward of which Cetni/Carrowkeel/Clogharevaun are a part in Galway. This is corroborated by local tradition and in the 'Dindsenchas of Maen Magh' which refers to its early dense population. The *'rhetorici dominicati'* would surely have set up a major church and monastic school there. Doherty asserts that "despite the claims of Armagh, it is clear that most of the clergy associated with these churches were independent bishops of the early missionary period. Many were no doubt aristocratic clergy of Gaul (who apparently came even before

---

[345] Walsh/Bradley, 'A History of the Irish Church 400-700AD', p. 4
[346] St. Patrick, 'The Confessions of St. Patrick', 13.
[347] Eoin MacNeill, 'St. Patrick', under population centres visited by the saint.

Palladius)."[348] Tirechan knew of this tradition in 690 AD. He referred to Gaulish missionaries, naming Bernicius, Hernicus and their sister Nitria who came to Ireland in the early 5th century led by Bishop Sachellus. Some worked from a basilica under his care, monastic fashion.

Ancient records refer to a very early (pre-7th century) monastery in the Clogharevaun/Kiltulla (*Cill Tulach*) area. "Some *tulach* sites were originally pagan religious centres."[349] Such sites most often became Christian sites. Within this Clogharevaun/*Cill Tulach* area there are springs, a stream dissappears underground, there is regular flooding in low areas and there is a deep pit which may be a ritual shaft. "Many (Celtic) native deities are associated with water, and in particular with springs or rivers. Ritual pits or shafts occur quite frequently (filled with artifacts) and there may be a close association with the (Celtic) water cult (which the Church Christianized). Some ritual shafts show signs of sacrifice."[350]

In the reign of Briun, son of Eochaidh Muigh Mhain, Maine Mor, ancestor of the Hy Many, led a massive invasion from Ulster into Connacht right to the E edge of the Turoe/Knockndala oppidum core while its Overking and army were campaigning against the Cruthintuatha of Roscommon. A massacre of the Fir Belg ensued. This spelt the end of Fir Belg rule from Turoe/Knocknadala oppidum in central Galway. Briun discarded it and set up his new centre of power on Loch Hacket near Loch Corrib (*Loch Orbsen*) in the territory between the new Kingdom of Ui Maine and the Cruthin kingdom of Magh Ai. Sachellus faithfully followed Briun. Tirechan noted that Sachellus erected churches in Briun's newly-won lands along the S boundary of Magh Ai in Roscommon and established Basilica Sanctorum at the place still known as Baslic (SW Roscommon) today, "so called because so many of the foreign saints died there." Sachellus' brother, Cethecus, became Bishop of Oran. Other Gaulish missionaries set up churches in this territory won over by Briun from the Cruthin. The exodus of Sachell from Domnach Shachell in the train of Briun parallels St. Patrick's later expatriation from Armagh to Downpatrick in the NE of Ireland following the overthrow of the Cruthin at Emain Macha.

This desertion of the monastic site and later land clearances left little trace of the urban extension, of Domnach Shachell and of the ramparts through Clogharevaun and Kiltulla. Stone-core outer ward ramparts through Kiltulla South and Greyford were built into 12-ft. high demesne walls by the Darcy landlords and maintained as a deer reserve for the medieval aristocratic hunt season.[351] Tons of stone were carted away from the massive walls and ruins of ancient houses and forts to build the castle, big houses and fuel lime-kiln and road-making operations, and the remainder carted off to the stone crushers of recent times.

In Kiltulla North the embankments ran on to Kiltulla Bog, one skirting the stream from Kiltulla bog to the W side of Kiltulla House (in ruins), taking advantage of the higher inner bank of the stream built up into a high rampart known as Lady's Walk, which still survives. This is a fine example of how streams were utilized with the higher inner bank built up as the main rampart. The outer rampart formed the W boundary of Kiltulla North to the edge of the bog where the set swung ENE. A-25 ft wide stretch of partially leveled rampart some 400 yards N of Kiltulla graveyard runs to the outer rampart along the edge of the bog. It gives an excellent idea of the original size of such ramparts. It is shown on the O.S. 6" map Sheet 96 with other nearby surviving isolated segments. The set ran ENE from the hilltop

---

[348] Charles Doherty in 'Irlande et France du Nord' ed. by Jean-Michel Picard p. 62-65.

[349] Dómnall Mac Giolla Easpaig, 'Early Ecclesiastical settlement names of Co. Donegal and Co. Galway' p. 165.

[350] Peter Salway, 'Roman Britain', p. 669-70.

[351] The victorious English army on its way to Galway after the Battle of Aughrim encamped in the lawn of Darcy's House. All the deer were killed for a feast. The deer-reserve never recovered from this episode.

sentinel forts in Kiltulla North across Knockatogher, along the edge of Gortakeeran bog to the S tip of Knockroe skirting the Ballinasloe road through Knockatogher to Raford. Low stretches of rampart survived along the N side of Raford road (shown on OS 6" Map, Sheet No. 96; Figures 23 and 24) built along the filled-in fosse. Transverse ramparts knit the parallel ramparts into a cohesive set. Vestiges of the rampart along the S verge of Gortakeeran bog and Campbell's Wood are shown on the OS map, but not those S of Raford road through an area known as 'the Rooans' where the ramparts were leveled in living memory. *'Roo'* is O. Irish for 'fossed earthen embankment', *'rooan'* is the plural form. The *Slí Mhór* highway from Athenry swung SSE along the Gortakeeran road to Knocknadala (shown on the OS map through Gortakeeran and Raford). It zigzagged on entering a wooded area through the set of ramparts. The road from Killimor Cross Roads (Raford Bridge) to Knockroe (*Cnoc Roo*) was built along an embankment fosse.

From the N of Brackloon River at the edge of the bog the set swung SSE straddling the river, forming Brackloon/Cloonsheecahill boundary. Belgic military engineers exploited the marshlands within the river loop and straddling the E stretch to enhance the complex defences. Within the river loop a stretch of rampart survives as a fine example of the original rampart width and of how this former right-of-way was leveled out for a railway line which never materialized (Figure 27). The embankments were lowered and narrowed to fill in the fosse. Bill Joe Craven of Cloonsheecahill walked to school along this right-of-way. He pointed out its route SSE through miles of townland from Brackloon, Killescragh and Sraheendoo en route to Ben More, Ballymurry, Bellayarha North and the starting point at Bellayarha South (Oosigh Bog) SE of Bullaun, 5 miles from his home. This is well above the usual extent of the older generation's knowledge of the double-ditches, as they refer to the embankments. People know of a one or two mile stretch at most. None today are able to point out the entire circumvallation.

The narrow road through Killescragh and Brackloonbeg was built on a leveled rampart passing by Lisheenahassy fort (Embankment fort) in the W of Carramore. *Shassaigh* is the plural form of *Shass/Shess*, another O-Irish word for a defence dyke. A nearby embankment is known as 'The Green Road'. An excellent example of the 18th century employment of these linear embankments is the section of road which forms the Brackloonbeg/Benmore boundary with wide banks on either side of the road. These are vestiges of the embankments which were lowered and narrowed from the inside to fill the fosse to lay the projected route of the Loughrea/Attymon railway line en route through Brackloon to Attymon, known as 'The New Line'. It was abandoned and a road built on it instead. The unsafe high narrow road through Ooshigh Bog in Bellayarha (Bel Dha Dhearg) is built on a high linear embankment. Horse carts caused considerable deterioration to numerous surviving vestiges used as right-of-ways. Landlords passed laws forbidding the use of carts on them. Thereafter, only horse and rider or people on foot were then allowed to use them (Fig 29).

At first sight short vestiges of these embankments may look medieval or later (Figure 30). But when one follows through and comes upon segments which retain their original width (approximately 60 ft) and design (25 ft wide inner embankment, deep 15 ft wide fosse, and 12ft wide outer lip) and becomes aware of the fact that there are three or more parallel lines of these linear embankments running for miles across the countryside welded into a set by transverse ramparts, one realizes that the medieval lords had no use for such embankments. Stories are still told of greedy landlords quarreling with one another as they moved markers back and forth between the main rampart and the outer-lip embankment to guide workmen engaged in levelling them and keeping part of the embankments as field enclosures. This explains why a number of these still run in zig zag lines. When one discovers that these sets of linear embankments circumvallate an important inner core such as the Turoe/Knocknadala royal complex and expand out, set after set, across the whole Galway landscape and far into adjoining counties, one begins to question one's first impression and ask what possibly could have necessitated such an extraordinary feat of human endeavour. If one then discovers that only the early Belgae ever erected such a complex system and that this is a mirror copy of the Belgic defensive system surrounding Belgic oppida in SE Britain and in Belgic areas of the Continent, one shouts '*Eureka*" and finally reinstates the denigrated Fir Belg. The Fir Belg expanded rapidly against weaker neighbours as they did on the Continent and in Britain where their expansion was cut short by Roman invasion and Catuvellaunian aggression. In Ireland they extended their oppida over several centuries at the expense of the aboriginal peoples. Each new Turoe outer ward set of embankments marks the several stages of their expansion paralleled by several regressions of the Cruthin defence lines. Vestiges of these still scar the face of the Irish Celtic landscape.

FIRST EXTENSION OF THE TUROE/KNOCKNADALA OUTER WARD

Reconstruction of a further extension of the Turoe/Knocknadala oppidum begins at the SE corner of the oppidum in the N half of Kincullia. The ramparts (shown on OS maps) headed W through the S sectors of Bushfield, Curraghroe, Coorbaun, Lackalea, Cahernamuck East and West, the N segments of Raruddy East and West, and along the Cahernaman/-Caherhenryhoe boundary. In Raruddy East opposite Lynchfort Castle the stream was banked up and floodgates fitted to enhance the defence system by inundation. Cuttings ('claishes') to extend the area of flooding survive. This system is still operative and is used for land-fertilization purposes. The embankment-set raced W along St Cleran's river, forming the boundary of Caherhenryhoe. As shown on the OS map, riverbanks were built up into ramparts with floodgates fitted to inundate an extensive area along the stream through Cahertinny, Cahernaman, Raruddy West, Caherhenryhoe, Cahernamona and Cahernamuck West. Fir Belg military engineers developed a system to turn this otherwise humble stream into a defensive sheet of water, as they invariably did whenever the topography obliged and danger of invasion loomed. The ramparts ran into Cahertinny, the fort of Tinny, a demoted king of Connacht and paramour of Queen Medb.

The set swung NNW through Doogeraun, skirting Faelan's Well and Killilan Bridge (Cill Fhaelan), named after 7th century St. Faelan's monastery. It straddled the Carrowbaun/-Carrownagower boundary with St.Cleran's. From their passage through the W of Dunsandle, vestiges survived in strips of woodland. Banks of the stream were built up and floodgates fitted to inundate the area in time of danger. Cuttings extended the area of flooding. The ramparts sped through the W of Lisnadrisha, the E of Carrowrevagh and Skeagharegan, through Raherneen and Caherakileen. Land reclamation demolished the ramparts along the Cahernalee/Raherneen boundary near the Dughiortach (*Dur*) River skirting the ringfort and Caherakilleen stone fort. This area known locally as 'Ceallagh Bui' was a lake before the new river channel was cut. Floodgates further W served to flood an extensive area for defensive purposes.

On the N bank of the new river channel stand two adjacent odd-shaped fortlets facing one another on the edge of both banks of the old river channel which funneled to a very narrow point between the two. They played a strategic role in controlling floodgates set on the river between these fortlets backed up by raised banks along the old channel and stout banks of the linear embankments to enhance the flooding of extensive areas along the river behind them, extended further by shallow cuttings. Did they control river transport! The floodgates could have been utilized for that purpose. The set ran NNW from Caherakilleen fort straddling the Greyford/Curragh More/Beg boundary. The embankment forming the boundary survives as a long stretch of thornbush-covered rampart, a sample of the original obstacle. The set skirted the W of Greyford (*Lis an Chlaidh*, Dyke fort) to Curragh More where they marched with the outer-ward ramparts of Athenry oppidum straddling the Brusk road and skirting the E of Loughan Escir, Dominic's hill and Carnakelly boundary with several Gloves' Tlds. The section skirting Curragh More fort to the Kiltulla/Athenry road and the Brusk road was leveled for the laying of a projected railway line from Limerick to Sligo via Loughrea and Monivea in the 19th century. It was known as the New Line. The 19th century famine quashed the plan.

The set ran between Dominic's hill (*Bru A Scail*) and *Cruach Chian* in Brusk (*Bru A Scail*) and swung ENE through Carnakelly South. Cruach Cian's cone-shaped hill was demolished in gravel mining. It was the Otherworld abode of the god Cian, alias Scail Balb. Embankment vestiges survive ENE through Carnakelly South/North, Laragh, Lisduff, Killimor and Lenamore (Figure 28). Ned Burke of Laragh recounted the route of the embankments back through Carnakelly, Brusk SSE to Dunsandle and Carrowbaun, and forward via Laragh, Lisduff, and Killimor Church to Lenamore. Vestiges survive through Laragh, Lisduff and the S of Killimor bog. They straddled the Lenamore/Killimor boundary to the NW elbow of Raford River which dictated their course SSE along the Cloonsheecahill/Derrynamanagh boundary following the loop of the river. Marshlands within the loop and along the edge of Derrynamanagh bog were exploited to enhance the defences. The river banks and its floodlands were embanked to form a formidable obstacle, making this stretch a treacherous place for any attempt at crossing.

From Tormaun, Island and Gortnaboha they ran through Caraun, Knockaboley, Bellafa and Grange (*Grainseach;* corn repository). An embanked cattle-krall north of the Bellafa/-Ballinasloe road occupied the area between Grange and Knocknaboley (*Cnoc na Buaile*) as the name clarifies. "It is the law of the Feini that cattle should be in an enclosure (*i mbuaile*) by nightfall".[352] Few survive. Bellafa (*Bel an Fheadh*, Forest gateway on the route of the *Slí Mhór* Eiscir Riada) heralds its strategic importance for Turoe/Knocknadala oppidum's forest periphery. This is highlighted by traditions of Fianna camps in the vicinity. Townlands around Bellafa's *Slí Mhór* passage through this forest gateway bear the names of 3 Fir Belg septs of Fianna warriors, the Clann Ui Conain (Mac Morna), the Mac Rin of Crossmacrin and the Mac Lane of Turmacleane on the N slopes of Rahally overlooking the *Slí Mhór*. John O Donovan claimed that the Lane clan (Mac Leane) alone survived the massacre of the Fir Belg of Connacht by Maine Mor. He erred by misreading the location of the invasion and his unawareness of the Turoe/Knocknadala oppidum. The life of St. Grellan, quoted by him, tells how Maine Mor went with an Airghiallan army from Ulster to seize the land of Cian in Magh Seincheineoil (Clann Cian territories in East Galway Tiaquin area).[353] Before the Clann Cian buffer states were established the territory of the Cruthin of Ulster reached this Bellafa entrance to the Fir Belg oppidum through the forest periphery. This excellent boley was recently bulldozed into oblivion to make way for the Third Millennium.

The set crossed the NE of Caraun, Cross, Cloonyconaun and the NE slopes of Toormaclean and the outer embankments of Rahally hill fort, straddling Slievedotia. On the Cross/Benbeg boundary near the route of the *Slí Mhór* there is a Toberdoney. Near this holy well is a large moated site (early temple site?). An old man remembers hearing of Donaherneen there. Doney/Dona is Irish *Domhnach*, a very early church. 'Herneen' would appear to be the founder's name. Across river from Donahachell in Kiltulla South on the W flank of the first extension of Turoe/Knocknadala oppidum is Caherakilleen (Church Fort) beside Raherneen. Was he the same Herneen of Donaherneen? Hernicus was an early missionary who came in the train of Palladius and Sachellus of Donahachell. Is his name linked to this early church? Toberdoney adjoins Cross (*Crois Chriost*) Tld., the site of an archaic church. This should be investigated before a proposed superdump at the site destroys all the

---

[352] A. T. Lucas, "Cattle in Ancient Ireland', p. 25. 'Ancient Laws of Ireland', Vol 4, p. 96.

[353] John O Donovan, 'Tribes and Customs of Hy-Many', p. 8 ff.

evidence, especially in view of the fact that the ancient church which gave nearby Kilreekil its name brings Palladius into the picture. He was the Bishop sent to Ireland by Pope Celestin in 431. St Rechil who gave her name to Kilrekill is said to have been a sister of Palladius "who was also known as Patricius." Croch, the sister of Bishop Felert of Domnach Mor Magh Seola at Loch Seola near Tuam, had a *Crois Chriost* church which gave its name to the village of Cross, between Cong and Headford in Galway. Felert was consecrated Bishop of Magh Seola by Sachellus.

The embankments set straddled Boleymore and Ballinphuill bog. It ran on into Carra where it swung SSW along Carra's south running boundary with Carrowmore. Fine vestiges of ramparts survive along this line. A stream from Carra bog forms the Doon/Cahernagarry boundary. It had floodgates and raised banks to inundate large areas behind, including Carra bog, to enhance the defences. The set ran on through Cahernagarry and Kilboght to the N tip of the Ballybroder/Kilmeen boundary where it swung W at the starting point. The embankments skirted the boglands and ancient forested periphery of the oppidum along the N and E flanks just as they did on the S and W flanks.

SECOND EXTENSION OF THE TUROE/KNOCKNADALA OUTER WARD
Reconstruction of a new extension of the Turoe/Knocknadala oppidum starts from the SE corner 5 miles SE of the Turoe Stone from Carra just S of Kilreekil. The set ran W straddling the Cooleeny/Ballynahistil, Drought/Ballydoogan boundaries. From the Black Wood (*Coill Doo*, Dyke Wood) it ran astride the Kilmeen/Moyleen boundaries with Ballybroder. It left its trail W through Kinkullia, Fairfield and Caheronaun, skirting a string of sentinel forts commanding wide vistas. Ramparts in Graigue were effaced in the development of Loughrea Golf Course. So too was the site of an archaic village complex of stone-slab housing and a narrow-gauge sunken road system with 4 ft. wide walls (shown on the OS map; partly preserved outside the Golf Course) linked to the Slí Dála. A bulldozer uncovered an underground bunker above the linear embankment (Figure 38). Tusks of the mythological wild boar rooted up the ramparts racing W through the S segments and bogs of Curraghs, Ballygasty, Raruddy East and West, and the N parts of Monearmore, Cosmona and Gorteennabohogy. Vestiges of the ramparts cross the surviving segment of the Slí Dála, shown on the OS map, in the SE corner of Ballygasty opposite Loughrea rugbyfield.

The set raced W across the N of Caherlavine and Cahernagormuc. It crossed Ardnadoman East/West (Ard na Domnann, Tinny's Domnann sept defended this oppidum flank). It skirted Cahertinny, Gortsheela and Cahernaman as it ran through Carrowmore. It swung NNW at Ballnamucka along Knockdaumore (Dyke hill), Cloghastookeen and Doogaraun. It skirted St Cleran's boundary with Derryhoyle Beg, Coolraugh and Srah. Riverbanks through these townlands were raised and fitted with floodgates to enhance the defences. Departed elders, Martin Quinn, Pat Curley and Michael Martin related traditions of the Dumnann leader, Tinny, and his fighting men at Cahertinny, Ardnadumnann, Caherlavine and Cahernaman, centres of the Dumnann and Manapi of the Colla Mann branch of ancient Moycola in the service of Cormac mac Art. The old Yellow Bog Dublin/Galway road through Ardnadoman West and Cloonoo East was built on a linear embankment.

The set sped through Lickerrig, along Lacarrow/Ballynahivnia boundary to Glebe and its boundary with Lisalondoon, traversing Cahercormac (where Cormac Mac Art retired from the Kingship on being blinded in one eye and on his rejection by the Druids for becoming Christian) and Garrakyle. Cahercormac is at the E edge of the ancient forest of Achaill Oichne. Pseudo-history transferred Cormac's place of retirement from Achaill of Garrakyle in Galway to Achall of Arraklye near Tara of Meath. Lisalondoon retains the name of London, British capital of the Trinovantes. Originally called *Lud Dun* after Lud who rebuilt it for his brother Cassivellaunus who overran the lands of the Trinovantes. Lud was buried beside the

London gate which bears his name, Ludgate. As Trinovanten aristocrats fled Britain with the Iceni, they followed the exiled Dumno, King of the Trinovantes, to Ireland with his Canti followers. Townlands of the Canti (*na gChanti*), Iceni and Dumnann dot the area adjoining Lisalondoon. The area along the E edge of Achaill Oichne forest is *Coill Clann Iceni* (Iceni Forest, corrupt Kilconicny). Part of the forest east to Lisalondoon is *Treanchoill* Tld., 'Trinovanten Forest' perhaps. These placenames are pregnant with important geopolitical messages for early history.

The set sped on through Hollypark, Cregg, Kilconierin and Carrownamorrissy along the Dughiortach (*Dur*) River to Rathgorgin where they marched with the outer-ward rampart of Athenry oppidum. Carrownamorrissy is one of several placenames, like Lisnamorrissy, along this W front of the Turoe/Knocknadala oppidum, named after the Belgic Marrasi. Their name is variously listed on Continental records as Marasci, Marezaten or Maresaci, neighbours of the Menapi, Morini and Cannan Fatad (Fotads/Votadini). The Marasci were forced inexorably into the Rhine/Meuse delta at the SW of Holland before disappearing entirely from the early Continental maps. They may have come with the Votadini and Manapi from ManauGoddodin in SE Scotland together with Tuathal or Lughaid Mac Con.

Rathgorgin (Ailech Gorgin) was the palace of Gorgin (Corc), son of Lugdech, greatgrandson of Eoghan Mór of Munster. Corc's palace, encircled by the old river channel and converted by the Normans into a moat and bailey, survives. At the S of Rathgorgin, across river from Carrownamorrissy, is Lis na Gal (foreigner's fort), so named after the foreign fighting men brought in by Lughaid Mac Con. With the Marasci (Morrissy) to the N and S, Fotads (Votadini) of Moyode (their royal seat was Clochar na ngFhotad) to the W and the Menapi to the S, SE and W of him, Lughaid Mac Con and his vassal-allies proved difficult to dislodge from their strongholds of massive stone forts at the NE end of Achaill Oichne forest. Some who came with Mac Con went with him to Munster. Some remained behind along the west coast. After numerous battles against him, they eventually slew Cormac Mac Art at the Battle of Moyvilla. Those who remained were ruled first by Lughaid Laga and later by Corc. Corc led these vassal-allies into Munster and conquered Cashel where he was surrounded by these vassal-allies. They survived in Munster as the Deisi and Uaithni of historic times. Cormac mac Art suffered defeat earlier when he went to aid his Munster allies who were being overrun by these exiles.

On the Dur's opposite bank this extension marched with the outer ward of Athenry oppidum which ran NNE from Rathgorgin through Esker, Killascaul and the W of Gloves South/-Middle. From there the Turoe/Knocknadala set ran ENE astride the Gloves East/Cloonbrusk boundary. Carnakelly bog road zigzags between two embankments, the outer forming the Cloonkeenmore South/Carnakelly North boundary (Figure 31). The many 'Gloves' townlands ('*Na gChlaidhbh*e', The Dykes) proclaims the presence of the dykes where they have been for the most part demolished. Along these Gloves Tlds. the outer-ward dykes of the Athenry oppidum, to be reconstructed anon, rendezvoused with those of Turoe/-Knocknadala oppidum overlooked by Dominick's Hill (Brugh A Scáil) and Cruach Chian, 2 coliding oppida with different alignments, accommodating the other. The phenomenon of bringing bog, forest and other natural defensive features within the oppidum defence fortifications is a military strategy encountered again and again in later extensions. Parallel transverse ramparts survive along the E edge of the bog along Laragh road running N to Laragh Cross Roads (Figure 36). One is known as the Carriage Way across the road from Ned Burke's house in Laragh whence it ran NNE to the E-bound rampart on Laragh Hill. The Lisduff/Attymonmore neck of land was a strategic passage-way into the oppidum. There was no other entrance across the expanse of boglands for miles on either side. So it was heavily defended by several ramparts instead of the more usual three.

The set raced across Attimonmore South (*Ait Ui Maine Mor*, the place of Maine Mor's people who overran the Clann Chian, forcing them into the forested boglands). It ran astride the Cappanashruhan/Killimor boundary, through Cappananool, the S of Clooncah and Streamsford with the linear embankment forming its N boundary and turret-like forts. It swung SSE through Skehanagh, Coppanagh and Gortmore, straddling their boundaries with Beefield and Gortlemon. It sped through Tooreen and Castlebin North, South and East, skirting Castlebin and other forts on this defence line along the E side of New Inn's Knockbrack and Knockmore. It ran through Treanbaun, Highpark and the E of Ballyglass into Glennaskehy bog and swung SW through Ballintubber West/East into Newgrove. Impressive vestiges of linear and transverse ramparts shown on the OS Map survive in Balintobber and Newgrove (Figures 32, 33, 34 and 35). In the latter Tld. one low vestige is "wide enough for 2 lorries to run side by side on its surface," as people remark. Most fine vestiges are being wiped out by modern machinery in land-reclamation. The set straddled the Doon/Carnaun boundary, leaving vestiges along the Dublin/Galway road. Transverse ramparts survive along the Bullaun/Kilreekill road forming the Doon/Wallscourt boundary. Lecarranagappogue in Kilreekill is a sentry post.[354] It skirted Toberahoney (Tober a Shonnaigh) and Wallscourt fort. It straddled the Wallscourt/Meanus, Dartfield/Glenmeen boundaries and ran by the W of Carra back to the start.

As the Turoe/Knocknadala oppidum expanded a new development was taking place on its NW flank. A new Belgic oppidum emerged centered on Athenry. Its inner ward embankment, in typical Belgic style, circumvallates the present Norman-walled town (along its N and E walls). Vestiges of several outer-ward extensions survive. Athenry (*Rath Cruacha/Magh Muc Dhruim* in Dindsenchas lore) and Turoe/Knocknadala oppida collided as they expanded. This point has now been reached in the reconstruction. It will affect, and be reflected by, further reconstruction. The two oppida accommodated each other. The Craughwell/Dunkellin/Raford (Dur) River and the NNW line of embankment from Greyford in Kiltulla along the west boundaries of Carnakelly and Cloonkeen to the Killaclogher river and Roundfield in Monivea became the boundary line between the two oppida. It reflected a satisfactory solution when the two oppida collided. Later extensions of Turoe/Knocknadala oppidum enveloped the Athenry oppidum.

---

[354] So named after St Rechil, sister of Palladius who was sent by Pope Celestin as the 1st Bishop to Ireland in 431.

Figure 27: Arrows on OS map pointing to a 20 meter wide embankment in Brackloon levelled for a railway line ('New Line') but never completed, and a parallel short stretch of raised bank at a bend of the Raford River on the edge of Knockroe (*Cnoc roo* = Dyke hill) higher ground to inundate lowlands behind, obviating the need for an extra line of embankment and extra defence forces.

Figure. 29: **Numerous vestiges of the Turoe/Knocknadala linear embankments have been preserved as tree-lined avenues just as has been done with Ulster's Black Pig's Dyke. Examples here are at Cornamuclagh near the River Suck NE of Ahascragh (lower), at Benmore/Benbeg (centre) and at Turoe (top).**

Figure 30: Rivers and streams were brought into the sophisticated Belgic defence system. Embankments were built on one or both banks and floodgates set to enhance the defence mechanism to inundate large areas in time of danger as seen here in Kiltulla North (lower), Raford River (centre) and Bellayarha (top).

Figure.31:Vestiges of linear embankments forming the Dooghcloon/Streamsford boundary (top; a mile-long stretch), through Carnakelly/Laragh (centre), and a leveled-down section in Kiltulla North to the edge of the cut away bog (lower).

Figure 32: Linear embankments leveled in the 1870/80's for the laying of a road (top: Rathglass) and for a railway line ('The New Line', 2 lower photos in Brackloon) E Galway but never completed. In the top photo notice how part of the main embankment was preserved as a field ditch and how the filled-in fosse fell below the partly leveled-down embankment.

Figure 33 Vestiges of weathered embankments run across Baunoge/Tonnaroasty (Bottomland dykes; a parallel line formerly ran along the tree-lined brow of the hill; top) E of Loughrea lake; through Kilconierin into Moyode (2nd top); through Killimordaly (2nd lower) and along the Galway/Mayo border (lower).

Figure 34: Typical examples of how linear embankments were levelled down for the laying of roads or as winter platforms for farm animals in wet lands.

Figure 35: Vestiges of partly leveled out linear embankments at Turoe, Co. Galway (left), on the Galway/Roscommon border near Creggs (centre), and at Newgrove, Kilreekill, Co. Galway (lower: this latter linear embankment is "wide enough for two lorries to run side by side on its surface").

Figure.36: Wide vestiges of partly dismantled linear and transverse embankments at Turoe (lower), at Cornamuclagh (Hill of the Magic Boar's Dyke) near
Galway/Roscommon border on the River Suck NE of Ahascragh, (centre), and
at Laragh/Knockroe (*Cnoc roo* = embankment hill, top) NE of Turoe.

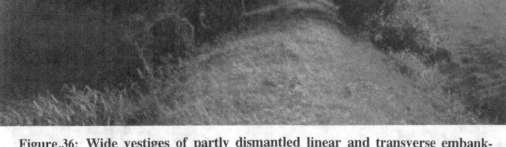

Figure 37: A linear embankment along the brow of a hill just E of Loughrea lake (top two photos). A stone wall separating two adjoining farms has replaced the outer-lip rampart. A line of embankment leveled-down to almost ground level has a drain cut along its centre through Rahroody townland just N of Loughrea lake (lower).

Figure 38: Embankments on hill slopes E of Loughrea (top). Cave entrance (centre) and interior (lower) on the line of embankments at the SE of Loughrea Golf Course. Several such hideaways exist along the linear embankment sets.

THIRD EXTENSION OF THE TUROE/KNOCKNADALA OUTER WARD

Reconstruction of the next extension of the Turoe/Knocknadala oppidum begins from the NW corner and proceeds clockwise. Starting (4 miles ENE of Athenry) from the N tip of the Cloonkeen/Ballyboggan boundary straddling the Cloonkeen River where it marched with an outer-ward extension of the Athenry oppidum, the rampart set ran ENE. Its alignment was dictated by the narrow strip of land between the bogs embracing Cloonkeen through Cloonkeenmore North. The name Cloonkeen on several townlands is a corruption of Clann Chian, descendants of Cian, the leader of vassal tribes of fighting men (Collaibh Oige, corrupt 'Colla Woge'), who came from Eli in N Munster seeking military service with Queen Medb in the expansion of the Turoe/Knocknadala and Athenry oppida. Their task was to erect and defend the fortifications of the outer wards along their N flank in lieu of lands given for their services. They formed an expansive buffer state between the Fir Belg and the Sogain branch of the Cruthin. The Cruthin then occupied the country from this outer ward of the Fir Belg oppidum at the centre of Co Galway right up across NE Connacht and the whole North half of Ireland. With each extension of these outer wards the Cruthin territory contracted apace. After Maine Mor's 5th century invasion of their lands, the Clann Chian bitterly complained of being driven into this strip of forested boglands and had to fell the ancient forests: "hewers of wood and drawers of water."[355] Cian's descendants, one of the 3 Colla branches of young fighting men (Colla[ibh] Oige), marched with Cormac mac Art against the Cruthin of Ulster. They were awarded prime lands for their military service and became known as the Chiannachta. They survived well into the middle ages along the N Leinster coast. Cian's Connacht territory was drastically decimated to 14 Clann Chian townlands after Maine Mor's invasion.

From Cloonkeen village on the N bank of Cloonkeen River the set cut its way E through Cloonkeenmore North, Ballynanulty, Attimonbeg, Gortnalone South, Cappanasruhan and Clooncah. The Dublin/Galway railway line swung more ENE to commandeer this rampart section. The names Ballynanulty and Attimon are of 5th century provenance. They make a statement of political significance to Connacht history and to the wider Irish context. Suffice it to say here that Attimon (Ait Ui Maine) is named after Maine Mor descendants. His Airghiallan army from Clogher in Ulster (na nUltaigh) overran these lands of the Clann Cian in the 5th century. Early sources give Maine Mor as a son of Niall of the Nine Hostages, founder of the Ui Niall Dynasty. The later pedigree invented for him is fictitious. There was originally but one kingdom of Maine, son of Niall, E and W of the Shannon.[356]

According to the invasion story preserved in the Life of St. Grellan, Maine Mor's army marched towards the centre of the Fir Belg stronghold along the passage through these bogs leading in from Gurteen to Knockaboy (Victory hill), site of one of the placenames mentioned, Knockasheefraigh (Cnoc an Shee Fraoich). It states euphemistically that the bogs swallowed up the Fir Belg. Some of Maine Mor's followers settled in Attimon area but were later pushed east. The adjacent townland of Ballnanulty (Baile na nUltaigh) pinpoints the area where a segment of the Ulstermen settled on the NE side of the Turoe/Knocknadala oppidum, keeping the stretch of bogs as a buffer between them and the latter. Gortnalone (*Gort na Lann*, field of the spears) is named from the number of spears found there after the massacre. The Attymon hoard of bronze La Tene horsebits and pendants in the National Museum was found at the bog's edge at Cappanashruhan. Pointed stakes planted in the bog to impale cavalry horses were found in turf-cutting operations. Countless burials were unearthed on gravel hills near the scene of the massacre of the Fir Belg. In the shadow of Knockaboy lie Air Cealtragh (Cealtra massacre), Clooncah (battlefield) and Moyarwood

---

[355] Martin Finnerty in his *'Punan Arsa'* relates this local oral tradition.
[356] Byrne, Op. Cit. p. 92; T.F. O Rahilly, Op. Cit. p.97, p. 479-80; P Walsh in J.G.A.H.Soc, xvii, p. 124ff

(*Maigh air*, plain of the massacre). All announce the killing fields of Maine's massacre of the Fir Belg of this former Clann Chian territory.

The set ran from Clooncah to Dooghcloon ('doo', O-Irish for dyke) and Derrydoo (Dyke oakwood) Lough. Vestiges survive. It sped through the S tip of Moyarwood and Greenhills and ran astride the Carrowholla/Carrowmore boundary with Woodlawn to the railway station area. It swung SSE straddling the Woodlaun road partly built on a leveled rampart which formed the Cloonahinch/Kilaan boundary with Woodlawn. It cut through Cloonymorris, Lisnamoltaun, Escirgclaidh (sandhill dyke) and Killagh More where large vestiges survive. It ran through Ballymabilla (forest) skirting Ashbrooke, Turksland, Toormore and Doonaree as it ran into Eastwell. Several of these names proclaim that these ramparts ran through a forested periphery surrounding the Turoe/Knocknadala oppidum, corroborating Caesar's description of the classic Belgic oppidum. Doonaree (Kings' fort), Cartron Sheela (the fertility goddess Sheela, associated with royal sites) and Tooree (king's hill) signal a minor royal centre here. The rampart set straddled the Ballydonnellan, Cloonmain, Lissalumma and the Carrowreagh/Corbally Mor/Lisheenahevnia boundary with Ballyhogan. It sped over Finnure (Cnoc Findabhair = Hill of Findabhair, the youngest daughter of Queen Medb and consort of Fraech mac Fidaig, King of Connacht). It raced across Castlenancy to Ballynamurdoon (*'Mur Doon'* was a Cruthin term referring to the dyke defence line corresponding to the Fir Belg *Dun Cladh*). The Dal nDhruitne (ngChruthine) were a Cruthin clan descended from Celtchar mac Uithechair. Isolated in the Fir Belg invasion they had a large settlement area here SE of Loughrea.

From Gortymadden the rampart set sped W through Carrowroe, Ballydavid along the slopes of Ballydoogan (Dyke set), Knockbaron and Carrowmore. It straddled Carn/Knockadikeen boundary (*'dikeen'*/*díg*, corrupt Gaelicization of 'dyke), Tonnaroasty (*Tonna rooasty*, dyke bottom-land). Vestiges survive in Baunoge. Surface traces of linear embankments survive along the slopes on the Baunoge/Gorteenapheebera boundary. The set straddled the Tonnaroasty/Gorteenapheebera and Farranalynch/Caherwalter boundaries and skirted the N shore of Loughrea Lake. The building of this Norman-walled town demolished the ramparts. The North Wall fosse may be a vestige of the Iron Age Belgic fosse. The dyke set ran W from the lake through Cuscarrick, Cosmona and Pollroebuck (*Poll Roo*, Dyke Bog). It ran W through St. Lawrencefields and Tullagh Upper and Lower. Like the magic wild boar mythologically associated with the erection of the fortifications, the ramparts cut through Cloonoo, Knockauncoura (*Cnoc an couragh*)/Glenatallan and Ballnamuca. Sheamus Callanan of Knockauncoura village pointed out rampart vestiges running through Knockauncoura and Cloonoo and flexed his knowledge of similar dykes in widespread areas in which he hunted often as a youth. Long memories such as his have saved many ancient linear fortifications from being forgotten forever.

The set straddled the Gortawullaun/Lurgan, Boherduff/Tonbaun/Carrowclogh and Cartron/-Carrowmunna (of the Manapi)/Moycola boundaries, skirting Gortnabarnaboy (victory gap). Moycola, plain of the Colla Menn (Menapi fighting men), a mere shadow of its former extent, stretching from Loughrea to the inner harbour of the Iron Age seaport of Ath Cliath Magh Rí. This extended inland when the sea was 6 to 8 feet higher from the 3nd to the 5th century to the strongforts along the shores of Dur Loch (Turlough of Rahasane on the *Dur fluvium* of Ptolemy's record, *an Dughiortach*) between Craughwell, Clarenbridge and Maree. Vassal allies manning this sector of the Belgic oppidum were made up mainly of Belgic Manapi (Manach) who left their name on many townlands, such as Mannin, Manninard, Carrowmanen, Clann Manach, Ard na Managh (corrupt Monksfield), Ballymannagh, Newmannin (*Mannin Uagh*, Manapi necropolis) and Carrowmunna. With higher seas in the early centuries wide areas S of Rahasane, Craughwell and NW of these around Foirchoill ('wood of the sailor's rest'; wrongly anglicized as Coldwood) and

Moyveela (Magh Mell, sea plain) were regularly inundated by sea. It resembled the lands of the Manapi in the Rhine Delta and on the shores of Loch Erne. Being geese farmers and fishermen, these wetlands were ideal for the livelihood of the Manapi. These Colla Mann were one of the 3 Collas (*Collaibh Oige,* young warriors), repaid in the lands of their buffer states for their military services to the Turoe/Knocknadala Kings.

From Ballymoneen the set swung NNW through Seefin, Knockroe and Toorclogher boundaries. Toorclogher (Temhair Clocher) was known as Temhair Clogher Nath I (nDhathi), palace of Dathi mac Fiachrach, the 5th century king of Connacht and Fir Belg Overking. Pseudo-history made him High King of Tara. His 'Temhair' was in Galway in the West, not in Tara in the East. Toorclogher/Seefin area was the centre of Ui Fiachrach Aidne, the kingdom of Dathi, the son of Fiachra son of Eochaid Muigh Mean, Fir Belg Overking of the Turoe/Knocknadala oppidum. Toberneighey (nDhathi, Dathi's Well) is in adjoining Blackgarden. Toorclogher was the site of Diarmad and Grania's Bed. It is alledged that it was arranged for Grania, daughter of King Cormac Mac Art to wed Finn Mac Cool. She eloped with Dermot Mac Morna, brother of Gol Mac Morna, leader of the Connacht Fianna, but was ambushed by Finn in their forest hideout which became known as Fidh Mac Cool (Cool's Grove today; no grove survives).

From Blackgarden (*Garra doo*: Dyke park) the set ran through Derryhoyle More (Forest) and Reaskmore (marsh; the Belgic oppidum incorporated both forest and marshlands). It traversed Crossderry, Capanraheen, Creggaun, Loughgill and Coolraugh on the bank of the Craughwell River and in the fork of Dunkellin River. Ramparts across river belong to the outer ward of Athenry oppidum with which they collide along the Dur (Dunkellin) river here, an area of dense forest as the names of the Tlds. proclaim. The next 3 townlands along the route make their own political, geographical, historical or topographical statements. Treankyle (*Trean Coill*, Trenovanten forest) lies within the two arms of the Dunkellin River. The vast Tld. of Ganty (*na gCanti*) preserves the name of the Belgic Canti tribe who came with Verica/Ferach, grandson of Commius. Caherkinmainwee (*Caher Chinn Main Mhuigh,* fort at the head of the Plain of Maine, son of Queen Medb) makes its own significant political, historical, geographical and topographical claim. Maine's residence stood at Clogharevaun at the core of Turoe/Knocknadala oppidum at the centre of Main Magh to which he gave his name.[357] Main Mhaigh (The Plain of Maine) was then co-extensive with the Turoe/Knocknadala oppidum enclosed within the embankments of the present outer ward under reconstruction. Maine succeeded his mother Medb as monarch of Connacht. They did not reside at Rathcroghan of Roscommon which pseudo-history claimed to be the royal capital of Connacht in Medb's time. They resided at the centre of Galway. Rathcroghan was then a dependency of Emain Macha of ancient Ulster. The profound statement made by this tiny Tld. is a time bomb under the Rathcroghan myth. Coill Winard (Winard Forest) in adjacent Cappagh further corroborates the fact that this was a heavily forested area in archaic times. Doonard overlooking Craughwell, Caherdangan and other strong-forts in the area manned the linear embankments. Across river these ramparts marched with those of the Athenry oppidum back to the starting point.

FOURTH EXTENSION OF THE TUROE/KNOCKNADALA OUTER WARD
From Templemoyle near Newcastle church, where the Athenry/Rath Cruacha outer ward marched with that of the Turoe/Knocknadala oppidum (shown on OS Map, some 4 miles NE of Athenry), embankments of a new outer ward extension of Turoe/Knocknadala oppidum began. It ran E through Shoodaun, skirted the forested bogs astride the Cloonkeen Beg/Cormacuagh boundary through Clough (*Pollacladh,* Dyke Bog; early OS Maps show the dykes) parallel to the E stretch of Killaclogher river. It sped over Tample, Knockaboy,

---

[357] The Dindsenchas of Main (Maen) Magh.

Sheeaun, and Caltragh (*Aircaltra*), skirting Attimany. Each of these, and nearby Caltraghbreedy has its story to tell. Sheeaun was the Otherworld Abode of the god of eloquence and learning, Ogma, son of Dagda who was Father and Ruler of the Celtic gods. In Celtic literature Ogma retired to his 'sidhe' on Airceltra (Caltragh). Local elders claim this was on Knockaboy, originally known as Sheeaun hill, near its summit shrine or military encampment (moated site) on the line of embankments. Caltragh became known as *Air* (Massacre) *Celtragh* from the massacre of the Fir Belg by Maine Mor in this arena between Clooncah and Temple. Cian's Fir Belg people were euphemistically said to have been swallowed up by the surrounding bogs.

Ogma's sister, Brigid, the goddess of fertility, poetry, healing, and smiths, had her Otherworld Abode in nearby Caltraghbreedy (sanctuary of the Briganten goddess Brigid). This sanctuary was in the lands of the Clann Cian, descendants of Tadg Mac Cian from Eli in Offaly who were Briganten and worshipers of the goddess Brigid. Before their decimation by the invasion of Maine Mor, the Clann Chian buffer state had expanded out to this frontier at the expense of the Cruthin of the 6 Sogain. In this sanctuary of those Celtic deities, Ogma and Brighide, early churches were erected to suppress their pagan worship, one at *Teampail* (Temple) and one at Caltrabreedy in honour of St. Brigit (the site survives). In all-but-lost local tradition, Tample was associated with Cormac Mac Art and pointed out as the place of his burial mound in the Tample cemetery (destroyed except for the mound) as attested by the name Cormacuagh (Cormac's tomb) which included part of present-day Clogh (Poll an Cladh) and Temple Tlds.

The set crossed Lenareagh and straddled the Clooncah/Caltraghbreedy/Dooghcloon/Moyarwood boundary with Gortronnagh/Fahy/Shanballard and Corskeagh. It skirted Greenhills, Carrowholla, Carrowmore and Moneyveen boglands, and swung SSE through Moneyveen. It straddled the Clooncalleen/Hillswood, Clooncallis/Ballyglass, Corraneena/Ballintober and Killagh Beg/Hazelfort boundaries. It cut through Ballinphuill and Ballynaclogh. It straddled the Sliaun Beg, Gortnahimrissan and Mountain boundaries with Cappataggle, the Pollatlugga/Brackloon boundaries with Rooaun (Dykes)/Tooree, the Chelsea, Poppyhill, Ballinrooaun (Dyke) boundaries with Ballydonnellan East, Lissacullaun, Carrowreagh. It straddled the Corbally More, Corbally Hogan boundary into Mullagh More (east of School) and Lismacteidg, the Foxhall Little (*Sonnagh Beg*) boundary with Cappanaghtan and Foxhall *Sonnagh* rampart. Vestiges of linear embankments survive there and in Lurganshanny (Lurgan Shonnagh). It crossed Liscoyle, Drumeyre, Drumhogan, Boleyroe, and Coolagh.

The set swung W through Killnamullaun, Rahyconor/Cormick/Lisduff/Garaunnameetagh (Moote lands), Cloonprask, Gortaneare, Shanvoher, Ballindrimma/Shangarry boundary, Cloghbrack, Clogharoasty and Lissaphuka. It straddled the Rathfarn/Kilmacrah and Srahdoo/Carheendoo boundaries. Floodgates were set in the stream. Skirting Lissheenahasty, it straddled the Glenaslat/Traskernagh boundary. Across Masonbrook several forts stood sentinel, notably Rathsonny (Dyke Fort). It proceeded through Moanmore and Loughaunlea into Moanmore East. The Moanmore stream, forming the S boundary of Moanmore East, had raised banks and floodgates to enhance the defences. The Masonbrook/Loughrea area was a major centre of the Dal gChruthine (Dal nDruithne), a Cruthin enclave related to the Sogain of E Galway and the Cruthin of NE Connacht and Ulster, descended from the Ulster hero, Celtchar mac Uitechair. Sanctuaries and necropoli here, and the 7 monuments in Moanmore East and Doon Hill, were theirs. Monoliths in Masonbrook over Rathsonny and in Earlspark above Brickloch are two of many. After Maine Mor's invasion Loughrea's archaic landscape became part of Hy Many. The Dal ngChruithne revived their fortunes, defeating the Ui Maine E of Loughrea in 802 with the aid of their kinsmen, the Sogan of Tiaquin.

The set ran W across Earlsparke and along the slopes of Mount Pleasant and Knockanima to the SE of Loughrea Lake (Figure 37 and 39). The Slí Dála formed the Mount Pleasant/-Knockanima boundary, climbing up from the E side of Loughrea town to the heights above the lake. It swung ESE forming Earlspark's boundary with Mountpleasant and Moanmore West, heading off to Roscrea. A branch road bifurcated from Slí Dála, heading S over Aille along the E slopes of the Aughta Mountain. At the NE end of the lake another branch headed S along the W side of Aughta Mt. A local man, Joe Dunne, pointed out the different routes. Loughrea lake was a sacred lake in Queen Medb's day. It was also known as Lind Lir. Ailill Mac Mata, made keeper of the lake by Medb, later became Medb's consort and King of Connacht. Medb had a Royal Crannog on the lake, one of numerous crannogs on the lake. It was while bathing there during the great festival of the lake that she was eventually assassinated. An ancient sprawling urban-like complex enfolded this lake. In 1997 Loughrea town officially marked the 1200th anniversary of the sacking of Loughrea in 797 by Muirgius.

This set skirted the S lakeshore as the previous set did the N shoreline. Transverse ramparts run down to the lake. A rare example of a linear embankment facing uphill forms the field boundary below Shield's house in Grange on the slope to the lake. The set ran W on the slopes above the lake through Grange and Grange Park. Numerous forts studded the route along this belt above the lake. Twelve are shown on the 1840 OS Map, eight on the 1933 OS Map. Most have disappeared. Embankments overlooking the lake in Grange and Curheen are not marked on OS maps. Their line curved following to the curve of the lake's S shoreline. It continued W through Curheen and Glenaclara East and West. Vestiges survive in Curheen and Cuscarrick.

The set ran from Loughrea W to Kilchreest through Glennaclara, Aille, Cahercrea East/West, Ballingarry, Gortnamacan, and Killaspugmoylan, along the marshlands of the W stretch of Kilchreest river to its W zigzag curve where it swung away SW. Hard to find traces in Kilchreest and Gortnamacan ran along the river whose floodlands were utilized superbly. Short sections of the river were banked up and floodgates fitted to the S end of Ballygarraun to induce inundation for defence purposes. This is corroborated by the 1844 OS Map which shows vestiges on both sides of the river in Kilchreest, Gortnamacan, Ballingarry and Ballygarraun. Some became right-of-ways and later local roads. Most were leveled before the revised 1933 OS Map was published and were not recorded. The 1844 map shows the complicated web-like nature and interrelation of onward and transverse ramparts giving a fine example of the confusing and classic nature of the Belgic defensive system.

The set swung NW from the N tip of Roxborough through Pollnashinnagh *(Poll na shonnagh*, Dyke Bog), Ballyshea, Caherskeehaun, Creggmulgreny and Lakyle. It skirted Lough Kinlea (Cinn Chlaidh) and Lough Burke at the N of Ballyshea and Knocknamanagh. It traversed Carheen and Emlagh, skirting Killogilleen and Caher Gal. It ran through Ballynascragh, Ballylin West and Bauttagh, skirting Ballymanagh. It sped through Ballynamannin and Mannin, all named after the Manapi *(Manach)*. The set raced through the W side of Roo (Dyke) in which there is a Lisdoo (Dyke fort), Aggard Beg with its Lisroo (Dyke Fort) and Lissindragan on the line of fortification. Skirting Aggard More, it cut through to the marshlands to the edge of the original Rahasane Lake (Dur Loch) and the Dooeyertha/Dur (Dunkellin) river in Carrigeen East and West. Across the lake and river stood the ramparts of the outer ward of the Athenry oppidum in line with the latter as they ran NNW to Carnmore and Lisheenavalla, welding the two oppida of Turoe/Knocknadala and Athenry/Magh Muc Dhruim into one joint oppidum.

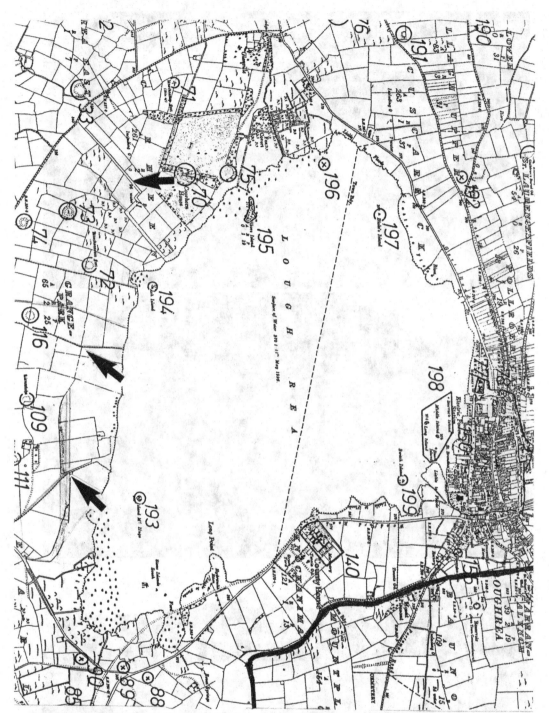

Figure 39: Loughrea lake where Queen Medh had a royal crannog (destroyed by King Muirghius of Rathcroghan in 802) and where she was assassinated, has a high concentration of ringforts (many shown on early maps) along the curving embankments on the heights above the lake's S end. The Norman-walled town and suburbs have obliterated all trace of forts and embankments along the north side of the lake. The Slighe Dala (dark line) from Turoe converged on Loughrea, climbing up the heights overlooking the lake from the east before swinging ESE to the Shannon.

Figure 40: Spoilt vestiges of linear embankments run down the W side of Cruach Magh Seola towards Lough Corrib near Headford (top), and skirt Coldwood (Foir Choill in nFhochoillut Oichne = wood of the sailor's rest/watch) Lake near Clarenbridge (centre). Escir Uí Manachain in Culferne (lower) in the buffer state defended by the Manapi near Ballinlough, Ballyhaunis and Loch Mannin. Escirs were utilised in the defence system.

THE ATHENRY/RATH CRUACHU/MAGH MUC DHRUIM OPPIDUM

It is now opportune to reconstruct the Athenry oppidum. More appropriate are its archaic names, Rath Cruacha/Cruachan and Magh Muc Dhruime (Plain of the Magic Pig's Dyke) of dindshenchas history. The significance of the names and their location are not understood because pseudo-history hijacked and transported them to an entirely new scenario. When Ui Briuin spin-doctors transferred Queen Medb from Rath Cruacha of Athenry to Rathcroghan of Roscommon, they also expropriated the name of Rath Cruacha/Cruachan for Rathcroghan. The latter was never known as Rath Cruacha/Cruachan except in pseudo-history. Residents within a 20-mile radius of Rathcroghan insist that Rathcroghan is not, and never was, known as Rath Cruachan. Pseudo-historians deliberately concocted this confusion. O Rahilly noted "the Irish name of Rathcroghan, Co. Roscommon, may in origin have been a tribal name,"[358] Rath Cruthin. It was the NE Connacht stronghold of the Cruthin of the West of Ireland, and as such, was known as Rath Cruthin. Rathcroghan as pronounced by local residents sounds very much like Rath Cruthin. Rath Cruacha of Athenry, not Rathcroghan, was the Fir Belg stronghold of Queen Medb. Rath Cruacha and Magh Muc Dhruim are better known in Dindsenchas history than Turoe or Knocknadala which were suppressed. Until the 1940's the ramparts round the walls of Athenry were referred to as the Inner Dun and their corrosponding sets of outer ward embankments as the 'Great Dun', 'Dun Cladh', 'Muc Cladh' or 'Muc Dhrum'. The ramparts of Athenry's inner ward, wrongly ascribed to the Normans, were erected 1200 years before the Normans came. Pseudo-historians say Athenry had no history before the Normans. Ramparts of the inner ward survive outside the E and N walls. Country-folk confound the 'official doctrine' of pseudo-history by claiming these ramparts were erected by the Fir Belg.

Sixty years ago, long before any author wrote about the unique nature of the Belgic defensive system, one local elder, Martin Finnerty, wrote a treatise entitled 'Punan Arsa' ('Archaic History Notes')[359] on aspects of the early history of the area ages before the coming of the Normans. He described a long stretch of the 'Great Dun' which ran all round Athenry 4 miles out from the town. Without using archaeological terms such as 'Inner' or 'Outer Ward', he claimed people of his young days were well aware of outer expansions of the ramparts around the medieval Norman-walled town. He claimed the common knowledge among countryfolk in his young days was that these ramparts were erected by the Fir Belg 2000 years ago. He noted a 7-mile stretch of rampart from Greyford in Kiltulla to Roundfield in Monivea. He described the section in Roundfield on which he played as a boy some 100 years ago. Only surface traces survive. His groundbreaking document lies buried in the National Library, Dublin.

This present reconstruction, then, does not claim to be original. It owes much to oral history handed down by countryfolk, such as Mr. Finnerty, covering a wide area not only around Athenry, but the whole of Galway and beyond. It is not the intention to present a definitive reconstruction of the Athenry oppidum, but to show how it stands as an oppidum in its own right in relation to the Turoe/Knocknadala oppidum, how it merges with, and was subsumed by the latter. Full credit for putting the Athenry oppidum on record long before similar Belgic Capitals with their unique defence systems in SE Britain and in Belgic areas of the Continent were placed on record will not be taken from Mr. Finnerty. While his documentation of the Athenry oppidum is rudimentary, he was actively gathering information and carrying out research to produce a fuller account, not only of the Athenry oppidum, but of that of the Turoe/Knocknadala oppidum also, when he passed away. He was ahead of his time in putting on record the existence of the unique Fir Belg defensive system, however simply expressed.

---

[358] T. F. O Rahilly, 'Early Irish History and Mythology', p. 26, n. 2.
[359] Martin Finnerty, 'Punan Arsa' in the National Library, Dublin.

INNER WARD OF ATHENRY: RATH CRUACHU: MAGH MUC DHRUIM

Inner ward embankments run outside Athenry's Norman walls. The walls on the N side were built on the rampart, leaving the fosse and outer lip outside the walls. Vestiges of 2 embankments and a fosse survive along the E wall. This line of rampart is well known (Figures 41, 42, 43). There are surface traces of another parallel rampart some 400 feet outside the latter and of transverse ramparts linking both. As these might have served as cover to protect the advance of invaders, these were leveled when the Norman walls were built. The Normans made a most astute move when they fortified this ready-made strategic site for their conquest of this part of Connacht. They were emulating their British kinsmen who fortified the inner ward ramparts of Belgic oppida and the walled earthworks of large Roman forts in similar fashion in England.

Athenry's ramparts along the townwalls form its boundary with Gorteenacra and Knockanglass on the E, Baunmore (where Queen Medb held war-games and a pre-war Assembly) and Prospect on the S, Raheen and Ballygarraun South on the W, and Culairbaun and Caheroyan on the N side. Before the Memorandum of July 7th in the 33rd year of Henry the Eight (Record Office, Dublin) in which Athenry is rendered as Athenrie, it was never known as Baile Ath An Rí. Athenry is not Ahenry (Atha an Rí, Ford of the Kings, a false rendering of late provenance). The 'At' of Athenry as ever pronounced, is the Irish word *'ait'* meaning 'home', 'place of residence'. **Athenry is the 'AUTEINRI' of Ptolemy's Irish record**. The Greek 'AYT-EIN-PI ', like the name Athenry itself, when broken into its components spells Aut ein ri = 'Ait en Rí', Residence, Seat or **Home of the Kings**. As it was in Ptolemy's day, so it is today. 'Experts', believing they knew better, tried to 'gaelicize' this Old Irish name as 'Baile Atha na Rí. If this were correct, it should be called Ahenry, not Athenry as spoken. It was also the Home of the gods. Not only were kings and queens interred there, Celtic gods and goddesses had their Otherworld Abodes in Athenry's vast ancient necropolis, each allotted their places in the four Mountain (Cruachan) segments surrounding Athenry. The chief place allotted to this sprawling royal cemetery of Releg na Rí in the archaic necropolis texts and the vast area this necropolis occupies should alert one to the fact that ancient Athenry was a very much larger and more important site than the snug little town is today.

THE FOUNDING OF ATHENRY'S RATH CRUACHA:

The name of Caherroyn (site of the Norman Castle; *Caher Roighan* retains the O. Irish form of *Caher Righain*, Queen's Palace) makes its own royal statement which Athenry has ignored to its utter detriment. At the W end of Caherroyan Tld. is *Lis na Reena* (*Righiona*, 'Fort of the Queen'), a later form of *Roighan*. Both speak of a Queen (O. Irish *Roighan*), not a King. Who was this Queen? As this book grows on the reader so will this Queen of Rath Cruacha. Athenry, not the Norman town, but the Belgic oppidum, was her father's creation. When Medb's father, Fir Belg Overking (Rí Temhro) Eochaid Ferach (Eochaid Felech), commissioned Tinni mac Cónrach to erect defensive embankments around Rath Cruacha it was not at Rathcroghan of Roscommon, seat of the Cruithintuatha, that he erected the ramparts but at Rath Cruacha of Athenry of Galway. Tinni was king of the Domnann sept spearheading the Fir Belg expansion at the expense of the Cruthin. The Domnann were placed in buffer states on the S, W and N flanks of the outer ward defence line of the expanding Belgic Oppidum. In repayment for so speedily erecting the fortifications around Rath Cruacha, the Fir Belg Overking made Tinni first king of Ól nÉgmacht at Rath Cruacha. Rath Cruacha/Cruachan was the royal Capital of Ól nÉgmacht, which was archaic Connacht in embryo. The name 'Connacht' came into existence several centuries later. As Tinni soon became embroiled in conflicts, as *'Cath Boinne'*[360] relates, Eochaid Felech (Rí Temhro) demoted Tinni and placed his own daughter Medb on the

---

[360] *Eriu ii, 178;* Pseudo-history transferred it to Croghan of Roscommon, T.F. O Rahilly, Op. Cit. p.96

throne. In the earliest texts she is recorded as Queen of Ól nÉgmacht, not of Connacht which had not yet come into being. Rathcroghan of Roscommon was never part of Ól nÉgmacht. From Rath Cruacha she reigned not only over the Fir Belg of Ól nÉgmacht, but led the combined Fir Belg forces of Ireland against the Cruthin of Rathcroghan and the North. Tinni bided his time at his stronghold, Caher Tinni, some 2 miles NW of Loughrea at the N side of Ardnadooman (Ard na Domnann; height of the Domnann sept of whom Tinny was king), but continued to be a frequent guest of Medb at Rath Cruacha. The outcome will be related later.

ATHENRY/RATH CRUACHA/MAGH MUC DHRUIM OPPIDUM OUTER WARD

From Mount Shaw in Ballygarraun just W of Athenry ramparts of the first outer ward ran E through Raheen, the S of Moanbaun and Ballydavid South to Culairbaun and Caherroyn. They swung SSE through Kingsland (*'Ait na Rí'*) North/South and then SW straddling Baunmore/Rahard boundary area. They ran W straddling Boyhill's (*Cnoc Boidbh* = the god Bodbh's Otherworld Abode, alias *Sidhe Buidbh, Sidh Cruacha, Sidh Connacht, Sidhe nOchaill* or *Relig na Rí*,[361] where traces of tumuli survive) boundary with Loobroo (Otherworld abode of the god Lug), Bottom (*an tShonnagh*, embankment) and the N of Toberconnelly, to Farranablake. They swung NW through Newford back to Mount Shaw. The fort in Athenry cemetery was known as Rath Cruacha. So were other nearby forts.

FIRST OUTER WARD EXTENSION OF ATHENRY OPPIDUM

An extension of the outer ward ran ENE from Moanbaun, a mile NW of Athenry, through Park and Ballydavid to Carrowntobber West where it swung SSE through Kilcornan, Pollacappul, Blean and Backpark where vestiges survive. Traversing Deerpark, it straddled the stream which forms Moyode's boundary with Loobroo, Bottom and Mountain South (one of the 4 *Cruachans* wrongly anglicized as 'Mountain' around Athenry), as it ran WSW. Across the road in the NE tip of Clamparpark is the ruin of a double-ringed stone fort, Clochar Chonail Chruachna, palace of Conall, King of Temhair[362] (Turoe) where Conn of the Hundred Battles, a later King who gave Connacht its name, was fostered. Conall was Conn's uncle. This was one of the finest stone forts in Ireland before it was badly defaced by a bulldozer. Following the banks of the Escir River, the rampart set straddled the Clamperpark/Turloughalanger boundary to Cahereenascovoge. It swung NNW through Castleturvin and along the Millpark/Mulpit/Cloran boundaries. It crossed Ballygarraun West, Rathmorrissy and Pollnagroagh on its way to its Moanbaun starting point. Several stout forts guarded its route (Figure 44).

SECOND OUTER WARD EXTENSION OF ATHENRY OPPIDUM

Reconstruction of a 2nd extension of the outer ward starts some 3 miles NW of Athenry. It ran ENE from the Pollagooil/Deerpark boundary via Tobernavean (Fianna Well), Carnaun, Pollagh and Fahys-village, astride the latter's boundary with Mountain North (*Cruachan Thuaid*) and Castle Ellen. It sped through Loughaunenaghan, Skeaghadereen and Knockbaun into Montpelier. In Carrowantobber East it swung SSE through Gregabbey. It ran astride the Gloves West/Gloves Middle boundary. This Irish name of the many Gloves Tlds. is *'Na gChlaidhbhe'* (the Dykes), a name which spells out the character of this area of strategic defence. The prevalence of so many Gloves Tlds here is because the Athenry and Turoe/-Knocknadala oppida outer wards met and marched together through this region.

The set ran through Killascaul, Esker and marched with the Turoe/Knocknadala outer ward at the foot of Dominic's Hill (*Brugh A Scail*) and Cruach Chian (Otherworld Abode of Cian,

[361] *De Gabail an tSida'/'De Chopur in da Muccida'* in Bk Of Lein, 246a 32931-5; 290a 37234-7; 155a 20348-50

[362] Dindsenchas Cnoc na Dala'; "Conall Cruachna...robo rì ar tuathaib Temrach", line 22-4.

father of Lugh). The forest of *Coll A Scail* (O-Irish name of the adjoining Tld) was extensive in early times. It bears the name of the god *'A Scail'*, alias Lugh. Lochaun Escir and Escir River forming the N boundary of Killascaul were known as *Loch A Scail* and *Abha A Scail*. The upper River Scheld in Belgium in the lands of the Atrebates and Morini was known as 'A Scail' *(A Scaul* shown on early Roman maps). From there the Belgic Atrebates (Aitreabh) and Morini (Mac Morna) came to Ireland via the SE of England. From Escir School area the ramparts swung WSW through Rathgorgin and Cruachanaine (*Cruachan Aine* = Otherworld Abode of the goddess Aine, Cian's consort). The presence of the sacred shrines of Cian and Aine on the boundary between the oppida is significant. On the Continent sacred shrines of Celtic gods/godesses often stood on tribal boundaries which were also places of fairs and markets. On the boundary between the two oppida at the S foot of Dominic's Hill there is a raised rectangular earthen embankment with outer fosse, marked on the OS map as 'moated site'. Was it a Celtic Temple on the boundary where the oppida met? Several *fulachtai fia* stood above it.

Rathgorgin (*Ailech Gorgin*) was the Palace of Gorgin (Corc), son of Lugdech, ancestor of the Eoganacht of Munster. Corc's Mother was a Scottish Manapian princess. Corc left descendants in Mag Gorgin (Gergin or Circin), named after him, in Scotland. Corc returned to Ireland and settled, not at Tara, but here at Ailech Gorgin (Corc) where he became overking of the Deisi tribes. When King Cormac Mac Art reclaimed his rightful throne and subdued these, Corc left with his followers and went forth to found Cashel, which become the Capital of Munster.

From Rathgorgin's surviving vestiges, the set sped WSW along the Moyode/Tallyhoe Cross boundary. Moyode (Magh Fotad), the plain of the Fotads, makes a political statement which deals a devastating blow to the Tara Myth. The Fotad warriors came in the war band of Lughaid Mac Con from the Votadini tribe in the SE of Scotland. Pseudo-history claimed three Fotad Kings reigned as High Kings of Ireland after Lughaid Mac Con at Tara of Meath. The Fotad royal palace, *Clochar na ngFho*tad is in Moyode (Magh Fhot) Co. Galway, but is not shown on the OS Map. The story of the Fotad kings, together with that of Lughaid Mac Con and Corc (Gorgin), will be told in a later chapter. It will tug the rug from under Tara's pedestal, destroying its pseudo-historical glory.

From Moyode the ramparts, many with stone cores, ran through Slieveroe (Sli Bhrugh, Avenue of the Otherworld Abode of the gods), Rockfield, Knockatoor and Cahercrin into Moneyteig. They swung NNW parallel to the NS stretch of the Escir/Lavally River and commandeered Caherfin Esker. From Greethill they straddled the Gortroe (Dyke park)/- Derrydonnell More boundary and the Rathmorrissy/Tobberoe boundary. Through Caraunduff and Knocknacreeva the set ran back to the starting point at Pollagooil and Deer Park. At the centre of Carnaun (traces of satelite carns) are the ruins of what is called King John's Castle by some, or Clogher Goill (palace of Goll Mac Morna, leader of Connacht's Fianna fighting men who manned sections of the ramparts and were given lands for their services) by others. O-Irish 'Cloghar' was 'a royal residence'. There are many examples. In Carnaun district there are a number of local place-names referring to the Fianna, such as Tobernavean (*Tober na bhFhianna*).

Figure 41: Inner ward embankments of the classic Belgic defensive system outside the Norman E town walls of Athenry (top and middle). They swung west round King John's Castle (under renovation at top of photo) and ran along the north wall of the town. Legendary history tells that they were erected by Tinni and his Domnann tribe at the command of King Eochaid Felech, Queen Medb's father.

Figure 42: **Rath Cruacha's (Athenry) linear embankments were erected by Tinni and his Dumnann tribe at the command of Fir Belg King, Eochaidh Fedlech, the father of Medb (he elevated her to the Queenship of Ól nÉcmacht). They have the classic Belgic defensive system dimensions: main embankment is 25ft wide at base, the fosse is 15ft wide, the outer-lip is 12ft wide, and outer ditches**

Figure 43 The Normans built the walls of Athenry on the inner bank of the Graigabbey/Athenry River which originally flowed between the wall and the Belgic embankment enclosure along this E wall. A new river channel was cut within the walled town. Cattle give some idea of the height and width of the Athenry embankments and the depth of the fosse before it was filled in.

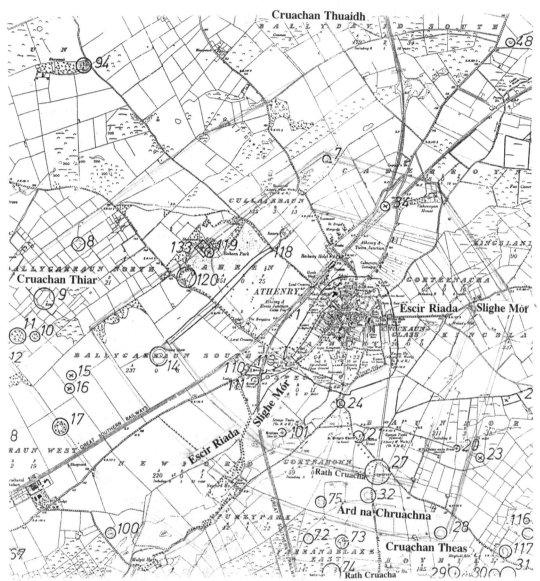

Figure 44: Athenry's inner ward embankments outside its east and northwest walls are well known. Not so well known are vestiges of sets of outer ward linear embankments out the countryside surrounding Athenry. Many were robbed of their stone core fill in the great stone rush when the Normans came to town. The alignment of outer ward embankments dictated that of the field grid around Athenry as the OS map shows. As at the Knocknadala/Turoe oppidum, there was a sprawling semi-urban complex at Athenry around the concentration of forts in the Ballygarraun, Farranablake and Ard na Cruachna areas.

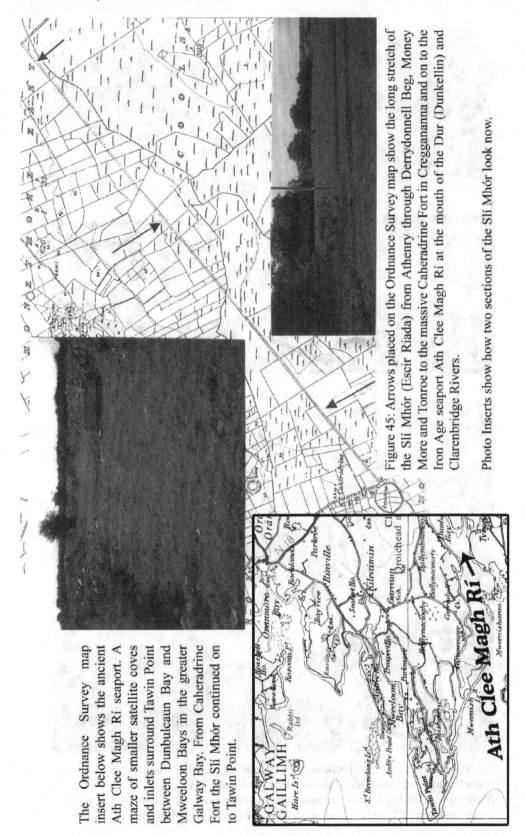

The Ordnance Survey map insert below shows the ancient Ath Clee Magh Rí seaport. A maze of smaller satellite coves and inlets surround Tawin Point between Dunbulcaun Bay and Mweeloon Bays in the greater Galway Bay. From Caheradrine Fort the Slí Mhór continued on to Tawin Point.

Figure 45: Arrows placed on the Ordnance Survey map show the long stretch of the Slí Mhór (Escir Riada) from Athenry through Derrydonnell Beg, Money More and Tonroe to the massive Caheradrine Fort in Cregganama and on to the Iron Age seaport Ath Clee Magh Rí at the mouth of the Dur (Dunkellin) and Clarenbridge Rivers.

Photo Inserts show how two sections of the Slí Mhór look now.

Ath Clee Magh Rí

Figure 46: Vestiges of embankments in Escir gChlaidh/Killagh Mor near Kilconnell (top), on the Derrydonnell Beg/Mountain West marsh boundary (2nd from top), a section on the Moyode/Kilconierin boundary resembling Athenry's inner rampart (2nd lower), and at the edge of dried up Coldwood lake (lower).

THIRD EXTENSION OF ATHENRY/MAGH MUC DHRUIM OPPIDUM.

Fom Rathgorgin and Oldcastle where the Athenry outer ward met the Turoe/Knocknadala outer ward, the last outer ward extension of Athenry oppidum commenced. Marching with an extension of the Turoe/Knocknadala oppidum, the two merged into one joint oppidum. It ran WSW through Moyode Demesne, straddling it to the *Dughiortach* (*Dur*/Dunkellin) river to which it ran parallel through Ballywinna, Temple Martin, Parkroe, Shanbally, Killeely and along the Ballywullagh/Crinnage boundaries to the NE end of Rahashan lake (*'Dur Loch'*), and river (*an Dughiortach;* the "Dur" of Ptolemy's record). These archaic names are reflected in the name of an ancient road, *Boher Dughiorthaigh* (Boherdooroghy on old OS maps), running NW from the W end of the lake to an inner harbour in Oran Beg when the sea was higher in the 4th/5th century. There is evidence that the sea, at high tide, flowed into *Dur Loch* which served as an inner harbour. Vestiges of landing ramps survive. Seashells on the undersides of rocks in the area can only be explained by the presence of the sea in former times. British experts have shown that the sea was 6 to 10 feet higher in the Roman period (2nd to 5th century AD).

On high ground above the original N shores of Rahashan (*Dur Loch*) from Scalp, Ballynagran, Caherfurvaus, Carheenadivane, Caheradine to Kileeneen Beg/Mor stand a line of strong forts, their main concentration being close to a natural landing place. A nearby fort bears the significant name of Caherfurvaus, (*Caher Foir Mhas,* fort of the sailors haven whilst waiting for high tide to set sail). The same O-Irish word 'Foir' is found in nearby Foorkill (Foir Choill, wood of the sailor's haven), wrongly anglicized as Coldwood, the O. Irish *'foir/faire'* being confounded with modern Irish word *'fuar'*. Late Iron Age high sea levels reached Foir Choill along the Clarenbridge river channel as seashells found on the undersides of rocks there as at Rahashan prove. Beside the wood of Foorkill, there was also a Fochoill, Eochoill and Achaill. The entire area from Rahashan N to Athenry was known as Achaill or Ochaill Oichne as referred to in ancient legend and *dindsenchas* texts.

Local lore says Patrick, fleeing from slavery on Slieve Mish and guided by an angel, rested here before sailing home. In his 'Confessions' he named 'Foculut' as the place where he waited. He noted that it was not on, but close to, the western sea 200 Roman miles from his place of slavery, a point ignored by commentators. This inner Ath Cliath Magh Rí harbour beside Fochoill (O-Irish gen. form *Fochoillut*) **is** 200 Roman miles from Slieve Mis, unlike Kilalla on the N Mayo coast, the alleged 'traditional site of Foclut' according to the pseudo-historic record of Tirechain. Ath Cliath Magh Rí, 2 miles W of Rahashan and Coldwood, was the illustrious "seaport of ancient Ireland visited by all ships sailing the high seas" Coldwood Turloch, was a large lake. After deepening the channel only Pollnacirca bird-haven remains. Landing sites survive at the original inner E end of Foorkill/Coldwood lake.

From the NW of Rahashan, a lake within the defence line, the set ran NNW from Kileeneen through Caherbulligin (Fir Belg fort), Cregananta and Brochagh to Coldwood. Watered-down ramparts survive in the N of former Coldwood lake (Figure 46). They crossed Moyveela (sea plain), Shantallow, Derrydonnell Beg, Mountain West (*Cruachan Thiar*) and Derrydonnell North (Figure 40). A lengthy 25-ft wide stretch of rampart cut through by the railway line from Derrydonnell Cross runs NNW astride Mountain West/Derrydonnell North boundary. Lisroughan (*rooaun:* dyke) manned the set S of the railway. The SSE section of the Dublin/Galway road at this cross was built on this rampart. Transverse ramparts survive in Mountain West Forestry plantation. The set straddled Carnmore E/W boundary to Lisheenavalla. It swung ENE through Ballymoneen, Grange East and Peakroe, straddling the Caherteemore N/S boundary. It crossed Sheeaun Park and Cossaun, straddling its boundary with Mount-browne (*Cnoc Roo*)/Saint Ellen and Caraun boundary with Castle Ellen and Belleville. Ned Ruane of Monivea Road had a wide knowledge of several sets of ramparts and a store of folklore from the older generation. Irish speakers in his young days claimed

Saint Ellen was a corruption of *Sidh nEthelann* (Abode of the goddess Ethlenn). It sped on through Loughaunenaghan and Hundred Acres to Roundfield. It marched with an outer ward rampart of Turoe/Knocknadala oppidum from Corrabaun/Roundfield in Monivea SSE to Curraghmore/Greyord in Kiltulla, through Knockbrack, Tisaxon, Bingarra, Binn/Lisdoran, Ballyboggan, Cloonbrusk, and the Gloves/Carnakelly N/S boundary to Curraghmore/-Greyford boundary. This completes the expansion of the Athenry/Magh Muc Dhruim oppidum in its own right. The expansion of the two oppida will now be reconstructed as a joint oppidum.

Local tradition noted in Finnerty's "*Punan Arsa*"[363] sixty years ago spoke of "the ancient dun that exists to the present day and runs alongside of the town" of which the outer ward Greyford/Roundfield extension circumvallating Athenry 4 miles out from the town is the 'Outer Dun' or 'Great Dun.' A wide vestige ran from Greyford in Kiltulla through 7 miles of countryside to Roundfield in Monivea. There it swung W around Athenry and back again to the starting point in Greyford (Rath Chlaidh). He named the stretch running W through Mountbrowne and Carheenlea to the Clare river as the "*Dun Cladh*' of Athenry.

Mr. Finnerty claimed these outer ramparts and those immediately outside Athenry's walls were attributed by the old people, not to the Normans, but to the Fir Belg. He noted "'authorities' have written that this town had no civil history before the arrival of the Normans." Against this, he put forward the tradition handed down by countryfolk 100 years ago: "Let it well be borne in mind that Athenry had an ancient name, with a storied past and a background of antiquity when Ptolemy wrote about it" in the 2nd century AD. Had it not, Athenry would not have figured on his geographical record as Auteinri (*Ait na Ri*; Home of the Kings)." His *'Punan Arsa'* preserves a valuable description of a section of rampart in Roundfield as it was when he played on it over 100 years ago. This is all the more precious as the rampart has since been obliterated, nor is there another in such excellent condition with fosse intact. At the close of the 19th century as he stood on a section of rampart in Roundfield "a feeling of awe came over me on looking down." He describes its construction: "10 feet wide on top and more than 10 feet high above ground level with a sloping stone revetment on either side. The deep fosse added another 10 feet to its outer face presenting a formidable high obstacle to an invader." It was erected by cutting "a canal at least 10 feet deep" on the outer side. Old people claim the height of the rampart varied according to the type of terrain it traversed. So much leveling has occurred in the course of time that it is difficult to have an exact gauge on the original height of the ramparts. The height of the embankment facing the enemy from the outside, whether on the hillslope or in a lowlying bog, would have been formidable.

Mr. Finnerty claimed the 'Great Dun' corroborated Ptolemy's record: the "Dun of Athenry is evidence of the fact that it was the work of the Fir Belg (the Belgae). No other tribe did such marvelous work," This has since been corroborated by British and Continental archaeologists who have analyzed this unique type of defensive system developed by the Belgae. The Cruthin built the 'Great Wall of Ulster' known as the 'Black Pig's Dyke'. This was in answer to the advance of the Fir Belg using an idea learnt from them for their defence, but of a different style. The Cruthin at first relied on a single massive rampart unlike the Fir Belg. It ran from one coastline to another cutting off the area occupied by the Cruthin rather than circumvallating their Capital like that of the Fir Belg. Later Cruthin defensive embankments became more like those of the Fir Belg. The parallel Muclahs (*Muc Cladh*) at Croghan of Roscommon are almost on a par with Fir Belg ramparts. Mr. Finnerty was well ahead of his time in recognizing that the Belgae alone developed this unique type

---

[363] Martin Finnerty, *'Punan Arsa'*.

of elaborate defensive system encircling their capitals, a fact that has only been recorded in Britain and the Continent in the last 35 years.

FIRST EXTENSION OF THE JOINT TUROE/KNOCKNADALA/ATHENRY OPPIDUM Yelp with the hounds in the mythological chase. Bound up hill and down dale. Be hot on the heels of the storied Wild Boar entrenching the landscape in mythical fury. Nip at its heel. Thrill to its squeal. Relish the zest of the hunt's reckless pace. Cut to the chase.

The first extension of the joint outer ward of Turoe/Knocknadala/Athenry oppidum commences from its NW corner on the N banks of the Clare River. From Rooaunmore and Kiniska (head of Turloughmore lake) it ran E to Claregalway and straddled the Lacaghbeg/-Cahershilleeny, Coolaran/Grange East, Carheenlea/Caherateemore and Rathfee/Glenmore boundaries to Killsceagh. It straddled the Gortavaura/Mountbrown boundary to Farravaun, Corralea (Dyke)/Roundfield and Pollavullaun/Corrabaun boundaries with Pollboy. It crossed *Cnoc a Farra*, (Mac Morna sentry post), Glennagloghan and Corrantarramud (*Carn Dhearmait*), tumulus of Diarmait Mac Morna, brother of Goll Mac Morna, the Mac Morna Fianna leader. His tumulus is on the hill beside Newcastle road near its west end.

Belgic military engineers no longer recognized a division between the Athenry and Turoe oppida. The two fused into one joint oppidum as the ramparts ran straight on along Corantarramud/Glennaslat boundary, Lenamore, Tiaquin, Cormacuagh/Derroogh boundary, Shan - ballymore and Ballyglass where *'na curraigh'* ran on to Gurteen church. They straddled the Cloonbornia/Gurteen, Gortnahultra/Creeraun Corskeagh/Kinreask, Ballinlough/Carrownakelly boundaries, Carrownea, Tullawicky, Liscune and Gortyroyan to Callow Lough (*Loch Acalla*). The Curha Dyke swung SSE through Cartrondoogan beside the railway line to Kilconnell (Figure 47) through Ballyglass, straddling the boundaries of Abbeyfield and Corraneena, into Gortadeegan (Dyke field; *'dig'* and *'dickeen'* are Gaelicized forms of 'dyke' common in Connacht and Ulster). The ramparts ran parallel to the W side of the first half of the Kilconnell/Aughrim road and thence on for 12 miles to Killimor.

Rampart vestiges remain along that section of the Kilconnell/Aughrim road which was partly laid out along the fosse through Ballinderry, Killareeny, and Ardross. It ran through Garrymore, Lavagh, Newcastle, Moat, Cloghagalla, and Ballynamuddagh. *Muddagh* (Móta) is a gaelicized rendering of mootes, the word commonly used in SE Galway for the ramparts. From Lurgan Great it ran to Lurgan More, both names referring to the earthen embankment. From Derrew and Lisdelingy it cut through Derrysiskal, Corry, Rusheeny and Ahanduff to Moneenaveena (Fianna bog). Vestiges of linear and transverse embankments survived in these Tlds. The old name of the Kilcrow river was Abha an Doo (Dyke River, corrupt Ahanduff) because stretches of the river were banked up into dyke ramparts in the classic Belgic defensive system style, as shown on the OS 6" Sheet N. 99. Legendary history links Killimor with the Fianna and Fir Belg. It was known as Killimor Belga (corrupt 'Bologa', Killimor of the Fir Belg), a stronghold of the Fir Belg fighting men. The Cruthin of Ulster and NE Connacht held them at bay along this defence line for a long period before they were pushed back behind the Suck River. The Fianna left their name on Moneenaveena. Ardanena at Killimor was a Fir Belg stronghold.

South of Killimor the set swung W along Garryduff/Treananearla boundary through Killeen, Cloonacusha, Tynagh, Derryfrench, Bracklagh Grange, Ranamackan, Limehill, Leitrim Beg/More, Dalystown, Ballyknock, Knockash, Knockroe, Bookeen, Curhoor and Killeennadeema West overlooking Killeenadeema/Aille road. It ran through Burroge, Kylegarriff, Ballynacurragh, Gortnamannagh East/West, Gortnagleav, Cloghaun, Cregganore and Castleboy, its forested line of defences enhanced by extensive Aughta boglands. Belgic engineers erecting these fortifications utilized all natural defences along the route, such as forest, bogs, hillslopes, mountains, lakes and streams, incorporating them into the unique expansive defensive system.

The set swung NNW through Pollacurra, Ballinrooaun (dyke), Isertkelly, Moneen, Furzeypark/Fiddaun, Shantallow, Cloghroak and the NE of Ballybaun and Toberacreggaun. It straddled the boundaries of Gortroe, Parkalaughan, Fawnarevagh, Lavallyconnor Pollnagarragh, Carrowmaneen, Caheraloggy West, Parkroe, Garraun and Rinn. It crossed the Dunkellin River, straddling the narrow neck of land between Rahashane and Dunkellin Turloughs linked by a narrow channel. It sped through Caherapheepa, Fahymactibbot/-Roevehagh/Killeeneen More/Ballygarriff road, known as *Boher Dur Abha* and built on the rampart. It is Ptolemy's *Dur*. Residents along this road to Oran Beg claim it as the oldest road in Ireland. It may not be as old as Slí Dála and Escir Riada (Figure 45), but that does not detract from its ancient pedigree. The set crossed Toberbrackan, Lavally, Tarramud, Ballinillaun, Coolsrahra, Moyveela (sea plain), Moneymore East, straddling the Bally-nageeha/Bushfield boundary, through Oran Beg to Frenchfort. It traversed Glennasacul, Carnmore West, the Lydacan/Lissarulla/Cregboy boundary, Gortagleva and Lakeview at the Clare River, returning to its starting point, straddling the Clare River bounding Claregalway, Kiniska and Rooaunmore (Great Dyke).

SECOND EXTENSION OF THE JOINT TUROE/KNOCKNADALA/ATHENRY OPPIDUM

The Fir Belg expanded as the population grew and the need for more land arose. Each new set was farther apart from the last, following the lines of rolling hills of this landscape. As they extended deeper into the Aughta Mts., the ridges, wider and farther apart, dictated the alignment and distance from one outer ward set to the next. Reconstruction of the second extension of the outer ward of the joint Turoe/Knocknadala/Athenry oppidum begins from the top NW corner. From Liscananaun in the fork of the Cregg and Waterdale Rivers a new extension ran ENE for Knockdoe, straddling the Waterdale River as it headed through Cloghaun, Mullaghruttery and the S of Carheeny. It sped through Peak, Knockdoemore, Knockdoebeg West in which stands Knockdoe (Dyke hill). It ran E along the edge of the former Turloughmore Lake (*Tír Loch Mór*) into Knockdoebeg East and Lackagh More. It crossed Turloughmore Common and Ballyglass. It continued E through Monard, Ballynasheeog and Garraun into Mira. It straddled the Cloonnavaddoge/Laragh More boundary into Laragh Beg, and the tips of Carrowreagh East, Farravaun, Caherlissakill, Crooroe, Park, Ballyskeagh/Corralea and Pollboy boundaries. It sped through Monivea and Glenagloghaun North into Monivea Demesne. It crossed Knockcorrandoo/Corrandoo, Aghafadda, Laghtonora, Cudoo and Derroo. Skirting boglands on its S flank, it sped through Colmanstown and Cloonkeenkerrill. It straddled Kilooaun/Glennamucka/Creeraun/-Ballygrany/Gortbrack/Garrymor boundaries. Martin Finnerty was a veritable storehouse of knowledge regarding the Gurteen, Cloonkeenkerrill and Glennamucka areas which he referred to in his 'Punan Arsa'.

Glenn na Muice Duibhe (Black Pig's vale) alludes to the Magic Boar which mythically rooted up these defence embankments. Many parts of Ireland hoard legends of the Magic Boar rooting up boundary embankments. Mr. Finnerty noted an ancient roadway covered by bog, running N from Attymon and Gurteen through Cloonkeenkerrill bog discovered in turfcutting operations. Whence? Whither? From Hampstead and Cave the set crossed the Mountventure/Alloon/Ballymacward boundaries across Annagh, Cloonatleva and the S of Fohanagh. It swung SSE straddling Ballydoogan/Cloonatleva/Cartrondoogan/Clonbrock Demesne boundaries. It crossed Doon Upper/Lower to Aughrim Hill via Cloonigny (manned by Clann Ickny), straddling the Dundoogan/Gortnaglogh boundaries. From Aughrim Hill it raced on to Doocreggaun, passing to the W of Kiltormer. It skirted Ardultagh (stronghold of Ui Maine Ulstermen). It sped through Killadulisk, Cloonoolish and Derrew SE of Killimor, to Fairfied forest.

Figure 47:Vestiges of linear embankments at Carrowmanagh, Kilconnell (lower and centre). Decayed embankment at Roundfield, Monivea (top), Co. Galway.

Figure 48

Cairn Cesra (top), the massive burial cairn of Cesra, the Gaulish Queen of the Briganten King, Ugaine Mór, on the summit of Cruach Magh Seola in Galway. Tirechan
alleged that St. Patrick blessed the Ui Briuin lands from here. Vestiges of linear
embankments on the N brow of Cruach Magh Seola (lower) and to the NE of it (centre)

Some 2 miles N of Portumna it swung W, skirting Sheeaunrush, Capira, Cooldorragha and Cloghatanna. The Curraghmore embankments ran W through Lickmolassy, Drumsgar, Kilcorban, Pallas and Lisdoora. This Magic Boar tore across Aughta mountain range through Pollagh, Tomany, along Duniry River, Curragh, Tonroe Dyke, Derrygarriff, Barratoor, Callatra, Allygola, Larraga, Drumkeary, Cullenagh, Drummin, Coppanagh, Funshadaun, Bohaboy, Toormacnevin, Drummucdhruim and Sonnagh Old. The names of the last two Tlds. Drum Muc Dhruim and Sonnagh, proclaim the passage of the Dykes. which cut through forests and bleak boglands. Forestry plantation work has left little trace of the great rampart network through the Sonnagh Tlds. where long stretches of the 'Sonnagh' (Dykes) are shown on the early OS maps. Rampart vestiges overlook scenic Loch Belsrah swan lake and the Boleyneendoorish (rampart set) river on the S cutting its way W to complete the enclosure of this 20 mile S flank straddling the Gortnagchlaidhbhe (Dyke field)/Coillbeg, Derryvokeel/Gortadraghaun/Kilcarrooraun (Embankment set) boundaries. The set swung NNW skirting the Coill More forest round Aughta's Scailp SW shoulder on the heights above Peterswell and Castle Daly, with spellbinding panoramic views over Galway Bay. It slid down the slopes skirting forts along its route through Lissadoill, Lecknabegga, Lissnadulta, Blackrock (*Clogh/Cladh Doo*), Limepark and its boundaries with Turlough na Cloch Doo and Bullaunagh on the slope of Giant's Hill, Grave and Grannagh. It crossed Rahaly, Cookstown, Caheratrim, Rathbaun, Lackan and Creggaclare Demesne E of Ardrahan. It ran through Rooghaun (Dyke set), straddling the boundaries of Barratrena, Tonroe, Cregmore, Kiltiernan and Caranavoodaun, Caherpeak and its boundary with Carraghadoo, bringing Tullaghnafrankagh Lough within the defensive net. It straddled the Kilcolgan/Killeely More boundary up to the inlet of the Dunkellin River.

Crossing the Dunkellin river, the set straddled Stradbally S, N and E and its boundary with Kilcornan on to the banks of the Clarenbridge river along the inner banks of streams which linked both rivermouths near their inner recesses at late Iron Age high sea levels. Ath Cliath (Claidh) Magh Rí was the seaport at the mouths of the Dur (Dunkellin)/Clarenbridge rivers, the most renowned seaport of Iron Age Ireland, "the port of call of all ships sailing the high seas, the port through which all the invasions of Ireland came."[364] Among the invasions through this port recorded in legendary history was that of Lughaid Mac Con who led a massive force from N Britain, comprising Manapi (Manach) and Votadini (the Fotads of Moyode) from Manau Goddodin (Manapi and Votadin territory) of SE Scotland. After King Art's assassination, Lughaid Mac Con marched from there via Achaill Oichne S of Athenry to Cnoc Temhro (Turoe) to become Rí Temhro. Pseudo-history made him march to Tara and become High-King of Ireland. This pseudo-historic manipulation of facts is blatantly anachronistic. There were no High Kings of Ireland then, nor for centuries thereafter. The throne of Art which Lughaid usurped was at Turoe, not Tara. Later Lughaid's cousin Corc (Gorgin) returned from Scotland through the same seaport. He settled at Rath Gorgin among the Fotads and Manapi in Galway. He led them S to set up his seat at Cashel of Munster. Tuathal, grandfather of Conn, led his invasion through this same seaport of Ath Clee Magh Rí and marched to Cnoc Temhro to retake the throne usurped from his farther and re-enact the Feis Temhro. Menapi mariners settled on the headland facing Tawin Island along Ballynamanagh River to Kilcaimin at the head of Mweeloon Bay. They brought in a much wider area including the Sraid Baile with its Rath an Aonach on the point between the Kilcolgan/Dunkellin and Clarinbridge rivers in Dunbulcaun Bay protected by the forested *Coill Managh* and *Manavaghan* (Manapian Forest) between Kilcolgan and Clarenbridge. The

---

[364] "*gur ab e an cuan so (.i.Ath C.) aonchuan gabhala na hEirionn mar do frioth a n-ar leabhraibh, oir is ann as mionca do hionnsuighe Eire riamh.*" Hogan's *'Onomasticon Goedelicum'* p. 56 follows 'St. A'.; Irish Ms. at Stonyhurst College c. 1700 A.D. p. 124, wrongly accredits this modernised text to Ath Cliath (Dublin) which would only have meaning if referring to the period after the coming of the Danes and Normans. The editor of this late Ms. was unaware of the existence or singular importance of the Iron Age western Ath Cliath Magh Rí.

defence line continued NW through forested lands of Tonroe and Rinville (*Rinn Mhíl* on which Míl, son of Dela, erected his beach-head fort, Murvoch Mhíl) to Rusheen Point in Oranmore Bay. Later Míl settled on Rathville on Knocknadala. This Manapian headland was heavily fortressed and larger than the Manapian promontory fort of Dun Forgall Monach, Drumannagh at Loughshinny near Lusk on Dublin's N coast.

'Ath Claidh' Magh Rí in Galway Bay has the same meaning as the British Ath Clied, Rath Clied or Firth of Clyde from which the Clyde River took its name. The N British '*Claidh*' refers to the Roman Rampart on which the Antonian Wall, from the Clyde to the Firth of Forth, was built. The Irish *Ath Claidh Magh Rí* refers, not to Ath Cliath (hurdle ford), but to the river mouth port of the great *Claidh* (pronounced *Clee)* circumvallating 'Magh Rí', Plain of the Kings of the Turoe/Knocknadala/Athenry/Magh Muc Dhruim oppidum. Among its Regents who used this port was Maine who, before becoming King of Ól nÉgmacht, defended this seaport and its hinterland by erecting the dyke *(Claidh)* against marauders. Other Regents were his mother Queen "Medb of cold Aidhne" (the name of this SW Galway area), her father Eochu Ferach Mhor who set up his residence, Rath Ferach Mhor, on Turoe hill, and his great grandfather Dela who led his invasion force through this seaport and set up his royal residence on Knocknadala. There were also King Art, who lost his life trying to repel invaders through this port, Art's assassinator, Lughaid Mac Con and Art's great grandfather Tuathal Techtmar, both of whom led invasions through this seaport, Art's grandfather, Fedlimmid Rechtaid, Art's father Conn of the Hundred Battles and Art's son Cormac Mac Art, all alleged High-Kings of Ireland in pseudo-history. Art and Cormac were assassinated close to this seaport. Their home and thrones were there in the West of Ireland in Co. Galway, not at Tara of Meath.

From Clarenbridge River mouth in the E of Ballynamanagh East, the rampart set ran along Hill Park, Slievaun, Tonroe turlough and Gortard. It sped through Cregganna More skirting the massive Caheradrine fortress manning the W head of the Escir Riada, Parkroe (Dyke field), Moneymore West, Lisroe (Dyke fort), Rock Hill and Rockland, Oran Hill, Moneyduff and Oranmore along its boundary with Rinn. It sped through the W of Oran Beg and Frenchfort, crossing inner Oranmore Bay to Mill Plot, Carrowkeel, Carrowmoneash, Deerpark, Glennascaul and their boundaries with Garraun. It cut through Glennrevagh and the W of Carnmore W, Kiltulla and Cregboy. It straddled the Pollaghrevagh/Cahergowan boundary, heading through Montiagh into Gortcloonmore back to the starting point in the fork of the Cregg and Waterdale rivers. The intention of the military engineers who erected this oppidum was to close off the span of countryside bounded by Galway Bay on its W flank, backed up by extensive forests, mountains and lakes on its landward side just as their kinsmen did with the Atrebatic oppidum at Chichester/Selsey in S England. It was the same Belgae who erected the Chichester/Selsey oppidum in England who migrated to W Ireland and set up their new oppidum there without any further Roman or outside interference. Their defensive strategy was the same.

THIRD EXTENSION OF THE JOINT TUROE/KNOCKNADALA /ATHENRY OPPIDUM
The embankment set of each new extension of the outer ward become more elaborate. One notices a shift in alignment along the different flanks of the oppidum. The earlier squat alignment has given way to a more NW/SE alignmemt. The N and S flanks have taken on a more direct EW alignment. Topography was the gauge. Hills, mountains, rivers and bogs all played their part in dictating the shift in alignment. By now the long list of placenames, increasing with every extension, has become such that one is in danger of being drugged into torpidity by the sheer deluge of townland names. So from here on intermediate linear embankment sets will be skipped while the numbering will continue uninterrupted, and only names of pertinent points and places of note or items of special interest along the route will be recorded to delineate the overall route of the outer ward. Reconstruction of the next

extension of the outer ward begins from Annaghdown on the E shore of Loch Corrib. The embankment set ran E across Tonamace and Tonagarraun. Had all vestiges vanished, these *An tShonnagh* tlds. would continue to proclaim their ancient character. It crossed Corrandulla, Gortroe and Carrownrooaun chasing E across country for 28 miles from Loch Corrib to Garafine and along the N of Foghenagh/Pallas boundary to Clonbroc Demesne in E Galway. It swung SSE just W of Ahascragh, to Sonnagh, Caltraghlea, Eskerroe, Knockroe and Curragh Grange (all vaunting their Dyke onomastic origins). Commandeering the Urraghry Hill, it sped SSE along the Kiltormer-facing slopes of Ballydonagh hill past Skycur, Feagh, Stowlin, Longford House, and Derryhiveny South to the bank of the Shannon at Portland NE of Portumna, skirting Derryhiveny Castle.

Vestiges of defence dykes survive along different sets of linear embankments. Few of the calibre of the noteworthy specimens along this last section SE of Kiltormer, such as in Feagh, Skycoor, Timsallagh, Stowlin and Cappakeela (between 5 and 12 miles N of Portumna) have been allowed to survive. Those near Stowlin House and crossing the old Eyrecourt-Stolin-Killimor road are avenue-like embankments. One in Cappakeela S of the latter, crossing the Portumna/Laurencetown road near Longford House (6 miles NNE of Portumna), is a raised wide embankment. Further back beside the far end of the Curragh Grange village lane E of Aughrim is an almost fully intact embanked *buaile* or *grainsech*.

This set ran down the Shannon to Lough Derg and swung W above the lake's N shore, skirting Abbey and Ballynakill. It cut across the Aughta Mountains along the Owenda-lulleegh River through Derrybrein along the S foothills of Cashlaundrumlahan, skirting Loch an Chlaidh (Dyke) and Pollduff (dyke bog). Owendalulleegh (*Abhainn da luilioch*) River through Derrybrien carries its own story back to Queen Medb's time as related in the Dindsenchas of Sliab nEchtga (Aughta Mt.). In her time, two royal Cruthin princes, Fergus Mac Ruidh and Cormac, son of Conor Mac Nessa, fled from Conor Mac Nessa's Ulster Capital to Medb at Rath Cruacha. A princess of the pre-Celtic Cruthin of SW Galway area (isolated by the ongoing Fir Belg expansion), Echtga, daughter of Urscothach, resided at Cuil Echtair beside Sid Nenta SW of Loughrea. Scions of Gann and Sengann were seeking her hand. Queen Medb saw an opportunity to win over the Cruthin of this region by arranging a royal wedding between Fergus and Echtge. Echtga consented on condition that her bride-gift would be a permanent estate. She had chattels but little land while Fergus had been given a large tract of land by the King and Queen of Connacht (Ól nÉgmacht in O-Irish version)[365] from Maen Magh to the sea (*o Maen co fairrgi*). Fergus gave her the mountain section which ever since is named *Sliab Echtga* (Aughta) after her. Her dowry of 2 young cows (*luilioch*) gave the name to the river along which they grazed, Owendalulleegh (*Abhainn da luilioch*) in Derrybrien, evidence of the tale's great antiquity. It is interesting to observe the influence this and other archaic events exerted upon the topographical nomenclature of the country and of how it survived to this day.

Delve in anywhere along the linear embankments and be amazed by the rich oral toponomy whose profuse names of hills, fields, rivers, not just those recorded on the OS map, but those enduring in local memory, proclaim the passage of the defensive dykes in many varied ways. In Derrybrien local names such as Cnoc an doo (Dyke hill), Claidh Sceagh, Clee Thorn (Thornbush Dykes), Loch a' Chlaidh (Dyke lake), Ming an dooan, Ming a' dooroge (dooan/dooroge dyke sets), Curraugh, Currach, Garrai na Clais, Claidh na Cille, Roo, Cul Roo, Cnoc na nDhoo, all refer to the dykes. This holds true at almost any point along the defence lines where old folk with long memories hand on unrecorded oral toponomy. This grass roots history, like the rampart vestiges, is a history more authentically passed on through the Celtic memory and bloodstream than that in the 'history books'.

---

[365] Whitley Stokes: The Rennes *Dindsenchas Sliab n-Echtga,* No. 60.

The ramparts swung NNW along Slieve Aughta's SW shoulder overlooking Lough Cutra, passing 2 miles S of Peterswell. They ran 18 miles to Rinville West on the outer tip of Oranmore Bay crossing the fork of the Dunkellin/Clarenbridge river and inner Kilcammin Bay. Townlands en route boldly proclaim their former dyke defensive role in the expanding oppidum: Lissatunny (Liss an tShonnaigh, Dyke fort), Rooaunmore (Dyke set), Carraghadoo (Dyke rocky land), Cuildooish (Dyke wood) and Knockawuddy (móta/dyke hill). In Dunbulcaun Bay on Stradbally (Sráid Baile), named after the Fir Belg whose invasion force landed here, on the tip of land in the fork of the Dunkellin and Clarenbridge Rivers stood Rahaneena (Rath an Oenach emporium, market fort) overlooking the landing places of Manapian ships. There were shop docks at the inner mouths of these rivers, one still intact at the Ballynamanagh rivermouth beside the massive Dunbulcaun fort entrepot. A brisk market prospered here. Dun Bulcaun and numerous forts manned the harbour. Ramparts crossed Stradbally West and Roy More. The seafaring Manapi had a powerful presence here in the many Ballynamanagh Tld's (named after them) and Stradbally (market town) in this Iron Age seaport of Ath Clee Magh Rí. Straddling Ballynamanagh West/Lisdoo (Dyke fort) and Knockawuddy (móta/dyke hill), the set ran on to Rinville West down to the edge of the sea. From the N shore of Oranmore Bay they ran NW from Curra Grean and Roscam to the starting point. Vestiges survive between Doughiska dyke inpark and Twomileditch, a rampart right-of-way developed into a road. Vestiges through Carrowbrowne, Muckrush and Ballylee (Baile Chlee, Dyke Tld.) are shown on the OS Map along the E of the Corrib.

FOURTH EXTENSION OF THE JOINT TUROE/KNOCKNADALA/ATHENRY OPPIDUM
From Murroogh (Seaboard Dyke) on Galway Bay's N shore 2 miles E of the city a new set of embankments ran NNW past Menlough to the SE of Loch Corrib 3 miles NE of the city, bringing the lower Corrib into the defence system. From Annagh and Grange below the E protrusion of lower Loch Corrib 2 miles NE of Annaghdown, and skirting Tonamace, it ran E for 30 miles to the NE of Clonbrock Demesne, straddling Ballintleva and Kilglass. It swung SSE from Cornamucladh (Magic Boar's Dyke hill: Figure 49), skirting the Ahascragh/Bunowen River to the Suck River which it skirted through Derrymullen NW of Ballinasloe. Skirting the W of the town the set ran SSE through Pollboy, straddling the Gannaveen road to Laurencetown. Cutting through Rooghan, Ballynamuddagh (Mootes Tld.), Redmount (*Cnoc roo*) and Lisdooan (Dyke fort) the set sped past Eyrecourt to the Shannon at Muckanagh below Big Island. It ran down the Shannon to Lough Derg. From the Cloonmoylan/Cregg Pt. area on Loch Derg this set straddled the Woodford River to Lough Atorik. It bounded W across Aughta Mt. along the S slopes of Knockauneaneagh and Slieveanore. From Corlea Bridge area it chased down the Bleach River to the N of Lough Graney, 18 miles from Lough Derg. It swung NW through Ballardiggan at the NE of Lough Cutra. It pressed on via Kilbeacanty and Kiltartan to Mulroog, Ringeelaun and the sea at Killeenaran, 18 miles from Lough Greany. Mulroog (Rout hill) above Dunbulcaun Bay was the scene of a rout. Legend tells of numerous incursions of invaders. The set ran along the coast across the tongues of land which protruded into the sea.

DINDSENCHAS MENTION OF A DYKE DEFENCE SYSTEM AT CLARENBRIDGE
The *Dindsenchas* of *Ath Claidh Medraige (Magh Rí)* records a raid by the Munster Clanna Dedaid following the *Táin Bó Dartaid*. It describes Ath Claidh Magh Rí (Clarenbridge, SW of Athenry) as a place of "defence dykes *(claidhbha is coibhden*, not *cliathatha)* and warriors" where "the Clanna Dedaid waged red strife on a foray against the 7 Maines. Bloodstained were the braves on raids on the kingly Maines." The Maine sons of Queen Medb had erected blackthorn and redthorn-covered dykes *(claidhbha draigin is derg-sciatha)* as defences against invasion. "From these defences is named Ath Claidh Magh Rí with its dense population: '*Ó na claidhbha-sin* (not *cliathaib-sin* take note) *amne is Ath Claidh co*

tresse trebh.'"[366] *Claidh* (dyke) sounds like *cliath* (sword). One sees how confusion crept in. Transmittors of oral dindsenchas heard *Claidh*, but wrote *cliath*. Rennes version rendered it as a 'wall-hurdle of thorns' *(falcliatha draigen)*, others as 'thornbush covered spears'. Just imagine! The original word was *claidh (clee)*, not *cliath* (sword). Similar confusion reigns in the transmission of the stratagems of Lughaid Mac Con's invasion through Ath Claidh Magh Rí, as told in *Cath Magh Muc Dhruime* where the transcriber wrote *cliath* instead of *claidh (clee)*. This was deemed 'obscure' and misunderstood by editors as was the name of the place where Lughaid's army landed, Ath Clee Magh Rí. The *'Claidh'* (Dyke) has been anglicized correctly as a thornbush-covered dyke even by editors who adopted the O-Irish *cliath* (Modern Irish *claiomh*) but confounded by other authors who attempted a literal cleith/cliatha/claiomha (sword) interpretation.[367] The great Iron Age port will therefore be given its correct original *Ath Claidh Magh Rí* title here.

FIFTH EXTENSION OF THE TUROE/KNOCKNADALA/ATHENRY OPPIDUM

An extension of the outer ward embraced the expanse of Galway city from Dyke Road at its E end to Cladagh at its W end. It ran NNW along the River Corrib to the forested SW shore of Upper Corrib between Aughnanure Castle and Carrowmoreknock, a distance of 12 miles. It ran E from Clydagh on the NE shore of the Lower Lake. Clydagh and Cladagh, names at the top and bottom of Lower Loch Corrib, have the same meaning. Cly (Claidh as in Clybaun), Cla (Cladh) and Clee are common local names for dyke defences. Clydagh on the N scruff of the neck of Loch Corrib, 4 miles SW of Headford, was a place of dykes. From there it ran E for 36 miles through Doolough (Dyke Lake), Cluidrevagh (Dyke), Laurclabhagh (Dyke), Corrofin, along the Abbert River and N slopes of Abbeyknockmoy and Ballinrooaun (Dyke set). It skirted Castleblakeney, Caltra and Clonbrock River 4 miles NE of Ahascragh. Skirting the S of Gowla bog it swung SSE through Cloonshee, Knockaunroe (Dyke hill) and Addergoole. It crossed the Suck 4 miles N of Ballinasloe and ran SSE on its E side. Cleagh Beg, Cleagh More, Cleagh Garve and Rooaun (all Dyke Tlds) announce its passage there. It straddled the Suck and along its SSE stretch to Meelick on the Shannon, passing E of Laurencetown and Eyrecourt.

It incorporated the N half of Lough Derg into its defence system. It ran WSW from Doorosbeg Point (mid-lake) up the Coos River, down the Corra River W of Scalp along the S slopes of the Pollagoona/Corrakyle and Cappaghabaun Mts. to the S of Loch Greany. It swung NNW through Dooglaun (Dyke set) and the Fianna Forest (*Coill na bhFhianna*). It crossed Dromadoora (Dyke mount) and Killafeen (*Coill na bhFhiann*, Fianna Forest) to Loch Cutra. Hugged by forts from Lough Greany, it ran NW via Gort, Lough Coole and Curra to the promontory fort of Rath Durlais by Dunguaire, manning the inner port of Kinvarra Bay at the SE end of Galway Bay. Guaire, the renowned 7th century King of Connacht, resided here. The defence line now overlooked the entire inner Galway Bay. All of the hinterland facing Galway Bay has been turned into a powerful Belgic enclave resembling the Chichester/Selsey oppidum on the S coast of England whence these same Belgic (Fir Belg) tribes came to the West of Ireland.

SIXTH EXTENSION OF THE TUROE/KNOCKNADALA/ATHENRY OPPIDUM

From the W of Salthill (and Galway city) a new set ran NW through Rahoon and Tonacurragh (Dyke) to Clydah (Dykeland) at Ballycuirke Lake. Along Moycullen/-Oughterard road it straddled a line of inter-connecting lakes to Ross Lake linking them into the oppidum defence line. It ran NNW along Knocknalee past Oughterard to Drumindaroo (2 dyke mount) at the head of Cappagarriff Bay on the W shore of Loch Corrib 17 miles NW of Galway city opposite upper Inchiquin Island. From the mouth of the Black River and

---

[366] Dindsenchas of Ath Cliath Medraige, p. 315f; Cath Magh Mucrime ed. from the Bk. of Leinster; cf. p.177f
[367] See p. 166 for further examples of this confusion.

Slieveroo on the E shore it ran ENE skirting Killursa, Headford, the N Cloonkeens (Clann Chian) and the S slope of Knockmaa (*Cruach Magh Seolgha*). It sped on to Ardawarry (*Sliabh Fuirri*, abode of the sun god Mac Greine, son of Ogma), Barnaderg, Polladooey (Dyke bog), Cooloo and Mullaghmore. Passing S of Moylough and N of Mountbellow it straddled the Castlegar/Shiven River to the Suck River N of Ballyforan. It swung SSE along the SW stretch of the Suck River and crossed into Roscommon 38 miles from Lough Corrib. It ran SSE to Old Town and Cloonfad recrossing the Suck 2 miles W of Shannonbridge. It ran past Clonfert to Rooaun, Shannongrove 2 miles W of Banagher, and down the Shannon to Lough Derg. Friendly Fir Belg kingdoms lay to the east. From forested Rinbarra to Farra (sentry post) Hill Pts. in mid-Loch Derg around Whitegate a new set of dykes ran W by WSW above the lake past Mountshannon along the S foothills of the Cappaghabaun Mt. and slopes of Sheeaun. It ran along the N side of Scarriff River to Loch O Grady. It swung NNW past Feakle, Glenbonniv, along the S slopes of Maghera Mountain to Ballynakill Loch, past Sheeaun and Roo east of Tulla. It ran parallel to the Galway/Clare boundary. It sped over Knockancaura (Dyke hill), Roo, Roo Demesne and Inish Roo to Corranroo (all *roo* dykes) Bay at the SW coastal tip of Co. Galway 3 miles W of Kinvarra. The frequent occurences of Roo (rampart) in Tld. names along this 27-mile stretch from Loch O Grady proudly proclaims the presence of the early Belgic defensive system ('*Roo*') here.

SEVENTH EXTENSION OF THE TUROE/KNOCKNADALA/ATHENRY OPPIDUM

From the N shore of Galway Bay the last complete circumvallation of a further extension of the outer ward commenced from Knocknacarragh 3 miles W of Galway City. It ran NNW via Clybaun dyke, Tonabrocaigh and Attyshonoch up along the W side of the Moycullen/Oughterard road along forested Knockaunranny and Knocknalee to the NW tip of Upper Loch Corrib in line with Inchagoill Island 20 miles from Galway city. The entire Corrib was now part of the defensive network of this outer ward extension. From the E of Loch Corrib on the N side of the Black River at the S tip of Co. Mayo, it ran E, skirting Moyne Castle, bringing Loch Hacket into the defence system. It utilized the steep N slopes of Knockmaa (*Cruach Magh Seolgha*) on top of which stand the *Dumha Seolgha*. The massive Cairn tumulus, the tomb of Cessair, the Gaulish princess and consort of King Ugaine Mor, exerts its awesome presence on the hill summit (Figure 48). From the middle ages Knockmaa, as known locally, has been said to be the Otherworld Abode of Finnbheara, King of the fairies. Vestiges of defensive dykes endure along Knockmaa's N slopes and in Turloughnarovey (Dyke Turlough) in Belclare. Crossing Claretuam, Cloontooa and Barrnacurragh it skirted Tuam, Summerville Lough, Moylough, Newbridge and ran from Ballaghlea (Dyke Tld), skirting Ballygar, to the curve on the Suck River below Mount Talbot. It crossed S Roscommon to the Shannon between Clonmacnoise and Shannonbridge, leaving vestiges and place names recording its former presence there.

By now the Turoe/Knocknadala oppidum outer ward incorporated Lough Derg to its S tip at Killaloe, 40 miles S of Balinasloe, into its defensive system. From Balboru Fort near Killaloe it swung NNW through Glennagalliagh pass NW through Slieve Bernagh Mtn. to Bodyke and Glendree pass, to Ballinruan (Dyke set) along the SW slopes of Mahera to Tulla. It formed the Clare/Galway boundary along the NE slopes of the Burren running to the NW tip of the coast of Aughinish Bay at Finavarra across Galway Bay from its starting point. This last section of the boundary line is recorded as the N boundary of the 4th/5th century Menapian kingdom founded by Lughaid Meann, overlording the earlier Fir Belg buffer states of Clare which were part of ancient Connacht and its expanding oppidum. A line of Mac Umhor and Manapi buffer states centered on Magh Adhair, Maughaun, Mullagh Mor, Cahercommaun and Burren defended this 37-mile stretch from Killaloe to Finnavarra. The Burren Fir Belg buffer state was founded by Irgus Mac Umhor whose fort, Dun Irgusa, stands at Cenn Bairne on the Black Head NW tip of Clare.[368] South of this is Caher Bolg Fir Belg Fort facing the Aran Islands. These forts, including those of Aengus and Conchuirn on the Aran Isles, were part of the defensive system defending the seaward side. Mac Umhor buffer states defended the S and N flanks. The Mac Umhor site of Magh Adhair founded by Adhar Mac Umhoir controlled the SE of Clare NW of Limerick city and the Corcobascin peninsula from the mouth of the Fergus River to Liscannor Bay. Magh Adhair's coronation pillar beside the sacred oak tree was the inauguration site of the Fir Belg kings of Thomand, including Brian Boru. In 877 Lorcan, King of Thomand, defended the site in a fierce battle against the Ui Neill warlord, Flann, alleged High King of Ireland, who tried to impose his superiority. The sacred oak tree was cut down in 982 by High King Malachy to assert his superiority. Connacht's Aed O Connor cut it down again in 1051 in retaliation for the destruction of the ancient royal residence of the Ui Briuin Kings of Connacht on Loch Hacket in Galway by Brian Boru.

Dun Meann (Maughaun), the largest prehistoric hill-fort, so massive it can only be viewed completely from the air, was named after the Manapi, allies of the Mac Umhor branch of the Fir Belg. They commandeered the inner recess of the mouth of the Fergus River in the Shannon estuary. The history of the dramatically situated cliff-edge Cahercommaun is not known, but it so closely resembles Dun Aenghus on the Aran IIs. that it is thought to have been constructed by the same Mac Umhor clan. Mac Umhor and Menapi clans formed a line of vassal states from Kilalloe to the extreme NW tip of the Burren. The 5th century Menapi leader, Lughaid Menn, cut off Clare with its extensive Corcobascin peninsula and part of Limerick S of the Shannon estuary as far as Carn Fheradaig (Cahernarry), the original Gangani kingdom, from the Turoe/Knocknadala/Athenry oppidum of which it was originally a part. Cormac Mac Art's kingdom extended from Carn Fheradaig in Limerick to the Drowes River in Donegal.

This vast oppidum with line after line of defence dykes incorporated Galway Bay in its system. Numerous strongforts along the coast indicate its need to be defended tenaciously. The Aran Islands were part of the seaward defence system of the Fir Belg Turoe/-Knocknadala/Athenry oppidum, stretching now from the N tip of Loch Corrib to the Suck River, to the S tip of Loch Derg, to the Burren. The sea protruding into Galway Bay was an open invitation to any invading force, a vulnerable point on the W flank of this oppidum which had to be robustly defended. Dindsenchas lore, relating that all the early invasions of Ireland came through the Iron Age seaport of *Ath Clee Magh Rí* in Galway Bay, underlines its vulnerability from the seaward side. Hence the Aran Islands guarding the passage into Galway Bay were heavily defended with massive stone forts in a manner altogether out of proportion to their tiny size or importance. These Island defences played a vital role, as did those along this coast, and as did the ancient forests there. They were by no means the least strategic part of the defence system of this oppidum which was now over 1500 sq. miles in extent and growing. 'Muck' Tlds. such as Muckinish (Boar Isle), Muckcoort (Boar pass) and Muckrush (Boar forest) along the Galway coast and Lough Corrib fronting this oppidum, are a reminder that the Galway Bay area was forested in the Iron Age. Ossianic tales tell of Finn Mac Cool "hunting the forested harbours of Galway Bay." The forest of Ochoill Oichne (Eochuil or Achaill, Yew forest), later Coill Ua bhFhriachrach, in this coastal area E and S of Galway Bay, survived into late medieval times. Forests were the greatest defensive shield (as seen in Caesar's invasion of Britain) and were heavily incorporated into the defensive network of this oppidum in typical Belgic fashion.

---

[368] Met. Dindsenchas, iii, 444, 1; F.T. O Rahilly, 'EIHM' p.146.

This is the final complete circumvallation of the oppidum for the reason that it had now reached the outer wards of the Fir Belg oppida of Munster on the opposite banks of the Shannon. The entire area from the top of Loch Corrib through Tuam to Clonmacnoise on the Shannon and along its course through Lock Derg to the mouth of the Shannon was warded off by an elaborate defensive system into a vast Belgic enclave. Its core was at the centre of Co.Galway. It was known as nÓl nÉgmacht (Oppidum Enclave). Clare was part of ancient Connacht from the Iron Age into early historic times. This was the extent of Ól nÉgmacht until the time of the celebrated Conn, King of Connacht, after whom it was named Connacht. Henceforth, it expanded N and NE at the expense of the men of Ulster. The territory to the N and NE of these defensive outer wards was firmly in the hands of the Cruthin of Ulster. Rathcroghan of Roscommon, pseudo-history's alleged Capital of Connacht, was not even part of nÓl nÉgmacht, Queen Medb's kingdom. Rathcroghan was the power centre of the retreating Cruthin, Medb's bitter enemies, within Connacht. Rath Cruacha of Athenry at the centre of the Magh Muc Dhruim oppidum was the royal seat of Queen Medb and of the Kings of early Connacht. The expanding Turoe/Knocknadala oppidum was the power centre of the Fir Belg Overkings.

Each outer ward extension, representing enormous outlay in time and manpower, advanced forward a mere mile or two at a time instead of taking a giant leap forward and thus eliminate the almost superhuman effort of erecting line after line of extensive outer ward fortifications. Remember this was originally a tiny enclave (*'égmach'*). Hence the name Ól nÉgmacht. Fir Belg fighting men were advancing against a fiercely determined implacable enemy, the Cruthin of the North, the Ulstermen. Greater by far than the effort to erect the defensive fortifications was that expended in pushing back an enemy. They were, in their own words, "unwilling to yield an inch of ground unless it were barricaded against them by a blood-reddened embankment covered with bodies," that is, unless they fought to the death along it's barricades. The Battle of Airtech is a pertinent example. Connacht's Fir Belg armies, spearheaded by their Fir Domnann fighting men, tried to advance to the NE of the Suck River. They were driven back by the Cruthin who declared they would not halt their pursuit until such a red fortification was erected against them. Each extension of the outer ward represents a bloody victory by an equally determined and consistent Fir Belg power in the battle for territorial conquest against the older inhabitants. This is potent history written in sweat and blood across the Celtic Irish landscape. It does not lie like the so-called 'history books'. It is not surprising then that so many compound townland names along the route of each extension carry the component 'boy' (*buaidh*, victory), *-cath* (battlefield) or *fuil* (blood). How precious land becomes when it is bought in blood and defended by one's ancestors' lives. It is not surprising either that early Fir Belg Kings, when their oppidum was but a tiny enclave, befriended the Cruthin through marriage alliance. Eochaid Ferech, Ideal King of the Fir Belg, married off 3 of his daughters to Conor Mac Nassa of Ulster, purportedly to appease him for the death of his father by Eochaid's hand. When the first died in childbirth, he gave the hand of his younger daughter Medb to Connor. She, out of pride of mind promptly returned to her father's palace complaining, "who could stand that man." When Conor tried to take revenge, Medb exploded. This resulted in bitter all-out war between Connacht and Ulster. Eochaid kept his promise to Conor and gave him another of his daughters as his consort to replace the sullenly aloof Medb.

To show this oppidum's relation to the Rivers Suck and Shannon, and the passage across the Shannon as mentioned in legendary history, in relation to the relative positions of both the Cruthin of Ulster and the Fir Belg of Connacht, more extensions of this oppidum could only take place on the N, E, and NE front as it was hemmed in by the S and SE Fir Belg oppida across the Shannon. The lower Shannon now formed its E and SE extremity.

FURTHER EXTENSIONS OF THE TUROE/KNOCKNADALA OPPIDUM

Conmaicne septs of the Manapi set up bases along the Connemara coastal inlets for whose defence they were responsible as they were along the outer wards from the Aughta foothills above Loughrea to the seaport of Ath Clee Magh Rí, their early settlement area. They extended up the valleys and habitable lakeland districts of this densely forested mountainous region, squeezing the earlier Partrige decendants of Gann and Sengann northwards. They were the great sea traders and hence were known as *Conmaicnamara* (young sea hounds) which gave its name to Connemara. This suggests they were especially responsible for the defence of Galway Bay and its Aran Islands. The Manapi were late-comers in comparison with the Belgic Atrebates and Morini. These renowned fighting men who refused to submit to Caesar and the Romans set up widely scattered settlements of the Manapi. Their Conmaicne septs formed a string of buffer states through the habitable areas of Connemara and along the N extensions of the outer ward. The Turoe/Knocknadala/Athenry oppidum was defended on this W flank by the Conmaicne whose buffer states ran from the coast at Knocknacarragh through Clybaun W of Galway City. Along the Connamarra seaboard there are vestiges of defensive dykes, Cladh Mor, Clynagh and 'An tShonnagh Mor' as known to local Gaelic speakers. The Conmaicne had a powerful presence all the way from Na Forbacha (Furbogh) just W of Galway city to Mannin (named after the Manapi) Bay near Clifden. These Manapi buffer states were the W extensions of the Turoe/Knocknadala oppidum right across Connemara. They have not been examined in detail.

The reconstruction of the N expansion of the oppidum commences from the shore of the NE extremity of Loch Corrib SE of Ashford Castle in Cong above Inishmacatreer. An embankment set ran E just S of Shrule, skirting the N sides of Tuam and Ballygar to the Suck River NW of Mount Talbot, a distance of 40 miles. The Suck from Mount Talbot N to its source in Loch Ui Flynn remained the boundary along which the Connacht Fir Belg oppidum of Connacht was held at bay by the Cruthin of the North. It straddled the Suck past Mount Talbot and ran SE, skirting Rooskagh and Cornafulla (hill of the blood) on its way to the Shannon at Inchinalee (Dyke Isle) above Clonmacnoise. The Suck/Shannon fork from Ballinasloe to Athlone had been taken by the Fir Belg in the time of Medb, but had been retaken by the Cruthin. The Fir Belg won it back in mile by mile of bloody warfare.

A new extension ran ESE from Rosroe at the outer tip of Killary Harbour along its S slopes via Derrynachlee (Dyke wood) and Leenaun to its inner recess. Before roads were built, these dykes served as right-of-ways. Vestiges of a parallel defence line ran along the N shoreline of this narrow channel, *Caolaire Rua (roo)*, converging on Killary's inner recess. This defence line ran to the SW tip of Lough Mask as shown on the 'Map of Co. Galway' from actual survey by W. Larkin,[369] as an "undetermined boundary." Like a Great Wall of China, climbing from Boheross at the mouth of the Owen Errive up along the ridge of the wrongly anglicized Devil's Mother Mtn. (correct *Maghair Chlee an Deamhain*, Devil's Dyke Ridge) above Glennagevlagh and Glenanane rivers at its W and E foot. It hugged the ridge of Knocklaur and Benwee to the sacred mountain-top lake on Mam Trasna. Having paid obeisance it swung down by Dooletter River between Sliabh Chlaidh na Bruicca (Badger's Dyke Mtn) and Mam Trasna Mtn. to Loch Nafooey and down the Derryveena River to the SW tip of Loch Mask. This mother of all dykes, devised to deter even the devil, presents heavenly panoramic views and became the Galway/Mayo boundary. The Partrige na Locha, descendants of Gann and Sengann, defended this outer ward and the land between Loch Corrib and Loch Mask. Hence their sobriquet.

As this set continued E from the SE shore of Loch Mask skirting Neale, Clyard (High Dyke), Doora E of Kilmain, to Kilconly, it shows that Connemara was part of the

---

[369] William Larkin, 'Map of the Co. of Galway' from actual survey, pub. by Phoenix Maps 1989

Turoe/Knocknadala Athenry oppidum, adding hugely to its size. It skirted Clonbern and Kiltullagh Loch, the N slopes of Slievemurry (Abode of war god Mac Greine; wrongly named Sliab Muire) and Creggs. Ardawarry (*Arda Mhóri*) near Tuam and this Slieve Mhóri are named after the Morini, the Mac Morna who manned this N flank of the oppidum).[370] The set straddled the Galway/Roscommon border and Suck River S to Rookwood, W of Atleague. It crossed into lower Roscommon and ran SE by the N side of Cladh na Shade Loch (Shad Lake Dyke), the NE face of Funshinagh, Corralea (dyke), and S side of Funshinagh Loch. It ran through Moyvannan (Plain of the Manann), named after the Manapi who manned this stretch along the SW side of Loch Ree to its tip above Athlone. The Shannon crossing at Athlone is featured in many legends dating back to the Iron Age, as will be encountered in a later chapter. This extension of the N and NE flank of the oppidum covered more than 70 miles. Can one imagine the amount of time, man-power, sweat and blood involved in erecting just this one stretch alone? It should be noted that not every outer ward extension is recorded here. There are intermediary sets of defensive dykes which are passed over in silence for the simple reason that it would be too taxing for even the most tenacious reader and unnecessary for the overall design of this book.

The next extension to be reconstructed ran from the Promontory fort above Kinnadooh (*Ceann na doo,* Head of Dykes) on the S Mayo coast 4 miles N of Killary Harbour. From Rooankeel (dyke set) it followed the curve of the mountains and the slopes of Tawnydoogan (Dyke set). It ran ESE via Doo Loch Pass (Dyke Lake) between Mweelrea, Ben Creggan and Sheeffry Mts. It straddled Glenummera and lower Glendavoch River valleys, Tawnyard (*an tShonnaigh ard*) Loch and Owenduff Rivers NE to Shrahlea bridge where it swung SE via the Toormakeady gap in the Partry Mtn. range to the shore of Loch Mask S of Toormakeady. The Partrige, descendants of Gann (Commius) and Sengann (Tincommius), who gave their name to Partry Mtn., expanded their buffer state N across this region from Cong on the S to this mid section of Loch Mask. From the Robe (*Roobhagh,* Dykes) river mouth on the E of Lough Mask, along its S side through Gorteenlynagh to Ballinrobe the dyke set sped E through Urracly (*Iubhraighe Claidh*, Yew Wood dyke) and the 2 Ummercly (*Ummer claidh*). Vestiges survive where it skirted Singking River, Miltown, Dunmore (manned by the Mac Morna), Glenamaddy, Creggs and the Suck River loop from Passage SE to Atleague. Through lower Roscommon it traversed Curraghboy, Carrowmoney, Funshinagh Loch, Red Hill (Cnoc roo) and Carnagh Bay on Loch Ree. This expansion from the Suck to Loch Ree took place later date than those W of the Suck as the Manapi expanded N from the Plain of the Manapi (Moyvannan) along the SW shores of Loch Ree where they had a strong presence at this time. Components of placenames along the linear embankments such as '(ch)lea', 'clee', 'roo' and 'doo', do not always mean grey, red or dark respectively as claimed by Joyce in his 'Irish Names of Places'. Placenames constructed with the component 'lea' with the definite article '*na*' before '*lea*' show clearly that '-lea' was a noun, not an adjective (Coolicknalea=*Cool lice na Chlaidh*, Dyke standing-stone) and Gortnalea (*Gort na Chlaidh*, Dyke field). 'Roo' and 'doo' are O. Irish words for dyke still clinging to vestiges. 'Rooan' and 'dooan' refer to a set of these. Cooladooan (*Cool an dooan*, dyke end) has its peculiar Irish way of proclaiming the passage of the former linear embankments.

Another set ran ESE from Emlagh Point between Roonah (Dykes) and Roonah Quay at the SW tip of Clew Bay. From Dooghmakeon and Formoyle na bhFhiann (Fianna Herbel Hospital) the dyke set straddled Derryrascurra and Tangincartoor. Passing through Srah na Claidh and Cregganroo (both announcing dykes) it skirted the Bunowen River around the S slopes of the hill. It straddled Loch na Corra, Lenanadoortaun and Oughty hills on the S slopes of Croagh Patrick. The lands from Croagh Patrick to Loch Carra and S to Cong at

---

[370] In the southeast of Britain the Morini left their name on Moridunum, fort of the Morini (Mori).

the N end of Loch Corrib formed the Partrige buffer state which grew with each expansion. Once the next set took the 760 metre high coned-shaped Croaghan Aighle (Croagh Patrick) into its defence line, it became known as Croagh Phartraig (Partraige Mountain after Gann's and Sengann's Partraige descendants), uniquely confoundable with St. Patrick's name (*Patraig*). Pseudo-historians saw a golden opportunity to subtly rename this outstanding cone-shaped Mountain as Croagh Phatraig and promptly concocted an enthralling 'Moses on Mount Sinai-like' episode in the Tara/Patrick Myth.

The set ran via Bracklagh, Rooghan, Loch Moher and swung ENE to Tonlegee to round the N slopes of Partry Mtn. It swept down to Loch Na Corralea (Dyke) and along the N of Lough Mask to upper Loch Carra (*Loch Cera*). The Partraige of Cera claimed descent from Genann mac Dela mac Gann, leader of the Fir Belg invasion. From Doonwood promontory fort on the E shore of Loch Carra, it ran ESE through Drumnashonnagh, Rooghaun, Ballynaglea, Drumshonnagh, Knockanroo and Sessiagh (all 6 Tlds proclaim the dykes) along the N of the EW stretch of the Robe (*Roobhagh* Dyke set) River between Claremorris and Ballindine. Passing between Cloonfad and Dunmore it ran via Curragh West, Glenroughra and Sonnagh to Loch Doo on the Suck where the Galway/Roscommon border and Suck parted company for a stretch. On the E of the upper Suck no attempt was made to carry this outer ward through Roscommon to upper Loch Ree. Ramparts E and N of the upper Suck belong to the Cruthin whose stronghold was Rathcroghan of Roscommon. These stood on slopes facing S or SW against those of the Fir Belg, confirming legendary tradition and early history that the Cruthin of Ulster held the Fir Belg of Connacht at bay along this stretch of the Suck River well into historic times.

There were many more extensions of this Fir Belg oppidum, taking a distinctly more SE alignment dictated by the lie of mountain ranges. Only one more will be summarily noted here, bypassing others, because of its association with legendary history and Cormac mac Art's time and because of well-known landmarks along its route. From the inner recess of Newport Bay N of Westport in Clew Bay a set of embankments ran ESE, skirting the S of Castlebar, straddling Knock (Cnoc Muire), Ballyhaunis and Loch Mannin, manned by the Manapi (Figure 51 and 53). It skirted the S of Loch Ui Flynn and N slopes of Sliabh Ui Flynn manned by Mac Morna fighting men in Cormac Mac Art's day. It ran on the S side of the upper Suck from Loch Ui Flynn and swung S at Castlerea to Ballymoe. Along the Roscommon side of the Suck from its source in Loch Ui Flynn to Atleague there are traces of defensive ramparts of the Cruthin of Rathcroghan facing SW against those of the Fir Belg. The first pointers to genuine archaic Irish history are found in Ptolemy's 2nd century record. Some say Cormac mac Art stands on the border-line between semi-historical personages and Ireland's emergence into the light of history. One can put names and rough dates on royal personages who carried forward the development of Connacht to its widest extent, and name events which had widespread implications not only for Connacht but for Ireland as a whole. Were these linear embankments erected in China, they would have taken precedence over the Great Wall of China as famous historic Tourist attractions because of their vast extent when taken as a whole.

But this is Ireland!

From its source to Atleague and Athlone the Suck River was the border between two great adversaries, the Cruthin of Ulster and NE Connacht and the Fir Belg of nÓl nÉgmacht, the burgeoning Province of Connacht. Scraps of legendary history retail sagas of great battles fought along this boundary. These are encapsulated in the many Clooncah (Battlefields) and Victory Hills (*Cnoc buaidh*) along the route. The Cruthin held the Fir Belg at bay along, and within the arms of, the Suck and Ox Mountain range for centuries, fiercely defending their territory centered on Rathcroghan of Roscommon. The Fir Belg expanded N along the

W of N Mayo. For a long time an E expansion had been taking place at the expense of the Cruthin of N Mayo spearheaded by the Fir Domnann from their primary settlement area on Erris, Irrus Domnann, and NW Mayo. The followers of Domno, a Canti king of SE Britain, came with Iuvor whose fort stood on the N of Achill, in the van of Verica (Ferach). The Gamanrad of Irrus fighting men were celebrated in legend for their martial qualities as one of the three warrior-races (*laech aicmi*) of Ireland. Their territory included all of NW Mayo and W Sligo from the Robe to Drumcliff River in Sligo (*'o Rodba co Codnaig'*).

Roscommon from its boundary with N Galway east to the Shannon, Leitrim and NE Mayo were in Cruthin hands in Queen Medb's time. Her forces, spearheaded by the Domnann, attempted to overrun this territory. *Cath Airtech* tells that the Domnann were almost annihilated. They were driven back with great slaughter behind a line of rampart (*mur roo*) running NW along the Moy from the Loch Mannin E of Knock up along its forested plain of Kiltimagh to Loch Conn. In their weakened state this stretch of Connacht's defence line was vulnerable. To strengthen this line of defence fronting the decimated Domnann, Manapi buffer states were introduced from Loch Mannin up the W side of the Moy River through Derrymannin Loch between the Moy and Loch Conn to Killala Bay. They gave their name to many places along this line, such as Loch Mannin and Derrymannin. The area SW of Killala Bay was Magh Domnann. Eochaid Felech made the Domnann king, Tinny, king of the Connacht Fir Belg tribes reigning at Rath Cruacha of Athenry before replacing him by his own daughter, Queen Medb. Alongside the Menapi (Mannagh) and Morini (Mac Morna), Domnann buffer states were dispersed in various parts of Galway manning segments of the outer wards, such as Tulcha Domnann (Dunmore), Ardnadomnann NW of Loughrea and along the Suck. The Gamanrad, Gabraige and Cattraige along the Suck were claimed to be of Fir Domnann warrior stock.[371] This Fir Belg oppidum founded by Dela, son of Gann, was still in the process of expansion. It took in not only all of present-day Connacht but expanded across the Shannon. The Fir Belg Turoe/Knocknadala/Athenry oppidum expanded E of Athlone up the E shores of Loch Ree leading Leinster Fir Belg kingdoms from their original bases N of a line across the centre of Ireland. Vestiges of advance boundaries of Leinster tribes straddle Moate and its environs in the centre of Ireland running NNW from Clara (*Cladhra*). Others ran NNW by Horseleap and W and E of Kilbeggan from the vicinity of Tullamore, W and E of Tyrrellspass running NNW to Loch Ennell. Others are near Enfield, Kilcock and Maynooth. These are the footmarks of Fir Belg septs expanding N across the central plain led by the Fir Belg Kings of Connacht.

Though there were several more extensions northwards (as seen in surviving vestiges), this will bring to an end the reconstruction of the several sets of outer ward defensive dykes of this joint Turoe/Knocknadala/Athenry Fir Belg oppidum. This is adequate to link legendary history to known historic or semi-historic figures who carried on the further expansion of this massive oppidum to the conquest of the entire present Province of Connacht and well beyond as will be related in the next chapter. From scraps of legendary history this was the extent of the joint oppidum in the time of Cormac Mac Art in the 3rd century before he led the Colla and Chianacht contingents against Ulster. Battles for territorial possession between the Cruthin of Ulster and the Connacht Fir Belg under Queen Medb and later kings are described as taking place on the boundaries of the outer wards along these front lines. The SE portion of Roscommon just NW of Athlone was in dispute between the men of Ulster and Connacht in Medb's day. A wide slice of Cruthin territory known as the 'The Six Sogains' or *'sinchineal seanclair Sogghain'* (ancient plain of the older population of Sogain) was isolated by the expansion of the Fir Belg in NE Galway. Their one-time royal seat was in the barony of Tiaquin, Co. Galway. Numerous Cruthin enclaves were isolated by ongoing Fir Belg expansion in Connacht and beyond.

---

[371] F.T. O Rahilly, 'Early Irish History and Mythology' p. 96-97.

At the time of Cormac Mac Art, the Mac Morna branch of the Fir Belg fighting men had been allotted buffer states in W Roscommon across the North Galway border, along the last outer ward reconstructed above, in exchange for their military services. They had one of their Herbal Hospitals, known as Formaoil na bhFiann, on Slieve Ui Flynn in W Roscommon which indicates that the front-line was then at least that far north.[372] The front-line Formaoil na bhFiann referred to earlier was on the line of ramparts in the Clew Bay area of Mayo. The Cruthin country of Croghan of Roscommon still remained unconquered by the Fir Belg. It was known as 'Cruithintuath Croghain'. Countryfolk there insist its correct name is Rathcroghan, not Rath Cruachan as pseudo-history would have it. As they pronounce it, it sounds like Rath Cruthin. This may indeed have been its original name, as O Rahilly suggested. It was never the royal seat of Queen Medb and remained in Cruthin hands until the 8th century as will be shown in a later chapter. The implications of these early traditions emphatically contradict the 'official doctrine' of the history books which dance to the pseudo-historic tune. The territory E and N of the River Suck and N of the line of fortifications to Athlone as described above was firmly in the hands of the Cruthin of Ulster. Queen Medb could not then have reigned from Rathcroghan, nor her father from Tara of Meath, as pseudo-history claims they did. How then did it come about that there is nothing about this massive Belgic oppidum in the history books? How is it that Commius and his descendants, and the Fir Belg of this and other oppida in S Ireland, are all but lost and forgotten? How did it come about that Queen Medb was transferred from Rath Cruacha of Athenry to Rathcroghan of Roscommon? What led to her being turned into the goddess of Tara? How did her father, Eochaidh Felech, the Ideal King of the Fir Belg, together with Kings Tuathal, Conn, Art and Cormac Mac Art, come to be High Kings of Ireland reigning from Tara of Meath? How did Tara of Meath and Croghan of Roscommon come to be called the Capital of Ireland and Capital of Connacht respectively from time immemorial? The surprising answers will come in the course of the following chapters. First it is appropriate to continue with the further expansion of the Fir Belg of Connacht in a chronological manner as related by legendary history which contradicts the 'official history' of the history books.

---

[372] J. H. Lloyd, M.R.I.A,. 'Formaoil na bhFiann'; and in the Scottish Highland lay *'Losgadh Tigh Farmaile'*

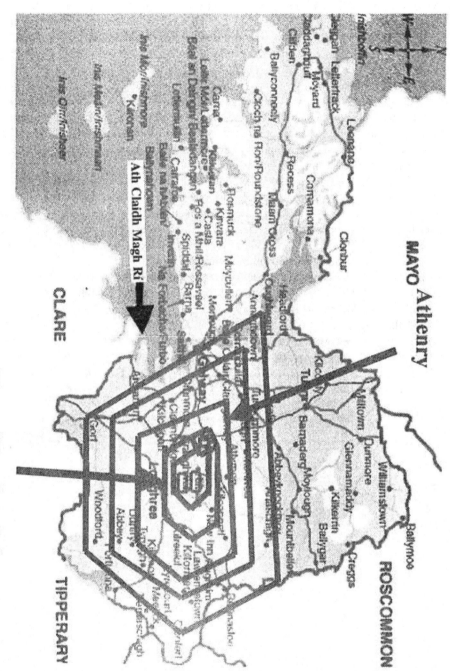

Turoe/Knocknadala

Figure.51 An approximate alignment drawing of several sets of linear embankments surrounding the Belgic Turoe/Knocknadala/Athenry oppidum in Galway which gives a fairly good rough general overview of the expanding oppidum defensive complex, courtesy of Kieran Jordan. Further expansions into NW Connacht took on a much more NW by SE alignment.

Figure 50: Galway's Iron Age seaport of Ath Clee Magh Rí in Dunbulcaun Bay. From the top;
(1) Looking inwards towards the mouths of the Clarin River (left) and the DunKellin River
(right); (2) View of the inner mouth of the Dunkellin River; (3) A dock built up with revetement
stones and raised loading banks at the mouth of the Ballynamannagh River equiped with piers
fitted for floodgates to control the water at high-tide levels. Here sleek Manapi long-ships could
ride secure from storms - ideal for loading. Beside it is the massive marine warehouse of Dún
Bulcaun surrounded by the Ballynamannagh (Mannapi mariners) townlands. Similiar port
docks existed in the Stradbally (Sráid Baile) harbour towns at the inner recesses of the mouths
of the Clarin and Dunkellin Rivers.

Figure 52 Magh Adhair in S Clare was named after Adhar Mac Umor, the most southerly of Connacht's Mac Umoire (Iuvor) Fir Belg leaders who formed buffer states around Dela's Turoe/Knocknadala oppidum. It is a miniature copy of the Belgic defensive system. The raised inauguration mound is surrounded by a fosse and embankment. It sits at the bottom of a saucer-like space whose outer rim is partly man-made. A raised bank on the inside of the stream (lower photo) skirting the mound had floodgates fitted. A cutting (right lower corner of centre photo) channelled floodwater into the saucer-like surround to enhance its defences.

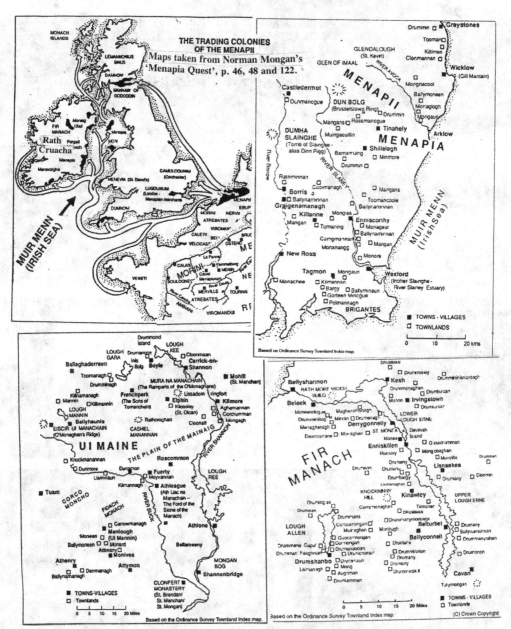

Figure 53: Belgic Continental Manapi mariners established trading colonies and hinterland settlements along British and Irish coasts (top left). With fighting men from their Galway and Wicklow/Dublin (top right) colonies, Cormac Mac Art set up a line of advanced buffer states against the Cruthin of Ulster up through Monaghan and Fermanagh (named after them; lower right) to Donegal. Fifth century Maine Mór led their hosts back down into Connacht (Ui Maine; lower left). Numerous Manapi family names (Mannin, Mannion, Mangan, Minnan, Menamin, Monaghan, Mongan, Mooney) and placenames (Fir Managh, Fir Monagh, Ui Maine, Attymon, Ballymanna, Dunmannagh, Graignamanna) survive in SE Ireland, in Loch Allen/Erne areas, and particularly in Connacht. Their great seaport was *Ath Clee Magh Rí* beside their Ballynamanna home in Galway Bay. The Irish Sea was named *Muir Menn* after them.

Figure.49 Linear embankments in the Kilglass/Runnymede area of Ahascragh (lower 2 photos). A Cornamucklagh embankment, parallel to a tributary of the Suck between Ahascragh and Ballyforan/Roscommon border), running up Cornamucklagh (Hill of the Magic Boar's Dyke) where the road was built along the filled-in fosse (top 2 photos)

CHAPTER 3

CAPITALS OF IRON AGE IRELAND
VIS-À-VIS
TARA, RATH CROGHAN AND
CASHEL MYTHS

TARA OF MEATH
vis-a-vis
TUROE OF GALWAY

RATH CROGHAN OF ROSCOMMON
vis-a-vis
RATH CRUACHA OF GALWAY

CASHEL OF MUNSTER
vis-à-vis
EARLY CAPITALS OF MUNSTER

TARA OF MEATH VIS-A-VIS TUROE OF GALWAY

Tara of Meath and Turoe of Galway are but two of several similarly named hills derived from the O. Irish *Temhair* (*Tur* or *Chaur,* the *'m'* being eclipsed by the *'h'*). Tara derives from the dative form as in *'i Temhra'* (in Tara). Turoe derives from the genetive form, *'Cnoc Temhro'* (Hill of Turoe), whether *'Cnoc'* is spoken or implicit. The confusion of Turoe with Tara is understandable. Medieval Ui Neill chroniclers deliberately exploited it. *'Temhair'* means 'hill with a panoramic view'. Ptolemy's *Regia E Tera* in Western Ireland is as close a rendition of *Regia e Temhra* (minus the silenced *'mh'*) as one could achieve in Greek letters. F.J. Byrne noted, "unlike the acropolis of Cashel of Munster, Tara (like Turoe) is by no means an impressive site on its low ridge in the heart of Meath. But (like Turoe) once the ridge has been climbed an astonishingly wide panorama is unfolded"[373]

The misappropriation of the history and traditions of Turoe to Tara sparked the rise of the Tara/Patrick Myth. In the late Iron Age Tara was the centre of a minor kingdom of the Over-kingdom of Ulster. Conor Mac Nessa, Ulster's Overking at Emain Macha, had his daughter succeed his son, followed by a grandson, as regents of Tara. From the 5th to 7th century, due to the defeat of the Cruthin of Ulster, the loss of their Capital, Emain Macha, and their retreat E of the Bann, Tara became the seat of the Overkings of the Cruthin of Ulster and Scotland. In 637 it was conquered by Ui Neill warlords. Tara is as conspicuous by its virtual absence from the earliest reliable tradition of Ireland, the Ulidian legendary history, as it is from the 2nd century record of Ptolemy. This is in direct contrast to the paramount position of importance given to Tara by pseudo-history, a glorificatory fame cast back into prehistoric times by Ui Neill eulogists. On the other hand, the names of Turoe and Knocknadala are unknown today. The reconstruction of the Belgic defensive system of this Iron Age oppidum corroborates the 2nd century record of Ptolemy of Alexandria which equates the great Turoe/Knocknadala oppidum with his 'REGIA E TE(MH)RA' (Capital in Temhair at the centre of Galway; Turoe today) and his 'NAG NA TA[L]' ('Cnoc na Dal') which he described as "the most extensive and illustrious city in all Britannia." This is not to say that Tara did not have its era of glory in the far distant pre-Celtic past - 3000 to 100 BC. It sure did. But this is another story altogether.

The deliberate misappropriation of the traditions of Turoe of Galway to Tara of Meath has deceived even the greatest historians of this, and previous, centuries and prevented them from drawing the logical conclusions to their analysis of Iron Age Irish history. So sophisticated was the work of medieval manipulators of Iron Age and early Irish history that a historian of the calibre of O Rahilly, who did so much to expose the Tara/Patrick Myth, was nevertheless misled into vigorously insisting that "the Midland Goidels ('Gaels of Tara') were the Connachta, 'descendants of Conn', that the Connachta were the men of Tara, and vice versa. He hammered home his belief that "the Midland Goidels established themselves in Tara and this remained their capital down to the seventh century,"[374] so much so that it is still accepted as 'dogma' today. This absurdity led him to numerous false conclusions. Prominent among these was his claim that the long drawn-out warfare between the Connachta and men of Ulster was directed from Tara of Meath, capital of the Connachta, and that the Connachta of Tara of "the race of Conn, were an expansive people who were not content with ruling a moderate-sized area in the Midlands. Some of them pushed west across the Shannon, and made themselves masters of what is now known as the province of Connacht. In the course of time the name Connachta ceased to be applied to them and was restricted to the Gaelic conquerors of the west."[375] History is thus turned back to front. The

[373] Francis John Byrne, 'Irish Kings and High Kings', p.56
[374] T.F.O Rahilly, 'Early Irish History and Mythology', p.173.
[375] Op. cit., p. 173-174

myth-buster became a myth-maker in his own right. Due to the power of his arguments, historians have accepted his new myths as sober history.

O Rahilly concocted modern myths based on that false premise: *"The restriction of the name Connachta to the men of the western province had important consequences for the Ulidian Tales. The Ulaid preserved traditions of the long-continued struggle thay had waged against the original Connachta, i.e. men of Tara, and these traditions were introduced into the tales of the Ulidian cycle, more especially the 'Tain Bo Cuailgne'. By the time the tales were being given literary shape the name Connachta was applied only to the men of the province of Connacht, whose capital was Cruachain in Roscommon. Genuine tradition of the Ulaid, before it became conventionalized in the literature, must have recognised quite well their enemies in ancient times were the men of Tara on their southern border; but the literati judged it more diplomatic to represent the struggle as one between two provinces, and not between the Ulaid and the King of Ireland, for in their day the king of Tara would inevitably be regarded as king of Ireland. Accordingly Medb, the goddess who typifies the sovereignty of Tara, is made to reign, not in Tara, but in Cruachain. And so in the 'Tain Bo Cuailgne' the narrator has first to bring Medb and her forces from Cruachain to Tara before they can march north against the Ulaid."*[376] **O Rahilly had finally to humbly admit in his almost unnoticed 'Additional Notes' that at that time the power of the Ulaid extended south of the Boyne and included Tara.**"[377] Sadly, by then his life was cut short before he had time to absorb the vast implications of his all too late admission and correct his errors. His string of medieval and modern myths in a marriage of confused convenience must be unraveled. What O Rahilly put forward as a possibility with his "must have" has been accepted as sober 'history'. As will be shown, the original Connachta were the Fir nÓl nÉgmacht whose stronghold was the Turoe/Knocknadala/Athenry oppidum in Galway who expanded N and NE in a several-centuries long expansion. Their 8th century descendants made themselves masters of Tara district at the expense of the Cruthin of Ulster.

COICED nÓL nÉGMACHT VIS-A-VIS CONNACHT AND RATHCROGHAN DISTRICT

Fortunately Ptolemy of Alexandria's 2nd century record of Ireland has been preserved as has been the early name of Connacht in Ireland's oldest stratum of legendary history, the Ulidian Tales. The isolated nucleus of the Turoe/Knocknadala/Athenry oppidum gave ancient Connacht its unique name, *Coiced nÓl nÉcmacht (nDháil/nDeól nÉcmacht)*, the 'embanked province'. In its earliest days it was but an embryonic enclave in the SW of the great Cruthin kingdom of the Northern Half of Ireland. In archaic texts Knocknadala (*Cnoc na nDáil*) is referred to simply as *'Dáil'* as in the *Dindsenchas of Carn Conoill* text *'Míl for Murbeach, Daelach for Dáil'* (Fir Belg leaders Míl settled on Muirbeach, Dela on Dáil. *Deól* is an archaic form of *Dáil*).[378] *'nDhál'*/*'nDeól'* sounded like 'nÓl' to a transcriber. O Rahilly's attempt to explain *'nÉchmacht'* is more unsatisfactory than that of others he dismissed as "childish attempts to explain it." Even had he known of the O-Irish Law Tract *'Bech Bretha's'* usage of *'écmacht'*, referring to an 'embanked territory', he would still have been unaware of its significance as the earliest name of the Western province, *Coiced nÓl nÉcmacht*, since he was unaware of the Belgic defence system enclosing the Knocknadala/Turoe oppidum to which *nÓl ('nDeól) nÉcmacht'* referred. It was a tiny hemmed-in enclave within a vast Cruthin territory. Thus he failed to absorb the significance of this name in the Ulidian Tales. Otherwise he could not have so erroneously conjectured that "the genuine tradition of the Ulaid (the Cruthin), <u>must have</u> recognized quite well that their enemies in ancient times were the men of Tara on their southern border!"[379]

---

[376] Op. cit., p. 175-176

[377] T.F.O Rahilly, 'Early Irish History and Mythology', p.485.

[378] Sa., 46 a; cf. Onomasticon Goedelicum.

[379] T.F.O Rahilly, 'Early Irish History and Mythology' p.176.

Ulidian tradition never speaks of 'the men of Tara on their southern borders' nor of the 'Connachta' as the enemy. Again and again early Ulidian tradition speaks of 'the men of Ól nÉcmacht' (*Fir nÓl nÉcmacht/Coiced nÓl nÉcmacht*) as the enemy. Coiced nÓl nÉcmacht is equated with Coiced Medba & Aililla (the Province of Queen Medb and Ailill). Moreover, far from Coiced Medba referring to Rathcroghan of Roscommon area as it does in pseudo-history, it is expressly stated that Medb's kingdom extended from Bealach Conglais in Limerick to the Black River (Abha Dubh) on the Mayo/Galway border. Coiced nÓl nÉgmacht is also equated in many references with Coiced nGaind (Gann), Coiced Genainn (Sengann) and Coiced Sreing mac Sengainn in Connacht, the original Fir Belg leaders.[380] These significant references mean that the Fir Belg kingdom established by Gann and Sengann along the Shannon estuary had expanded north into Connacht as far as the Mayo/Galway border, but not into Roscommon, by the time of Medb. Coiced Medba =Coiced nGaind=Coiced nÓl nÉcmacht. Ulidian tradition speaks of the enemy, not 'on their southern border', but 'way to the southwest', as seen from Emain Macha, the capital of Ulster. Ulidian tradition always describes the armies of Ireland being led from Coiced nÓl nÉgmacht, never from Tara of Meath, against the province of Ulster. The archaeological record of the defence earthworks of Ulster and Connacht shows a corresponding decline of the borders of ancient Ulster in a NE direction as the outer defences of 'Ól nÉcmacht' expanded. This tradition is corroborated by Ptolemy's record.

Early tradition explicitly shows that Tara, far from being the Capital of the Connachta was in fact a satellite seat of the Cruthin Kings of Ulster right up until 637 AD. The early *Táin Bó Cuailnge* refers to a daughter of King Conor Mac Nessa as the Queen of Tara, to Conor installing his grandson Erc as King of Tara, and to Conor's sons mustering at Tara before setting off westwards to attack Medb's forces. It refers to a Tara king, Luighaire, a cousin of Conor, and ancestor of the Ui Luighaire sept of Tara district, which pseudo-history re-invented as Laoghaire, a son of Niall of the nine Hostages. The saga of *Cath Rúis na Rí* described Tara as in the possession of Connor mac Nessa and his grandson Erc. The legal tract, *'Bech Bretha'*, which exhibits the fact that Tara was still a royal seat of the Cruthin kings of Ulster as late as the 7th century AD, survived suppressor and shredder despite the best efforts of the Ui Neill eulogists to extirpate this solid fact of history. *'Cath Crinna'* falls halfway between these two tales and corroborates the evidence of both at different levels, adding further facts in its own right. The authenticity of the Ulster Tales is verified in the unmistakable evidence they provide that Tara of Meath was never the seat of the High-Kingship of all Ireland. It was but a satellite seat of the Cruthin kings of Ulster. These and other pertinent materials will now be examined.

ANCIENT CONNACHT (Ól nÉgmacht) NOT A BACKWATER BUT CENTRE STAGE

Like Tara, Rathcroghan of Roscommon is conspicuous by its absence from Ptolemy's map which designates Rath Cruacha of Galway as *Aut-ein-ri (Ait en Rí* = Home of the Kings). Referring to early Connacht, James Charles Roy encapsulated the political content of the *Táin*. *"The Táin Bó Cuailgne reflects one of the earliest historical realities of Celtic Ireland - the constant warfare between the Connachta from Cruchan (in the SW) and the Ulaid (Cruthin) from Emain Macha in Ulster. The outcome of their rivalry marked the end of the Heroic Age, though certainly not the Heroic tradition, the spirit of which survived for hundreds of years. With the destruction of Emain Macha, however, and the re-arrangement of so many boundaries, the balance of power altered fundamentally. The men of Ulster gave way to the men of Connacht, who in turn found themselves beleagured from within by one of their own, the Ui Neill. The ramifications bleed into the historical period. The real centres of power - Cruchan and Emain Macha - occupy centre stage. Tara is virtually unmentioned whereas levies from Leinster and Munster are described as allies of Connacht. We approach*

---

[380] Bk of Lecan 23, 553, 17 a; 556 ; Bk of Ballymote 4 a, 16 a, 17 a; Ar. 242-3; Lebor na hUidhre 41 b

the true Berlin of ancient Ireland, the city of Cruachan. The immediate urge for expansion among the Connachta was neither greed nor desire for new dominions per se, but a response to overpopulation - too many people on too little land. The usual recourse of Celts in similar difficulties had been to gather their herds and travel west, but nothing lay beyond Ireland. They turned north to the traditional enemy, the men of Ulaid (Ulstermen).[381] The early 'Táin' was allowed to survive, even in its later rescinded forms which manipulated its earlier content, in spite of its adverse reflection on the glorification of Tara.

"Connacht is of importance prior to the 11th century for its function as a supply-base and manufactory of tribes."[382] This claim by Byrne is corroborated by the archaic demographic description of the Belgic oppidum of that province which defined it as densely populated: *"o Maen na treibh tuillte co rein na fairrgi"* ('from densely populated Maen Magh to the sea'). The Plain of Maen (*Maen Magh/Magh Main*) is the central plain of Galway with Turoe at its core, named after Maine, King of Connacht, son and successor of Queen Medb. No other area of ancient Ireland earned such a demographic accolade for density of population. Byrne referred to areas of the province "crowded with small tribes" and tribal movements due to pressure of peoples, one upon the other. This offsets the trend among historians who downgrade the politico/historical role of early Connacht, portraying it as outside of the mainstream of Irish history until the high middle ages. Far from being a backwater, Connacht was, in fact, dynamically at centre stage throughout the Iron Age.

One name, and its geographic position, needs to be clarified forthwith, namely, Rath Cruacha/Cruachan of Connacht. Roy, O Rahilly and Irish historians have been conned by the 'Cruachan' of pseudo-history. A correct interpretation of 'Cruachan', 'the true Berlin of Ireland,'[383] is vital to any real understanding of the pristine history of early Ireland. The Cruachan of Queen Medb was not Rathcroghan of Roscommon, but Rath Cruacha of Athenry, Co. Galway.

In Chapter 2 the defence system of the Fir Belg oppidum centred on Turoe and Athenry ('REGIA E TERA', Royal Seat at Te[mh]ra, and 'AUTEINRI', *Ait na Rí* (of Ptolemy's record; pronounced with a distinct 'ait' sound), the Rath Cruacha of Galway, was reconstructed with its extensions encompassing archaic Connacht. Numerous vassal groups defended the various segments of its frontier. These colonies of fighting men were rewarded for their mercenary services with lands further afield facing the Cruthin of Ulster by the Kings of Connacht (ancient Ól nÉgmacht). These formed 'buffer states' of the ever-expanding realms of that province at the expense of the Cruthin. It is now expedient to take a closer look at Connacht's Iron Age Capital, its Kings and Queens, their wars and the colonies or 'states' of fighting men whom they employed. One must "trace these back as far as possible" as well as forward into the new acquisitions of the growing Connacht Fir Belg power in which they were awarded lands for their military services. It must start with the reality and position of 'Rath Cruachan'.

The Rathcroghan Myth is a mirror-replica of the Tara Myth. Only by the 8th century did Connacht's Fir Belg Ui Briuin ruling dynasty finally conquer the Rathcroghan district of Roscommon and thereafter use the Carnfree mound as the inauguration site of their kings. Until then the Rathcroghan territory had been the power centre of the 'Cruthintuatha Croghain', a Connacht branch of the Cruthin of Ulster. In Medb's time the 'Cruthintuatha Croghain' centered on Rathcroghan and embracing East Mayo, almost all of Roscommon, Sligo and Leitrim were still attached territorially to the main body of the Cruthin of Ulster.

---

[381] James Charles Roy, "Celtic Ireland", p.74-77.
[382] Francis John Byrne, "Irish Kings and High-Kings', p.230
[383] James Charles Roy, Ibid, p.74

No Celtic Fir Belg King could have ruled Connacht from Rathcroghan of Roscommon before the 8th century. This startling fact will become clearer as this chapter progresses.

MAGH MUC DHRUIME AND ITS RAMIFICATIONS

A question immediately poses itself: Where then did Queen Medb and Connacht's Iron Age kings reside? In the reconstruction of the defensive system of the Fir Belg oppidum of Connacht it was shown that a seperate oppidum centered on the present town of Athenry was eventually enveloped by and incorporated into the larger oppidum centered on Turoe as the latter expanded. The area enclosed within the confines of this smaller oppidum around Athenry was known in ancient times as *Magh Muc Dhruime,* Plain of the Magic Boar's Dyke. It referred precisely to the defence ramparts of the inner and outer wards of the oppidum, a Connacht Black Pig's Dyke, corruptly Magh Mucruma, Mucramma or Muccrime in variant texts. The startling significance of this name and of legends associating it with Queen Medb and her consort, Aillil, Regents of Ól nÉgmacht, were deliberately suppressed by medieval pseudo-historians. So too has the broader ramifications of this archaic tale in particular, *'Cath Magh Muc Dhruime'* in which is embeded a legend purporting to give the origin of its name. The only extant copy of the tale is preserved in a poem in the 12th century Book of Leinster, a manusript noted for its blatant interpolations, manipulations and synchronisms in its recensions of variant earlier texts. One catches the Leinster interpolator in the act of subtly changing the name of the Plain and its implications in the course of the poem. He begins by giving the correct version of the name of the plain of the Chase of the Magic Boar and its linear embankments:

> *"Magh Mucrama molas cach...magh na tigi is na trebthach*
> *Ro gab fini findEchdach.... Clar i tát claidib cressa...."* [384]

> *"Famous Plain of Muc Dhruim (Magic Boar's Dyke), Plain of many houses and tribes*
> *Conquered by the Fianna of Eochaid (Fedlech). Landscape of linear embankment Dykes."*

After opening what appears to be a typical wild boar chase to mythologically relate the erection of the linear embankments as dykes thrown up by the Magic Boar's tusks, he slipped into a fictional variant and altered the purpose of the chase to a counting of wild boar. He subtly changed the name to Magh Mucríma (the pig counting). Hence the Plain was so named, he alleged. The mythological origin of the linear embankments around the Athenry oppidum and its associations with Queen Medb's family were suppressed. Irish speakers some 50 years ago knew snatches of the original and insisted the correct form of the name was *Magh Muc Dhruim.*

By the use of the false variant, 'Mucríma', which carries an insignificant meaning, a new origin was given to the name, thus suppressing the true reality behind the tale. Variants of the original name *'Magh Muc Dhruim'* in manuscripts and pseudo-Dindshenchas, are 'Mucroma', 'Mucroime', 'Moghchruime', 'Mucraime' and 'Mucruma'. The opening stanza of the Book of Leinster poem, unmistakably spelling out the archaic character of the plain around Athenry, was left unaltered: *"Magh Mucrama molas cach...Clar i tát claidib cressa"* [385] *"Famed Plain of Muc Dhruim. Landscape of linear embankment Dykes."* The *'Magh Muc Dhruim'* of Athenry of Galway, carries the same mythological significance as that of Dun Mucrum (Muc Dhruim), the name of an unrecorded (now obliterated) section of a later more northerly segment of the Black Pig's Dyke above Ballyshannon (Donegal). It specifically refers to the earthen linear embankments. It resembled the rotund rump and broad-shouldered back (*'Drum'*) of the mythological Magic Boar that allegorically tore up the fosse entrenchment, like the 'Black Pig's Dyke' of Ulster or the 'Boar's Back' of the plain of

---

[384] Book of Leinster, Dindsenchas of Mag Mucrama, 162b, line 21559 ff.
[385] Book of Leinster, Dindsenchas of Mag Mucrama, 162b, line 21559 ff.

Athenry. The '*muc*' refers to the 'Magic Boar'. The *motif* of 'rooting up of the defensive entrenchment and its adjoining embankment' attributed to this 'Magic Boar' is common to both Ulster and Connacht and to other parts of Ireland.

Mythological origin-legends have survived in Ulster and Connacht relating the original erection of the great defensive earthworks in this allegorical and mythological manner. De Vismas Kane in his reconstruction of the Great Wall of Ulster, 'The Black Pig's Dyke', recorded several.[386] "*Throughout Ireland legends about Swine are extremely numerous, survivals of the chase of the wild boar which may be relegated to one of two groups of ancient legends. The first belongs to the mythological division of Celtic tales as is preserved in the Dindshenchas of Dumae Selga (Cruach Magh Seolgha in Galway). To this group evidently belong the various episodes of the hunting of magic pigs by Aillil and Medbh in Croghan (read Rath Cruacha), by Manannan Mac Lir's hounds, and by Mod (Mac Umhor), killed at Mucinis (Boar Island) on L. Conn, Co. Mayo. The other group of traditions connected with the boundary entrenchment between ancient Ulster and Connacht, which is the subject of this paper, centre round an earlier tale entitled 'The Fate of the children of Tureann'. From this, legends relating to the Race of the Black Pig (Black Pig's Dyke) in the N of Ireland and in Louth and Meath derive their motif.*"

Kane placed the Chase of the Magic Boar by Aillil and Medb in Magh Muc Dhruim in his first group which no longer had any connection to defensive linear earthworks. He did so because the story in its present form in the Book of Leinster has been deliberately robbed of its original mythological re-enactment of the 'digging up of the earthwork entrenchments of Magh Muc Dhruim/Athenry oppidum'. This was re-enacted through the medium of the chase of the Magic Boar by Ailill and Medb around whose royal residence at Rath Cruacha of Athenry this 'Black Pig's Dyke' was erected. Kane's interpretation of the various episodes of the hunting of the magic boar by Ailill and Medb was as much distorted by his infatuation with the Rathcroghan Myth as his directional alignments and terminals of Ulster's 'Black Pig's Dyke' were by the Tara Myth. His use of 'Croghan' instead of 'Cruacha' shows he believed that the episode referred to Rathcroghan. Yet, the milieu of even the most corrupt version of the Magh Muc Dhruim Wild Boar Chase by Medb is always anchored in the plain of Athenry underlining the fact that here was the 'Plain of the Kings', of Medb and Ailill and Connacht's Iron Age Kings.

Before it was interpolated, this mythological tale related the erection of the defence embankments of the Athenry oppidum. Some oral versions survive which give the lie to the Book of Leinster version, relating what is substantially the original version, although more succinct in the telling. The most pertinent version is that related by an elderly farmer accosted beside Cruach Cian on the Bresk road near Esker, 4 miles E of Athenry where the defensive fortifications of the Turoe and Athenry oppida met and marched together. In discussing a decayed dyke along the edge of the bog, he suddenly asked, as if something way at the back of his memory ignited: "Hold on! Would that have anything to do with the dyke leveled by Miss Ford in Curragh More (half a mile away)?" Without waiting for a reply, he said: "Did you ever hear of the Magic Boar chased by Queen Medb? The seanachies used to say Medb chased a Magic Boar around Magh Muc Dhruim encircling Athenry. The boar tore up a trench with its tusks as it was chased and thus formed the dyke. As it headed this way to Greyford (Rath Chlaidh), completing a circle of the countryside around Athenry, it tired. Medb caught up with it and speared it beside the Curragh More dyke which Miss Ford leveled recently. The Boar turned into stone. It is still there. Ask Miss Ford to show you the

---

[386] W. F. De Vismas Kane, "The Black Pig's Dyke: The Ancient Boundary Fortification of Ulster' in the 'Proceedings of The Royal Irish Acaemy', Vol. xxvii., Sect. c., p.322-328

track of the double-ditch she leveled on her own and the stone with the hole where Queen Medb's spear transfixed the boar."

In haste and excitement at the prospect of seeing Medb's Magic Boar frozen in stone, the name of the gentleman who so graciousely gave of his time and memory to relate this nugget from legendary history went unrecorded. The track of the leveled-out dyke in Curragh More was still fresh on the ground some 30 years ago. The large stone with the hole in its side lay there beside the route. Miss Ford knew nothing of the significance of the stretch of rampart she had leveled single-handedly, nor was she aware of any story relating to the stone except that it was used as a Mass rock. Half a century ago many people knew that this double-ditch ran all the way from Greyford and Curragh Mor to Monivea, 7 miles to the NW, where it swung W and rounded Athenry some 4 miles out from the town all along its route. It swung back to the starting point to complete the circle. This was the outer-ward entrenchment *('Dun Cladh')* of the Athenry/Magh Muc Dhruim oppidum. Vestiges survive and are shown on the OS Map. It left its name on Tlds. along its route, such as the nearby Gloves *(Na gClaidhbhe)* Tlds. Other versions of Medb's Wild Boar chase in the general area do not mention the boar's transmorgrification.

Similar tales were told in parts of Leitrim, Longford, Granard, Mohill and Drumsna by the Upper Shannon, relating the erection of The Black Pig's Dyke, the Ulster frontier fortification. Kane noted a version he heard in Mohill in the early 19th century: A druid used to turn his disciples into magic swine and hounds. Having transformed the sons of a red-haired widow, one chasing the other, she turned the Druid into a black pig. He fled through the country cutting a trench (Ulster's boundary) until he reached the Shannon at Rooskey. There the infuriated red-haired mother slew him on Crook na Muck (Mound of the Magic Pig) where the pig was petrified. A large stone marks the spot. Tales like those relating to Magh Muc Dhruim, are mythological origin-tales re-enacting the erection of the frontier embankments. Variant versions in the upper Shannon area claim the Magic Boar was magically transmorgrified.

Kane's Louth legend names the Druid turned boar which dug up the boundary fortification, involving the 3 sons of Tureann. Cian mic Cainte was a druid who changed children into swine for the purpose of setting dogs after them, thus amusing himself. The sons of Tureann resolved to take revenge on him. Once when he magically transformed himself into a black pig they pursued and killed him near Cnoc Cian Mic Cainte (Killeen Hill) near the Dane's Cast Dyke at Meigh, Co Armagh, on its border with the far north of Louth. Cian's tumulus cairn gave its name to the hill. The original tale of the children of Tureann relates that Cian being chased from the Tara district by the Cruthin king of Tara arrived at Magh Murthemne (N of Dundalk near Kileen Hill, Sliabh Gullion and Dane's Cast) and found himself being chased by the sons of Tureann. Brian turned his brothers into hounds who chased the magic pig northwards. He transfixed the pig with his spear. This mythological re-enactment of the erection of boundary earthworks running N from the W side of the Tara district, defending the territory of the Cruthin King of Tara along the E slopes of Sliabh Gullion and thence N (Dane's Cast) to Lough Neagh, delineates the last defensive frontier of the ancient Ulster.

Like the mythological origin-tales told along the different alignments of Ulster's Black Pig's Dyke, the origin-tale re-enactment of the erection of defensive embankments of the Athenry oppidum, which gave it its name, Magh Muc Dhruim, belongs to the same genre. The 'official' literary Tara Myth was unable to displace the much older Ulidian tradition which is diametrically in conflict with it. So too the interpolated mythological tale purporting to explain the name of Magh Muc Dhruim of Athenry embedded in the 12th century Book of Leinster version of 'Cath Magh Mucrime' failed to suppress the oral tradition handed down. The implication of Medb's association with the Magic Boar Chase around the Plain of

Athenry is highly significant. It corfirms that the Rath Cruacha of Queen Medb was Rath Cruacha of Athenry of Galway, not Rathcroghan of Roscommon which came into the possession of the Kings of Connacht only in the 8th century. Resulting from the erection of the embankments of the Athenry Belgic oppidum allegorically dug up by the tusks of the magic boar, the plain was named Magh Muc Dhruim, Plain of the Magic Boar's Back, the broad-crested linear embankment resembling a huge hog's back. The mythological origin-tale of Medb's Magic Boar chase symbolically records the erection of the embankments of the Rath Cruacha/Magh Muc Dhruim oppidum. It is the clearest statement linking Medb directly to this Galway Rath Cruacha. No Queen would go to the time-consuming effort of erecting such extensive linear fortifications were she not residing there. The fortified area forming the oppidum of Rath Cruachu of Athenry, was named Magh Muc Dhruim by Medb's eulogists who allegorized for all time the laborious task of constructing the linear defences in the Dindsenchas of Magh Muc Dhruim. The Book of Leinster version, begun perhaps with a Rathcroghan Myth effort to suppress the original meaning and change the name to 'Muccrime', is hogwash. This was not the only attempt to suppress Connacht's archaic capital in favour of Rathcroghan of Roscommon. The Rathcroghan Myth needs to be dealt with with the same vigour as the Tara Myth.

All Medb's associations are with Rath Cruacha of Athenry. Hence, all the Dindsenchas lore which refers to Rath Cruacha, Medb and her family, name associated places in Galway, but not in Roscommon. Take for example the *Dindsenchas of Áth Cliath Medraigi*. It tells that Medb's sons erected defensive 'thornbush covered dykes' near the sea port of Ath Clee Magh Rí in Galway. Medb sent help from Rath Cruacha. The *Dindsenchas of Sliabh nEchtga* Mountain on the Galway/Clare border tells of Sidhe Nenta near Loughrea and the lands between Maen Magh (Turoe/Knocknadala) and the sea being given by Ailill and Medb of Rath Cruacha, to Fergus Mac Ruidh. The *Dindsenchas of Carn Conaill* lists the sons of Umhor who went to Medb at Rath Cruacha. They 'set up there beside her', Oengus on Inish Mor and Conchuirn on Inish Meann, Cutra at Loch Cutra, Cimbe at Loch Cimbe, Mil at Muirbech Mil, Dela on Dáil, Lathrach on Laragh Hill, Tawan on Tawin Point, Conall at Aidhne, all in Galway, not even one in Roscommon. Their message is startlingly clear.

Attempts fail to fill Roscommon's lacuna. One hijacked Cnoc na Dala from Turoe and transferred it to Rathcroghan. Pseudo-verses interpolated in the *Dindsenchas of Carn Fraich* state that "Cnoc na Dala was its name in the days of Medb, great and glorious." Verses preserved in the original text clarify where Rath Cruachan stood: "The foster father of the great Conn Mac Felim was Conall of terraced Cruacha (*Conall Cruachna*); though he dwelt in stone-built Cruacha he was king over the tribes of Temhair (*tuathaibh Temrach*)." The double-ring stone fort, Caher Cruachan Chonaill Ceadgin, the royal residence of King Conal Ceadgin/Conal Cruachna stands in Clamper Park just S of Athenry. The Temhair over which he reigned was Turoe of Galway (Cnoc Temhro), not Tara of Meath. The Rath Cruacha where he resided was at Athenry, not Rathcroghan. His nephew, Conn, subsequent King of Connacht from whom Connacht was named, was in fosterage with him there. In the adjacent townland is Tobar Chonaile. Several forts around Athenry are known as Rath Cruacha. One or two have garbled versions such as Rath Croca (a corrupt 'Hangman's fort'). The OS Map has a similar garbled version of the Farranablake fort with the remarkably huge souterrain. The hill on which the fort in the new cemetery stands and another across the road from it in Farranablake East (bulldozed to make way for housing 40 years ago) was well known as *Árd na Cruachna*.

Medb's associations with Croghan of Roscommon belong to the realm of pseudo history which did a superbly sophisticated job on the Rathcroghan Myth. As with the Tara Myth, it was so sophisticated as to hogwash more than a millennium of Irishmen and their men of learning to this day. Numerous pointers to the original capitals, history and political geography of Iron Age Ireland have survived to set the story straight and solve the inconsistencies that damn the pseudo-historic record. There is an abundance of material which closely associates Medb and her royal family to the Athenry and Turoe areas. Yet, there is none which link her to Rathcroghan of Roscommon apart from the bald statements of pseudo-history which are seriously flawed. Rathcroghan of Roscommon was the seat of Medb's bitterest enemies. Many wars between Ulster and Connacht were led by Medb and her Fir nÓl nÉgmacht against the Cruthintuatha of Croghan of Roscommon and the Cruthin of Ulster. From this material may be cited a Book of Leinster poem, *'A Fhir theit i mmag Medba'*. It bears the usual Leinster hoax of appropriating Tara for itself, with Eochaid Fedlech reigning there as High King of Ireland, holding Connacht as Tara's special demesne over which he placed his daughter Medb as its Queen. It unequivocally anchors Medb squarely to the Rath Cruacha of Galway:

"Ingen Echach Fedlig Fail   *"Daughter of Echaid Fedlech, King of Fail*
Medb a hEdnig uair imshlan"   *Medb of cold clear healthy Aidhne"*

'Ednig' is the Aidhne territory of the O Hynes (Edhnigh) SW of Athenry, a far cry from Rathcroghan of Roscommon. The Ui Fiachra gave it its compound name of Hy Fiachra Aidhne. Achaill Oichne was the name of the forested area of SW Galway from Athenry to Clarenbridge.

GEO-POLITICAL LOCATION of QUEEN MEDB'S RATH CRUACHAN

The wild pigs of Fraechmagh, *'mucca fiatta i Fraechmaigh'* chased by Medb in the mythological tale of the Magic Boar Chase of Magh Muc Dhruim issued from the caves of Cruachan (*"a huaimh Chruachan"*), the Otherworld Abode known as 'Sid(h)e Cruachan'. A prose tale in the Book of Leinster, *'Do Chophur in da Muccida'*, anchors **'Side Cruachan', alias 'Side Connacht', just SE of Athenry. In referring to *'muccid Ochaill Oichni'* it states emphatically that the Otherworld Abode or Royal Cemetery of Ochall Oichne is the Otherworld Abode of Rath Cruachan, "*Sid nOchaill is ed Sid Cruachain.*" It then refers to it as 'Sid Connacht'. The startling implications of this *'Do Chophur in da Muccida'* text are devastating for the Myth of Rathcroghan of Roscommon.**

The redactor who copied this into the Book of Leinster did not understand its crucial significance or did not have the same incentive to suppress this evidence so incriminatory to the 'official doctrine' of the Tara and Rath Croghan Myths, as did the Ui Neill and Ui Briuin redactors. Just as *'Bec Bretha'* was a timebomb waiting to explode the Tara Myth, so too *'Do Chophur in da Muccida'* explodes the slippery slimy Rathcroghan Myth. This prose text speaks in the same context of *'Dun Chruachan'* and *'dun i Cruachnaibh'* referring to the embankments encompassing the inner ward of the Athenry Oppidum in the same sense in which elderly people in the vicinity referred to the outer and inner-ward embankments as the Dun or Duncla of Athenry.[387] People in the midlands refer to vestiges of the Black Pig's Dyke as *Dun Cladh*. Archaic material in the Book of Leinster's *'Táin Bó Fraich'* and in other Annals, distinguish between 'Dun Cruachan' and 'Rath Cruacha'. Rath Cruacha refers to the fort. When a large company arrives, too many for the fort to accommodate, they are admitted to 'Dun Cruachan'. This seems to refer to entering the inner ward but not entering the 'Rath' which implicitly stood within the inner ward. Archaic topographic material like that preserved in *'Do Chophur in da Muccida'*[388] clarifies that before the original tradition was manipulated to accommodate 8th/9th century political propaganda, it was well known that the Rath Cruacha of Queen Medb stood within the Athenry oppidum. To this day the townland adjoining the North Gate of Athenry, which sits snugly within the inner ward of

[387] Martin Finnerty, 'Punan Arsa', p. 2ff. National Library, Dublin (print by Galway Observer, 1953).
[388] Book of Leinster, 246a, line 32931-32935.

the Fir Belg oppidum, is no other than Cather Royan *(Cather Roighan,* the Palace of the Queen). The Tld. also has a Lis na Reena (Rioghna, Queens fort). Who was the Queen who resided there, indeed, if not Queen Medb? *'Roi'* and *'Roighan'* are archaic forms of modern Irish *'Rí'* and *'Righan'*, meaning king and queen respectively.

SIGNIFICANCE OF MAGH MUC DHRUIM

It is implicit in the Book of Leinster version of *'Cath Maige Mucrima'* that the Cave of Cruachan and the Otherworld Abode of Sidhe Cruachan are in Magh Muc Dhruim of Athenry. Disembarking at Ath Cliath (Claidh) Magh Rí in Galway Bay, Lughaid Mac Con led his army NE to Mag Mucrima in *'Crich Oc mBethrae fri Aidne atuaid,'* the N part of Aidne around Athenry. The itinerary of Mac Con's army is suspended in order to relate how Magh Mucrime got its name. "*Magh Mucrima di .i. mucca gentliuchta dodechatar a huaim Cruachna*"[389] (Magh Muc Dhruim got its name from the magic pigs which issued from the Otherworld Abode of Cruachan) and rooted up the embankments enclosing the plain. The redactor renders *'uaimh'* as 'cave'. 'Uaimh Cruachna' refers to underground passages of the cairn tumuli. 'Cruachan' invariably denotes cairns or tumuli. *'Senchas na Releg'* listed the Fir Belg gods/goddesses who had their Otherworld Abode in Sidhe Cruachan. Pseudo-history found a cave some distance from Rathcroghan to project as the so-called 'Cave of Cruachan' from which the magic swine allegedly issued. The tumuli cairns of Oenach Cruacha of Athenry have been stripped of their stone fill exposing kerbstones and the tumuli underground passages tombs ('caves'). It is implicit in this mythological tale that Queen Medb resided within Magh Muc Dhruim and that the erection of its Belgic Defence System dated back to the time of Medb.

SIDHE BUIDBH = SIDHE CRUACHA = SIDHE nOCHAILL = SIDHE CONNACHT
THE PRE-EMINENT ROYAL NECROPOLIS OF PRE-CHRISTIAN IRELAND:

The Otherworld saga *'Cath Magh Tuired'* recounts Ireland's Celtic Pantheon and the inter-relationships between the deities of this and similar Celtic Otherworld Tales. *'De Gabail an tSida'*, *'De Chopur in da Muccida'*, *'Senchas na Releg'*, and *'Shighud Tellaig na Cruachna'* (Necropolis of Cruacha), when restored to their original Iron Age geo-political context (hijacked by pseudo-history), show that Ireland's oldest tradition located the chief Otherworld Abodes of Celtic gods and goddesses at the core of Ól nÉgmacht, Medb's province, of which Rathcroghan was not a part. It is shattering to realize that the area round Rath Cruacha/Athenry oppidum is classed as one vast Necropolis of greater extent and importance than the Boyne Valley Passage grave megalithic cemetery. In *Senchas na Relec* Cruacha heads the short list of the pre-eminent Royal Cemeteries of pre-christian Ireland ("*primhreilce Herend ria cretim .i. Cruachu, in Brugh, Talltiu*"): 1) *Releg na Rí lamh le Cruacha* of Athenry, 2) *Brugh na Boinne* megalithic Necropolis on the Boyne (Newgrange), and 3) Tailtiu, the megalithic Necropolis on Loughcrew *(Slieve na Calliagh)* in the NW corner of Co. Meath. High honour indeed for Cruacha of Athenry! It is corroborated by the archaeological sites (mostly stripped down to kerbstone level and denuded of their stone fill, but recognizeable for what they were). Local toponomy loudly proclaims the character of this Abode of the Gods, Home of the Kings.

Otherwold Abodes of the pre-christian gods were well-known realities. Cairns, passage graves and royal burial mounds marked by pillar stones were enshrined in early literature and legend with reference to their residents and otherworld affinities. Yet they became lost worlds like the now famous Boyne Valley Bru na Boinne due to historical circumstances. Pseudo-history played a major role in their 'disappearance'. It spoke of The Bru as referring only to Bru na Boinne Passage-grave complex at Newgrange, alledging that almost all the High Kings of pagan Ireland were interred there. It concocted fictitious explanations as to

---

[389] Book of Leinster, 290a, , line 37234-7.

why some 'High Kings' were not interred there. Clare O Kelly, the Newgrange archaeologist, corrected this false view projected by pseudo-history. She noted that archaeology had shown that these passage graves on the bend of the Boyne had never been opened after being sealed for millennia before the earliest alleged 'High Kings' reigned and that none of those High Kings were buried therein.

Two poems in Lebor na Huidre (Book of Dun Cow), *'Senchas na Releg'* (Necropolis History) and *'Shighud Tellaig na Cruachna'* (Necropolis of Cruacha) list the names not only of the interred Kings and Queens but also of the gods and godesses who had their Otherworld Abodes there. They preserve the geo-political essence of Iron Age Ireland totally at variance with the fraudulent projections of medieval pseudo-historians. Amazingly, they escaped medieval shredders. The 12th century interpolator subtly manipulated part of the texts in favour of Tara and Rathcroghan. The titles *Temair na Rí* (Turoe of Galway) and *Rath Cruacha* of Athenry were transmuted to Tara of Meath and Rathcroghan of Roscommon respectively. The poems corroborate the evidence of Ptolemy and the Ulidian Tales that Ireland was divided between 2 great powers, each with its own Acropolis and Necropolis. These precious histories of the royal cemetries of pagan Ireland, despite the violent hand of the interpolator, retain the Iron Age dual division of Ireland. They project the 2 *'Priomh Relec'* (Chief Necropoli) of Ireland, Cruachu, the burial place of Connacht's Kings and of alleged High Kings of Ireland ruling at Tara (read Temhair na Rí, Turoe), and Tailtiu, burial place of Ulster Kings. *Senchas na Releg* states that every green mound (Cruacha) in the plain was a tumulus of one or other royal family or regent. There were so many in Cruacha's Necropolis that the author of *'Shíghud Tellaig na Cruachna'* had to admit that he could not enumerate them all: *"Ni thic dim a n-airimh uile."*

The archaic Necropolis Texts, *Senchas na Releg*, *De Gabail an tSída* and *De Copur in da Muccida*,[390] anchor Ireland's Chief Iron Age Necropolis, *Relig na Rí lamh le Cruachain*, at Athenry's Sidhe Boidb, alias Sidh nOchaill, not at Rathcroghan of Roscommon as claimed by 8th/9th century pseudo-historians. With the *Shíghud Tellaig na Cruachna* text, they refer to Cruachan Necropolis as *'na Cruachna'*, not only in the genitive case, but in the plural also, indicating a plurality of contexts. It had 4 compartments around Athenry, *Cruachan Thuaidh, Cruachan Theas, Cruachan Thoir* and *Cruachan Thiar*, erroneously anglicized as Mountain North, South, East and West, as shown on the OS maps, standing back some distance from the town. These are not the usual designations of townlands. There is no mountain to warrant such names. O-Irish *Cruach/Cruachan* refers to Necropolis burial mounds, not mountains. The necropolist texts *Shíghud Tellaig na Cruachna, Aided Nathi* and *Releg na Rí*, call *Releg na Rí lamh le Cruachain'* the Chief Necropolis of Ireland, ahead of Newgrange. Not only the early Kings of Connacht, but the Kings of Tara (*Temhair*) too, were interred at this *Releg na Rí* according to these texts. Gods and goddesses of the Celtic Pantheon had their Otherworld Abodes at Releg na Rí. They were divided into different groups with each allotted their own otherworld abode (*Sidhe*) in these Mountain North South, East and West cemetery (Cruachan) complexes by the Daghdha, father of the gods and goddesses. Their names still ring out across the Celtic landscape around Athenry.

Something of the archaeological significance of *'na Cruachna'*, referring to these archaic cemetery complexes around Rath Cruacha, was recalled by long-memoried elders up to 40 years ago. That old tradition corroborates the archaic texts that formerly these *Cruachna'* were not anchored to a single townland as the Mountain townlands now are on the OS maps. They were much larger, covering several adjoining townlands in their respective areas.

---

[390] Bk of Leinst, 246 a 32931-5; 290 a 37234-7; 155 a 20348-50). *'De Gabail an tSida'* and *'De Copur in da Muccida'*

Cruachan Thoir (Mountain East) cemetery complex covers the townlands of Brusk, Esker, Rathgorgin, Moyode, Deerpark, Backpark and Killascaul, east of Athenry. Dominick's Hill in Esker was *Brugh A Scáil* (Lugh's palace; Lugh and his father Cian are called '*Scál Balb*'/'*A Scál*)',[391] of which Brusk is the rough rendering. In mythological tradition Lugh reigned as King of the gods/goddesses of Ireland and had his Otherworld Palace on Brugh A Scáil. He retired to his Abode at Lugh Bhrugh (Loovroo) E of Boy Hill at Athenry. Dominic's hill area was known as Coill A Scáil (Killascaul). The lake was *Loch A Scáil,* a sacred cult lale. The O-Irish name of the Clarin River was 'A Scáil', the same as the Scheld River (Ascaul) in Belgium in the land of the Atrebates. At the S foot of Dominic's hill is a fossed earthen platform, perhaps a Celtic Temple site (marked on OS maps as a moated site). On the hillslope above are several 'fulacht fiadh', indicating a busy cult centre. The fame of Dominic's Well, fed from a powerful sacred spring at the foot of the 200ft high Dominic's Hill, goes back to pagan times when its waters were sprinkled on farms and animals. "Many deities are associated with water, and in particular with springs or rivers and there may be a close association with the (Celtic) water cult."[392] On the E of Dominic's Hill stood the cone-peaked Cruach Chian (demolished). Cian was the father of Lugh. Lugh's mother was the goddess Ethniu (Ethlenn). On the W of Dominic's hill in Killascaul is Cruachan Aine, sung of by the poet Raftery. Aine was goddess of sovereignty and consort of Cian. Brugh Aine was one of the *'Dighna Ereann'* royal sites. Aine was a daughter of the Daghdha, the principal deity in the Celtic Pantheon. Ancient cemetery roads survive intact in this area leading to different burial mounds and Otherworld Abodes. A section of one from Athenry to *Cruachan Thoir* survives in Backpark. *Bothar Bodb* branched off from it to *Cruachan Theas*. Ancient cemetery roads were important features in the Celtic landscape.[393] Munster's Royal Fir Belg centre's version made Aine of Knock Aine in Limerick the divine consort and sovereignty goddess of Eoghan Mór, King of Munster.

Cruachan Thiar (Mountain West): Local lore tells that the area from Pollnagroagh (*Poll na gChruacha*) extending west to Derrydonnell was known as *Cruachan Thiar*. It included Pollnagroagh, Poll na Brugh (Otherworld Abodes), part of the Ballygarraun, Cloran, Gortroe, Rathmorrissy, 3 Derrydonnell Tlds, the north of Moyveela, Palmerstown, Lisheenacoill, Toberroe, Carraunduff, Caherbriskaun, Cnocnacreeva and Castleambert. Mountain West on the OS map is at the west of this complex. There is a *Dirna in Daghdha/Cloch an Dagda* on a hillock in this area west of Athenry. The Daghdha was the father of the Celtic Pantheon. His massive club used to "dig up a dyke as wide as a provincial boundary." He was the father of Bodbh Dearg, Aine, Ogma and Brighid. Tradition claims Derrydonnell was originally Doire Danann after the Mother goddess Danu. A more recent account, ignoring its original name, claims Derrydonnell was named after Red Hugh O Donnell whose army encamped in the oak forest there before sacking and burning Athenry in 1596. The Daghdha's consort, Danu, was the *Mor-Rioghain* of Rath Cruacha. Little is remembered concerning her or the Daghdha or the Otherworld Abodes of Poll na Brugh in the vicinity of Pollnagroagh in *Cruachan Thiar*.

Cruachan Thuaidh (Mountain North) covered Ballydavid, Mountain North, Pollagh, Carnaun, Sheeaun, Park, Mount Brown, Saint Ellen, Castle Ellen, Caraun, Knockbaun, Knockbrack and Montpelier. Carnaun, Sheeaun and Saint Ellen's cairns went into the Norman Castle. Archaic texts refer to Sheeaun's Otherworld Abodes. The Book of Leinster preserves startling data about Sidhe Cruacha's *Relig na Rí* (Cruachan Necropolis), calling it *Dorus iffirn na Herend* (Ireland's gate of Hell) because it emitted magic swine, birds of

---

[391] Bk of Leinster, 9 a 43; Rev. Celtique, xv, 317.
[392] Peter Salway, 'Roman Britain', p. 269-70.
[393] Anne Ross, 'Everyday Life of the Pagan Celts' and 'Pagan Celtic Britain'.

blight and the Mythological Three-headed Monster, *'in t-Ellen Trechend'*. The magic swine were chased by Medb around Rath Cruacha of Magh Muc Druime of Athenry, not around Rathcroghan of Roscommon. Part of *Cruachan Thuaidh* complex is Sidhe nEthelenn (*Ellen*: corrupt St. Ellen). One of the most frequently repressented gods on Gaulish monuments was Tricephalus, a three-headed, three-faced god, *'in t-Ellen Trechend'*. More than thirty of his effigies have been discovered in Belgic North Gaul.[394] Tricephali were found at Turoe's Iron Age *Fearta* cemetery. Sidhe nEthelenn of the Mountain North *(Cruachan Thuaidh)* Necropolis some 3 miles N of Athenry, may rather have been named after the goddess Ethelenn (Ellen), daughter of the Fomorian god Balor whom Lugh deposed. Ethelenn and Cian were the parents of Lugh. Tradition tells that Sidhe nEllen (nEthelenn)/Carnaun area was a military complex of the Fianna where Finn had his military camp and residence, Clochar Fhinn. Pseudo-history transmuted this to Allen of Kildare.

Cruachan Theas (Mountain South) stretches S from Baunmore and Rahard through Farrana-blake, Boyhill, Turloughalanger, Clamper Park, Loovroo, Mountain South, Slieveroe and part of Moyode and Rockfield. The Daghdha succeeded Lugh as King of the Tuatha De Danann and was succeeded by his son, Bodb Dearg, lord of the Brugh of Cruachan who reigned over the gods and goddesses of Ireland. At the highest point of the Necropolis of Cruacha (*Sidhe Chruacha*) SE of Athenry is *Sidhe Boidb* which gave its name to Boy Hill (*Cruach Boidb*). *'De Gabail an tSida'* and *'De Chopur in da Muccida'* refer to it as Sidh nOchaill, Sid Connacht and Sidh Cruachan [395] (Figures 54, 55, 56, 57, 58, 59 and 60). In it resided the Celtic war goddess trio, Badb, Morrigan, and Nemain. A bush-covered cluster of large stones on Boy Hill's S slope was known as *Brugh Morrigan*. Badb (to be distinguished from Bodb) is the *Badbhcath* or *Cathu-badhua* of the Continental inscription of Haute-Savoie.[396] Archaic literature claims this Home of the gods was the Necropolis where Queen Medb, her father Eochaid Ferach, her husband Ailill, Connacht Fir Belg Kings and Rí Temhro (Turoe) were interred. Medb's tumulus (*Fert Medba*) stands out in Rahard across the road from Boy Hill. *'Senchas na Releg'* names other kings interred there. It contradicts the claims of pseudo-history which falsely relocated *Releg na Rí* at Rathcroghan of Roscommon, a site at which these Fir Belg gods and kings would have been totally out of place before the 9th century.

On Boy Hill's E boundary is Loovroo (*Lugh Bhrugh*). *'Senchas na Releg'* named Lugh as a resident of Sidhe Boidb. Lugh Brugh is the Otherworld Abode of Lugh, most renowned of all Celtic gods who gave his name to the Celtic cities of Lyons, Leyden and London, Lugh Duns one and all. Loobroo of Athenry reverberates with all the startling pagan significance of these great Celtic Centres. Lugh was a bitter enemy of evil-eyed Balar, king of the old gods before the arrival of the Fir Belg with their own gods. Lugh slew Balar in a battle between the old gods and the Fir Belg Tuatha De Danann. Lugh was adopted as 'ard ollamh' (professor) of all arts and crafts and installed by Eochaid Ferach, Fir Belg Overking, in Lugh Brugh of Temhroit (Turoe) and by Queen Medb at Loobroo of Athenry. Kerbstones and carn fill survived in Loobroo to the 19th century. Tons of stone were carted off to lime kilns. Some large cairn stones remain. Its sacred spring and pool, Loughan Ellis, played an important part in the cemetery cult rites of Relig na Rí of Rath Cruacha.

Apart from the gods/goddesses who resided in Sidhe Cruacha, malevolent animals and birds such as the terrifying cats mentioned in *Fled Bricrend*, the fiery *Ellén Trechenn*, the magic pigs described in *Cath Magh Muc Dhruime*, and the three werewolves described in *Acallam*

---

[394] Marie-Louise Sjoestedt, 'Gods and Heroes of the Celts', p.28

[395] Book of Leinster, 246a lines 32931-32935; 290a lines 37234-7 and 155a, lines 20348 and 20350..

[396] Marie-Louise Sjoestedt, 'God's and Heroes of the Celts', p.4.

na Senórach issued from their Otherworld Mounds there,[397] Olc Aiche was the 'divine Herdsman' who presided over the Otherworld Feast as described in Scéla Éogain is Cormaic. His prodigious appetite and large cauldron recall those of the Dagda.[398] He and his daughter Etain/Achtan played a decisive role in the birth tale of Cormac Mac Art.

Archaic texts diametrically contradict the Rathcroghan Myth by their unadulterated claims that Sidhe Boidbh is Sidhe nOchaill is Sidhe Chonnacht is Sidhe Cruacha, which is the illustrious Releg na Rí lamh le Cruachan.[399] Sidhe Boidb is Cruach Boidb (Boy Hill) of Athenry. Sidhe nOchaill is the Otherworld Abode in the district south of Athenry where Sidhe Boidb is situated, a far cry from Rathcroghan of Roscommon. The heights of Boy Hill and Farranablake surrounding the new cemetery was well-known as *Árd na Cruachna*.

Vestiges of satellite cairns around Boy Hill stretch into adjoining Tlds. Royal Cemetery roads are still remembered by name as *Boher Bodibh*, *Bealach na Fert* (Tumulus Avenue) and *Sligh Bhrugh* (Slieveroe), partly overlaid by present day roads, and formerly bounded by cairns and burial mounds. Medb's tumulus is close to *Boher Boidbh*. The poems *'Relig na Rí'* and *'Aided Nathi'* and others state that there were over 50 royal burial mounds of kings and queens in the plain, not counting the otherworld abodes of the gods which usually took centre stage. The Magic Boars chased by Queen Medb (as told in *'Cath Magh Mucdhruime'*), otherworld birds and the evil *'in tEllén trechend* (three-headed god) issued from the cairn caves of Cruachan and devastated Ireland. "There was a Celtic concept of a supreme or high god and a multitude of lesser deities, some widely worshipped, others very local indeed. Notable features are 'triads' or groups of three, some animal, others human, such as the very popular Matres or Mother-Goddesses particularly common in the Rhineland,"[400] like Danu or the war goddess trio, the Morrigan, above. The area around Athenry, including the 4 Mountain (*Cruachna*) complexes, was known as Magh Muc Dhruim after the encompassing linear embankments allegedly torn up by the tusks of the Magic Wild Boar from the cairn caves of Cruachan chased by Queen Medb.

Pagan religions are concerned with death as with life, hence the cemetery cults. "The duality of chthonic/fertility deities is illustrative of this preoccupation with these two extremes of human experience. This concept makes it natural for burial sites to serve as a focal point for ritual and religious games, tribal gatherings and festivities, in which the Celts indulged. The evidence suggests the custom of performing tribal rites about the graves of divine ancestors, the grave mounds constituting the visible focus of belief. The burial mound was regarded as one of the entrances to the otherworld of which the Celts were so conscious. The *Sidhe* mounds which are a regular feature of the early Irish world, originated in beliefs associated with burial mounds. A provocative description suggestive of the veneration of the dead is given in the prose dindshenchas. Lén Línfiachlach, a craftsman of *Sidhe Boidb*, was accustomed to cast his anvil each night east as far as the grave mound."[401] Carefully preserved groves of trees, individual trees and wells in the proximity of the grave mounds were sacred to the Celts. A square embanked 'shrine' once stood at the summit of Sidhe Boidb but the site has become a feeding place for cattle and has been trampled out. It is said that a stele standing stone stood within this enclosure but was taken away to serve as a gate post. Such enclosures were common elsewhere.[402]

---

[397] Tomas O Cathasaigh, 'The Heroic Biography of Cormac Mac Art', p. 35-6.
[398] Tomas O Cathasaigh, 'The Heroic Biography of Cormac Mac Art', p. 31.
[399] Bk of Lein: *'De Gabail an tSida'*, *'De Copur in da Muccida'*246 a 32931-5; 290 a 37234-7; 155 a 20348-50).
[400] Peter Salway, 'Roman Britain', p. 669.
[401] Anne Ross, 'Pagan Celtic Britain', p. 65-6.
[402] Anne Ross, 'Pagan Celtic Britain', p. 66-7

NW of Athenry is Carn Cesra, tomb of Cesra, King Ugaine Mor's Queen, on the summit of Knock Magh Seola (*Sidhe Magh Seolgha*), overlooking Loch Corrib. The Celtic sea god, Mannanan Mac Lir (alias Oirbsiu), like Olc Aiche, was another Lord of the Otherworld. His Abode was under the waters of Loch Corrib (*Loch Oirbsen*, to which he gave his name), while his father, Lir, had his under those of Loughrea lake. In the absence of Mannanan Mac Lir, the god Fionbharr was allotted the care of *Sidhe Magh Seolgha* by the Dagda, the great god and ubiquitous lord of all the Otherworld abodes. *Sidhe ngChethelenn* (Dun Kellen) stood at the Iron Age sea port of Ath Clee Magh Rí at the mouth of the Dunkellin (*Dur/Dughiortach*) River just as Templum nEhelennia stood off Lyden at the mouth of the Old Rhine in Holland. *Sidh Finn* lies some 6 miles SE of the town. *Sidhe Finnachaidh* and *Sidhe Lir* are 4 and 5 miles S of the town. *Bruidhen Mac Ceacht Mac Da Reo*, a son of the god Ogma, the most famous hostel in Ireland, stood on Sliabh Fuirri (corrupt Sliabh Muire) in NE Galway. *Sidhe Ogma* stood on Sidhaun Hill 5 miles E of the town on the N height of Knockaboy (*Aircealtra*). Ogma (Continental Ogmios) was god of eloquence and literature and husband of Etain. Nearby is the tumulus of King Cormac Mac Art in *Cormach Uagh*. Ogma's sister Brigid had her Abode in nearby *Cealtra Brigde*. Bui (Boi), wife of Lug, sister of Brigid, had hers on nearby *Cnockboi*. Turoe holds the Otherworld Abodes of Lugh and Shile near the burial tumulus of Art Mac Con.

A further significant reference links Ochall and Cruachan to Sidh Buidbh (Boy Hill) which locates them at this Cruachan at Athenry of Galway, not at Rathcroghan of Roscommon: *"Ochaill a Cruachain chroeabaig...oc Sid Buidb"*.[403] This text anchors the true position of Rath Cruachain of Releg na Rí around the hill of Sidhe Boidb or Cruachan Boidb (Boy Hill) in the N of Ochaill Oichne, over-looking Athenry from the S. It is a chief segment of the Iron Age Necropolis of Sidhe Cruacha, a vast, much denuded, megalithic complex. From the NE of Athenry, E of Laragh Gate, an ancient cemetery avenue, *Boher Bhoidb* (corrupt 'Bothar Vov' or 'Wob'), veered off from the Escir Riada. "It was a popular and lovely walk early in the (20th) century."[404] It ran SE to Sidhe Buidbh, the *Relig na Rí lam le Cruachain*. It followed the Lady's Well/Rahard road route and swung S to Boy Hill (Cnoc Buidbh), site of the ancient necropolis,[405] bounded by rounded banks. Adjoining farms replaced these with walls and narrowed its original width. It now stands forlorn and forgotten (Figures 54, 55, 61).

The Athenry, Lady's well, Rahard road is built on the ancient *Bealach na Fert* (Tumulus avenue), formerly bounded by cairns and burial mounds. It is mentioned in the tale of Queen Medb's Chase of the Magic Boar. The *Dindsenchas Maigh Muc Dhruime* tells that the plain was called Magh Fraech before it was renamed Magh Muc Dhruim. The Athenry/Craughwell road running NS along the W side of *Slighe Bhrugh*, Mountain South, and Boy Hill is built on the ancient *Slighe Bhrugh* Necropolis Road after which the townland is named. Clochar na ngFhota (Palace of the Fotad vassals of Lughaid Mac Con from SE Scotland) kings stood in nearby Moyode (Magh Fot). A massive stone fort across the river from Lios na Gal (foreigners' fort) at the E side of Moyode adjoining Kilconierin was known as Cloghervaconierin (*Clocher Mhac Chon Erainn*), Palace of Lughaid Mac Conn who usurped the title Rí Temhro. Ailech Gorgin (Rathgorgin) was named after Gorgin/Corc who founded Cashel of Munster. Slieveroe (*Slighe Bhrugh*) adjoins Moyode and Mountain South. The name on the OS map shows it was misunderstood as 'Red Mountain'. The absence of a mountain should have alerted the experts to the significance of its archaic name, corroborating all the texts in ancient records referring to this area surroundding

---

[403] Book of Leinster, 155a, lines 20348 and 20350.

[404] Aggie Qualter, 'Athenry', p. 61. She knew Sidhe Bhoidb/Cnoc Boidb (Boy Hill) was referred to in the Book of Leinster, without being aware of its startling significance.

[405] *Cf*, the ancient poem *'Relig na Rí lam le Cruachan', Senchas na Relec*.

Athenry. A long-departed Patch Kennedy and others insisted that the OS toponymists recorded the incorrect form of the name. The original name was *Slighe Bhrugh*, not Slieve Rua (Red Mountain). Ancient burial cairns, denuded of their cairn fill, reveal the real significance of the name, *Slighe Bhrugh*. It corroborates the fact that this was part of Ireland's extensive Chief Iron Age Necropolis of Sidh Cruachain.

Local lore claims enormous quantities of stone stripped from numerous cairns, even from the stone circle round Queen Medb's tumulus, were carted off by poor peasants under the heel of the Norman Lords of Athenry to build townwalls, streets, castles, churches and town houses. Just to take the Dominican Friary of Athenry alone, its University buildings, Theological College and the Quarters of the English Bachelors of Theology (House of Scholars) run by it in the early days, enormous quantities of stone were required for its many very large buildings. The first Provincial Chapter was held in 1242. The Friary buildings alone accomodated 280 Friars at the Provincial Chapter in 1482 and 360 Friars at the Provincial Chapter in 1542, not counting the very large number of servants. A large herd of over 60 cows were required to keep it supplied with milk. The Friary's vast size (not to mention the other buildings) and importance is underlined in several Pontifical Briefs showing that it was held in very high esteem by several of the Popes in those centuries. The Bermingham Barons of Athenry were the great benefactors. One of their gifts included very many horses and carts for the drawing of enormous quantities of stone for the buildings.[406] The 'mere Irishry' were hired for a pittance to draw stone from the nearest supply bases which were the ancient cairn tumuli of Releg na Rí lamh le Cruachan. This explains why they were stripped of almost all their stone fill. Only kerbstones remain at ground level to show where the cairns once stood. Many were known to local farmers who broke plough-shares and damaged hay machines on protruding stones. They cleared many of the vestiges of satellite mounds in an effort to remove these obstacles. Only a few on the W side of the Boy Hill have any carn fill left to indicate what they originally were and silence the pseudo-historians. Now the vast archaeological site is more seriously endangered by 21st century civilization such as by the proposed N6 dual carriageway to be bulldozed through the core of Cruachan Thiar, Cruachan Theas and Cruachan Thoir (Mountain W, S and E) and the new housing it will bring in its wake, obliterating for ever Ireland's Chief Iron Age Necropolis. Who cared then? Who cares now?

Before finally relegating the early kings and queens of *"Relig na Rí lamh le Cruachan"* to their disturbed final resting place it is appropriate to see something of them in real life.

---

[406] These facts are culled from Ambrose Coleman's O.P. work based on manuscripts dating back to 1619.

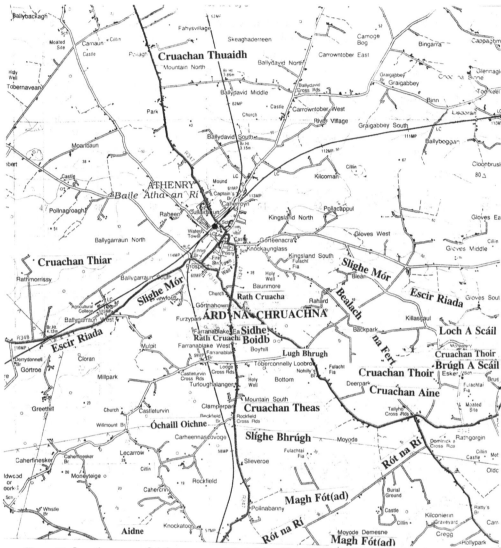

Figure 54   Location map of Athenry area (*Magh Muc Dhruim / Rath Cruachain / Ard Na Cruachna*). **Mountain North and South** (*Cruachan Thuaidh/Theas*) **stand some distance out from the town. Mountain East** (*Cruachan Thoir*) **covers the Esker, Brusk, Tallyho, Moyode, Deerpark, Backpark and Killascaul areas. Mountain West covers the Ballygarraun, Derrydonnell, Rathmorrissy and Pollnagroagh areas. The medieval Normans strategically built their walled town of Athenry within the inner ward embankments of this Iron Age Belgic oppidum core.**

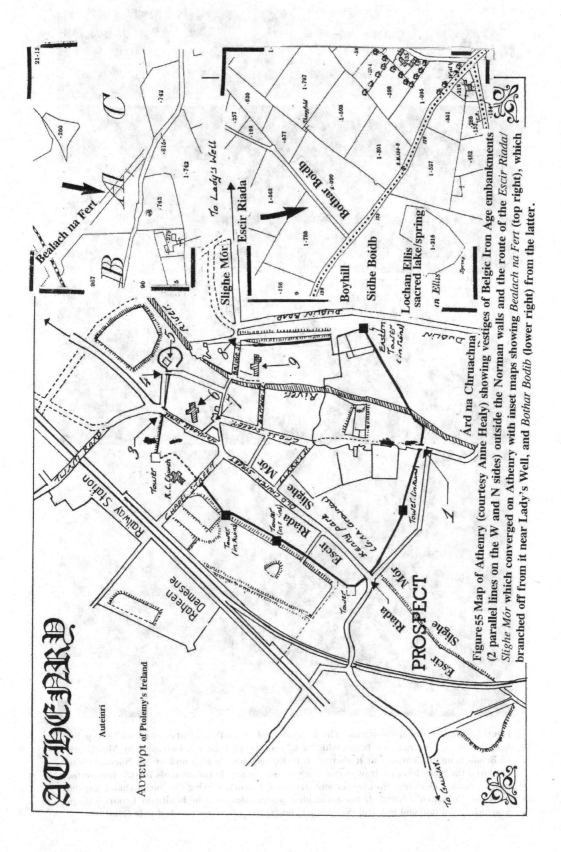

Figure 55 Map of Athenry (courtesy Anne Healy) showing vestiges of Belgic Iron Age embankments (2 parallel lines on the W and N sides) outside the Norman walls and the route of the *Escir Riada/ Slighe Mór* which converged on Athenry with inset maps showing *Bealach na Fert* (top right), which branched off from it near Lady's Well, and *Bothar Bodib* (lower right) from the latter.

Figure 56 Abomination of Desolation! The destruction of Ireland's ancient chief Royal Necropolis, *Releg na Rí lamh le Cruachan*, began with the 8th century Vikings, was continued by Muirghius, Ui Briuin King of Connacht at Rathcroghan in Roscommon, in 802, and by the Normans who employed the mere Irish to draw stones from its many cairn burial mounds for the townwalls, towers, castles, churches, townhouses and streets of Athenry, leaving the burial chambers, the 'caves of Cruachan', denuded. Some chamber portal stone remain in situ in Loobroo (*Lugh Brugh*; 2nd from top) and Boy Hill (*Sidhe Boidh*; lower) but others are knocked over (centre).

Figure 57: Example of Kerb stones around some stone fill of stripped-down cairns in the Lugh Bhrugh (top), Moyode (centre) and Boyhill areas (2nd from top and lower) of Athenry's ancient sprawling Releg na Ri cemetery complex.

Figure **58** Boy Hill (*Cnoc Boidbh, Sidhe Boidbh*) just SE of Athenry is named after Bodbh, son of the Dagda, King of the gods and goddesses of Pagan Ireland. In Dindshenchas texts it is equated with Sidhe Cruachain, Sidhe Connacht, Sidhe nOchaill (the district S of Athenry), and *Relig na Ri lamh le Cruachain*, Ireland's archaic Cemetery of the Kings. Vestiges of cairn tumuli dot the plain around Boy Hill, extending into adjoining townlands. The curb of their kerbstones indicate their original size.

Figure.59:Burial sites: Lugh Bhrugh on Turoe (top); its stepped escarpment (2nd from top); Cormac Mac Art's tumulus in Tample cemetery between Cormacuagh (Cormac's tomb) and Knockaboy (3rd from top); Cairn Dearmait (Carntarramud, Newcastle; 4th from top), the tomb of Dermot Mac Morna, leader of the Fianna; Queen Medb's tumulus (*Fert Medba* surrounded by a ring of bush-covered large stones; lower) near Athenry, before it was desecrated and turned into a dump site.

Figure 60 Echoes of the severed heads of early Irish myth and of a pagan past above the portal of the Romanesque jewel of Clonfert Cathedral Clonfert, Co. Galway (taken from 'Exploring the World of the Celts' by Simon James, p. 179). It was not alone. Such reminders of the pagan past are common occurrences.

Tiny head trophies surround a central solar boss in this horse trapping from Manerbia sul Mella, taken from 'Celtic Mysteries' by John Sharkey, Figure 34.

Shrines of the triad of mother goddesses expose the high respect and belief in these in the Celtic cults: altar shrine to Matronae Aufaniae in Cologne area of Germany (lower) and a shrine of the triple mother goddesses at a spring well from High Rochester fort in Northumberland, England (centre; from 'Exploring the World of the Celts' by Simon James p. 144). These cults were practiced at Releg Na Rí lamh le Cruacha at Athenry and in many other places in Ireland.

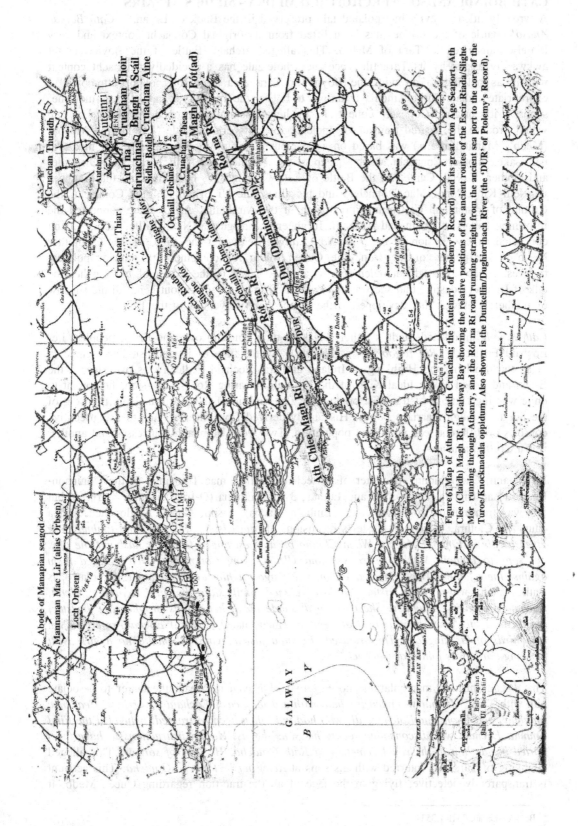

Figure 61 Map of Athenry (Rath Cruachan; the 'Auteinri' of Ptolemy's Record) and its great Iron Age Seaport, Ath Clee (Claidh) Magh Rí, in Galway Bay showing the relative positions of the ancient routes of the Escir Riada/Slighe Mór running through Athenry, and the Rót na Rí road running straight from the ancient sea port to the core of the Turoe/Knocknadala oppidum. Also shown is the Dunkellin/Dughiorthach River (the 'DUR' of Ptolemy's Record).

CATH BOINDI ANDSO - FERCHUITRED MEDBA - MEDB'S AFFAIRS

A wrongly titled, heavily interpolated tale preserved in the Book of Lecan,[407] *'Cath Boinde Andso'* (Battle of the Boyne) has been lifted from its original Connacht context and very loosely transferred to Tara of Meath. This alleged archaic 'Battle of the Boyne' is set awkwardly askew by its Tara tilt since the whole tale has a decidedly Connacht context which has nothing to do with the Boyne or Tara area. The interpolator attempted to expropriate archaic Turoe/Athenry traditions to bolster the Tara Myth and, at the same time, suppress it's original Connacht conext. Its medieval manipulator hoped the change of title would procure the desired transfer of ancient glory. Its original title 'Ferchuitred Medba' (Medb's Marrital affairs) was based on a salacious attack on the character of her medieval namesake, another Connacht Medb, queen of the Northern Ui Neill King, Aed Oirdnide, and mother of Niall Caille. At the Battle of Leth Cam in 827, Niall defeated the Southern Ui Neill King Conor Mac Donnchad and his allies, the Ui Briuin King of Connacht, the Cruthin of Ulster and Ui Cremthainn branch of the Airghialla. All of these supported the reforming abbots of Louth and Armagh. In anger and disgust at Niall Caille, Abbot Cuanu concocted a new version of the *Táin Bó Cuailgne* degrading the name of Niall's mother Medb in the person of the Iron Age Queen Medb for contemporary ulterior political motives. Medb's marital entanglements were embellished to the extent of making her the talk of Ireland, boasting that she was never married to one man without being in the shadow of another. This was later developed further in the Leinster version of the Táin.

Cath Boinde introduced Medb's father: "A king took kingship over the Erann peoples, i.e. Eochaid Fedlech" *('Rig rogob rigi for Erind')*. By the time of its recension this came to mean that Eochaid was Highking of Ireland at Tara. Eochaid Fedlech was overking of the Erann and hailed as the Ideal King of the Fir Belg. Fearing Roman invasion, he sought to unite warring factions of the Irish population, the Cruthin of the North and the Fir Belg of the South, through marriage bonds. His family derived from his marriage to 3 consecutive consorts of different sections of the population. Two were Domnann princesses and another was a Cruthin princess.

By Cloann (Cloithfhionn), daughter of Airtech Uchtlethan mac Tomanten of the Domnann, Eochaid had triplets, Breas, Nar and Lothar, 3 Find Emhna (O-Irish *emhain* = triplet, but this was transmutated to link them to Emhain Macha), a son, Conall Anglondach, and a daughter, Clothra. "*Within (*Leinster's recensions of*) the Ulster Cycle the Find Emhna were given a role at Emhain Macha. When Cloann became estranged from her husband she took her sons to Emhain Macha where she and Ulster's king Conor Mac Neasa urged them against their father. They mounted an offensive against him at Cruachan* (interpolated as Rathcroghan) *where their sister Clothra reigned until slain by her stepsister Medb, Eochaid's youngest daughter. She tried to dissuade them, her druids prophesying disaster, but to no avail. When they arrived at Temhair* (interpolated as Tara) *Eochaid offered them two thirds of his kingdom. They refused. Eochaid fasted against them (to no avail). Next morning battle was joined at Cummer*"

This *P*seudo-historic manipulation chose Comar of Navan in Meath the better to associate him with Tara.[408] *Lothar wounded Eochaid with a deadly cast. Eochaid's warriors, Ceat mac Maghach and Raon mac Roicheadail, who had until then been restrained, beheaded the Find Emhna. Eochaid was disconsolate seeing his sons' heads. He left instructions to have them buried beside him at the royal cemetery of Rath Cruacha. He died of sorrow.* This alleged Highking of Tara was interred with his sons at *Releg na Rí lamh le Cruacha*. This account is transparently defective, flying in the face of all the tradition regarding Queen Medb. It

---

[407] Book of Lecan, 351b - 353a
[408] Daithi O hOgain, 'An Encyclopaedie of the Irish Folk Tradition', p. 211

alleged that Eochaid was slain during Clothra's reign as Connacht's Queen whereas in the tradition of Medb, who succeeded Clothra as Queen of Connacht, Medb was installed in that office by her father Eochaid who lived into her reign as other tales admit. A variant version claims the Find Emhna fell much later at the hand of their father when, on the side of the Ulstermen, they opposed him at the Battle of Druim Criad (Drumcree, Westmeath) for territorial control between the Ulster Cruthin and Fir Belg of Connacht, a war the latter won. The triple imagery of the Find lore was extended in the fictitious claim that the Find triplets fathered Lughaid Reoderg on their sister Clothra. 'Serglige Conculainn' alleged he became High King of Tara, a claim Leinster pseudo-historians loved, making him High King in succession to Eochaid. Variant traditions contravene this, stating that Cairbre Cennderg and Conaire Mor succeeded Eochaid. What O Rahilly labeled as an interpolation in 'Serglige Conculainn', represented Lughaid Reoderg growing up in Ulster's Capital Emain Macha with his tutor Cuchulainn at the time of his election to the High Kingship of Tara,[409] placing powerful leverage in the hands of the pseudo-historians by lingking his grandfather Eochaid and aunt, Medb, to Tara. Eochaid's other son by Cloann, Conall, became ancestor of the Conailli of Louth. Cormac Conloingeas is variously given as son of this same Clothra by Conor Mac Nessa.

The earliest tradition represents Clothra as Queen, not of Rathcroghan, but of Ól nÉgmacht residing with her consort Cairbre on their royal crannog on Loughrea Lake in Galway. This lake was heavily barricaded by sets of dykes, vestiges of which survive to this day. Rath-croghan of Roscommon was never part of Ól nÉgmacht. Rath Cruacha of Athenry was yet to be founded by Eochaid Ferach. Cairbre and Clothra were regents of this embryo of ancient Connacht until slain by the Ruadchoin of the Mairtine of Munster.[410] In other versions Cairbre appears as an elder brother of Cett and Ailill mac Magach while the latter was a defender of Loughrea Lake. When Eochaid Ferach extended Ól nÉgmacht to include Cruthin-held Athenry he founded Rath Cruacha with the aid of Tinni Mac Conrac and his Domnann vassals. Tinni was made King of Ol nEgmacht until Eochaid replaced him with his daughter Medb.

After Cloann's estrangement, Eochaid married her sister, Onga, by whom he had two daughters, Mumain Etanchaithrech (Etain) and Eithne. Mumain was married off to Conor Mac Nessa, by whom she had a son Glaisne who became King of the Cruthintuatha at Rathcroghan of Roscommon and later Overking of Ulster. Her sister Eitne had earlier been married to Conor in settlement for her father's slaying of the Ulster King Fachtna, father of Conor Mac Nessa. By Conor she had a son Diarmaid, called Furbaide. He was born by caesarean section (furbad) from the womb of his mother who drowned as her child was due to be born, in the Inny (Ethni) River, so named after her on the Westmeath/Longford boundary. Intriguing evidence that caesarian section was practised in ancient Ireland! Eile, another daughter of Eochaid by his first wife, married Fergal Mac Magach whose royal seat was Croghan Hill near Birr in the kingdom of Eile (embracing Offaly and Tipperary as far south as Cashel). Later she married Sraibgend Mac Niuil whose son, Mata, was father of Ailill who much later became consort of her much younger half-sister Medb. Ailill was Medb's consort at the time of the Táin Bó Cuailgne.

Conor Mac Nessa was Medb's first husband. Through pride of mind the quick-tempered Medb forsook Conor before giving birth to his son, Amalghad. She spat out the words "Who can stand that man!" as she stormed home to her father's palace, Rath Ferach Mhor, on Turoe of Galway. Leinster pseudo-historians transferred Eochaid and Medb to Tara of Meath. This medieval Myth is perpetuated by authors who turn history back to front, such

---

[409] T F O Rahilly, 'Early Irish History and Mythology' p.487. IT i, 213.
[410] Ibid, p. 144; R.C. xii , 448; ZCP xvii, 145.

as O Rahilly: "Cairbre Cennderg may in origin be Cairbre Nia Fer artificially shifted from Tara to Cruachan, like Medb and Ailill." Daithi O hOgain concurred, claiming that Medb "is said to have been reared at Tara, and there is little doubt but that Medb of Tara and Medb of Cruachan were one and the same personage."[411] Tradition tells that Medb's father resided at Rath Ferach Mhor beside the original site of the Turoe Stone on Temhair (Turoe). The Medb of Turoe (Temhair) and Medb of Cruachan (Rath Cruacha of Athenry) was one and the same person. Once Medb was expropriated from Turoe by minters of the Tara Myth her role was transmutated by Leinster pseudo-historians into that of her namesake, Meadhbh Lethdherg, the Tara goddess of sovereignty. She is represented in this role as a personification of sovereignty, having numerous royal husbands, "for she would not allow any king in Tara unless he had her as Queen." So Medb was made queen of a suitable number of kings. Leinster pseudo-genealogists converted her consort, Ailill, into a brother of Finn, alleged contemporary king of Leinster. This association of a Leinster Ailill and Medb with Tara was a powerful weapon in their claim that Tara belonged to Leinster from time immemorial, the Leinster version of the Tara Myth.

Conor mac Neasa was not Medb's choice of husband. It resulted from a debt incurred by her father, Eochaid Ferach. It was by his hand that Conor's father, Fachtna Fathach, King of Ulster, was slain at the Battle of Corann. "It was as his *eric* (peace debt) that his daughters were given to Conor together with the forcible seizure of the kingship of Ulster over Clan Rudraidhe. Conor Mac Nessa cheated Fergus Mac Roi of the Clann Rudraige out of the Kingship of Ulster. The first cause of the stirring up of the Cattle-raid of Cuailgne *(Táin Bó Cuailgne)* was the desertion of Conor by Medb."[412] The Corann where Fachtna was slain was thought to be Corann of Sligo by the editor of the tale.[413] Since Corann of N Connacht was still well within the Cruthintuatha kingdom centered on Rathcroghan of Roscommon at that time, it is probable that the Ulster King was slain at one of the N Galway Coranns. These were still part of the Cruthin kingdom at this early period of the Fir Belg conquest of Cruthin lands in Connacht until they were brought into Ol nEgmacht by Eochaid Ferach. Medb's father contracted Tinni mac Conrach, king of his Fir Domnann vassals, to raise up the Fir Belg defensive ramparts surrounding Rath Cruacha of Athenry.

In return for his subject's military service in that battle and for promptly erecting the earthen ramparts, Tindi (Tinni) son of Conra Cas of the Fir Domnand was rewarded with the Kingship of this Fir Belg kingdom centered on Rath Cruacha of Athenry. Eochaid Dala and Fidig Mac Feicc of the Gamanrad lay claim to its kingship. Fidig went to Temhroid (Turoe) to win the kingship for himself. He asked for the hand of Medb in marriage. Tinni was furious and lay in ambush. The interpolator made them meet across the Shannon, insinuating that Eochaid reigned as High King of Ireland at Tara. Tara was then a minor stronghold of the Cruthin of Ulster. Fedheilm, daughter of Conor mac Neasa, reigned as Queen of Tara. Eochaid's Temhair was Turoe of Galway. All the action of this wrongly titled *Cath Boinde* took place in Connacht. The sons of Conra and Monodar, Conra's son, slew Fidig. This resulted in war between the children of Conra (Domnainn) and the Gamanrad. So Eochaid Ferach demoted Tinni and placed his own daughter Medb on the throne of nÓl nÉgmacht at Rath Cruacha of Athenry. Before then the seat of the Fir Belg kings of Ól nÉgmacht was on a royal crannog on Loughrea Lake at the centre of Maen Magh (Magh Main). Eochaid Ferach set up his residence as Overking of the Fir Belg of Connacht and Munster beside the original site of the Lia Fail, Turoe Stone, at Rath Ferach Mhor (Ferach was his real name, Mor his royal title) on Turoe. Tinni bided his time at Caher Tinni, two miles SW of Turoe. Eochaid designated Rath Cruacha of Athenry as the new seat of the Kingship of Ól

---

[411] Dr. Daithi O hOgain, 'An Encyclopaedia of The Irish Folk Tradition', p. 293.

[412] ''Cath Boindi Andso', ed. by J O'Neill, p.2.

[413] Joseph O''Neill, *Cath Boinde;* note on Corran.

nÉgmacht. It so happened that Tinni was a surreptitious visitor with Medb for a long time after that. Thereby lies another intriguing tale.

CONTEXT OF FEIS TEMHRO AND OENACH CRUACHA

"It was at Rath Cruacha with Medb that the fairs of Ireland (Oenach Cruacha) were wont to be held. Sons of kings came to Rath Cruacha to Medb to see if they might exchange war with the Northern Cruthin. Amongst those who came were Sraibhgend mac Niull and his son Mata to see if they could make war on Conor Mac Nessa for all the ill feeling between him and Medb and so win swordland for themselves. 'Feis Temhro' (Festival of Turoe) was held by Eochaid Felech, with the provinces of Ireland about him, all but Medb and Tinni. They bade Eochaid bring Medb to the Festival. Eochaid sent his female messenger, Searbhluath, to Rath Cruacha for Medb. Early on the morrow Medb came to Temhroid (Turoe). The Feis Temhro began and progressed for a fortnight and a month."[414]

Pseudo-history gave a different impossible geo-political context to the Temhroid and Cruacha of this tale from what it originally had. In the pseudo-context Temhair is Tara and Cruacha is Croghan of Roscommon. Obviously in 1st century Ireland it would have been impossible even for a male messenger to travel the distance of over 200 miles (roundtrip) between Tara of Meath and Rathcroghan of Roscommon in a day and for Queen Medb to arrive at Tara from Croghan 'on the morning of the morrow' (*'arna marach'*) as the tale specifies. She needed time to doll herself up for such an occasion and choose her regalia and a change of regal attire for a month of public festive exposure in the presence of the royalty of Ireland. She would show up at her stunning best as the *piece de resistance* of the Fair to pique the pomposity of her forsaken consort, Conor Mac Nessa, who was inevitably invited, being so closely related to her father and family. No king would send a female messenger on such a long, hazardous journey through enemy territory. Only in the original context of Turoe and Rath Cruacha of Galway, a mere 6 miles apart, the capitals of the Fir Belg oppida in W Ireland, could the exigencies of this text be met and make perfect sense. The interpolator left these details unaltered to his own unmasking.

When Feis Temhro had run its course it disolved in a disturbing episode: *"the men of Ireland dispersed, all except Conor Mac Nessa. He stayed on after the others at the winding down of the festivities, his heart aflutter, his eyes locked on stunning Medb. As she went to the river to bathe* (the recensionist interpolated *'in abhaind'* to *'ind Bhoind'*, the Boyne River to transport the context to Tara with a stroke of the pen) *Conor accosted and violated her. When this scandal broke across the Iron Age landscape the kings of Ireland (of the Erann/Fir Belg) assembled in Temhair against Conor, spearheaded by Tinni Mac Conrach and Eochaid Dala. The banners of King Eochaid Fedlech were raised to redress the infamy. Festivities foundered on fury.*

Cath Boindi claimed "Conor Mac Nessa won the battle of the Boyne over Eochaid Fedlech." It thus tried to link the episode to the Tara/Boyne district despite the fact that all persons, peoples and places mentioned, apart from Conor, Sraibhgend and Mata, and the interpolated 'Boyne', belong exclusively to Connacht and warrant a Connacht, not a Tara, context. The fact that Conor Mac Nessa's daughter Feidhelm reigned at Tara is suppressed in favour of Eochaid Fedlech, whose royal seat was Turoe. Eochaid was ancestor of the Ui Neill whose pseudo-historians attempted to push the late tendentious Ui Neill tenancy of Tara further back in time. That the kings rose up from Temhair (interpolated to Tara) to attack Conor, represented as an odious outsider, is a contradiction of the geo-politics of Iron Age Ireland. Conor was at home in Tara. It was part of his Ulster kingdom. His daughter

---

[414] *'Cath Boinde Andso'*, ed. by J O'Neill.

Feidhelm reigned there, succeeded by her son Erc. Only in Turoe of Galway, not Tara of Meath, can this tale find its true context.

Having stated that Sraibhgend and his son Mata fell sustaining the battle, the interpolator concocted a shameful retreat from the Tara/Boyne district by Medb and the Connachta. "Eochaid Dala took up the yoke of battle across Meath, over the Shannon, and brought Medb and Connacht safe by dint of fighting, so that he was not dared from the Boyne to the Shannon." Were Eochaid, Medb's father, really King of Ireland at Tara of Meath, his daughter Medb whom he placed on the throne of Connacht would not have had to suffer such an ignominious retreat from Tara. This awkward rescension has all the hallmarks of interpolation for the purpose of lifting a Connacht episode out of its original context and expropriating it for Tara's glory. It recoils on the Tara Myth and the interpolator's head.

The editors of *'Cath Boinde'* recognized as false the placing of this episode in the Tara/Boyne context. The hand of the interpolator is all too obvious. Before being manipulated to boost the Tara Myth, the episode was located at Turoe of Galway. It shows how far pseudo-historians were prepared to go to glorify the alleged Tara High Kingship. O Rahilly considered the placing of Medb on the throne of Connacht as "the Goidelic conquest of Connacht" by the Gaels of Tara. *"According to 'Cath Boinne', Eochaid Fedlech, king of Tara, banished Tinni, the Domnonian king of Connacht, from Cruachan into the wilds of the province before bestowing the kingdom on his own daughter, Medb. This is apparently based on a popular memory of the Goidelic conquest of Connacht. The Domnainn, driven into the wilds of Connacht suffered the same fate as they themselves had meted out to the Fir Belg a few centuries earlier."*[415] O Rahilly is guilty of numerous errors here, the most blatant being his failure to recognize that 'a few centuries earlier' the Fir Belg/Belgae had not yet crossed the Rhine westwards into Belgic lands in the NW of the Continent, let alone have set foot in Ireland. Equally erroneous was his obsession with his "popular memory of the Goidelic conquest of Connacht," a gross misconception. He saw the Gaels and Fir Belg as two different people, the one expelling the other. In fact the Irish Fir Belg were the Gaels and the Celts who invaded 1st century BC Ireland. The Connacht context resurfaces after the attempt to locate the action in the Boyne/Tara area. The Fir Domnann of W Mayo and N Galway (Tulcha Domnainn, Dunmor, was one of their strong-holds) were in the front line of the Fir Belg expansion into Carra, Erris and Tirawley in Mayo, Tireragh in Sligo, and temporarily in the Airtech (Frenchpark) area of Roscommon. The Fir Domnann, Dal n-Dhruithni of SE Galway, and Fir Chraibi (from the mouth of the Shannon up to and including Magh Muc Dhruim of Athenry, were 3 divisions of the Fir Belg Kingdom of Ól nÉgmacht (early Connacht). Each had their local king. Most of the north of Connacht was still firmly in the hands of the aboriginal Cruthintuatha peoples of the North of Ireland.

Cath Boinde tells that when the kings came to Rath Cruacha, Queen Medb stated that the peoples of the 3 divisions of Ól nÉgmacht (archaic Connacht) were all Fir Belg tribes. O Rahilly, without support, consistently claimed erroneously that the Fir Domnann were a Laignian tribe who conquered the Connacht Fir Belg. Medb and later kings employed Laignian tribes, such as the Galioin, as mercenary vassals. They never conquered Connacht. In *'Cath Boinde'* she declares: "For though they were three tribes through division, they were one tribe by origin, ie., the followers of Genand Mac Dela of the Fir Belg." Gann, Sengann, Dela and his son Genand were the leaders of the Fir Belg invasions of W Ireland. Ptolemy located the Gangani, Gann's descendants, along the Shannon estuary. Dela carried this Fir Belg invasion north and set up his throne on Knocknadala in Galway. He staged his Feis Temhro on Cnoc Temhro. In archaic texts his kingdom is variously named *Coiced Gann, Coiced Sengann, Coiced Genand, Coiced nÓl nÉgmacht* and *Coiced Medba.*

---

[415] T. F. O Rahilly, 'Early Irish History and Mythology', p.96. Eriu, ii, 178.

Gann's 'son', Verica (Ferach Mhor), brought Domnovellaunus, Umhor (*Iuvor*) and their followers with him when they fled from the Belgic areas of SE Britain. Domno's followers, the Fir Domnann, and Iuvor (Umhor)'s, the Mac Umhoir, formed interspersed buffer states up along the W Connacht coast and N boundary of the expanding Fir Belg oppidum of Ól nÉgmacht. Umhor (Iuvor) set up his own stronghold at Dun Iubhoir (Umhoir) on Achill Island while his sons set up thiers at strongpoints from the Aran Isles to the NW tip of Mayo. Aengus Mac Umhoir had his stronghold, Dun Aengus, on Aran Mor. Mod Mac Umhoir had his at Dun Mod Mac Umhor in Belmullet on the NW Mayo coast. "Seven sons of the majestic Iuvor"(Umhor) and his daughter Umna were at Dun Iuvor on Achill when Queen Medb led her forces to Dun Flidais in Erris.[416] The Domnainn were settled mostly in NW Mayo, W of Killalla Bay and in Erris (*Irrus Domnann*). According to *Táin Bó Flidais* the Gamanrad of Irrus Domnann were celebrated as one of the three warrior-races of Ireland and held a string of buffer states from "Drobhais (Drowes River on the Sligo/Donegal boundary) to Boirinn (Burren in NW Clare)". The Fir Belg Overking Eochaid Fedlech contracted the Fir Domnann king, Tinni Mac Conrach and his people to expand N from the then Turoe/Knocknadala oppidum enclave against the Cruthin and erect the inner-ward linear embankments of Rath Cruacha of Athenry. For the speed with which he carried out the work, Eochaid made him the first Connacht king to rule over Rath Cruacha, only to demote him later in favour of his own daughter, Medb.

'*Cath Boinde*' is primarily concerned with the election of a new Connacht Fir Belg King which should be conducted at its Fir Belg strongholds, Cnoc Temhro or Rath Cruacha of Galway, not at Tara of Meath. The council appointed Eochaid Dala to the kingship of Connacht with the consent of Medb on condition he would be her consort. Eochaid Dala was crowned king but stayed only a very short time at Rath Cruacha with Medb. She was too overbearing for his liking. He took up his residence at Knocknadala which gave him his sobriquet "Dála". At that time Ailill mac Mata mac Sraibgend of the Fir Belg of Eli came to Cruacha as a youth with the sons of Sraibgend to be fostered by Medb because of their kinship. Ele (Medb's stepsister), daughter of Eochaid by an earlier marriage, was his grandmother. Ailill grew up in Rath Cruacha into a high-spirited warrior, a battle-sustaining tower against Conor Mac Nessa. He was made chief of Medb's household and a caretaker of Loughrea's sacred lake on which Medb, like her sister Clothra, had a royal crannog. When pseudo-history much later expropriated Medb as alleged Queen of Rathcroghan of Roscommon, suppressing the fact that Glaisni Mac Conor Mac Nessa was king of the Cruthintuatha Croghain then, the site of her royal crannog was fictitiously transferred to Loch Ree on the Shannon. It camoflagued the fact that Medb could not have resided in this enemy territory. Medb loved Ailill for his many virtues. It evolved that Ailill replaced Eochaid Dala as her lover. Eochaid Dala grew jealous. So did the Fir Domnann because of their affection for him. They tried to banish Ailill and the Erna of Ele from Connacht. Medb forbade it, for she loved Ailill better than Eochaid Dala. Eochaid, seeing Medb's partiality was constrained to challenge Ailill to a duel for kingdom and consort. Eochaid fell by Ailill Mac Mata through the intrigues of Medb. Ailill assumed the kingship as Medb's consort. He was king of Connacht when Conaire Mor succeeded Medb's father as Overking of the Fir Belg tribes at the initiation of the cattle-raids against Ulster. Medb bore 7 Maine sons to Ailill. Their names were Feidlimid Aithreamail, Cairpri Maithreamail, Eochaid Andaoi, Fergus Tai, Ceat Morgor, Sin Milscothach, and Daire Mo-epert.

At the *Oenach Cluichemnuigh* (War-Game Festival) called to prepare for a counter-battle from Conor Mac Nessa which soon took place at Finn Chorad (Corrofin) in N Galway along the outer-ward embankments of the oppidum. Medb asked her Druid: "By which of my sons shall Conor fall?" He replied, "You have not given birth to him yet, unless your sons be

---

[416] T. J. Westropp, "Notes on the 'Táin Bó Flidais'in RSAI, 1912, p.154

renamed." "Why so?" asked Medb. "It is by Maine that Conor shall fall!" said the Druid. Medb then renamed all her sons Maine in the hope that Conor might fall by one of them. Medb thought the Druid meant Conor (Mac Nessa), son of Fachtna Fathach, Cruthin king of Ulster. However it was not he, but a Conor Mac Arthur Mac Bruidi Mac Dungaili, the son of the Cruthin King of Scotland who fell there by Maine Andaoi, the son of Ailill and Medb. Conor mac Nessa was slain by the great warrior Cet mac Magach. Thus ends the ill-titled *'Cath Boindi'*.

Cath Boinde tells that the Picts of Scotland marched with Conor Mac Nessa's Cruthin army. The Conor slain by Maine Andaoi was a grandson of Bruide Mac Dungali. Bruide was honorary title of Cruthin kings of Scotland and Ireland. As recorded in the Annals of the Picts, 30 kings named Bruide ruled the Cruthin of Scotland and Ireland jointly. They marched into battle together when the seriousness of occasion so demanded. The Cruthin of Ulster joined the Cruthin of Scotland in their frequent hit and run raids against the Belgae and Romans of S Britain as recorded in Roman records. That they marched with Conor in this attack on the stronghold of Medb shows that this was a desperate attempt by Conor to take revenge on Medb for her wars against his great Ulster Kingdom.

In one Fir Belg expansion against the Cruthin, with the Fir Domnann in the front line, the territory of Airtech (Frenchpark) NW of Croghan of Roscommon was overrun. At the fierce Battle of Airtech the Cruthin of Ulster and Connacht retook their territory with a great slaughter of the Fir Domnann who were driven into the wilds of W Mayo. The Ulstermen were ready to fight to the death to save Rathcroghan of Roscommon, seat of their ancestral Connacht territories. Far from it being the seat of the Fir Belg Queen Medb, part of the Rathcroghan district held by the Fir Belg was forcibly surrendered, after a hotly disputed tenancy, by none other than Medb herself to her great enemy Conor Mac Nessa as part of the agreement to bring about a peaceful settlement to the destructive 7-years war with Ulster. It will be examined in detail in analyzing the implications of *Cath Artig*.

IMPLICATIONS OF 'BRUIDHEN DA CHOCAE'

Fergus Mac Roigh (Roy) was deprived of the Overkingship of Ulster by a trick. Conor Mac Nessa then became Overking of Ulster. When Conor treacherously killed the sons of Uisnech, Fergus his predecessor, and Conor's own son Cormac, with their fighting men, migrated in anger to Connacht where they were hospitably received by Cormac's aunt, Queen Medb, and her consort Ailill. They were involved in Connacht's wars against Conor Mac Nessa. A passage in *'Cogad Fergusa & Conchobair'* (War between Fergus and Conor) tells of a war of revenge for a raid on Louth by Fergus and his forces allied to the Connachta and the *Rí Temhro* (Overking of Turoe of Galway, interpolated as Tara by pseudo-history), Eochaid Ferach. The exiled Ulstermen ravaged the W of Meath, Tailten (Lough Crew of NW Meath, Uisnech (Barony of Rathconrath in Westmeath), South Teffia (Westmeath SW of Lough Sheelin), River Inny ('Eithne', running SE from Loch Kinale to Loch Derravaragh, a boundary of ancient Ulster), then along the Boyne River to Tara and thence homewards. The above-named territories, including Tara, belonged to the Cruthin of Ulster at this time. Here was an attempt by the pseudo-historians to make it appear that the Tara district was in the possession of Eochaid Ferach who, it insinuated, was King of Tara. Several early tales corroborate this story of bands of Connachtmen invading these same Ulster territories precisely at this time.

After Conor Mac Nessa's death, the Ulstermen held council to choose a king. Some wanted their former king, Fergus Mac Roy. Others said they had suffered great evil from Fergus while in exile in Connacht and would not have him as king. Others said it should be Cormac Conloinges (so-called because he brought his warrior-bands into Connacht), son of Conor Mac Nessa, who was best fitted to rule over them. Conall Cernach sought the kingship for his fosterling, Cuscraide, another son of Conor. Bitter was the dispute. Ulstermen prepared to fight each other. Cuscraid refused to fight for the crown on the grounds that the Cruthin clans would mutually fall. Then Genann Mac Cathbad spoke up: "I know the makings of a king, Cormac Conloinges son of Conor. He is endowed with all the gifts of shape and valour, hospitality and truth. 'Tis to him, moreover, that Conor on the point of death commanded the kingship be given, for Cormac was his eldest son. He is the bosom-fosterling of Fergus who, note, never plundered us when he was with Cormac." Ulstermen united in agreement at this word of Genann and resolved to make Cormac their king. Great Ulster excitement grew apace.

Envoys were sent to solicit Cormac's return to Ulster. As the interpolated *'Bruidhen Da Choca'* tells it, "The charioteers fared forth till they were in Croghan Ai. Ailill, Medb and Fergus made them welcome." As seen above, Croghan of Roscommon belonged to the Cruthin of Ulster. Archaic texts speak of the *'Cruithentuatha Cruachain'*, the Cruthin clans of Rathcroghan of Roscommon. The Rath Cruacha of Queen Medb, was the Rath Cruacha of Galway. Only in this context could they find tidings of Cormac, unless Fergus and Cormac were not with Medb at all, but with their own kinsmen, the Cruthintuatha of Rathcroghan of Roscommon then ruled by Glaisni, son of Conor Mac Nessa. When they announced that they had come for Cormac to make him king to succeed his father they learnt that he was away hunting at Sid Nenta south of Loughrea lake on the foothills of the Achta Mountains. There was another Sid Nenta NE of Lough Ree on the Shannon, near Lanesborough in Longford, 10 miles NE of the Croghan of Roscommon. Pseudo-history claimed Cormac was hunting at the latter despite the fact that this was within Ulster's territory from which he deliberately exiled himself. A messenger was sent for Cormac. He came to Rath Cruacha. Medb pleaded for peaceful coexistence with the new king of Ulster on account of the hospitality he had received when he came to her as an estranged exile from Ulster. He promised: "It will be a pleasure for us to grant it to thee." He sent messengers to his bands of fighting men billetted on the Connachtmen. They came quickly from Irrus Domnann (Erris of Mayo in the land of the Fir Domnann) and outlying districts of Connacht. Irrus Domnann belonged to the Turoe/Knocknadala oppidum, not to Cruthin held Rathcroghan. Cormac set forth from Rath Cruacha with his 300 warriors, their families and hounds and servants, decked in purple and gold.

Cormac's return journey is elevated in an Exodus-like event to the dramatic heights of Greek tragedy foredoomed with calamity. As he left Rath Cruacha the druids uttered fore-boding ill omens that Cormac's journey would be slow and perilous. Craiphtine the harper vowed revenge because his wife, Scenb, daughter of Scethern, the wizard of the Connacht, had been Cormac's paramour during his stay. Cormac unwittingly violated his tabus one after the other, one of which was that he should not visit Da Choca's Hostel (Breenmore in Westmeath). Besides, he broke his peace covenant with Medb. Hence, Cormac was assassinated by Connachtmen at Da Choca's Hostel, 6 miles NE of Athlone, an area E of the Shannon captured by Connacht from the Cruthin of Ulster. It ends with a lament by Fergus, who had been hindered, by Medb's allurements, from marching with Cormac.

What has historic implications for the political geography of Iron Age Ireland is Cormac's baffling itinerary. Like that of Queen Medb in the early *Táin Bó Cuailgne* Cormac is said to have set out, like Medb, from Croghan of Roscommon to journey to the Capital of Ulster, Emain Macha, near Armagh. Yet, instead of heading NE, taking the shortest and most direct route by crossing the upper Shannon in its Longford/Leitrim stretch, he, like Medb, inexplicably headed south to Athlone, dragging women and children in his train. This glaring quandary has never been solved. O Rahilly recognized the problem but had no solution: "(Cormac) urgently left Rathcroghan to return swiftly to the Ulster capital; yet unaccountably made a long round-about journey SE to Athlone to cross the Shannon."[417] As is steadily being clarified, if the Rath Cruacha of Medb were the Rath Cruacha of Athenry in Galway, the itinerary via Athlone would have been the most natural and direct one. An awkward pseudo-historic enigma solved! This is the one and only solution.

Moreover, at least two archaic placenames on the tale's itinerary are not on the route from Croghan of Roscommon to Athlone but on that from Rath Cruacha of Athenry to Athlone. First was a forest called *Fidh Cunga*. Near Bellafea (*Bél an Feadh*; 'mouth of the forest') 7 miles E of Athenry, was *Fidh Cunga (Cinga),* named after the Fir Belg leader, Cing Mac Umhor as told in the dindshenchas tales of Cairn Chonail (cf. p234). He resided at Rath Cinga on Rahally, overlooking the Slí Mhór highway at Bellafea. The pseudo-historian tried to change the name by claiming that when Cormac's chariot-yoke broke as he went through Fidh Cinga it was replaced by an ash yoke (*cunga*) and so was called Fid Cunga. It was called Fidh Cinga before that. Further along the route Cormac violated one of his tabus by pursuing the birds of Magh Da Cheo, later known as 'Loch na n-en' (Lake of the birds). This is the lake known as En-Loch on the river Suck near Ballinasloe, mentioned in early tales at the crossing point on the Suck. Had Cormac set out from Croghan of Roscommon he would have had to go way off course to cross the Suck at Ballinasloe. Had he set out from Rath Cruacha of Athenry, these two places were on his direct route to Athlone.

As Cormac unyoked his chariot at Druim Airthir (Garman) on the brink of Athlone a red-haired woman was washing a chariot, cushions and harness at the edge of the ford. When she lowered her hand into the water the river became red with gory blood. Ominous! "Horrible is what that woman does." said Cormac. "Ask what she is doing!" One of his men went and asked. Standing on one foot with one eye closed, the Badb Catha chanted: *'I wash the harness of a king who will perish" etc*. The messenger brought back the evil prophecy which the Badb Catha (goddess of war and destruction) gave him. The Badb resided in the Otherworld Abode of Oenach Cruacha of Athenry. Pseudo-history alleged this was Rathcroghan of Roscommon, seat of the Cruthintuath. The pre-Celtic Cruthin had no association with the Badb except in pseudo-history, whereas the hill at the centre of the great necropolis of Oenach Cruachna of Athenry, Boy Hill, was the Otherworld Abode of Badhbhcatha. She accosted Cormac on his journey in her usual ominous manner, in the interests of the Fir Belg, not of the Ulster Cruthin. This pinpoints Rath Cruacha of Athenry as Cormac's point of departure rather than Rathcroghan of Roscommon. When Cormac went to the edge of the ford to ask her whose harness she was washing, she bluntly uttered this ominous lay: *"This is thine own harness, O Cormac..."*

Just then a division of Connacht warriors, returning from raiding Ulster, pitched camp nearby in Mag Derg, east of the Shannon. Amongst them were Maine Athremail, Medb's son, Sanb Mac Cet Mac Magach from Maen Magh (future Overkings who reigned at Turoe of Mean Magh), and Eochaid Becc Mac Eochaid Ronn, king of the Fir Craibe division of Ól nÉgmacht, together with a hosting of Connachtmen. Cormac's 300 warriors, in deference to his pledge of peace to Medb, unfurled the banners of war against the Connacht raiders of Mag Derg. Connacht was then in the process of consolidating its hold on lands E of the Shannon. The armies met in fierce combat. Cormac's 300 fighting-men defeated the Connachtmen. Cormac and his followers resolved to spend the night in the Hostel of Da Choca. Da Choca welcomed them. That night a hideous hag appeared foretelling doom and destruction by delirious keening.

Medb's forces went in pursuit of Cormac. It attacked Da Choca's Hostel and set it on fire. Cormac and his men sallied forth against the attackers. Cormac slew Mug (Cu) Corb, king

---

[417] T.F. O Rahilly, 'Early Irish History and Mythology', p. 134.

HAND OF HISTORY, BURDEN OF PSEUDO-HISTORY

of Medb's Gailioin Leinster mercenaries, as told by the 9th century poem of Orthanach. Cormac was then assassinated by Corb Gaillni (of the Gailioin) and Cett Mac Magach. An anonymous poem on the exploits of the Laigin claims that Mug Corb slew (not 'was slain by') Cormac Conloinges. The same statement is made in a gloss in Egerton 1782.[418] Only 3 Ulstermen and 5 Connachtmen, including the future kings, escaped the slaughter. "Significant is the fact that Craiphtine, the harper, is numbered among Cormac's enemies. Elsewhere Craiphtine is friend of Labraid Loingsech, leder of the Laignian invaders."[419] Fergus Mac Roi came from Rath Cruacha and bewailed his dead Ulster kinsmen.

IMPLICATIONS OF CATH ARTIG - THE BATTLE OF AIRTECH

Just how fierce battles between the Fir Belg of Connacht and the Cruthin of Ulster were is shown by the long list of chiefs slain in the Battle of Airtech. This and other startling revelations in *Cath Artig*, an archaic text with huge implications of a geo-historical nature, relate the vast extent of ancient Ulster and the fact that Tara and the Boyne area were then part of Ulster, that the territory of East Galway and Roscommon between the river Suck and Shannon were still in the hands of the Ulster Cruthin and ruled by Glaisne, son of Conor Mac Nessa, and that the Cruthin district of Roscommon near Rathcroghan was under seige by the Fir Domnann of the Connacht Fir Belg. *Cath Artig* is the natural sequel to *Bruiden Da Choca* in time and circumstance.[420] It is prefaced by a reference to Cormac Conloinges' death at the Hostel, steps taken to appoint his successor, the lamentation for the dead king, and finally the *'Teccosc'* (Instruction) given to a newly elected prince as part of an inauguration ceremony. The tale drips with widespread ramifications for the geo-political state of Iron Age Ireland. It describes the vast extent of Ireland ruled by the Cruthin of Ulster stretching S to the midlands and well into Connacht at that time. It gives details of the partitioning of Ulster amongst Cruthin princes, the cause of the battle, and the devastating defeat of the Connacht Fir Domnann at the Battle of Airtech.

The Battle of Airtech resulted from a dispute over the territory of Fir Maland (Malonn) adjoining Athlone just east of the Shannon in Co Westmearh which had been conquered by Medb's father and held by Medb from the Cruthin of Ulster. Connacht forces were permanently stationed there. Medb vigorously disputed this land with the new Ulster power after the death of Conor Mac Nessa. She maintained that it had been made over by her to Conor, and to him alone, in compensation for the destruction of Ulster and its people in the Táin Bó Cuailgne in order to bring a peaceful settlement to that bitter episode. R.I. Best noted that the historical background of the Conor Mac Nessa era is perfectly maintained, despite its late transmission. This "would argue in favour of some antiquity, as would the brief and unadorned narrative, the account of the actual combat, a palpable interpolation in H.3.18.397 *Cath Artig* in the nature of a chronicle"[421] is preserved in the Book of Lecan[422] and the Annals of Tigernach,[423] where it is an interpolation in the hand of **H,** the interpolator of Lebor na hUidre.[424] **H's** interpolation preserves and summarizes the essence of the tale: "The Battle of Artig waged against the province of Ól nÉcmacht by Cuscraid Mac Conor Mac Nessa, king of Ulster. Mac Cecht assassinated Cuscraid, Conall Cernach assassinated Mac Cecht. The Cruthin were victorious. Glasni Mac Conor Mac Nessa reigned thereafter for 9 years' as Cruithin King of Rathcroghan of Roscommon." *Cath Artig* tells that "After the death of Cormac (mac Conor mac Nessa) at Da Choca's Hostel a great assembly of the

---

[418] Egerton 1782, *'Mug Corb righ Laigin ro marb Corbmacc Conn Loinges',* RC xxiii, 324.

[419] T.F. O Rahilly, 'Early Irish History and Mythology.', p. 135.

[420] In Manuscript H.3.18 in Trinity College, Dublin, bound up with Part 11, p.724 ff (16th century)

[421] R.I. Best, ed. 'Cath Airtig', in preface p. 171.

[422] Book of Lecan, fol. 169 v, p.342a in the Royal Irish Academy.

[423] 'Annals of Tigernach', Rawl. B.502.

[424] R.I. Best, Ibid. p.171. See Eriu vii. 114.

Cruthin of Ulster was held. It placed the kingdom under the control of Conall Cernach. He refused: "I will not take it, but give it to my fosterling Cuscraid Mend Macha (of Emain Macha), for it has surpassed my strength and skill to control. Whoever will share equal portions of power and prowess, go round forest and plain night and day in the gap of danger against your enemies, so numerous in every place, he is the man to have as your battle-chief." Thereupon Cuscraid mac Conor mac Nessa, was proclaimed king. He bound the Cruthin princes of Ulster with pledges.

VAST EXTENT OF ANCIENT ULSTER IN THE TIME OF QUEEN MEDB

Cuscraid divided Ulster among his brethren, the Red Branch Knights and sons of Conor Mac Nessa. Those to whom various districts are given are named. It is difficult to precisely circumscribe the boundaries of each district of Ulster from the scarcity of particulars given. What is startling about this list of tribal territories of ancient Ulster is its massive extent - vastly more extensive than present-day Ulster, stretching down to the midlands and W across the Shannon into Connacht as far as the River Suck forming the Galway/Roscommon border. "To his foster-father, Conall Cernach, he gave the lands from Inbher Colpa at the mouth of the Boyne to Coba, i,e., the baronies of Upper and Lower Iveagh, Co. Down. To Furbaide Fer Bend, Conor Mac Nessa's son, the territories of North and South Tethba, which included Longford and the W half of Westmeath, down to the Midlands. To Glaisni Mac Conor Mac Nessa, who was to succeed Cuscraid as Overking of Ulster, were given the lands of Fir Maland and Finclair na Bredcha." Fir Maland was the territory adjoining the E shores of Lough Ree on the Shannon running from Athlone N into Longford, including the Hill of Uisnech. Within this area stood Da Chocha's Hostel on Sliabh Maland, Breenmore today, where the Ulstermen halted after defeating Medb's forces on Magh Derg. Amairgen objected on the ground that the territory then belonged to Medh. Fir Maland and Findclair na Bredcha was the territory disputed between the Fir nÓl nÉgmacht and the men of Ulster which resulted in the Battle of Airtech.

Findclair na Bredcha (Bredach) was the territory W of Lough Ree on the Shannon. It stretched from Athlone to the River Suck at Ballinasloe in Galway. It ran N from Moy Finn, bounded by the River Suck which formed the stretch of the Galway/Roscommon border N to the boundary of Airtech (Frenchpark) and the *Cruithintuatha na Chroghain* district around Rathcroghan. The Shannon separated it from the lands of Fir Maland and South Teffa. The name *Cruithintuatha na Chroghain* denotes this territory's possession by the Cruthin. Far, indeed, from Medb having her royal throne at Rathcroghan, it belonged to her bitterest enemy, the Cruthin King of Rathcroghan. Glaisne, son of Conor Mac Nessa, later to become Overking of Greater Ulster at Emain Macha, was king of this territory with its capital at Rathcroghan at the time of the Battle of Airtech. The vast extent of the Kingdom of Ulster in Medb's time underpins the significance of the archaic name of the Fir Belg embryonic province of Connacht, namely, *Ól nÉcmacht*, 'the isolated ramparted Enclave', surrounded by Cruthin territory, with its back to the sea.

Among those to whom territorial lands were granted, as recorded in *'Cath Airtig'* were 8 sons and a daughter of Conor Mac Nessa, some not recorded elsewhere. Yet, conspicuously indicating interference by pseudo-historians, Conor's daughter Feidhelm, her alleged consort Cairbre and son Erc, who succeeded one another as Queen and Kings of Tara of Meath, (Cairbre is unknown in the Ulster Tales) are excised from this list. The redactor of the tale, under the sway of the Tara Myth, studiously suppressed the fact that the Tara district and the eastern lands as far south as the Liffey were then and for a very long time after the Battle of Airtech, part of the tribal territories of ancient Ulster. The excision is a glaring lacuna in the interpolated version of *'Cath Artig'* in the hand of **'H'** whose portfolio was to glorify Tara's alleged High Kingship. Tara figured prominently on the original list.

The nobles of Ulster requested that Fergus Mac Roigh should be brought back from Connacht and peace be made with him for then they would be much stronger against their enemies; "for the illdeeds of the Erann (Fir Belg) were mighty against them. They were being raided, maimed and slain on all sides." Fergus later left Medb, returning to Emain Macha with a great retinue. He made peace with the men of Ulster. He and Cuscraid bound one another by covenant. Among the vaguely-delineated lands given him were Cric Rois and Brug Mna Elcmaire, the first partly in Meath, the second entirely so in the Boyne/Tara district, including Tara. All mention of Tara itself is excised from the text. However, Fergus returned to Medb after the death of Flidais. There he met his death through the jealousy of Ailill Mac Mata, Medb's consort. And thereby lies still another juicy tale.

Large tracts of Ulster territory allotted to his Cruthin princes by Cuscraid were won over by Medb's Fir Belg forces. She retook Crioch Fir Maland E of the Shannon. Medb and her Fir Domnann allies had taken the adjoining territory on the W bank of the Shannon stretching across Roscommon to the River Suck and N to the boundary of Cruthintuatha Chroghain and Frenchpark of Roscommon, known as Findclair na Bredcha, from Glaisne son of Conor Mac Nessa. A great contention between Ol nEgmacht and Ulster arose concerning these territories, particularly Crich Fir Maland. For it had been given back to Conor Mac Nessa by Medb in settlement, on account of those who were slain around him in the great hosting of the Táin Bó Cuailgne expedition. Medb insisted she made over the land to none save Conor alone, and that now on his death it must revert into her possession. The Ulstermen were insistant they would not yield an inch of land unless it was won from them on the field of battle. Awful, hitherto unheard of, was the fury of battle which broke out between them because of their counter-claims. Savage warfare was fought, gigantic deeds were done, by swift-slaying heroes who fell in that fierce fight. Many were the men of Ulster who fell around their king, Cuscraid, and the princes of Ulster. Numerous were the renowned heroes of Connacht who lay still on Airtech's killing fields.

It was then that the great hosting of Ulstermen led by Cuscraid crossed the Shannon W to join the Cruthintuatha of Croghan against the Fir Belg of Ól nÉcmacht who had taken possession of Findclair na Bredcha. They hacked and harried all before them until they came to the place of Airtech Uchtlethan Mac Tomanten Mac Fer Choga of the Fir Domnann which they had taken from the Cruthin. The 3 branches of the Fir Belg (the 3 Connachts), the Fir Domnann, Fir Craibe, and Tuatha Taiden, assembled to deter the Cruthin. The lords of the Fir Ól nÉgmacht were Tinni (Mac Ceacht), Cet mac Magach, Sanb son of Cet who was later to become king of Connacht and Maine who became King of Connacht after his mother's assassination. Ulster heroes are named. Both let slip their dogs of war. The uproar and tumult of battle, clash and clatter of swords, whizz and whirr of wardogs' spears and arrows, is told in gory detail. Mighty the din of war, quaking of earth under the feet of mighty men heaving one another heavily to the ground, "for never have there been heroes from that day to this like those heroes for vigour, strength, valour, daring and prowess." The names of those who died are given. Ulster and Connacht suffered frightful losses. The battle went against the Fir Belg of Ól nÉgmacht. The Ulstermen pursued them out of battle. It was at the Battle of Airtech that the Fir Domnann were all but annihilated. They were driven into the wilds of the west behind a line running from the inner recess of Killala Bay SE along the Moy to an earlier defence line from Loch Mannin to Loch Ui Flynn, source of the river Suck. The Fir Ól nÉcmacht made a 'red wall' (*'mur roo'* linear embankment) against the Ulstermen who never followed up a slaughter when such were raised against them. The Ulstermen halted. Glaisni Mac Conor Mac Nessa who reigned over Rathcroghan, Crich Fir Maland and Fianchlair na Bredcha was recalled to be Overking of Ulster, having regained possession of their lands E and W of the Shannon.

The erection of the 'red wall' against the Ulstermen by the Connacht Fir Belg is signifycant in the light of what has already been seen regarding the Belgic defensive system and that of the Cruthin of Ulster. The word used in the original *Cath Artig* text is *'Mur roo'* (*'mur derg'* in late texts). Its significance is not further explained except by way of stating that this was sufficient to deter the Ulstermen from advancing further SW. To deter the fiercely determined Ulstermen nothing less than the unique Belgic defensive system would suffice. The *'roo'* of the original version was misunderstood by the medieval redactor as *'ruadh'* ('red'), a frequent error in modern times, who substituted the word 'dearg' meaning 'red', as being more appropriate in his mind. The O-Irish word *'roo'*, used on its own or in compound placenames, refers to a fossed embankment of the Fir Belg defensive rampart, as frequently noted in the reconstruction of the Fir Belg oppida in Chapter 2. Vestiges of a set of outer ward embankments of the Turoe/Athenry oppidum straddled the upper Suck River from the vicinity of Castlerea, 10 miles SW of Frenchpark (site of the Battle of Airtech) and W of Rathcroghan. It skirted the territory along the N slopes of Sliabh Ui Flynn to the Suck's source at Loch Ui Flynn on past Ballyhaunis across Mayo to Loch Mannin and thence NW past Kiltimagh parallel to the Moy River to its mouth in Killala Bay. This may well be a vestige of *Cath Airtig's 'mur roo'* defence embankment erected against the Ulstermen. It skirted the W boundary of Airtech and Rathcroghan leaving both within the territory of the Cruthin of Ulster. Domnann survivors retreated W and S of this Suck/Moy boundary line. Vestiges of ramparts on hillslopes N and E of this facing S and W against Ól nÉgmacht's lands (archaic Connacht) belonged to the Cruthin.

From Medb's time one Connacht king after another narrowed the extent of ancient Ulster until "finally, the older, powerful Ulster of the hero tales was smashed into fragments by the family of Niall of the Nine Hostages. Yet, in the hero tales themselves there is no trace of any of this. There, Ireland consists of a great Ulster on the one hand, and the rest of the country under the hegemony of Connacht, on the other. There is no sign of a High Kingship of Tara, or the Southern dynasty of the Eoghanacht. Ulster is ruled from Emain Macha."[425] Tara was then a dependancy of Emain Macha as was Rathcroghan (Figure 61, 62 and 63).

THE TRUE PURPOSE OF THE SO-CALLED 'DUN OF DRUMSNA'

As *Cath Artig* relates, the Battle of Airtech resulted from a dispute over the territory of Fir Maland adjoining the E banks of the Shannon in Westmeath and Longford which had been conquered by Queen Medb's father, Eochaid Férach, from the Cruthin of Ulster. Connacht forces (Fir Ól nÉgmacht), auxiliaries from the Kingdom of Eile of which Medb's sister was Queen, and Leinster mercenaries were stationed there. *'Bruiden Da Choca'* tells that the Fir Ól nÉgmacht were actively engaged in that territory. The 'original Táin' tells that "a time arrived when that portion of Ulster territory E of the Shannon now represented by Co. Longford had been virtually wrested from her (Ulster) by Connacht."[426] Hence, an early Great Wall of Ulster defence embankment was constructed, namely, the Duncladh from Loch Kinale north to Loch Gowna an thence to Drumsna. Certain passages in the 'Táin' support this. This meant that the whole NE of Connacht, the territory of the Cruthintuatha Croghain which was then part of ancient Ulster, was not only being narrowed in extent West of the Shannon but was now also under pressure East of the Shannon by the Fir Ól nÉgmacht. The 3 mile linear embankment across the great loop of the Shannon at Drumsna was erected by the Cruthintuatha to defend themselves on this flank from Connacht's advancing Fir Belg power. Archaeologists Tom Condit and Victor Buckley reckon the whole complex would have required 60,000 trees and taken 10,000 men a couple of years to erect it. This was the only point on the Shannon River north of Athlone where attacking forces

---

[425] Kenneth Jackson, 'The Oldest Irish Tradition - A Window on the Iron Age', p. 47.
[426] W.F.De Vismes Kane, 'Additional Researches on the Black Pig's Dyke', R.I.A Proc., 0p. 549,452-3.

could have crossed without difficulty. These great defence embankments on the Roscommon side of the Shannon at Drumsna continue upriver along the shallows for a considerable distance. At least part of the Fir Maland territory was retaken by the Ulstermen when Glasni, the son of Conor Mac Nessa, reigning as king of Rathcroghan of Roscommon, brought his brother Cuscraid Mac Conor and the forces of Ulster to his aid at the Battle of Airtech. Although Queen Medb's Fir nÓl nÉgmacht were badly defeated in that Battle, she later retook the territory of Fir Maland and fiercely defended it.

A pseudo-historic interpretation is put forward by some researches who peddle the pseudo-view that these defensive earthworks at Drumsna were built by Connacht to defend itself and its seat of Government at Rathcroghan 14 miles to the SW from attacks from the Ulstermen. Glasni would not erect such a defence to protect himself from his father, Conor Mac Nessa or his own brother Cuscraid who were successive Kings of Ulster. Surely Conor Mac Nessa or his sons would not attack their kinsmen, the Cruthintuatha who were ruled from Rathcroghan. Connacht did not exist as a name or an entity then nor for a long time afterwards. Nor was Rathcroghan and its kingdom part of what is often referred to as archaic Connacht, namely, Ól nÉgmacht. Rathcroghan was then part of archaic Ulster just as Cashel of later Munster was then part of archaic Leinster. Ancient texts such as *Cath Artig* show just how agressive was the hostility between archaic Connacht and Ulster. Only fierce determination could lead the Cruthintuatha of Croghan to expend the enormous effort required to erect the massive defensive earthworks of the 'Dun of Drumsna' against the Fir nÓl nÉgmacht advancing up the east side of Lough Ree.

TARA IN THE LIGHT OF 'CATH RUIS NA RIG'

There was constant war between Connacht and Ulster from Queen Medb's day. The saga of the Battle of Rosnaree (*Cath Rúis na Ríg*) is a good example. Connacht's warlike Queen Medb was intent on improving the breed of cattle in Western Ireland. Wealth was counted in cattle. Not their quantity, but their pedigree, were clues to one's status. She sent envoys to Ulster to Daire, king of Sliabh gCullion district in Louth, to ask for a loan of his celebrated brown bull, offering a chariot worth 50 cows and a tract of choice land in Connacht. The envoys gained Daire's consent. To seal the transaction the envoys were entertained at a banquet. One Connachtman drank a wee drop too much, lost control of his tongue and boasted that if Daire did not loan the bull, Medb would come to take it by force. Ulstermen were galled by this drunken remark. Daire lost control of his temper. The envoys were rudely sent home without the bull. Medb was indignant. War! Hastily mustering her forces, she crossed the Shannon at Athlone into Ulster territory. In a season unsuitable for campaigning with early spring snow on the ground, Ulster's warriors were taken by surprise before they could man Ulster's defences. Medb's forces wasted Ulster right up to the gates of King Conor Mac Nessa's palace at Emain Macha in Armagh.

In the great war-expedition saga which became known as the 'Táin Bó Cuailgne' (Cattle Raid of Cooly/Sliabh gCullion), an embellished amalgam of many war-lording expeditions, Medb led her Connacht forces, Munster allies and 3000 Gailion warriors from Leinster, in an invasion of Ulster. A cattle-raid was a declaration of war. The cattle-raid of Sliabh gCullion was a success in so far as Ulster had been ravaged and Connacht succeeded in carrying off Daire's prized Brown Bull. Yet, it was a military disaster for Medb long celebrated in song and story in Ulster. King Conor Mac Nessa's forces pursued Medb's army, overtaking it where it set up camp for the night on the then S boundary of Ulster. He routed her army with great slaughter at the battlefield of Gairech and Illgairech east of Athlone on the Shannon. The Ulstermen allegedly suffered too heavily in the fight to recover the famed Brown Bull of Cooly but succeeded in driving Medb's forces headlong across Ulster's boundary at Gairech/Ilgairech and across the Shannon into Connacht at Athlone. *Cath Rúis na Rí* tells of the aftermath of the battle at Gairech and Ilgairech. Conor

Mac Nessa could not eat, drink, or sleep. Cathbad diagnosed his malady. Conor's memory of Medb's invasion of his territory and loss of the bull was undermining his pride, peace of mind, health and happiness. Conor swore to wreak vengeance on Medb and exact reparation from her Munster and Leinster allies. Cathbad sought to comfort him, telling him he had already inflicted loss enough on his foes. He counseled him to wait until summer, the best season for warring, to give his warriors time to heal their wounds. Meanwhile, Conor should send for Conall Cernach, the great Ulster hero who was then aiding his kinsmen in Scotland, and call on foreign auxiliaries to aid him in the coming war.

Conor swore that should Conall and the foreign hosts not arrive he would ravage Leinster, Munster and Connacht unaided. He summoned all Ulster's forces to prepare for war. He called the Cruthin of Scotland to his aid. News of his preparations spread throughout Ireland. Kings of the southern and western provinces summoned their forces to their side. The Galioin of Leinster were summoned by their king, Finn File, at Dind Rig on the Barrow. The Clanna Dedad Fir Belg of Munster were summoned by their king, Eochaidh Mac Luchta, at his royal seat of Temhair Erann in NW Munster. The muster of Connacht was held by Ailill and Medb at their oppidum stronghold at Rath Cruacha. In the list of kings and various capitals where their armies mustered to await Ulster's wrath it is conspicuous that no High King of Ireland (of Tara) is mentioned in *'Cath Rúis na Ríg'*. As with all Ulidian Tales, the most ancient stratum of Irish legendary history, the idea of High King of all Ireland was unknown. On the rare occasion when Tara was ever mentioned, as in this saga, Tara belongs to the Cruthin of Ulster, not to Leinster, Munster or Connacht. This was subtly suppressed in later rescensions. In early tales Connor Mac Nessa's daughter Fedhelm reigned as Queen of Tara in Queen Medb's day. In the 'Tain' her son Erc, grandson of Connor, brings aid from Tara to the beleaguered Ulstermen. Late Leinster recensions of *'Cath Rúis na Ríg'* claimed that a Leinster Cairpre was father of Erc and resided at Tara. Although Cairpre played no part in the Tain, as O Rahilly noted,[427] he played a significant role in its sequel of late Leinster provenance. Cath Ruis na Rig, Lebor Laigin and other late versions contain clear indications that his role was rigged and manipulated by Leinster pseudo-historians to lay claim on Tara as the Capital of Leinster from time immemorial.

From being Conor's consort, Medb became his bitterest enemy. Late Leinster interpolators concocted a fictitious marriage alliance with Ulster by claiming that Cairbre, brother of the Leinster King, Finn mac Rosa, who reigned at Dind Rig near Leighlinbridge on the Barrow, married Feidhelm Noichruthach, daughter of Conor Mac Nessa, Queen of Tara. In late recensions of 'Cath Rúis na Ríg' in the Book of Leinster, Cairbre Nia Fer is reckoned as a provincial king, but (as in the Book of Leinster's 'Táin') he is king of Tara only, not of Leinster which is treated as a distinct province ruled by his brother Finn mac Rosa. "Cairbre of the Ulidian Tales is little more than a name. His connection with them is artificial. Original Ulidian traditions knew nothing of him. Some Leinsterman invented the idea that Cairbre, Finn and Ailill (Medb's consort) were 3 brothers, who ruled contemporaneously in Tara, Ailenn (of Leinster), and Cruachan (of Connacht) respectively. This proved very popular among Leinster writers. It was taken up by the redactor of the Book of Leinster Tain and *Cath Rúis na Ríg* and introduced by him into these tales."[428] *Cath Rúis na Ríg* represents Finn mac Rosa as having his headquarters in Dind Rig in Carlow. Yet, in verses quoted later he rules at Ailenn (Knockaulin, largest hill fort in Ireland and residence of Leinster kings to the 7th century) in Kildare as he invariably does in other texts.[429]

---

[427] F.T.O Rahilly, 'Early Irish History and Mythology', p.178, n.3.

[428] Ibid, p. 179

[429] Ibid, p. 179 footnote 4.

Figure 63 *Táin Bó Cuailgne* **route from Rath Cruacha (Athenry) & pseudo-route from Rathcroghan (top). Map (lower) of Medb's route from Rath Cruacha to Dun Flidhais (NW Mayo) in** *Táin Bó Flidhais* **& pseudo-route to & from Rathcroghan. It shows Dun Iubair (Umhor) on Achill and Dun Mód Mac Umhor on Belmullet.**

Figure 62 The map (top) shows the vast extent of archaic Ulster and its traditional receding boundaries, first from the Dublin/Wicklow border to Athlone, then from the upper Liffey to Lough Boderg on the Upper Shannon via Lough Kilale and Granard (C. Duncla), then from Dublin's Upper Tolka to the Drowes River in Donegal bay via the Cavan Lakes (B, Worm Ditch), then via the Erne Loughs, and finally from the Boyne to Lough Neagh (A, Danes Cast). As the boundaries receded, not only were the Fir Belg of Ól nÉgmacht advancing from the Connacht side, but east of the Shannon too, separating the Cruthin of Upper Connacht from their kinsmen E of the Shannon necessitating the construction of the Doon of Drumsna (lower map) for their protection.

Auxiliaries summoned from Scotland by Conor mac Nessa and Conall Cernach landed in 3 divisions in NE Ireland, at Murlough Bay, Larne, Co. Antrim, and at the mouth of Castletown River, near Dundalk. Conor met them there. They were entertained at Cu Chulaind's castle. News of Conor's resolve reverberated round Ireland. Eochaidh mac Luchta, King of North Munster, sent a proposal to Medb that full reparation should be made to avoid war. She first refused, then yielded on the advice of Ailill, her consort. Meanwhile Finn mac Rosa's forces, in this rigged Leinster version, marched from Dind Rig allegedly to join his brother Cairbre at Tara. Envoys were sent to Conor with offers of full reparation. Conor refused them and swore to pitch tent in every province in Ireland, beginning at Rúis na Ríg (Rosnaree) S of the Boyne that night. The intention of the Leinster writer was to insinuate that the area S of the Boyne including Tara then belonged to Leinster as it finally did in later medieval times when this fiction was concocted. The envoys reported Conor's refusal to Cairpre and Finn. They resolved to give battle and solicited aid from Medb, promising help should Conor march on Connacht. "Surely you don't require aid against **him**" she said. They marched N to Rosnaree. Conor's forces marched S to Accaill and encamped at Slige Breg near Ardee on hearing that Rosnaree had been taken by the Leinster men. Typical Leinster fraud! Cu Chulaind stayed at Dundalk enlisting men and provisions for the campaign. Next morning Conor marched to Rosnaree. Feic and his men, sent by Conor to reconnoiter enemy positions, crossed the Boyne and attacked the Leinster men. He was wounded and drowned. Daig was then sent only to suffer a similar fate.

Iriel, 'prudent in outpost duty, brave in battle, fierce in pursuit' was then sent. He made an accurate survey of the number and position of the enemy. He and his men were attacked. They retreated, advising Conor to await reinforcements before attacking. Conor is likewise counseled by the Ulster captains, Cathbad and Eogan, as they brought their fighting men to join him on the N banks of the Boyne. Daire, owner of the celebrated bull whose loss caused the hostilities, was bent on fighting at once. Conor checked him. When Loegaire, Conor's cousin, founder of Tara's Ui Loegaire sept, brought up his fighting men, Conor's combined forces crossed the Boyne and engaged the Leinster men (Leinster's alleged claim on Tara). Conor's warriors were worsted as they strove to withstand the Leinster onslaught (a Leinster boast). Fortunately in their moment of greatest need, as Ulstermen were being forced to retreat, the hero Conall Cernach arrived from Scotland with Pictish reinforcements. They and the Ulster heroes prevented retreat from turning into a rout.

As Cu Chulainn arrived with more Ulster heroes he swore he would slay any Ulsterman who turned his back on the foe. The tide of battle turned. Conall Cernach and his men slew a thousand Leinstermen. Confronted by Cairbre, he was reluctant to slay him because of his (alleged) marriage to Conor mac Nessa's daughter. Connall and Cairbre were separated by a charge of Leinstermen. Cairbre and his men slew an equal number of Ulstermen. Carnage was colossal. Cairbre confronted Conor, his alleged father-in-law. Four hundred Ulster warriors rushed to Conor's aid. Cu Chulainn routed the Leinstermen and challenged Cairbre to single combat. He cut off Cairbre's head and shook it at the Leinstermen. They fell back before the fierce onslaught of Ulster's heroes, Cu Chulainn, Conall Cernach and Iriel. Retreat ran to rout. Leinstermen were chased south by Iriel's men as far as the River Rey near Leixlip and the Liffey, which formed the SE boundary of ancient Ulster and marched with the then N border of Leinster. There Fidach called a halt to the pursuit. Here was the SE border of ancient Ulster, a fact subtly suppressed by later fraudulent Leinster recensions. That this true prejudicial snippet of archaic history was allowed to be recorded in the Book of Leinster vouches for its veracity.

Whatever amount of historicity survives in this Leinster adaptation of the tale, the whole significance and weight of argument rests on what follows. The fact that it is preserved in the Book of Leinster vouches for the veracity of the original essence of the tale on the grounds that no Leinsterman would ever have admitted such details, such as the southern extent of Ulster, so prejudicial to their political interests at the time they were written unless they were well known to be historically true. Late versions tell that when Cu Chulainn brought Cairbre's head to him, Conor praised Cairbre who is then buried. The Ulstermen go home in triumph. The Book of Leinster version of *'Cath Rúis na Ríg'* tells that Conor Mac Nessa went straight to Tara after the battle where his daughter Fedhelm was Queen. Apart from the fact that it was only natural that he would want to visit his daughter while in the vicinity, the Leinster claim that she was Cairbre's Queen was made to appear all the more plausible in that Conor allegedly went to console her on Cairbre's death. The true reason was that Tara was his and the Sli Midhluachra road to the North ran north directly from Tara to Emain Macha.

The Book of Leinster saga preserves a detail which has enormous implications for Iron Age Irish history. After a week at Tara, Fedelm's son, Conor's grandson, Erc, came and "placed his head on the breast" of Conor who then bestowed the Tara kingdom on him. The fact that Conor could bestow Tara on his grandson confirms that it was in his possession to do so. That this adverse detail for the political interests of Leinster, which was then beginning to make its own claims on Tara, is admitted by the Book of Leinster surely indicates that this was an indisputable fact of history. From Conor Mac Nessa's day until the Battle of Moyrath in 637 Cruthin regents alone reigned at Tara of Meath. A final detail corroborating the fact that Tara then belonged to Ulster was that Erc, grandson of Conor Mac Nessa, new king of Tara, took the hand of Cu Chulainn's daughter, Findscoth, in marriage. An all Ulster affair! Conor took Erc to visit the battlefield where his alleged father was beheaded by Cu Chulainn. He tells Erc that his alleged father Cairbre prevailed until Conall Cernach's arrival, and was beaten only by superior numbers. On their return to Tara, Conor praises Erc's father and uncles. The fictional details implicating Cairbre and Leinster are self-laudatory glorification of Leinster provenance, laying claim to Tara. They have not been given the careful analysis they deserve. The admission of the fact, in a late work of Leinster provenance, that the descendants of the Ulster heroes ruled at Tara surely speaks volumes in its own right in the stream of Irish history. It is a glaring contradiction of the claims of the Ui Neill that they and their Fir Belg ancestors alone, great enemies of the Ulstermen, ruled at Tara from time immemorial. Cairbre's alleged role is a subtle late Leinster attempt to suppress the fact that Tara had always belonged to Ulster until 637. Cu Chulainn allegedly cut off the heads of the Leinster heroes Cairpre, Calatin, and the Munster hero Curoi because Curoi had beaten him in a fair fight, bound him and shorn off his hair. Sons of these princes formed a league of revenge, ravaged Ulster, and decapitated Cu Chulaind. "And so the beheading went on for years, because a (tipsy) Connacht gentleman did not hold his tongue, and an Ulster chieftain foolishly mislaid his temper."[430]

THE BLACK PIG'S DYKE AND SOUTHERN EXTENT OF ANCIENT ULSTER

The defended borders of ancient Ulster, the land of the pre-Celtic Cruthin, were pushed back NE by the men of Ól nÉcmacht (archaic Connacht). The Cruthin made extraordinary efforts to hold their ground and defend every inch of their lands. Vestiges of massive fortifications erected along their S borders to defend themselves from their aggressive enemies survive to this day. Eoin MacNeill was aware of just a single line of frontier fortifications when he penned the words: "there is a period during which the Ulster power stood at bay. Of this state of things we have a very remarkable record, not written on paper, but graven on the face of the country. The Ulster kings endeavoured to defend themselves against further aggression by fortifying their entire frontier except where it was already protected by strong natural obstacles such as lakes, forests or rivers. Linking these natural

---

[430] Edmund Hogan, in his 'Preface' to 'Cath Ruis na Rig for Boinn', p.xix-xx.

barriers they raised a massive earthen rampart which, with these barriers, formed a continuous line of defences from the Irish Sea on the east to Donegal Bay on the west."[431]

In this enormous effort they fought every inch of the way, not only to defend their lands, but also to recover lands lost to the enemy. Some of their efforts at recovery of lost lands are recorded in legend and history such as when they drove King Cormac Mac Art from Cnoc Temhro (Turoe of Galway) or when Congal Caech, 7th century Cruthin Overking of Ulster, became the aggressor advancing well into lost territory in an attempt to win back their former lands in Derry. Not once, but time and again they resolutely took on the superhuman task of erecting fresh frontier fortifications after having been driven back. "These very remarkable records not written on paper, but graven on the face of the country" do not lie. In fact, they underpin the suppression of vast tracts of early Irish history.

Judging by extant remains, Cruthin fortifications differ from those of the Fir Belg. Cruthin versions consist of a single massive rampart linking natural barriers. The Fir Belg system, also incorporating natural defences, differed in that it consisted of sets of 3 less massive parallel ramparts, linked by transverse ramparts. Less sophisticated than the Belgic system, massive Ulster dykes display a daunting determination to resist aggression. Details of extant remains of the 'Great Wall of Ulster' and popular traditions connected with them are found in Kane's paper on the Black Pig's Dyke in the Proceedings of the Royal Irish Academy.[432] He reconstructed 3 separate sets of the Great Wall of Ulster. He involved himself "in the progress of the Ordnance Survey work in Monaghan with the object of getting the surviving ancient remains correctly entered on the new maps. My attention was especially arrested by vestiges of a great embankment and ditch along the county verge, most of which has been leveled, but sections of which still remain in fair condition, and challenge notice by their huge size."[433] They continued into neighbouring counties. Aided by Canon Lett's work[434] he researched the extant remains of Ulster's defence frontier which he published in 1909. They are in urgent need of reanalysis.

Kane published 'Additional Researches on the Black Pig's Dyke' in 1917, correcting his earlier work. He referred to "apparently the final frontier of the kingdom of Ulster previous to the conquest of the province by the Collas." He made additional discoveries of earlier sets of the Great Wall of Ulster further south. "I propose to set out the line of 2 other boundaries to which the same name is popularly attached, which seem to indicate there were 2 consecutive recessions of Ulster territory,"[435] before the final recession caused by the loss of Emain Macha at the hands of the Airghialla. Although they drove the Ulstermen back with Connacht aid, the Airghialla took credit for having conquered Emain Macha on their own. The Ulstermen fell back on Tara as the seat of their overkingship. Kane's research was spoilt by the preconceived ideas about Tara which ruined O Rahilly's work, that the Iron Age Kings of Tara, rather than Fir Ól nÉgmacht from their stronghold in Connacht, warred against the Cruthin of Ulster. This accepted belief in his day was based on pseudo-history. Tara's Regents in Queen Medb's time were members of Conor mac Nessa's family, Overking of Ulster at Emain Macha, Fedhlem, his daughter, and Erc, his grandson. Referring to a fragment of defensive earthwork 4 miles S of Armagh, marked on the OS map of Armagh, sheet 16, as "Dane's Cast", to which Westropp directed his attention, Kane quoted passages from 'Táin Bó Cualnge' which refer to this defensive barrier "dug in Tir

[431] Eoin MacNeill, 'Phases of Irish History', p.131.
[432] Op.cit., p.131.
[433] W.F. De Vismes Kane, 'The Black Pig's Dyke: The Ancient Boundary Fortification of Uladh' in the 'Proceedings of the Royal Irish Academy', for May 1909, p.301.
[434] Canon Lett and other researchers in the 'Ulster Journasl of Archaeology, vol. iii., 1897.
[435] W.F. De Vismes Kane, 'Additional Research on the Black Pig's Dyke', R.I.A 'Proc.', p. 540, 1917.

Marcceni in Cualnge." "It is possibly a detached inner line of defence near the capital, where a last stand could be made in case a Southern enemy succeeded in forcing its way N by the Forkhill Pass. Emain Macha fell to the invading Collas."[436]

The Tara Myth syndrome led Kane, as it did others, to expect that the SE terminal of this Great Wall of Ulster should reach the E coastline somewhere north of Tara. Hence, he guessed the mouth of the Newry River at the head of Carlingford Lough was the E terminus of a later more northerly defensive frontier which had its W terminus near Bundoran in Donegal Bay. He guessed the mouth of the Boyne at Drogheda to be the terminus of his earlier more southerly Ulster frontier which he alleged had its W terminus at Athlone. In his 'Additional Researches' he referred to sections of earlier frontier fortifications W of the Boyne and Blackwater which were brought to his notice. Significant names were attached to them such as 'Worm Ditch' or 'Black Pig's Valley' indicating that they were authentic. Yet, from the sources of the Boyne and Blackwater NE to their mouth at Drogheda on the E coast he mentions no trace of frontier fortification at all. He simply took it for granted that the ancient boundary of Ulster followed the course of the Boyne in a NE direction. Pseudo-descriptions of the course of the Great Wall of Ulster which recognize only one frontier, claim it ran from Donegal Bay on the W coast to the mouth of the Boyne on the E, running in a NW/SE direction. This dances to the tune of the Tara Myth which excluded Tara from ancient Ulster and projected it as the capital of the alleged Highkings of Ireland who supposedly waged war on Ulster from Tara.

While Kane's additional researches corrected errors in his earlier work and showed that earlier frontier boundaries of Ulster stood further S, his research displayed much confusion and guesswork as regards the E terminals of different sets of frontier. Because of his adherence to the Tara Myth and consequent belief in a NE, rather than a SE orientation for the E half of the frontier line, he misaligned different sections and sets of frontier earthworks. Several frontier boundaries were erected by the Cruthin as they were being driven back by the Airghialla with Connacht aid. Kane confused several disparate sets of defence lines, as he admits to have done in his earlier researches, by arbitrarily attempting to tie them into a single set. Kane encountered a remarkable concurrence of traditional lore from widely separated areas corroborating legendary history indicating that an earlier frontier of ancient Ulster had its W terminus at Athlone on the Shannon. "It is evident that a tradition of Ulster territory having once extended to Athlone has survived. I hope to show from early sources that Ulster's sway once extended over at least the W half of Westmeath so far S and W as Athlone. In the Táin quest the hosts of Queen Medb retreated to Connacht by way of Athlone. A time arrived when the power of Emania (Ulster Capital) was weakening so that the portion of Ulster territory east of the Shannon now represented by Co. Longford had been virtually wrested from her by Connacht. Therefore an auxiliary line of defences was constructed from Loch Gowna to Loch Kinale and thence E. Certain passages in the 'Táin' seem clearly to support this hypothesis."[437] He quoted a reference from the 'original Táin' where Queen Medb accuses Fergus Mac Roigh, acting as guide into Ulster, of leading her army astray, turning S after reaching Granard:

Medb: "Fergus, speak, what shall we say? *Fergus: "Medb, why art thou so perturbed?*
    What may mean this devious way?   *There's no treacherous purpose here,*
    For we wander North and South   *Ulster's land it is, O Queen,*
    Over other lands we stray."   *Over which I've led the host."*

---

[436] W.F. De Vismes Kane, 'The Black Pig's Dyke', R.I.A.Proc., Vol., xxvii., Sect. C.

[437] W.F.De Vismes Kane, 'Additional Researches on the Black Pig's Dyke', R.I.A Proc., 0p. 549,452-3.

He proffered this as vital testimony that Westmeath and Longford through which Medb's army marched "were, at the epic's date of the compilation, considered within the bounds of the Ulster principality"[438] and that the barony of Rathconrath E of Athlone around Uisnech, formed part of what Fergus Mac Roigh claimed was within the confines of Ulster.

Kane gave another example of the S extent of ancient Ulster recorded in the Ulster Cycle relating the struggle between Ulster and Connacht. "In connection with the struggle between the armies of Medb and levies from Munster and Leinster (against Ulster), we are told that the Ulstermen pursuing Medb's retreating army arrived at "Slemain Midhe". The conical hills of Slane Beg and Slane Mor are 2 miles SW of Portloman at the S end of Lough Owel (W of Mullingar, 20 miles ENE of Athlone)."[439] The battlefield of Garech and Ilgarech stretched 9 miles W from Slane to "Clathra" (Killare?) near Ballymore (10 miles E of Athlone). Medb's hosts encamped there for the night: "It was then that the 4 great provinces of Erin (under Medb) established a dun and encampment at Clathra (*Cladh Rath*, dyke fort, W of the Hill of Uisnech)."[440] Fierce battle broke out. The 'Yellow Book of Lecan' says Cu Chulainn lay wounded at "Fedain Collna" (Ballymore), fastened to the ground to prevent him from joining battle because of his wounds. Fergus Mac Roigh, the Ulster prince in Medb's army, entered the fray roaring his blood-curling war-cry: "Hand me my sword. I'll send heads buzzing through the air like the flight of a swarm of honey-bees on a sultry summer's day." He truncated the 3 bald *('maoil')* hills of Meath in fury before retiring from battle. The hill in the neighbourhood of this battle-field between the Hill of Sciath and Rathconrath is Croc na Maoil. In the heat of the fray Fergus engaged the Ulster King Conor Mac Nessa in single combat, unaware who his antagonist was. He pressed his foe so furiously that the king's shield roared from the blows rained on it by the sword of Fergus, sending up showers of sparks. Finally recognizing the king from the sound of his shield, Fergus "retired, not wishing to slay the King of Ulster."

"Cu Chulainn, hearing the sound of Conor's shield burst the bonds fastening him to his sick-bed. His battlecry"[441] caused consternation in Connacht's camp. Medb's consort, Ailill, asked in alarm: "What cry is that?" Mac Roth, chief druid and soothsayer of Medb answered: "It is Cucullain striving to join the combat, sorely worn out where he lay in Fert Sciath, incapable of joining the combat after his fight with Fer Diad." The Stowe MS reads, "The Fert of Sciach (Sceth), daughter of Deagad", while Windisch's MS. 'H' reads, "The Fert of Sciach, daughter of Deghaidh". These placenames in the earliest versions of the Tain are prime guidelines in locating the S limits of ancient Ulster in this central part of Ireland. Vestiges of frontier fortifications corroborate them, not as Kane arbitrarily aligned them in a NE/SW direction obsessed by the pseudo-history of Tara, but in their true original EW and then NW/SE alignment.

In the course of his inquiries into the line of Ulster's boundary in this battlefield area, Kane was made aware of surviving traditions regarding the Magic Boar which rooted up the entrenchment. An upright pillarstone, a 'liagan' 4 foot high gravestone with a design of tiny cup-marks, sited on a ridge called 'Cnoc Skeagh' near Rathconrath, between Loch Owel and Ballymore, a few miles E of the village of Rath Skeagh (Skeah today), Sciach's residence. This is the site of 'Fert Sciach', Sciach's burial mound, and the site of Cu Chulainn's sickbed, according to the various MSS. On the Hill of Skeagh near the stone liagan which marks her grave stands a natural outcrop rock locally known as "Carraig na Muice" (Rock

---

[438] Op. cit., p. 555.

[439] Op. cit., p. 561.

[440] 'Tain Bo Cualgne' as translated by O'Looney and preserved in the Royal Irish Academy.

[441] W.F. De Vismes Kane, op. cit., p. 561.

of the Magic Pig). This has 2 marks allegedly made by the great Magic Boar which dug up the nearby frontier defence-works with its tusks as local tradition proclaims.

Old MSs. referring to Fert Sciach indicate that the position of Cu Chulainn's sickbed was near Medb's camp and this battlefield. Kane's discovery of traces and traditions of Ulster's ancient frontier defence-works nearby shows this battlefield stood on an early boundary of Ulster. The Tain's claim that Ulster's King and his forces came so far south to drive the invaders back across the border corroborates archaeological and oral evidence that at one time Ulster's borders reached down to Athlone. This and other legendary material was utilized by Kane to corroborate local traditions that the boundary of ancient Ulster had its W terminus at the SE protrusion of the S end of Loch Ree above Athlone, corroborated further by his discoveries of vestiges of that frontier heading towards Athlone. These constitute "a very remarkable record, not written on paper, but graven across the face of the landscape."

This grassroot history and its toponymic milieu of the battlefield were suppressed in later recensions of the Táin which were adapted to accommodate the Tara Myth. This led Kane to exclude Tara district from the territory of ancient Ulster even when he had substantial proof that at a very early period Ulster reached the Midlands. Two fixed points on the map designated the direction of his most ancient S frontier alignment 1) Athlone, on account of the frequent traditions he encountered among the peasantry earmarking it as the SW point of the ancient kingdom of Ulster, and 2) the Boyne mouth at Drogheda. A terminus S of Drogheda would have brought Tara within ancient Ulster, anathema to Tara's 'official doctrine'. He concocted a NE/SW direction for what he designated the more ancient frontier as against the NW/SE direction of his 2nd and 3rd frontiers. To obviate the need to include Tara in this vastly more expansive Ulster territory extending S to the central midlands, he made the lines of the S earlier frontier run from Athlone in the direction of, and following the course of, the Boyne river NE to its mouth at Drogheda passing W to N of Tara. He did not seek out any trace or tradition of it along that line or from among the peasantry, not even considering the possibility that the frontier from Athlone or further north might have reached the E coast south of Tara.

Pursuing this policy Kane took blind leaps from one frontier line to another, such as from Kilallon to Loch Derravaragh: "The most ancient frontier of the 3 commenced at Drogheda, with the river boundary of the Boyne and Blackwater. But at Tailteen it diverged to the W through Meath to near Kilskeer, passed S of Crossakiel (the Táin's "Ard Chuillend") through Killalon and thence to Loch Derravaragh **by a junction I am not clear about**, then past Multyfarnham to Lough Owel, to near Mullingar, Mount Temple, and Athlone." He persisted in this SW alignment even when reaching Navan on the Boyne he "found local traditions extremely confusing" (to his mind-set). They said "the line passing through Navan ran, not SW to Athlone, but NW along the Blackwater to Lough Ramor and through Cavan." Local tradition still insists that this line of fortification had no connection with Athlone but ran NW through Cavan and SE to the Tolka and upper Liffey to Dublin. The scholarly Rev. Conor McGreevy of Crossakiel, coversant with these traditions, supported this NW/SE alignment of the boundary fortifications from his study of local vestiges at Carnaross and along the Blackwater on the Meath/Cavan border which placed Tara within ancient Ulster. They were used as right-of-ways resembling raised tree-lined avenues just as were stretches of the linear embankments of the Fir Belg oppidum in Connacht. Traditions of a NW/SE alignment of the frontier through Navan and Loch Ramor correspond to the line of Airghiallan buffer states set up by Cormac Mac Art and referred to in poems proclaiming an early Ui Neill/Airghiallan alliance. Kane encountered traditions at Kells and Navan of an earlier frontier further S having its W terminus at Athlone.

One early frontier fortification ran SE from Killala Bay down the Moy River to Loch Mannin and thence to Loch Ui Flynn. It followed the Suck River SE to Mount Talbot. It ran SE to the Shannon at Athlone and thence E to the Dublin/Wicklow coast. Tara was part of ancient Ulster. The whole Cruthin-held NE of Connacht centered on Rathcroghan of Roscommon, where the sons of Conor Mac Nessa ruled in Medb's day, was part of the Ulster Overkingdom. The Connacht Fir Belg then captured lands E of the Shannon, N of Athlone, in Westmeath and Longford, as far as the Hill of Uisneach near Rathconrath W of Mullingar. Their new frontier-line then ran NW to the Shannon near Rooskey. Thus the NW/SE alignment of the Ulster frontier began to expand E of the Shannon. Segments of Ulster's retreating lines of frontier fortifications running in NW/SE alignments were reconstructed by Kane such as the Duncladh from Loch Kinale to Lough Gowna.

Ignoring local tradition, Kane claimed to "set out the alignments of 3 traditional boundaries following 'traditional routes' which are in some portions substantiated by the discovery of earthworks of more or less remarkable character. Their identification as frontiers has been corroborated by local names and surviving legends."[442] The authenticity of his "traditional routes", and his linking up of various vestiges are highly arbitrary, particularly as regards their East coast termini. His alleged Athlone to Drogheda alignment is the very antithesis of the true alignment of his so-called earliest frontier fortifications. As he was wearing the blinkers of his time well before the Tara Myth had been exploded, one must give him credit for his admission that, "no doubt if the early history of this part of Ireland was more reliable and definite," his research work would have been greatly facilitated.

Snatches of oral history and early literature tell that at one time the boundary of ancient Ulster reached not just Athlone and ran along the S boundary of Westmeath and Meath as far as S Dublin. Much earlier, the Cruthin peopled all Ireland before being pushed N by the incoming Brigantes and Fir Belg of the South, and later of W Munster and Connacht and their Airghiallan allies. Well into historic times isolated branches of the Cruthin were widespread in Leinster and Connacht such as the Loiges of Co. Laois and the Midlands, the Fothairt of Leinster who left their name on the baronies of Fort in Wexford and Carlow, the 6 Sogains of Galway and the Cruthintuatha of Croghan of Roscommon. So widespread were they that clearly they were masters of Ireland before the coming of the Celts who drove them north, isolating Cruthin enclaves in the process. These became subjects of the new masters. It is against this background that the Fir Belg power of Connacht and the South expanded at the expense of these aboriginal Cruthin. By Queen Medb's day S Connacht had been wrested from the Cruthin, as had most of the South of Ireland stretching in a rough line from Loch Corrib in Galway through Athlone to Dublin. Medb instigated her Fir Belg allies, the Fir Domnann and Mac Umhoire to expand against the Cruthin of North Connacht. They were driven back with great slaughter behind the defence line erected from Killala Bay along the Moy and Suck rivers to the Shannon at Athlone. Medb's forces crossed the Shannon at Athlone and conquered territory along the E banks of Loch Ree. A text in 'Revue Celtique'[443] shows that Breenmore, 6 miles NE of Athlone along Loch Ree near the S extremity of ancient Ulster, had been alienated by Medb's father. This was the earliest advance of the Fir Belg across the Shannon at the expense of the Cruthin of Ulster, not from Tara which was firmly in the hands of the same Cruthin.

Laud 610[444] tells how the Belgic invaders found the Cruthin dominant in the N half of Ireland and fought many wars with them, driving them north. It tells that "Conn fought numerous battles against them (hence his epithet *Cetchathach*, 100 battles), as did his son Art and

---

[442] Op. cit., p. 558
[443] 'Revue Celtique', xxi, p. 313.
[444] Confer 'Zeitschrift fur Celtische Philologie', viii, 313 f.

grand-son, Cormac."[445] This account, authentic in its relevant quotation, is seen through the eye of the Tara Myth. It is flawed to the extent to which it intercalated the original account to make these kings rule from Tara rather than from their power-centre in Connacht. It reflects the tradition of perennial warfare, not between the 'Goidels of Tara' and the men of Ulster, as O Rahilly and pseudo-history claimed, but between the men of 'Ól nÉcmacht' (early Connacht) and the Cruthin of Ulster whose territory stretched down to the midlands and across the Shannon into Connacht. It was being inexorably whittled away as Connacht's Fir Belg power expanded apace. The extent to which they had driven the Cruthin back along a NW/SE line of retreat by the time of Cormac Mac Airt can be guaged from the positions of the frontline buffer states of the Airghialla positioned by Cormac Mac Art along this frontier of ancient Ulster.

TUROE Vis-a-Vis TARA: THE AIRGHIALLIAN EVIDENCE

The well-known Great Wall of Ulster is gauged from the later positions of the Airghiallan states well into historic times when they had advanced considerably, over several centuries, further into the Cruthin territory of Ulster. These buffer states at the time of the original conquest and lands later won from Ulster in the following centuries were given to the Airghiallan allies of Connacht Kings, in reward for military services, while they remained tax-paying subjects. This is the meaning of the name 'Airghialla', which survived in its anglicized equivalent, 'Oriel', (from O-Irish 'Air Ghialla', Eastern Subject Peoples). It indicates in which direction lay the centre of power to which these peoples were subject - it was to the west, to Connacht. They could in no way be so designated had they been subject to the Kings of Tara, even when at a much later date they did in fact become subject to the Ui Neill Kings. Their name very conspicuously corroborates the fact that they were subject peoples, not of the king of Tara in the East, but of the king of Connacht. "The conquerors were the princes of the Connacht dynasty. Their army was drawn from Connacht. All this chain of events is the direct sequel of the old rivalry between Connacht and Ulster which forms the basis of Táin Bó Cuailnge and the Ulster Cycle in general. The inhabitants of the conquered parts of Ulster got the significant name of Airghialla, Oir Ghiala, 'eastern subjects'. In relation to Tara they were not 'eastern subjects'. The name Airgialla is based on the fact that the conquering power at the time when the name came into use was regarded as the western power, its home was Connacht."[446]

Perennial bloody warfare left deep permanent scars not only across the face of the Irish landscape in the form of boundary entrenchments, such as the Black Pig's Dyke, but on the lives of even the sturdiest heroes to this day. The great Cruthin warrior Conall Cearnach grew totally exhausted from his bloody campaigns against Medb. He finally made peace with her, as he thought. He went to recuperate to her court at Rath Cruacha where he spent a year. The somewhat aging Medb had noticed that her younger consort Ailill was keeping company with one of her ladies-in-waiting. Overcome with jealousy, the wily Medb prevailed upon Conall Cearnach to put Ailill out of her sight for good. He secretly acquiesced to her request with a deadly javelin-cast. Medb then treacherously announced to the Connachtmen that Conall was the culprit. Thus she encompassed his death also.

AIDED MEDBHA - THE ASSASSINATION OF QUEEN MEDB

Medb's own assassination is described in the 11th century *Aided Medbha*. Interpolated in favour of Rathcroghan Myth, it claims Medb's stepsister Clothra had her royal residence on Loch Ree on the Shannon. Scraps of local and legendary history tell that before Rath Cruacha of Athenry was established Clothra's royal seat sat on a crannog on Loughrea Lake in Galway, not on Shannon's Loch Ree. Medb led the Mairtine of Munster (Fir Magh Feine

---

[445] T.F.O Rahilly, 'Early Irish History and Mythology', p. 349.
[446] Eoin MacNeill, 'Phases of Irish History,' p. 125-126.

of Fermoy) to slay her stepsister Clothra and her consort, Cairbre Cennderg. Her father later elevated Medb to Connacht's throne at Rath Cruacha of Athenry. Legendary history, contradicting the interpolated version, tells that Medb's crannog was Clothra's former crannog on Loughrea Lake at the centre of the Fir Belg oppidum of Ól nÉgmacht, not on Loch Ree on the Shannon at the heart of enemy territory, the Cruthintuatha of Croghan. The *Dindsenchas Loch Riach* refers to Loughrea Lake as *Lind Lir* (of the god Lir). In the Celtic Pantheon Lir was the father of Manannan, alias Orbsen, who gave his name to Loch Corrib (*Loch Orbsen*). These were Fir Belg gods, not Cruthin gods. This dindsenchas text tells that the then Bailiff of Loughrea lake was from nearby Moyode (Magh Fot) on the famous Road of the Kings (*Rót na Rí*), a far cry from Loch Ree of Roscommon. He succeeded Ailill, Medb's consort, the previous bailiff.

"Fót, diata Magh Fót co fiar ar Rót na Ríg, is e in Fót-sin ba rechtaire lór don loch."

Aided Medbha tells that when the Seven Year Assembly was held at Loughrea Lake ("a seven-yearly cycle" is still remembered there), Furbaidhe, Conor Mac Nessa's son, saw Medb bathing at the spring in the lake beside her crannog. He recalled how Medb slew his mother Clothra and succeeded her as Queen of Connacht, and how he had been groomed from boyhood under *geis* by Conor to avenge the death of his mother on Medb. Unable to restrain the urge to take advantage of this auspicious moment, the force of the slingshot of this master in martial arts struck Medb a deadly blow on the forehead. Assassination! Revenge! *'Senchas na Releg'* and local tradition point to her burial mound on the N side of *Releg na Rí lamh le Cruacha* in Rahard on the N side of Boy Hill just SE of Athenry.

In late recensions of the *Táin*, Medb is presented as a proud, scheming, ribald *femme fatale,* "the result of increased dramatization of her personality. Her character as a power-hungry virago was very much the creation of medieval literati. (Her ongoing gross portrayal) whetted the appetite of medieval audiences. Accordingly more narratives were composed."[447] Through the medium of the Iron Age Queen Medb, Cuanu, the Abbot of Armagh, in his 8th/9th century recension of *Táin Bó Cuailgne,* concocted vicious character assassination of the medieval Medb, the mother of Niall Caille. In 784 the N Ui Briuin king, Tiprait mac Taidg, having established his dynasty at Rathcroghan, wrecked his SW Galway Ui Fiachra rivals for control of Connacht's Kingship. To add insult to injury he ransacked Medb's palace at Rath Cruacha which the Ui Fiachra upheld as Connacht's ancient Capital to erase it from popular memory in favour of Rathcroghan. He desecrated Medb's royal crannog on Loughrea Lake. With Cuanu's aid he made pseudo-historic claims that her throne was at Rathcroghan and her royal crannog was on Lough Ree. Her portrayal as a personification of the sovereignty of Tara appeared in the 12th century Leinster recension of the *Tain.* It claimed she would not allow a High King to reign at Tara unless he had her as consort. The alleged "love affairs of Medb have become multifarious and indiscriminate with unfortunate results for the character"[448] of Queen Medb.

Medb is on a par with nearly contemporary British Celtic Queens, Cartimandua or Boudicea. "Cartimandua is one of the outstanding women rulers of Celtic antiquity, comparable with her contemporary, Queen Boudicea, and with Queen Medb of Connacht. It is impossible to have any true understanding of either Celtic history or literature without realizing the high status of Celtic women, and something of the nature of their place in society, in Gaul, Britain"[449] and Ireland. Medb suffered malicious character assassination, almost demonization, by pseudo-historians, as did Boudicea by Roman authors. In stifling

---

[447] Daithi O hOgain, 'Myth, Legend & Romance, Encyclopaedia of Irish Folklore Tradition' p. 294ff
[448] T. F. O Rahilly, 'Early Irish History and Mythology', p. 131f.
[449] Myles Dillon and Nora Chadwick, 'The Celtic Realms' p. 25.

Medb's character, as they did to Palladius, pseudo-historians blatantly debased Celtic women and Celtic history. Pseudo-history claims Medb was reared at Tara and that the Medb of Tara and the Medb of Croghan "were one and the same personage."[450] Indeed, the Medb of Cnoc Temhro and the Medb of Rath Cruacha "were one and the same personage." Medb was reared on *Cnoc Temhro* of Galway, not Tara of Meath, at her father's palace, Rath Ferach Mhor. He elevated her to the Queenship of Connacht at *Rath Cruachan* (Rath Cruacha of Athenry, not Rathcroghan of Roscommon). Pseudo-history transferred Medb of Rath Cruacha of Athenry to the Cruthin-held stronghold of Rathcroghan of Roscommon and later made her the goddess of sovereignty at Tara.

Queen Medb of Rath Cruacha was never Queen of Rathcroghan of Roscommon or the goddess of sovereignty of Tara of Meath. Neither did her son Maine, her successor as Regent of Connacht, reside at Rathcroghan. Nor did her daughter Fionnura, later Queen of Connacht. Maine's residence was Clochar Ui Mhain (Clogharevaun) at the centre of Magh Mhain/Maen Magh forming the Knocknadala/Turoe oppidum core. The *Dindsenchas Main Magh* tells that this plain was named after Maine, son of Queen Medb. Maine's sister Fionnura, later Queen of Connacht, had her residence on Finnure Hill, named after her, 5 miles ESE of Turoe, in Maen Magh. Medb placed the Mac Umhor leaders in their buffer states along the perimeter of her Ól nÉgmacht (Connacht) oppidum, as told in the dindsenchas of *Carn Conaill*. "Oengus Mac Umhor was settled at Dun Oengus on Aran", "On Conall, son of Oengus Mac Umhor, Medb bestowed lovely Aidne." His was buried at Carn Conaill. "Cutra went to Lough Cutra" to the SE of Gort, "Cimbe to Lough Cime" (Lough Hacket) at the foot of Cruach Magh Seolgha SW of Tuam, "Adhar built his fortress at Magh Adhair" in Clare, "Mil built his at Murvech Mil" on Aran. Dela (Daelach, Mil's father and leader of the Fir Belg invasion) had set up his own royal residence at Knocknadala (Hill of the Great Assembly) and established the Oenach Dind (Feis Temhro, the inaugural celebration at the coronation site) beside him on Cnoc Temhro (Turoe). "Bir was placed at Rinn Burren" on the N Clare coast. "Mod was placed at Modlind" on the Mayo coast. "Irgus at Cend mBairne" in the Burren, "Cing on Aille (Rath Aille near Bellafea), Conchuirn in Inish Mean (Aran), Lathrach on the hill of Laragh" near Attymon. "Taman on Rinn Tawin" (Tawin Point) in Galway Bay, and Assail in lovely Druim Asail", S of Limerick city. Cet Mac Magach from Maen Magh acted as surety. These buffer states stood along the outer wards circumscribing Medb's province of Ól nÉchmacht. She acted as regent of this her own territory, not of Roscommon's Rathcroghan nor Tara of Meath

DINDSHENCHAS RATH CRUACHAIN: FERT MEDBA & DATHI

The *Dindshenchas Rath Cruachain*[451] refers to the tombs of Medb and Da Thi (Nathi) in the same phrase as being in Oenach Cruachain, *'a feirt Medbha & Da Thi mac Fiachrach.'* Medb belongs to the 1st century BC/AD, Da Thi (Nathi) to the 5th century AD. This is half a millennium of the Royal Cemetery of Cruachan usage by the Fir Belg Royalty. The reference to 'fert Medbha & Da Thi', the burial mounds of Medb and Dathi, draws attention to two necropoli tracts, *Senchas na Relec* (Lore of the Royal Cemeteries) and *Aided Nath I* (Death of Nath I) in *Lebor na Huidre* (Book of Dun Cow). The Book of Leinster *Senchas na Relec* gives pride of place to Oenach Cruacha with a stunning statement, the significance of which has never been fully appreciated: *"Oenach Cruacha chetus iss and no adhnaictis rigrad Temhrach no co tanic Cremthand mac Lugdech.'* This snippet astoundingly claims that the entire Royal Household of Temhair from the beginning right up to the time of Cremthann Mac Lugdech was interred in Oenach Cruacha. It then proceeds to name the most renowned royal personages interred there. They are Cobthach Coel Breg & Labraid Loingsech & Eochaid Airemh & his brother, Eochaid Feidlech, with his three sons and six

---

[450] Daithi O hOgain, Ibid, p293.
[451] Book of Leinster, 170a.

daughters including Medb, and her consort, Ailill and seven brothers, and the entire Connacht Royal household until the time of Cremthann. In pseudo history, this meant nothing less than that the Kings and Queens of Tara as well as the entire Connacht royal household were interred in Cruacha until the time of Cremthann.

Why the so-called royalty of Tara in the east of Ireland should be buried in Cruachan in the West has baffled one and all. Only the feeblest of explanations have been put forward to try to reconcile this statement, such as O Rahilly's claim that during that Iron Age period (more than 500 years) "Connacht was a dependency of Tara, its special demesne." Even were it true it would in no way solve the dilemma. The inclusion of two Leinster kings, Cobthach Coel Breg, alleged king of Tara, and Labraid Loingsech, leader of the Leinster invasion and slayer of Cobthach, was a late Leinster attempt to superimpose its own pseudo-version of history on this archaic tract. It claimed Tara for itself (with Cruacha as its Necropolis) from time immemorial by insinuating that the early Leinster king Cobthach ruled there. The tagging on of Leinster kings to the list of Fir Belg kings and queens interred at Sidhe Cruacha cemetery was part of Leinster's new-fangled claim on Tara's Kingship concocted under Dermot Mac Murrough's patronage. With Norman aid, he was priming himself to be crowned High King of Ireland at Tara. Earlier versions of pseudo history had pushed Tara's High Kingship back to Cormac Mac Art. Dermot's chroniclers pushed it back to the 1[st]century BC Eochaid Felech who was *Rí Temhro*, Overking of the Fir Belg tribes of the Southern half of Ireland reigning from Turoe of Galway. They appropriated the title Rí Temhro for Tara and made Eochaid Ferach a High King of Ireland there. By Dermot's day *Rí Temhro* had come to mean High King of Ireland at Tara.

Queen Medb's consort, Ailill, was a Leinsterman from Bri Eile. This presented the opportunity for introducing Ailill and Medb and their royal family into the Laiginian pedigree. Dermot's pseudo-chroniclers accordingly invented the idea that Ailill, Cairbre and Finn were 3 Leinster brothers who ruled contemporaneously in Rath Cruacha, Tara and Ailinn of Leinster respectively. This proved very popular in 12th century Leinster, allegedly making not only Tara, but Rath Cruacha too, part of Leinster's archaic possession. It was taken up by the redactor of the Leinster version of the *Táin Bó Cuailgne* and *Cath Ruis na Ríg*. As well-known Necropoli texts such as *Senchas na Relec* claimed King Eochaid Ferach, Queen Medb, her consort Ailill and their family and the entire Royal Household of Rí Temhro were interred at *Relig na Rí lamh le Cruacha*, the redactor of 'Senchas na Releg' had to be satisfied with simply tagging Leinster kings to the list of the so-called 'royal household of Temhair' buried at Releg na Rí. He did not realize that this inflated the Tara/Rathcroghan myth pseudo-bubble to bursting point.

The Temhair and Oenach Cruacha referred to were not Tara of Meath or Rathcroghan of Roscommon since both were firmly in the hands of the Cruthin of Ulster for a considerable time after the reign of Cremthann. The predicament is solved when it is understood that Temhair and Oenach Cruacha referred to Cnoc Temhro (Turoe) and Oenach Cruacha, (Sidh Cruachan) in Galway before pseudo-history reinterpreted this archaic material and engineered its structural transformation in favour of Tara and Rathcroghan. These two Galway sites are some 6 miles apart. It is no surprise that the kings of Turoe (Rí Temhro; 'rígrad Temhrach') of Galway would be interred in the presently unrecognized vast archaic Necropolis of Sidh Cruachu/Oenach Cruachna around the present town of Athenry.

Senchas na Relec names 3 notable exceptions to the general rule: "Three Rí Temhro (converted by pseudo-history to 'Kings of Tara') were not buried in *Releg na Rí lamh le Cruacha* because they had become believers in God, namely Connor mac Nessa, Morand mac Corpri, and Cormac mac Art." Following this Leinster intercalation it reverts to the original text and ignores Connor mac Nessa and Morand. It refers only to Kings who ruled at the Temhair of Galway (*Rí Temhro*), Cormac, his father Art and Conaire Mor. Niall of the Nine Hostages was added to a later rescension which is of Ui Neill provenance. The original text had no reference to Niall. Being unfavourable to the Ui Neill it was 'updated'. It states that before the time of Cremthand the Rí Temhro were interred in Oenach Cruachan and that from Cremthann's time until that of Loeguire mac Neill (note the Ui Neill provenance and fictitious claim) they were buried at Bru na Boinne, the megalithic necropolis of Knowth, Dowth and Newgrange on the Boyne, all except for the said four. It deals at length with Cormac in a clear manipulation of facts the better to bring him into close association with Tara. It does the same for Art and Niall in a more succinct manner insinuating that they were both Kings of Tara. Pseudo-history first claimed that Cormac mac Art founded the High Kingship of Tara. The founding of the High-kingship was pushed back in time in late versions to include Art and his ancestors.

Senchas na Relec gives an interpolated version of Cormac mac Art's burial. The politically motivated rehash created by the Tara Myth Syndrome made Cormac Tara's most famous monarch. It says he became a Christian. This is tantamount to proclaiming that there were Christians in Ireland, and that a High King had become a Christian, long before Patrick's time, a serious body blow to the Tara/Patrick Myth. That it was not suppressed is a clue that the original tale preserved the seed of truth in its claim that Cormac became a Christian. He was forced to resign from the kingship by the Druids after his conversion. He retreated to Achaill. Dying tradition in the Craughwell/Dunsandle area of central Galway claims that the double-ringed fort of Caher Cormic W of Dunsandle on the E side of the ancient territory of Achaill Oichne, 6 miles SE of Athenry and W of Turoe, was where Cormac mac Art retired. The interpolated version attempted to associate Cormac with an Achaill near Tara in order the better to accommodate the Tara Myth version.

This pseudo-version claims that before he died Cormac ordered that he should not be buried in the pagan cemetery of Bru na Boinne on the Boyne near Tara, but in a Christian cemetery (another hint that there were Christians in Ireland at that early date). As his bier was allegedly being carried thither the Boyne flooded. It was impossible to bury him there. So he was buried at Ros na Rí on the banks of the Boyne. Blatant fiction! Pseudo-history at its brilliant worst! Old folklore current in the Gurteen, Tample, Tiaquin and the central Galway area claims the tumulus burial mound known as Cormac Uagh (Cormac's Tomb), which gave its name to Cormacuagh beside the ancient *Teampaill* (very early church) which gave Tample (6 miles NE of Athenry and NW of Turoe) its name, is the burial mound (*'uagh'*) of Cormac mac Art. This preserves the older tradition that Cormac having become a believer requested to be buried at the Christian cemetery of the church of Tample N of Attymon. His burial mound still stands there in a section of Temple townland known formerly as Cormac Uagh South which was changed to Cladh (corrupt Clough) after the great outerward ramparts of the Turoe/Knocknadala oppidum passing through the area. When an O Kelly prince built his mansion on this ancient cemetery bones from smaller mounds were reburied at the side of this burial mound of King Cormac Mac Art.

Senchas na Relec in the form in which it has come down claims that Niall, ancestor of the Ui Neill dynasty, was interred at Ochain. This fictitious claim was concocted for the same justificatory reason as that of King Art and Cormac, the better to bring Niall, like Cormac, into close association with Tara. It is obviously erroneous since the territory of Ochain was still firmly in the hands of the Cruthin of Ulster for centuries after Niall's time before it finally became swordland of his much later descendants. *Senchas na Releg* similarly claimed that Conaire Mor, Rí Temhro (subtly manipulated by pseudo-historians to mean High King of Ireland ruling from Tara by the time of this redaction), successor of Eochaid Felech in Queen Medb's time, was interred at Magh Feic in Meath. This is contravened by the hand of the interpolator, **'H'**, who wrote in the space of the original text of Lebor na hUidhre, which he violently erased, that the Conaire interred in 'Fert Conaire' of Maigh Feic was not Conaire Mor, but Conaire Carpraige. Unaware that the earlier hand had deliberately transferred Conaire's burial place from Magh Feic[452] in Munster to Magh Feic in Meath the better to associate him to Tara as had been done to Art, Cormac Mac Art and Niall, **'H'** penned in his fictitious version of the 'official doctrine', in a note above the line, that Conaire Mor and Loegaire son of Niall were buried at *Temhair na Rí*[453] (understood by him and pseudo-history as Tara). Some 9 lines further on, a gloss attached to "Clanna Dedad hi Temhair Erand," in a hand labelled **M,** noted that this referred to the descendants of Conaire and the Erann/Fir Belg of West Munster. Conaire Mor of Temair Erainn was elected Overking of the Fir Belg tribes of Munster and Connacht at Temhroit (Turoe of Galway) a seat of the Fir Belg Overkingship, not High King of Ireland at Tara of Meath.

FIANNA FIGHTING FORCES OF THE FIR BELG KINGS AND QUEENS

The Fianna fighting force defended the High Kings of Ireland at Tara according to pseudo history. Why then were the branches of the Fianna fighting men, known also as the Colla/-Collaibh Oige ('young defenders': corruptly Colla Woga), placed in a wide circle along the periphery of the Galway/Mayo, Galway/Roscommon and Galway/Clare borders enclosing ancient nÓl nÉgmacht, and later along the perimeter of a greatly expanded Connacht? The question begs a definitive answer. There were various branches of the young Fianna defenders, Luigni and Gailenga, Mac Morna and Ciannachta, Fir Domnann and Menapi (Manach), Gammanrad and Catraige, to name a few. Well into historic times the Gailenga and Luigni were closely linked in S Cavan, N Meath and Dublin where they formed a line of buffer states with the Manapi, Ciannachta and other vassel states between the Cruthin and the far-expanded Connachta. Earlier segments of these tribes served a similar closely associated role in Mayo and Sligo. They were planted in N Connacht on the periphery of the Fir Belg oppidum of Ól nÉgmacht (to become known as Connacht), along the Ox Mountains and the Suck River. They formed extensive buffer states between the Fir Belg and Cruthin. They erected defensive frontiers further and further NE. The Mac Umhoire, Fir Domnann and Gamanrad were interspersed with the Mac Morna and Manapi fighting men stretching at one time SE from Loch Conn to Loch Mannin in Mayo to the source of the Suck through Loch Ui Flynn and Castlerea in Roscommon where they swung SSE along the Suck. They skirted the boundary of the Cruthin-held heights of Croghan of Roscommon. On the E banks of the River Suck vestiges of Cruthin defence embankments survive facing W against those of the Fir Belg of Ól nÉgmacht.

The Cruthintuatha Croghain were a major adjunct of the Cruthin of Ulster across the Shannon in Connacht. The Gailenga and Luigni expanded N dominating Cruthin subtribes until eventually they became an overkingdom in their own right in the later middle ages. Their ruling families, the O'Gara and O'Hara, were prominent until the 17th century. The baronies of Gallen in Mayo and Leyney in Sligo bear the names of these buffer states as did their later buffer states of the greatly expanded Connacht in the baronies of Lune and Mor Gallion in Meath. Medb had 3000 Gaileoin from Leinster divided into separate bands dispersed among her armies lest by their prowess they might take over the reins of power. They receive honourable mention in *Táin Bó Cuailgne*. Medb testified to their prowess but distrusted their loyalty. The historical tribes of the Gailenga of Mayo and Meath are identified with the Gaileoin. Meath and Dublin colonies retained the older form of the name 'Gallion'. Early colonies left their name in Laois and Offaly as Gailine (Abbeyleix) and Gallen (Ferbane). They were of Leinster origin. One colony granted lands in Antrim for their services to the Ui Neill were of Leinster origin.

---

[452] Magh Feic around the hill of Clarach near Millstreet and the upper Blackwater in NW Cork.
[453] Lebor na hUidhre, 51b, line 4102: *'hi Temraig he .i. Conaire & Loegaire'*

The Mac Morna descended from the Continental Belgic Morini, neighbours of the Attrebates and Menapi. They loom large in early Irish legend as leaders of the Connacht Fianna. In literature and legend the Fianna are linked to several areas along early frontiers of the Fir Belg oppidum, along the heights of the Aughta Mountains straddling the Clare/Galway border on the S, in the vicinity of Ballinasloe on the E, along the Mayo/Roscommon/Galway border on the N, and along the Galway coastline in the W along the defence lines around the Fir Belg oppidum. Legendary history is explicit about the places of residence of several of the leaders of the Fianna fighting men, who in pseudo-history allegedly guarded the High Kings of Tara. Far from residing near Tara in the E, they are found instead surrounding the Turoe/Knocknadala oppidum in Galway. Conan Maol Mac Morna had his home (*'baile'*) in *Cill Tulach* NE of Tuam in Galway. Garaidh Mac Morna's residence was in Formaoil beside Lough Ui Flynn on the upper Suck near the Galway/Mayo/Roscommon border. Goll Mac Morna, Chief of the Fianna fighting bands had his home in Maen Magh, the plain of which Turoe is the centre. This was the country of the Clanna Morna leaders of the Fianna forces of the Fir Belg of Connacht, both of Turoe (*Temhair na Rí*) and Rath Cruacha. The Fianna defended Kings of Turoe, not High Kings of Ireland at Tara which was then part of ancient Ulster. The Ulster Red Branch Knights defended Tara.

"FORMAOIL NA bhFIANN - A COUNTRY OF THE CLANNA MORNA"

The *Formaoil na bhFhiann* were Herbal Hospitals for the care of wounded warriors. Of the many Fir Belg Formaoil, one was in Caher River Valley near the Green Road dyke of Gleninagh in NW Clare. There was a Manapian Formaoil in Seefin, in SW Galway, and a Fir Domnann Formaoil in Louisburg WSW of Croagh Patrick in Mayo. In his 'Formaoil na bhFiann, a country of the Clanna Morna', J.H. Lloyd listed 4 Formaoil na bhFiann, one of the Luigni near Loch Arrow in Sligo, one in Fir Belg territory at Suidhe Finn in Tipperary, one in the Ui Bairrche area of Wexford and Formaoil na bhFiann on Sliabh-Ui-Fhloinn near the Galway/Roscommon border in Garadh Mac Morna's land, a renowned Fianna leader. This 500-ft hill, Breicsliab, was formerly Suidhe Finn, a convalescent seat of the Fianna. In *'Acallam na Senorach'* the district of Formaoil na bhFiann in W Roscommon and N Galway is described in detail, giving the names of many places in the area.

When Cailte Mac Morna reached the summit of this beloved hill he wept on "seeing the place where Finn Mac Cool was wont to sit, for a choice hunting ground of the Fianna was this mountain, and Loch Formaoile below. Cluain na Damraid (Kiltullagh) was the residence of Conan Mac Morna. Ros na nEcraide had a stud of the steeds of the Fianna. Carraic na fhUmhorach (Dunmore N Galway: Centre of the Umhoire and Clanna Morna), was in the distance." *'Laoidh an Duirn'* tells that Goll Mac Morna, Fianna Captain, was seriously wounded on *Cnoc Temhro* (Turoe). 1000 men of the Clanna Morna escorted him to Formaoil na bhFiann passing Rath Cruacha on their way. Pseudo-history distorted this episode making him travel from Tara via Croghan of Roscommon on his way to this Formaoil. The itinerary from Turoe necessitated going via Athenry (Rath Cruacha) before turning north because of the line of bogs blocking any passageway N for miles. Goll was placed in intensive care among the herb gardens of Formaoil na bhFhiann on Sliabh Ui Fhloinn. Nine weeks he languished there as he was nursed back to a state of convalescence. Prof. Connellan in his 'Dissertation on Irish Grammer' (1834) noted that Irish speakers called the many *'Formaoil na bhFiann'* hospitals of the Fianna. This is confirmed by the details of this arresting tale of archaic hospitalization and intensive care.

Wendy Davies of the Department of History, University College, London, overlooked this material and its significance in her 'The Place of Healing in Early Irish Society': "I have for some years been puzzled by the fact that there are relatively few healing miracles in the earliest Irish *Vitae*. Nor is there any strong tradition of sick care. It is notable that there is no large collection of charms or herbal remedies. These are puzzling omissions for one might expect to find traces of some early native tradition among the rich collection of early texts to come from Ireland. I am therefore stimulated to think about the significance of these lacunae: what did the early Irish do about care of the sick? Can it be that there was no tradition of healing in early Irish society? If so, what does this signify about that society? Determining the means of such provision is crucial to describing a social structure...I have been struck by Professor Binchy's emphasis, in his introduction to 'Bretha Dein Checht', on the absence of medical treatises from early Ireland."[454] Her low appreciation of early Irish society based on this alleged lacuna must be addressed. Early Ireland knew of numerous *'Formaoil'* Hospitals. This episode from 'Formaoil' tradition is evidence that there was care of the sick and wounded. Of the various Formaoil described, Lloyd noted that the Fianna of the Clanna Mórna "retired there to recover from battle-wounds."[455] In these sanatoriums, as noted, wounded warriors were placed in herb gardens to bring them speedily to a state of convalescence (the Clanna Mórna were connected with Loughrea/Leitrim in S Galway and in N Galway. They descended from the Morini whose Capital, Thorout/Thauroit near Brugge in Belgium, is cognate with Turoe (Temhroit).

CLOSE LINKS BETWEEN FIR BELG OF MUNSTER AND CONNACHT
Close ties existed between the ruling Fir Belg tribes of Munster and Connacht descended from Gann, Sengann and Dela, and between them and the Menapi. Fiachu Fir Mara was ancestor of the Muscraige, Corco Duibhne of Kerry, Corco Baschain of West Clare, the Dal Fiatach and Dal Riata of Ulster. This Menapi seaman set up trading colonies around the coast where dense clusters of Menapian family/place names survived, such as around Ath Cliath Magh Rí in Galway Bay. They expanded inland and formed settlements such as the Mendraige kingdom in Cork, Lughaid Meann's kingdom in Clare and Manapi settlements in Magh Colla and the Loch Corrib area in Galway. They became so strong as to be a threat to Gann's descendants. The 3 sons of Cairbre Mac Conaire,[456] Oengus Musc, founder of the Muscraige, Ailill Baschain of the Corco Baschain, and Eochaid Riata of the Dal Riata, were grandsons of the Conaire Mór, son of Eterscel, whose burial place was at Magh Feic near Millstreet, Co. Cork. Manapi princesses married into the Eoghanacht and Connacht aristocracy and vice versa. The mother of the three Cairbres was Sarait, daughter of Conn Cetchathach, Fir Belg Overking. In *'De Maccaibh Conaire'* Conaire is a contemporary of Eoghan Mór, ancestor of the Eoghanacht of Munster, and son of Conn's daughter Sadb. A gloss on the text represents Eoghan Mór as a son of Eterscel and brother of Conaire Mór, confusing Eoghan, son of Ailill Olum (Aulomm), with his grandfather who was also known as Eoghan Mór (Mug Nuadat), Eoghan Taillech or Eoghan Fitech (Fithecchach). Ailill Olum wed Sadb. In either case, Eoghan's mother was Sádb, daughter of Conn Cetchathach. Conn's daughter, Sádb, first wed Lughaid Loigde (Lága) of the Corcu Loigde of Cork by whom she bore Lughaid Mac Con. Lughaid Mac Con was fosterson and son to Oilill and Sádb, and grandson of Conn. "He and Eoghan Mór were reared on the same knee, at the same breast."[457] Eoghan's Queen was Moncha of Monapia[458] (of the Menapi). Eoghan Mór's granddaughter, Mongfhind, wed Eochaid Muigh Mhaen (Moyvane), Fir Belg Overking, ancestor of Connacht's medieval kings and dynasties.

Conaire Mór and his Clann Dedad descendants had their power base at Temhair Érainn as told in the necropolis text *"Clanna Dedad hi Temhair Érainn"* (Temhair Luachra, now Tara Luacra, Tara Hill or Friarstown Hill) overlooking Friarstown Abbey, 7 km. S of Limerick city.[459] As Fir Belg/Erann overking of Munster and Connacht, Conaire expelled the sons of

---

[454] W. Davies, 'The Place of Healing in Early Irish Soc' in 'Celtic Studies in honour of Prof Carney" p. 43-7

[455] J.H. LLoyd, 'Formaoil na bhFhiann', in 'Galway Archaeological and Historical Society' p.115.

[456] Eriu, vi, 133; LL 324, b 29-30.

[457] Myles Dillon, 'The Cycles of the Kings', p. 16.

[458] "The Menapia Quest", Norman Mongan, p. 129

[459] Eamon Kelly and Tom Condit in "Limerick's Tara" in 'Archaeology Ireland' Vol. 12, No 2, 1998

Désa from Ireland for marauding. At sea they met a British Menapi reaver, Ingcel (Ancel) of the Conmaicne.[460] They disembarked at Tracht Fuirbthi (Furbo today) in Galway Bay in the land of the Conmaicne (Connemara). With 5000 men they marched along the Slí Mhannin (Mannin/Manapi Road) to Temhair (Turoe) and assassinated Conaire who was being entertained at Bruiden Da Dhearg near Turoe. It is not stated whether they usurped the Fir Belg Overkingship or, if so, for how long. But the Menapi threat was now real.

The Book of Lecan and Book of Ballymote record the tradition that Eoghan Mór sojourned with Connacht's Conn Cédchatach, his father in law, to help curb the power of the Menapi by setting up his stronghold at Rath Fidech (Fidig, Fidich, Fidachi Regia) in the N of Aidhne S of Athenry at the heart of what had become a sprawling Menapi settlement stretching fom Ath Cliath Magh Rí to Loughrea near the Turoe oppidum core. He settled his bands of young warriors, the Oige Beatra/Ogaibh Bethra, which he brought from Crich Ealla (Duthaigh Ealla, now Duhallow on the Allow River near Kanturk in NW Cork) around Rath Fidech.[461] The Oga Beathra are recorded as one of the 4 tribes of archaic Aidhne, the other three being the Ciarraige Aidhne, Tradraige Dubrois and the Caonrige Árd Aidhne.[462] This Galway Rath Fidech was at the pivitol point of the 3 divisions of Ól nÉchmacht. Eoghan had two other strongholds, also called Rath Fidech, one in Huibh Liathain in S Munster and one in Coiced Conaire in N Munster.[463] All 3 had large souterrains (*'fithecc'*) which allegedly gave him his sobriquet, Fitecchach. When Lughaid Mac Con led his vast army of Menapi and Fotads from MannauGoddodin in the SE of Scotland to Áth Cliath Magh Rí in Galway Bay he slew the Fir Belg Overking Art son of Conn together with Eoghan Mór and his sons at the Battle of Magh Mucruime of Athenry and marched to Temhair (Turoe) to usurp the title of Rí Temhro, as told below. To dissipate this growing threat, Cormac Mac Art later led a large contingent of the Manapi fighting men (the Colla Menn)) against Ulster at the Battle of Crinna and settled them along its border as the Airghialla. The mother of Conall Corc, founder of Cashel's Eoghanacht line, was Bolga Manand Bretnach of pure Manapi stock.

By the 8th century the Ui Neill, who hived off from the Connacht Fir Belg stem in the 5th century, won unchallenged control of the N Half of Ireland. At the Terryglass '*Dáil*' in 737 (cf. p. 376f) the Ui Neill in concert with the Munstermen evolved the doctrine of two equal hegemonies of Ireland of Leth Cuinn (the N Half) and Leth Moga (the S Half) divided between them along the ridge of the Esker Riada across Ireland. Soon thereafter the Ui Neill publicly alleged many of their kings were High Kings of Ireland. The Munstermen followed suit but "did not succeed in evolving an 'accepted lie' which could give their cause the morale it needed in the eyes of the learned public."[464] Overkingship of the Fir Belg/Erann tribes had alternated between Munster and Connacht kings in earlier times. Now pseudo-historians made Conaire both succeed Conn Cedchathach as High King of Ireland of Tara (*Rí Temhro*) and precede him, splitting Conaire into 2 distinct Kings, Conaire Mór Mac Eterscela, hero of '*Togail Bruidhne Da Derga'*, and Conaire Mac Mogha Láma, Conn's successor.[465] And instead of the friendship and aristocratic intermarriage between their dynasties, Eoghan and Conn are suddenly turned into fierce rivals fighting for the High Kingship of Ireland, which incidentally did not come into being for two centuries after the Terryglass Dáil. It was alleged that Eoghan banished two Munster kings, Conaire mac Moga Lama and Macnia (Lughaid Mac Con) mac Lugdech and took the kingship himself. The

[460] R. 136 a 29-32
[461] Laud 610; ZCP viii 312f; Ml 20; Ca 302; Ai 84 b: Lec 164 Fy Tp; RC xvii, 7; Ml 20; Hc 568 a.
[462] Fy. 52; X. 48.
[463] Ml 20; Ca 302; Hc 568a.
[464] "Irish Kings and High Kings", Francis John Byrne, p. 202-203.
[465] F. T. O Rahilly, EIMH, p. 202-3; BDD 92; Tucait Innarba na nDéssi, (LU 4363) here Sarait, daughter of Conn, is consort of Conaire Mór and contemporary of Cormac Mac Art; Eriu vi, 147.

deposed kings took refuge with Conn at Tara. "Conn gave them his daughters in marriage." "An invasion of Munster follows. Eogan is defeated and Conaire and Macnia are restored. Eoghan went to Spain, married the daughter of Eber, King of Spain, and retrurned with an army of 2000 Spanish warriors. Conaire and Macnia submit to him. He stirred up the Laighin and the Ulaid to revolt against Conn. Conn was compelled to divide Ireland with him. Eoghan renewed the war against Conn, but on this occasion was defeated and slain in the battle of Magh Lena. Conaire and Macnia were once more restored to their kingdoms, the 2 provinces of Munster."[466] *Cath Maige Lena* developed this fiction. Earlier, Eoghan's Queen, Moncha[467] was manipulated by the Crecraige (a vassal-tribe of the King of Cashel) who made her a daughter of Triath (Dil) maccu Creca of the Crecraige to claim special privileges from Eoghan's descendants. Thus medieval anachronistic propaganda suppressed and obscured legendary history which told a very different story.

CATH MAGH MUC DHRUIME - LUGHAID MAC CON AS 'RÍ TEMHRO'

Lughaidh Mac Con's expulsion and later invasion of Ireland is told in *Cath Maigh Mucc Dhruime*. He assassinated Art son of Conn, father of Cormac mac Art, and usurped his throne as *Rí Temhro* (King of Turoe), Overking of the Fir Belg tribes. Eoghan Mór and Lughaid Mac Con were on their way to visit their uncle, Art son of Conn, Sádb's brother, not in Tara but Turoe, and quarreled over the ownership of Fer Fí under the sacred yew tree at Munster's coronation site, a dispute over the kingship. Lughaid challenged Eoghan to battle. Their armies met at Cend Abrat. Eoghan wounded Lughaid. Eoghan was victor. Lughaid fled to Scotland to a king related to his own Manapian people who inquired: "How are Lughaid's people (the Corco Loigde of Cork)?" Lughaid replied: "They are not prospering, but in subjection in the service of Eoghan." Hearing his grievance, the Scottish king helped him assemble a vast army from various tribes including Votadini and Manapi from MannauGoddodin in SE Scotland. Led by Lughaid Mac Con, the enormous fleet, forming a bridge of ships all the way from Scotland to Ireland, sailed to Ath Clee Magh Rí in Galway Bay and assassinated King Art. Lughaid Mac Con then marched on Temhair (Turoe) and usurped the Overkingship (Rí Temhro).

The route to Turoe led through Magh Mucc Dhruim, the plain of the Magic Pig's Dyke around Athenry. The tale digresses to explain how Magh Muc Dhruim got its name from the Magic Pigs from Cruacha chased by Medb around the plain of Magh Muc Dhruim - a classic mythological account of the erection of the defensive Dykes of the Athenry/Rath Cruachu oppidum dug up by the Magic Boar. Hence its name, Magh Muc Dhruim. This name was altered by pseudo-history to Mag Muccrime/Muccrama to distort its startling significance which anchored Queen Medb in Athenry. It is implicit that the "tombs of Cruachu" as well as Medb's palace of Rath Cruacha were in Magh Mucc Dhruim. After the 8th century conquest of Rathcroghan of Roscommon by Ui Briuin dynasts the mythological tale was stripped of its meaning. Rath Cruacha was re-interpreted as Rathcroghan. Art stalled the invasion force along the outer-ward dykes near Clarenbridge and called his Munster cousins from Rath Fidech to his aid, seeing the enormity of the invading force. It was led by Lughaid Mac Con, Lughaid Lága, and Beinne Bruitt (from Pictland near the Firth of Forth in SE Scotland). They concealed half their troops in the dyke's fosse.[468] The remainder ambushed the forces led by Art, Eoghan son of Oillil Olum and his 6 brothers. They turned Art's Belgic defensive system against him. Suddenly they (Menapi and Votadini from ManauGoddodin and Picts) emerged from the dykes and massacred Art's forces. Beine

---

[466] 'An Encyclopaedia of the Irish Folk Tradition', Dr. Daithi O hOgain, p. 183; O Rahilly, EIHM p. 186.

[467] "The Menapia Quest", Norman Mongan, p. 129

[468] Archaic details of Lughaid's stratagems are considered 'obscure' and misunderstood by editors & interpolators just as was the interpretation of the place where Lughaid's army landed, Ath Clee Magh Rí. The oppidum outer ward 'Claidhbha' (Dykes) are confounded with cleith/cliatha/(swords). cf p. 112.

Bruitt beheaded Eoghan Mór. Lugaid Lága, overcome with sorrow for his nephew, beheaded Beinne Bruitt. He then assassinated Art. The 7 sons of Oillil Olum, King of Munster, were slain. Mac Con marched on Temhair (Turoe) and reigned as *Rí Temhro*. His resided at the great stone fort of Clochar Mhac Con Erainn (Clocharvaconierin; Mac Con's Palace) in Kilconierin on the Moyode (Magh Fhót) boundary, 3 miles W of Turoe. The Votadini and Manapi set up buffer states around him, the Votadini in Magh Fót on his N flank, the Manapi in the Colla Mann district (Magh Colla) S of him. Cormac Mac Art later expelled Lughaid from the Overkingship when he delivered an unjust judgement. Lughaid Mac Con returned to Munster with a great following to serve under his foster-father Oillil Olum and his mother Sádb. Lughaid Lága refused to return to Munster since he had opposed his 'brother'. He entered the service of King Cormac Mac Art[469] as overking of the remaining vassal-allies from Scotland who remained behind in central and SW Galway.

Art was assassinated at a defence line of the Turoe Fir Belg oppidum near Carn Conaill to the NE of Clarenbridge and Ath Clee Magh Rí where Lughaid's army disembarked. The *Dindsenchas Ath Claidh Medraige (Magh Rí)* refers to "black-thorn and purple-thornbush-covered defense dykes."[470] Local elders point out the cairn where Art was interred near the place of his assassination at Lahart. When the Kingship was restored to Cormac, he had his father's remains brought for burial at the royal cemetery of Fearta on Turoe where his tumulus was erected. Cruachan Airt (Art's Burial Mound) stood out on the brow of Turoe until it was most unceremoniously bulldozed into oblivion in 1991, the last of the royal Turoe burial mounds to be destroyed. No more will Patrick Keane and local Turoe farmers point it out to their sons, nor their grandsons to their own children, as had been done by Turoe residents before them, proudly proclaiming: "There is Cruachan Airt, the burial mound of Art son of Conn, father of King Cormac mac Art." Old tradition sinks into oblivion having no visible garb henceforth. Pseudo-history substituted 'Treoit' of Meath for Turoit of Galway as the site of Art's tumulus to associate him with Tara. The blatant interpolation in the hand of **H** in Lebor na hUidre version of *Senchas na Relec* states that Art's body was carried east (from SW Galway to Treoit of Meath), where his *'fert'* (tumulus) was erected *'i nDuma nDergluachra ait hi fail Treoit indiu."* The tumulus of Dergluachra in which he was allegely buried is known as Denda Dimor, Moat of Dimor, near the Cavan/Meath border. The original tale told that his remains were carried E from Carn Conaill in SW Galway to Galway's *Temhróit* (Turoe).

In the 'Three Poems in Middle-Irish Relating to the Battle of Mucrama' (Magh Muc Dhruime) derived from a source known to the author of LU[471] existing in his day, and edited by Eoin MacNeill, it is insinuated by way of a gloss in an interpolation of the text that Art kept his favourite hunting seat there at Denda Dimor[472] while he was High King of Tara. The ulterior motive behind the interpolation was to secure a close association for Art to the vicinity of Tara the better to make him less conspicuously out of place there. "It is in effect a Christian interpolation in the form of an episode (inserted in the tale of the Battle of Mucrama, manipulated in the "Leinster Cycle") of a vision/prophecy which allegedly took place the day before Art marched against Lughaidh Mac Con in SW Galway. It is inserted, together with a corrupt version of the accompanying poem, in all the later copies of the tale.[473] It is a feeble effort on the part of the interpolator to transpose the context of Art's royal seat from Turoe (*Temhróit*) of Galway in the W to the vicinity of Treoit NW of Tara of Meath in the E. The vision of angels ascending and descending introduced by the

---

[469] Myles Dillon, 'The Cycles of the Kings',

[470] "claidhbha draigin is derg-sceach. Ó na claidhbha-sin amne is Áth Claidh co trese trébh." corrupt 'cliathaibh.

[471] *'Lebor na hUidre'*, ed. Best & Bergin

[472] *Cain do Denna Den'* with pseudo-gloss .i. *Denna Dimor fer grada Airt*, the Moat of Dimor, Art's favourite

[473] Eoin Mac Neill, 'Three Poems in Middle-Irish', in Proceedings of the Royal Irish Academy, p529.

monastic interpolator is, as Mac Neill noted, "manifestly founded on Jacob's dream. Stanza 27 contains an allusion to Art's secret burial like that of Moses or Patrick."[474] This 'secret burial' of Art belongs solely to pseudo-history in an effort to associate Art with Tara and bolster the Tara Myth. No secret burial of Art existed in the traditional lore of the West. His tumulus stood out on the brow of Turoe hill.

How Art, hunting in the E of Ireland, knew that invaders were preparing to disembark near Clarenbridge in Galway Bay is camouflaged by an anachronistic ecclesiastic intercalation. Poem A tells that the Holy Spirit gave Art prophetic insight to see this portentous event. He set off to join the Battle of Mag Muc Dhruim in which he was assassinated. Lughaid Mac Con, invasion leader, usurped his throne, allegedly at Tara of Meath. Were Art King of Tara, then why should Lughaid Mac Con sail his armada from a port in Britain all the way round the dangerous W coast of Ireland to a seaport in Galway to march all the way across the country to usurp the throne of Ireland at Tara in the East when he could sail the short distance across the Irish Sea to an eastern port convenient to Tara? The answer, of course, is that the throne of Art as Rí Temhro was not at Tara of Meath but at Turoe of Galway.

Pseudo-history avoided the question of how Art crossed Ireland to engage Lughaid's army before it marched inland. O Rahilly posed the question without giving a convincing answer due to his infatuation with Tara. Intriguingly, the name of Art's hunting-seat in Poem A is *'Sidhe selca'*, 'Sidhe Seolgha' near Loch Corrib NE of Athenry near the 'house' of Olc Acha, where Art spent the night before the battle. Had Art been in the E of Ireland at the time of the invasion in the W, the invaders would have been half way across Ireland before he knew it. The fact that Art was assassinated on the front line defenses near the landing site shows he was nearby when the invasion force was sighted. The purpose of the anachronistic justificatory Christian camouflage was to bolster pseudo-history's version of events in favour of Tara. The lateness of the interpolated 'Three Poems in Middle-Irish' is exposed by its anachronistic nature and by the germ of the medieval feudal system contained in it.[475] Angelic visions/prophecies were favoured by the medieval pseudo-historians.

Cóir Anmann tells that Lughaid Mac Con married Fuinche, daughter of Benne Brit, King of the British Votadini of Manau-Goddodin in SE Scotland. Benne came with Lughaid to Ireland. One of Lughaid's (Scottish Magh Gergin) sons by Fuinche was Fotad Caindia.[476] He became Leader of Lughaid Mac Con's Fianna, as told in *Reicne Fothaid Canainne*. The site of Mac Con's palace, Clogharmhaconierin, adjoining Magh Fhót (Moyode) SE of Athenry, corroborates Lughaid's close connection to the Fothads. Fothad Airgthech,[477] was a brother of Fothad Caindia. Finn is depicted as feuding with Fothad Caindia. Smirnat Mongfind, Caindia's daughter, was the first wife of Finn hUa Baiscne from the Ui Thairrsig of Offaly. After her death, Finn chose Grainne, daughter of Cormac Mac Art. She eloped with the Fianna leader Diarmait Mac Morna. Finn wed her sister Ailbhe. Finn was chief (*rigfeinnid*) of the 150 Fianna leaders appointed by Cormac Mac Art. Locals claim Cloghar Fhinn in Sidhe Ethlenn (Saint Ellens)/Carnaun area N of Athenry was Finn's palace. Leinster pseudo-history made him Finn Mac Cumhail of Allen in Kildare defending Tara's High King.

The historic descendants of the army led by Lughaid Mac Con from Scotland to Ireland, the Fotads and Manapi, resided W of Turoe of Galway, not Tara of Meath, before being driven S to Munster. The Dindsenchas of *Medraige* (Magh Rí, Maree and Clarenbridge in Galway Bay) states: "The folk of the ireful Mac Con seized all the land around Medraige

---

[474] Ibid, in Proc. of the R. Irish Acad., p.530 (1894). See E.O'Curry on this piece, MS. Mat., p.391.

[475] As in line 44 of Poem C. See MacNeill, Ibid, Proceedings of the Royal Irish Academy, p.531, 1894

[476] Fated Canine was the name of the tribe on the N Dutch Coast before being overrun by the Friesians.

[477] Kuno Myer's ed. of Voyage of Bran, vol 1, p. 45.

(Clarenbridge) and settled there"[478] as corroborated by *'Corpus Genealogiarum Hiberniae.'*[479] The Manapi (Managh) of the Ballymanagh Tlds were densely settled around Clarenbridge and Maree, and had a string of Tlds. stretching inland to Loughrea jointly known as Magh Colla, and along the Connemara coast to Clifden where they were known as the Conmacnamara. The Magh Colla buffer state defended the oppidum from the Cruthin of Ciarraige Aidhne to the SW. The Scottish King who provided Lughaid Mac Con with his vast army to free his people from subjugation was related to his Manapian Corco Loigde tribe. He was a king in Manau Gododin in SE Scotland inhabited by the Manapi and Votadini (Fotads) who were forced to vacate Continental coastal districts by invading Germanic Friesians. The Votadini and Manapi who came with Lughaid Mac Con settled around his palace (Cloghar Mhac Con Ierin) at Moyode (Magh Fhót) W of Turoe and adjoining Kilconierin, and the Manapi (Managh) Tlds. on its S border. Cormac Mac Art fought 7 battles with followers of Lughaid Mac Con in SW Galway after the main body went into Munster. Cormac Mac Art, Fir Belg Overking, Fergal, King of Connacht, and the sons of Munster's king were slain by them at the Battle of Moyvilla near Maree SW of Athenry,[480] near the assassination site of his father. Pseudo-history made Cormac die near Tara. "In historical times the Uaithni were located in the NE of Limerick and N Tipperary, but at an earlier period they had dwelt W of the Shannon. They descended from the Fotads (Votadini), the name of a British tribe near the Firth of Forth (Scotland)"[481] Tradition claims Fothad Caindia retreated to Munster with Lughaid Mac Con. This is corroborated by his death at the Battle of Feic (Clarach hill near Millstreet, Co Cork).

TARA IN THE LIGHT OF 'CATH CRINNA' WAS PART OF EARLY ULSTER

Traditions embodied in the Ulidian Tales and legends of Cormac Mac Airt and the Battle of Crinna *(Cath Crinna)* tell that throughout an extended period an aggressive warfare was waged against the Cruthin of Ulster by the Fir Ól nÉcmacht (Connacht Fir Belg). They were aided by vassal allies who were awarded with the conquered lands. Cormac's title, *'Rí Temhro'*, referred not to a King of Tara of Meath but of Turoe of Galway. The implications of the Battle of Crinna corroborate the fact that at the time of Cormac, and for centuries after, the power of the Cruthin of Ulster extended S of the Boyne not only to Tara but as far as the Tolka River which flows into Dublin Bay on the East coast.

Vassal tribes were planted by Connacht as defenders of the outer-ward fortifications, becoming vassal owners of the lands conquered. These formed buffer states between the Connacht Fir Belg and Cruthin of Ulster. As Connacht's power expanded so did the power and extent of these buffer states, so that Connacht kings feared certain vassel tribes had become too strong and populous and might overthrow the central power. To offset this danger it was deemed necessary to expand further afield, aided by the strong vassal states, splitting those which constituted a threat and rewarding them with distant lands, while expanding Connacht's territory. The Luigne and Gailenga were planted at an early date along Connacht's N boundary. In Cormac Mac Art's day the Cruthin were mounting lightning hit and run raids against Connacht's Fir Belg Capitals as they were doing in Roman Britain, by land and sea. "The chief historic feature of Cormac's reign which can be gleaned from tradition is his constant warfare with the Ulaid"[482] who drove him south into Munster. Deciding enough was enough, he led Fir Belg tribes of S Ireland in a massive invasion of Cruthin territory. *Cath Crinna* does not state that Cormac was king of Tara, or

---

[478] "Muintir Mac Con co mbarann, cor gab in tracht-sa uile ocon ath-sa Medraige" Dinsenchas Medraige
[479] M.A O Brien, 'Corpus Genealogiarum Hiberniae' "Gabsat crích Maine is crích Fiachrach Aidne.' P. 265
[480] Aggie Qualter's 'Athenry', p. 55.
[481] T. F. O Rahilly, Op. cit. p.10-11. He wrongly claimed the Uaithni were called Autenoi (Auteinri) by Ptolemy. Ptolemy's record is 2 centuries earlier than the arrival of the ancestors of the Uaithni in Galway.
For Fothad Canann's death at Feic see 'Fianaigecht' p. 9-10; O Rahilly, Op. Cit. p. 34.
[482] Francis John Byrne, 'Irish Kings and High-Kings', p. 68.

that he "established the Connacht dynasty there." A careful analysis of the tale and its political geography shows that Tara and the territory S of the Boyne as far as the Tolka river flowing into Dublin Bay was part of Ulster. Despite claims that this was the annexation of Tara, Connacht did not annex Tara. Cormac led his Conacht vassal allies and Fir Belg tribes from across the South of Ireland to the battle of Crinna against the Ulaid. His army consisted of the Colla Menn tribes of Galway, their kinsmen, the Fir Managh of Dublin and Wicklow, the Ciannachta of Taidg Mac Cein, and the Luighne and Gailenga. He planted these on lands each conquered from the Cruthin of Ulster along the new border running NW from the Tolka to Loch Ramor to the NW Connacht coast.

MacNeill wondered why the annexation of Tara is glossed over by historians. "In their histories generally Tara is the seat of the monarchy in remote antiquity. This location of the monarchy in Tara from time immemorial, like the assumed existence of such a monarchy, exemplifies a common tendency, to project the known present into the unknown past."[483] Tara's annexation is subtly insinuated in *Cath Crinna*. The cause of the battle "was the hostility of the Ulstermen to Cormac's line. One king after another of this Connacht dynasty which still ruled over Connacht, had fallen in fight with the Ulstermen. Cormac had forced Ulster to give him hostages. So unsubdued were they that they set fire to his beard. Ulster again took up arms and drove Cormac out of Meath (*Midh,* the Midlands, not Tara, insinuating that he resided there), forcing him to take refuge in his native Connacht"[484]

Cath Crinna depicts Cormac assembling his vassal tribes, including the Ciannachta of Éile. These had a long history as vassal-allies of Connacht. Croghan Hill (tomb of Éile of Brí Éile) in the NE of Offaly was their Capital. Brí Éile is named after Éile, daughter of Eochaid Ferech, stepsister of Medb. Her first consort was Fergal Mac Mágach, her second was Sraibhgent Mac Niuil. When her stepsister Medb become Queen of Connacht, Sraibhgent led his sons/grandsons to seek service with Medb in the hope of war against Ulster to win lands for themselves. One of those, Aillil, ousted Medb's consort and took his place by her side as King of Connacht. The Ciannachta became guardians of Connacht's borders and went to war against Ulster. They formed a branch of Cormac's Collaibh Oige (young defenders; corrupt 'Colla Woige'; 'bh' of Collaibh strung on to 'Oige') in Galway's many Clann Chian (Cloonkeen) townlands. They were planted there to defend the NE of the Fir Belg oppidum and check the Cruthin Sogain enclave in NE Galway. From Cormac Mac Art's time they became known as the Ciannachta when Cormac took Tadhg Mac Cian, prince of Eile, as an ally. They marched with Cormac to the Battle of Crinna where they won land on Ulster's then SE border. Tadhg mac Cein is the personification of the Ciannachta, Luighni and Gaileanga in '*Cath Crinna*': "Before the battle, Tadhg made a compact with Cormac that, if Tadhg (personifying the frontier colonies) came off victorious, Cormac would grant him as much territory as he could ride round in his chariot on the day of victory."[485] Witness pseudo history's insinuations: "Tadhg completely defeated the Ulstermen. Though wounded, he set out in his chariot to ride round the territory he desired to win, ordering his charioteer to bring Tara within the circuit. Overcome with loss of blood, he fell into a swoon and lay unconscious in the chariot." No attempt was made to camouflage the fact that Tara was part of Ulster which might be conquered. It insinuates that Cormac Mac Art foresaw that Tadhg would try to possess Tara. "Cormac desired Tara for himself and bribed the charioteer to leave Tara out of the circuit of the ride. At intervals Tadhg woke from his swoon. Each time he asked: "Have we brought in Tara?" the charioteer answered "Not yet." At nightfall, Tadhg came to his senses and saw that he had reached the banks of the Liffey at Dublin which is here seen as part of the Cruthin lands of

[483] Eoin Mac Neill, 'Phases of Irish History', p.120

[484] Ibid, p.121.

[485] Eoin MacNeill, 'Phases of Irish History', p.121

Ulster. "Have we brought in Tara?" he asked. The charioteer said 'No'. Seeing he had been cheated, Tadhg slew the charioteer.[486] It is thus insinuated that Tara fell to Cormac.

Intoxicated by the Tara Myth, MacNeill wrote: "the territory that fell to Tadhg's share extended along the coast from Ardee to Dublin and inward along the N frontier of Meath to Loch Ramor. In the angle of this L stands Tara, ancient capital of North Leinster, but henceforth the capital of Cormac's kingdom." Although the N of this territory was occupied by Connacht colonies after the fall of Tara to the Ui Neill in 637, such was not the case with Tara and the area around Ardee in Cormac Mac Art's day. MacNeill erred in thinking Tara previously belonged to Leinster and passed to Connacht. "Except for this story of the Battle of Crinna, there is no other story which explains how Tara ceased to be the seat of the Leinster kings and passed into the possession of Connacht kings. There is no other account which explains how the Leinster frontier, which formerly lay along the Boyne and the Blackwater was afterwards pushed back to the Liffey and the Rye."[487] *Cath Crinna* shows that the area S to the Liffey, including Tara, never previously belonged either to Leinster or Connacht, but solely to the Cruthin kings of Ulster. MacNeill had to admit: "Yet in the story itself, there is no mention of Leinster and Cormac's only enemies were the Ulstermen. The conflict seems to be altogether between Cormac and Ulster.[488] Thus he struck the core of the original truth, but ignored it because of his preconceived ideas about Tara which led him to believe that the tale was defective. He could not bring himself to believe that the tale of the Battle of Crinna was stating the emphatic truth that up to this time the territory of ancient Ulster stretched all the way down south to 'the banks of the Liffey'.

The long hostility between Ulster and Connacht is not in question. It is Ireland's earliest history. The assumption that Cormac was already King of Tara and High King of Ireland before he was driven out of Tara by the Ulstermen is a subtle insinuation of pseudo-history, a blatant interpolation. Infatuation with the Tara Myth led the 'old historians' to tacitly assume that the Battle of Crinna was the aftermath of his forced exile and resulted in the so-called annexation of Tara. Should Cormac have been forcibly exiled from Tara, then the aftermath of the Battle of Crinna could not be called an annexation, but rather a reconquest of Tara. The assumption in the Battle of Crinna that Tara was annexed by Cormac is as spurious as that other fiction of the Tara Myth which fathered on the same Cormac the building of the Mound of the Hostages at Tara. Modern archaeology has exploded this myth by dating this tumulus to more than two thousand years before Cormac Mac Art's day.

Cath Crinna insinuates that Cormac drove the Ulaid north of the Boyne and annexed Tara. "Too much credence cannot be given to the historicity of this account. It is no more than an 'origin-tale' to explain the political situation of the 8th century, when the Southern Ui Neill were overlords of Brega kingdom extending over Meath, N Dublin and S Louth, and ruled over the vassal states of the Luigni, Gailenga and Ciannachta. It particularly refers to the Ciannachta, who (only by the 8th century after Tara was wrested from the Cruthin, not the 3rd century) occupied territory on both banks of the lower Boyne."[489] The insinuation that Cormac had to bribe the charioteer to save his alleged High Kingship at Tara goes beyond the bounds of credibility. To suggest that all Taidg had to do to take Ulster land for keeps was to encircle it in his chariot is too childish for credence. It is an insult to the Cruthin to suggest they would allow anyone 'conquer' even an inch of their land without a fight. It is more ridiculous to suggest that the alleged High-King of Ireland, Cormac Mac Art, was reduced to bribery to prevent his ally Taidg Mac Cein from taking Tara, so-called seat of

---

[486] Ibid, p.122.

[487] Ibid, p. 122-123.

[488] Ibid, p. 123.

[489] Professor F. J. Byrne, 'Kings and High-Kngs', p. 68.

the High-Kingship, denying Cormac the one object for which the battle was allegedly fought. It is transparently and ludicrously spurious.

14 Clann Cian (Cloonkeen) Tlds. in Galway remained of their once extensive presence there after a large segment of these Collaibh Oige marched with Cormac to push back the extensive kingdom of Ulster. The Luigni and Gailenga, neighbours in Connacht defending territory conquered by the Connacht Fir Belg from the Cruthin, were associated with the Ciannachta when Cormac planted them along the new boundary of Ulster. "There is reason to agree with MacNeill that they were vassal tribes of fighting men whom the Connachta brought from the West and planted on the lands they had conquered."[490] *Cath Crinna* shows that Cormac was not reigning king of Tara of Meath but of a power base in Connacht from which he mounted the invasion of the lands of the Cruthin of Ulster whose boundary then stretched from Tolka River in Dublin to Lough Ramor in Cavan and NW-wards. Tara was then well within this boundary of ancient Ulster. Cormac was already 'Rí Temhro' at Turoe of Galway long before he crossed the Shannon to invade the lands of the Cruthin. Pseudo-history did its utmost to reinterpret this title as 'High King of Tara' and King of Ireland.

Byrne sensed an interpolation in the context of the royal seat of Cormac as 'Rí Temhro' of legendary history, a sly shift from a Connacht centre of power to Tara of Meath as insinuated in 'Cath Crinna'. "There are indications that the Ulaid, even after they had lost their ancient capital and forfeited their sway over central and W Ulster, still ruled as far S as the Boyne in the first half of the 6th century," 3 centuries after Cormac's time.[491] Discerning a hoax embedded in 'Cath Crinna' bolstering the Tara Myth, Byrne concurred with Mac Neill that the Luigni, Gailenga and Ciannachta were vassal tribes of fighting men whom Cormac brought from Connacht and planted in a group of tribal kingdoms stretching from Glasnevin to Lough Ramor in Cavan. "The Brega Ciannachta with the Setna, extending as they did (leaving Tara within the Ulster boundary), give the impression of a remarkably homogeneous body."[492] He exposed the alleged early planting of the Ciannachta along the Louth/Meath coast E of Tara to which they gave their name at a much later date by noting that they could only "have been planted here by the Ui Neill centuries after Cormac's alleged reign" at Tara.[493] A case of pseudo-history pushing later historic fact back to archaic times to justify the present. Byrne's qualification of 'Cormac's reign at Tara' by his use of the word 'alleged' exposes *Cath Crinna's* insinuation that Cormac reigned at Tara. **F. T. O RAHILLY HAD TO ADMIT IN HIS LATE 'ADDITIONAL NOTES' THAT 'CATH CRINNA' SUGGESTS THAT AT THAT TIME THE POWER OF THE ULAID EXTENDED SOUTH OF THE BOYNE, AND CONSEQUENTLY INCLUDED TARA.**[494] Wow! At last! Sadly, his life was cut short before he had time to absorb the full ramifications and vast implications of his all too late astounding discovery.

The Airghialla planted by Cormac mac Art in the aftermath of the Battle of Crinna carried the frontline buffer states NW from Glasnevin on the upper Tolka along the Blackwater to Loch Ramor through Cavan to the Foyle in Londonderry. This formed a new NW/SE frontier with Ulster. Byrne's line of buffer states, marching with Ulster's frontier, stretches from Glasnevin on the Tolka in Dublin to Lough Ramor in Cavan. It is identical with an alignment of buffer states along Ulster's border embedded in an 8th century poem illustrating the early relationship between the Ui Neill and Airghialla who had been weaned away from Connacht by Ui Neill dynasts. It describes "the line of Airgialla stretching from

---

[490] Op. cit., p. 69.
[491] Op. cit., p. 69.
[492] Op. cit., p. 69.
[493] Op. cit. p. 69.
[494] T.F.O Rahilly, 'Early Irish History and Mythology', p.485.

the Buaighne (Tolka in Glasnevin) to Lough Febail (Foyle at Derry)," through Loch Ramor, leaving Tara well within the confines of ancient Ulster. It records an early tradition after Cormac Mac Art's day but before the Northern Ui Neill had moved from their home in the NE corner of Ireland defended by Airgiallan buffer states along the River Foyle

CORMAC MAC ART'S EXPULSION OF THE DEISI

Of the massive army led by Lughaid Mac Con from Scotland some followed him into Munster when he was expelled from the Overkingship of Temhair (Rí Temhro, Turoe of Galway). Segments of the Fotad (Votadini) remained behind. They had their stronghold at Clochar na ngFhotad (Fotad Palace) in Moyode (Magh Fhót in Galway. The Votadini (O. Irish 'Fotad'), like the Cauci in Wicklow, were allied to the Manapi. They were a Germanic tribe which overran the Dutch coastal strip N of the Rhine estuary earlier held by the Manapi. They were overrun by a later wave of Manapi whose hinterland territory was overrun by Germanic hordes. A century later both had mostly disappeared off the Continental map, pushed out by the Friesians. They re-emerged in Manau-Gododin (Manau = Manapi, Gododin = gFhotadin) in SE Scotland facing their former homeland. They swelled Lughaid Mac Con's invasion armada which formed a 'bridge of ships from Scotland to W Ireland'. Fotad Kings ruled at Moyode between the Turoe and Athenry oppida, not at Tara. They usurped the Fir Belg Overkingship, until expelled by Cormac Mac Art.

Tucait Innarba na nDéssi (Expulsion of the Déisi), altered in favour of Tara Myth, had nothing to do with the Déisi of Tara. Contravening pseudo-history, it referred to the Manapi, Fotads and Picts expelled from Galway where they had increased under Lughaid Lága, former consort of Sádb, daughter of Conn (grandfather of Cormac Mac Art). They were later ruled by Fiachu Suidge, Conn's sibling and became known as Dál Fiachach Suidge. The Fotads left their name on Moyode (*Magh Fhót*). The Manapi left theirs on the numerous Ballynamanna -munna -mannin -man -Manach or -Monagh Tlds. stretching from Loughrea to Clarenbridge. Many of the Manapi joined their kinsmen from the Dublin/Wicklow coastal area under Cormac Mac Art in his expeditions against the Cruthin of Ulster. Known as the Colla Menn, they were settled on conquered lands as buffer states. They became the Fir Managh and Fir Monach (Fermanagh and Monaghan). "Analysis by county shows that Galway had the most resident Menapian septs"[495] noted Norman Mongan in his record of his research on the Manapi. *Tucait innarba na nDéssi* tells that Art Corb of the Dál Fiachach Suidge had 4 sons, Brecc, Oengus, Echaid and Forad. Ceallach, son of Cormac Mac Art, abducted Forad's daughter. Oengus and Forad went to Cormac's court to find her. In blind rage Oengus slew Ceallach. The linkchain of his spear struck Cormac, blinding him in one eye. He became known as Oengus Gaifhuilech. War broke out between them because of this. Cormac expelled him and his brothers, the sons of Art Corb, for his son's death and his own blinding. Cormac retired to Caher Cormaic 4 miles W of Turoe, on the E of Achaill Oichne in SW Galway from which he expelled some of the Déisi. Cormac fought 7 battles against rebel Déisi tribes and was finally slain in battle at Moyvilla[496] near the Galway coast like his father, Art. Local tradition tells that because he was a Christian, Cormac was buried at Cormacuagh (Cormac's tomb) near Tample church between Attymon and Gurteen in E Galway. Pseudo-history, frantic to bring Cormac, like Art, into close association with Tara of Meath, claimed Cormac resided at Achall SW of Tara and was buried at Ros na Rí beside the Boyne in Meath having choked on a salmon bone from the Boyne. Before the expulsion Oengus Gaifhuilech and son Duibne resided near Turoe. After the expulsion Oengus was king of the expelled Déisi tribes of the S of Ireland under the Corcu Loigde of Cork.[497] His son Duibne went on to found the Corcu Duibne of Kerry.

---

[495] Norman Mongan, 'Menapia Quest', p. 192.
[496] Aggie Qualter, local tradition recorded in her 'Athenry', p. 55.
[497] Y Cymmrodor xiv, 104; Eriu iii, 135; LU 4335ff; Anecdota i, 15; Laws iii, 82; ZCP xx, 174f.

DEISI ROLE IN THE LAIGHIN INVASION AND CONQUEST OF DYFED

The expelled sons of Art Corb and followers were unwelcome among Cormac's Munster Fir Belg cousins. Fiacha Ba Aiccid, son of Cathaoir Mar, leader of the Laighin (Leinstermen) invasion, welcomed and settled them on swordland seized with their aid from the Ui Bairrche of SE Leinster. Known as Deisi (rent-paying/vassal), they helped his new kingdom expand at the expense of the Ui Bairrche. They remained there until the time of Crimthann Mac Enna Ceinselach when the Ui Bairrche forcibly repossessed their former lands. The Ui Bairrche gave them battle at Gabran and Commur and routed them in 7 battles.[498] Thereafter some went to Ard Ladrann. Others accompanied Echaid son of Art Corb when he went with Crimthann Mac Fidaig, Overking of the Fir Belg tribes of Munster and Connacht, to Wales to established the kingdom of Dyfed, and ease the overcrowding of Fir Belg Munster. Echaid Allmuir Mac Art Corb of Dal Fiachach Suigde got his epithet 'Allmuir' (Overseas) from this emigration to Wales. The 8th century ruling dynasty of Dyfed was descended directly from Echaid Allmuir. Welsh genealogies corroborate the 'Expulsion of the Deisi' record which is one of the main sources for the history of the Irish colonization of Dyfed. Miller has shown Echaid's emigration should be placed within the years 400-420.

The sons of Art Corb were instrumental in helping the invading Laighin to establish themselves in Leinster by pushing the Ui Bairrche north, which pushed their Manapi neighbours up the Wicklow coast to the N Dublin coast. "In early historical times the Laghin are the dominant power in that part of Leinster which lies S of the mouth of the Liffey; but numerous remnants of the earlier population survived, though reduced in status or expelled from their original territory. In the Ireland described by Ptolemy, on the other hand, there is not a trace of the Laighin. Those people we find occupying a subordinate position early in the historical period are in unchallenged occupation of this part of the country, Manapi (Monaig) and Brigantes (Ui Bairrche)."[499] The Ui Bairrche Tire who occupied the barony of Bargy in Wexford were "shorn of all their power and reduced to a position bordering on insignificance. In historical times they settled well to the N in the barony of Slievemargy (named after them) in SE Laois and adjoining portions of Carlow and Kilkenny. They had settlements further N in Kildare"[500] around Naas and Enfield and in SE Ulster.

"The dispersal of the Ui Bairrche from their earlier home in Wexford was the result of the hostility of the Southern Laghin (Ui Chenselaig). The 'Expulsion of the Desi' tells that the Ui Bairrche were expelled by Fiachu ba Aiccid, king of the Laghin. He gave their territory to the Desi who continued to occupy it until the reign of Crimthann (son of Eanna Censelaig), when Ui Bairrchan Eochu Guinech expelled them. According to the Tripartite Life, Cremthann Mac Censelaig, king of the Laighin, oppressed the Ui Bairrche, so that they migrated from there. One of them, Oengus mac Macc Erca, slew Cremthann in revenge for his banishment (c. 485 AD). Elsewhere, his slaying is attributed to Oengus' son, Eochaid Guinech, king of the Ui Bairrche.[501] A few years later (c. 491) Eochu Guinech aided the N Laghin in the Battle of Cenn Losnada (Kellistown in Carlow), in which Oengus mac Nad Froich, king of Cashel, son-in-law of Crimthann, was slain."[502] This war between the Ui Bairrche and Cashel's king reflects an advanced stage in the expansion of Fir Belg from the West at the expense of the dominant Brigantes across S Ireland. The late 4th century capture of Cashel by Corc, the establishment of the Deisi as Munster buffer states protecting Cashel, and the E expansion of the Corcu Loigde, caused further disestablishment

[498] R # 16; L 100f.
[499] T. F. O Rahilly, 'Early Irish History and Mythology', p. 39.
[500] Ibid, p. 36.
[501] LL 39 b 5; AI 10 a 19; Chron. Scot. 487; Ann. Clon. 73.
[502] T. F. O Rahilly, Op. Cit. p. 36-37; RC xvii, 120; Chron. Scot. 487; Ann. Clon. 73.

of the Brigantes. The Deisi were a link between the invading Laighin and Cashel. They played a large role in Cashel's expansion under Corc's descendants.

A remark by Flann mac Mael Maedoc (+ 979) throws light on the 5th century northward trek of the Ui Bairrche which had a knock-on effect on their Manapi neighbours, pushing them in turn further N up the Wicklow and Dublin coast. According to Flann the migration of the Ui Bairrche followed the slaying of Laidcenn mac Baircheda, the poet, by Eochaid, son of Enna Censelach. "It was as a result of this that they (Ui Bairrche) turned N from Enniscorty."[503] The name of his father, Bairchad, implies that Laidcenn was of the Ui Bairrche. Other texts note that Laidcenn's brother, Bri mac Baircheda, the druid, was with Cathaer Mar (ancestor of the Lagin) afterwards as a faithful ally.[504] The invading Lagin befriended the Deisi (sons of Art Corb) and rewarded them with lands for their services in dislodging the Ui Bairrche. The 'Expulsion of the Desi' states that the Lagin placed these Deisi on the lands of the Ui Bairrche Tire. These Deisi were the sons of Art Corb expelled from Galway by Cormac Mac Art. They must not be confused with the Cruthin known as "the Fothairt and Loighes (from whom Laois is named) who were also faithful vassal-allies of the Lagin and were known as *cliathaire Lagen*."[505] The most important Fothairt settlements were *Fothairt in Chairn* represented by the barony of Forth between Wexford harbour and Carnsore Point, and *Fothairt Fhea* forming the barony of Forth in Carlow. The Cruthin, fighting on behalf of Crimthann, King of the Laghin, crushed in battle a people known as the Tuath Fhidga and took possession of their land.[506]

In their new position along the Dublin coast the Manapi found themselves right on the front line of the ever-expanding Belgic overkingdom spearheaded from Connacht. Aware of the renowned Manapi military prowess, the Belgic overkings offered them new lands in return for their military service. They formed the SE end of the line of buffer states between the Fir Belg of Connacht and the Cruithin of Ulster whose territory stretched down to the north Dublin coast. The Irish Monaig (Manaig) are the representatives of Ptolemy's Manapi.[507] Early in the historical period these latter are found surviving in two widely separated communities, one in the W of Co. Down, the other along the shores of Lough Erne where they gave their name to Fermanagh (Fir Manaig) and Monaghan (named after the Monaig). The tradition of these Monaig/Manaig was that they come from S Leinster, their original settlement area. O Rahilly noted, "A stage in the northward trek of the Monaig seems to be indicated by the tradition which associates them with the north of Co. Dublin. Forgall Monach had his Otherworld residence near Lusk. In the parish of Lusk is Druim Monach/Drumanagh. A ford on the River Delvin got its name from Scenmenn Monach. The practical idenity of their names authorizes us to believe that the Monaig were ultimately the offshoot of the Menapi, one of the group of tribes collectively known as Belgae."[508] From an early period the Monaig, like other Airghialla septs, were associated with the Connacht Fir Belg power in the conquest of the Midlands at the expense of the Cruthin. In the final defeat of the Cruthin at the Battle of Moy Rath in 637 the Monaig were given lands in Moyrath in Down for their military services to the Ui Neill. These may be a different branch which came instead from the Isle of Man, the Manapi island.

The Manapi and Votadini (Fotad) in the van of Lughaid Mac Con's army settled beside Lughaid's palace in central Galway, Caher Mhac Con Ierin, on the Kilconierin/-

[503] Flann mac Maicc Erca, ZCP viii, 118, # 23, '*ba de sain soiset fo thuaid o Inis Coirthi.*'
[504] R 116 c 6.
[505] T. F. O Rahilly, Op. Cit., p. 34; R 119 a 5.
[506] LL 15 a 22-30.
[507] Eoin MacNeill, 'Phases of Irish History', p. 58.
[508] T. F. O Rahilly, Op. Cit., p. 32-33.

Moyode/Rathgorgin border when Mac Con usurped the Fir Belg Overkingship. When Cormac Mac Art drove him and his rebellious followers S into Munster, Mac Con's tutor Lughaid Laga, son of Eoghan Mór and brother of Oilill Olum of Munster, remained behind in Connacht in submission to Cormac Mac Art. He was king of the remaining Fotad/Menapi vassals (Deisi).[509] Later Conall Corc (Gorgin), greatgrandson of Eoghan Mór was installed as their king by Queen Mongfhind, widow of Eochaid Muigh Maen, Overking of the Fir Belg of Munster and Connacht. Corc's (Gorgin's) residence was Ailech Gorgin, Rathgorgin today, near Mac Con's former fort. On his return from exile Corc bought off Menapian and Fotad vassals and led them into Munster. He settled the Fotad in NE Limerick and N Tipperary and the Menapi in Magh Manand in E Cork and N Clare in repayment for their services in his conquest of Cashel, later Capital of Munster. They are the ancestors of the Uaithni, Mendraige, Corco Daula and Gregraige of Munster.[510] The Cork Menapi kingdom, Mendraige, was centered on the plain of Fermoy, bounded by the Nagles and Knockmealdown Mountains along whose S foothills are vestiges of the Cleeroo Belgic defence ramparts. It opens to the sea between Cork and Dungarven Harbours. The Menapi controled the sea-trade. Menapi strongholds in Fermoy district are Dunmanann and forts in the vicinity of Manning Fort overlooking the Funcheon River. The Abha Managh (Womanagh) flowing into Dungarvan Bay is named after them. Corc's grandson Oengus Mac Nad Frioch aided by the Deisi and Corcu Loigde expanded east at the expense of the Ossraige. So did the Deisi buffer states expand E through Waterford and S Tipperary.

Lughaid Meann led the Deisi of Manapian stock to colonize Clare with Eoghanacht assistance and establish a Menapian kingdom in Clare which later seceded from Connacht (Ol nEchmacht)[511] in the 5th century. Known as the *In Deis* they split in two. The Deis Deiscirt (Dail Cais) were fictitiously attached to the Eoganacht genealogy from the time of their illustrious descendant, Brian Boru. The main branch was called Deisi Mumhan to distinguish it from others such as the Deisi Breg around Tara in the Barony of Deece who were never expelled despite the fictitious claims of pseudo-history. Some Deisi septs driven into Munster joined Crimthann Mac Fidaig in his conquests in Wales. In the chaos following his death the Ossraige expanded as far W as Pallas Green in Limerick. Descendants of Echaid Allmuir's brothers in Leinster were driven back into the S of early Munster to join other Deisi septs in the service of Cashel. "There are 50 migratory bands which are called Deisi."[512] The Deisi Muman retained the name of Dal Fiachach Suidge.

CORC THE FOUNDER OF CASHEL OF MUNSTER
Luigthech, greatgrandson of Eoghan Mór of Munster, wed Bolga of the British Menapi (*Bolga Manand bann Bretnach*) by whom he had a son, Conall Corc. Crimthann Mac Fidaig, King of Munster, adopted his cousin, the young Corc (Gorgin).[513] When Corc scorned the overtures of Crimthann's consort, she accused him publicly of seducing her. "Hell hath no fury like a woman spurned."[514] Crimthann tried to have him slain by sending him to subjugate the Ossraige and levy taxes from them. Corc fled to the Turoe/Knocknadala oppidum in Galway to Mongfhind, Crimthann's sister, Queen and consort of Eochaid Muigh Mhaen, Fir Belg Overking (*Rí Temhro*) residing in Maen Magh (hence his epithet Moyvane) in Galway. She made him king of the vassal states of the Fothads (Votadini) and Menapi fighting men brought in by Lughaid Mac Con from Scotland who remained in Connacht as vassals to the *Rí Temhro* after Lughaid Mac Con's expulsion.

[509] Myles Dillon, 'The Cycles of the Kings', p. 18 - 21.

[510] F.J.Byrne, 'Irish Kings and High Kings', p.185.

[511] Ibid, p. 76

[512] Ibid, p.

[513] F. T. O Rahilly, EIHM, p. 49-50f, *"Bolga Manand Bret[n]ach brass"*, RC xlvii, 304

[514] Shakespeare.

They were first ruled by Lughaid Laga, brother of Oilill Olum and uncle of Eoghan Mór who had shared in Mac Con's fosterage, exile and return.[515] They were then ruled by Fiachu Suidge, younger brother of Conn. Finally they were ruled by Gorgin (young Corc) whose palace was at Ailech Gorgin (Rath Gorgin) beside Moyode between Turoe/Knocknadala and Rath Cruacha of Athenry at the heartland of these vassal tribes, Menapi (-Man -Men - Mannin -Monach and Managh Tld's) and Fotads of Moyode (Magh Fhot). When Crimthann succeeded Eochaid as Overking of Fir Belg tribes of Munster and Connacht at Turoe, Corc fled to Scotland, sailing from Ath Cliath Magh Rí port. The text's editor Vernam Hull confused this Ath Cliath with Ath Cliath Culainn in Dublin under the sway of pseudo-history which made Crimthann reign at Tara of Meath instead of at Turoe of Gaway. Pseudo-history claimed Crimthann sent Corc to a King of Scotland with a secret ogham message which only the Pictish king of Scotland would understand requesting him to slay Corc. Instead of death, royal marriage and dynastic alliance were his lot.

Corc wed the daughter of Feradach, King of Cruthintuath of Pictland. One of Corc's sons was known as Cairbre Cruithnechan (Cairbre of the Picts). The Eoganacht of Mag Gorginn in Scotland between the Tay and Dee rivers descended from Corc. Oengus Mac Forggusso (+761), the most powerful Pictish king known to history, descended from this off-shoot of Corc. The Kings of Lennox and the Stuarts of Scotland, from whom descended the British Royal house of Stuarts, claimed descent from another son of Corc, Maine Lemna. On Crimthann's death, Corc returned to Ireland via Ath Clee Magh Rí in Galway, the seaport used by Lughaid mac Con when he usurped the throne of *Rí Temhro*.

Fierce rivalry broke out for the kingship of Munster following the assassination of Crimthann Mac Fidaig, Overking of the Fir Belg tribes. In the chaos, the Ossraige and Briganten descendants of Brasal Barrech crossed their W boundary which stood until then along the E perimeter of the Galtee and Knockmealdown Mts. The long defensive boundary dyke ran from Ardmore via Cappoquin along the Suir W of Cashel and Thurles to the Slí Dála on the early boundary near Portumna. They burst through the Glen of Aherlow and other passes to the W foothills of these mountain ranges, driving the Deisi vassal-allies of the Eoganacht headlong before them. They erected a new defence line from Cappoquin to Fermoy along the Blackwater and thence N via Pallas Green on Bealach Febrat in Limerick N to the Shannon. Vestiges of this defensive boundary survive. Corc's wealth bought off the Scottish vassals-allies (Deisi) and their hostages who, following the expulsion of Lughaid Mac Con remained behind in Connacht. Corc had been their king before he fled for his life from Crimthann to Scotland. The Deisi in S Galway and in Clare who supported Lughaid Mac Con's invasion and waged 7 wars on Cormac Mac Art, for which they were expelled, were led by Corc against Munster's invaders. They arrived in the nick of time to save Munster from being overrun by the Ui Bairrche and Ossraige.

Recent historians question the expulsion of the Deisi from the Tara district, since the Deisi tribe remained there long after Cormac Mac Art's day. The vassal tribes whom Cormac expelled, not from Tara but from Turoe district, were the Fotads, Menapi and Pictish Dal Fiachach Suidge forces who came with Lughaid Mac Con. He assassinated Art and usurped the Over-kingship of the Fir Belg at Turoe (*Rí Temhro*). When Mac Con was expelled from the Overkingship, these rebellious vassal tribes were not trusted. Those who did not submit to Cormac were expelled to the S of the Shannon. From Corc's time many of the vassal Fotads, Menapi and other Deisi septs are found E and S of the Shannon in Munster.

---

[515] Myles Dillon, 'The Cycles of the Kings', p. 18-21, *Cath Maige Mucrama,* Stokes, RC 13, 426-74

CONALL CORC SETS FORTH TO FOUND CASHEL OF MUNSTER

O Rahilly censured MacNeill for stating: "Let it be noted that Cashel, seat of Munster kings in Christian times, stands outside of ancient Munster."[516] Early Kings of Munster had their power bases in W Munster. One was Knockgraffon in SW Tipperary, residence of Eoghan Mór's descendants, who earlier resided in the Limerick district of Knockaine until they dominated the Mairtine of Emly. An early capital of Munster was Temhair Erainn (Tara Hill) near Friarstown 7.5km S of Limerick city.[517] Just as Rathcroghan of Roscommon was not part of Connacht until well into historic times so too what is now East Munster, including Cashel, was not part of Munster before the 5th century AD. Tales concocted and updated to meet changing political circumstances told how Cashel was "discovered" by Corc c 400AD.[518] Despite the fact that Cashel was still outside the confines of Munster, Eoghanacht chroniclers made it appear Cashel was always part of Munster, albeit not yet its capital. The pseudo-historic legend of Corc with its mythological content was concocted at the behest of the later Eoghanacht sept, of which Conall Corc was its august ancestor. It told that Corc on his return to Munster lost his way in a snow-storm. That day the swineherd of Aodh, king of the Muscraighe, had seen a vision of a yew tree on the great rock of Cashel. He informed his master. Aodh's druid interpreted this to mean that the kingship of Munster would soon be centred on Cashel. The first person to light a fire under the yew-tree would be king of the entire province. Aodh wished to go at once but his druid advised him to wait until morning. Corc arrived on the rock before him, unaware of the prophecy. He lit a fire there. Aodh arrived and submitted to him. Within a week Corc allegedly had established himself as king of Munster. Pure myth! Believe it if you dare.

A later version states that when Corc came to Magh Femhen in which Cashel stands tall "the kingship of Ireland closed around him." These fables are transparently false. Had Corc come to Cashel without a mighty army he would have been eaten alive by the wardogs of Eile. It is implicit in the 8th century version that Cashel, until its conquest by Corc's 'sons', lay in the territory of Conall Mac Nenta Con, king of Eili Deiscirt. Thurles, *Durlas Eile,* N of Cashel, proclaims its earlier origin. The reality was very different then. As Dáibhi O Cróinín noted "Traces of an older political situation can be found in the crudely stitched fabric of Eoganachta origin legends, and in the personnel of important churches"[519] such as Emly (Imblech Ibair, *'medon Mairtine'* of the early Mairtine).

The conquest of Cashel was a lengthy warlike affair. It took more than 2 centuries for Corc's descendants to establish themselves in Cashel as the ruling kings of Munster. Only with the connivance and subtle pseudo-historic annalistic support of Armagh did they succeed in giving the so-called conquest of Cashel and Kingship of Munster by Corc wide credence. Snippets of local and legendary history stitch together the more credible scenario of Cashel's hegemony. These tell that after Crimthann's death Corc gathered the unwelcome vassal tribes from the territory around his former palace of Ailech Gorgin, i.e. the Fotads and Menapi (Managh) in Galway and led a great hosting S into Munster. He linked up with his father's people, the Eoghanacht and Corcu Laigde of the Lee district of Cork. They began the task of pushing back the Ossraige. The Deisi sept, expelled by Cormac Mac Art and welcomed by Fiachu Ba Aiccid of Leinster were later driven back into Munster. They entered into an alliance with Oengus Mac Nad Froich, grandson of Corc. Corc's followers, a medley of Menapi, Fotads (Uaithni) and other fighting men brought into Ireland from ManauGoddodin of SE Scotland by Lughaid Mac Con, were welded into a cohesive fighting force under the Deisi Muman (fighting men of Munster) by Ethne Uathach, the dynamic

[516] Eoin MacNeill, 'Phases of Irish History', p. 127.

[517] Eamon P. Kelly and Tom Condit, 'Limerick's Tara' in 'Archaeology Ireland', Vol 12, No. 2, 1998

[518] A variant version makes Corc son of Lughaid Mac Con whilst in Scotland.

[519] Daibhi O Croinin, 'Early Medieval Ireland 400 - 1200', p. 58. 1998.

Deisi princess.[520] Not only did the Dal Fiatach Suidge branch of the Deisi provide rulers of Deisi Muman, they provided this Queen for Oengus Mac Nad Froich. Thus they avoided the Deisi tag. Under Ethne's leadership, Munster expanded at the expense of the Ossraige. Cashel became an Eoganacht centre of power. Although severely depleted in 7 wars against the Ossraige, Eithne regrouped the Deisi, who with Oengus and the Corcu Loigde drove back the Ossraige. The Ethne-led Deisi were rewarded for their services with extensive conquered lands in S Tipperary and Waterford.

With the 7 Muscraige septs allied to Corc, the Deisi formed a line of buffer states along the Munster border with the Briganten/Ossraige kingdom along the Blackwater from Youghal to Fermoy and N along the W front of the Ballyhoura, Knockmaeldown and Galtee Mts. via Pallas Green to lower Loch Derg. O Rahilly did not accept that Cashel and Thurles were part of the kingdom of Eile nor that Ossraigh extended as far W as Pallas Green in Limerick. He dubbed it erroneous "due to confusing Grian on the W boundary of Osraige (Greane Hill, near Urlingford in Kilkenny) with Pallas Grean in Limerick." Greater Munster came into existence slowly. Like Connacht's Ól nÉchmacht, it grew from a tiny embryo. As Munster expanded at the expense of Eile and Ossory so did the Desi buffer states along the new boundary and south of the Suir in Waterford. The Deisi Becc of Limerick were pressed by the Ui Fidgenti (descendants of Eoghan Mór) from the W. They lost lands S of the Shannon and were confined to E Clare. Galled by humiliation they finally emerged victorious over Danes, Eoghanacht and Fidgenti, as the 'Dal Cais' under Mathgamain Mac Cennetig and his brother Brian Boru.[521]

The Corcu Loigde ruled Munster alternately with the Eoghanacht. Oilill's son, Eoghan Mór, was ancestor of the Eoghanacht. Corc was great-great-grand-son of Eoghan Mór. "The legend which tells of the final break in the Eoghanacht-Dairine (Corcu Laigde) succession arrangement deals with the judgement given by Oilill Olum. This was when his sons disputed with his fosterson Lughaid Mac Con over the possession of the Otherworld musician Fer I son of Eogabul; Eogabul was slain and his daughter Aine ravished by Oilill Olum at Cnoc Aine."[522] Thus were the fortunes of the Eoghanacht and Corcu Laigde mythologically symbolized. The Eoghanacht faded when Toirrdelbach (ancestor of the Ui Thoirrdelbaig of Dal Cais and the O'Brien family) cut down an ancient yew-tree at Emly, thus symbolizing the future Dal Cais destruction of Eoghanacht power in Munster.[523] The Corcu Loigde and Deisi led the Eoghanacht advance on Cashel then belonging to the Ossraige. Ossory's decimation by Munstermen highlights the fact that earlier the Ossraige (Ui Bairrche) had spread across the S of Ireland from Wexford, Carlow and Dind Righ through Kilkenny and Tipperary to E Limerick.[524] Their Overkings such as Eanna Airgtheach had their power-centre at Rath Bethaigh on the Nore in Magh Airgead-Rois in Kilkenny. They made shields from the silver-wood forests. In the 2nd century Conga Mogh Choirb was king of Magh Airgead Rois. Ugaine Mor, whose rule ostensibly reached as far W as Galway before the arrival of the Atrebaten Fir Belg leaders Gann, Sengann and Dela, made Cunga (Cinga) king of this Nore plain. Under Breasal Bairrech the Ui Bairrech stormed SW across Abann an Riogh at Callan in Kilkenny over Magh Feimhin, between Sliabh na mBan and Slieveardagh. They settled on the Tipperary plain around Cashel. The Munster/Ossory boundary then stood along a line running from Silvermines and Slievefelim Mts. through Pallas Green on Bealach Febrat in Limerick along the W front of the Galty Mountain range to Fermoy and E along the Blackwater to Cappoquin and S to Youghall. To admit this

---

[520] Tomas O Cathasaigh, 'Deisi and Deyfed', in Eigse, p. 5 - 12
[521] Francis John Byrne, 'Irish Kings and High Kings' p. 181
[522] Ibid, p. 182.
[523] Ibid p. 182.
[524] Professor Padraig Mac Carthaigh, 'Naoimh agus Laoich na Feoire', p. 5-17.

would have been anathema to Cashel's pseudo-historians. 1000 years later the annalists still regarded Tipperary clans, such as the O Dwyers, as of Ossorian stock. They left their mark on clans and placenames right across this area.

Until Corc arrived from Connacht, the Eoghanacht had settlements chiefly in mid, N and W Limerick, SW Tipperary, Killarney, Bandon and E to their boundary with the Ossraige at Fermoy in E Cork, interlinked with the Corcu Loigde. Their fighting power was greatly increased by the arrival of vassal tribes led by Corc from Galway's Turoe/Knocknadala/- Athenry oppidum. Among these were the Fotads. Their historic descendants who formed a defensive flank for the Eoghanacht expansion at the expense of the Eile and Ossraige S of the Shannon were the Uaithni septs in NE Limerick and NW Tipperary. The Manapi who came with Lughaid Mac Con from Manau-Goddodin in SE Scotland stood beside the Fotads in Galway surrounding Lughaid Mac Con while he reigned there. Led S into Munster by Corc, they soon won over Co. Clare from Connacht for the Eoganacht and set up their own kingdom there extending into N Limerick under the leadership of Lughaid Menn. Another branch founded the Manapian Mendraige kingdom in Co. Cork. A large segment of Deisi expanded E along the S flank of the Corcu Loigde/Eoghanacht expansion on the Waterford side of the Suir River as a buffer state for the Eoghanacht in the southeast.

The Corcu Loigde/Eoghanacht/Deisi advance routed the Ossraige (Ui Breasail Bhric; O-Irish form of Brigantes) near Clonmel on the Suir.[525] They overran Cashel and Magh Femhin N of the Suir. East Munster came under Eoghanacht control in the lifetime of Oengus, grandson of Corc, leader of the Eoghanacht/Deisi/Corcu Loigde alliance. Pseudo-historians claimed this happened in Corc's day and dubbed Cashel, *'Caiseal Choirc na gCarthach'*. The Corcu Loigde /Eoghanacht expansion continued eastwards. Forming a four-pronged attack on the Ossraige, the forces of Nad Froich and Oengus (son and grandson of Corc) fanned out in a N arc from Cashel. The Corcu Laigde and Muscraige pursued the retreating Ossraige NE through the Golden Vale between Slieve na mBan and Slieveardagh. The Deisi expanded along the Suir and concentrated their attack on the Ossraige in the Calann district S of Slieveardagh (*Ardachaidh*), pursuing them to the Luininn River which separates Windgap in Kilkenny from Templeorum in Tipperary. "Here was drawn up forever after the boundary between Munster and Leinster."[526]

Corc's descendants continued their expansion NNW to Loch Derg, across the plain from Cashel to Thurles, Templemore and Roscrea, and NE to Urlingford and Durrow. Various peoples with Briganten pedigrees, such as the Arada Cliach in NW Tipperary and the Eili streching E through Offaly, were overrun by this Eoghanacht expansion. The original people of Tipperary's Airthir Cliach district were also of Briganten stock before coming under Eoghanacht control in the early 6th century. The Corcu Laigde advanced along the S of Slieveardagh to Magh Airgead Rois in Kilkenny and from Freshford through the pass of Bearna between Cul Chaisin and Slieveardagh along the Nore valley to Durrow, overruning the Briganten fortress of Rath Beathaigh. Another Briganten stronghold in this Plain of the Silverwood overrun by Corc's descendants was Ballyragget, its ancient name *Tulach Ua mBairrche,* proclaiming its Briganten/Ui Bairrech origins. The plain thereafter became known as *Ban O nDuach* from the branch of the Corcu Laigde led by Cucraidhe Mac Duach, which overran this district and became known as the Eoghanacht Ruis-Airget:

> *"It is that Cucraidhe, son of Duach of Cliu, who occupied that territory (Ossory) in spite of the sons of Condla, son of Breasal Bairrech; it was he who killed the chief of Ui Duach. Principle tribes of Ossory then were the Ui Bairrche, Ui Duach..."*

---

[525] Professor Padraig Mac Carthaigh, *'Naoimh agus Laoich na Feoire'* short history of Ossory, p. 2-10
[526] Professor Padraig Mac Carthaigh, 'Naoimh agus Laoich na Feoire,' p.6

In the Eoghanacht genealogy Duach is Corc's cousin. Six of his kindred succeeded Cuc-raidhe as Kings of Ossory. They were "The Seven Kings of the Corcu Loighdhe." The combined forces of the Eoghanacht, Deisi, Muscraige and Corcu Laigde swept through Kilkenny and Carlow to Cill Osna (Kellistown) near Tullow and the upper Barrow where their advance was stemmed. Their King, Oengus Mac Nad Froich, Corc's grandson, was slain in 490 AD. The 'Expulsion of the Desi' saga tells that having been driven from Temhair (Turoe) the Deisi were granted lands in Waterford and Tipperary by Oengus Mac Nad Froich for driving back the Ossraige and defending the new Munster borders which date from the 5th century. For ever after these separate Waterford and Tipperary from Kilkenny, Laois and Offaly. This co-operation made the conquest and vast expansion of Munster possible. It gelled the Eoghanacht and various branches of their allies into one.

A century later during Cenn Faeladh's reign, the Northern Ui Neill king, Aed Mac Ain-mire, tried to force the Cocu Loigde to pay tribute to him without success. He took Scanlan, the king's son, hostage. Due to the friendship of the Corcu Loigde saints, Canice of Kilkenny and Lachtin of Freshford, with their classmate Colum Cille, the latter persuaded his royal cousin Aed to free Scanlan and observe a truce with the Corcu Loigde. After Aed and the saints' deaths, before the capture of Tara in 637, his warlording successors, aided by the Ui Bairrche Clann Condla (Ossraige proper), renewed their assault on the Eoghanacht Ruis-Airget of Kilkenny and drove them out. The Ossorians re-emerged as rulers of their former Nore vale with the death of Scanlan son of Cenn Faeladh, last Corcu Loigde king of Ossory, between 620 and 630 AD. A small remnant remained by retreating into the forested fastness of the foothills of Slieveardagh and Cul Chaisin overlooking Freshford and Magh Airged-Rois in Kilkenny whence it was impossible to dislodge them.

Corcu Loigde kings appear in the Eoghanacht genealogy. The Corcu Loigde of Magh Airged-Rois in Kilkenny were known as Eoghanacht Ruis-Airged despite not being descended directly from Eoghan Mór. "In spite of the theory that the name Eoghanacht denoted descent from Eoghan Mór son of Ailill Olum, in practice it was confined to those septs descended from Conall Corc in the 5th century. Two important Munster dynasties, the W Limerick Ui Fidgenti (descended from Eoghan Mór) and the E Cork Ui Liathain, claimed to be of Eoghanacht stock". A *Frithfholaid* tract tells that Bressal Mac Ailello Thassaig, grandson of Eochu Liathan, Ui Liathain ancestor, was an early King of Munster. The Ui Fidgenti, descended from Eoghan Mór, produced only one claimant to the kingship of Cashel. The Ui Fidgenti, Ui Liathain and Corcu Loigde were descended from the Dairine of W Munster before Cashel became part of Munster and only later attached to the Eoghanacht genealogy after Eoghan Mór's time.

Eoghanacht Locha Lein kings of Iarluachair (W of Sliabh Luachra barrier between Cork, Limerick and Kerry) descended from Conall Corc by his Scottish wife through their son Coirpre, were regarded with hostility by the Cashel historians reluctant to admit any of them as kings of Munster. The Scottish Eoghanacht of Magh Gorgin (Gerginn - the Mearns), the Lennoxes and Stuarts (royal heirs to the British Throne), descended from sons whom Conall Corc (Gorgin) or his son Coirpre left behind in Scotland.[527] Corc's son Coirpre arrived from Scotland with 30 horsemen which he unyoked on Corc's land following the legal procedure for laying claim to property. Cashel historians and genealogists, in spite of their hostility to Coirpre's sept, had to admit that Coirpre was eventually buried in Magh Femhin near Cashel and that the stewardship of Iarluachair (Iarmumhu) was given to his son Maine, grandson of Corc. Daui Iarlaithe, Maine's son, succeeded him but refused to pay his dues to Cashel. This led to war between him and the King of Cashel, his cousin Oengus Mac Nad Froich, grandson of Corc. When Oengus was slain by the Ossraige in 490, Daui Iarlaithe

[527] Ibid, p. 194

became King of all Munster reigning not from Cashel but from Iarluchair in West Munster. Daui is recorded in a very old obscure passage as battling against the Uaithni of the Loch Derg district of Tipperary who were descendants of the Fotads expelled from central Galway by Cormac Mac Art.

The tract *De bunad imthechta Eoghanachta* tells that Cormac Mac Art went to Fiachu Munlethan son of Eoghan Mór, King of Munster at Raphaind (Knockgraffon in SW Tipperary), Capital of the Eoghanacht kings long before Cashel became part of Munster. The fragmentary obscure tract *Cain Fuithirbe* composed by Amairgein mac Amalgado mac Mael Ruain of the Deisi was named after the site of the Dail at Magh Fuithirbe on the Cork/Kerry border at the request of its king Cormac. It lists many Munster kings who never reigned from Cashel and are not recognized in later regnal lists. Donennach of the Fidgenti (+683), Congal of Iarluachair (+690), Finguine of SW Munster (+695), Cumscrad of Fir Maige Fene, Slebene of Corcu Duibhne, Dunlaing of the Ui Echach, and kings of Corcu Loigde and Deis Tuaiscirt. "In its present state the text reveals a distinct W Munster ambience."[528] Just as Rathcroghan was not the Capital of Connacht until the 8th century, snippets of legendary history show Cashel was not the Capital of Munster until this much later period, a fact studiously suppressed by pseudo-regnal lists favouring Cashel's glorification. It took centuries for Cashel to make its claim the 'official doctrine' with the conniving annalistic support of Armagh and Ui Neill dynastic support. The 8th century Terryglass *'Dail'* between Cashel's King Cathal Mac Finguine, the Ui Neill King Aed Allan and the Abbot of Armagh was a crucial step in its acceptance.

Cashel's pseudo-historians with Armagh's expertise suppressed the genuine traditions of the early capitals of West Munster in favour of Cashel. "The Eoghanacht who ruled Munster until the middle of the 10th century were distributed strategically throughout the province. The Eoghanacht of Cashel, late seat of the high-kingship of the province, had no prerogative claim to that office. Geographically they were outliers, the most easterly of the dynastic groups."[529] Just as the ancestral kings of archaic Connacht originated in the S of the province, Cashel's closest blood-relations, one and all, resided in the W of the province, the original archaic Munster where they originated. The Airthir Chliach resided on the Limerick/Tipperary border controlling the pre-Patrician church of Emly, the Eoghanacht Glendamnach, named after the Cork's Glanworth, seated to SW of the upper Blackwater near Fermoy, the Eoghanacht Aine Cliach at the site of the mythological traditions of the original Eoghanacht of archaic Munster in the Knockaney area in Limerick.[530]

BREAKDOWN IN RELATIONSHIPS BETWEEN MUNSTER AND CONNACHT
Following the rise of Lughaid Mac Con and Corc and the Deisi expulsion by Cormac Mac Art, the close relationship which existed between the Fir Belg rulers of Munster and Connacht broke down. War broke out between them. The background to this enmity must be analyzed to counteract the fictitious anachronistic concoctions of pseudo-historians. They pushed this worsening state of affairs back several generations to the time of Conn, grandfather of Cormac Mac Art, and Eoghan Mór of Munster, ironically the very time when their friendship had reached its climax through marital relationships. A series of events introduced foreign elements into Munster politics and consequently into the relationship between Munster and Connacht. Such were the usurpation of the Overkingship of the Fir Belg by Lughaid Mac Con as *Rí Temhro* at the Battle of Magh Muc Dhruim, Lughaid's expulsion from Temhair (Turoe), the eviction of the Deisi by Cormac Mac Art, Corc's 'adoption' by Crimthann Mac Fidaig and his reign over the Deisi. A disturbing episode

---

[528] Ibid, p. 176.
[529] Ibid, p. 176-177
[530] Ibid, p. 182.

which ended Crimthann's career brought this new reality to a climax. "Crimthann Mac Fidaig, first cousin in the genealogical scheme to Conall Corc,"[531] figures in the origin-tale of the Eoghanacht as uncle and fosterfather of Corc of Cashel. Following these events, Munster began to expand in more ways than one. Not only was Cashel and a vast segment of Ossraige territory brought within Munster's orbit, Crimthann is credited with conquests in Britain and consequently titled Overking of Ireland and Britain.

Roman Records attest that "it has generally been accepted that the early migration from the Northern half of Ireland (to Scotland) was paralleled by those from this Southern half to Gwynedd and Dyfed in Wales. These represent contemporaneous manifestations of an outward thrust from Ireland to the neighbouring island (Britain). The southern migrations left their enduring memorial"[532] on the ogham stones and placenames of Wales. They are deemed prehistoric since no contemporary records survive. So the testimony of later records has taken on an importance which it would not otherwise have. The origin-legend of the founding of the kingdom of Dyfed by the Deisi expelled from Turoe, not Tara, by Cormac Mac Art, as told in the 'Expulsion of the Deisi' details the conquests in Britain made under Crimthann Mac Fidaig, king of Munster. History corroborates prehistory.

Crimthann conquered parts of SW Britain with the aid of the Ui Liathain and the Deisi. "For when great was the power of the Irish over the British they divided Alba (Britain) among them in districts. The Irish dwelt on the East of the sea no less than in Ireland. Their palaces and royal forts were built there. *Inde dicitur* Dinn Tradui (*Dun Tre-dooibh*), the three-fossed fort of Crimthann Mac Fidaig, King of Ireland and Alba (Britain) down to the Ictian Sea, *et inde* Glasimpere na nGaedel (Glastonbury of the Irish) a (pre-Patrician) church on the border of the Ictian sea. There too is Dind Map Lethain (Dun Mac Liathain) in the lands of the Cornish Britons. Thus did each tribe divide, for there was an equal proportion in the East. They held their possessions there until long after the coming of Patrick."[533] Byrne added: "In the middle ages memories remained of the Irish settlements made during the 4th century in those parts of Britain (Wales, Cornwall and W England). The Welsh kings and saints of Brycheiniog (Brecknock) claimed Irish descent"[534] The 'Expulsion of the Deisi" saga preserves the genuine pedigree of the 8th century king of Dyfed, Tewdws ap Rhein. A prince of the Deisi expelled by Cormac Mac Art from Temhair (Turoe), Echaid Allmuir mac Art Chuirp, led his people to Demed (Dyfed/Demetae) in Wales. The saga adds that "from them are the people of Crimthann over there," i.e. they, like the Ui Liathain, were among the Irish led into Britain by Crimthann.

The Cycle of Crimthann Mac Fidaig tells how he became King of Ireland (meaning Overking of the Fir Belg tribes) in 366 AD (dates of medieval chroniclers are guesswork) in succession to Eochaid Muigh Mhaen (Moyvane) Mac Muiredach Tírech (Temhrach). Eochaid was Rí Erainn and Rí Temhro which then meant Overking of the Fir Belg tribes of Connacht and Munster, but was fictionally transmuted by pseudo-history to 'King of Ireland at Tara of Meath'. Eochaid's Queen was Mongfhind, sister of Crimthann Mac Fidaig. She bore four sons to Eochaid, namely, Briun, Fiachra, Ailill and Fergus. Eochu had a younger son, Niall, by a British slave girl, Cairenn, whom Mongfhind detested and expelled from Temhair (Turoe). Her favourite son was Briun, the eldest. When Eochaid died, Briun was too young to secure the kingship. Mongfhind persuaded the men of Ireland (*Fir Erainn/Fir Belg*) to give the Overkingship to her brother Crimthann until Briun was ready for it. Briun was sent into fosterage to learn the art of war for 7 years. When he was ready to lead the

---

[531] Francis John Byrne, 'Irish Kings and High Kings', p. 183.
[532] Tomas O Cathasaigh, 'Deisi and Dyfed', in Eigse XX
[533] Cormac Mac Cuilennain, King of Munster, in '*Sanas Cormaic*' circa 900 A.D.
[534] Francis John Byrne, Op. Cit., p. 183

Fir Belg armies forth into battle, Mongfhind was anxious to see her favourite son Briun on the throne of the Overkingship as Rí Temhro.

Old Crimthann was Overking of the Fir Belg of Connacht (the text retains its archaic name, Coiced nÓl nÉgmacht), Munster and Britain. He was on his royal circuit visiting his British subjects and taking his own sweet time, to Mongfhind's chagrin. She took the law into her own hands. After all was she not Connacht's Queen, Crimthann's elder sister and a *mulier fortis* to wit? Mongfhind's sons, with her connivance, availed themselves of Crimthann's auspicious absence to divide the kingdom among themselves. Briun took Cnoc Temhro, seat of the Fir Belg Overkingship. Fiachra took Rath Cruacha of Athenry, the royal seat of Connacht extending from Carn Feradaig (Cahernarry) in Co. Limerick N through Clare to the N boundary of Magh Muc Dhruime. Ailill, Fergus and Niall were to go N to cut out sword-land for themselves at the expense of the Cruthin. In later times Carn Feradaig was on the border between the N and S Deisi Begg, but until the time of Briun and Fiachra it was the border between Coiced nÓl nÉgmacht and archaic Munster.

News of these developments reached Crimthann. He hurried home, not to Tara of Meath but to Cnoc Temhro of Galway. He gathered his forces to expel his sister's sons. Mongfhind prepared a treacherous feast *i Temhra* (read 'in Turoe') to 'celebrate' his return as though to make peace between her sons and her brother. She offered him a 'welcome home' poisoned cup which he refused to drink until she first drank of it. She drank and Crimthann drank after her. She died at Temhair (Turoe). Crimthann died at Crathloe in Clare just N of the Shannon crossing at Limerick on his way from Turoe to the old capital of Munster, not from Tara to Cashel as pseudo-history rendered it. It forgot that crossing the Shannon at Limerick involved a problematic crossing into Connacht first. It also forgot that Cashel was not then, nor for a long time afterwards, part of Munster.

Pseudo-history reared its ugly head again. It manipulated the facts claiming that the treachery of Mongfhind and the sacrifice of her life were in vain. It alleged that it was Niall who took the High Kingship of Ireland at Tara in succession to Crimthann, and that Briun was his 'smiter in battle', seizing hostages and levying tribute from all parts of the kingdom. This blatant Ui Neill propaganda has no basis whatever. No High Kingship of Ireland existed before the 9th century AD. This has been recognized since the early 20th century. This stratum of pseudo-history did admit that Briun became Overking of Connacht's expanding Fir Belg province while Fiachra was king of Ól nÉgmacht, the division of archaic Connacht extending from Carn Feradaig to Magh Muc Dhruim centered on Rath Cruacha of Athenry. Peel off the outer pseudo-historic layer of Niall's High Kingship of Ireland and the inner core of truth remains. The enmity that arose between Fiachra and Briun is admitted but tied again to the pseudo-historic outer layer. It claimed that Briun defeated Fiachra and sent him captive to High King Niall at Tara and that Briun was slain by Crimthann Mac Enna Cennselach. It went on to allege that Fiachra was released by Niall who made him King of Connacht and his 'smiter in battle' to replace Briun.

Briun's Overkingdom took in a vast triangle of present day Leinster stretching N from the Colla Man lands on the Dublin coast along a line of Airghiallian buffer states running NW to the mouth of the Drowes river in Donegal. Crimthann Mac Enna Cennselach, King of Leinster, was experiencing severe pressure from the Briganten Ossraige driven E by the Corc-led Eoghanacht/Corco Laigde expansion of Munster. He began to expand north at the expense of Briun's Overkingdom with the aid of these Ui Bairrche, Ossraige and Airghiallan states who were of Leinster stock whom Crimthann swayed to join his cause. Briun sped east to defend the E sector of his kingdom. He was defeated and slain.

Fiachra succeeded Briun as Overking. He and Ailill defeated the Munstermen at the Battle of Caenraige and took their hostages who were buried around Fiachra's grave when he was later slain. When the Men of Munster heard of Fiachra's death, Ailill was seized by Eochaid son of Crimthann, king of Munster (not of Cashel). This was in compensation for the death of his father, Crimthann Mac Fidaig, "who brought Ireland and Britain (Alba) under the dominion of Munster" as Munster pseudo-historians proudly proclaimed, stealing the thunder from the Ui Neill/Armagh Syndrome. They slew Ailill. War broke out between Munster and Connacht, resulting in the struggle for the territory of Thomond (N Munster, Clare). A Menapian leader, Lughaid Menn, aided by Menapian septs of the Muscraige, Corco Baiscinn[535] of W Clare and Deis Begg. He took the territory from Carn Feradaig in Limerick to the Aughta Mountains (N Limerick and the whole of Clare) from Connacht and set up a Menapi kingdom. It became known as Tuadh Mumhan (North Munster/Thomond). "There are two territories which the Munstermen took and defended by force, Ossory which was seized in compensation for Eterscel who was killed by the Leinstermen, and North Munster in compensation for the death of Crimthann. But they are not lawfully entitled to them, for that territory of North Munster belongs by law to Connacht, since Connacht extends from Limerick to the Drowes River in SW Donegal."[536] It was so from Cormac Mac Art's day until the day when Connacht lost lower and upper portions of its province and large tracts of land E of the Shannon.

BREAKUP OF IRON AGE CONNACHT INSTIGATED BY NIALL and his sons

To further expose the fraudulent nature of the Tara, Rathcroghan and Cashel Myths, Connacht's early history and the origins of the Ui Neill dynasty must be analyzed carefully. Historians allege they are amazed at Connacht's apparent lack of an overkingship in the sources (pseudo-historic though these are). "If the sources for early Munster are meagre, those for Connacht in the centuries before AD 800 are almost non-existent. Connacht alone of all the provinces - appears to lack any strong pattern of over-kingship"[537] This apparent lacuna is due to the success of the Tara Myth Syndrome's suppression of Connacht's Iron Age royal oppida which plundered their history and traditions in favour of Tara's glorification. Connacht's early powerful Overkings were fictionally transmuted into High Kings of Ireland reigning at Tara of Meath, an institution which did not exist before the 9th century AD. Yet, as Professor Dáibhi O Cróinín notes "various bits and pieces allow some of the jigsaw to be reconstructed." An early law tract gives royal glory to Connacht, but not to Tara of Meath: "He is no highest king who does not magnify the Fifth of Ailill Mac Mata (Province of Connacht)." In Ptolemy of Alexandria's geographical record the only province in early Ireland outside of Ulster to be credited with a major royal Capital ('Regia') is Connacht. In the Ulidian tales, Connacht's Regents led the other provinces of Ireland against the might of Ulster. The archaeological site of the massive Iron Age Turoe/Knocknadala/Athenry oppidum reconstructed above lends indisputable support to these sources which project a Connacht dominating the rest of Ireland.

Eochaid Moyvane (Muigh Mhaen), grandson of Fiacu Sraibtine (from his residence at 'Dun Sraibtine in Ól nÉgmacht') was Rí Temhro, namely Fir Belg Overking of the Turoe/Knocknadala Oppidum in the late 4th/early 5th century. Eochaid's father was Muiredhach Tírech (Temhrach) whose epithet refers to his Ballymurry residence on the E side of Turoe, site of his demolished Rath Muiredhach. Eochaid's own epithet Moyvane (Muigh Mhaen; intercalated by pseudo-history to Mugmedon to suppress his true origin), proclaims that he resided in Magh Mhaen (Maen Magh) at whose core stood the seat of the

---

[535] Certain obscure texts make Fiachu Fer Mara, a Menapian sailor, ancestor of the Muscraige, Corco Duibhne of Kerry, and Corco Baiscinn of West Clare, and of the Dal Fiatach and Dal Riata of North East Ulster.

[536] Myles Dillon, 'The Cycles of the Kings', in 'The Cycle of Crimthann son of Fidach", p. 32-33

[537] Dáibhí O Cróinín, 'Early Medieval Ireland', p. 59 in the new Longman History of Ireland series.

Turoe/Knocknadala Fir Belg Oppidum in central Co. Galway. His epithet distinguished him from contemporary namesakes. Of his 4 legitimate sons, Briun, Fiachra, Ailill, and Fergus, Briun or Briunan was the eldest and thus first in line to the throne. Eochaid's fifth son by a British slave girl was Niall. "There is good evidence that his mother, Cairenn, was a British captive, so that Niall himself was half-British,"[538] illegitimate, and thus ineligible to the throne. Niall and his mother were treated accordingly. The Ui Neill spin doctors subtly surmounted this problem and glorified Niall.

Cuan O Lotchain (+ 1024) spuriously proceeded to make the illegitimate Niall more eligible than his eder legitimate step-brothers in his poem '*Echtra Mac Echdach Mugmedoin.*' He began by suppressing Eochaid Muigh Mhean's surname which anchors him in Magh Mean, the plain in which Cnoc Temhro (Turoe) stands in Galway in order to transfer him to Tara as its High King. He made his son Niall, hero of the poem, High King of Tara from 379-405. He converted Niall's mother, Cairenn, from a British slavegirl into the royal daughter of a British King carried off in a raid and kept as a slave, and Niall's Tara into a second Rome. He admits that Niall's elder step brothers conceived deep envy towards him through the ill-will of their mother who detested Cairenn. God took pity on Cairenn and her son Niall who grew up to be almost like a god, splendourous golden locks, lustrous princley countenance, bravest of the brave, noble descendant of Conn of the Hundred Battles. His stepbrothers are projected as scheming cowards. It was his right to speak before them at the Dal Assembly. Pseudo-propaganda!

Cuan concocted a series of tests to show how Niall was chosen over his step-brothers to be High King despite Eochaid's consort's determined efforts to secure the succession for her favourite son Briun. Cuan centres his poem round *motifs* which had their parallels in medieval romance, e.g. in the *Marriage of Sir Gawain* and in Gower's *Confessio Amantis*. There is a play on the words *túr dige* and *buaid do dig (LL)* which can mean a drink (*deog*) or a defensive dyke (*díg*). The brothers went to win the drink of kingship at the boundary (of Ulster) at Loch Erne. Niall alone bravely triumphs and drinks the cup of ale or mead bestowed by the goddess of kingship. Finally his step-brothers sent him to the border hoping he would be killed. Instead, he burst through the barriers and was victorious. Cuan uses Niall and his son's stamping ground by linking him to Fanad between Loch Swilly and Loch Foyle in the Inishowen peninsula of Donegal in the NW corner of Ireland where his sons won kingdoms for themselves. He also put Niall on Tailtiu, the assembly place of the S Ui Neill, his medieval descendants. As a result of the tests which had nothing to do with the Iron Age right of succession, and more to do with medieval intrigue, Briun, the eldest brother, would have a fleeting visit to Temhair but no posterity there, while Niall would be king of a counterweight Temhair in the East. The language is equivocal. Briun's reign at Temhair (Turoe) was brought to an end by Maine Mor's invasion. It never recovered from this disaster. Thus, Niall and his descendants were fictionalized into High Kings of Ireland at Tara. The High Kingship of Ireland did not come into being until the 9th century.

Younger siblings of reigning kings led their fighting men to new conquests and new kingdoms on the conquered lands. This was the role cut out for Niall. He could not succeed to his father's throne over the heads of his legitimate elder brothers. Much less could he be High King of Ireland despite all the justificatory tracts and tricks conjured up by pseudo-history to anachronistically seat him on Tara's throne. There was no such institution then nor for centuries thereafter. They tried to camouflage this obstacle. To gain a tiny kingdom for himself, Niall made swordland in Cruthin territory alongside his stepbrother Fiachra.

---

[538] T. F. O Rahilly, EIHM, p 234. Westropp, 'Ancient Forts of Ireland., p.139. Sean P.O Riordain, 'Antiquities of Irish Countryside' p. 64.

Connacht's ruling dynasty assumed it was acquiring a subordinate, not a rival.[539] But Niall cut loose from the parent stock. Bits of legendary history show him leading his sons NW, aided by Fiachra and Ailill, making conquests alongside them on the frontlines of the Fir Belg Kingdom in N Connacht as far as Donegal in the NW tip of Ulster. This expansion north by Niall predated the seizure of Tara by his descendants by some 2 centuries.

"A necessary preliminary to the settlement of the sons of Niall in Ulster was the breaking of the power of the Ulaid. A legend as to how this came about serves as a preface to the account of the Airghialla. According to the pseudo-genealogical convention, the Airghialla were descended from 3 brothers known as 'the three Collas' who were sons of Eochu Domlen, brother of Fiachu Sraibtine, (so-called) King of Ireland. They slew their uncle Fiachu at the Battle of Dub Combair. They were afterwards pardoned by Fiachu's son Muiredach Tirech, who, knowing their prowess as warriors, urged them to attack the Ulaid and make swordland of their territory. The Fir nÓl nÉgmacht provided them with 7 battalions of fighting men."[540] O Rahilly concluded: "Thus were established the Airghialla, who in early historical times were in occupation of half of the present province of Ulster. That the legend has a solid basis of historical fact is unquestionable, though there is every reason to treat with skepticism the details with which the story has been embroidered."

A detail which caused his skepticism is that recorded by pseudo-historians like Flann Mainistrech claiming Fiachu Sraibtine was slain by the Collas. Yet "in other texts the same Fiachu meets a different end - he is slain, along with his alleged brothers (Eochaid and Eochu Domlen) in the battle of Cnamross in which the Lagin under Bresal Belach defeated (their father) Cairbre Lifechair."[541] Tradition tells that the Collas were vassal allies of Connacht's kings in Fiachu Sraibtine's time just as they were in Niall's time. In *'Baile in Scail'* Niall's father Eochaid Muigh Mhean, not Fiachu, is slain by the Collas in the Battle of Dub Combair. O Rahilly claimed this version of the Colla legend is nearer the historical truth. The Airghialla were outlawed by Connacht's new Overking, Briun, when Niall encouraged them to follow his example and cut loose from vassalage to Connacht's Over-kingship. Niall won over their allegiance. Three of Niall's sons made conquests in NW Ulster in the lifetime of their father."[542] The details are given in legendary history. The policy placed on the lips of Niall's grandfather, Muiredach Tirech, spoken to the Collas, was carried out by Niall: "I see our children have grown numerous. Let each part from the other and take one of the enemy lands." O Rahilly lept to one of his fatal verdicts: "The conclusion is inevitable: the 3 brothers known as 'the Collas' were Eoghan, Conall and Enda, the three sons of Niall.[543]

This allegation that the 3 Collas were the 3 brothers, Conall, Eoghan and Enda, is false. The 3 sons of Niall merely carved out minor kingdoms for themselves in the extreme NW of Ireland in Donegal, which certainly did not amount to the overthrow of the Ulaid. When Cormac Mac Art went forth to the Battle of Crinna leading Fir Belg tribes right across the country to advance north against the Cruthin, his army consisted mainly of the 3 Colla bands of fighting men, the Colla Menn, Colla Fo Chri (Ochra) and Colla Uais. The O-Irish word *'Colla' (Collaibh)* referred to 'bands of fighting men', 'defenders of a realm'. The Collas were distinct tribal groups of defenders who formed buffer states between the expanding Turoe/Knocknadala Fir Belg oppidum and the Cruthin kingdom of Ulster. This advance under Cormac Mac Art was the beginning of the breakup of the archaic Ulster.

---

[539] Gearoid Mac Niochaill, "Ireland before the Vikings', p.10
[540] F.T. O Rahilly, 'Early Irish History and Mythology', p. 225-6
[541] Ibid, p. 228.
[542] Ibid, p. 229.
[543] Ibid, p. 230.

Magh Colla (Cola) on the Loughrea/Craughwell outer ward flank of the Turoe oppidum defended by the Manapi (Manach) is highlighted by the Manapi tell tale appendage -Manach, -Munna, -Menn, -Maine, -Managh or -Monagh in numerous place-names such as Ballymanagh. These Colla Mann were Manapi fighting men employed by the expaning Connacht Fir Belg oppidum. The Colla Fo Chri were descendants of the Manapi who appear on Ptolemy's record on Wicklow coast, later pushed N by the Leinstermen. The Lusk district on the N Dublin coast was a stage on their N trek when Cormac Mac Art who, in payment for their military services, gave them lands along the banks of Lough Erne to become the Fir Managh and Monachi of Fermanagh and Monaghan. The Colla Uais (Os) were the Ciannachta, still remembered in the several Clann Cian (corrupt Cloonkeen) townlands of NE Galway as the Collaibh Oige, young defenders. The Ciannacht Collaibh Oige marched with Cormac together with the Colla Menn and Colla Fo Chri bands inexorably expanding the frontier of the Connacht Fir Belg oppidum at the expense of the Cruthin of Ulster. Niall took control of them when he and his sons finally hived off from the Connacht Fir Belg dynasty and set up kingdoms for themselves. and placed the Ciannachta in their most northerly frontline buffer states in Derry and Louth.

The 3 Collas consisted, not of 3 brothers, but of 3 "congeries of tribes known as the Airghialla,"[544] as seen from their positions along the Airghiallian/Cruthin frontier following their advance against the Cruthin and the conquest of their Capital, Emain Mhacha. Collectively called Airghialla (Eastern Vassals), they consisted of the Mugdorna in Monaghan, the Fir Manach of Fermanagh and NW Monaghan (Menapi/Colla Menn), the Fir Li, Ui Crimthainn, 'ind Airthir' (Orientals of Armagh), Ui Meith, Ui Thuirtri, Ui Niallain and Ui Bresail descended from Fiachra Cassan of the Colla Fo Crith (the Mac Mahons were their chief representatives), the Luigni, Gailenga and Ciannachta/Ui Maccu Uais. The Colla Uais (Os) were the Ui Mac Uais Ciannachta of Meath and Westmeath. In later times the Mac gUidhir, Mac Mathghamhna and Mac Domhnaill claimed descent from them.[545] "The achievements attributed to the Collas represent a fact of history."[546]

Then came O Rahilly's fatal pseudo-historical flourish: "Niall Noigiallach and his father Eochaid are the earliest historical kings of Tara."[547] He was caught in the web of the 'pius fraud', the Tara/Patrick Myth which he did so much to unravel. Niall could never have been *Rí Temhro* at Tara then! Niall's father Eochaid Muigh Mhean, as his epithet proclaims, resided in Maen Magh, the plain round Turoe in Galway. He reigned as *Rí Temhro* of the Turoe/Knocknadala oppidum. His son Niall by a British slavegirl was ineligible to reign as Rí Temhro. The role of a younger son, born of a slavegirl to wit, was to serve his elder brothers and cut out sword-land for them. That is the role given to Niall by snippets of legendary history, not at Tara but at the Cnoc Temhro/Cnoc na Dail oppidum. This is the scenario in which Niall, the son of Eochaid Muigh Main and Cairinn, is anchored in a poem attributed to Torna Eices:

> *When we hosted forth to Dál (Cnoc na Dal) with the son of Eochail Muigh Mhain*
> *More golden than the golden sobairche was the hair of the son of Cairinn.*

One of Torna's poems on the rough treatment dealt out to the slavegirl Cairinn and her son Niall by the jealous wife of Eochaid Muigh Mhain glorifies Niall as *"the champion of Maen Magh"* (the plain round Turoe in Galway). This is a far cry from Tara of Meath.

---

[544] Ibid, p. 231.
[545] Ibid, p. 230, f.
[546] Ibid, p. 230.
[547] Ibid, p. 234.

While expanding Connacht's border northwards, Niall manoeuvred into a unique position, capitalizing on contemporary circumstances. He took hostages of the 9 Airghiallan tribes put at his disposal, or who placed themselves under him, weaned away from allegiance to his elder brother Briun, Overking of Turoe/Knocknadala oppidum. One poem makes Maine Mór a son of the Manapian leader Eochu Fer Da Ghiall, but another claims Niall fathered Maine on a daughter of Eochu Fer Da Ghiall of the race of Colla Fo Chrith (Colla Da Chrioch) of the royal house of Clogher. This Eochu was then *Rig Airghialla*, overking of all the Airghiallan tribes. He held the hostages of the Cruthin and Ulaid, as his epithet 'Fer Da Ghiall' announces. Colla Da Chrioch refers to the 2 branches of the Manapian Colla Fo Chrith under Eochu's care, the *ind Airthir* who controlled Armagh district, and the Manaig of Ui Cremthain on Lough Erne, the Fir Manach of Fermanagh overflowing into Tyrone and Monaghan.[548] As leader of Connacht's fighting forces facing the Cruthin of Ulster, Niall made himself overlord of the Airghialla along their front line buffer states. With the aid of their Airghiallan leader, Eochu, Niall persuaded all the Airghiallian tribes to place their hostages under his protection and rise up against Briun, the Fir Belg Overking, promising them independence and favourable terms. O Rahilly concluded that "From the hostages he held from the (9) vassal states Niall got the epithet *Noighiallach,* 'of the Nine Hostages'. His reign (as Airghiallan overlord, not as King of Tara) marked events which had a momentous effect on Irish history. Led by his sons (Eoghan, Conall, Enda) his forces overthrew the Ulaid and razed their capital Emain Macha"[549]

Niall earned a reputation as a raider of Roman Britain by which he gained considerable wherewithal to engage fighting men to win swordland for himself and his sons. Roman records tell that when Roman forces withdraw from Britain, Irish plunderers made devastating raids into Britain and carried off huge quantities of loot and slaves for sale. This greatly enhanced Niall's role. With the aid of his stepbrothers, Fiachra and Ailill, forces drawn from Connacht, and Airghiallan vassal allies in the buffer states, his warlording family made conquests against the Cruthin of Ulster. Numerous legends tell of the exploits of Niall and his sons in this sphere of activity. Niall led his sons, Conall, Eoghan, Cairbre, and Eanna, to carve out kingdoms for themselves in the NW of Ireland in the 5th cent., two of which played an important role in later history down to the 17th century. They became independent kingdoms which hived off from Connacht's parent dynasty contrary to its norms and expectations. Thus Niall redressed his lowly status by birth.

Legends tell that Conall was his father Niall's favourite son. Had Niall been High King of Ireland at Tara (which was not so) it is Conall, not Loeghuire as pseudo-history persisted, who should have succeeded him. Mac Niochaill questioned "whether (Niall) ever ruled in Tara." Noting that Niall is credited with 14 sons in all, he asked in disbelief whether at least some of "all these links with Niall are not perhaps fictitious."[550] Loeghuire of Tara had no link with Niall. He belonged to a pre-Ui Neill Cruthin sept, a cousin of Conor Mac Nessa. He was ancestor of the Ui Loeghuire sept of Trim and Tara district long before Niall was born. Loeghuire was anachronistically welded, by Muirchu, to the Ui Neill genealogical stem as son of Niall in an attempt to link Niall to Tara and its alleged High Kingship of Ireland, and to confer an early artificial association with Tara on the Ui Neill dynasty. The Loeghuire Myth has cast its pseudo-shadow over Niall's son Conall.

Niall's stepbrother, Fiachra, expanded the kingdom named after him, Ui Fiachra, from Connacht's Fir Belg oppidum frontier, as it stood at the end of Chapter 2, up through Mayo into Sligo. Niall ranged himself alongside Fiachra. He and his sons pushed further N from

---

[548] T. F. O Rahilly, EIHM, p. 31-32; R 146, f-g; Trip. Life (Stokes) 192; F. J. Byrne, Op. Cit. p. 115.

[549] Ibid, p. 234

[550] Gearoid Mac Niocaill, 'Ireland before the Vikings', p.12

the W periphery of the Cruthin-held W protrusion of Roscommon and W Leitrim up through Sligo to the Benbulben region, and finally into Donegal. Cormac mac Art's earlier conquests with his Airghiallian allies, the Collas, had pushed back the boundary of ancient Ulster stretching in a line running NW from the Dublin coastal Menapi kingdom along the upper Liffey and thence along the Blackwater through Kells to Virginia in Cavan. It continued NW along Loch Erne and thence along the Drowes River to the sea near Bundoran between Sligo and Donegal Bay. A line of Airghiallian buffer states defended this Connacht expansion. It ran from Forgall Monach's Menapian buffer state on the Dublin coast to the Menapian buffer states along Lough Erne and the Menapian Calraige buffer state round Benbulben in Sligo S of the Drowes River. It cut off the Cruthin kingdom of Rathcroghan of Roscommon (Cruithintuatha Croghain) from its Ulster kinsmen. The Luigne and Gailenga buffer states stretched through Cavan and Meath (Kells/Virginia). Connacht's border with Ulster lay along this defence line erected by the Ulstermen, the Great Wall of Ulster or Black Pig's Dyke ('Cladh na Muice Duibhe') stretching from the Drowes river on the western sea (Donegal) to the Tolka in Dublin.[551]

Niall, his sons and Airghiallan allies burst through the defence lines erected by the Ulstermen from the head of the Erne estuary at Dunmucrum (Dun Muc Dhruim, Fort of the Black Pig's Dyke) in Ballyshannon and along the Erne. This extensive boundary ran SE through Cavan to Loch Ramor and the Blackwater. With this boundary breached, the Cruthin of Ulster were sent reeling backwards. The boundaries of Airghiallan frontline buffer states, the Fir Manach, Ciannachta, Luigne, Gailenga and descendants of Colla Da Chriach, between the Connacht and Cruthin overkingdoms moved forward apace.

Niall's son Conall got his epithet 'Gulban' from the conspicuous Sligo precipice in the shadow of which he spent his youth. Conall's father, occupied with war-lording against the Cruthin and hit-and-run raids in the N of Roman Britain, placed Conall in fosterage with Fiachra. Fiachra was too busy with the expansion of his own kingdom and trouble in the south to take proper care of his foster-son. He sent Conall to be educated by Muiredach Meann, Menapi king of the Calraige sept around Benbulben in Sligo. His military training in this scenario involved a daily run from a pillarstone up the sheer slope of the SW face of Benbulben (archaic 'Beann Gulban'). Each day Muiredach marked the place where Conall halted to draw his breath. Day by day he was made to run faster and further until finally he could reach the peak without rest. Hence Muiredach's druid named him Conall Gulban. When Conall's uncle, Briun, Fir Belg Overking, on his royal rounds visited Muiredach, his burly army captain boasted out of bravura that he could climb to the top of Benbulben without halt for rest just as well as Conall. Challenged to justify his claim, he dropped dead from the effort. Conall's military prowess endeared him to Niall. It cut him out for a life of warlording in his father's footsteps. At the expense of the Cruthin, he made swordland, and left behind rulers, of the greater part of Donegal, called Tir Chonaill (Conall's land) after him. This Sligo/Donegal scenario, not Tara of Meath, was Niall's family stamping ground.

Their conquest of the Cruthin-held NW tip of Ireland began in retaliation for a defeat in the wars between the Fir Belg of Connacht and Cruthin of Ulster when the latter burned down the fortress of Muiredach Meann, Conall's fosterer/teacher, in the shadow of Benbulben. Conall sped S to Rath Cruacha of Galway (not Rathcroghan of Roscommon which was in the hands of the Cruthin) to seek the assistance of his first fosterfather. Fiachra and his son Dathi (Nath I) led their forces to Conall and his brothers' aid. Niall counseled his sons that compensation should be accepted from the Ulstermen instead. This was over-ruled by Fiachra, reigning King of Connacht, who urged Conall against this. In the bloody battle which ensued at Ath Cro (Ford of the Blood at Ballyshannon in Donegal), near the then

[551] Francis John Byrne, 'Irish Kings and High-Kings', p244

Cruthin 'Wall of Ulster' through Dun Muc Dhruim, Conall and his Airghiallan allies, assisted by Fiachra and Dathi leading Connacht's forces, drove back the Cruthin from the N shores of Lough Erne. They made significant gains in the NW lands of the Cruthin converting NW Fermanagh and SW Donegal and Tyrone into Menapian buffer states protecting Conall's kingdom. The victory was left to Niall's sons, particularly Conall. Fiachra and Dathi returned to their Fir Belg capital at Rath Cruacha of Athenry in Galway.

Niall's sons Conall, Eoghan, Cairbre and Eanna, aided by the Airghialla, pursued their campaign against the Cruthin, carving out kingdoms for themselves, until N Sligo, Donegal (Tir Chonaill) and Tyrone (Tir Eoghain) were in their hands. They later absorbed Eanna's kingdom. Eoghan "penetrated as far as Inishowen"[552] (NE Donegal peninsula), aided notably by Conall. In the ferocious battle of Cruachan Droma Luighean large numbers of the Airghialla were slaughtered at Lifford in the inner recesses of the Foyle Estuary which forms the E boundary of Donegal. Conall's brothers led by Eoghan faced certain defeat. Conall rose from his sickbed to their rescue and led them to rout the Cruthin. The Foyle Estuary and river as far S as Clady served as the new boundary line along which the Cruthin held the sons and grand-sons of Niall at bay for a considerable time. From Clady ('Claidhe, Dyke) Niall's sons advanced the line of Airghiallan buffer states against the Cruthin of Ulster. The Manapi and Ciannachta of Derry were the furthest N followed by the Ui Maic Cairthinn of Lough Foyle, the Ui Fiachrach of Ardstraw and the Ui Thuirtri (these 3 were known collectively as the Ui Macc (Colla) Uais. These were followed by the descendants of Colla Da Criach, a Menapian state in Clochar Damhain of Tyrone and the Fir Manach (Menapi) of Fermanagh extending into Monaghan. They were followed by the Luigne, Gailenge and Saitne through Cavan and Meath on the W banks of Loch Ramor and the Blackwater. The Ciannachta and Menapi on the Dublin coast completed the NW/SE Airghiallan buffer state defence line begun by Cormac Mac Art.

A text embedded in a 14th century genealogy of Fiachu, alleged son of Niall, lists Niall's division of the conquered lands between his sons. Conall's portion lay between Lough Foyle and the Drowes River at Bundoran, i.e., Tir Chonaill. "He placed Eoghan on the territory of Ailech," i.e. Inish Eoghain in the N of Donegal. Tyrone (Tir Eoghan, land of Eoghan) conquered - at least in the person of his descendants - was also named after Eoghan. "Niall placed Fergus with each (Eoghan and Conall). He placed Cairbre (Cairpre), his eldest son, between Conall in his land in the N and Fiachra, his stepbrother, at the sea (Sligo and NW Mayo) between Ess Ruaid and Rót Ua Fiachrach." Benbulben district lay between the lands of Conall and Fiachra. Cairpre left descendants, the Cenel Cairpre, who expanded E from Sligo across the Shannon into areas overlapping Leitrim, Longford and Westmeath, and later as far as the barony of Carbury in Kildare, named after them. The kingdom of Maine, younger son of Niall by a Menapian princess from Cloghar, formed a parallel belt W of the latter down along both sides of the Shannon. Descendants of Niall's 4 elder sons - Cairbre, Conall, Eogan and Eanna - became known as the Northern Ui Neill.

Briun, the *Rí Temhro* Fir Belg Overking, became alarmed by his brother and stepbrother's refusal to submit their new kingdoms, won over with the aid of his vassal-allies, to his Over-kingship. They had weaned away his Airghiallian buffer states to serve their own burgeoning overkingdom, encouraging them to revolt against Briun. Briun organized an all-out assault on Fiachra for supporting Niall and his sons against his over-kingship. He defeated Fiachra's forces at Damhchluain in Magh Seola on the E shores of Loch Corrib N of Rath Cruacha of Athenry. The location of the battle shows Briun was the aggressor. He set up base on Loch Hacket near Loch Corrib, punching a wedge through the heart of Fiachra's new kingdom, cutting it into two Ui Fiachrach kingdoms, Northern and Southern.

---

[552] Gearoid Mac Niocaill, 'Ireland before the Vikings', p. 12

He moved to do the same between the Northern Ui Fiachra and the kingdoms of Niall and his sons to choke their close co-operation. Briun took Fiachra into custody. Pseudo-historical versions of these events, which are of Ui Neill provenance, claimed that Fiachra was sent by Briun as captive to High King Niall at Tara. This claim, apart from being at odds with the Fiachra/Ui Niall alliance, is altogether anachronistic. Niall could not have been further from Tara than he was in Donegal.

Fiachra's son, Dathi (Nath I), sped N to Donegal to seek support from his uncle, Conall, to free his father. Conall's forces joined Dathi's and reassembled his father's defeated army, determined to dislodge Briun from Magh Seola, the mid-section of Fiachra's kingdom. Their combined forces defeated Briun in a second battle at Damhchluain. Briun fled, was pursued and slain, according to the pseudo-history of Ui Fiachra/Ui Neill provenance. Elsewhere, he is said to have been slain by Crimthann Mac Enna Cennselach and the Leinstermen. There may have been a temporary setback for Briun. Snatches of legendary history show that his descendants succeeded in holding on to Magh Seola despite this alleged reverse. They still had their royal residence on Loch Hacket to the NE of Loch Corrib in the late 7th century when Tirechan wrote. A fierce struggle began at the heart of the Connacht dynasty. According to Ui Fiachrach records, Daithi and Conall led their victorious forces around Briun's overkingdom, subduing all of Connacht and defeating a N Munster king, Lughaidh Meann, a Menapi cousin of Briun's mother, Briun's ally. Clare's Fir Belg kingdoms had been loyal to Briun and part of Connacht. Fiachra became Fir Belg Overking after Briun with the complicity of his stepbrother Niall, so-called High King of Ireland. The new Ui Neill/Airghiallian alliance drove a wedge between the branches of the Connacht dynasty and cut off its overkingship of territories outside the province E of the Shannon. The Ui Neill were then free to expand into these territories at will.

The pseudo-versions of these events bear the hallmarks of the suppression of genuine history and the fabrication of different strata of fictitious history by the Ui Fiachra/Northern Ui Neill Syndrome. It was further manipulated from the 9th century on as the result of a conspiracy between the descendants of Briun, the Sil Muiredaig (Ui Briuin Ai) after they gained possession of Rathcroghan of Roscommon, the monastic chroniclers of Armagh and Louth and the Southern Ui Neill who were by then in possession of the Tara district. Loaded with inconsistencies and anachronisms, they project Briun as taking the captured Fiachra to Niall, fictional High King of Tara. Daithi (Nath I) was supposedly elevated to the throne of Connacht at Rathcroghan of Roscommon in the absence of his father. Daithi and Conall allegedly traveled to Tara to be reconciled with Niall. Fiachra was released and reinstalled as King of Connacht at Rathcroghan of Roscommon. Since Tara did not come into the possession of the Ui Niall until the mid 7th century and Croghan of Roscommon did not come into the possession of the Ui Briuin until the 8th century, this pseudo-historic scenario was impossible. The nearest Niall came to the High Kingship of Ireland at Tara was a mere foothold in North Connacht and Donegal in the far NW of Ireland.

After Briun's assassination, Fiachra led his forces into Munster to present himself as the new Overking of the Fir Belg tribes, levy tribute and take hostages. Eochaid son of Crimthann and Maide Mescorach leading the Munstermen against him. Fiachra won the battle of Caenraige and returned to Rath Cruacha (Athenry).[553] Thus began the long drawn-out warfare between Munster and Connacht for the territory which ever since is known as Thomand (*Tuadh Mumhan,* North Munster). In 7 battles, Lughaid Menn led former Manapian followers of Lugaid mac Con in Clare and Munster, faithful allies of the Fir Belg Overkings until the assassination of Briun in the fifth century and wrested the south of

---

[553] Mac Firbisigh, *Leabhar Buidhe Lecan, 900*: "Gabais Fiachra o Carn Feredaig co Magh Mucrama.."

Fiachra's kingdom, Clare and north Limerick, from Connacht which then became Thomand, North Munster.

The boundaries of Lughaid Menn's kingdom extended "from Berna Tri gCarbad at Carn Feradaig, S of Limerick city, to Ath na Boraimhe at Cenn Cora, the Shannon ford at Killaloe at the S of Loch Derg. The boundary ran NW along the Clare foothills of Sliabh Achta. Thence it skirted the Burren to Luchad, Bealach-an-Luchaid (Bealaclugga) between Kinvarra (Co. Galway) and Ballyvaughan at the NW of Clare and N tip of the Burren, forming the SW Galway/NW Clare boundary. Thence to Leim an Chon (Leim Conchulainn) at Loop Head at the SW tip of Clare and back to Carn Feradaig"[554] near Bruff and Knockaney SE of Limerick city. An ancient road, Bealach an Luchaid, ran along the height of this natural boundary forming an outer ward of the Fir Belg Turoe/Knocknadala oppidum expanding S into Clare. The S border of Lugaid Menn's kingdom is less clear. Had it run from Loop Head to Carn Feradaig (Bruff/Knockaney) north to Ath na Boraimhe at Killaloe it would have taken in much of Limerick, including the former territory of the Gangani, descendants of Gann. Well into historic times the Partrige na Locha (Cong district on the Galway/Mayo border between Lough Corrib and Mask) claimed to be displaced descendants of Gann, Sengann, and Sreng. The Partraige of Cera in Mayo claimed to be descendants of Genann, son of Dela son of Gann (Commius). Bruree (Brugh Righ) near Carn Feradaig in the archaic part of Limerick, was the royal seat of Ailill Olumm, Fir Belg King of Munster. His large fort and circular wall defended by square towers survives. Here one is at the heart of Iron Age Belgic Munster long before Cashel was annexed. Co. Clare thus ceased to be part of Connacht and became part of Munster, allegedly in compensation for the assassination of Overking, Crimthann. It was the cause of later wars between Connacht and Munster.

Munster kings withdrew former allegiance under Briun. Fiachra took his Munster hostages as he crossed the Shannon to Mullingar to make it known to the Airghiallian vassal-allies that he was now their Overking. The territory around Mullingar was known as Magh nAsail from Asail, a descendant of the Fir Belg leader Umor, who cleared the plain in the service of the Overking Conn of the Hundred Battles. Loch Ennel (Ainninn) got its name from Ainninn, a descendant of Umor. Slighe nAsail ran through Magh nAsail via Delvin, NE of Mullingar, and the famous ford over the river Inny just N of Loch Derravaragh heading through Longford to Loch Boderg on the upper Shannon. Built by Asail's people along Connacht's frontier facing Ulster it ran parallel to the earlier Longford Corlea Road some 15km to the south. The name is retained by the Barony of Moyashal of Mullingar. A tract of Cruthin land E of the Shannon, NE of Athlone, had been won, lost and won from the Cruthin by Connacht in Queen Medb's time. Conn Cedchathach in his numerous campaigns against Ulster extended his Overkingdom NE to the Mullingar/(Delvin)/Longford frontier. His son Art and grandson Cormac extended the frontiers ENE. Cormac's massive advance against the Cruthin, leading the Colla/Collaibh Oige, the Clann Chian, Menapi (Managh), Delbhna, Luigne, Gailenga, Saitne, and others, classed under 3 major Colla groups of fighting men, Uais (Os), Menn (Menapi), and Ocre ('Colla Fo Crith'), to form a new line of buffer-states between the Connachta and the Cruthin.

The Colla Fo Crith branch of the Monach (Menapi) were part of this line of buffer states when they moved forward from Wicklow up the Dublin coast which formed the SE tip of Ulster at this time. The Menapi leader Forgall Monach had his stronghold on the N Dublin coast. Cormac Mac Art placed the Fir Monach (Menapi) along the top NW end of the line of buffer states stretching in a NW alignment from the River Tolka in N Dublin through Lough Ramor in Cavan and thence along the Erne Lakelands to Drowse River in Donegal.

---

[554] Keating's History of Ireland, 159 b.

They established a major buffer state which became known as the Manaigh Locha hEirne or Fir Managh, Fermanagh. They slowly moved further north into N Fermanagh, S Tyrone and Monaghan to which they also gave their name. They were still moving into these regions from Leinster and expanding in their new homelands a century later.[555]

The *'Tripartite'* text acknowledges that the lakelands of Magh nAsail around Mullingar and Multyarnham, named 'Magh Locha' in the 'Book of Rights,' had been a Connacht possession, ruled in Patrick's time by Briunan (Brenain), son of Eochaid Moyvane (Muigh Mhean). This was the Briun who succeeded to the Fir Belg Overkingship after the death of his father Eochaid's successor, Crimthann Mac Fidaig, as Rí Temhro (Highking of Tara in pseudo-history). Fergus, his elder brother, ruled there first, but died young. Briunan (young Briun) ruled the territory until recalled to succeed Crimthann. This Briunan is not to be confused with the Brenain son of Briun, a prince of Maine Mor's household in the adjoining territory of S Tethbae whose obit is given under 576.[556] A text of Ui Neill/Armagh provenance would not give such facts so damaging to their interests were they not authentic. It exhibits its biased nature in favour of the Tara/Patrick Myth by claiming that Briunan resisted Patrick when he tried to build a church at Agh Maigne. Patrick allegedly cast his curse on him declaring that he would neither have son or successor in the kingdom. One can rest assured that this curse never issued from Patrick's lips but rather from the chroniclers of the Ui Neill who made sword-land of this territory in the wake of Maine Mor's conquests down along both banks of the Shannon. During Briun's lifetime the territory of Magh nAsail of which he was king before Crimthann's death remained faithful to him. When Fiachra appeared on Magh nAsail to take it under his wing he was promptly assasinated. The 50 Munster hostages he brought with him as proof that he was the Fir Belg Overking were buried with his corpse at Forrach (Farrow near Mullingar).

In pseudo-history Fiachra's son, Daithi, who succeeded his father as king of Connacht, is glorified as a hero who allegedly conquered Scotland at the Battle of Magh Circinn (Gorgin) and swept through Britain and France receiving submission from all and sundry until struck dead by lightning in the Alps. In reality he and his son Amhalghaidh (perpetuated in the Mayo barony of Tirawley of which he made swordland) suffered a fate similar to that of Fiachra. The saga of his death states that Amhalghaid died in the territory of the Deisi Temhro S of Tara with his father after fighting several battles. Daithi (Nath I)'s body was taken home for burial. He was interred at Oenach Cruacha, the *'Relec na Rí lamh le Cruacha.'* Pseudo-history re-interpreted this as Croghan of Roscommon. The *'Relec na Rí'* Cemetery "back home" was Rath Cruacha of Ochall Oichne of Galway, close to Dathi's royal palace, Clogher nDhathi ('Naghi') S of Athenry. The tale of the red sandstone pillar at Rathcroghan said to mark the grave of Daithi (Nath Í) is pseudo-historic. The excavation of so-called Dathi's Burial Mound at Rathcroghan by archaeologist John Waddell in 1981 contradicts the pseudo-historic claim that it was Dathi's 5th century burial mound. Although it had the appearance of a burial mound, the excavation confirmed that the "mound was natural and carved out of a small gravel ridge. No graves were found."[557] The prominent pillar stone on the summit sets it apart indicating that it had a ceremonial rather than a funerary purpose. Charcoal samples taken from the mound "gave a calibrated date range between 350 BC and AD 230,"[558] long before the time of Dathi. In Dathi's day the latter site was then, and for some centuries thereafter, firmly in the hands of his fiercest enemies, the Cruithintuatha of Croghan, not of the Fir Belg of Ól nÉgmacht.

---

[555] Norman Mongan, 'Menapia Quest', p. 70-75
[556] AU s. annis 552, 575.
[557] Professor John Waddell, 'The Prehistoric Archaeology of Ireland,' p. 350.
[558] Professor Barry Raftery, 'Pagan Celtic Ireland', p. 71.

Daithi's son Ailill Molt, Fir Belg Overking, is "universally recognized in the records as king of Tara,"[559] a pseudo-historic deliberate misinterpretation of the original Irish *'Ríg Temhro'*. The anglicized title 'king of Tara' did not come into being until a few centuries ago. The O-Irish title, *'Ríg Temhro'* was well known in Ailill's time. It referred to the Fir Belg Overkingship seated in the Turoe/Knocknadala oppidum of Galway, not to Tara of Meath. Ailill Molt crossed the Shannon to revenge the deaths of his father and grandfather and address the loss of Connacht's former vassal-states, attempting to revive the great Fir Belg Overkingship. He was no more welcome than Daithi and Fiachra. Records of Leinster origin, claimed he fought several battles against the province of Leinster. The name 'Laigin' in this and similar contexts has been misunderstood and needs clarification. The Leinster of that date did not reach up into the N Midlands, nor did it include Tara. Leinster pseudo-history projected the fiction that Tara was part of Leinster 'from time immemorial', conning historians.[560] Mac Neill's misconceptions are the epitome of this fallacy as he wrote of "Tara, the old capital of N Leinster" until the time of Cormac Mac Art, and of "a zone of colonies transplanted from Connacht into Leinster to guard the conquests of the Connacht Kings *c* AD 250-300 (Cormac Mac Art's time). These states, when we trace them back as far as possible, are native to Connacht."[561] These states included not only the Luigni, Gailinga and Cianachta, but also Partraige, Delbna, Sogain, Corcu Roide and Grecraige of Meath and Westmeath, and Conmaicne Rein of Leitrim.[562]

The Cianachta claimed descent from Tadhg mac Cian of Bri Eile from Leinster Fir Belg stock before Bri Eile became part of Munster under Corc (Gorgin). Tadhg and his followers joined Cormac mac Art at the Battle of Crinna. After victory over the Cruthin, Tadhg's forces were planted along a line of frontier buffer states running from Dublin in a NW alignment up through the Midlands to guard Connacht's conquests. Various Fir Belg tribes of Leinster origin S of a line from Athlone to Dublin were led by Cormac in a massive NE bound advance making swordland across this line spear-headed by the Fir Belg Overkings of Connacht at the expense of the Cruthin. For those with an eye to historical precedent, the steady whittling away of the great Kingdom of Ulster by Connacht's Fir Belg over-kingdom over several centuries was an early precedent of Rakosian "salami tactics, one slice at a time."[563] Vestiges of line after line of boundary dykes erected by Leinster septs expanding N across the Athlone/Dublin line corroborate this fact of history. Vestiges survive E and W of Moate, Clara (*Cladhra*, dykes), Kilbeggan, Tyrrellspass, and Miltownpass. Vestiges also survive E and W of Kinnegad, along the edge of the nearby bogs. Further vestiges survive along the upper reaches of the Boyne in Moyvalley. Others survive E and W of Enfield, Maynooth and beyond. Although these septs were of Leinster origin and these swordlands conquered by them were granted to them for their military services, they remained rent-paying subjects of the Fir Belg Over-kingship at that time. They did not constitute a North Leinster Province until very much later.

Ailill Molt did not go to war with the province of Leinster. When he crossed the Shannon into territories which much later were to became North Leinster he was crossing into what, until Briun's time, had been his Fir Belg Overkingship realms won over from the Cruthin of Ulster and defended by Airghiallian buffer-states. These extended from Loch Foyle SE through Loch Ramor and along the Blackwater to Navan in Meath, and thence along the Tolka river to the N Dublin coast. The name applied to this conglomeration of vassal tribes, *'na hAirghialla'* (Eastern Vassal-allies of Connacht, not of Tara) underpins this fact.

---

[559] Francis J. Byrne, 'Irish Kings and High-Kings', p. 85.
[560] E. Mac Neill,'Phases of Irish History', Cormac conquering Tara from the Laigin, p. 120
[561] Ibid, p. 121-125.
[562] E. Mac Neill,"Colonization under early Kings of Tara' in 'Jrnl. Galway Arch. and Hist. Soc.'xvi,101
[563] Matyas Rakosi, former Premier of Communist Hungary, re. Communist tactics.

The Airghialla of Leinster origin were drafted by the expanding Connacht Fir Belg power, way back in the time of Medb who employed the Gaillioin to fight alongside her Connacht armies and continued up to the time of Niall of the Nine Hostages. At the instigation of Niall and his sons, the Midland Airghialla with the support of their kinsmen from Leinster defeated Ailill Molt in several battles, as they had defeated Fiachra and Daithi before him. In reprisal for the deaths of his father and grandfather, Ailill laid waste the lands of the Airghialla and their kinsmen southwards into the Leinster areas from which they originated. He partly redeemed his defeat by a victory over the Leinstermen in 475. Mac Niocaill wrote: "It seems not impossible that Ailill's misfortunes were in part due to a less than wholehearted support by the Ui Neill." This is shown by the surprising combination which opposed him and brought about his death at the battle of Ochae (Cath Fhocha at Faughan Hill, Kells) in 482. The Airghialla, in whose lands the battle took place, were supported by Niall's descendants. They were prepared to join forces with their later enemies, the Leinstermen from the SE led by their king, Crimthann, in their determination to put a stop to Ailill and the Connachta from having any further say in affairs E of the Shannon. What is remarkable and shows to what extent they were prepared to go, was that they joined their bitterest enemies, the Cruthin of Ulster led by their overking Fiachra Lond (reigning at Tara, a fact studiously suppressed by the pseudo-historians). The territory of the Fir Li (Lee) in Derry which had recently been taken from the Cruthin by the Ciannacht branch of the Airghialla was given back to Fiachra Lond in reward for his participation in the defeat of Ailill at the Battle of Ochae. In 563 the Northern Ui Neill retook it from the Cruthin.

The Ui Neill, having won over the Airghiallia, ensured that the rival branch of the Fir Belg of Connacht would never again exert power E of the Shannon. Mac Ercae, the son of Ailill Molt, was slain by Tuathal Maelgarb, grandson of Cairpre son of Niall of the S Ui Neill at Ardbraccan in 543, 60 years after the death of his father. Tuathal's epithets, Maelgarb (fierce one)/Oengarb (rough one) indicate the ferocity with which the kingdom founded by Cairpre "thrust deep into the midlands from a base in NE Connacht and Longford." Ailill Molt's death at Faughan and the massive defeat of his forces mark the end of the Connacht Fir Belg Overkingdom east of the Shannon. It was also the beginning of the end for segments of the Airghialla, a paving of the way for the Ui Neill and Ui Maine.

West of the Shannon Briun's descendants exacted revenge on Fiachra who had taken over a major part of Mayo and Sligo at the expense of the vassal allies of the Fir Belg Overking, the Luigni and Gailenga, with the assistance of Conall son of Niall and the Northern Ui Neill. The Ui Fiachra and the Northern Ui Neill were vigorously supporting each other against them. The Ui Briuin liberated Luigne and Gailenga lands from Ui Fiachrach domination. These formed a wedge in N Connacht between the Ui Fiachra and the N Ui Neill. Thus the Ui Briuin ended the early dominance of the Ui Fiachra and won back the kingship of Connacht. A number of early Ui Briuin kings lost their lives in doing so. Daui (Dui/Duach) Galach Tenga Umai,[564] son of Briun, wrested Connacht's kingship from the Ui Fiachra after the death of Ailill Molt. He lost his life in the Battle of Segais (Battle of Ui Fiachrach), along the Boyle river, rescuing the territory of the Luigne of N Connacht. Forggus and Domnall, sons of Muirchertach of the Cenel Eoghan joined Ainmere mac Setnai and Ninnid mac Duach of Cenel Conaill to defeat Eogan Bel, son of Daui Galach,

---

[564] Duplication of the name Daui, son of Briun confuse his genealogy. In some lists he appears as Duai Galach and later as Dui Tenga Umai. According to O Rahilly in EIHM, 398, N, "the historical Duai succeeded Ailill Molt (as King of Connacht); the unhistorical Daui is represented as succeeding a later namesake." In LL 350 a 29-31 Dui Galach Tenga Umai is made son of Fergus, son of Muiredach, son of Briun. In LB, 17 c ad calc., he is Duach Galach Tengai Umai son of Fergus, son of Muiredaig Mail, son of Eogan Sreb; Lec. 43 a 1.10-15 distinguishes 2 Daui: "Duach Tenga Umae son of Fergus, son of Muiredaig Mail, son of Eogan Srem, son of Duac Galaig, son of Briuin. His epithets, Bel and Srem both refer to a deformity of the mouth.

slaying him at the Battle of Sligo on Luigne territory (barony of Leyny) in 543. The same combination slew Eogan Bel's son, Ailill Inbanda, at the Battle of Cul Conaire in Cera (Carra in Sligo) in 550. Eogan's royal residence on a crannog on Inish Eogain in the SE of Loch Mask at the N head of Magh Seola, now expanding N under the Ui Briuin resurgence, shows that Eogan Bel belonged to the Ui Briuin Seola. Most regnal lists attach Eogan Bell to the Ui Briuin genealogy, but some of Ui Fiachra provenance link him to the Ui Fiachra dynasty. Had he belonged to the Ui Fiachra, this battle would be inconsistent with the trend in mutual relations between the Ui Neill and the Ui Fiachra of Connacht.

Swordlands won by Niall's sons cut off the Cruithinthutha of Connacht bounded by the upper Shannon and Suck rivers and centered on Croghan of Roscommon from their Ulster kinsmen, leaving them vulnerable on all sides. Niall cast a cold eye on this Cruthin territory. If his sons did not benefit from the weakened circumstances of the Cruthin W of the Shannon, Briun's descendants would. There was bad blood between Niall and Briun since Niall's manipulation of the Airghialla and territories won by his sons with their aid, setting themselves up independently of Briun's Overkingship. Niall, with forward insight, deemed the best way for his dynasty to advance would be at the expense of the Cruthin but especially at that of the Fir Belg Overkingship of lands E and W of the Shannon. As this plan hatched in Niall's mind it greatly expanded his ambitions for himself and his sons.

MAINE MOR'S INVASION - MASSACRE OF CONNACHT FIR BELG

Maine Mor is usually given as son of Eochu Fer Da Ghiall. Variant versions make him a son of Niall Noigiallach and an Airghiallan princess, the daughter of Eochu Fer Da Ghiall of the race of Colla Da Crioch of Clogher of Tyrone. The genealogy of the virgin martyr St. Dymphna, patron saint of Gheel in Belgium, records her as a daughter of Damhan, son of Cairpre son of Eochu Fer Da Ghiall of Clogher Damhain (Clogher of Tyrone near the Monaghan border). She was born at the royal palace of *Rath More* of *Clogher na Riogh* (King's Palace), chief stronghold of the Airghiallan Overkings. Eochu Fer Da Ghiall was Airghiallan Overking in Niall's day as was Dymphna's father, Damhan, two generations later. Niall's alliance with Eochu's family gave him a weighty say in Airghiallan affairs. Eochu gained political clout in thus being closely associated with the leader of Connacht's frontline forces. Niall incited Maine to lead a massive invasion with the descendants of Colla Da Chrioch and segments of the Airghialla and their Cruthin subjects. They cut a wide swath down along both banks of the middle Shannon and through Cruthin lands in S Roscommon and E Galway back into the original lands of the Colla tribes. This effectively cut off the Fir Belg Overking, Dui Galach, from his Airghiallan frontline buffer states and the Midland territories subject to Connacht. Niall's sons could step in where the Connacht Fir Belg power failed. The tradition that the Ui Neill claimed suzerainty over the Ui Maine (descendants of Maine) of Connacht is genuine. Maine Mac Cerbaill of the S Ui Nell was slain in his attempt to enforce this suzerainty at the Battle of Claenloch near Gort in S Galway in 538. The parting of the ways between the Ui Neill and the Connachta in the course of the 6th century led to the total separation of the Ui Maine and Cenel Maine.[565]

In the *Life of St.Grellan* (in *Tribes And Customs Of Hy Many*[566] and *Book of Rights*)[567] Maine Mor's invasion took place in the reign of Duach Galach. His elders spoke thus: *"'Numerous are our heroes and great is our population, our tribe having multiplied. We cannot well bear to be confined. Let us see in which province we can make room for ourselves and in which the Fir Belg race is most expansive. Let us go and narrow it on them.'* Those who held this conversation were Niall, Maine Mor, his father/father-in-law, Eochaid Fer Da Ghiall, who

---

[565] Francis John Byrne, in 'Irish Kings and High Kings', p. 92-93.
[566] Tribes and Customs of Hy Many, ed. O Donovan, 8ff
[567] Book of Rights, ed O Donovan, p. 106n.

held the hostages of the Ulidia and Cruthin with him." The hostages of the Cruthin refers to Cruthin areas won over as sword-land by the Airghialla, not the free Cruthin kingdom of Ulster. The Cruthin population which remained behind was subject to Airghiallan lords. They provided fighting men for them. This accounts for the over-population of Eochaid Fer Da Ghiall's over-kingdom. The decision to invade the "province in which the Fir Belg race is most expansive," i.e., the Overkingdom of Connacht, was not from hatred of the Fir Belg since the invaders themselves were mostly Fir Belg tribes. It was because of Niall's hatred of Briun and his mother, Mongfhind, for the way he and his slave-mother Caireann had been treated by Niall's stepmother. It was aggravated by the antagonism between Niall and Briun because of Niall's takeover of the Airghiallan states, inciting them, and Briun's younger brothers, against Briun.

Maine's invasion is told thus: "These multitudinous superior hosts suddenly and heroically proceeded in orderly battalions, with enormous flocks and herds, from Clochar Mac Damhain (Tyrone) to Druim Clasach in Tir Maine (in Connacht) between Lough Ree and River Suck."[568] This had formerly been Cruthin territory ruled by the Cruthintuatha of Rathcroghan of Roscommon. In NE Galway there were Cruthin lands, the 6 Soghains, stretching from Attymon to Moylough (the Barony of Tiaquin). It had been made sword-land by the Fir Belg, aided by the Ciannachta, the ancestral parent tribe from which some of the Airghialla had gone forth 150 years earlier in the van of Cormac Mac Art to establish buffer states against the Cruthin of the NE. The parent tribe still inhabited their original homeland, Magh Seincheineoil (Plain of the parent stock). Maine's hosts overran these lands as far as Magh Seincheineoil. From there they sent messengers to Cian, Ciannacht king of Magh Seinchineoil, not the Fir Belg king of Connacht nor the Fir Belg Overking, to inform him that the descendants of Colla Da Chrioch had come to demand tribute and territory from him. Connacht's Fir Belg army was at that time fighting against the Cruthintuatha of Croghan, unaware of the invasion, leaving its oppidum core poorly defended. Maine marched his massive army almost to the edge of the inner ward of Connacht's oppidum before meeting any opposition. Cian came out on the plain of Magh Seincheineoil to meet the enemy. St. Grellan, patron saint of the Ui Maine (Hy Many) repressed both parties, checked their animosity, and ratified a peace between them. He ordered that Maine Mor give three times nine persons out of their nobility to Cian, as pledges to observe the peace. Cian was induced by his lawgiver to kill the hostages and resist.

Cian met Eochaid Fer Da Ghiall and Maine Mor at Magh Seimhni on the confines of Magh Seinchineoil and Maen Magh (the plain around Loughrea and the Turoe/Knocknadala core of the Fir Belg overkingdom in Galway). According to the Life of St. Grellan (of Airghialla/Hy Many provenance), Cian pretended he had a feast prepared for them. What he had prepared was treachery. This 'perfidious design' was made known to St. Grellan, the guarantor between them. By this time Maine Mor's forces had marched as far as Bearnach na nArm in Maen Magh and Seisidh Beg[569] at Knockaboy (Cnoc an Buaidh) between Temple and Attymon, former Clann Cian lands in East Galway which were taken over by these Ulstermen (as Bail-na-nUlta and local names attest) 5 miles N of Turoe.

Maine's invasion recorded in the *'Tribes and Customs of Hy Many'* manifests its Airghiallan bias. It states that "St. Grellan raised his hands in prayer. His request was answered by God, for the great plain softened into a quagmire under the feet of Cian and his people so that they were swallowed up into the ground." The surviving Mss. of St Grellan's Life[570]

---

[568] 'Life of St Grellan" published in part by John O Donovan in 'Book of Hy Many', The complete Life was published by the Bollandists from surviving Mss. in 'Acta Sanctorum," Tomus 1V, p.483-95

[569] Seisidh Becc; alias Bearnach na nArm in Maenmagh in central Galway, Onomasticum Goedelicum

[570] ed. by Edmund Hogan, p. 594. One Ms. in Brussel's Burgundian Library, aother in the Royal Irish Academy.

refer to his biased interference in this affair. O Donovan, editor of *'Tribes and Customs of Hy Many'* in which this Hy Many origin-tale is found, remarked: "it is to be lamented that no Fir Belg writer survived to relate the true account of this transaction. For every acute investigator of history will suspect that the treachery was on the side of the conquerors, the Clann Colla," that is, the Hy Many branch of the Airghialla. Cian's army was defeated by Maine's vast army. O Donovan misinterpreted the Ms. account taking Cian as the Fir Belg Overking. He believed the entire Fir Belg race of Connacht was wiped out and that not a single Fir Belg "survived to relate the true account." Elsewhere he claimed that only one Connacht Fir Belg family, the Ui Lane, survived. The language of the origin-tale in the *'Book of Hy Many'* is highly glorificatory of Maine Mor and his descendants, seeing that it appears only in their own Annals specifically written for their own people. Despite having lost the E half of Galway to the Ui Maine, not only did the main branch of the Connacht Fir Belg survive, they provided the medieval Kings of Connacht and the first authentic monarchic High Kings of Ireland in the middle ages.

St. Grellan's father was Cuillin, son of Cairbre Cluaisderg of the Colla Uais Airghialla who went with Maine, an Ui Bairrche sept of Bri Eile. His mother was Ethne, daughter of Cairbre Musc, granddaughter of Conn. She was mother of Cairbre Cluichechair, an Ui Bairrche poet given land in Munster for his services. His descendants were known as Dal Cairpri Arad Cliach in W Tipperary. As such St. Grellan was related to the Airghialla on both sides, and a descendant of Tadhg Mac Cian, ancestor of the Airghialla. Hence his interest in this invasion. He was an elderly cleric by the time of Maine Mor's invasion.

The story of Maine Mor's massacre is frozen in placenames in the area where the Fir Belg were "swallowed into the ground" near Bealach na nArm 5 miles NE of the Turoe/Knocknadala oppidum core. 'Bealach na nArm (Army Route) in Maen Magh' is a narrow passage through widespread boglands running into the centre of this oppidum. It ran through Attimany (Ait Ui Maine, Place of Maine's descendants), Clooncah (Cloon Cath, the Battle Field), Caltragh (Air-Caltragh, Cemetery Massacre), Knockaboy (Victory Hill), Seisidh/Seasaidh Beg/Mor (name of the linear embankments) running across upper and lower Knockaboy, Attimon More (Ait Ui Main) and Ballnanulty (Baile na nUltaigh, Ulstermen's place). These names proclaim Maine Mor's victory. His descendants were later forced to move further E in Galway. Their kingdom, named Hy Many (Ui Maine) after him, was more extensive in the earliest period. In it were the Sogain in Galway's Barony of Tiaquin, and the Dal nDruithne (ngChruithne) of Maen Magh around Loughrea, descended respectively from Conall Cernach and Celtchar mac Uithechar, implying that they were both of the same stock as the Ulstermen (Cruthin). In the reorganization of the Irish Church in the 12th century the Diocese of Clonfert was coextensive with the kingdom of Hy Many. This origin-legend of the Hy Many people and the topography of the massacre of Cian's people emphatically corroborate the legendary history of the Fir Belg Capital in Connacht. Far from it being at Croghan of Roscommon as pseudo-history persists, it was at the centre of Galway at the end of the 5th century AD as it was in the early 2nd century when first recorded by the renowned geographer, Ptolemy of Alexandria.

The itinerary of the final stage of Maine's invasion led right through the territory of Ciannachta (Clann Chian, still referred to as the Colla Woige, corrupt form of Collaibh Oige, young fighting men) and the lands of their subject people, the 6 Soghain. The latter were an isolated Cruthin enclave, kinsmen of the Cruthin of Ulster, cut off in NE Galway in the early stages of the Fir Belg invasion. The Ciannachta, descendants of Tadgh Mac Cian's Fir Belg followers from Brí Eile, were drafted to defend this section of the defensive frontiers of the Connacht Fir Belg oppidum and subdue the Cruthin enclave which they cut up into the six Soghains. They occupied an extensive buffer state along the outer ward of the Fir Belg oppidum in the NE of Galway between itself and the then vast Cruthin Kingdom which stretched from Ulster all the way across the Shannon to the banks of the River Suck which forms the E boundary of Co. Galway. A large force of Clann Chian fighting men marched with Cormac Mac Art across the Shannon to set up a new line of buffer states to defend Connacht's territories in the Midlands of which they formed the lower S section alongside the Manachi (Menapi) and Luigni. Much later under Niall's descendants they became the Ciannachta of the coastal strip of Louth and Meath. Just 14 townlands of their parent tribe in Galway survived the invasion of Maine Mor and are still known as the Cloonkeen (a corruption of Clann Chian) townlands in NE Galway today.[571]

The Cian named in the Maine Mor invasion story was not the Fir Belg King of Connacht or Fir Belg Overking who ruled from Turoe of Galway. Dui Gallach, son of Briun son of Eochu Muigh Maen, was the Fir Belg Overking, after Ailill Molt. With the aid of the Luigni and Gailenga, he was expanding his over-kingdom further N in Connacht at the expense of the Cruthin and carving out swordland along the boundary of the Cruthintuatha N of the upper Suck in the Creev district near Airtech (Frenchpark) in Roscommon when the invasion of Maine Mor took place. St. Grellan allegedly visited his camp site and brought his son Eogan Bel (Beal) back to life, albeit with a deformity of the mouth which gave him his epithet. Eogan Bel succeeded his father as Fir Belg Overking of Connacht.

Cian was the Fir Belg king of the Ciannachta of Magh Seincheineoil of NE Galway in whose lands this massacre took place which Maine Mor and his descendants occupied thereafter. He had to deal with Maine Mor from his meagre resources since the Fir Belg Overking, Duai Galach, was warlording in Roscommon and had the main Fir Belg forces with him. Reference to the plain being "turned into a quagmire which swallowed up Cian and his Fir Belg people" alludes to the brutal massacre which took place in bogs along the narrow neck of land, Bealach na nArm, through which Maine's army marched. Much of the Clann Chian (Cloonkeen) lands in NE Galway were covered by forests and boglands which girded the outer perimiter of the oppidum. Turf-cutters in these killing fields often found skeletons along a line of sharp-spiked stakes sunk in the turf hidden below the surface pointing in an outward direction to transfix horse and rider in a cavalry charge. The Attymon La Tene-carved bronze horsebit set now in the National Museum in Dublin was found in this same bog. Local farmers like Enda Ryan tell of findings of axes and spearheads by turf-cutters in the area. Others in gravel-mining operations found mass burials in shallow graves on the sandhills in the surrounding area.

ALIGNMENT OF GREAT WALL OF ULSTER AFTER CORMAC MAC ART
The realignment of the Great Wall of Ulster after Cormac Mac Art's time is corroborated by an 8th century poem attributed to Mael Mura. It refers to an early, but not the earliest, line of Airgiallan buffer states along the boundary of Ulster after the time of Cormac Mac Airt when the Ui Neill were no more than a tiny princedom at the extreme NW corner of Ireland far from Tara of Meath. This delineation of the Ulster boundary running in a SE direction from the inner recess of the Foyle river in Londonderry to the upper Tolka river (*Buaighne*) in Glasnevin, Dublin, corroborates the historic fact that Tara was still part of Ulster at this late period, in fact until the 7th century, as revealed by *'Bech Bretha'*. This frontier ran in the true traditional NW/SE direction, diametrically opposing the NE/SW alignment of De Vismes Kane and followers who took their cue from the Tara Myth.

Between the time of Cormac Mac Art and the welding of the new relationship between the Ui Neill and Airgialla a further recession of the boundary line of ancient Ulster took place along the NW frontier. Under Niall and his sons' expansion with Airghiallan aid, its NW terminus moved N first from the Drowes River in Donegal Bay where it stood in the time of

---

[571] Martin Finnerty, "Punan Arsa', 'The Clannkeen Townlands'

Cormac mac Art, to the Erne River and Lakes and later to Loch Foyle. It was within this time-period, place and politico-dynastic anchorage, according to legendary history, that three sons of Niall of the Nine Hostages carved out swordland in Donegal and later W Tyrone pushing Ulster's boundary line NE to Lough Foyle. Niall's sons, Eoghan, Conaill and Eanna gave their names to Tir Eoghain (Land of Eoghan, Tyrone), Tir Chonaill (Land of Conaill, Donegal) and Tir Eanna (Land of Eanna). Thus, it is obvious that later medieval Ui Neill eulogists were making the absurdly anachronistic, fraudulent, claims of an Ui Neill High Kingship of Tara way back at a time when the Ui Neill were no more than a tiny, burgeoning, princedom at the extreme NW corner of Ireland. By the time the Ui Neill moved into overdrive from the 6th century on, on their way to becoming the most powerful dynasty, all Ireland stood aghast. Through a series of superbly orchestrated military moves, the Ui Neill, aided by the Airghialla, particularly the Ciannachta and Menapi, brought the erstwhile Connacht Fir Belg dominance of a large part of Iron Age Ireland to an abrupt end. They then used this vacuum as a stepping stone to their own rise to medieval power across almost the entire northern half of Ireland.

Pseudo-history concocted a noble justificatory tale for Niall, making him High King of Ireland at Tara, an institution which did not come into existence for centuries thereafter. With Connacht forces drawn from the Ciannachta and others he won swordland for himself and his sons at the SW tip of the Cruthin kingdom of Ulster. He made mutually favourable alliances with the Airghialla along Ulster's border, relieving them of burdensome rent-paying vassal status in favour of a more friendly alliance with himself. Once he had weaned them from their vassal status to Connacht's Fir Belg power, he set them against their erstwhile masters. Niall's instigation of Maine Mor's invasion, which decimated Connacht's Fir Belg power in the 5th century, was to the advantage of the Airghialla who gained considerable tracts of land on both sides of the Shannon, known originally as Ui Maine (Hy Many). "There once existed a single overkingdom of Maine lying E and W of the middle reaches of the Shannon which was fragmented when the Ui Neill finally organized themselves in the 6th century as a separate dynasty from the rest of the Connachta."[572] In this vacuum the Ui Neill rose to power, taking over the mantle which previously belonged to their Connacht ancestors. It created an alliance which should have united the Ui Neill and Airghialla more closely than that which prevailed later.

Niall's sons reduced Connacht's Overkingdom with the aid of Airghiallan allies, and weakened the latter who were now overstretched because of their massive invasion of Connacht. He orchestrated carefully planned military operations against the Cruthin of Ulster. All this played into his hands. After the massacre of the Fir Belg, the Ciannachta were involved in the 2 major military operations mounted by the Ui Neill which brought about the final defeat of the Cruthin of Ulster and their confinement to a much reduced kingdom E of the Ban and Lough Neagh. When the Ui Neill invaded the Cruthin territory of Derry they placed the Ciannachta in a buffer zone between themselves and the Cruthin. Until then the Menapi had provided protection and seaports along the Foyle Estuary. When the Ui Neill finally wrested the Tara district from the Cruthin after the battle of Moyra in 637, the Ciannachta moved N from their earlier position won under Cormac mac Art and were given extensive lands along the Louth/Meath coastal strip for their services in this definitive defeat of the Ulstermen. These became known as the 'Ciannachta,' The Menapi (Manach) stood alongside the Ciannachta in this Ui Neill expansion.

'Mael Mura's' 8th century poem is in accord with the blatantly ambitious contemporary Ui Neill propaganda describing the places allegedly reserved for princes of Munster, Leinster and Connacht (Ulster's princes are omitted because the Ui Neill were by this time masters

---

[572] Paul Walsh, 'Tethbae and Ui Maine' in 'Eriu' xiii.

of Ulster) in the banqueting hall of the Ui Neill overking, referred to as 'Lord of Tailtiu', (not Lord of Tara be it noted). Tara is conspicuous by its absence: "Let us establish the position over which the Lord of Tailtiu presided, let us recount the relationship of the (Ui Neill) nobility with that of the Airghialla." It harks back to the early flowering of the alliance between them enshrined in its verses: "Afterwards the children of the Collas (Airghialla) undertook service in the battle-camps (of the Ui Neill) against the king of the North (Cruthin overking of Ulster)." In the early period this alliance was mutually advantageous to both parties. But the Ui Neill were masters in the art of manipulating peoples.

An event which soured relations between the Ui Maine W of the Shannon and the Cenel Maine of the E bank allied to the Ui Neill is told by Tigernach. In 538 Maine Mac Cerbaill of the S Ui Neill fell at the battle of Cloenloch near Gort in Galway, slain by Goibnenn mac Conaill, king of Connacht's Ui Fiachrach dynasty, while attempting to assert hegemony over the Connacht Ui Maine. The latter promptly suppressed the Ui Neill side of their genealogy and stressed their Airghiallan descent through Eochu Fer Da Ghiall. "Once the Ui Maine were incorporated into the Connacht overkingdom they were awarded a pedigree of flattering affinity to the true Connachta."[573] Cenel Maine E of the Shannon stressed the Ui Neill side of their descent and "were accepted as Ui Neill *pur sang.*"[574]

Having narrowed Connacht's powerbase, the Ui Neill and their Airghiallan allies turned their attention on the Cruthin of Ulster as related in poem: "Afterwards the children of the Colla (Airghialla) undertook service in the battle-camps against the king of the North." The Ui Neill had become masters of the North when this poem was penned which harks back to a time when the Cruthin were still masters of greater Ulster stretching S as far as the Tolka and Glasnevin. They inexorably narrowed the territory of the Cruthin. When the Ui Neill took control of the Tara district from 637 the Ciannachta branch of the Airghialla moved forward into the vacuum left by the retreating Cruthin and were granted the lands known as Ciannachta on both banks of the lower Boyne along the coastal strip half-way up into Louth. Although planted by Cormac further SW along an earlier boundary of Ulster which then stretched all the way down to the Tolka (Buaigne) of Dublin, only in the 7th century did they occupy their lands on the banks of the lower Boyne. "The Ciannachta may thus have been planted here by the Ui Neill some centuries after Cormac's alleged reign (at Tara), as the N branch (of the Ciannachta) almost certainly were"[575] in Derry. *Cath Crinna* relates that Cormac Mac Art, with the assistance of the Ciannachta under Tadg Mac Cian, drove back the Ulaid who were under the leadership of the three Ferguses. Cormac rewarded Tadg and his Ciannachta with the conquered lands.

Before leaving this 8th century poem, note that nowhere does it mention an Ui Neill High King of Ireland, or a High King of Ireland reigning at Tara despite ambitions riding high. Tenth century Leinster pseudo-historians made Cormac the founder of Tara and its High Kingship. When their myth-makers got to work, pushing the conquest of the Tara back achronistically to Cormac Mac Airt's time, they subtly interpolated the facts, making Cormac bribe Tadhg mac Cian's charioteer to allegedly save his own 'seat' at Tara.

A whole series of tales were concocted the better to bring Cormac into close association with Tara. After the assassination of Cormac's father Art at the Battle of Magh Muc Dhrum by Lughaid Mac Con near Athenry, Cormac's real mother, Achtán (Etáin), was taken as consort by Lugna Fer Trí, king of the Luigne in Sligo. There she gave birth to her son

---

[573] Op. cit., in 'Eriu' xiii; O Rahilly, 'EIHM', pp, 96, 406, 479.

[574] Paul Walsh, in 'Eriu' , xiii.

[575] Francis John Byrne, 'Irish Kings and High-Kings', p. 69.

Cormac, conceived by Art before his assassination. In *Scéla Eogain is Cormaic* and in *Genamuin Chormaic Ua Chuind*, Cormac's birth-tale, abduction, suckling by a she-wolf in the cave (*brugh/bruidhion*) of Céis Chorainn in the territory of the Luigne of N Connacht, his rescue and fosterage are all part of the build-up of pseudo-historic myth. According to *Genamuin Chormaic,* Cormac is fostered by Lugna until he goes to Temhair (alleged to be Tara) to depose Lughaid Mac Con, alleged usurper of the High Kingship of Ireland. *Scéla Eogain is Cormaic* alleges that Cormac was fostered by Lugna for a year. Lugna then warned Achtán that her life and that of her son would be forfeit should Lughaid Mac Con find out about Cormac's whereabouts. Achtán fled to the N Leinster territory of the same Luigne tribe on the Cavan/Meath boundary to Fíachra (Fíachnae) Cassán who was allegedly the foster-father of Cormac's father Art.[576] As Achtán crossed the mountain at midnight the wolves of Ireland came and took the child Cormac from her by force and suckled him in the cave of Slieve Conachla in E Luigne near Kells while she was given protection by a wild herd of wolves across the border in Meath in Lisnagcon. Cormac was rescued and brought up by Fíachnae until he was thirty years of age when he went to Tara to succeed the usurper of the High Kingship, Lughaid Mac Con.

Genamuin Chormaic transferred Cormac to the Luigne of N Leinster the better to bring him close to Tara, overriding the historic fact that there was no Highkingship of Ireland based at Tara before the 9th century. The interpolator did not realize the blunder he was making when he concocted the tale that Cormac and his mother went to N Leinster to distance themselves from Lughaid Mac Con. If Lughaid indeed were reigning at Tara, instead of distancing themselves from him they were walking straight into his hands. Perhaps the myth-maker could not forget that Lughaid usurped, not the High Kingship of Tara, but the Fir Belg Overkingship of Turoe (Temhroit) in Galway. If so, he would be more consistent. Some claim that the better to glorify Tara[577] the lupine and suckling elements in the Cormac saga "underline an implied comparison by making Cormac, regarded as the founder of Tara, be suckled like Romulus (the founder of Rome) by a wolf-bitch. Tales in the 10th century Leinster strand of pseudo-material such as the charming tale, *The Melodies of Buchet's House* and *Ectrae Cormaic*, concocted a Leinster consort for Cormac, Eithne Thóebfhota, daughter of their ancestor Cathaer Mar, alleged King of Ireland. This again was an attempt to associate Cormac, the alleged founder of Tara, as closely as possible with Leinster. *Esnada Tige Buchet* curiously claims that "Kells was then the royal seat, and Cormac, when he became King, founded Tara on the land of Odran, a herdsman." This conflicts even with all established pseudo-tradition.

DIRE CONSEQUENCES OF DYNASTIES DIVISIONS AND FIERY FEUDS

Niall and his Northern Ui Neill dynasty championed the cause of his half-brother, Fiachra, and his dynasty against their elder brother, Briun, Overking of Connacht's widespread territories. This sowed the seeds of a fierce dynastic feud which flared for centuries after the invasion of Maine Mor and would eventually lead to dire consequences for the archaic Capitals, history and peoples of Iron Age Ireland by the 8th century. The Turoe/Kncknadala Fir Belg capital was absorbed into Maine's new kingdom, whereas, very significantly, it's nearby sister oppidum of Athenry/Rath Cruacha, seat of the Kingship of Connacht where Fiachra, his son Dathi (Nath I) and early Ui Fiachrach descendants reigned, was spared. Maine's takeover of a large tract of Connacht land halted just E of Athenry forcing the expulsion of the Fir Belg Overkingship from the Turoe/Knocknadala oppidum core. Briun's sons made Magh Seolgha, N of Athenry, E of Loch Corrib, their new power-base, residing on a royal crannog on Loch Hacket. They were still there when Tirechan wrote in the 7th century alleging that Patrick visited them there, baptized them, and erected the basilica of

---

[576] Tomás O Cathasaigh, 'The Heroic Biography of Cormac Mac Art, p. 52.
[577] Professor J. Carney, in 'Irish Sagas', 156.

Domnach Mor Magh Seolgha on the lakeshore. Briun had cut Fiachra's kingdom into two separate entities, the original *Ui Fiachrach Aidne* in SW Galway, and the more recently conquered *Ui Fiachrach in Tuaisceirt*, which had 2 main lines: Ui Fiachrach Muaidhe of the Moy estuary in N Mayo and Fir Chera around Castlebar.

The Ui Fiachra/N Ui Neill alliance against Briun and his descendants and the consequences of Maine Mor's invasion for Connacht's Fir Belg Overkingdom fuelled a perennial feud between the descendants of Fiachra and Briun, fanned by Niall's descendants as it would accrue to the glory of their own burgeoning dynasty. The groundwork was laid for the feud which tore the Connacht dynasty in two. It was exploited by the N Ui Neill until it backfired on them. The ferocity of the hostility between the two branches of the Connacht dynasty, Hy Fiachra and Hy Briun, led to all-out suppression of the old history and traditions of the Fir Belg and Cruthin of Connacht in particular and Ireland in general, and of the lost capitals of Iron Age Ireland. It led to the alarming accretion of pseudo-history. This has not been fully understood nor appreciated.

In the swift-changing political situation in the N Midlands where, after Maine Mor's invasion, Niall's descendants made inroads into these territories in the guise of saviours, encouraging the Airghiallian vassal-allies of Connacht to throw off their subject status and become independent. Niall and his sons vowed to support their cause. A rash of Ui Neill lands given to the sons of Niall by the Airghialla for their services against Ailill Molt, or won by force, broke out across the face of the Midlands like fairy mushrooms on a summer cowpie. The 14th century genealogy of Fiachu claims Niall gave his son Maine the lands "from Cruachain Feda in Chrioch Briuin to Loch Rí mic Maireda as well as the overlordship of all Ireland" *('ardchomairchi hErend uli')*. This meant from Croghan near Killeshandra in Cavan (Breifne) to Loch Ree on the Shannon. In fact it reached Loughrea, the SW extremity of Hy Many, in Galway. By the time this was written in the 14th century the kingdom of Maine W of the Shannon had long since cut its link to Niall and been welded to the genealogy of the Connacht dynasty. The title 'Overlordship of all Ireland' is a glorified redaction of Briun's 'Overking of the Erann/Fir Belg people', a title which could not apply to Maine without some spurious form of emendation.

A spurious tract embedded in the genealogy of Fiachu's descendants enumerates the alleged sons of Niall whose descendants became known as the Southern Ui Neill. "Niall placed Conall Err Breg on the land of Brega; from him descended Sil Aeda Slaine in Fir Breg, and Clann Cholman Mhoir of Mide. He gave the supremacy of Tara to Laeghaire. To Clann Leagaire half a 'triucha cet' to the W of Tara. To Enna Ilchrotach and Laegaire Beg he gave land NW of Loch Ennel. He placed Fiachu in Uisnech of Mide (Westmeath)." This territory was won over by the Southern Ui Neill long after Niall's sons to whom he allegedly divided it out. "Hagiographical sources have preserved an anecdote that an important sept of the S Ui Neill, the Cenel Fiachach, had been satirized by poets who claimed they were of plebian origin." The Clann Cholman, not Cenel Fiachach, claimed the title *'Rí Uisnig,'* 'kings of Uisnech'. As late as the 11th century their alleged Ua Maelshechlainn Kings of Tara dwelt, not at Tara, but at Dun na Sciath beside Loch Ennell or Croinis near Uisnech. "The foundation of the kingdom of Uisnech in Westmeath, between Mulingar and Athlone, antedates the foundation of the Ui Neill kingship of Tara."[578] Princes of the Sil nAedo Slaine resided, not at Tara, but at Oristown and Lagore. The text claims Niall had 2 sons named Laeghaire. Even were it true, neither of them ever reigned as High King of Tara. The Loeghuire of Tara and Cenel Loeghuire W of Tara had no connection with Niall. They were a pre-Ui Neill Cruthin sept descended from Loeghuire who was a cousin of Conor Mac Nessa as recorded in the Ulidian Tales. Clann Colman and Sil nAedo Slaine were the two

---

[578] Gearoid Mac Niocaill, 'Ireland Before The Vikings', p. 12.

great branches of the Midland Ui Neill dynasty which had burgeoned forth from the eastern perimeter of Maine's and Cairbre's kingdoms.

RISE OF THE UI NEILL DYNASTY AT THE EXPENSE OF THE AIRGHIALLA

The Ui Neill expanded into Connacht's territories in the Midlands at the expense of the Airghialla. After Ailill Molt's death at Faughan Hill, Cairpre, son of Niall, expanded SE into Airghiallan lands aided by his cousins. Finnchad, king of Leinster, marched N to aid his Airghiallan kinsmen but fell at Granard in Longford in 485. Granard became Cairpre's base close to Maine's at Ardagh. Cairpre advanced into Arghiallan lands winning battles against them, at Teltown in Meath in 494 and at Loch Slevin in Westmeath in 499. The Airghialla regretted their desertion of the Connacht Overkingship in favour of that of the Ui Neill. Cairpre determined to put an end to the constant intrusion of Leinster kings into the Midlands in support of their Airghiallan kinsmen who acquired these lands for their services as vassal-allies of Connacht. He and his Ui Neill cousins claimed that as descendants of the Connachta they were entitled to be there since this was Connacht's sword-land conquered from the Cruthin! Cairpre, following up his previous advantage, struck S into the heart of Leinster to make it known he would not tolerate interference in his affairs. He inflicted a defeat on Leinster at Cenn Ailbe in S Kildare in 501. In 503 and 507 the Leinstermen rallied to defend their Airghiallan kinsmen in the Midlands, and inflicted defeats on the Ui Neill. In 510 Failge Berraide, a ruler of the Leinster Ui Failge marched up into the lands of Fiachu, alleged son of Niall, and defeated him at Frevin Hill W of Loch Owel in Westmeath. In 516 Fiachu went south to Druim Deirg and inflicted a crushing defeat on Failge Berraide which put a decisive end to their interference in Ui Neill affairs.

In pseudo-history the Ui Neill possessed Tara to the exclusion of all others; this was contested by the later Leinster strand of pseudo-history which claimed it for 5th century Bresal Belach and later Leinster kings. Neither possessed it before the 7th century when the Ui Neill, with the aid of the Airghialla, finally wrested it from the Cruthin of Ulster. In this Battle of the Books "a precise chronology was assigned to the high points in the struggle between the Laigin and the Ui Neill" for the alleged possession of Tara. Mac Niocaill noted, "On this warfare was later superimposed, not earlier than the 8th century, a tradition of tribute, the *Borama,* payable by the Laigin to the (so-called) kings of Tara. By the time the tradition reached the 11th century the amount payable had reached fantastic proportions. The tale may be dismissed as pure fiction devised to legitimize Ui Neill aggression against the Laigin retrospectively. It has no place in the history of the 5th and 6th centuries."[579]

Following the hiving off of the Ui Neill from the Connachta, Maine Mor's invasion and the rise of Ui Neill kingdoms in the 5th/6th centuries, a new set of political alliances took shape. This appears in the struggle between the N and S branches of the Ui Neill, and between Connacht's Ui Briuin and Ui Fiachra. In 520 Ardgal, son of Conall Cremthainne, of the S Ui Neill was slain in the Battle of Detnae in the N Midlands by Muirchertach Mac Erca of the Northern Ui Neill, with the support of Colgu, king of the Airghiallan kingdom of Airthir in which Armagh was situated. He was the same Muirchertach, grandson of Eogan son of Niall, who organized the remarkable combination which slew Ailill Molt in 482.[580] He was active in this area for a long time, 40 years if these dates are correct. The Airghiallan St Cairnech, founder of Tuilen (Dulane of Kells) church "made peace between Muirchertach and Tadg Mac Cein's descendants, the Delbna, Ciannachta, Gailenga, Luigni, and Saitne."[581] His war-alliance with the Airghialla in the defeat of Ailill Molt and his cousin Ardgal strengthened his own and the N Ui Neill hand. After their subjugation by Muirchertach, the

---

[579] Gearoid Mac Niocaill, 'Ireland before the Vikings,' p. 15-16.
[580] F. J Byrne, 'Irish Kings and High-Kings', p. 85
[581] *Aided Muirchertaig Meic Erca";* F. J Byrne,'Irish Kings and High-Kings' p. 101

Airghialla regretted taking his side against Connacht's Ailill Molt. "Kings of Ailech in N Donegal, descended from Eogan son of Niall, extended their territory S and E at the expense of the Airghialla. A notable event in the history of Ulster was the Battle of Leth Cam in 827, in which Niall Caille (Muirchertach's descendant) defeated the Airghialla and slew many of their kings."[582] This vastly expanded Ui Neill power. Victories in the Battles of Ochae and Leth Cam were looked back on as major events in the rise of the Ui Neill. "It is certain from the entry in the *Annals of Ulster* that the battle of Ochae was a significant event, for chronological calculations are given dating it from the death of Conor Mac Nessa and Cormac mac Airt."[583]

CONNACHT'S POLITICAL MELTING POT

The war-lording feats of Niall's descendants E of the Shannon mirrored those of the descendants of his brothers W of the Shannon, particularly the descendants of Briun Orbsen son of Eochaid Muigh Mhean, over the same timespan. In this W scenario there is confusion, when there should not be, over the kingship groups to which the putative kings of the two branches of the Connacht dynasty belonged. This resulted from the Rathcroghan Myth created by the Ui Briuin with the connivance of the Southern Ui Neill in concert with the Abbots of Armagh and Louth. A carbon-copy of the Tara Myth, it needs debunking so that what follows can be understood and appreciated for its dire implications in the concoction of the pseudo-history which suppressed the history of Iron Age Ireland.

Ailill Molt and his son Mac Erca failed to reclaim Connacht vassal-lands E of the Shannon. Their descendants consolidated their hold on Magh Seola to which they were confined by Maine Mor's invasion. They overran lands of former allies. A century later they were encroaching on the lands of the Cruithintuatha of Croghan. Confusion is caused by the erroneous belief that the Ui Briuin spread out from Rathcroghan of Roscommon, despite the fact that the Ui Briuin Ai branch of Rathcroghan, known officially as the Sil Muiredaig, established themselves there only in the 8th/9th centuries. The pseudo-fiction blatantly proclaimed by the Ui Briuin was that their ancestors had always reigned from Rathcroghan, thus becoming the 'official doctrine' of their "descendants who in the 12th century came nearest to transforming the High-Kingship into an effective monarchy."[584] From the 9th century on they were arm-in-arm with Armagh and the Southern Ui Neill in mutually proclaiming the twin Myths, that of Tara of Meath and that of Rathcroghan of Roscommon.

The eponymous ancestor of the later Ui Briuin dynasty, Briun Orbsen, never set foot on Rathcroghan nor did any of his ancestors. It was then the capital of their most powerful enemy, the Cruithinthuath of Croghan, kinsmen of the Cruthin of Ulster with whom the Fir Belg of Connacht were constantly at war. The boundary of the Cruthin kingdom of Ulster stretched down to the banks of the Suck which forms the Galway/Roscommon border and included Rathcroghan district until well into historic times. Briun's epithet gives the lie to the preconceived idea that Briun resided at Rathcroghan and that the Ui Briuin branched out from there. He got his epithet, Briun Orbsen, from Loch Orbsen, the ancient name of Loch Corrib[585] beside which he and his descendants resided. Many anecdotes locate him and his descendants there on the royal crannog on Loch Hacket near the E shores of Loch Corrib in Galway. In the early 11th century King Brian Boru desecrated this Ui Briuin royal crannog on Loch Hacket due to the Ui Briuin refusal to support his campaign. Deliberate desecration of royal sites threatening the political destruction of a people or dynasty was endemic during those centuries. It was the highest form of insult which could be cast on a people or

[582] F. T. O Rahilly, EIHM, P. 224.
[583] F. J. Byrne, Ibid., p. 85.
[584] F.J Byrne, Ibid, p.86.
[585] Loch Corrib is the corrupt form caused by erroneously attaching the 'ch' of Loch to Orbsen.

dynasty. After Brian's demise at Clontarf in 1014 his brother repaired the desecrated royal crannogue of the Ui Briun of Magh Seola and made reparation for this blatant insult.

When Tirechan wrote about them at the end of the 7th century, the descendants of Briun still resided on Loch Hacket, known as Loch Seolgha or Loch Cime, in N Galway. In his 'Breviarium' he brought Patrick into contact with the sons of Briun because they were the reigning power in Connacht in Tirechan's time. He did not honour them with the title of 'Kings of Connacht' because his own tribe of the Hy Fiachrach were contesting this title with them. It was a bone of contention. The descendants of Fiachra were masters of Connacht at first with the aid of the sons and descendants of Niall from the NE. Then the Ui Briuin took over the reins of power by dispossessing the smaller independent tribes of their lands. Hence, Tirechan's purpose of concocting a tale linking Patrick with their ancestors. A seat was allegedly made for Patrick at Dumha Seolgha on the summit of Cruach Magh Seolgha (Knockma) with its panoramic view. Tirechan did not miss this opportunity to take Patrick to its summit to bless the sons of Briun and their lands from this vantage point (Figure 65). He claimed Patrick erected the Basilica of Domhnach Mor Magh Seola and baptized the Ui Briuin there near the shore of Loch Seola for the purpose of winning over this fast-burgeoning ruling Connacht dynasty (late 7th cent.) for Armagh. The Ui Briuin patron, Bishop Sachellus, had moved with this dynasty from Domhnach Shachell of the Turoe/Knocknadala oppidum when it was forced to move to Magh Seola by the invasion of Maine Mor. Bishop Sachellus or his immediate successor, Bishop Felartus, were the true founders of the basilica of Domhnach Mor Magh Seola.

When Patrick visited Croghan of Roscommon the Ui Briuin were not there nor anywhere near. They were not yet there even in Tirechan's day. Had they reigned there in Patrick's or Tirehhan's day, Tirechan would have concocted a graphic account of their baptism by Patrick at Rathcroghan. The Cruthin still ruled at Rathcroghan although coming under pressure from the Ui Briuin. It was more than a century after Tirechan's time before the Ui Briuin finally made swordland of Croghan Ai and the hitherto Cruthin stronghold of Rathcroghan. In Patrick's (5th cent.) and Tirechan's day (7th cent.) the Ui Briuin were the Ui Briuin of Magh Seolgha of Galway, not of Croghan of Roscommon. Understanding this is vital to ending the massive misconceptions regarding the Ui Briuin King's of Connacht in general and their later role in the deliberate suppression of genuine Iron Age and early history of the lost Fir Belg Capitals and oppida of Connacht and the conspiracy between the Ui Briuin, the S Ui Neill and Armagh in the concoction of the pseudo-history of Tara, Rath Croghan and Ireland as a whole (Figure 64).

Paul Walsh pointed out that the term 'Ui Briuin' in even the late 11th century *Book of Rights* stands exclusively for Ui Briuin Seola of Galway, never for the Ui Briuin of Croghan Ai of Roscommon.[586] The 'Ui Briuin' are mentioned in 'Vita Tripartite' as the Ui Briuin of Domnach Mor Magh Seola in Galway.[587] The 7th/8th century descendants of Briun who were only then in the process of making swordland of Croghan Ai district of Roscommon were exclusively named the Sil Muiredaig in the Book of Rights.[588] The Síl Muiredaig derived their name from Muiredach, King of Connacht 696-702. He was the first of this dynasty to conquer the central plain of Roscommon, Croghan Ai, from the Cruthintuatha. He lost his life in the process.[589] It took more than a century and 5 generations of Muiredach's family to conquer Croghan Ai. This shows that far from the Ui Briuin spreading out from Croghan Ai

[586] Rev. Pasul Walsh, "Connacht in the Book of Rights' in 'JGAHS', Vol. XIX, Nos. i & ii, 1940, p. 13.
[587] V.Trip. l. 1079: 'alaile i nDomnach Mor Maigi Seolae la Ui Briuin Seolai; Lib. Ardm. fol. iiv.: aecclessia magna campi Saeoli.
[588] Rev. Paul Walsh, Ibid, p. 13.
[589] Book of Rights, 'Muiredach Campi Ai moritur'

of Roscommon down into the Magh Seola district of Galway, exactly the opposite is true. A branch of the Ui Briuin from their true ancestral homeland in Galway expanded NE into the Croghan Ai district and finally made this their centre of power in the course of the late 8th/early 9th centuries. The pseudo-historic Iron Age Gaelic High-Kings of Tara of Meath were in fact the Fir Belg Overkings of Turoe of Galway. So too, the pseudo-historic Iron Age and early medieval Gaelic Kings or Queens of Croghan of Roscommon were in fact the Fir Belg Kings and Queens of Turoe, Rath Cruacha of Athenry and Magh Seola of Galway. Let it be noted that they were the most hostile perennial enemies of the Cruthin Kings of Tara and Rath Croghan.

Late highly anachronistic pseudo-history and hagiography welded two Ui Briuin kings, Eogan Bell and Ailill Inbanda, onto the Hy Fiachra genealogy. This would require that relations between the Northern Ui Neill and the Ui Fiachra were the opposite of what the were. The highly fictitious and anachronistic Life of St Cellach, alleged son of Eogan Bel, was concocted to portray Guaire, the most prominent figure in the Irish king sagas and the most renowned Ui Fiachra king of Connacht, in an embarrassingly unfavourable light to win over the Northern Ui Neill to the side of the Ui Briuin and of Armagh. It was claimed that after being slain by the Northern Ui Neill, Eogan Bel was buried standing upright at Rath Ua Fiachrach on Knocknarea mountain facing N with his red spear in his hand. As long as he remained thus the Northern Ui Neill could never defeat the Ui Fiachra of Connacht. "Eventually the Ui Neill disinterred his body, burying it face downward at Oenach Locha Gile, the assembly place of Lough Gill, Co. Sligo".[590] From Fiachra and Conall's time, and for a very long time after Eogan Bell, a strong mutual relationship existed between the Ui Fiachra of Connacht and the Northern Ui Neill. Eogan Bel's own royal residence was on Inish Eogan, named after him, at the SE end of Loch Mask, the NW perimeter of Magh Seola in the territory of the Ui Briuin Seola in N Galway.

Eochu Tirmcharna of the Ui Briuin succeeded Ailill Inbanda as King of Connacht. His son Aed later became King of Connacht. In revenge for the slaying of Aed's son, Curnan, by Diarmait mac Cerbaill of the S Ui Neill in violation of Colum Cille's protection, Aed joined forces with the N Ui Neill led by Forggus and Donald to defeat Diarmait in the Battle of Cul Dreimne at the foot of Benbulben near Drumcliff in Sligo in 561. Diarmait had incurred the wrath of saints and kings by his kinslaying and warlording. Medieval records claimed that "Colum Cille was so incensed that he incited his Cenel Conaill cousins, Ninnid and Ainmere, to ally with Forggus and Donall of Cenel Eogan and Aed Mac Echach, King of Connacht," to defeat Diarmait. Revenge for the death of Connacht's King's son under Colum Cille's protection, an excellent excuse for enlisting Aed's support in this rare alliance, was but a cover for the real reason for the Battle of Cul Dreimne. Its purpose was to ensure that the leading advantage and over-kingship of the rising Ui Neill dynasty would remain with Colum Cille's own branch of the Ui Neill at the expanse of Diarmait and the S Ui Neill. Colum Cille repented of the slaughter he had caused at Cul Dreimne for which he went into penitential exile in Scotland. That Aed, of Ui Briuin stock, should have allied himself with the N Ui Neill is against the trend in developing political alliances of the day. Exasperation at the death of his son under Colum Cille's protection, as well as the latter's powers of persuasion, might explain Aed's paradoxical stand.

The *Annals of Inishfallen* say Aed gave Annaghdown on Loch Corrib to St. Brendan of Clonfert. Aed was of the Ui Briuin Seola in whose lands Annaghdown lies. The empathies of the Ui Briuin Seola were beginning to lean strongly in the direction of the S Ui Neill in reprisal for the hostility of the Ui Fiachra/N Ui Neill alliance. Siding against the notorious Diarmait did not strain these relationships. Diarmait warred against his own S cousins and

---

[590] F. J. Byrne, Op. Cit. p. 244.

their N counterparts and against the Cruthin of Ulster and the men of Leinster. Following his defeat at Cul Dreimne he went to war with his own S Ui Neill cousins only to be defeated again at Cul Uinsen by Aed mac Brenainn mac Brion of Maine's household in Tethbae. "The annals show the hostility of the other Ui Neill to Diarmait mac Cerbaill's rise to power."[591] After Tuathal Maelgarb's assassination in 544 all Ireland stood in awe at the spectacle of the warlording Diarmait and his sons crashing around the Midlands in an all-out attempt to capture permanent hegemony of the S Ui Neill, a feat they eventually accomplished. Aed's action was laudable in Ui Briuin circles

The epithets of Briun's early descendants anchor them exclusively in the Loch Corrib/Loch Hacket/Magh Seola district of Galway. Such pertinent clues pinpoint their continued occupation of the territory of Magh Seola between Athenry and Tuam in Galway, not Rathcroghan of Roscommon, by the Ui Briuin in the early middle ages. The kingship of Connacht passed to Ragallach mac Uatach mac Aed Mac Echach who reigned until his assassination in 649. "He was the true founder of the Ui Briuin fortunes".[592] He gained the kingship by slaying his predecessor Colman Mac Cobhthaig, head of the Ui Fiachrach and father of Guaire, at the Battle of Ceann Bugha (near Roscommon) in 622. The site of this battle shows that Colman was the aggressor. He paid the price with his life. In an early saga verse attributed to his wife Muirenn, Ragallach is styled *'Rí Selga'('Seolgha')*, that is Magh Seola of Galway. There was no Shelga, Seolgha, or Magh Seola in Roscommon in spite of pseudo-history's contortions to try to invent one or, failing that, confuse the name.

Ragallach resided on the royal crannogue of Loch Seola (early Loch Cime, Loch Hacket today). An early saga told that one day he spied a stag grazing beside his crannog. His spear transfixed his prey. The startled stag staggered away as Ragallach lept into his boat and paddled ashore in hot pursuit. He sprung onto his white steed and chased after his fatally wounded prey. When he caught up with it he himself was startled to discover that his wounded stag had been slain by estranged vassal peasants cutting turf in a nearby bog. Ragallach demanded the deer's carcass, claiming it was his by right of chase. As their Overking, they owed him this respect. They, however, bitterly resented the fact that Ragallach had overrun their lands. In the ensuing quarrel they slew him with their turf-cutting spades as he sat enthroned on his white steed. The deer brought death in its wake.

The *Annals of Tigernach* say Ragallach was slain by Mael Brigte mac Mothlachan and the Corco Cullu, a deliberate error for Corco Cuile of Cuile Tollad (Kiltulla on the Mayo/Galway border) whose lands had then been overrun by the Ui Briuin Seola. Corco Cuile was changed to Corco Cullu of Croghan Ai to bring Ragallach into close association with Rathcroghan. A fatally wounded deer could not have been chased all the way from Loch Hacket in Galway to N Roscommon, a territory in the hands of the Ciarraige, a branch of the Cruithintuatha, the most hostile enemies of Connacht's Fir Belg power. Ragallach would not dare encroach on their territory even with a vast army. The claim that he was brought for burial to the Basilica of Croghan Ai is part of the 9th century pseudo-historic myth that Croghan Ai was the royal Capital of Connacht and home of the Ui Briuin from time immemorial. This church was in the hands of the Ciarraige until the end of the 8th century. The Corcu Cuallu were a vassal-tribe of the Ciarraige.[593] Neither would have allowed the burial of a bitter enemy in their cemetery. Ragallach was interred in his own royal cemetery of the Ui Briuin Seola at the Basilica of Domnach Mor Magh Seola. This was near his royal crannog on Loch Hacket in Co. Galway.

---

591 F. J. Byrne, Op. Cit., p. 105.
592 F. J. Byrne, Op. Cit., p. 239.
593 F. J. Byrne, Op. Cit., p. 246-247.

A pernicious pseudo-historical narrative in which the story of his assassination was embeded ridiculed Ragallach, founder of Ui the Briuin fortunes in retaking Connacht's kingship from the Ui Fiachra by slaying Colman, father of king Guaire. It was invented.[594] The 9th century tale was concocted for the highly motivated purpose of discrediting the Ui Briuin. It was elaborately embellished until the 11th century to defame their reigning Ua Conhobhar (O Connor) kings, direct descendants of Ragallach. Scurrilous retaliation for this earlier defamation of Ui Briuin kings was embedded in the 9th century Táin Bó Cuailgne. It exposes the Ui Fiachra and Northern Ui Neill in an embarrassingly unfavourable light in the persons of their so-called High King Aed Ordnide and his Ui Fiachra consort, Medb, cast in the role of the *Táins's* Iron Age Queen Medb, while extolling the S Ui Neill king Connor mac Donnchad cast in the role of the Iron Age King Conor Mac Nessa. The spurious recension alleged Ragallach slew his nephew and slaughtered all his relations.[595] Because of his alleged kinslaying his death was destined to be brought about by his own daughter. Hence he ordered her to be slain at birth. The swineherd commissioned to carry out the deed pitied the infant and left it to be reared by a holy woman. "Hearing of her great beauty, without knowing who she was, the infatuated Ragallach took her to himself. This caused the jealousy of his queen, Muireann, who promptly swam across the Shannon (from the Rathcroghan of Roscommon side) and fled to the Southern Ui Neill High King Diarmaid mac Aodha Slaine, allegedly reigning at Tara." Note the anachronisms.

St. Feichin of Fore, cousin of the Ui Neill King, was drafted into this justificatory fiction to add the weight of the church to the pseudo-historic mix. He and other saints allegedly rebuked Ragallach for slighting his queen for a young beauty. They declared a fast against him, praying passionately that he would perish shamefully before the feast of Bealtine. As May Festival Day drew near their prayers were answered in the deer chase and disgraceful death of Ragallach.[596] Nothing of this was known to genuine early meagre annalistic references. Numerous inconsistencies bedevil the medieval concoction. Different layers of pseudo-historic material and strands of political propaganda superimposed on the original historic content are perceptible here, as in so many other tales, to bolster the Tara and Rathcroghan Myths.

"This dramatic lore of Ragallach's career is quite contrived. It is noticeable that neither his nephew nor daughter are named. The episode of his nephew is borrowed from the Leinster story of Cobhthach, while that concerning the daughter is based on the well-known plot of a child foretold to kill its tyrant grandfather." Early annals made no reference to such events concerning Ragallach, merely recording his death by Maolbhrighde mac Mothlachain, Muireann's mourning him, and his death avenged by his son Cathal.[597] The fraudulent narrative of the alleged nephew and daughter was invented to discredit the Ui Briuin Seola and the O Connor king. The N Ui Neill engaged in a war of words with the Ui Briuin. Character assassination and other elements of a pseudo-historic nature were built around the death of Ragallach. His alleged burial in the Basilica of Croghan Ai was part of the 9/10th century Battle of the Books, concocted at a time when the pseudo-historic claim that Ragallach, his ancestors and those of the Sil Muiredaig, resided from time immemorial at Rathcroghan, not Magh Seola of Galway, had become the 'official doctrine'.

594 D O hOgain, "Myth, Legend and Romance," p.371; (Annals) O Donovan 1 258-61.
595 Ibid, p. 371, 'Revue Celtique' 17, 188-9; Paul Walsh in JGAHS, 17, 132.;(Narrat.) S H O Grady 1, 394-6..
596 Ibid, p. 371.
597 Ibid, p. 371

Figure 64: Apart from Athenry's Rath Cruacha, pre-8th century kings of Connacht resided elsewhere in Galway: Dun Guaire in Galway Bay faces the royal crannog-residence of the 6th century King Guaire (lower) of the Ui Fiachra dynasty which vied for the Kingship with the Ui Briuin Seola who had their royal crannog on Lough Seola (centre) and their Basilica, Domnach Mór Magh Seola (top) above the lake near Lough Corrib.

Figure 65: Carn Cesra (burial cairn of Cesra, Queen of King Ugaine Mor) crowns Cruach Magh Seola (Seolgha) (top) overlooking Loch Corrib and Loch Seola (Hacket) SW of Tuam where the early Ui Briuin Kings of Connacht had their royal crannog. A satelite cairn beside Cairn Cesra was modified (centre) with inner 'rooms' and a stairway (bottom). This was Tirechan's "resting place for Patrick among the rocks" when he posthumously dragged the saint to the summit to bless the Ui Briuin kingdom of Connacht in an attempt to bring its churches under Armagh's Monastic Federation.

After Ragallach's reign Connacht's kingship passed to Guaire of Ui Fiachra Aidne, whose residence was Dun Guaire at Kinvara in the S of Galway Bay, and to a son of his before reverting to the Ui Briuin Seola in the person of Cenn Faelad mac Colgan. Apart from his defeat of the Ui Maine in 653, he and his cousins took revenge on the Corco Cuile, the Conmaicne Cuile Toladh (Kiltulla) near Galway/Mayo border for the assassination of Ragallach. He drove them from their lands into the barony of Kilmaine. Cenn Faelad was himself assassinated in 682, like Ragallach, by the same Corco Cuile Toladh, with the help of the Ui Maine, led by Dunchad Muirrisci of the Ui Fiachra who became Connacht's next King.[598] "The fact that these early Ui Briuin kings fell at the hands of subject tribes reveals the extent to which they were intruders in their territories."[599] They were extending their power-base, not SW from Croghan of Roscommon, but NE from their primary settlement areas in Magh Seola of Galway.

TARA IN THE LIGHT OF 'BECH BRETHA'

An archaic untampered miniscule Law Tract on honeybees, *'Bech Bretha',* carries a time-bomb that explodes the Tara Myth, as no other historical statement does, by the weight of its dynamic implications. That it escaped the shredding scissors of Ui Neill chroniclers and Armagh fabricators may be accredited to its miniscule size and innocent looking title. Who would ever suspect that a tiny innocuous-like tract on honeybees could carry the lethal political clout it does? Byrne noted "It is odd that only once in the voluminous mass of Old Irish legal tracts is Tara mentioned, and then in terms which contradict the official history. An 8th century law tract on bees *('Bech Bretha',* 'Judgement on Bees') asserts that Congal Caech, the Cruthin Overking of Ulaid who fell in the battle of Moira in 637 had been king of Tara until deprived of sovereignty through the loss of an eye"[600] when stung by a honeybee. It quotes as a leading case the judgement arrived at concerning the damages caused by bee-stings: the bee-owner bears responsibility: "This was the first case of judgement ever pronounced concerning a serious wrong committed by bees against Congal Caech whom they blinded. He was king of Tara until this deprived him of the kingship".[601] Until then Tara of Meath was in the hands of the pre-Celtic Cruthin people (the Ulstermen), not of the Celtic Fir Belg, the Connachta, and least of all the Leinstermen. This is a lethal timebomb for the Tara Myth in a law tract written at a time when Ui Neill chroniclers and Armagh's fabricators alleged that the Ui Neill and their ancestors were High Kings of Ireland from time immemorial. It is important for the rediscovery of the lost history of Tara of Meath and Turoe of Galway in particular and of Ireland in general. Byrne stressed the attenuating evidence that the statement of *'Bech Bretha'* is the sole passage citing Tara in the Law Tracts and "runs directly contrary to the accepted doctrine that (Tara) was a monopoly of the Ui Neill. This is the only reference in the law-tracts to Tara. It does not declare that the (Tara) kingship entailed sovereignty over all Ireland."[602]

What is the significance of this brief statement from the miniscule Law Tract *'Bech Bretha'?* Byrne noted "The accident which preserved this text in a tract whose archaic language was obscure even to medieval Irish scholars has secured for us an untampered version of the legend"[603] and the truth of the blinding of Congal Caech, Overking of the Cruthin of Ulster and Picts of Scotland, reigning at Tara. It is an original version which miraculously escaped the attention of Armagh and the Ui Neill. It accurately articulates and clearly corroborates the claims of the Cruthin of Ulster, the ancient Ulaid, that they themselves had been the

---

[598] G. mac Niocaill, Op. Cit. p. 117.

[599] Ibid, p. 247

[600] Francis John Byrne, 'Irish Kings and High-Kings', p.58.

[601] 'Bech Bretha': "*Air is si cetnae breth inso cet-ara-cet im chinta bech for Congal Caech caechsite beich, bach Rí Temhro conid-dubart assa fhlaith*"

[602] Op. cit., p.113.

[603] Francis John Byrne, 'Irish Kings and High-Kings', p.113.

perennial rulers of Tara of Meath until it was finally wrested from them in the course of the 7th century. So too, it emphatically explodes the bombastic claims of the Ui Neill that they and their ancestors alone monopolised the High-Kingship of Ireland from Tara of Meath up to the time of its compilation in the 8th century. The statement in *'Bech Bretha'* was dealing with fact, not pseudo-history. It does not offer the slightest suggestion that the king of Tara was King of Ireland, or that the position of Tara "was one of peculiar importance." The fact that this is the sole reference to Tara in the entire voluminous corpus of Irish Law Tracts which deals to such an extent in the affairs of kings and overkings, and the fact that it explicitly contradicts the fraudulent 'official history' blatantly propagated by the Ui Neill and Armagh henchmen regarding the position of Tara speaks volumes for the fact that Tara was conspicuous by its lack of any special importance other than its role as seat of minor kings of Ulster and, for a short time, its Overkings. It served as the seat of the Cruthin Overkings of Ulster and Scotland after the loss of Emain Macha. Tara's glory days lay in the far distant pre-historic BC pre-Celtic past. Were Ptolemy writing then, it would have been conspicuous in his Irish record.

THE HIGH NOON OF TARA OF MEATH: 2500 – 300 BC

The Tara of 2500 – 500 BC is an altogether different story. A Discovery Programme survey of the Hill of Tara was carried out between 1992 & 1996 under archaeologist Conor Newman. Using sophisticated technology, his team mapped what was underground. What they discovered directly beneath the crown of the Hill of Tara was a massive, oval-shaped monument measuring about 170 meters at its widest point. This enormous temple was once surrounded by 300 huge posts, 2 meters wide, made from an entire oak forest and indicating a massive human effort involved in the construction. This astounding archaeological discovery brings out the pre-historic importance of Tara and helps to anchor it in the context of time and culture. Conor Newman notes that the discovery made sense of the distribution and positioning of other sites and monuments in the area. "It probably dates from 2500 to 2300BC. It fills a very important place in the jigsaw"[604] of Tara of Meath. The Turoe/-Knocknadala/Athenry oppidum in central Galway fills another. The true historic dimensions and unique place in history of Tara of Meath will never be fully understood while the Tara/Patrick Myth survives.

EARLY MEDIEVAL DYNASTIC DIVISIONS AND ALLIANCES

Mutual bonds developed between the Ui Briuin Seola and the Southern Ui Neill against the Ui Fiachrach/Northern Ui Neill alliance. "It is not until the joint reign of the sons of Aed Slaine, Diarmait and Blathmac, that the S Ui Neill dynasties which controlled Tara were firmly established. Their reign came to be regarded as an epoch in Irish history,"[605] because Tara after 637 was finally in the hands of the Ui Neill for the first time ever, though the lateness of this fact was consciously whitewashed by psudo-history. Sechnasach mac Blathmac, the S Ui Neill king of Tara and the Midlands, was slain by Dub Duin of the Cenel Cairpre branch of the N Ui Neill in 671. Sechnasach's brother, Cenn Faelad mac Blathmac, sought the aid of his namesake Cenn Faelad mac Colgan of Magh Seola of Galway in return for aid to him against the Ui Maine and the Ui Fiachrach. A combination of Ui Maine, Corco Cuile Conmaicne, Cenel Cairbre and Ui Fiachrach were led by Finsnechta Fledach, Cenn Faelad mac Blathmac's cousin, against Cenn Faelad Mac Colgan to help the Ui Maine retake their lands in Galway. This included the old Turoe/Knocknadala Capital and its title *Rí Temhro*, which he had won back from the Ui Maine at the Battle of Air Cealtra (near Attymon, *Ait Ui Maine,* 5 miles N of Turoe in Galway) in 675. Cenn Faelad Mac Colgan was stripped of his earlier gains against the Ui Maine and Corco Cuile. Finsnechta's ulterior motive for opposing his cousin was to gain the kingship of Tara and

---

[604] Conor Newman, archaeologist in charge of the survey; The Irish Examiner, November 12, 2002.
[605] F. J. Byrne, Op Cit., p. 105.

the title *Rí Temhro* for himself. In the ensuing massacre Finsnechta Fledach slew Cenn Faelad Mac Blathmac and became king of Tara. The title *'Rí Temhro'* was back in currency but with a new import, as he took the Ui Maine half of Connacht and usurped its old Turoe/Knocknadala title, *Rí Temhro*. These events bonded the Ui Briuin and S Ui Neill.

THE BIRTH OF IRISH PSEUDO-HISTORY: TARA/RATHCROGHAN MYTHS

Fraudulent history was flagrantly fabricated during the reign of Finsnechta Fledach (Snechta Fina 675-695) and with his blessing. Adomnan and Muirchu had his full support. Towards the end of his reign the earliest fictitious king-list of Tara, *Baile Chuind,* was concocted. It chronicled Muirchu's fable alleging that Loegaire, son of Niall, was the High King of Ireland at Tara of Meath in Patrick's day, and Adomnan's allegation that other Ui Neill warlords, especially Finsnechta's own ancestors, were 'destined by God to be High Kings of Ireland.' *Baile Chuind* does not explicitly state that the descendants of Conn Cedchathach down to Finsnechta Fledach were High Kings of Ireland.[606] The implications of the claims of Muirchu and Adomnan were still too blatantly revolutionary to be projected in this more sober text. Finsnechta's name appears near the end of the list as Snechta Fina. His uncles, sons and cousins make their appearance on this Tara king-list. It is significant that the name of Cairbre mac Niall is given here as succeeding Loegaire in the High Kingship. His descendants were in league with Finsnechta when he assassinated his cousin Cenn Faelad and won the Tara kingship for himself. Thus he rewarded them. Cairbre's name was deliberately expunged from the later Middle Irish lists. Later hagiographers set their seal on his absence from these lists and the decline of his dynasty by having this prophesied by Patrick who cursed him and his descendants from the High Kingship for having attempted to kill him.[607] Thus, early pseudo-history could be interpolated at will as later circumstances changed. God could not alter history but Irish 'historians' could. The Rathcroghan Myth had not yet made its appearance because Muiredhach had not yet conquered the Rathcroghan district of Roscommon. But the atmosphere was ready for it.

Connacht's kingship reverted to the Ui Fiachrach in the person of its N representative, Dunchad Muirrisc, after Cenn Faelad mac Colgan's death. "With him, the entry of the Ui Fiachrach of the North on the scene marks the start of a new phase in the history of Connacht in which the early reigning Ui Fiachra of Aidne (and the old Capital of Rath Cruacha of Athenry) gradually drop out of the running. Dunchad was slain in 683"[608] by a conspiracy between the N Ui Neill and the Ui Fiachra Aidne. Fergal, a grandson of Guaire, succeeded to the kingship. "His reign was no more than the last flare-up of the power of the Ui Fiachrach of Aidne. His death (+696) marks the end of his lineage's intermittent possession of the kingship of Connacht".[609] His successor was the Ui Briuin Muiredach Muillethan, grandson of Ragallach, founder of the Sil Muiredaig. He made swordland of the Croghan Ai district of Roscommon at the expense of the Cruithintuatha Croghain. His father, Muirgius, slain by the Ui Fiachrach Aidne in 654, was wed, if the report be true, to Cred, daughter of Guaire, who had previously been consort of Marcan son of Tomain, king of Ui Maine. Muiredach's own queen was Cacht, daughter of Mael Brigte mac Mothlachan of the Corco Cuile branch of the Conmaicne, the slayer of his grandfather Ragallach. This marriage alliance to the formerly hostile Conmaicne was a stepping stone to the later conquest of the Cruithintuatha Croghain of Roscommon. Muiredach was slain in his attempt to conquer the Rathcroghan of Roscommon territory in 702.

---

[606] Ibid, p. 254.

[607] F. J. Byrne, Op Cit. p.91.

[608] G. mac Niocaill, Op. Cit., p. 117.

[609] Ibid, p. 117.

He was succeeded by Cellach, son of Ragallach of Magh Seola, known as Cellach Locha Cime, an old name of Loch Seola (Loch Hacket) in Galway. This corroborates the fact that this Galway scenario NE of Rath Cruacha of Athenry, not Rathcroghan of Roscommon, was still the residence of the Ui Briuin Kings of Connacht. Saga projects Cellach as aged, yet as nimble as a mountain goat. His father, Ragallach, was slain 55 years before his own demise. The N Ui Neill king, Loingsech of the Cenel Conaill of Donegal, felt a noose closing round his dynasty's neck, outflanked in the far NE corner of Ireland by the Cenel Eogan expansion into Derry and Tyrone. The Ui Briuin of Magh Seola were driving a wedge through the Ui Neill kingdom of Cairbre on Cenel Conaill's SE flank. Seeing the only outlet for expansion of his dynasty was S through Connacht, Loingsech marched his army S into the Moy district of Sligo in 704. Indrechtach, son of Dunchad Muirisci, the Ui Fiachrach king of the Moy, sped S to Cellach in Magh Seola to seek aid against Loingsech. Old King Cellach, after bathing in herbs and being anointed with oils, sat himself, not between the 2 Dunchads as claimed, (Dunchad Murisci had already been slain 20 years earlier), but between the two Domnalls, one his son, the other his nephew, as he rode forth to war. He promised his kingdom to both in turn. His ancient bones rattled as he lept from his chariot on the Sligo battlefield of Corann. Loingsech was decisively defeated and slain together with his sons and a host of Ui Neill princes. This was the closest Loingsech came to being High King of Tara and of Ireland (*rex Hiberniae*), the title conferred on him by the pseudo-historic *Annals of Ulster*. Cellach retired to a monastery and was ordained cleric before he died. Indrechtach son of Dunchad Muirisci, succeeded Ceallach but was assassinated 3 years later by the N Ui Neill led by Fergal son of Loingsech in revenge for his father's death. He was succeeded by Cellach's nephew Domnall in fulfillment of his uncles' promise. Cellach's son, Domnall, succeeded to the throne in fulfillment of the same promise after the reign of Indrechtach mac Muiredaig, grandson of Ragallach. All these Connacht kings ruled from Magh Seola or from the Ui Fiachrach Aidne royal site of Rath Cruacha in Galway.

From the Fir Belg invasions in the last century BC until the early 8th century AD, not one of these Fir Belg kings of Connacht ever reigned at Rathcroghan of Roscommon. Yet, the pseudo-historic claim of Ui Briun/Muiredaig provenance was that Rathcroghan of Roscommon was the royal seat of Connacht from time immemorial. The Cruthintuatha Croghain of Roscommon held on tenaciously to their territory. Muiredaig and many of his descendants fell waging dogged warfare to wrest Croghan Ai from these Cruithintuatha Croghain. The reign of Indrechtach mac Muiredaig, grandson of Ragallach of Magh Seola, from 707 to 723 witnessed the beginning of the conquest of the Croghan Ai district of Roscommon and the consolidation of the Sil Muiredaig branch of the Ui Briuin as the later dominant dynasty of Connacht. An archaic poem portrays Indrechtach faring forth from Magh Seola to make swordland of the Cruthin territory of Croghan Ai of Roscommon - Muirenn of Magh Seola in Galway was Ragallach's consort and Connacht's Queen:

> *'Indrechtach of the lands of Briun (Magh Seola), warring far with heroic feat,*
> *Flaming firebrand of the offspring of a hundred kings, soaring hero, dreaded wolf,*
> *Subduer of the dogs of war, scion of Muirenn (Ragallach's Queen in Magh Seola)'*

Indrechtach died at Clonmacnoise, a monastery which favoured the acceptance of Ui Briuin rule in S Connacht.[610] The descendants of Muiredach and Indrechtach (Sil Muiredaig) were most opportunely aided by the decline of their dynastic colaterals, the Ui Ailello, descended from Ailill, Briun's brother, into whose lands and that of their vassal-allies they now expanded. A series of battles for the unchallenged possession of the Croghan Ai district of Roscommon followed Indrechtach's reign. The Ui Ailello waged war against their vassal-allies, the Calraige Muighe Luirg on the plains of Boyle in 743 for possession of their lands.

---

[610] Ibid, p. 248.

As the Ui Ailello waned the Sil Muiredaig completed the conquest of Calraige lands N of Croghan Ai in 752. In 789/90 the Ui Ailello overthrew the Luigni at Achad Ablae and Ath Rois in the vicinity of Corann and slew the king of their 3 septs. This was their undoing. They were brought to terminal decline by the combined forces of Luigni, Gailenga and (Cruthin) Gregraige. The Ui Muiredaig stepped into the void left by the Ui Ailello by overrunning their lands and that of the Gregraige, Luigni, Gailenga and Cailraige of Magh Luirg. After the battle of Ard Maicrime in 792 the Ui Ailello faded from history while the Sil Muiredaig branch of the Ui Briuin accelerated apace. They defeated the Ui Neill branch of the Cenel Cairpre in 754 and drove a wedge between the Sligo, Leitrim and Longford divisions of its extensive kingdom. They expanded into Breifne east of the Shannon where they become known as the Ui Briuin Breifne.

As Indrechtach was making headway in N Connacht, his brother Cathal, a later king of Connacht, branched out E from Magh Seola where he engaged in winning unchallenged possession of vassal-lands. His descendants, under their ruling family, the Ui Flanagain, carved out swordland for themselves in S Roscommon at the expense of the Ui Maine. For a century thereafter the Sil Cathail proved strong rivals of the Sil Muiredaig for the Kingship of Connacht. The Ui Briuin of Magh Seola tried to expand W and NW but suffered defeat at the hands of Connacht's Ui Fiachrach king, Ailill Magh Righe (Medraige), at Drumrovay in S Mayo in 758. Ailill's epithet links him to Maree in Galway Bay, the land of the Ui Fiachrach Aidne. The site of this battle in the lands of the N Ui Fiachra, rival colaterals for the Kingship of Connacht, indicates that the Ui Briuin were on the offensive in this SW direction.[611] They felt the Ui Fiachra might succumb as happened to the Ui Ailello. After the death of Ailill Magh Righe in 764 the Kingship of Connacht reverted to Dub Indrecht mac Cathail of the Ui Briuin Seola who continued his father's wars to gain unchallenged possession of the district between Croghan Ai and the original Ui Briuin homeland of Magh Seola. His crushing defeat of the Conmaicne Cuile Toladh at Shrule in Mayo is another indication of the ruthless advance of the Ui Briuin from their Galway home base.

The Ui Briuin turned their attention on the Ui Maine who had driven them from the E of the province in Maine Mor's invasion. This was logical in the light of present political circumstances. The Ui Maine had allied themselves closely with the descendants of Fiachra (Ui Fiachra Aidne) whose old capital was Rath Cruacha of Athenry. Guaire, King of Connacht, gave the Ui Maine access to the sea-port at Clarenbridge/Maree (Ath Clee Magh Righ) in the S of Galway Bay where their Manapi (Managh) kinsmen maintained a marine colony, in order to keep their alliance against the growing power of the Ui Briuin. Their 7th century king, Marcan mac Tomaine, son-in-law of Guaire, was titled 'King of Ui Maine and Maree'.[612] When the decline of the Ui Fiachra Aidne set in, this alliance crumbled. This breakdown in relationships is evidenced by the battle between the Ui Fiachrach Aidne and the Ui Maine in 743. The Ui Briuin Seola, witnessing this cooling of relations, put pressure on the Ui Maine. The Sil Cathal branch of the Ui Briuin moved E encroaching on Ui Maine lands in S Roscommon. This came to a head in 775 when the Ui Briuin routed the Ui Maine at Achad Liac (Athleague). Artgal, the son of Cathal and next King of Connacht, routed the Ui Maine again three years later.

Having weakened the Ui Maine and thrived on the decline of the Ui Fiachra, the Ui Briuin kings felt they were in a position to deliver the death blow to the descendants of Fiachra and revenge the ancient disgrace Fiachra and his son Daithi inflicted on their ancestor Briun. When Artgal abdicated in 782 all-out war broke out between the Ui Briuin and Ui Fiachrach dynasties. An odious campaign of black propaganda boiled over, having respect neither for

---

[611] Ibid, p. 249.
[612] Ibid, p. 250.

truth nor for the ancient capitals and their traditions. The next Sil Muiredaig king (of the N Ui Briuin) finally overrunning Croghan Ai of Roscommon, Tipraite mac Taidg, Indrechtach's grandson, ranged N and S to inflict deadly blows on the S Ui Fiachra of Aidne at the historic battlefield of Carn Conaill near Gort in SW Galway in 784, and devastate their cousins, the N Ui Fiachra on the Moy in 785. Tipraite's accession to Connacht's new throne at Rathcroghan was marked by a very significant visit of Dub-da-Leithe, Abbot of Armagh. King and Abbot established the Cain Phatraic (Law of Patrick) in Connacht. This marked the mutual recognition of the pseudo-historic claims of Armagh and of Connacht's Sil Muredaig. A succession of Armagh Abbots visited Sil Muredaig kings at Rathcroghan of Roscommon at frequent intervals during the next 40 years (in 799, 811, 818, 825 and 836) to cement this new relationship in advancing the Tara/Patrick and Rathcroghan Myths. In 802 the new Connacht king Muirgius went S to Ui Fiachra Aidne to stifle dissent to the 'official doctrine' of the Rathcroghan Myth, suppress the memory of the archaic royal site of Queen Medb at Rath Cruacha of Athenry in favour of Rathcroghan and lay waste Medb's royal crannog on Loughrea Lake.[613] Connacht's record of its early history, the *Lebor Balb* (the Silenced Book) 'disappeared' for ever.

TARA VIS-A-VIS 'THE BLACK PIGS DYKE'

The Cruthin (Picts to the Romans) were more prominent in Scotland in historic times where they preserved their independence to the 9th century. Before the Dal Riata invasion from Ireland they possessed the whole of Scotland. In early times when the origin of the different ethnic strata of the population of Ireland was still remembered, the Cruthin were conscious of the fact that their ancestors had inhabited the country before the coming of the Fir Belg and other Celts. Ireland's oldest stratum of legendary history is full of the sound and fury of the warfare between the pre-Celtic Cruthin, at the losing end, and the incoming Belgae (Fir Belg), spearheaded from their chief centre of power in Connacht. This warfare is fossilized in the most famous of all legendary epics, the *Táin Bó Cualgne*, portraying the armies of Ireland under the leadership of the indefatigable Queen Medb of Connacht marching against the Cruthin of Ulster. The scars of this centuries-long warfare still show across the face of Ireland in isolated fragmentary segments of consecutive recessions of the continuous frontier fortifications which defined the shrinking S boundaries of ancient Ulster (Ulaidh) at different periods of its history. The final frontiers of the kingdom of the Ulaidh are well known as 'The Black Pig's Dyke'/'Great Wall of Ulster', the so-called penultimate defensive line, and 'The Danes Cast', the ultimate frontier of the defeated Cruthin of Ulster, which ran from the foot of Slieve Gullion up the Newry valley to Scarvagh. In his 'Additional Researches on the Black Pig's Dyke' published in 1917 De Vismas Kane recorded his 'discovery' of vestiges of earlier more southerly boundary fortifications with local traditions referring to them as the 'Black Pig's Dyke' or 'Duncla' (Dyke fortification). Traces of earlier frontier fortifications are still being 'discovered' as far S as the Midlands. Isolated segments of these ancient scars of history now receive the modern technological face-lift which wipes all trace of these monumental works of war from the face of Ireland, even by land owners aware that these are historic fragmentary relics of earlier versions of the Black Pig's Dyke. History is being bulldozed into oblivion.

Mythological origin-legends re-enact the erection of various alignments of boundary fortifications that corroborate the legendary and historical data in an amazing manner. Kane recorded a legend of the erection of the S terminus boundary fortification of a greatly reduced Ulster running from the Boyne N along the Louth boundary with Monaghan and Armagh to the N of Louth. It linked up with the 'Dane's Cast', the well-known section of the ultimate boundary of Ulster running from Sliab Gullion up the Newry valley to Lough Neagh after the final collapse of Emain Macha. It is carried S to include the Tara district in

---

[613] Francis John Byrne, 'Irish Kings and High-Kings', p. 250-251.

the versions of the legend in the vicinity of Drogheda and the Boyne recorded by Kane at the beginning of the 20th century. He misinterpreted the evidence and made no attempt to reconstruct it. He noted that the King of Tara changed a Magician into a Black Pig and chased him, not west across the country, but North. The Pig's tusks tore up a furrow running North. These local legends in the Tara district preserved the pristine truth that the King of Tara who erected this ultimate defence line of the final decimated Cruthin kingdom of Ulster was an Ulster Cruthin, not a Gaelic Ui Neill King. As noted by Kane and others, not just written and oral tradition, but archaeological evidence of the extant remains of the boundary fortifications of Ulster, proclaim that the fossed embankments were the defence work of the Cruthin, not of the advancing Fir Belg power. The early Cruthin kings of Emain Macha directed their workforce in this massive construction work. The mention of a King of Tara in these Boyne district versions of the legend indicates that it refers to a time after the loss of Emain Macha when the pre-Cruthin Kings of Ireland and Scotland reigned at Tara. This awkward alignment, as seen by pseudo-history, running north along the west side of Tara district goes altogether against the doctrine of the Tara Myth Syndrome.

The Louth and Dundalk versions present a true description of the final frontier before the final collapse of the Cruthin at the battle of Moy Rath in 637. It included Tara district within its defence line. It ran N along the extant remains of the ancient boundary on the present border of Louth with Monaghan and Armagh, along the Dane's Cast to Lough Neagh and along the Bann to the N Antrim coast. It is corroborated by another boundary origin-legend implicating Glass, son of Nuadu Argetlamh, in a boar chase running S from the W of Tara to the Wicklow border. Despite legendary evidence and extant vestiges of an ancient boundary running in a N direction from the upper Liffey near the Dublin/-Wicklow/Kildare borders, skirting the W perimeter of Tara and Hill of Lloyd and swinging NE near Carnaross in Meath to the NW Louth boundary, this had not even been suspected by Kane or other researchers as being the ultimate Ulster frontier. They have yet to be reconstructed. In recent times a lady from Carnaross, discreety inquiried whether she might level a section of what she and her neighbours called the Black Pig's Dyke running N through her land. Neighbours had bulldozed vestiges through their lands without asking questions, making it more difficult by the day to rediscover the original alignment. A time will come when there will be nothing left to reconstruct. All too soon, indeed!

Kane's interpretation of these origin-legends under the influence of the Tara Myth, made "the alleged flight from the Boyne to the N of Louth, then W across Ireland to the Shannon at Rooskey, so preserving the historical alteration of the boundary from the Boyne to the N limit of Louth, and thence by a devious route to the Shannon."[614] Very different sets of boundary fortifications, in time and place, are confused in this 'identification', an error he was guilty of more than once and confessed to in his later Papers. One refers to an earlier boundary fortification of ancient Ulster that had its W terminus at Rooskey on the Shannon above Longford town, whereas the traditional W terminus of a better-known later boundary is commonly given as much further N at Bundrowes in Donegal Bay. The other gives a very different later S terminus of a boundary fortification of a greatly reduced Ulster from the W perimiter of Tara and the Boyne N along the Louth boundary with Monaghan and Armagh to the N of Louth where it joined the 'Dane's Cast', the well-known section of the ultimate boundary of Ulster after the final collapse of Emain Macha.

The Louth legend tells of a Druid changed into a Black Pig that dug up the boundary forti-fication with its tusks. Cian mic Cainte was a druid who was wont to change children into swine and set his wolfdogs after them to amuse himself. The sons of Tureann resolved to take revenge on him. Once when he magically transformed himself into a black pig they

---

[614] Ibid, p.326

pursued and killed him near Cnoc Cian Mic Cainte (Kileen Hill) near the Dane's Cast near Meigh, Co Armagh, on its border with the far N of Louth. Cian's tumulus cairn crowned the hill to which it gave its name. This cairn was carted off to a lime kiln by a local farmer named Dickie in 1836 according to local tradition, a fate that befell all too many ancient burial-cairns all over Ireland well into the 20th century, as available material for limekilns.

The tale of the Children of Tureann tells that Cian was chased from Tara by its Cruthin king and arrived at Magh Murthemne (N of Dundalk near Kileen Hill, Sliabh Gullion and Dane's Cast). Brian, son of Tureann, turned his brothers into hounds who chased Cian, changed into a magic boar, northwards. This mythological origin-legend re-enacting the erection of the earthworks running N from the W of Tara, defending the territory of Tara's Cruthin King along the E slopes of Sliabh Gullion and N as the Dane's Cast to Lough Neagh, delineates the last frontier of the reduced Cruthin kingdom before its final collapse in 637. It is amazing that this mythological frontier origin-tale from early Christian times, and versions from Ulster and Connacht, except for the highly interpolated version in the 12th century Book of Leinster, have been allowed to survive with all their damning ramifications for the Tara Myth. They preserve a large amount of pagan myth even in their modern oral form as told today. The literary Tara Myth was unable to displace the old oral tradition that so diametrically contradicts it.

TARA: SEAT OF THE CRUTHIN OVERKINGS OF ULSTER AND SCOTLAND

Tara belonged to the Cruthin of Ulster before the coming of the Fir Belg and long after. Until the battle of Magh Roth (Moira of Down) in 637, the turning point in the history of Tara which was then lost to them, they were still a power to be reckoned with in Londonderry, Antrim, Down, Louth, Meath and to Dublin's Tolka river. *'Bech Bretha'* corroborates their claim that Tara was theirs until then. They cherished memories of their former dominance of the N half of Ireland and their overkings who ruled Tara. "They considered the Ui Neill recent upstarts."[615] In the 5th to 7th centuries the alleged Ui Neill High-Kings of Ireland ruling from Tara, were in fact warlords newly emerging from their NW lair and expanding E from their isolation in Donegal, while the Cruthin Overkings of Scotland and Ireland reigned from Tara of Meath.

Before Emain Macha was lost to the Cruthin of Ulster and Tara became the seat of Cruthin Overkings of Ulster and Scotland, extant records relate that at least one son and daughter, a grandson and a later cousin of Conor mac Nessa, as well as several other Cruthin Kings of Ulster and Scotland, reigned at Tara of Meath. Chroniclers of the Ui Neill Dynasty who later hyped the 'history' of the monopoly of Tara by the Ui Neill and their ancestors from way back in prehistoric times knew that Congal Ceach and many of his ancestors had been overkings of the Cruthin of Ulster and Scotland reigning at Tara. Long after their final defeat, the Cruthin continued to claim that many of their overkings ruled at Tara up to 637. This found its way into the early chronicles. The genealogical account of the Cruthin overkings preserved in the 'Book of Lecan', in the 'Chronicles of the Picts', and elsewhere,[616] states that "thirty kings of the Cruthin (of Ireland and Scotland) ruled Ireland and Scotland, from Ollam Fotla to Fiachna mac Baetain (+626)." It claims that "seven kings of the Cruthin of Scotland ruled at Tara."[617] This statement borrowed from the 'Irish World-Chronicle' has the significant addition of *'Alban'* after *'Chruithnibh'*, as O Rahilly noted:[618] and "is based on the 'Pictish Chronicle' that 30 kings named Bruide (Cruthin Overking title) ruled Ireland and Scotland. Skene claims the Picts of Scotland and the

[615] Francis John Byrne, 'Irish Kings and High-Kings', p. 113.
[616] ZCP xiv, 62ff; Skene, 'Chronicles of the Picts', 318-321.
[617] Lec. "*Secht rig do Chruithnibh Alban rofhallnastair Erind i Temair*".
[618] F.T.O Rahilly, 'Early Irish History and Mythology', p.347.

Cruthin of Ireland were 'governed as one nation' until AD 626"[619] *'Bech Bretha'* updates this to 637. The "seven kings of the Cruthin" of Scotland (and Ireland) who ruled at Tara fill the gap between the loss of Emain Macha and their collapse in 637.

Ui Neill eulogists were past masters in the art of manipulating history. Mael Mura of Othain (+887) was their genius. The Ui Neill canonized him for eulogizing their dynasty and Capital, Grianan Ailech in Donegal in the NE of Ireland, and glorifying Tara as their Capital of an imaginary All Ireland High Kingship. Whatever was written by Mael Mura has to be stripped of its fictional, anachronistic, wrappings. He claimed Ellim mac Conrach, the Dal nAraidi Cruithin King of Ulster, ousted High King, Fiachu, from *Temhair* which he projected as Tara, and reigned there. Anachronism undoes Mael Mura's statement. Firstly, the institution of the High Kingship of Ireland did not exist in Ellim mac Conrach's time or for centuries thereafter. Secondly, Ellim reigned as Over King of the Cruthin of Ulster from Emain Macha, Capital of Ulster, not from Tara of Meath eventhough Tara was part of Ulster at the time. By the time Mael Mura wrote, Tara had been wrested from the Cruthin of Ulster by the Ui Neill who were then endeavouring to make the High Kingship of Ireland a reality and transmute the title *'Rí Temhro'* of their Iron Age ancestors in Connacht to mean High King of Ireland by transporting it from Turoe of Galway to Tara of Meath, a subtle sleigh-of-hand since both bore the O. Irish name *Temhair*. O Rahilly was duped by Mael Mura: "In Mael Mura's time the titles 'king of Tara' (*Rí Temro*) and 'king of Ireland' meant the same thing."[620] They did not, despite the attempts by Ui Neill dynasts' to make them do so. *Rí Temhro*, meaning King of Turoe, and *Rí Erenn*, meaning Over King of the Erainn/Fir Belg peoples, did mean the same thing.

Taking his cue from Muirchu's fictitious King Loeguire of Tara, Mael Mura made Ellim of Emain Macha usurp the Kingship of Tara. Tara was the last capital of the Cruthin Overkings of Ulster and Scotland before they met their Waterloo at the Battle of Moira in 637. He glorified Tara by transferring the ancestors of the Ui Neill from Turoe of Galway to Tara. Early legendary history told that Ellim made a lightning strike SW against the Fir Belg Capital of Connacht, as his Scottish kinsmen were doing against the strongholds of Roman Britain. He captured *Cnoc Temhro* in W Ireland (Turoe) and ousted Tuathal, *Rí Temhro,* a title Mael Mura promptly transmuted to mean 'King of Tara and King of Ireland.' But vital clues indicate that the Temhair referred to was the Temhair of Galway: Ellim sailed round the coast to Inver Domnan in the West of Ireland. Tuathal was the grandfather of Conn who gave his name to Connacht. Roman author Tacitus claimed that an exiled Irish king fled to the Roman Commander Agricola in Scotland for help to recover his throne. The exiled Tuathal raised a N British fleet, sailed round the coast to Iorrus Domnann in the West of Ireland where he linked up with allies and marched on Turoe, the Temhair taken by Ellim. 'High-King Loegaire' of Muirchu's account, who alegedly accosted Patrick on the Hill of Tara, was not a son of Niall of the Nine Hostages. This is an interpolation of the name of the Ui Loeghuire, a pre-Ui Neill Cruthin sept residing in Tara district in the 5th century (as Doherty noted) descended from Loeghuire, cousin of Conor Mac Nessa. There never was a King Loegaire, High King of Ireland at Tara, other than that hoax hyped by Muirchu. He anachronistically inserted the name of an alleged son of Niall into the stem of this Cruthin Ui Loeghuire sept, insinuating he sprung from Niall in the time of Patrick. The Ui Loeghuire sept had come under the overlordship of the Ui Neill by Muirchu's time. They were glorified by this high honour bestowed on their ancestor. The descendants of Niall, who had only gained their first firm foothold of swordland in the far NW corner of Ireland at the time of Patrick and had just begun to establish their dynasty,

---

[619] Op. cit., p.345.; Skene, 'Celtic Scotland', iii, 126.
[620] F. T. O Rahilly, EIHM, p. 164f.

were even more glorified by this anachronistic honour conferred on them by the power of Muirchu's pen.

Fierce warfare was carried on by the Ui Neill warlord, Diarmait mac Cerbaill, on the one hand, and the Northern Ui Neill on the other, against the Cruthin of Ulster who dourly defended their still extensive lands. Clearly the fiercely aggressive Ui Neill war-lords had not yet taken control of even the North of Ireland, let alone be Kings of Ireland, as late as the 2nd half of the 6th century. In the battle of Moin Dairi Lothair in 563 the Cenel nEogain branch of the Northern Ui Neill, with the assistance of the Ciannachta, crushed the power of the Cruthin W of the Bann and expanded E into that area of Co. Derry. Seven kings of the Cruthin fell in that battle. Another fled. Far from being High-Kings at Tara, this was the first time the Ui Neill dared to step out from their homeland in Donegal and Tyrone in the NW corner of Ireland. Having crossed from Magilligan's Point in N Derry, they spread out, first driving the Cruthin E of the Bann with the help of the Ciannachta whom they planted in mid-Derry as a buffer between themselves and the Cruthin. Then they encroached on the Airghiallan Ui Mac Uais, until, by as late as the 9th century, they were firmly entrenched in the heart of the North. They moved into a position from which to make a bid, for the High-Kingship of Ireland.

The Dal nAraidi emerged as the single dynasty ruling the Cruthin in a strip of territory E of the Bann running S through Louth and across the Boyne into the Tara district. Aed Dub mac Suibni Araidi, overking of the Cruthin of Ulster and Scotland at Tara, Diarmait's slayer, was recorded by later chroniclers as King of Tara. Had there been any truth in the claim that Diarmait took over the kingship of Tara, it would have been at the expense of the Cruthin. His son Colman Mor was slain by Dubsloit, Cruthin King of Tara. The fiction of Diarmaid's High-Kingship of Ireland, monopolized by the later Ui Neill, is exposed by the fact that different factions of the Ui Neill were then at war with one another. In 561 Diarmait suffered his greatest defeat at the hands of his own Northern kinsmen at the battle of Cul Dreimne, not accepted by his own Ui Neill kinsmen, let alone by the whole of Ireland. His savage warlording incurred the wrath of the Church. The battle for dominance between the N and S Ui Neill raged. So too did the battle for the defeat of the Cruthin of Ulster and the capture of the seat of their overkingship at Tara. It was a battle for the dominance of the N half of Ireland, not for the High-Kingship of Ireland

COLM CILLE INCITED AN UI NEILL DRIVE FOR DYNASTIC DOMINATION

Colm Cille (Columba), a scion of the princely line of the Ui Neill dynasty of Cenel Conaill in Donegal, was too deeply enmeshed in goading his kinsmen to overlordship for their own liking. He was the cause of the battle of Cul Dremne. He foresaw that were the different Ui Neill factions united in purpose and win over the powerful Dal Riata as allies, they were in a position to dominate Northern Ireland as overlords, and, as such, claim the 'imperium' as the most powerful overkingship in Ireland. The pseudo-legend of the Battle of Cul Dremne is of Ui Neill provenance. It tells that Colm Cille surreptitiously copied a manuscript of St. Finnian. "When the latter appealed to the High King, Diarmait delivered the famous judgement: 'To every cow its calf, to every book its copy.' So incensed was Colum Cille that he incited his cousins of Cenel Conaill to join Forggus and Domnall of Cenel nEogain and Aed mac Echach Tirmcharna of Connacht, to defeat Diarmait. The encounter took place at the foot of Benbulben above the Columban church of Drumcliff"[621] in N Sligo. The 'Life of Mo-Laisse' of Devenish on Loch Erne tells how Colm Cille repented of the slaughter at Cul Dremne and went into exile to Scotland where he founded Iona in obedience to penance imposed on him by Mo-Laisse.

---

[621] Francis John Byrne, 'Irish Kings and High-Kings', p.95.

Colm Cille's biographer, Adomnan, abbot of Iona, glorified Diarmait for ulterior motives. He drew a very different picture which covered up any hint of enmity between Colm Cille and Diarmait. He referred to a synod at Tailtiu, the newly adopted centre of the S Ui Neill, where a "sentence of excommunication was passed on the saint for certain trivial and very pardonable offences."[622] He condemned Aed Dub mac Suibni, unashamedly recorded as Cruthin Overking of Ulster and Scotland reigning at Tara, for slaying Diarmait who had wreaked widespread destruction on his Ulster territory. "Aed the Black, verily a man of blood, who had slain Diarmait the son of Cerball, who had been ordained by God's authority as ruler of all Ireland." In view of the savage nature of Diarmait's war-lording and that he made kin-slaying a bye-word for his dynasty, the condemnation of Adomnan is extremely biased. This glorificatory political and ecclesiastical propaganda at its basest had ulterior self-interests at stake. Adomnan felt it expedient, in view of his monastic federation's ulterior motive of winning over the patronage of the Southern Ui Neill, to posthumously put in the mouth of Colm Cille a warning to Diarmait's son Aed Slaine against the crime of parricide. It is couched in carefully calculated, precisely-worded, political propaganda: "Take heed, son, lest by the crime of parricide you lose the prerogative of monarchy over the kingship of all Ireland, predestined for you by God."[623]

Adomnan referred to Diarmait as "ordained by God's authority as ruler of all Ireland", and to Aed Slaine's "prerogative of monarchy over all Ireland, predestined for you by God." What is this worth against the background in which it was written and against Adomnan's other propagandist statements of this nature? When one learns that Adomnan referred in similar terms to Oswald of Northumbria as "ordained by God as emperor of all Britain" it is obvious that this is high-flown extravagant propagandist language meaning vastly less than it appears to say. Byrne noted: "In neither case does the imposing title correspond with reality. It is Adomnan who is the first to ascribe an *Imperium* to an Anglo-Saxon Bretwealda. Her office was at least as vague a concept as that of the Irish high-kingship."[624] The summit of glorificatory propagandist language concocted by Adomnan must be viewed vis-a-vis the identical politico-ecclesiastical propaganda of his contemporary, Muirchu, glorifying Loeguire 'son of Niall' as High-King of Ireland. Muirchu tried to win the patronage of the N Ui Neill for the monastic community of Armagh. Adomnan concocted his to wean over to Colm Cille's monastic federation the patronage of the Northumbrian kings and of the S Ui Neill power, represented by Diarmait. Historic fact was out. Political propaganda for monastic patronistic expediency was in.

Muirchu and Adomnan strove to outdo each other in the art of highfaluting, political propaganda in an all-out effort to win over the powerful patronage of the Ui Neill war lords. Oswald was simply king of Northumbria who in no way could be considered a King of all Britain. Similarly, Diarmait and his son Aed Slaine were unable to lord it over their own Ui Neill kinsmen, let alone over the Cruthin of Ulster or the provinces of Connacht, Munster and Leinster. The highbrow flattery had the desired effect. It was highly politicized propagandist language ingeniously concocted and eminently calculated to win powerful patronage rather than a sober statement of fact. It has to be seen in the light of developments taking place elsewhere. Muirchu and Adomnan had ample justificatory Continental precedents for their historical aberrations. Alcuin described Charlemagne's rule as an 'imperium' long before it became so.[625] In the light of the rise of Armagh to a monastic federation, it made gargantuan efforts to wean over Ui Neill patronage. Adomnan was more concerned to preserve the patronage of his own Ui Neill kinsmen for Colm Cille's monastic

---

[622] Op. cit., p. 96.

[623] Op. cit., p. 96

[624] Op. cit., p. 259.

[625] Op. cit., p. 259.

federation than for strict historical accuracy. Adomnan is conspicuously silent about Tara, which in view of the extent of his writing and wide range of place-names listed, he could not have omitted naming Tara had either Diarmait, Aed Slaine or any Ui Neill Dynast reigned there. "Adomnan and Muirchu afford us the earliest unequivocal statements of the Ui Neill claims to Highkingship of Ireland."[626] These "claims to High-kingship of Ireland" are blatant politicized patronage-seeking propaganda concocted by Adomnan and Muirchu without the slightest foundation of historical truth, yet articulated in such a sophisticated manner as to confound even the most astute scholars of history.

The real reason for the battle of Cul Dremne was far more political than that mentioned in the legend handed down. The 'Annals of Tigernach' do not even mention the case of the copied manuscript, but that one of the causes of the battle was the slaying of Curnan, son of the king of Connacht, by Diarmait in violation of Colm Cille's protection. "Secular and hagiographical literature relate how Diarmait slew another Connacht prince, Aed Guaire of Ui Maine (of Galway), in violation of the sanctuary of St Ruadan of Lorrha."[627] These slayings tell of the far-flung atrocities perpetrated by Diarmait not only against his own kinsmen, but against the princes of Connacht and those of the Cruthin of Ulster, in his attempt to gain dominance of the N half of Ireland. The outcome according to pseudo-history was that St. Ruadan assembled the '12 apostles of Ireland' to fast against him; they solemnly cursed Tara. "Since then the site has remained desolate and abandoned." This 'cursing and abandonment of Tara' in the reign of Diarmait has no historical justification. It is contradicted by many texts which unashamedly make Aed Dub mac Suibni Araidi a Cruthin king of Tara, or, in the light of the 'Bech Bretha' account, of another Cruthin overking reigning there in the 7th century. When a text of Ui Neill provenance admits that a king from the enemy camp, a hated Cruthin overking at that, ruled at Tara, however fictitious the balance of the text, this singular acknowledgement bears all the marks of authenticity. After the 7th century overthrow of the Cruthin overkingship of Ulster by the Ui Neill and their Airghiallian allies Tara was, indeed, finally abandoned and no High-King of All Ireland, neither Ui Neill nor any other, ever reigned there again.

CONVENTION OF DRUIM CEAT A RUSE TO DOMINATE NORTHERN IRELAND   The Convention of Druim Ceat (Daisy Hill, Limavaddy in Derry) in 575 is pure hype. It was said to be a great assembly of all the kings of Ireland under the High-King of Ireland, Aed mac Ainmuirech of the N Ui Neill. It was attended by Colm Cille leading a delegation, including Aedan mac Gabran, King of the Scottish Dal Riata. Its aim is camouflaged by clever ploys. The matter of urgency to be settled was the relationship of the Dal Riata of Scotland and Ireland to the Ui Neill. The Irish Dal Riata was to ally itself to the Ui Neill king and to march with his armies. The Scottish portion of the kingdom would be independent except for the obligation to serve with the Ui Neill fleet when required. This was the plan to crush the Cruthin of Ulster and gain dominance over the North of Ireland.

The Convention story suffers from major defects. If it were held under the presidency of an Ui Neill High-King, why was it not held at his residence at Tara rather than far way in the NW of Ireland? There was no High King ruling at Tara or elsewhere then. This is one more articulation of the Tara Myth. Aed mac Ainmuirech was not High-King in 575 even in the official doctrine of the Ui Neill. The list of all the Kings of Ireland who allegedly attended the convention is full of errors and blatant anachronisms akin to those committed by 10th/12th century pseudo-historians. "The annals and king lists admit to thorough confusion concerning the succession after Diarmait's death. Aed could not have become king until after the death of his cousin Baetan mac Ninnedo in 586. He and his predecessors on the

---

[626] Francis John Byrne, 'Irish Kings and High-Kings', p. 97.
[627] Op. cit., p. 95.

throne, Baetan mac Muirchertaig and Eochaid mac Domnall of Cenel nEogain are non-entities. *'Baile Chuind'* admits none of them, not even Aed mac Ainmuirech."[628]

Adomnan's celebrated biography of Colm Cille tells how the saint blessed the boy Domhnall, son of the alleged High King, Aed, at the Convention of Druim Ceat and foretold he would excel over his brothers/stepbrothers to become High King. Later texts tell that this pleased Domhnall's mother but angered Aed mac Ainmhuirech's legal queen because her own son had been superseded. She called Colm Cille a 'crane-like cleric'. He retorted that she and her maid servant who assisted her in plotting against him would themselves be cranes until doomsday. "There they stand in a nearby river to this day." The queen's son, Domhnall's stepbrother, Conall, who was destined for the 'High-Kingship', incited the rabble to throw stones at Colm Cille and his monks at Druim Ceat at her behest. The saint cursed the High Kingship from his grasp. Instead he became a defender of the nearby S Donegal border against Connacht by day, and by night a royal jester at **High King Domhnall mac Aed's court at Dun Chinn Craoibhe just S of Ballyshannon, Co Donegal,**[629] **not at Tara, let be it noted. Thus, inadvertently, they let slip the Ui Neill High Hoax to their shameful undoing. Far indeed from ruling at Tara as High Kings of Ireland, the nearest these 6th century Ui Neill kings came to Tara's High Kingship was a puny princedom in Donegal.** The fraudulent anachronistically interpolated tale of the Convention of Druim Ceat tried to hide the secretive Ui Neill ambitious plan to crush the Cruthin of Ulster and dominate the North of Ireland, not to gain the High Kingship of All Ireland. All this shows up the blatant fiction of the so-called Ui Neill claims to the High-Kingship of Ireland at Tara at a time when there was considerable confusion and disunity in the camps, claims, and genealogies of the Ui Neill warlords.

TARA BELONGED TO THE CRUITHIN OVERKINGS OF SCOTLAND AND ULSTER

There is no such confusion in the Cruthin claims to a united over-kingship of the Cruthin of Ulster and Scotland from Tara of Meath long before, during and after the time of Diarmait, Aed, Domhnall and other Ui Neill king's alleged reigns at Tara. Apart from Mael Mura's claim that Ellim mac Conrach, Cruthin King of Ulster, ousted Highking Fiachu, from Temhair, there were several other Cruthin Kings of Ulster who ruled from Tara. Pseudo-historians of Ui Neill provenance reluctantly admitted the Cruthin kings, Fergus Dubdetach, Fiachu Araide and Eochaid Gunnat, did rule from Tara, alleging each ousted Cormac Mac Art from Temhair.[630] As to Cormac's alleged reign's at, and exile from, Tara, O Cathasaigh was forced to admit that "There is a conflict of evidence, and it is as well to admit that one is puzzled by it all." Mythological elements in Cormac Mac Art's Birth Tale and other texts in the Cormac cycle, such as *Esnada Tige Buchet,* were concocted specifically to transfer Cormac from his original Connacht context and bring him to a convenient locale close to Tara from which to launch his alleged reign at Tara. Cormac never reigned at Tara. He was *Rí Temhro* at the Temhair of Galway.

If Diarmait mac Cerbaill ever set foot on Tara it could only have been on a short warlording raid. Most conspicuously, the Ui Neill themselves unashamedly admitted that Diarmait's slayer, Aed Dub mac Suibni Araidi, Cruthin overking of Scotland and Ulster, reigned at Tara. The less ostentatious *'Baile Chuind'* claims Faechno (Fiachna mac Baetan) succeeded Aed Dub as Cruithin King of Tara. He was the Dal nAraidi Overking of the Cruthin of Scotland and Ulster. Other middle-Irish Sagas state that Faechno was king of Ireland and Alba (Scotland), ie., of the Cruthin of both lands. Pseudo-historians deliberately confused the Baetan who was Faechno's father and predecessor as king of Tara. Ui Neill

---

[628] Francis John Byrne, 'Irish Kings and High-Kings', p.110.
[629] Brian O Cuiv in *Eigse* II, 183-7, 290; Whitley Stokes in *Revue Celtique 20, 426-8.*
[630] Tomas O Cathasaigh, 'The Heroic Biography of Cormac Mac Airt', p. 87-91; O Rahilly, EIHM, p. 284.

chroniclers by design replaced his name by Ui Neill alleged high-kings Baetan mac Ninnedo and Baetan mac Muirchertaig of the Cenel nEogain. They substituted these two non-entities in place of Baetan, Faechno's father, subtly insinuating that the Baetan who ruled at Tara was an Ui Neill High-King of Ireland. The fact that they picked on 2 nonentity Ui Neill princes named Baetan to fill an awkward gap in their fake regnal list indicates how desperate they were to disguise the actual tenure of the kingship of Tara by another of that name, Baetan of the Dal nAraidi, over-king of the Cruthin. Ui Neill chroniclers were guilty of blatant bias and fraud. In many and various ways they subtly and ingeniously insinuated themselves into the regnal list of the alleged High-Kingship of Tara of Meath over a lengthy period spanning centuries.

To compound the confusion, another prominent Ulster king, Baetan mac Cairill (572-581), king of the Dal Fiatach, asserted suzerainty over the Dal Riata of Scotland and the Isle of Man. Historians confused matters further by styling him *Rí Erenn ocus Alban,* (king of the Dal Fiatach and Dal Riata of Ireland and Scotland). The real purpose of the Convention of Druim Ceat was to create a powerful alliance between Aedan mac Gabrain, ordained as king of the Scottish Dal Riata by Colm Cille, and the N Ui Neill king Aed mac Ainmuirech against the 2 Baetans, Baetan mac Cairill of Dal Fiatach and Baetan, the Cruthin overking of Scotland and Ulster reigning at Tara. Colm Cille welded the alliance. "Colm Cille's earliest biographer, Cuimmene Ailbe, tells us ('Life' by Adomnan) he warned Aedan against breaking this alliance. He laments Aedan's grandson, Domnall Brecc's folly, bringing disaster on Dal Riata in 637" by joining forces with Congal Caech, the Cruthin overking of Ulster and Scotland, in the Battle of Moira, thus ending up on the losing side.[631]

Baetan, the Cruthin overking at Tara was succeeded first by Aed Dub mac Suibni Araidi (581- 588), the slayer of Diarmait in 565, and then by his own son Faechno (Fiachna 588-626). The latter was a great seafarer and made several expeditions overseas. The title of a lost saga relates his expedition to *Dun Guaire i Saxanaib* (Bamborough in Engand), which the Welsh historian Nennius refers to as *Din Guayroi* and may well be that referred to in the annalistic entry at 623 *'Expugnatio Ratho Guali la Fiachnae mac Baetain'*. Faechno was succeeded by yet another Dal nAraidi overking of the Cruthin of Ulster and Scotland, namely, his own grandson Congal Caech, a historic fact fossilized in *'Bech Bretha'*. He fell at the great watershed battle of Moira in 637. Tara was finally lost to the Cruthin of Ulster.

The manner in which this historic event was interpolated to their own advantage by Ui Neill eulogists is sophisticated. Looking at the historic background against which this distortion of history was perpetrated, Congal carried on the work of his predecessors defending the diminishing lands of the Cruthin agaist the ever-encroaching Ui Neill. In 628 he slew Suibne Menn of Cenel nEogain, another alleged Ui Neill High King of Ireland. In the following year he was defeated by 'High King', Domnall son of Aed mac Ainmuirech at Dun Ceithirnn in Derry. The site of the battle shows Congal was the aggressor attempting to retake former Cruthin lands in Derry recently won over by the Ui Neill. This shows that Domnall, the alleged king of Tara, far from being at Tara, was way up at the NW tip of Ireland. On his N frontier Congal had to ward off aggression by the Dal Riata now fighting on the side of the Ui Neill since their alliance signed at the Convention of Druim Cett through the 'good' offices of Colum Cille. He dealt them a devastating blow. As Byrne recounts, "by 637 Congal had persuaded the Dal Riata to reverse their alliance. Together with Domnall Brecc of Dal Riata he met (Ui Neill king) Domnall mac Aedo at the great battle of Mag Roth (Moira, Co. Down). Congal was slain and Domnall Brecc fled to Scotland to be slain a few years later by the Strathclyde Britons whose song of triumph over the death of 'Dyfnwal Vrych' found its way into the *'Canu Aneirin'*. On the same day a

---

[631] Francis John Byrne, 'Irish Kings and High-Kings', p. 111.

naval battle was fought between the Dal Riata and the Cenel nEogain (Ui Neill) on the one side and the (alleged) highking's forces of the Cenel Conaill (Ui Neill) on the other. Congal succeeded in playing off factions within the Northern Ui Neill"against one another.[632]

The facts of history were ingeniously distorted by Ui Neill chroniclers. Their version of events promulgated in the 'history' books, claimed that Congal had been fostered by the Ui Neill 'High-King', Domnall mac Aedo, allegedly reigning at Tara, but in fact, in S Donegal. This fiction claimed that Congal nursed a grudge against the alleged High King because a bee stung him in the eye - hence his cognomen Caech (the half-blind). Observe the preservation here of innocuous truth and the suppression and manipulation of facts disadvantageous to the self-interests of the Ui Neill. Having thus suppressed the truth and rendered the evidence of history harmless to their forgery of the Ui Neill High Kingship of Tara they pressed on nonchalantly with what had the appearance of sober history. Congal, they claimed, resented the occupation of his Ulster (Cruthin) lands by the N Ui Neill with the aid of the Airghialla who had been thier allies since the 5th century. They alleged that the so-called High-King, Domnall mac Aedo, had promised to restore these lands to the Cruthin. This is an explicit acknowledgement that the lands of the medieval Ui Neill in Ulster had been taken from the Cruthin by force. Yet, by an almost imperceptible interpolation their 'men of learning' turned the story round making the Ui Neill king, Domnall mac Aedo of S Donegal, High-King of Ireland residing at Tara with Congal Caech in fosterage with him. Thus they bolstered the Tara Myth with their powerful cocktail of truths, half-truths and interpolated facts mingled with fabricated fraud. Ingenious!

The law-tract on bees, *'Bech Bretha'*, preserves the earlier "untampered version."[633] It has profound historical implications. It tells how Congal Caech, Cruthin Overking of Ulster and Scotland, not the Ui Neill Domnall mac Aedo, reigned at Tara. It corroborates Cruthin claims that their kings, and theirs alone, ruled at Tara up to the battle of Moira in 637. This fact and its attendant ramifications are vital to the rediscovery of the lost history of Iron Age and early Christian Ireland. By many devious distortions of history, such as that perpetrated on Congal, which are far too many to describe here, 'historians' of the Ui Neill and of their allies, the Airghialla of Armagh, conned all Ireland with their persuasive Tara/Patrick Myth. The raucous roar of the rising Ui Neill warlords smothered the humble truthful voice of the Cruthin. Thereafter all Ireland rode on the back of a fiendish fraud reverberating with profuse repercussions, civil, social, religious, political, cultural and historical, affecting all Ireland, past, present and future. It is still being taken for a ride.

The Battle of Moira brought an end to the Cruthin tenure of the overkingship of Northern Ireland and Scotland from Tara. It fell into the hands of the Ui Neill. Since the Cruthin kings styled themselves 'overkings of Ireland and Scotland', though this was restricted to their Cruthin subjects, the Ui Neill claimed they too had a right to be called 'kings of Ireland', a grandiose pretension. Domnall mac Aedo died in 642. The 8th century 'Annals of Ulster' which began the process of propagating the Tara Myth accorded him the title 'king of Ireland'. Later Annals equated 'King of Tara' with 'High-King of Ireland'. "These early annals are extremely sparing in their references to the high-kingship. Domnall is the first to be so honoured by them."[634] In the 9th century an Ui Neill king, Maelsechlainn mac Maele Ruanaid, made the High Kingship of all Ireland a reality for the first time.

---

[632] Op. cit., p. 112-113.

[633] Op. cit., p. 113.

[634] Op. cit., p. 114.

WHAT HAPPENED TO HISTORY? THE UNASKED QUESTION GOES A-BEGGING
In the light of the forgoing, the question arises: If Kings Cormac mac Art, his father Art, grandfather Conn, Conn's grandfather Tuathal, Queen Medb and her father Eochaid Fedlech did not reign at Tara of Meath or Rathcroghan of Roscommon as pseudo-history says they did, then where in all Ireland did they reign, if reign they did? O Rahilly, not finding a trace of any of those royal personages at Tara or Rathcroghan, with a stroke of the pen consigned them to the realm of pure myth, all except Tuathal. His infatuation for Tuathal drew from him an entire chapter of pseudo-history. He claimed that the "province of Connacht's capital was 'Cruachain of Roscommon,'" and that "Medb, the goddess of Tara, is made to reign, not in Tara, but in Cruachain. And so in 'Táin Bó Cualgne' the narrator has first to bring Medb rapidly from Cruachain to the Tara district before she can march N against the Ulaid." His strong statements, such as "Of the kings who ruled in Connacht in pre-christian times history knows nothing,"[635] can now be seen for what they really are, pure pseudo-history. He was duped by 'medieval myth'. What then happened to history?

Having debunked O Rahilly's claims that "the men of Tara were the Connachta"[636] and that "the enemies of Ulster were the men of Tara on their S border," it now remains to explode the rest of this web of early and modern myths. The Connachta have been traced back to their original homelands in W Ireland. Their original Capital was not "Croghan of Roscommon," but Turoe/Rath Cruacha of Galway. Far indeed from the men of Tara being the Connachta, they were the pre-Celtic Cruthin of Ulster against whom constant warfare was waged by the Connachta. Their Fir Belg ancestors set up their power centres there at the heart of their primary settlement areas. This is the thrust of Ireland's legendary history, the 'Ulster Tales', and archaeological material, corroborated by the early geo-political account of Ireland left by Ptolemy and by the Turoe/Athenry Fir Belg oppida.

The earliest legendary history tells how various tribes of Connacht fighting men, such as the Luigni, Galenga, Collas and Ciannachta, marched with the Fir Belg Overking, Cormac mac Art, to the Battle of Crinna, against the Ulstermen. Present-day N Leinster was still in the possession of the Cruthin and reckoned as part of Ulster. O Rahilly had finally to admit that the entire area of N Leinster as far S as the Boyne and Tara was reckoned as part of Ulster even to the 19th century.[637] Eoin MacNeill claimed, despite O Rahilly's disparaging remarks, that the Luigni, Gailingi and Ciannachta were transplanted from Connacht to Leinster "to guard the conquests of the Connacht kings."[638] In these tales, notably the Battle of Crinna, the territory conquered from the Cruthin of Ulster stretched NW from the Liffey and Rey of Dublin. Mac Neill suffered from a preconceived idea that this territory belonged to Leinster. The territory wrested from the Ulstermen "extended along the coast from Ardee to Dublin and inland along the N frontier of Meath to Loch Ramor"[639] and back to the Rey cutting off an extensive triangle of land. These tales imply that those lands belonged to Ulster, although "in later times they were occupied by Connacht colonies,"[640] before becoming N Leinster. They remained in the hands of the Luigna, Gailenga and Ciannachta into the later middle ages as is still known there.

Local historian, Philip O Connell, summed up the tradition in the area surrounding Loch Ramor. "The Luigni, like the Gailenga, was one of the frontier colonies/buffer states estab - lished about the 3rd century to guard the frontiers against the forces of Emain (Macha – Cruthin). They belonged originally to Connacht. Here (Meath and Cavan) as in Connacht

[635] T.F.O Rahilly, 'Early Irish Hiatory and Mythology', p.176.
[636] Op. cit., EIHM, p. 175.
[637] T. F. O Rahilly, 'EIHM', p. 485
[638] Eoin MacNeilll, 'Phases of Irish History' p.121; T. F. O Rahilly, 'EIHM', p. 479
[639] E. MacNeill, Ibid, p. 122
[640] Ibid, p. 122

they occupied neighbouring territories. The territory occupied by the Luigni and Gailenga races extended over a large area in E Co. Cavan and N Co. Meath. It included the district around Loch Ramor, and extended along the valley of the Blackwater. The baronies of Lune and Mor Gallion in Meath derive their titles from the Luigni and Gailenga; the extent of these baronies as now defined represent only a small section of their ancient territories. They retained their territorial rule, although much restricted, as late as the 11th century. With the coming of the Anglo-Normans towards the close of the 12th century the Luigni and Gailenga pass from the historical record."[641] This is grassroot oral history!

Eoin MacNeill was not the only one who could not accept the fact that ancient Ulster stretched down to the Liffey in Dublin as implied in 'Cath Crinna'. He is in distinguished company duped by pseudo-history into believing that N Leinster inclusive of the territory between the Boyne and the Liffey was one of the ancient Provinces outside of Ulster that already existed before the time of Cormac Mac Art. The story of the Battle of Crinna shows that the territory between the Liffey and the Boyne belonged to the Cruthin of Ulster until Cormac Mac Art and the Collas, wrested part of it from them. Later the Ui Neill leading their new allies, the Ciannachta and Airghialla, won over the remainder. The territory never before belonged to Leinster, nor, indeed, for a long time afterwards. The story of the Battle of Crinna preserves this historcal fact - an amazing preservation of historical truth in the circumstances. It was manipulated at a time when the Ui Neill chroniclers put forward the idea that the Monarchy at Tara of Meath was founded by Cormac Mac Art after he had annexed the district from the Cruthin of Ulster but before the time when the idea that "Tara was the seat of the Monarchy from time immemorial" was concocted. True history is corroborated by ancient boundary fortifications.

Cormac was already *Rí Temhro* (King of the Turoe in Galway) and *Rí Erann* (Overking of the Erainn/Fir Belg peoples) before he led his Connacht armies E across the Shannon. This, of course, is suppressed in the interpolated story. The idea that he became *Rí Temhro*, interpolated to mean High King of All Ireland at Tara, only after he had allegedly annexed the Tara district from the Cruthin of Ulster, is ingeniously insinuated in this piece of pseudo-history. The claim that he was High King of Ireland is an anachronism pointing to the lateness of its concoction as there was no such institution before the 9th century. The claim that he annexed the Tara district and became King of Tara is fiction. Legendary history tells that he placed a line of frontier colonies as "buffer states" of Ciannachta, Luighni, Galienga, Manachi and other tribes stretching all the way from the Liffey to Lough Ramor and Lough Erne. This is supported by the historic presence there of these tribes and by their origin-legends. These frontier colonies stood well back from Tara until the downfall of the Cruthin at the Battle of Moy Rath in 637 when Tara was finally lost to them. The Cruthin claimed they drove Cormac mac Art from *Midh* (the Midlands), not from Tara of Meath. This defeat did not affect his title 'Rí Temhro'. Buffer states set up by him remained in place well into historic times. The Ciannachta welded a new alliance with the Ui Neill and moved forward into more extensive areas up the coastal strip of Meath and Louth after the Cruthin collapse there in 637, as they did in Derry.

Cormac Mac Art's role East of the Shannon was that of aggressor. His role in Connacht was that of Overking administering the province as its regent, a role he did not play in any other province outside of the realms of the extended Connacht of his day. Gratianus Lucius[642] noted that Cormac defeated the Cruthin of Ulster twice near Granard, slaying a considerable number of them with their king, Aengus Finn, son of Fergus Dubdedach, at the Battle of Crinn-Fregabail (Crinna). He moved the frontline of Airghiallan buffer states forward to a

---

[641] Philip O Connell, M.Sc., Ph. D. 'On the Territory of the Luigni' in his paper on 'Castle Kieran' p.12

[642] Gratianua Lucius, c. 8. p.70

new frontier line from the Blackwater to Lough Ramor and Lough Erne. Due to loss of lands many of the Cruthin fled to the Isle of Man and the Hebrides of Scotland.

Within Connacht, Aidh, grandson of Conall-Cruachna (foster-father of Cormac's grand-father, Conn), who succeeded Kedgin-Cruachna as king of Rath Cruacha (of Athenry), was deposed by Cormac for acting against his interests. He replaced him with Niamor, son of Lugna Fer Tri (by Achtan, Cormac's mother whom Lugna wed after the assassination of Cormac's father Art at the Battle of Magh Muc Dhruim). When Niamor was later assassinated, Cormac placed Niamor's brother, Lugadh, on the throne. Here Cormac is seen in his role as overking of the expanding province of Connacht. Turoe of Galway was the seat of the Fir Belg overkings. Rath Cruacha of Athenry was the royal seat of a satellite, albeit central, kingdom of the province of Connacht. A similar supreme overkingship role over the extended territories of Connacht on both sides of the Shannon is carried out by his father Art, and grandfather Conn from whom Connacht is named, clearly implying his association with Connacht rather than with Tara. His great-great-grandfather Tuathal, and predecessors, Queen Medb and her father Eochaidh Fedlech, 'ideal King of the Fir Belg' played similar roles in Coiced nÓl nÉgmacht (archaic Connacht) but not elsewhere. Recognizing the precise milieu and role of each of these regents, before the older tradition was transported from its original context for the glorification of Tara and Rathcroghan of Roscommon is vital for a true understanding of the political geography of Iron Age Ireland. Connacht colonies, the Collaibh Oige (the Luigne, Gailenga, Ciannachta and others) "in Meath and Ulster were frontier colonies planted to guard the conquests of the Connacht kings" at Ulster's expense. Why then do the history books tell a diametrically different story? Does the question go a-begging? The next chapter will give the surprising answer and shocking truth.

CHAPTER 4

SUPPRESSION OF
IRISH IRON AGE HISTORY

ARMAGH'S ROLE IN THE BIRTH
AND
GROWTH OF PSEUDO-HISTORY

THEIVES AND ROBBERS
OF EARLY IRISH
HISTORY AND TRADITIONS

ARMAGH'S ROLE IN HISTORY'S DEMISE AND PSEUDO-HISTORY'S BIRTH

The uprooting of pseudo-history, of which the Tara/Patrick Myth is the epitome, is a first step to undo the suppression of genuine Irish Iron Age history and its political geography.

"From the 8th century on a succession of learned Irishmen devoted themselves to the task of reconstructing the history of their country in pre-christian times. The result of their labours is seen in Lebor Gabala Erenn (Book of the Conquest of Ireland). It may be described as a deliberate work of fiction."[643] *"The history of pre-christian Ireland as related in 'Lebor Gabala' imposed itself on our ancestors. It was accepted unquestioningly as historical truth by scholars despite its generally spurious character. A fiction, which necessitated a long series of fabrications to support it, was their claim that the dominant Goidels (the Irish) had been in occupation of Ireland from a very remote period (2000 BC) and that their kings had ruled Ireland from Tara of Meath from time immemorial. It is precisely this 'pious fraud' that has been most readily accepted by many scholars in recent times."*[644] *"The pedigree-makers and the authors of Lebor Gabala worked hand in hand. Their object was to provide a fictitious antiquity for the Goidels and a fictitious Goidelic descent for the Irish generally. Accordingly, they filled out the prechristian part of the pedigrees of the Kings of Tara with names drawn from the traditions of the Erainn (Fir Belg). The inventors were very far indeed from being animated by a desire for historical truth and accuracy. Their object was rather to disguise the truth."*[645]

They stole or suppressed the early history of Ireland. The truth which was disguised and not found in History Books was that pre-christian Ireland was being progressively dominated by Fir Belg tribes who set up primary settlements in the Southern half of Ireland and had a chief centre of power at Turoe (Cnoc Temhro) and Athenry (Rath Cruacha) in Galway in Western Ireland. Thence they spearheaded their conquest and domination of the N half of Ireland at the expense of the aboriginal Cruthin peoples, the Ulaidh (the men of Ulster) of history.

Roy sums up the Tara/Patrick Myth: *"Tara is a place of supernatural confusion, not physically in terms of the site itself, but factually, historically. The end result has been a final hardening of fable into fact. For an age that should know better, we seem to be losing our ability to arrive at some bearing that approximates reality. Few spots in the world have been, in popular imagination, more abused. The single overwhelming force in Tara's case has been the legend of Patrick - to imagine Patrick as he approached the Royal Palace of Tara on a 5th century Easter Sunday to do battle with the druids. Most visitors couldn't escape this if they tried, so persistently has the tale been repeated. The sequel is rigorously maintained throughout the Republic in every school, church and tourist bus: how Laoghaire, High-King of Ireland, son of Niall of the Nine Hostages, allowed his followers to convert. A Christian tidal wave ensued with Patrick in control, sweeping all before him. In the span of 30 years his mission stood complete, the island won for Christ."*[646]

Truth is often bitter, fact stranger than fiction. Tara, contrary to widespread belief, was never the Capital or Royal Seat of an Iron Age or medieval united Ireland. The projection of a High-Kingship of All Ireland at Tara in Patrick's day is pure fiction perpetrated for political propaganda with perennial repercussions. What then was the root cause of the great medieval conspiracy which suppressed the archaic history of the Turoe/Athenry oppidum of Galway in particular, and of Ireland in general, in favour of Tara of Meath and Rathcroghan

---

[643] T. F. O Rahilly, 'Early Irish History and Mythology', p. 193.
[644] T. F. O Rahilly, 'Early Irish History and Mythology', p. 263-264.
[645] T. F. O Rahilly, 'Early Irish History and Mythology', p.267-268
[646] James Charles Roy, 'The Road Wet, The Wind Close' or 'Celtic Ireland', p.55-56

of Roscommon? These were exalted and glorified out of all proportion as the Royal Seats of the High-Kingship of Ireland and of Connacht respectively from time immemorial. This fiction flies in the face of Irish and Continental Iron Age and early history. This chapter will address the who-what-when-where-and-why of this hoax. Just how was this 'pious fraud' conceived? How did it come to birth and grow apace? When and where were the seeds of this pseudo-history sown? Who fathered this monumental hoax of history? And what are its short and long-term consequences? This chapter will give a more comprehensive answer to all these questions.

To answer these questions satisfactorily one needs to be a detective who digs deep into the doings of the dark and distant past. Much of this work has already been done and the culprits identified. It needs to be restated. Authors who have done the digging and brought many pertinent facts to light will be quoted directly. Much spadework remains to be done. The roots of this pseudo-history must be dug out once and for all. What is exposed, such as in Chapter 2, presents a radical reinterpretation that will revolutionize the science of Iron Age Irish history, political geography and archaeology. It will bring to an end the curious irony that still exists. While the historicity of the Iron Age Irish record remains open to serious question, the political geography of Tara of Meath and Croghan of Roscommon as the Capitals of Iron Age Ireland continues to be taken for granted without question. Scholars still look for evidence of Celtic Iron Age Ireland in the wrong places and from the wrong premises. They take the political geography of pseudo-historical Annals for granted while questioning the veracity of its history. A more fruitful approach would be to reverse the order. In so doing the historic traditions and political geography of Iron Age Ireland plundered by the 7th to the 9th century pseudo-historians could rightly revert to their original context. Then the truth would become obvious.

By assuming that the stream of Irish history evolved and revolved around Tara from time immemorial genuine history is sidetracked, a myriad of questions left unanswered and countless others crop up because of the resulting ambiguity. Hence many historians have thrown Irish prechristian history overboard as pure myth, having failed to find place for it in the context of Tara of Meath and Croghan of Roscommon. Shift the political geography of Tara of Meath to Turoe of Galway, and of Croghan of Roscommon to Rath Cruacha of Athenry. Then reconstruct the ancient records and legends from within this geo-political context. One will be overwhelmed at how history fits into its rightful place. The historical panorama will become crystal clear instead of being the cryptic puzzle it now is.

One must understand how Irish Pseudo-History came into being and usurped the place of genuine history. One must go all the way back to the coming of the Celts to Ireland, something of which has been elucidated in the first two chapters. To analyze the manufacture of this myth in motion one must go back to Patrick's mission and re-examine how he was resurrected, reanimated, inflated and elongated the length and breadth of Ireland by the blatantly ambitious monastic federation of Armagh, and adopted by the Southern Ui Neill Dynasty, for its own aggrandizement. Armagh's programme of Patrician supremacy would have been impossible without, on one hand, the simultaneous rise to power of the Ui Neill who from the 7th and 8th centuries it enticed by calling their warlords, past and present, High-Kings of Ireland reigning from Tara of Meath from pre-christian times, and on the other, the total collapse in see-saw fashion of Columcille's rival monastic federation.

THE CHRISTIANIZING OF PRE-PATRICIAN IRELAND: PATRICK'S ROLE:
J. Walsh and T. Bradley made the sober remark: "Traditionally, the humble St. Patrick has been credited with converting the entire Irish race from paganism in the very short period between 432 and 461. However, there were certainly Christians in Ireland before Patrick

arrived. He worked as an evangelist only in a part of the island."[647] The coming of Christinity to Ireland is obscure, yet, there are certain indicators as to how it arrived in a number of cases, not the least being the Roman Mission of Palladius. The Corcu Laigde of Cork claimed to have been the first Irish Christians. They carried on an extensive wine-trade with Gaul, a partly Christian land by then. There was considerable trade between Britain and Ireland in that same period that would have been another channel for Christianity.

The lost 'Leiden Glossary', a 12th century document based on 6th century Gaulish accounts, told that a migration of Christian 'learned men' fled from France to Ireland due to the invasion of Gaul by Germanic tribes at the dawn of the 5th century. There are references in Irish records to Gauls and Gallic missionaries working in Ireland before Patrick's time. Patrick's own mention of the presence of '*rhetorici*' ('learned men') is a reference to these fugitives.[648] The may have come to Ireland aboard the Belgic Corco Laigde wine ships and have been responsible for the conversion of this Cork tribe. Kuno Meyer elaborated the arrival of earlier Gauls who allied themselves to older Irish tribes in the E and S of Ireland.[649] Their established tribal groups survived into early historical times. "Of the presence of Christianity in Ireland by the start of the 5th century we can be in no doubt for there is indisputable evidence that Christianity had reached Ireland before Patrick began his mission."[650] In response to Pelagius' damage to the Church in Britain, Germanus of Auxerre was sent there in 429. "An offshoot of this excursion was the subsequent mission of Palladius to the Irish believing in Christ: incontrovertible evidence that from at least the 3rd decade of the 5th century, there were sufficient Irish Christians to justify the appointment of a bishop for them by Rome." In his 'Chronicon' under the year 431 Prosper of Aquitaine noted: "Palladius, ordained by Pope Celestin, is sent to the Scotti believing in Christ, as their first bishop." The influential Palladius, deacon at Auxerre, was instrumental in having Germanus sent to tackle Pelagianism in Britain. Writing of Celestin in his 'Contra Collatorem', between 434-437 in Rome, Prosper recorded another piece of highly germane information that throws light on facts suppressed by the concoctors of the Tara/Patrick Myth. "By ordaining a Bishop for the Scotti (Irish), while he strove to keep the Roman island Catholic, Celestin also made the barbarous island (Ireland) Christian."[651]

Scholars agree this not only refers to, but is positive proof of the success of Palladius's work in Ireland, 'the barbarous island', and that Pope Celestin also preserved Britain, the 'Roman island' from the Pelagian heresy by sending Germanus. Written several years after the commissioning of both men by Pope Celestin, this is first hand crucial confirmation of the success of both missions. Had Palladius been murdered or left Ireland within a year of the start of his mission, as various Armagh-inspired attempts to glorify Patrick at the expense of Palladius claimed, Prosper could not have written what he did about the Christianization of Ireland as a result of the sending of Bishop Palladius with a routine retinue of Continental missionaries by Pope Celestin. Indeed, if one were to take Prosper's highly relevant statement seriously at face value it would indicate that both Prosper and Rome considered Ireland to be already Christian, or largely Christian, by the time these words were written. This was well before Patrick ever set out on his mission to Ireland. According to the more trustworthy scholarship, Patrick's mission began as late as 461, a quarter of a century after Prosper penned these highly pertinent words. Prosper's record unreservedly places the stamp of success on the Roman/Celestin-inspired mission of Palladius to Ireland. On the strength of Prosper's entry, Palladius was still successfully

---

[647] John R. Walsh and Thomas Bradley, 'A History of the Irish Church 400 - 700 AD.', p.1
[648] St. Patrick, 'The Confessions of St. Patrick', 13.
[649] Kuno Meyer in 'Eriu', Vol 4, p.208.
[650] J. R. Walsh and T. Bradley, Op. Cit. p. 4.
[651] Prosper of Aquitane, in his 'Contra Collatum'.

active in Ireland several years after his commission by Celestine. This gives the lie to the fabulous Armagh/Muirchu and Tara/Patrick Myth allegations to the contrary.

While Armagh's mentor, Muirchu, admitted that Palladius was sent by Pope Celestin, his suppression of the success of Palladius' mission and manipulation of facts to glorify Patrick is transparent: "They knew for certain that Palladius had been consecrated and sent to this island." No one could deny this well-known recorded fact. However, unaware of Prosper's later pronouncement on the success of Palladius' mission, Muirchu twisted the facts regarding Palladius and brought his mission to a sudden inglorious end with a notoriously villainous excuse. "Neither were these wild harsh men (the Irish of Palladius' day) inclined to accept his teaching, nor did he himself wish to spend a long time in a foreign country, but decided to return to (Celestin) who sent him." If Palladius returned to Rome within a year of his commission by Celestin, as Muirchu claims, Prosper would have known this and could never have written what he did. Prosper consulted Celestin concerning contemporary ecclesiastical affairs of which he wrote profusely before penning the highly pertinent statement quoted above. He assisted Popes Celestin and Leo I, whose secretary he was, with their correspondence. He had his finger on the facts. Muirchu did not. Muirchu alleged that on his way home Palladius died in Britain. The lameness of Muirchu's claims is glaring. Rome would never have appointed Palladius as Bishop to the Irish were he unwilling to spend his life as a Bishop in Ireland. Neither would Rome have sent someone on his last legs. A man in his full vigour was what this mission demanded. Unperturbed at having so slyly suppressed Palladius and cleared the decks, Muirchu brought Patrick on stage and concocted a fiction of his alleged splendid success of converting Ireland single-handedly in the course of 30 years. This travesty of the truth is transparent. One moment the 'wild Irish' are not inclined to accept the teaching of the Gospel. Next moment as Patrick steps ashore the same 'harsh men' are wildly enthusiastic. This is typically Muirchu's mean manipulation of the facts. Pure Muirchusation!

Thus the activities of Palladius and Patrick became confused. Much of the missionary work of Palladius ('Patricius' in Ireland), has been attributed to Patrick. 'Patricius' was a Continental honorary title. O Rahilly claimed Palladius laboured in Ireland from 431 until 460. Recent scholars claim Patrick worked in Northern Ireland from 461 until his death about 492. Bieler noted that any Bishops sent by Rome had the assistance of a suitably large staff. A mission with Papal backing would be constantly reinforced. He located the scene of Palladius' labours in SE Ireland. Secundinus, Auxilius, Iserninus and other Continental miss-ionaries who had no contact with Patrick, are believed to have been part of the Roman Palladian mission and to have continued Palladius's work. Armagh's chroniclers, having consigned Palladius to the trash-can of history, placed these Gaulish missionaries directly under Muirchu's newly minted Patrick who allegedly assigned each to his respective area of work. "The Church of Kildare may have been a relic of the effectiveness and independence of Palladius and his followers."[652]

In his 'Confessio' Patrick showed himself aware of episcopal activity elsewhere in Ireland and the administration, independent of his own ministry, of the sacraments of Baptism, Confirmation and Ordination. He traveled to places where "no one else had ever penetrated, in order to baptize, ordain clergy, or confirm" - thus insinuating that there were places in the country which had received spiritual ministrations from other sources.[653] Having based the centre of his missionary work at Armagh, adjoining the Cruthin Capital of Ulster, it is clear that his missionary work was confined to the Cruthin of Ulster who controlled Tara at

---

[652] Walsh and Bradley, Op. Cit. p. 8.
[653] Op. Cit., p. 8.

that time. He spoke their language from his time of slavery among them. This may have decided why he chose or was sent to work in that area among them.

The Cruthin of Ulster were among the last peoples to be evangelised in Ireland as were their kinsmen, the Picts of Scotland. The Picts were in the process of being evangelized as much as a century later by Colum Cille and others. In Northern Ireland Patrick "clearly considered himself as essentially a pioneer, not anybody's successor," as Walsh and Bradley noted. This slotted him into this neglected niche in the evangelization of Ireland among the Cruthin of Ulster. Patrick's role among them is confirmed by his retreat with them to their centre around Downpatrick after their capital of Emain Macha was overrun by Airghiallian forces. What cannot be denied is that Christianity had already taken firm root in the rest of Ireland before Patrick's time. "By the time the saint had begun his mission, the ground work had been done and the foundations had been laid for a Celtic Church in Ireland that over the next few centuries would become one of the most vibrant parts of the Body of Christ."[654]

A NEW ERA UNFOLDS WITH THE PASCHAL CONTROVERSY

The great plague of 548 AD brought prodigious changes to the Irish Church and its Roman system of episcopal authority introduced by the early missionaries. It cut a swath through the religious community in Ireland. It led to a radical re-arrangement of religious organization which proved seminal to the great medieval fraud of Irish History and political geography. At the head of this new tide was Columcille, born in 524 AD from the Ui Neill royal sept of Clann Conaill in Donegal in the NE of Ireland. Being son of an Ui Neill chieftain, directly descended from Niall of the Nine Hostages, founder of the great Ui Neill Dynasty which dominated the Irish political scene from the 7th to the 10th century, he was eligible to the throne. As such he had no small interest in the rise of his dynasty and played a part in its political and ecclesiastical affairs. Even after his alleged expulsion to Scotland in the year 565 because of his too divisive involvement in its war-lording affairs, he continued to be deeply enmeshed in its political advancement. Completing his priestly formation in Moville and Clonard, Columcille founded his 1st church at Derry. From 546 to his exile in 565 he trod across N Ireland oozing with energetic spiritual fire setting up churches and christianizing, not just the bottom layer of society, but the top echelon. He spoke the language of the kings, not as a stranger but as an equal. Celtic honour demanded he be listened to. Soon he was surrounded by powerful followers. In each church he founded he left behind a religious community. He belonged to the monastic system, not to the Roman episcopal system of Patrick. The scales tipped in his favour.

The absolute contrast between Patrick as Bishop and Columcille as Abbot must be seen to understand the background to later developments. Columcille's effectiveness derived from his royal heritage in two respects. First, his enormous prestige as a member of a royal dynasty, son of kings and elegible to the throne. Second, his intuitive sense of the Celtic system, which had proved a stumbling block to Patrick. Unlike the Patrick of Roman background, often severely confronted by the Celtic system, Columcille was able to turn this to his benefit. Columcille had the unfair advantage that he was a Celt, not a Briton of Roman background like Patrick, a Royal Prince, not a former slave, as Roy noted.[655] Patrick came as a Bishop of the Roman system and so had no source of power in pagan Ireland. He was confined to one 'tuath' (petty kingdom) at the mercy of pagan kings. He had to pay the Brehons for his freedom to travel and for safe passage from one petty kingdom to another, to preach in each. His disadvantage was that he was a stranger to the system, a prisoner of his own Roman diocesan system.

---

[654] Op. Cit., p. 8-9.
[655] James Charles Roy, 'The Road Wet, The Wind Close', p. 111-114 et al.

Columcille, by contrast, was scholarly and eloquent. As his fame spread, kings sought to ingratiate themselves with him by granting him property on which to settle his growing number of followers. There gradually evolved across the North of Ireland numerous monastic communities with a great feeling of solidarity between them - a true monastic family. The common thread was Columcille - after his death, the memory of Columcille - out of which came the notions of *'paruchia'* and *'coarb'* (successor) which sealed the fate of the bishops.[656] In 561 Columcille's overwhelming success was temporarily halted when he became too involved in the affairs of his dynastic family. He was 'excommunicated' from the Irish Church for his leading role in the battle of Cul Dreimne between the N and S Ui Neill. His biographer, Adomnan, glossed over the affair so that little is known of what happened. In 563 Columcille, aged 42, went into 'permanent' penitential exile in Scotland. He embarked on the task of converting the Picts with spectacular success which brought him enduring fame. His 'paruchia' spread the length and breadth of Scotland and across the border down to Northumbria, and back again to Ireland. Iona was his centre. It had links throughout the Celtic world, becoming the most renowned monastery ever founded. While Columcille's monastic 'paruchia' multiplied, in seesaw fashion the Roman episcopal See of Armagh founded by Patrick sunk into insignificance.

Roy made the rise of Columcille's monastic system and "the demise of Patrick's still-born episcopal system a fascinating study."[657] He noted that the year 575 AD when Columcille returned triumphantly to Ireland with a host of bishops and princes for the Convention of Druim Cett, marks the tipping of the scales when the fate of the bishops hung in the balance vis-a-vis that of the monastic paruchiae. This was the watershed where the Columcille-style Celtic system pulled away from the Roman Patrician-style episcopal system to which Armagh belonged. The tidal wave of monastic paruchiae with their spider-web network of confederations were a growing humiliation for the older established episcopal communities like Armagh which found themselves struggling to survive outside the orbit of ecclesiastical developement in poverty and isolation. Armagh's former patrons, the Cruthin of Ulster, had fled from Emain Macha, Ulster's capital, never to return. With Patrick in tow, they were confined in their decimated kingdom between Downpatrick and Tara. After this debacle, Tara became the seat of the Cruthin Overkings until their final defeat in 637. Tara's King led Cruthin resistence against the Ui Neill. In these lean times for the episcopal see of Armagh, she was driven to think of survival. The solution was simple but stark: emulate the monastic paruchiae or die. She decided to become predator rather than prey.

Columcille befriended Scotland's kings, Aedan Mac Gabrain whom he crowned King of Dal Riata in 574, and Brude Mac Maelchon, King of the Scottish Picts. They became his powerful allies and patrons of Iona. Baetan Mac Cairell's election as Overking of the Cruthin of Ulster and Scotland at Tara alerted Colmcille to the dangers which faced his *paruchiae* in Ireland. Baetan, in time-honoured tradition, called for pledges of submission and hostages. The Dal Riata of Antrim were legally required to submit to their ancient Overlords. Contention arose when the Dal Riata septs in Scotland, of considerable size and importance by then and technically speaking still men of Ulster (Dal Riata of Ulster and Scotland were ruled by one Over-king), were considered by Baetan as his subjects. Determined to restore the greater Cruthin Kingdom of Ulster, Baetan demanded control of their fighting men and their powerful fleet. This was highly alarming not only for the Dal Riata but especially for the Ui Neill, particularly Columcille's branch. Were the Scottish and Irish branches of the Dal Riata to pledge support to Baetan, both branches of the Ui Neill would feel threatened. To ignore this demand of their rightful king would provoke retaliation from Baetan who for now was stronger than they. Aedan sought the advice of

---

[656] Ibid, p. 116.
[657] James Charles Roy, 'The Road Wet, The Wind Close', p. 107 - 119 and ff.

Columcille whose own paruchiae of daughter monasteries among the Irish Dal Riata were in danger of falling apart in the event of a Dal Riata disaster at the hands of Baetan. Baetan's warlike posture elicited a powerful response.[658]

DRUIM CETT: WATERSHED IN THE HISTORY OF ULSTER AND IRELAND

Columcille's response was decisive. He re-entered the Irish political swirl with a vengeance and convened the Council of Druim Cett in N Ui Neill lands near Limavady in Derry in 575, well out of Cruthin earshot.[659] The Scottish King Aedan was invited. Columcille's cousin, Aed Mac Ainmuirech, King of the N Ui Neill was the most important king present. The now estranged S Ui Neill were not invited. Neither was the Cruthin Overking of Ulster and Scotland, Baetan Mac Cairell. Aedan presided over the Convention with Columcille as spokesman. Columcille persuaded the Dal Riata to side with the N Ui Neill for their own protection. Otherwise the N Ui Neill King, Aed, would destroy what was left of the Dal Riata in Ulster. He played this political pawn to perfection. He impressed upon them that if they or their Scottish fleet submitted to Baetan they would be crushed. This became the official N Ui Neill policy. The Convention of Druim Cett achieved its goals pro tem, at least. The agreement was dicey but utterly self-serving on political and monastic grounds, clandestinely confidential and camouflaged with literary smoke screens.[660] "Loose lips sink ships" was their tight-lipped motto.

As Ulster King Baetan's overlordship of Scotland was rendered void, "the submission rightly owed him by the Dal Riata, of troops, was recognized by Aed in such a way as to save face for Baetan. In reality the message was made even plainer: the Dal Riata, as far as Aed was concerned, were now wards of the Northern Ui Neill. Baetan lost out in just about every way."[661] By allying the Dal Riata to his cousins, Columcille had forged a link which assured survival of his extensive monastic federation. His cousin, King Aed, guaranteed at Druim Cett that the abbacy of Iona, head church of the entire federation, would forever be the heirloom of the Cenel Conaill branch of the N Ui Neill. The responsibility of protecting and patronizing Columcille's investments in Ireland was thus transferred from the weak to the strong, from the Dal Riata to the N Ui Neill. With the signing of this agreement Columcille had drawn the lines of contention. There was no longer any pretence of alliance between the N and S Ui Neill.[662] How then could there have been an Ui Neill High King of Ulster, let alone of all Ireland?

Armagh's good fortune was that the Ui Neill dynasty split into Northern and Southern factions, each seeking supremacy over the other. The Southern faction alienated itself from Columcille's monastic paruchiae. Adomnan, Columcille's successor in Iona, did his utmost to coax it within Columcille's monastic federation by ingratiating their war-lords with highfalutin political propaganda which had worked on the King of Northumbria whom he called High-King of Britain. He used similarly loaded language on the S Ui Neill, unashamedly claiming they "were ordained by God to be over-kings of all Ireland," the first time this idea was ever broached in Ireland. It was highly politicized propaganda dangled before the astonished Southern Ui Neill and well calculated to warm the hearts of these fierce warlords who were fighting for supremacy over their own kinsmen in the N and over the Cruthin of Ulster, but not over all Ireland. Would this subtle aggrandizing propaganda be heady enough to win over the patronage of the Southern Ui Neill as it had done with the King of Northumbria in the NE of England? With the wiley Muirchu waiting in the wings, could he rise to the occasion and out-cajole Adomnan?

---

[658] James Charles Roy, 'The Road Wet, The Wind Close - Celtic Ireland', p. 131
[659] Ibid, p. 131-5.
[660] Ibid, p. 131.
[661] Ibid, p. 135.
[662] Ibid, p. 135.

The logical strategy for the episcopal church of Armagh was to nail its fortunes to those of the S Ui Neill. How might it counteract the blatant overtures of Adomnan? How could it outdo the sophisticated propaganda of Columcille's monastic federation? What would win over the patronage of the S Ui Neill? Enter the wily Muirchu with his magical wand! If Adomnan could get away with such highfalutin propaganda, just watch Muirchu! This cunning cleric somehow, anyhow, by hook or by crook, would conjure up a subtly sophisticated scheming stew of sheer wizardry that would outscore and overawe the overtures of Adomnan and bowl over the S Ui Neill. In brewing up the most sophisticated political propaganda ever devised in their war of words to win over the hearts and minds of the Ui Neill potentates, Adomnan and Muirchu became inebriated by the exuberance of their own high-flown, bombastic and luxurious language which had no relation whatever to reality. In fact, all Ireland was bowled over and has still not recovered its senses. Muirchu rose to heights hitherto undreamt of in glorificatory propagandist flattery that set Ui Neill hearts aflutter. He enlisted the supernatural power of a Moses-like Patrick. Hitherto Patrick's cult was purely local in the Armagh and Downpatrick districts and embarrassingly associated with the defeated Cruthin isolated in the petty kingdom round Downpatrick. Muirchu would change all that and aggrandize Armagh. The Ui Neill had no previous association with Patrick, Armagh's founding father. Muirchu minted an Ui Neill connection to Patrick which was like a dream almost too good to be true. Move over Adomnan!

In 637 AD the Ui Neill defeated the Cruthin and won control of Tara district. Tara of Meath and Turoe of Galway share the same O-Irish name, *Temhair*. The *Rí Temhro* Overkings of the Fir Belg tribes who ruled from Turoe were ancestors of the Ui Neill. Turoe was a long-forgotten relic of the past. Muirchu re-opened this goldmine. Tara, in lieu of Emain Macha, became the seat of the overkings of the Cruthin. Muirchu wiped it clean of all its Cruthin associations and insinuated that the ancestors of the Ui Neill reigned there. He made Loeghuire, an alleged son of Niall, father founder of the Ui Neill Dynastly, reign at Tara as so-called High King of All Ireland when Patrick allegedly went there to begin his mission. The Loeguire of Tara, far from being a son of Niall, was a cousin of Conor Mac Nessa and ancestor of the Ui Loeghuire sept of the Tara and Trim districts whom Muirchu welded to the genealogical stem of Niall. Muirchu raised Tara to the level of ancient Babylon, and Patrick to the level of an all-conquering hero-prophet from the humble saint that he was. The confrontation between High King and Patrick is raised to the level of a Biblical drama at the court of King Nabuchodonazer.

To follow this embryonic fraud and understand its implications, one must analyze the work of Muirchu, Tirechan, Bishop Aed of Sletty, Ferdomnach and others on behalf of Armagh's monastic federation vis-a-vis that of the other monastic paruchiae of the day. One sees a glaring contrast between what Muirchu says about Patrick and Patrick says about himself in his 'Confessions'. The Armagh-minted Patrick replaced the real Patrick of the Confessions, just as Tara replaced Turoe, thanks to Muirchu's magic.

GREAT ARMAGH AND ITS HOST OF VENERABLE HEROES

'Great Armagh remains with a host of venerable heroes....
The name of Patrick, glorious, illustrious, this is the one which grows'.
(Prologue to 'The Martyrology of Oengus', c. 800 A D)

"The name of Patrick, glorious, illustrious, this is the one which grows". Grow it did, and grow and grow. The 'venerable heroes of Armagh' who fathered and perpetuated the phenomenal growth of the name of their newly minted 'Patrick' must be investigated. The twin myths, that of 'Patrick' and that of a 'High-Kingship of Ireland sited at Tara of Meath from time immemorial' are so inextricably intertwined as to form a single entity so tightly knit together that to undermine one would collapse the other. The Tara/Patrick Myth was conceived by those 'venerable heroes' of Armagh, Muirchu, author of 'Vita Patricii' (Life of Patrick), Tirechan, compiler of the 'Breviarum' (Brief Account of Patrick) and Co. In their 'History of the Irish Church 400 - 700 AD', Walsh and Bradley present pertinent personal information on them. They examine their writings and the light they and other relevant sources from the period, such as the infamous 'Liber Angeli' (Book of the Angel), throw on Patrick's association with Armagh and his role, significantly, not in the conversion of Ireland, but in that of Ulster.

MUIRCHU AND TIRECHAN

Muirchu moccu Machtheni was a priest of Armagh. Doherty noted that "Muirchu's tribal territory may have been an obscure Tuath Moctaine close to Armagh,"[663] a branch of the Airghialla. "Muirchu's biography (of Patrick), following the model of the 'Life of Martin', is coherent, polished and dramatic. He is particularly strong as a storyteller, his anecdotes are gripping, vivid and real. Steeped in the Bible, quoting often, he is widely read, slipping quotations into his narrative from Virgil, Sedulius and Ovid."[664] Muirchu compiled his 'Life of Patrick' at the insistence of Bishop Aed of Sletty (Co. Laois) who had affiliated his church to the Patrician church of Armagh when it was in danger of losing its independence between 661 and 668. Doherty offers good reason to believe that Muirchu's biography of Patrick was written after 668 when the retired Bishop Aed moved his residence to Armagh to be close to his co-conspirator, Muirchu, and where he died in 700.

Barring Cogitosus' 'Life of Brigit' c. 650, Muirchu's 'Life of Patrick' is the earliest example of Irish hagiography. In its own right it set a precedent, giving to this genre of Irish literature an utterly unenviable reputation. Muirchu was writing 200 years after the death of Patrick without any record of his activities and little else to rely on. Rather than being an obstacle, this was looked on as a blessing, allowing his lively imagination free reign to concoct a detailed 'Life of Patrick' full of gripping anecdotes which no one could gainsay. While Muirchu's 'Life of Patrick' was offered as a major document projecting a primary aspect of Armagh's 7th century agenda of ecclesiastical and political propaganda, it is a subtle cocktail of fiction and manipulated materials plundered from various sources. It was Armagh's answer to Adomnan's highly articulate political campaign on behalf of Columcille's monastic federation. Muirchu, following the example of Cogitosus whom he calls his 'father' in this genre,[665] regarded his biography of Patrick as a precedent. Walsh and Bradley claimed that "this (reference to Cogitosus as his father) can be viewed as a statement of gratitude for intellectual inspiration and the provision of a prototype."[666] What this 'inspiration and prototype' consisted of will be clarified as it had profound implications

---

[663] C. Doherty, 'The Cult of St. Patrick', in 'Ireland and Northern France' ed. Jean-Michel Picard, p. 82
[664] Op. Cit., p. 39.
[665] Walsh and Bradley, Ibid, p. 39 ('Preface ii').
[666] Ibid, p. 39.

in the development of Irish secular and ecclesiastical pseudo-history. For an insight into the nature of Muirchu's inspirational springboard to his monumental fraud one must isolate in Cogitosus' work what it was that most inspired Muirchu.

There is a "noticeable similarity" between the 'Life of St. Brigit' by Cogitosus and Muirchu's 'Life of Patrick' as J.F. Kenny noted. Cogitosus acknowledged that he was intellectually indebted to the author of an earlier piece of Continental hagiography, the 'Life of St. Samson'. Cogitosus' 'Life of Brigit' is one of the products of the 7th century scriptorium at Kildare's monastery which reflect its growing importance in the religious and secular life of Leinster. Works from this centre influenced Muirchu. It is a window which affords a peep into the social, political and ecclesiastical life of Ireland circa 650 AD, a preview of the type of claims Armagh would shortly make through Muirchu. Kildare was then making exorbitant claims of a secular and ecclesiastical nature. In his 'Life of Brigit', Cogitosus wrote that the Bishop of Kildare's double monastery, which he called the "Episcopal and Virginal See", is "Chief Bishop of all Irish Bishops" and its abbess is the "Abbess whom all the abbesses of the Irish venerate." Here was Muirchu's inspiration. This blatant expression of Kildare's expansionist ambitions was toned down later due to the harsh realities of the day. One can hear Muirchu mumble: "Well, if Kildare's Cogitosus can get away with such grossly inflated claims, why not Armagh's Muirchu?" This propagandist language promulgated by Kildare in 650 AD has close affinity to the hyper-ventilated claims to All-Ireland metropolitan hegemony Armagh made later the same century through Muirchu. Kildare did not persist long with its blatant claims. Armagh crowed louder and longer as it strutted on the stage of medieval history, drowning out Kildare. Armagh co-operated superbly, in a sophisticated manner, with its powerful patron, the burgeoning S Ui Neill dynasty, in making the expansionist ambitions of both a reality.

Kildare's ostentatious claims sparked Armagh's ambition under the influence of Bishop Aed of Sletty whose independent church was just then under severe pressure from Kildare. This is the meaning of Muirchu's acknowledgement of "gratitude for intellectual inspireation and the provision of a prototype." Hence his claim of Cogitosus as his literary 'father. Muirchu hijacked Kildare's metropolitan claims to put forward Armagh's claim to an All-Ireland metropolitan hegemony. It was necessary to flesh it out and give it substance as a measure of credence. To achieve this the patronage and support of the expanding Ui Neill dynasty, and the cumulative co-operation of coworkers such as Tirechan, were indispensable. Muirchu gained Ui Neill support by glorifying their war-lords in claiming that the Loeguire of Tara was the son of Niall of the Nine Hostages, and that he was the High-King of All Ireland when Patrick arrived there to begin his mission. He widened the scope of Armagh's claim to metropolitan hegemony by tying it to the claims to political and secular hegemony for its Ui Neill patron. To this end he built on the high-flown propagandist language of Adomnan, without acknowledging his gratitude for the intellectual inspiration thus provided. Events were unfolding which made Armagh feel it had more right to its claim than Kildare, although Armagh had entered the lists of monastic aggrandizement late in the day. Armagh and Patrick would grow at Kildare's expense, and at Columcille's, Adomnan's, Iona's and everyone's expense. Armagh expanded the prototypes provided by Cogitosus and Adomnan into a more broadly-based, mesmerizing and gripping claim than Kildare or Iona had ever dreamt of. His 'Life of Patrick' shows just how well the imaginative Muirchu was eminently capable of achieving this.

"Scholars have found it difficult to reconstruct Muirchu's 'Life of Patrick' because no complete manuscript survives." One suspects that the original version has been substantially modified and updated as it was being penned into the Book of Armagh by Ferdomnach, the Armagh scribe, at the beginning of the 9th century. Ferdomnach drastically censored the copy of Patrick's 'Confessions' he penned into the Book of Armagh, thinking it was the only copy in existence. Hence, nobody could gainsay him. He interpolated Muirchu's 'Life of Patrick' to meet contemporary 9th century circumstances. He was unaware of the existence of copies of the original of Patrick's 'Confessions' on the Continent that one day would explode the Tara/Patrick Myth by exposing the blatantly odious nature of his censorship, and the underhand manner in which Armagh was prepared to treat the real Patrick to make way for its newly-minted glorified Patrick. One's suspicions are sharpened when one learns of Ferdomnach's lame excuses for not recording Patrick's second work, the 'Epistola' (Letter to Coroticus) and replacing it by blatant spurious material fathered on Patrick. One is convinced that both Ferdomnach and Armagh had ulterior motives for deliberately suppressing the entire Letter to Coroticus which he claimed he 'forgot' to record. That he still failed to record it after this omission and negligence was pointed out provides every reason to believe that Ferdomnach would have no hesitation in eschewing or concocting material which went into the Book of Armagh, whether from Patrick, Muirchu or Tirechan, for the most favourable articulation of Armagh's contemporary ambitious agenda. Muirchu's 'Life of Patrick' gives more historical facts about the circumstances of the late 7th and 8th centuries than it does about Patrick and his times. It must be examined against the secular and ecclesiastical background against which it was written. Doherty noted: "For historians of early Ireland the 7th century is a watershed." It was an era of tumultuous change and massive upheaval. For Early Irish History it was the beginning of the end, the dawn of Pseudo-History. Muirchu, Ferdomnach and Armagh agents laid the foundation stone upon which was built the enduring edifice of Pseudo-History.

C. Doherty created "a picture of developments since the introduction of Christianity in the 5th century. When the struggle of the church for survival was past it became possible for churchmen to turn their attention to more worldly matters. As a means of establishing the rights and prerogatives of their respective churches some clergy became more interested in the history of the church, particularly their own, during the course of the 7th century. Some monastic schools in the forefront had been successful in attracting the patronage of major dynasties."[667] Armagh picked a winner in the potent Southern Ui Neill Dynasty. The 7th century was a watershed for the declining petty tribal kingdoms and their churches which were being swallowed up by the burgeoning dynastic powers. These churches of the now insignificant subject peoples found themselves being fiercely fought over and being put under powerful political pressure from the major monastic federations who were engaged in cutthroat competition and aggressive aggrandizement.

"It is clear that major monasteries such as Clonmacnoise and Iona were building up their paruchiae by taking over old independent, or non-aligned, churches of the missionary period. Many of these were among peoples who were, by the 7th century, politically weak or irrelevant, even though some may have been dominant in the 5th century when a church had first been established in their territory."[668] Doherty noted: *"The rise of Armagh to ecclesiastical dominance was certainly stimulated by the problems of the churches in the midlands and Leinster. It is evident that free independent bishoprics, some founded by the Gaulish mission (led by Palladius) found themselves under threat by the 7th century. The petty 'tuatha' or tribes of which they were a part were now in political decline. New dynasties favoured their own churches. Churches without powerful patrons were in danger of being absorbed into the paruchiae of major monasteries. They needed protection."[669]*

---

[667] Charles Doherty,'The Cult of St. Patrick and the Politics of Armagh in the 7th Century', ed. by Jean-Michel Picard in 'Ireland and Northern France 600 - 850 A D. p.53.

[668] Ibid, p. 65-66.

[669] Ibid, p. 73.

Here Armagh came into its own. On the back of the Roman party in the Paschal controversy and the consequent defeat of the Columcille (Columban) federation of monasteries Armagh leap-frogged into the breach on the national stage on which it strutted throughout the medieval period crowing down the fighting cocks of all the major monasteries. It claimed to be the champion of these endangered independent churches. It projected itself as their God-sent national hero and saviour. Having almost shared the same fate as many of these which were taken over by the major monasteries, Armagh understood their plight and was more acceptable to them, before it became too almighty arrogant.

The Airghialla controlled Armagh. They were in alliance with the expanding Ui Neill dynasty, a 5th century offshoot of the Connacht dynasty. With the massive defeat of the Ulster Cruthin at the battle of Magh Roth (Co. Down) in 637/639 the Airghialla entertained grossly inflated ambitions for territorial overlordship. During the remainder of the 7th century they enjoyed a period of independence alongside their erstwhile Ui Neill allies until 827 when they were subjected to the Ui Neill. Doherty notes that during the time of independence "the surge of Armagh to the fore must surely be due, in no small measure, to the political patronage of the Airghialla during the course of the 7th century and to the fact that Armagh's Airghiallan clergy were astute politicians".[670] The history of Armagh from this time forward shows that she began to take the initiative among the northern churches and strove vigorously for pre-eminence. All too aware of the rising power of the Ui Neill, Armagh set itself the task of weaning away the S Ui Neill warlords from the Columban monastic federation to Armagh's Patrician federation of churches. Armagh knew that thus she was in the best position to play the politico-ecclesiastical game to her advantage. The Cruthin stronghold of Downpatrick had been the major centre of Patrick's cult in Ireland. It is not without significance that Armagh, controlled by the Airghialla, suddenly assumed the leadership of the Patrician cult, albeit that of its own newly-minted Patrick, taking over the role of the Cruthin following their massive defeat at the battle of Moira. It did so soon after Kildare's aborted attempt to assume ecclesiastical hegemony.

Old churches (*senchell*) which retained the link with Roman Christianity through Palladius' Gallo-Roman mission found it convenient to look to the growing cult of Patrick dressed up as Roman. They were led to believe that Palladius and Patrick were one and the same man sent by Rome to christianize Ireland and were discreetly directed to rationalize the situation by joining Armagh's federation of churches. Notes supplementary to Tirechan's 'Breviarum' insinuate that "Pope Celestin first sent Bishop Palladius, who was Patricius by another name." Armagh, struggling for the control of the cult of Patrick, was only too willing to develop this propaganda. The paruchia of Armagh expanded as old independent churches in Connacht and Leinster looked to her for protection in the course of the 7th century. Much of the rivalry among major churches in the 7th century was over the question of rights over independent non-aligned churches. Against this background Armagh evolved from being an episcopal church towards one that was monastic with a far-flung paruchia and eventually embraced the whole island.[671]

MUIRCHU, BISHOP AED AND THE SLETTY SYNDROME

F. J. Byrne, Kim McCone[672] and C. Doherty[673] present this process in action as can be seen most clearly in the case of Sletty (Sleibhte, a mile NW of Carlow town, but in Co. Laois). Muirchu wrote his 'Life of Patrick' at the behest of Bishop Aed maccu Brocain (of the Ui Bairrche) of Sletty. In the 'Additamenta' to Tirechan's 'Collectanea' in the Book of Armagh

---

[670] Ibid, p. 68.

[671] Charles Doherty, Ibid, p. 74.

[672] Kim McCone, 'Pagan Past And Christian Present in Early Irish Literature', p. 242-243, 245.

[673] Charles Doherty, Ibid, p. 75.

there is a document telling that Bishop Aed went to Armagh during the abbacy of Segene (661-668) and offered his church and kin to Patrick (Armagh) for ever. What lay behind this move by Aed? Why were the facts of history manipulated to accommodate it by the concoction of a fictitious episode? This blatantly transferred the glory of the conversion of the Southern Laighin, the consecration of their first bishop, Fiacc, and the foundation of Sletty, from the Continental Bishop Iserninus to Patrick who never set foot there.

The answer to these questions presents a classic example which exhibits the politico-ecclesiastical propaganda game being played by Armagh. One catches a glimpse in this episode of the methods of Muirchu as he and Armagh's other agent, Tirechan, elongated Patrick posthumously the length and breadth of Ireland, aggrandizing Armagh and Tara in the process as they laid the foundation stone of Irish Pseudo-History. The Carlow/Laois branch of the Ui Bairrche who dominated the area were being squeezed out and put under severe pressure by the later Northern Laigin. In desperation, with their church in danger of being swallowed up by Kildare, they turned to Armagh which jumped at the opportunity to become their saviour. The facts of history were manipulated to justify this move and confer on it a veneer of permanence to satisfy the aims of both parties concerned.

Sletty's bishop, Aed, went to Armagh to offer it his bequest before the death of its abbot Segene in 668. Later he retired as anchorite to Armagh where died in 700, after providing invaluable information of the circumstances in SE Ireland, not least of Kildare's high-handed methods, to Armagh's agents, notably Muirchu. His successor and grandnephew, Conchad, died as bishop of Sletty in 692. Conchad ratified Aed's agreement with Armagh by personally submitting to its new abbot, Flann Feblae. "It was the presence of Conchad in Armagh that provided the stimulus for Aed (in Armagh) to engage Muirchu in the work" of writing the blatantly manipulated biography of Patrick".[674] Aed and Muirchu became bosom friends. Together they attended the Synod of Birr in 697 which brought the Paschal Problem to its conclusion. Armagh, glowing in the victory of its pro-Roman stance, made known its 'God-given' role as saviour of Independent churches, with Aed's Sletty bequest before their eyes as an awe-inspiring example to follow. After Armagh's success at this Synod, Muirchu put the final touches to his 'Life of Patrick'. One is led to believe that Ferdomnach 'upgraded' the original with his own deft touches to accommodate contemporary 9th century political circumstances and developments as he penned its earliest-known copy into the Book of Armagh.

Sletty, chief church of the Ui Bairrche (Brigantes), was still powerful in S Leinster in the previous century. Early in the 2nd half of the 7th century the Ui Bairrche were under severe pressure from the Ui Chennselaigh and the dominant Ui Dunlaing of N Leinster. The latter were supporting the claims of Kildare to All-Ireland metropolitan status by the mid 7th century before Aed persuaded Muirchu to hijack that claim for Armagh. "In turning to Armagh, the Church of Sletty was outflanking her traditional enemies in an attempt to maintain some independence."[675] This episode encouraged Armagh and its mentors, Muirchu and Tirechan, to effect similar transactions elsewhere in Armagh's favour. It set its community agog, its ambitions soaring. It set Muirchu's imagination on fire.

Bishop Aed mac Borrachain of the Ui Bairrche was a mine of information on Leinster and S Ireland which Armagh exploited. Pertinent information regarding the churches founded by Isserninus and other pre-Patrician Gallo-Roman missionaries who came in the train of Palladius was readily available from Aed at Armagh where it was mulled over and manipulated as in the case of Sletty. Mac Neill claimed Isserninus worked in central

[674] Charles Doherty, Ibid, p. 78
[675] Charles Doherty, Op. Cit. p. 78.

Leinster ranging N from Sletty. His main church was Ahade in Carlow. Isserninus was closely associated with the Dal Cormaic, a sept of the Ui Bairrche who dwelt in S Kildare and the vicinity of Carlow town.[676] Their churches were under the authority of Sletty. Those people among whom Isserninus laboured were exiled by Crimthann, the ancestor of the Ui Chennselaig, "for believing before everyone else" (a reference to their early conversion). The fictitious entry in the 'Additamenta' in the Book of Armagh,[677] claimed that Patrick, having baptized Crimthann, besought him to allow Isserninus and the Dal Cormaic to return to their lands. Here Aed and his Armagh agents are caught in the act of concocting Patrick's alleged baptism of Crimthann in order to forge a fictitious devious link to the Ui Chennselaig. "This link with Patrick would have suited the Ui Cennselaig whose rivals for the control of the province, the Ui Dunlainge, were dominant in Kildare. The Sletty formula was used to admit the churches of Isserninus to the 'paruchia' of Armagh."[678] This forged link served the double purpose of boosting Armagh's ambitions while delivering the knockout punch to Kildare's claim to metropolitan hegemony. With this magic formula Armagh began to quickly mount the metropolitan pedestal.

The newly minted Patrick is a far cry from the humble saint of the 'Confessio'. He is hewn into a hero fit to stand alongside the great Biblical heroes or those of Celtic secular saga. He orders kings to obey his wishes and becomes a national saviour, not only for his contemporaries, but for those converted long before he set foot in Ireland as a missionary, and for 7th century independent churches under pressure from major monasteries and dynasties. Muirchu converted his monumental fraud into a gripping epic to rival that of the old Celtic hero tales. One gets a taste of the drama to come in Muirchu's prologue to his 'Life of Patrick' addressed to his patron, Bishop Aed of Sletty. "I have my little talent, a boy's paddle-boat as it were, out on this deep and perilous sea of sacred narrative, where waves boldly swell to towering heights among rocky reefs in unknown waters, on which so far no boat has ventured except the one of my 'father', Cogitosus."[679] This prologue addressed to Aed was written before Aed's death in 700 AD. Thus Muirchu declares that no one had written about Patrick before him. He, then, under Aed of Sletty, must take full credit for minting the new Patrick, and take full responsibility for laying the foundation of the hoax of Irish pseudo-history, the infamous Tara/Patrick Myth that substituted Patrick for Palladius and Isserninus. Aed and Muirchu were among Ireland's pioneer pseudo-historians who took medieval Ireland by storm and hold all Ireland in thrall.

Muirchu's narrative goes into greatest detail for his home area around Armagh, Antrim and the N Down area of Slemish, Saul, Downpatrick and churches around Strangford Lough. Colman mac Murchon, Abbot of Magh mBili (Moville in Down) who died in 763 was Muirchu's son. Doherty noted that the cult of Patrick, through the evidence of Colman and Muirchu, in its earlier stages was located in the area between Slemish in Antrim and Louth - the key churches being Saul and Downpatrick, denoting the heartland of Patrick's working ministry. Initially, Armagh attempted to define the territory within which she assumed leadership of Patrick's cult to the exclusion of Saul and Downpatrick in the territory of her political enemies. Armagh assigned Muirchu to link Patrick intimately to these areas and peoples he knew best. "The essential task of Muirchu was to harmonize relations between Armagh and the cult of Patrick at Downpatrick and Saul (enemy territory). He is the one who mends the rift in the cult. With harmony within the home territories, the ultimate success of the cult of the national Apostle with his seat at Armagh was assured"[680] Muirchu

---

[676] Eoin MacNeill, 'St. Patrick', p. 122-126.

[677] 'Additamenta', 12, 1-8, p. 174-176.

[678] Charles Doherty, Op. cit., p. 78.

[679] Muirchu maccu Mocteine, 'Vita Patricii', Prologue 2, p. 63, in Charles Doherty's art., Op. cit. p. 83.

[680] Charles Doherty, Op. cit. p. 94.

declared that the area which Patrick loved most, apart from Armagh, was Mag nInish, the barony of Lecale in which Downpatrick stands. There was a strong admixture of Ui Bairrche, kinsmen of Aed's tribe at Sletty, stretching from Downpatrick to the Mourne Mts. (Benna Boirche after the Ui Bairrche). Muirchu concocted a legend that it was there that Patrick had his first convert, Dichu at Saul, an episode designed to link Patrick to the ancestor of the family which controlled Saul in the 7th century, but not in Patrick's day. Dichu was of the Dal Fiata who now controled the churches of Saul, Downpatrick, Nendrum, Moville, and Kilclief around Strangford Lough.

Muirchu felt obliged to fabricate an elaborate account of Patrick's death and burial to hide Armagh's embarrassment at not having his tomb. He explained why he did not die there but at Saul and was interred at Downpatrick in the heartland of the Cruthin of Ulster who were confined there following the fall of Emain Macha. Patrick founded his original church at Armagh near Ulster's Cruthin Capital, Emain Macha, before the Cruthin were driven E of the Bann and Loch Neagh by the Airghialla. Patrick, the apostle of the Cruthin, fled with them to Saul and Downpatrick. Muirchu built up Patrick into a Moses-like hero replete with burning bush. He told that when Patrick tried to go to Armagh, "the place he loved more than any other," the Angel Victor appeared in a burning bush on his route and sent another angel to tell him to return to Saul. When Patrick died his body was placed on a cart yoked to untamed oxen. They halted at Downpatrick where he was buried - a Biblical motif borrowed from the earlier 'Life of Foillan' on the Continent. There was a lively correspondence between the Continental monasteries of Foillan and Ultan, and Armagh in the time of Muirchu. In another episode Muirchu is once again caught attempting to win over the churches of the Ui Chonaill. He alleged that the oxen which pulled the cart carrying Patrick's body were specially chosen "from a place called Clocher, east of Findhabhair (near Downpatrick) from the cattle of Conall, ancestor of the Ui Chonaill. As Doherty noted, "while this may seem an obscure location, it is exactly in line with Muirchu's efforts to include local families of the Saul and Downpatrick area as with his mention of the family of Dichu." Muirchu was a master in the art of winning unsuspecting peoples and churches from the clutches of major monasteries.

Muirchu spun a tale to create a semblance of credence alleging flames of fire sprung from the earth above Patrick's grave when workmen attempted to dig the foundation of a church. The message was clear. The Cruthin of E Ulster around Downpatrick would not allow the grave of their apostle to be desecrated. Muirchu was at pains to prevent war between the Cruthin and Airghiallian/Ui Neill alliance over the remains of Patrick. He was anxious to prevent a split in the widening federation of Patrician monasteries across the lands of these warring peoples. He indicates that there had recently been warlike attempts instigated by the Ui Neill and their allies, the Airthir of Armagh, against the Cruthin to gain possession of Patrick's remains. It would have been a powerful boon to Armagh and to the Airthir who provided its abbots at this period to possess Patrick's remains. When one considers the 7th century obsession with relics, one can understand how readily these parties were prepared to go to war over the remains of Patrick. The Southern Ui Neill had just adopted Patrick as their patron saint and so were obliged to give mutual support to Armagh which they had been subtly lured into patronizing. The Cruthin of Ulster were ready to fight to the last for their beloved apostle, Patrick, who stayed with them through thick and thin and had taken permanent abode among them. The Airthir ('most easterly' vassals) who attempted to steal Patrick's remains occupied the area around Armagh, controlled its monastery and monopolized its abbatial office in the late 7th century. Had they succeeded in bringing Patrick's remains to Armagh, Muirchu would have provided gripping annecdotes, replete with miracles to convince the world that it was there Patrick died. The Annals of Ulster at 618 recall "the incursion of Armagh" which, Doherty says, reflects the struggle for the control of its church in the early 7th century and for the control of the cult of Patrick. The attempted invasion of Armagh, before the defeat of the Cruthin at Moira, represents a late attempt by the Cruthin to recapture their ancient stronghold. It gave the Ui Neill/Airghiallian alliance an excuse for the battle of Moira and for the attempted theft of the remains of Patrick in Downpatrick. At this time the Cruthin were making incursions deep into parts of Ulster which formerly belonged to them to recapture lost territory.

Tirechan ingeniously established a direct link to Patrick for the Airthir, although they were far from Armagh and Patrick, when he established his original church there. Muirchu, unwilling to be upstaged by anyone, even by Tirechan, established a far more ingenious and illustrious link to Patrick for the Ui Neill although they were much further from Armagh at the time Patrick was active there. Tirechan felt it more natural to allow Loeghuire, fictitious son of the Ui Neill ancestor Niall, so-called High-King of Ireland at Tara when Patrick allegedly visited him there, to refuse baptism by Patrick, preferring to die a pagan like his ancestors. Muirchu, on the other hand, made doubly sure that he had Loeghuire himself and early Ui Neill dynasts and their families baptized personally by Patrick. He was not going to pass up this golden opportunity to forge a glorious link to Patrick for this dynasty of all others which he was determined to win over to the cause of Armagh and Patrick. Patrick may well have baptized members of the early Ui Neill dynasty before they expanded from Donegal and Tyrone where they were settled in the NW of Ireland in Patrick's time. The Loeguire of Tara whom Muirchu fictionalized into Laoghaire, son of Niall, was ancestor of the Cruthin Ui Loeguire sept of Tara who were bitter enemies of the Ui Neill in Patrick's time. Muirchu's 'Life of Patrick' implies that Patrick's history is intimately tied up with the decline of the Cruthin, the ancient dominant people of Ulster, and the triumph of the Ui Neill. Muirchu was a superbly shrewd politician and, according to K. Hughes, a supreme realist too. As such he was intent on acknowledging and glorifying the contemporary superiority of the Ui Neill in his own day to whom he linked Patrick so intimately. Yet he was extremely careful not to dissociate him from the Cruthin of Ulster, enemies of the Ui Neill. After the massive defeat of the Cruthin in 637 by the Ui Neill/Airghiallan alliance, the Ui Neill were now in control of most of former Cruthin Ulster and North Leinster, including Tara. The geo-political map of Ireland had radically altered.

Muirchu's 'Life of Patrick' reaches its climax at Tara. In order to cement the Ui Neill link with Patrick, Muirchu felt obliged to backdate the fall of the Tara district to the Ui Neill from the 7th century to before the time of Patrick in the early 5th century. During the following centuries Armagh pushed the conquest of Tara by the ancestors of the Ui Neill further and further back in time. Muirchu made Tara the royal seat of Loeguire, anachronistically making him 'King of the Irish' and fictitiously welding him genealogically to the line of Niall of the Nine Hostages, ancestor of the Ui Neill dynasty. Muirchu took up the idea of High-Kingship, invented by Adomnan for both the King of Northumbria and an Ui Neill warlord in seeking their patronage for Columcille's monastic federation. Muirchu carried it a step further, calling Loeguire, 'son of Niall', 'High-King of the Irish'. He forged the meeting between Patrick and the High King of Ireland at Tara. He concocted the baptism of High-King Loeguire and his followers for the sake of establishing a fabulous link which glorified both Patrick and the Ui Neill. The implication was that the Ui Neill were obliged to claim Patrick as their patron saint. It is in no small measure due to Muirchu's flattery that the Ui Neill fell for his bait. Armagh found itself patronized by the now most aggressive secular power in Ireland. Muirchu's meticulous manufacture of motifs as links to Patrick and subtle manipulation of secular and Biblical history to boost his so-called High-Kingship brewed the potent cocktail of Irish pseudo-history. It went straight to the hearts of the Irish. "The highlight of Muirchu's biography is undoubtedly the confrontation between Patrick and High-King Loeguire at Tara."[681]

---

[681] Charles Doherty, Ibid, p. 86.

Borrowing from the Book of Daniel,[682] Muirchu modeled his drama on Nebuchadnezzar's court, comparing Tara to Babylon. The scene is dramatic. Patrick, having arrived in the vicinity of Tara, lit the Paschal Fire on the Hill of Slane. The pagan Irish had a festival that same night. No one could light a fire before one had been lit in the King's house. Patrick upstaged the High-King by lighting the Pascal Fire before the King's own cult-fire was lit. He was brought before the King. A dramatic confrontation follows. For Muirchu's 7th century audience this was so arranged as to have supercharged implications and ramifycations on a number of levels as the Pascal controversy had reached a climatic stage. It was built into a dramatic confrontation between the power and light of Christianity and the darkness of paganism. It was a grossly exaggerated facelift for Tara which could not be called a city, let alone be compared to Biblical Babylon. Dressed out as a grandiose royal palace for the so-called High-Kingship, it was elevated to a level of significance which neither it nor its kings had ever known. The Iron Age glory accredited to Tara was plundered from ancient Turoe of Galway, seat of the well-known Rí Temhro, such as Eochaid Felech, Conn, Art and Cormac mac Art, ancestors of the Ui Neill dynasts. In a supreme effort to win over the S Ui Neill to Armagh's cause, Muirchu grew intoxicated with his Tara/Patrick Myth as he had earlier done with his magic Sletty formula, satisfying all sides concerned at the expense of the truth. The Ui Neill became even more obsessed by the idea of High-Kingship although it was still no more than a hallucinating dream. Armagh saw the aggressive Ui Neill warlords, as they saw themselves, the most likely dynasty to make this dream come true. They set this as their future agenda.

Armagh's 'venerable heroes' were adept in the art of flattering those whom they wished to win over, be they meek like Sletty or mighty like the Ui Neill. Armagh's assertively sophisticated propaganda blitz had succeeded in gaining a patron and ally like no other monastic federation had, i.e., the warlording S Ui Neill dynasty, the most aggressive and expansive secular power in Ireland from the 7th to the 9th century. She could now coast to new conquests by riding on the back of this burgeoning dynasty as new territories and their churches came under its sway. An example of one such roughshod ride in monastic empire building is found in the Ui Neill overrunning of the midland area in which the monastery of Rahan stood. Abbot Carrthach Mo-Chutu of Munster origin was expelled. He founded the monastery of Lismore in the lands of the Desi. Ui Neill appointed Abbots usurped his place at Rahan and Armagh Abbots ruled there henceforth. Thus many other churches came under the sway of Armagh. As Ui Neill warlords won more sword-land, Armagh's monastic federation grew apace. While Muirchu ruled the roost, the Cruthin of Ulster become isolated in Co. Down, surrounded by the Dal Riata and Airghiallan buffer states subordinate to Ui Neill warlords fighting to expand in all directions.

The Paschal Fire episode and deliberate choice of Easter for the dramatic confrontation between Patrick and the alleged Ui Neill High-King of Ireland at Tara was another subtly loaded motif introduced by Muirchu which must be read against the background of the paschal controversy then raging. During the course of the 7th century it built up into an acrimonious climax. Armagh aligned itself with Rome against the stance of the Columban monastic federation. Again it backed the winner. It is uniquely against this background that one can appreciate Armagh's over-eagerness to concoct the alleged visit of Patrick to Rome to boost its Roman link in this bitter controversy. Armagh's deepest ambition was to win Rome's approval of its new claim to be the metropolitan church of all Ireland. As part of this self-canonizing process it had to go to the extreme limits of glorifying itself through a glorified Patrick to be successful. As Armagh's mouthpiece, Muirchu exploited archaic secular and ecclesiastical history to under-pin her aggrandizement. He flattered Bishop Aed of Sletty, his patron, and won Leinster support for Armagh. He invented the episode

---

[682] Book of Daniel, 2,2; 3,2-3.

alleging that the pagan 5th century Leinster poet, Dubthach moccu Lugir, was the only man to rise before Patrick as he entered the banqueting hall at Tara, and that he was the first to believe in God. Muirchu manipulated historical information gleaned from Aed of Sletty by alleging that Dubthach had with him a boy called Fiach who afterwards was consecrated first bishop of Sletty by Patrick. Doherty noted: "Here again the link between Patrick and an allied church was further cemented using the familiar formula." Muirchu alleged that the pre-Patrician Leinster bishops, Auxilius, Iserninus and Secundinus, were conferred with lower orders on the day Patrick was consecrated bishop and were sent by Rome as his helpers, although they had come in the train of Palladius a whole generation before Patrick's missionary work began. And so "The name of Patrick, this is the one which grows" while all others were made to rise and bend the knee before him like Dubthach.

Muirchu minted a blatantly bombastic claim: In return for his obedient retreat to Saul to die the Angel told Patrick that 4 requests made by him to God were granted, that (1) his pre-eminence would be in Armagh, (2) whoever recites his hymn on his death-bed will have his sins judged by Patrick, (3) the descendants of Dichu shall not perish, and (4) Patrick will judge all the Irish on the Day of Judgement. This developed into the full-fledged 'Liber Angeli' (Book of the Angel), carrying a much wider, politically-loaded message. One stands aghast at the audacity of Muirchu. It is abhorrent to imagine the humble Patrick[683] demanding the usurpation of the role of God at such a critical moment, a reason why the 'Confession' of Patrick had to be so drastically censored when copied into the Book of Armagh by Ferdomnach. "The message of Muirchu is clear. Patrick was bishop of all Ireland by beginning his missionary campaign from Tara, Armagh was firmly allying with the Ui Neill dynasty, the most powerful in the country in the late 7th century. By emphasizing her 'Roman' status she was indicating a special relationship with the oldest churches in the country and by proclaiming her orthodoxy on the Easter Question she could gain the support of the southern churches. All traditions of independent missionaries, or independent bishoprics, were brought within the cult of Patrick by making them subordinate to him, or by bringing them into association with him."[684]

In his 'Aggrandizement of Armagh'[685] Liam de Paor remarked that her activities among the midland churches are relevant as being part and parcel of Armagh's agenda of subordination of earlier missionary bishops to Patrick. The most remarkable aspect of Armagh's rise to power is the interest taken in the cult of Patrick by the midland churches as cultivated by Armagh. This can be seen in the ascription of the most famous medieval hymn in honour of Patrick, the 'Audite Omnes' to the pre-Patrician missionary from the Continent, Secundinus, whose name is preserved in Dunshaughlin (Domnach Sechnaill in Meath). In a marginal gloss to a reference to this hymn in the notes supplementary to Tirechan's work in the Book of Armagh the poem was originally ascribed to Colman Elo (+ 611). Scholars have now debunked Armagh's anachronistic ascription to the early 5th century Secundinus, agreeing that it was written in the early 7th century by Bishop Colman Elo. Colman came from the Dal nAraidi branch of the Cruthin of Ulster who vigorously claimed Patrick as their Apostle. Leaving his home at Lough Neagh near Slemish in Antrim he founded a church for a Cruthin enclave at Lynally SW of Durrow in Offaly. Though far removed territorially, it maintained a close klink with the Church of Connor in his Ulster home territory, sharing the same abbots for centuries. He brought the cult of Patrick to this region at the turn of the 6th/7th century. He also visited the Picts of Scotland, kinsmen of the Ulster Cruthin. He called on Columcille at Iona, an embarrassment to Armagh. The 'Vita Colmani' calls him the second patron of Connor. Coming from the heartland of 'Patrick country', a poet to wit,

---

[683] St. Patrick, *'Ego Patricius'*, 'The Confession' of St Patrick.

[684] Charles Doherty, Ibid, p. 88.

[685] Liam de Paor, 'Aggrandisement of Armagh', p. 101

it is apt that he should have written a hymn in honour of Patrick. Professor Carney has pointed out the similarity between this poem and others attributed to Colman.[686] Another bodyblow to Armagh's Tara/Patrick Myth! Armagh purposely ascribed this hymn to the 5th century Continental missionary, Secundinus, as part of its agenda of subordination of early missionary bishops to Patrick. "Given the close connection between Armagh and Domnach Sechnaill, the ascription to Secundinus must belong to a literary package created during the 7th centuries when relations between the two churches were being established."[687] If Armagh's 'venerable heroes' were prepared to treat sacred history thus, then what were they not prepared to do, and how far were they not prepared to go, with secular history?

The Cruthin were in no doubt about the authorship of the hymn 'Audite Omnes'. It was held in great veneration in Colman's own church in Lynally as reflected in his 'Lives' and among the Ulster Cruthin. Unlike Armagh, they gave Patrick the highest respect as reflected in this hymn. Nothing was too sacred for Armagh's ambassadors, Muirchu, Tirechan and their successors, to manipulate for their own ulterior motives. Colman's hymn with its Roman and Apostolic flavour neatly fits into the pontificate of Pope Gregory the Great - the Pope most admired by the Irish - which provides a fitting background to the general sentiment expressed therein. The Patrick it portrays is not the arrogant, proud, saga-like hero of Muirchu and later hagiographers, but one who breathes the spirit of the humble, gentle, saintly Patrick of the 'Confession'. Certain linguistic phrases of the hymn lent themselves to being exploited by Armagh's hagiographers. In terms of 7th century religious ecclesiastical mentality the hymn elevated Patrick to 'Apostolic' status, making him, like St. Paul, an apostle to the gentiles, not of all Ireland. Where this noble sentiment left itself open to the kind of abuse to which Armagh subjected it was in the last stanza where it suggested that, as a reward of his immense labour, Patrick would reign, like the Apostles over Israel (in the Biblical sense). This exalted sentiment sparked Armagh's imagination to claim the Angel granted Patrick's exorbitant request that he judge all the Irish on the Day of Judgement because "all had been given to him by God." The hymn's description of Patrick as the Gospel-light on a candlestand to give light to all sparked Muirchu's fiction of shafts of brilliant light shining from Patrick's fingertips

TIRECHAN

Muirchu worked his own NE of Ulster where Patrick had been most active. Tirechan trekked Meath and the NW of Ireland, notably his home area of N Connacht, as far as time, political and ecclesiastical constraints permitted. Tirechan was a native of Tirawley in N Mayo, coming from Caille Conaill between Lackan and Rathfran Bays, a sept of the N Connacht dynasty of Ui Fiachrach which took the side of the N Ui Neill in a bitter alliance opposed to the ruling Ui Briuin dynasty. Tirechan was a disciple of Ultan, Bishop of Ardbraccan in Meath, then under Armagh's sway. Under Ultan's tutelage, he was imbued with prevalent Armagh propaganda and with the Sletty mode of monastic aggrandizement. Tirechan assertively made the transparently anachronistic claim alleging that his own area of N Mayo had been incorporated into Armagh's federation of Patrician churches in Patrick's day. The idea of a federation of churches did not exist in Patrick's day under the old Roman diocesan system. It belonged to the unique ecclesiastical circumstances of the 7th century monastic church of Tirechan's day. That did not deter Tirechan. By devil's hook or bishop's crook he would give his local church a respectable pedigree linked to Patrick and Armagh. As a Connachtman he emphasized Patrick's alleged missionary labours in that area. He went to great efforts to link churches, especially in N Connacht which he knew best, to Patrick and projected Armagh as saviour of churches of petty tribes in danger of losing their independence, bringing them under Armagh's wing.

---

[686] Professor James Carney, 'The Problem of St. Patrick', p. 40-46.
[687] Charles Doherty, Ibid, p, 88.

Tirechan's work is not a Life of Patrick but a record of Patrick's alleged activities. He begins by recounting Patrick's Irish captivity and his escape. Patrick's alleged travels through Gaul and Italy are plundered from the life of Palladius and are basic to the latter's confounding with Patrick. Tirechan, abetted by Ferdomnach, fused Palladius and Patrick by having one believe that Palladius was also known as Patricius. He made Patrick and his alleged retinue of subordinate Gaulish bishops arrive at an island off the Dublin coast. Patrick went to Tara. His first baptism, unlike that of Muirchu's account, is that of the infant Benignus, whom he there and then appoints as his 'heir', as Patrick's successor in the church of Armagh.

Why this contradiction between Muirchu and Tirechan regarding Patrick's first baptism? Both wrote specifically for home consumption within their respective areas and addressed their work accordingly. Muirchu's work was aimed at his home area in NE Ireland and Ui Neill dynasts. Tirechan wrote for the Ui Fiachra dynasts and their allies in his home area of N Connacht and for the Cruthin churches of the Croghan district of Roscommon which were in danger of being swallowed up by the advancing Ui Briuin and the monastery of Clonmacnoise. When their works were copied into the Book of Armagh some two centuries later they became public property on a national scale. However, as will be seen, neither did Armagh nor her Ui Neill patrons attempt to press their exorbitant claims such as the alleged Ui Neill High-Kingship of Ireland or Armagh's metropolitan hegemony on the other provinces even as much as a century later. It was solely for home consumption. This is strikingly transparent. Tirechan focused on Benignus and his alleged baptism and immediate nomination by Patrick as his successor at Armagh since Benignus was an early Connacht Bishop. This was a blatant attempt on the part of Tirechan to link Connacht intimately with Armagh by means of Benignus. The message is clear: Connacht should follow its first Bishop Benignus and throw in its lot with Armagh. After this attempt to woo Connacht into Armagh's arms, Tirechan related the alleged arrangements made by Patrick regarding the foundation of churches in Meath. Patrick is then brought to Tara for the dramatic encounter with the alleged High-King Loeguire who, Tirechan claimed, refused baptism in contrast to Muirchu. Both had their ulterior motives for alleging that High-King Loeguire refused baptism from Patrick (Tirechan) or received baptism from Patrick (Muirchu). In a matter of such importance for the conversion of Ireland one would have expected Armagh's two 'venerable heroes' to have agreed on this crucial point. Both were writing for different ulterior motives. The fictitious acts attributed by both to Patrick were solely for home consumption within their respective territories.

Following the well-established Continental hagiographical model, in the form of an 'itenerarium', Tirechan led Patrick on a circuit, first of the North and then of the South of Ireland. The latter was cut short by the death of Tirechan and to await better accounts of 5th century Munster's geo-politics and history to manipulate them in favour of Armagh. Tirechan forged a Patrick founding churches and appointing clergy in places where the real Patrick never set foot. He imbibed this ruse from Ultan, following the model of Continental pseudo-hagiography which had not long before done a similar elongation of Martin of Tours, dragging him posthumously to places he had never visited all over France. As part of the process of subordinating all missionary bishops to Patrick and confounding him with Palladius, Tirechan made Patrick appoint bishops as he moved from place to place, including Gallo-Roman missionary bishops in the retinue of Palladius commissioned by Pope Celestin a generation before Patrick's day. This approach of employing the 'itinerary' or 'circuit' proved highly appealing in Ireland, as it had done on the Continent in similar circumstances. There was a much-loved native oral, and later written, literature about famous places of interest, the well-known '*Dindshenchas*'.[688]

---

[688] Charles Doherty, Ibid, p. 56.

To concoct his record of the missionary journeys of Patrick, Tirechan stopped off at churches to collect pertinent data, inquiring about their past histories and present allegiance. He was keenly interested to find out who founded each church and what records existed, if any. Where none existed, as was most often the case, or the memory of its founder had faded, Tirechan sprung into action with astounding aplomb. He filled the lacuna with an ever ready supply of fascinating 'missing facts' taken from Armagh's alleged 'great Library' on such matters, 'recorded' by Patrick's 'assistants'. This would allegedly show how each church was founded by Patrick and incorporated by him into Armagh's alleged federation of churches. Tirechan was adept at brewing the most beguiling episodes regarding the alleged foundation of each church which charmed one and all as well as flattered, and captured the hearts of, local rulers.

Where records did exist or the memory of the founder was still strong, particularly if that church was not yet bound to any monastic federation of churches or was under unwelcome pressure from such, Tirechan posed as a God-sent saviour recommending the following of Sletty's example to place itself under the 'very lenient friendly protection' of Armagh. A master at concocting charmingly convincing episodes he would relate how the founder was Patrick's favourite, travelling in his retinue, who then appointed him to establish a church there. Each founder was an alleged subordinate of Patrick. Tirechan, like Muirchu, falsified facts congenial to the parties concerned. Each in his own effusive and inimitable manner knew best how to suppress or distort the truth in Armagh's favour. Tirechan masterminded the creation of links to Patrick for Connacht, Leinster, North Munster (Cashel) and parts of Ulster. Walsh and Bradley noted: "it is difficult to avoid the conclusion that Patrick's association with these places, for the most part, is fictitious. Tirechan conveniently identified his hero with all the major centres in Ireland. Tirechan's work is of value as a rich source of information which tells us much about the toponomy and politics of the late 7th century,"[689] but nothing about the real Patrick and his times. His "references to Patrick tend to confuse rather than enlighten. (His) 'Account' is undoubtedly of much less value than Muirchu's 'Life' as a source of information regarding the real St. Patrick."[690] Tirechan's Patrick commences his missionary itinerary from Tara and terminates it there. He has an abundance of material from Meath, but provides the greatest detail for his home area around Killala Bay in N Mayo, Sligo, and around Croghan of Roscommon where he resided for a long time and wrote at least part of his narrative there.

TIRECHAN'S VITAL EVIDENCE ON RATHCROGHAN OF ROSCOMMON
Rathcroghan was the seat of the '*Cruithintuath Croghain*', the Cruthin of NE Connacht adjoining the lands of their kinsmen on the Ulster side of the Shannon. They held on tenaciously to Rathcroghan until the 8th century. Pseudo-history tried to enlist the support of Tirechan in proclaiming Rathcroghan of Roscommon as the Capital of Connacht from time immemorial. Tirechan cannot be held responsible for this fraud. It is clear from his work that Rathcroghan of Roscommon was not the Capital of Connacht either in Patrick's day or in Tirechan's day. Nowhere does he state that the Fir Belg Kings of Connacht ever reigned there. His evidence regarding Rathcroghan is vital. In Chapter 2 it was shown that the royal seat of the Fir Belg Kings of Connacht until Patrick's day was at Rath Cruacha of Athenry in Galway, not Rathcroghan of Roscommon. When Tirechan brought Patrick into the presence of Connacht's chiefs, the Ui Briuin princes, whose ancestors had been Overkings of the Fir Belg, and were still the dominant power in Connacht in Tirechan's day, and from whom all the later Kings of Connacht descended, it was not at Rathcroghan the encounter took place. Significantly, it was at their royal crannog on Loch Seola (Hacket), NW of Athenry near Lough Corrib in Galway. These chiefs were sons of Briuin Orbsen, the son of

---

[689] John R. Walsh and Thomas Bradley, 'A History of the Irish Church 400 - 700 A D', p. 41.
[690] Ibid, p. 42.

the Fir Belg Overking, Eochu Muigh Mhain. The location of these Connacht chiefs as given by Tirechan corresponds to the facts of history and portrays a very different picture of Connacht from that of pseudo-history.

Patrick met no King of Connacht at Rathroghan in Tirechan's 'Account'. Tirechan knew that they were not there because he had worked there for a considerable time. Had they reigned there either in Patrick's or in Tirechan's day, he certainly would not have omitted to mention this as a crucial fact. By the early 7th century Connacht's Fir Belg Kings were subjugating the Ciarraige Ai Cruthin of the Croghan district. Ui Briuin princes, bitterly opposed to Tirechan's dynasty, the Ui Fiachra, were extending NE in the direction of Croghan of Roscommon in his day, putting unbearable pressure on the Ciarraige Ai, *Cruithinthuath Croghain,* and their churches. Pressure to submit their churches to Clonmacnois' monastic federation, patronized by the Ui Briuin, led to serious frictions. Tirechan stepped in to 'rescue' these endangered churches by offering the protecting hand of Armagh. It became fertile ground for Tirechan's operations. Ui Briuin Kings over-ran the Croghan district of Roscommon only after Tirechan's day. They made it their new power-base, alleging it had always been the ancient capital of Connacht from the time of Queen Medb, by suppressing traditions of Rath Cruacha of Athenry in the hands of their rival collaterals, the Ui Fiachra, from whom the Ui Briuin had wrested power. Tirechan did not live to see Rathcroghan become the Capital of Connacht. His activities among these declining peoples, advertising Armagh as their only saviour, won over a multitude of churches for Armagh's monastic federation. He concocted clever episodes linking their foundations to Patrick to give a semblance of credence to his blatant fabrications.

Tirechan claimed two daughters of Loeguire, King of Tara, were in fosterage at Rathcroghan where Patrick baptized them. More has been read into his statement than what it simply says. It has been interpreted to mean that "in Patrick's day the King of Tara was automatically King of Connacht," as Byrne noted.[691] This interpretation is based on the totally inaccurate belief that Croghan of Roscommon was Capital of Connacht in Patrick's time. The text does not state this. In fact, it shows it was not so. In Patrick's time, the Airghialla with the aid of the Connachta overran Emain Macha, ancient capital of the Cruthin of Ulster. From Patrick's day until 637 Cruthin Overkings of Scotland and Ireland (of Ulster and isolated Cruthin enclaves, including those of the Croghan district of Roscommon) reigned from Tara of Meath which until then had been a satellite site of Emain Macha. The Cruthin King of Tara was overking of the Cruthin of Croghan of Roscommon, but not of all Connacht. If his daughters were in fosterage at Rathcroghan this would support the fact that the *Cruithinthuatha Croghain* were still in possession of Rathcroghan in Patrick's day. Had Fir Belg Kings been ruling there, a Cruthin King of Tara would not have placed his daughters in fosterage with his bitterest enemy. As apostle of the Cruthin, Patrick might very well have visited the *Cruithinthuatha Croghain* at Rathcroghan and even baptised the daughters of the King of Tara there. Tirechan fabricated the most endearing encounter between Patrick and the two royal damsels. The tale demonstrates how adept Tirechan was at capturing and enrapturing his audience with a semblance of truth.

When Tirechan led Patrick to meet the chiefs of Connacht it was not at Rathcroghan of Roscommon that the encounter took place but at Lough Hacket, ancient Lough Seola (Seolgha/Selga) NW of Athenry (ancient *Rath Cruacha*) near Headford and Loch Corrib in Galway. They had retreated thither from the Turoe/Knocknadala oppidum after the invasion of Maine Mor from Ulster. These Connacht chiefs were the family of Briun Orbsen (who took his sobriquet from nearby *Loch Orbsen*; Corrib) son of Eochaid Muigh Mhean (who took his own sobriquet from Maen Magh), the plain around Loughrea, Co. Galway, at the

---

[691] Francis J. Byrne, 'Irish Kings and High Kings', p.232.

centre of which stood the core of the Capital of the Fir Belg Overkings, Cnoc Temhro. They were the ancestors of the medieval Kings of Connacht who would capture Croghan of Roscommon from the 8th century onwards, already a threat in Tirechan's day. Hence, he established a link between them and Armagh. It was still beyond his ken that they would make Croghan of Roscommon the new royal seat of Connacht and suppress the names of the archaic capitals. The sly 9th century Ferdomnach who penned Tirechan's work into the Book of Armagh could not substantially alter what Tirechan had written in this regard since it was common knowledge that the Ui Briuin were losing one king after another in their desperate attempt to make Croghan of Roscommon their new Capital of Connacht. These facts, and the invasion of Maine Mor towards the end of Patrick's missionary career, display a very different geo-political map of Ireland from that developed by later pseudo-history, the implications of which will be elaborated later. Tirechan knew the Ui Briuin Seolgha residing at Lough Seolgha (Loch Hacket) were the ruling elite in Connacht. Hence, he astutely assembled this alleged encounter between Patrick and Connacht's Fir Belg dynasty to link them to Patrick and Armagh. He orchestrated their baptism and the erection of their basilica by Patrick. Thus their basilica known as Domnach Mor Magh Seolgha was 'rededicated and renamed' in Tirechan's record as 'Domnach Padraig'. Tirechan blatantly manipulated the facts of history in Armagh's favour. Yet, it is equally true that he based his gross manipulations upon genuine contemporary facts of history to give a semblance of credence to his blatantly concocted claims. The fact that the Ui Briuin Seolgha who ruled Connacht in Tirechan's day resided on Lough Seolgha (Loch Hacket) was later suppressed.

In the early 20th century Archbishop Healy of Tuam made a voluminous study of Patrick's travels as recorded by Tirechan, the Tripartite Life and other Lives of Patrick. He had to admit that the missionary journeys of Patrick along the Galway/Mayo border, especially in the Loch Hacket area of Galway, were not clearly set out. Tirechan who laid the foundation for other works of fiction on Patrick's travels was unfamiliar with the area.[692] Working in the interests of Armagh, Tirechan was a *persona non grata* in Magh Seolgha. His presence there would have been unwelcome by the monastic authorities of Clonmacnois who now controlled the churches of the area. Dependent on indirect information, his description of the area was erratic. He was active in the district of Rathcroghan still in the hands of the Cruthin, kinsmen of the Cruthin of Ulster. Their territory formerly stretched further S but was now being narrowed and coming under increasing pressure by Connacht's Fir Belg dynasty of the Ui Briuin Seolgha ruling from Lough Seolgha of Galway. The Rathcroghan Cruthin kingdom was in danger of being overrun by the Ui Briuin. Many of its churches had already been taken over by Clonmacnois under the patronage of the Ui Briuin. This was bitterly resented by Tirechan and Armagh. Clonmacnois strongly resisted Armagh's claims. Tirechan endeavoured to bring as many churches under Armagh's wing as possible, and win over the Ui Briuin Seola dynasty itself in Patrick's name for Armagh into the bargain just as the S Ui Neill had been won over by Muirchu and Armagh. Tirechan did not succeed but later Armagh Abbots did win over their descendants.

Tirechan's description of the territory where the princes of the dominant Connacht Fir Belg power resided has caused considerable confusion. The aspirated 'mh' of Dumha and 'gh' of Seolgha are missing in the Ulster records, beginning with the work of Tirechan in the Book of Armagh, thus changing it to Duma Sealga or Selca). This may be due to Ferdomnach who entered Tirechan's record into the Book of Armagh some 2 centuries later. The dropping of the 'h' aspiration became common from this time. There are numerous examples of this in O-Irish words which had a silencing aspirated 'g' (*gh*) or 'm' (*mh*) originally, but where the aspiration was later dropped and the name wrongly pronounced as if it never had an aspirated 'g' or 'm'. The original name of the Fir Belg Mac Umhor is

---

[692] Most Rev. Dr. John Healy, 'The Life and Writings of St. Patrick" (Dublin 1905), p. 221-222.

later given as *Umor* and pronounced accordingly due to the loss of aspiration. Similarly, the aspiration in *Seolgha* was dropped and it was written and pronounced as *Sealga* or *Selce*. The guide to Old Celtic name pronounciation at the beginning of this book cites several examples. The name *Magh Seolgha*, *Seoghla* or *Seola* was henceforth rendered as Selga/Selce and Latinized and anglicized as Moyshalla or Moyselga. The aspirated O-Celtic 'gh' silenced the 'g' sound. It is thus pronounced 'Sheola'. In the Book of Armagh the name is written with an unaspirated Celtic '*g*' or '*c*' as *Sealga* or *Selce*. The error may date from the Latinized form of *Selcae Inscae*. What is certain is that the Ui Briuin who, once they conquered the Rathcroghan district, fictitiously claimed that they and their ancestors reigned at Rathcroghan of Roscommon from time immemorial. They attempted to suppress the original name of Magh Seolgha to vadidate this false claim and suppress the fact of their long-standing residence on the royal crannog on Lough Seolgha (Seola) in Galway. Their pseudo-historians renamed an indiscriminate mound at Carnfree some distance from Rath-croghan of Roscommon as *Dumha Sealga* or *Selce* to bolster their fictitious claim.

Copied into the Book of Armagh and all Annals of Ulster provenance, Tirechan says: "Patrick came to Magh Sealga, that is Dumha Sealga, where the six sons of Briuin resided. With a multitude of holy bishops they encamped among the burial mounds and readied a bed and seat for him among the stone monuments on which his own hand inscribed the saviour's name in 3 languages, *'Jesus', 'Soter', 'Salvator'* (Hebrew, Greek and Latin). He founded a church above *'Selcae Inscae'* (Lough Seolgha's crannoge) and baptised the sons of Briuin there." There is no Magh Seolgha or Sealga in Roscommon. There is no lake near the fictitious Dumha Sealga at Carnfree. There is no site of any church founded by Patrick above the non-existent lake in the district. There are no great stone monuments in the area apart from a few small *dumha* and standing stones. The only scenario where all of these are in place, Magh Seolgha, Domnach Mor Magh Seolgha basilica above Lough Seolgha at the foot of Cruach Magh Seolgha crowned by the Dumha Seolgha tumulus cairns, is at Lough Hacket (Lough Seolgha) near the shores of Lough Corrib and Heardford, Co. Galway. There the descendants of Briun Orbsen (named from Lough Orbsen/Corrib), resided for centuries before conquering Rathcroghan of Roscommon. Tirechan referred to the plain, lake, cairn and church of Lough Seolgha in Galway.

The text clarifies that Briun's sons resided on 'Selcae Inscae'. It is a well-known historic fact that the descendants of Briun Orbsen, then Connacht's regent, resided on the crannog on Loch Seolgha (Hacket) from the 5th to the 8th century before they finally wrested Croghan of Roscommon from the Cruithintuatha Croghain and ruled Connacht from there. Paul Walsh pointed out that the term 'Ui Briuin' in even the late 11th century *Book of Rights* stands exclusively for Ui Briuin Seola of Galway, never for the Ui Briuin of Croghan Ai of Roscommon.[693] The 'Ui Briuin' are mentioned in 'Vita Tripartite as the Ui Briuin of Domnach Mor Magh Seola in Galway.[694] The Ui Briuin Seolgha continued to rule from Lough Seolgha for centuries. When they refused to submit to and support Brian Boru in the early 11th century he marched N, not to Rathcroghan, but to Lough Seolgha of Galway. He desecrated their ancient royal crannog, the highest insult one could offer any dynasty. So damaged was the kinship between these Fir Belg kinsmen as a result that after Brian's demise at the Battle of Clontarf, his brother felt obliged to travel to Lough Seolgha to restore both royal crannog and the broken relationship. Yet, once the Ui Briuin Kings had overrun Rathcroghan, they began to claim that their ancestors had ruled there rather than at Turoe or Lough Seolgha from time immemorial. They persuaded Armagh to have this Rathcroghan Myth documented as the 'new official doctrine' in the Book of Armagh and all

---

[693] Rev. Pasul Walsh, "Connacht in the Book of Rights' in 'JGAHS', Vol. XIX, Nos. i & ii, 1940, p. 13.

[694] V.Trip. 1. 1079: 'alaile i nDomnach Mor Maigi Seolae la Ui Briuin Seolai; Lib. Ardm. fol. iiv.:
aecclessia magna campi Saeoli.

Annals within Armagh's influence. They demanded that their ancient Capital of Rath Cruacha of Galway (Athenry), now in the hands of their Ui Fiachra collateral dynasty with whom they were in fierce rivalry for the Kingship of Connacht, as well as their royal crannog on Loch Seolgha, be suppressed in favour of Rathcroghan. In return, they proclaimed the '*Cain Padraig*' (Patrick's Rent paid to Armagh) throughout Connacht. One mass-media deal merited another. Armagh, mistress of manipulation of the medieval media, obliged only too sanctimoniously. The Rathcroghan Myth, like the Tara Myth, endures

Tirechan noted that after leaving the lands of the Ciarraige, Patrick went S to Magh Selce. This compounds the confusion. When Tirechan wrote, the Ciarraige tribe had not yet been driven N into Croghan Ai district. As in Patrick's day, they resided much further south, adjoining the northern boundary of Magh Seolgha which lay between Athenry and Tuam in Galway. Pseudo-history took Tirechan's statement to mean that Magh Sealga was further north and, hence, different from Magh Seolgha, but was the "by then a forgotten name" of some vague area in Croghan Ai. Briuin Orbsen, whose sons resided on Loch Seolgha could not have taken his sobriquet from the Rathcroghan area but from Lough Corrib by virtue of the fact that he resided on Lough Seolgha beside Lough Corrib (Lough Orbsen, genuine name of the lake; hence Briuin Orbsen) in Magh Seolgha, not on any vague lost mythical Loch Sealga.

Overlooking Magh Seolgha is Cruach Magh Seolgha on whose summit stand the *Dumha Seolgha* mounds, one being *Cairn Cessra* (stone burial tomb of the Gaulish Celtic princess Cessair, Queen of the Brigantan King, Ugaine Mor, the *'Rí Temhro'*, whom pseudo-history transferred to Tara. Nearby is a satellite mound whose turret-like circular stone structure may represent Tirechan's alleged 'seat and bed' structure set up for Patrick. Tirechan's imagination on this score are as fabulous as his claim that Patrick inscribed the name of the Saviour in Greek, Hebrew and Latin on the stone monuments and that a multitude of bishops accompanied him. Tirechan used many motifs to glorify Patrick, not the least being this pretence that he knew Hebrew and Greek. The real St. Patrick knew neither. The "multitude of holy bishops" in his train was an attempt to create a Pope-like figure with a college of Bishops. Like the feeble attempt to give a semblance of credence to the claim that Palladius' train of Gaulish prelates were under Patrick's authority, this hoax is part and parcel of the glorification of Patrick.

Tirechan, astute political propagandist that he was, had Patrick climb conspicuous heights to bless kings, tribes and territories. He packed a benediction for Patrick so potent that when he stretched out his hand on a conspicuous hill summit to bless the territory below Satan and all Serpents were dispelled beyond the farthest horizons. The territory as far as the eye could see was made over as spiritual swordland for God, Patrick and Armagh. Thus, it was claimed, powerful kings and dynasties were linked to Patrick while his authority, and that of Armagh, was extended to its utmost limits without his ever having to walk the territory. Tirechan's real mission was to win over as many churches and peoples for Armagh as he could by pseudo-history's hook or bishop Patrick's crook. His real motive for bringing Patrick posthumously to the summit of Cruach Magh Seolgha, home of the gods and goddesses, near whose foot Connacht's Ui Briuin princes resided, was to place them and their extensive kingdom under Patrick and Armagh in perpetuity. It is insinuated that his exalted all-encompassing blessing bestowed on the territory of the Ui Briuin from the heights of Dumha Seolgha placed it under Patrick's eternal care and that of Armagh. Known as Sidhe Magh Seolgha ("Cruach Maa"), this celebrated cemetery of the gods was, since the middle ages, renamed the 'Hill of the fairies of Ireland' over which the Celtic god Finvara (Finn Bheara), now reduced in status to 'King of the Fairies', resided. His exploits are the stuff of tales told all over Ireland. Tradition claims that Cairn Cesra stands beside Sidhe Finn Bheara. Cairn, dumha and shee (sidhe) refer to ancient aristocratic burial mounds or otherworld abodes of the gods. Although he had a hand in the Tara/Patrick Myth and tried mightily to win over Connacht's reigning dynasty to Armagh's cause, Tirechan, to his credit, did not confuse Rathcroghan of Roscommon with the royal seat of the Kings of Connacht either in Patrick's day or in his own. That was the work of later pseudo-historians who modeled the glorification of Rathcroghan on that of Tara.

The 'Tripartite Life of Patrick' adds further details to what took place on Patrick's alleged visit to Magh Seolgha. It names the sons of Briun and some of the bishops who allegedly assisted Patrick. Tirechan's fictitious claims were canonized by the 'Tripartite' which bolstered his literary rededication of the basilica of Domnach Mor Magh Seolgha to Patrick. Furthering his hoax that Palladius was known as Patricius, it was subtly claimed that Domnach Mor Magh Seolgha, Domnach Palladius, was Domnach Padraig and that it was in this basilica that Patrick baptized the Ui Briuin princes. One has to take off one's hat to the exquisite skill with which the entire episode was concocted by Tirechan and expanded by the 'Tripartite Life'. Its imaginative artistry is captivating especially when one knows the setting of the ancient basilica of Domnach Mor Magh Seolgha and has climbed Cruach Magh Seolgha to enjoy the panoramic view from the summit of Queen Cessair's cairn tumulus. This latter compares more than favourably with the great cairn cemeteries on the Boyne, at Knocknarea, and Carn D at Loughcrew.

This episode is on a par with Tirechan's account of Patrick's alleged activities on conspicuous hills in territories of dominant princes of other provinces. An example of his subtle use of notable hilltops was Patrick's alleged blessing on the summit of Finnine hill in Limerick which, thanks to the weight of this fiction, was renamed Knockpatrick. It was the most conspicuous hill in that historic locality from which Tirechan's Patrick could obtain a far-reaching view across the Shannon over Clare as far as Slieve Elna and Aughta on the borderland between Clare and Galway. The sole purpose for Patrick's alleged trek to the summit of this steep hill was to perform a powerful benediction reaching the farthest limits of the Fir Belg tribes of Munster and N to Fir Belg Connacht. The message was clear. Since the earliest 'Lives' and 'Itineraries' did not bring Patrick on a tour of this extensive Fir Belg/Erainn territory, the Knockpatrick blessing substituted for the latter. The heartland and dynamic powerbases of Fir Belg tribes which stood around and between Knockpatrick and Cruach Magh Seolgha remained untouched by Patrick in the earliest 'Itineraries' apart from these two hill-top benedictions. These were deemed powerful enough to win over this vast territory for Patrick and Armagh.

So persuasive was the pseudo-history of "the Kingship of Connacht based at Rathcroghan of Roscommon from time immemorial" that historians and antiquarians, including Archbishop Healy who encapsulated the 'pure milk of tradition' in his 'St. Patrick',[695] tried to locate Mag Sealge in the vicinity of Rathcroghan. They did so despite the fact that no Mag Sealge ever existed in Roscommon. This was due to the fact that Tirechan had Patrick operating along the S limits of the Cruthinthuatha and Ciarraige Ai of the Croghan district prior to bringing him into the Magh Seolgha district to meet the Ui Briuin princes. Pseudo-historians sought to locate the royal residence of the Ui Briuin princes who ruled Connacht as close to Rathcroghan of Roscommon as possible the better to accommodate the Rathcroghan Myth. Since no Magh/Lough Sealga could be found anywhere in Roscommon, the fanciful antiquarians of the 19th century had no scruples in allocating legendary names to all the monuments, not only at Tara of Meath, but at Croghan of Roscommon too. Hence their ludicrous explanation that Lough Sealga was originally located on the hill of Croghan but was later magically transferred to another site. They pointed to Shad Loch, claiming it was a corruption of Sealga. The old church site of Aghclare, though some distance from Shad

---

[695] Most Rev. Dr. John Healy, Op Cit.

Loch, is still pointed out as the site of Domnach Mor Mag Selce. This 'identification' dates only from these 19th century antiquarians. They noted that Magh Sealga (Shalla, almost identical in pronunciation to Seolgha), "is not generally known now and is applied vaguely to no definite lands." Brilliant balderdash!

For those who refuse to be swayed by the force of pseudo-history and for the country-folk who passed on the true tradition century after century, the Basilica of Domnach Mor Magh Seolgha (anglicized Moyshalla) still stands today to the E of Loch Corrib, NW of Rath Cruacha of Athenry, above Lough Seolgha (Loch Hacket) and SW of Tuam, Co. Galway. This lake enfolds the royal crannog of the Ui Briuin Seolgha, descended from Briun Orbsen, who dominated early medieval Connacht. No amount of pseudo-history can alter these facts as Archbishop Healy admitted: "It has been said, indeed, that Magh Selce was the plain around Castlehacket (Loch Hacket/Seola), SW of Tuam"[696] in Co. Galway.

Northern Records, including the Book of Armagh, the Tripartite, Annals of Ulster and related texts such as the Annals of Ulster and of Tigernach refer to Ragallach, the Ui Briuin King of Connacht in the early 7th century, as 'Rí Sealga'. He resided on the royal crannog of Loch Seolgha near the banks of Loch Corrib in Galway. Ragallach failed to wrest Croghan Ai of Roscommon from the Cruthin. Many of his successors lost their lives in their attempts to conquer the Croghan district before one of his Ui Briuin descendants finally succeeded in the 8th century. Only then did this dynasty finally succeed in making Croghan of Roscommon the new royal seat of Connacht. Only then did this ruling dynasty which hived off from that of Magh Seolgha become known as the Ui Briuin Ai. From them descended all the later Kings of Connacht. Dating from their conquest of Rathcroghan the Ui Briuin Ai dynasty suppressed Connacht's archaic royal Capital at Rath Cruacha of Athenry, which was in the hands of its rival Ui Fiachrach collateral dynasty descended from Eochaid Muigh Main. Traditions of their ancestors at Turoe/Knocknadala, Rath Cruacha of Athenry and Loch Seolgha were transferred to Rathcroghan of Roscommon, claiming Rathcroghan had been the home of their ancestors and royal seat of Connacht from time immemorial. In collusion with Armagh they bartered the proclamation of this new official doctrine in the Book of Armagh and other Annals under its influence in exchange for the proclamation of 'Cain Padraig' throughout Connacht.

As the location of Dumha Sealga was unknown to 18/19th government-employed antiquarians, they likewise unscrupulously renamed a mound at Rathcroghan as Duma Sealga. There are three pillarstones several hundred yards apart on the same hill which they claimed were three stone monuments on which Patrick allegedly inscribed the name of the Saviour in Hebrew, Greek and Latin. To justify their absurd claims and explain away the fact that there is not the slightest trace of markings on any of the stones they added that "in the course of time these inscriptions faded." One of these pillar-stones is inside a circular bank with traces of a rectangular building which they claimed as the site of Domnach Mor Magh Selce. They conveniently forget that the medieval records indicated that this basilica stood above the shore of Loch Sealga, unaware of the fact that the true Domnach Mor Magh Seolgha where the Ui Briuin princes were baptized stood beside Lough Seolgha (Hacket) of Galway some 50 km far away to the SW from Rathcroghan. Domnach Mor Magh Seolgha still stands there today.

Aware of the tradition that Tirechan's Magh Sealga was Magh Seolgha, Dr. Healy admitted, "It has been said that Magh Selce was the plain around Castlehacket, SW of Tuam in Galway; but the whole course of the Tripartite narrative points to it as part of Magh Ai

---

[696] Most Rev. Dr. John Healy, Op. Cit. p.222.

(Roscommon)."[697] It was not the 'whole course of the narrative here' which points to it as part of Magh Ai, but rather his own and pseudo-history's preconception that "Carnfree, near Tulsk and Rathcroghan of Roscommon, was from time immemorial the place where the Kings of Connacht were inaugurated,"[698] which falsely points in that direction. He continued, "It (Carnfree near Rathcroghan) was the centre of their (Ui Briuin) royalty, and hence we find that Patrick erected this memorial (basilica of Domnach Mor Mag Selce) close to the place." His wildgoose chase led to an alternative site for the elusive misnomer, Magh Sealga, another example of how guesswork, preconceived ideas and false premises have pulverized history and compounded the confusion in the academic world regarding the residence of the Ui Briuin princes on Loch Seolgha. "We conclude, therefore, that it (Magh Sealga) was somewhere in Magh Ai. The parish of Killukin included Carnfree; in that parish is a lake, Ardakillin lake; on its shores stood the old church of Killukin, and that we believe was the place where the Ui Briuin were baptised and where Patrick set up the memorial stones. Moreover, we know that the princes of the O Connor line (descended from the Ui Briuin) had in after ages a famous castle at this very place. The ancient mounds still remain near the shore of the lake in Ardakillin; so there can hardly be a doubt that these mounds are the Dumha Sealga referred to in the Tripartite, which continued to be for many centuries a stronghold of the O Connors".[699] 'Hardly a doubt'! Yet, scarcely 7 lines further on, in a footnote, the Archbishop's erstwhile certitude evaporated when he stated that "there is another lake now called Clonfree nearer to Strokestown which may be the place indicated."[700] To highlight the futility of following the dictates of pseudo history, a recent definitive work on the sites of Rathcroghan and Carnfree, added that Selce was "probably the ecclesiastical site at Cairns, close to Carnfree."[701] Pseudo-history has no leg to stand on.

Dr. Healy and others were taken in by the Selce misnomer of Tirechan and the Tripartite and by the weight of the Rathcroghan Myth. Yet, he wrote: "Then again, St Patrick's church at Castlehacket (Magh Seolgha) is referred to later on in the Tripartite as Domnach Mor Maige Seolai."[702] He believed Magh Selce was S of Oran, near Rathcroghan, whence Patrick came S to meet the Ui Briuin princes. He believed that the Ui Briuin princes Patrick allegedly baptised were the Ui Briuin Ai, unaware of the fact that the Ui Briuin Ai only came into existence in the 8th century as an off-shoot of the Ui Briuin Seolgha. In that century, they conquered the Croghan district and began to celebrate the inauguration of their Kings at Carnfree. There is no record, nor could there have been, of an inauguration of an Ui Briuin Ai King of Rathcroghan at Carnfree before the 8th century. Dr. Healy was aware that Domnach Mor Magh Seola was the basilica of the Ui Briuin Seola when he quoted the Tripartite. He noted that the coppersmith Essa or Assach made patens, one of which was "in Domnach Mor Maige Seolai, on the altar of Felart, the bishop of the Hy Briuin Seolai, far west from Elphin"[703] - in Co Galway.

To reverse Dr. Healy's claim that "the whole course of the (Tripartite) narrative here points to it (Domnach Mor Mag Selce of the Ui Briuin) as part of Magh Ai (Rath Croghan district)", one has only to show that the narrative in question could hardly point more directly to the Magh Seolgha district of Galway. After stating that Patrick blessed the Ui Briuin princes from Dumha Sealga, the Tripartite narrative gives a list of bishops and priests who were with Patrick there together with a list of their respective basilicas. The list of

---

[697] Ibid, p. 211.

[698] Ibid, p. 212.

[699] Most Rev. Dr. John Healy, Op. Cit. p. 212

[700] Most Rev. Dr. John Healy, Op Cit., p. 212

[701] Professor Michael Herrity, 'RATHCROGHAN and CARNFREE', p.7

[702] Ibid, p.212.

[703] Most Rev. Dr. John Healy, Op. Cit. p.197.

place-names and churches proceeds S from that of Bron in Sligo to that of Sachell at Baslic in the former lands of the Ciarraige Ai in the W tip of Roscommon on its border with Galway and Mayo, to Bennen of Tuam and finally to bishop Felert and his two sisters in the Lough Corrib district. Felert is recorded as bishop of the Ui Briuin Seolgha and his basilica as Domnach Mor Magh Seolgha in this area. The Tripartite states that one of Felert's sisters, a nun, "Croch of Cuil Conmacne, was on an island in the sea of Conmacne," the Manapian sea/Lough Corrib, round whose shores the Manapi Conmacne dwelt. The island on which Croch had her anchorite site on upper Corrib is known as Deer Island or Crochan Coelann. The site of her church survives. She had another church at Cross (*Crois Chriost*) near the lake which gave her her sobriquet, Croch of Cuil Conmacne, the village of Cross between Cong and Headford in the district of Conmacne Cuil Toladh, the barony of Kilmaine, 7 miles NW of Felart's basilica of Domnach Mor Magh Seolgha. Roscommon's Rathcroghan is 50 km far away to the NE. Dr. Healy stated that "the nun in question would naturally like to be near her brother, Bishop Felert, at Donaghpatrick (Tirechan's misnomer for Domnach Mor Magh Seolgha), near Headford."[704] The Rathcroghan Myth blinded him to the fact that the narrative pointed directly to Domnach Mor Magh Seolgha near Cuil Conmacne of Lough Corrib. The basilicas of other bishops mentioned are named. After naming bishop Felert, and referring to his sister Croch of Cuil Conmacne close to Domnach Mor Magh Seolgha, the narrative immediately concludes by stating that Patrick then "founded a church at Lough Selce, namely Domnach Mor Maige Selce, in which he baptized the Hy Briuin." The signposts could hardly be clearer for anyone not blinded by preconceptions.

Loch Seolgha was dubbed *Loch Thechet* (Hacket) after the retreat thence of the Ui Briuin. O-Irish *'teic'* means flight as from an enemy. The Ui Briuin princes took refuge there in the late 5th century from Maine Mor's massive invasion. There they had their royal crannog and slowly worked their way back to the Overlordship of Connacht. The name Thechet (Hacket) led to confusion in the Tripartite text which stated that after founding the basilica above Lough Hacket Patrick then went to the Gregraidhe of Lough Techet. These Cruthin descendants of the 1st century Oengus Finn, son of Fergus MacRoy, King of Ulster, defended the S frontiers of the Cruthin kingdom which stretched down into present-day Connacht. In the 5th century the Gregraidhe had become one of the isolated Cruthin enclaves overrun in the expansion of the Fir Belg. Due to the invasion of Maine Mor and the flight of the Ui Briuin kings and their followers NW into the Loch Hacket district of Galway, the Gregraidhe, Ciarraige, Conmacne and subject tribes, were pushed north into E Mayo and NW Roscommon. In Tirechan's day, and particularly by the time the Tripartite was written, the Gregraidhe were long settled between the Moy river and Loch Gara on which their kings took refuge near the Cruthintuatha of Croghan, thus giving this lake too its name *Loch Techet*. The Tripartite substituted this Lough Techet of Mayo for Lough Thechet (Hacket) of Galway. The error is evident in making Patrick go north and retrace his steps south again to Loch Glynn and Magh Airtig before turning north. Dr. Healy admitted that it was "not easy to trace Patrick's movements here."[705]

Dr. Healy exposed his reliance on pseudo-history and abetted it at the expense of genuine history of the entire area in his work: "We find from various entries in the Annals that princes of the line of Heremon (pseudo-historic) dwelt in Cruachan of Magh Ai (Rathcroghan) from the beginning down to the Norman invasion. It was the scene of the loves and wars of the renowned Queen Meave during the 1st century of the Christian era and always continued to be the chief royal residence of the Gaelic kings of Connacht. The enchanted cave of Croghan, the royal cemetery of Relig-na-righ and Dathi's pillar above the

---

[704] Ibid, p. 211.

[705] Ibid, p. 216.

hero's grave can still be seen."[706] This is the cream of the Rathcroghan Myth. Unaware of the presence of the Cruthin at Rathcroghan he failed to realize that had Queen Medb or King Dathi or the Ui Briuin of Magh Seolgha of Patrick's day dared venture into the Magh Ai district of Croghan of Roscommon, royal seat of their fiercest enemy, they would have been massacred, as were those who tried.

In his *'Ogigia'*, the learned 16th century historian, Roderick O Flaherty, took issue with this particular brand of pseudo-history then in full bloom. He listed the territories ruled by the descendants of Briuin in the 2 centuries after they were forced NW in the wake of Maine Mor's invasion, before they finally overran the Croghan district of Roscommon. He was born in Magh Seolgha, a direct descendant of the Ui Briuin Seolgha. Though conned by the Patrick Syndrome which claimed that Domnach Mor Magh Seolgha was erected by Patrick and hence was known as Domnach Padraig, he decried the name 'Mag Selce'. Noting variations such as Sealga or Shalla, corrupt forms of Seolgha, he proclaimed emphatically the 16th century belief that the Domnach Mor Mag Selce of the Tripartite was the basilica erected, allegedly by Patrick, above Lough Seolgha (Lough Hacket), near Headford and Lough Corrib on his own ancient plain of Magh Seola (Seolgha) NW of Athenry, Co. Galway. It was well known that the Ui Briuin princes, direct descendants of Connacht's archaic Kings, had their royal residence on this Lough Seolgha from the time of Patrick, biding their time before once again exerting their dynastic Kingship over Connacht and, eventually, the High-Kingship of Ireland in the high middle ages. Akin to the confusion of the name of Magh Seolgha and the accruing of its traditions to Rathcroghan of Roscommon was the transfer of the name and traditions of *Rath Cruacha* of Athenry, Co. Galway, to Rathcroghan by pseudo-history. The Ui Briuin Ai chroniclers did their utmost to confiscate these renowned names for Rathcroghan with the aid of Armagh's media moguls. Elderly residents in the Rathcroghan district of Roscommon insist that *Rathcroghan (Rath Cruthin)* is not, and never was, known as *Rath Cruacha/Cruachan*. So too elderly residents around Athenry of Galway insist that the area and forts around the town were well known as *Rath Cruachu, Cruacha, Cruachan* and *na Cruachna*.

Tirechan was equal to the challenge. He was adept at 'finding' alleged bits and pieces of Patrick all over Ireland, a tooth here, a limb there, a bell yonder, shreds of his vestments all over the place, giving the distinct impression that Patrick had evangelized the entire Island of Ireland. Making him as old as Moses, in order to place him on a par with the latter, gave him ample time to loose his apendages in every corner of Ireland to be discovered for future use as precious trophies in Tirechan's arsenal in that relic-mania era. Tirechan went into overdrive by claiming for Patrick all the oldest independent churches known as 'Domnach' or 'Sendomnach'. These names belong to the most archaic stratum of O-Irish religious terms referring to the earliest churches. They are Irish forms of the Latin 'dominicum' ('house of the Lord'), a word brought in, not by Patrick, but by his predecessors, the Continental missionaries. These churches were founded by the Gaulish mission of Palladius, sent to Ireland by Pope Celestin to oversee the work of the already developing Irish church long before Patrick began his Irish mission. That they were pre-Patrician did not deter Tirechan but made him all the more determined to claim them for Patrick. Domnach Mor Magh Seolgha was a case in point. Such basilicas on the doorstep of royal residences, like the latter, made them all the more desirable to Armagh.

THE BLOSSOMING GRAPES OF WRATH: 'LIBER ANGELI'
Tirechan worked from a 'sendomnach' near Rathcroghan of Roscommon as Mac Neill noted. His own native church in N Mayo was a 'sendomnach'. He scoured the country for more. With Armagh's agents, he singled out such churches as of vital significance to

---

[706] The Most Rev. Dr. Healy, Archbishop of Tuam, in 'The Life and Writings of St. Patrick.' p.205-6

Armagh's burgeoning ambitions. The *'Liber Angeli'* (Book of the Angel) underlines just how vital these were to Armagh's inflated interests. The 'Liber Angeli' could not have been concocted without many of these having been 'claimed' by Armagh. It blatantly boasted:

"Every free church in Ireland seen to have been founded by a bishop, and every church any where which is called 'domnach', aught, in accordance with the mercy of the mighty Lord towards holy Patrick and the word of the Angel, to belong to the special federation of churches of Patrick and the heir to his See at Armagh. For, as we have already said, God gave him the whole island."[707]

This text seethes with the specialized parlance of 7th century monastic federations, not the ecclesiastical language of Patrick's 5th century. Doherty dated *'Liber Angeli'* to c 640. This appears too early unless one can show that Tirechan and Muirchu were riding the crest of Armagh's success at this date. *'Liber Angeli's'* claims are far too blatant without Tirechan and Muirchu's conquests to flesh out these exorbitant claims in Armagh's favour. It would have clashed violently with Kildare's claim to metropolitan hegemony at a time when it was without peer. It would flow more naturally from the claims, successes and failures of Tirechan and Muirchu than precede them. Rather than those men quoting from *'Liber Angeli'*, the author is summing up the essence of their statements and achievements, their foiled efforts and bitter frustrations, in forwarding Armagh's agenda. Certain phrases, statements and styles of expression from both are compounded into this infamous work. The authorship of this notorious work could not be fathered on any 7th century author but on the Angel who allegedly spoke to Patrick. Hence its title, *Liber Angeli*, the 'Book of the Angel'. It is obvious from Tirechan's Notes that many churches allegedly belonging to Armagh were under the control of Armagh's rivals. He complained bitterly that Clonmacnoise forcibly held many of Patrick's churches since the plagues of 664 and 680. These were former independent churches of declining tribes, erected, not by Patrick, but by the Continental missionaries in the train of Palladius. Tirechan, attempting to win them over for Armagh, renamed them after Patrick, as in the case of *Domnach Mor Magh Seolgha* which he renamed *'Domnach Padraig'*. After the great plagues, new rising dynasties, and some old ones, crushed weakened tribes which formerly were strong independent septs. Their churches fell prey to the respective monastic federations which the dominant dynasties patronized. It is inconceivable that 'Liber Angeli' could have been written before these events took place. The resultant bitter frustrations from Armagh's failure to salvage them from the claws of major rivals is reflected in almost every angry statement of that indignant work which might well have been titled 'The Grapes of Wrath'.

Armagh might have been swallowed up by another monastic federation had she not taken the radical step she did. She become aware of the full extent of the take-over of independent churches or of those under severe pressure from various monastic federations as Tirechan came into contact with them personally. To seek out those under pressure and salvage those already taken over by offering Armagh's protection and 'Patrick's friendly sway' was Tirechan's roving portfolio. It would have taken time for the anger caused by the forcible takeover of Patrick's so-called churches by Clonmacnoise and other monastic federations after the 664 and 680 plagues to vent itself in the blatant, bitter, tendentious claims of 'Liber Angeli'. Some of these contested churches were in the Donegal and North Connacht regions which were still under Cruthin control at the time of Patrick, the apostle of the Cruthin tribes. He may well have visited these areas and founded churches. Racoon, between Donegal town and Ballyshannon, was in dispute between Iona and Ardstraw (Co. Tyrone). To Armagh's extreme annoyance the monastery of Devenish held Sirdruimm church near Donegal town while Clones held the church of Carrac.

---

[707] 'Liber Angeli', 2 1 p. 188.

Tirechan minted one of his many intriguing tales to link Patrick to Cell Toch in Carra Co. Mayo. It opens a window onto the type of pressure put on independent churches of the subject peoples, as well as on Armagh's subtle methods of salvaging such churches and offering them 'refuge' for its own ulterior motives. He claimed "Patrick went to Magh Tochuir (in Donegal) and built a church there. In that place a bishop of the tribe of the Corcu Theimne came to him from Cell Toch in the territory of the Temenrige in Carra, together with one Sister, both being persons in religion attached to Patrick. Their place (church and lands) is (now in 7th century) under the community of Clonmacnoise, and the people of that place suffer great hardships." The implications intended by Tirechan in inventing this tale, based partly on historical fact, is that already in the time of Patrick these subject people through their bishop, conveniently unnamed, came and offered their church, and attached themselves personally, to Patrick, Sletty-style. This is a stark admission that the people of that territory in the West were already baptised and had their own bishop before they ever allegedly came into contact with Patrick. It accuses Clonmacnoise of having stolen this church from Patrick. Clonmacnoise did indeed 'steal' this independant church, not from Patrick in the 5th century, but from its 7th century independent owners. That did not deter Tirechan. He insisted that "they should immediately return themselves now to Patrick" through Armagh's kind services. Internal evidence shows the frame of thought of the entire episode is endemic to the 7th century quarreling parlance of monastic federations, certainly not to the time of Patrick in the 5th century.

In Patrick's day the Temenrige of Cerae were a subject people. After the massacre of the Fir Belg by Maine Mor, a branch of Connacht's Ui Fiachra dynasty moved North, overrunning Temenrige lands and subjugating their churches. Doherty noted that "under the name of Fir Cherae, the N Ui Fiachra (collaterals of the Ui Briuin Seolgha with whom they were partly dislodged from their primary areas round the centre of Galway by Maine Mor's late 5th century invasion) were to occupy their lands in the course of the 7th century."[708] The Ui Fiachra patronized Clonmacnoise in the 8th century, based on the discovery of the graveslab there commemorating an Ui Fiachrach king, Aillil Medraige, who died in 764, two generations after Tirechan's time. Clonmacnoise took over the chief church of the Fir Cerae in the latter half of the 7th century when Tirechan was writing. Doherty describes Tirechan's devious methods to salvage the Temenrige church which are in line with the recommendations of the 'Liber Angeli' requesting former independent churches to leave the monastic federation of churches which have assumed control over them and return forthwith to 'Patrick's church'. When the Temenrige came under political pressure from the Ui Fiachra and Clonmacnoise, the ousted Temenrige bishop of Cell Toch and a nun took refuge in a Patrician church in Mag Tochuir in Donegal. This is the scenario envisaged in the statements in 'Liber Angeli'.

> *"One ought to know: any monk of any church, if he returns to 'Patrick', does not deny his own monastic vow, especially if he devotes (himself to Patrick). Therefore whosoever goes over to (Patrick's) church for the love of him must not be blamed nor excommunicated, because he (Patrick) himself will be judge of all the Irish on the great day of the terrible judgement in the presence of Christ."[709]*

Mention of 'political and ecclesiastical pressure' is the peculiarly petty parlance that uniquely belonged to 7th century monastic bickering. The 'Liber Angeli' text reflects a situation that did not exist in Patrick's day when the Ui Fiachra and Ui Briuin were themselves under severe pressure following Maine Mor's massive invasion. It was composed close to the time and temperament of Tirechan's concoctions to wrest the Fir Cerae church

[708] Charles Doherty, in 'Ireland and Northern France' ed. by Jean-Michel Picard, p. 63.
[709] 'Liber Angeli'

from the grasp of Clonmacnoise. Tirechan was endeavouring to establish 'a dossier of churches and property' which he was determined to convince the world 'belonged by right' to Armagh. His portfolio was to work within a framework with an agenda to project Armagh as the chief church in Ireland with legal precedence over all others. He, like *'Liber Angeli'*, decried others as arch-robbers and warlords. From the language of the *'Liber Angeli'* it is evident it was written within this same biased agenda. Tirechan, as Doherty remarked, was "clearly under some frustration that this (agenda) is not universally accepted:"

> *"My heart is full-sore with a love of Patrick because I see the deserters, arch-robbers and warlords of Ireland hate Patrick's territorial supremacy, because they have taken away from what was his and are now afraid, for if the heir of Patrick were to investigate his supremacy he could vindicate for him almost the whole island as his domain, because God gave him the whole island with its people through an Angel of the Lord. They do not love his community because it is not permitted to swear against him or overswear him because all the primitive churches of Ireland are his; on the contrary, he overswears whatever is sworn. "*[710]

The anger and frustration boiling over in this ostentatious *'Liber Angeli'* text is the result of toil, conflict and failure in the teeth of fierce opposition to win over more churches for Armagh following her initial successes. It is a blatant accusation thrown in the face of the rest of Ireland. The 'arch-robbers and warlords' refer to all the other monastic federations which were then in opposition to Armagh and almost all the dynasties which were in conflict with the Southern Ui Neill, including their cousins, the Northern Ui Neill. They patronized monastic federations which were putting pressure upon and taking over ('robbing') the independent churches of the now submerged petty tribes. This opposition was enormous then. It embraced most of Ireland, notwithstanding *'Liber Angeli's'* tendentious claim of 'almost the whole island as his domain'. The surprising *'hate Patrick'* bit of the above narrative was a very awkward admission let slip artlessly by the Armagh author that even by the end of the 7th century most of Ireland had conspicuously not accepted Patrick as the Apostle of Ireland nor Armagh as its metropolitan Church. It would take more than two centuries of incessant hammering home of this fiction with the full weight of the 8th/9th century Ui Neill High-Kingship behind it to make this spurious claim begin to stick as the 'official doctrine' throughout Ireland.

The mentality reflected in the *Liber Angeli* and the nature of its parlance could only have been expressed in the way it is after Armagh had already gained at least some 'territorial supremacy'. It rode on the back of S Ui Neill Kings to overawe and outwit the Kildare, Columban, Clonmacnois and other federations in their claims and counter-claims, in its all-out bid for supremacy and metropolitan hegemony. Binchy has shown that the claim for Patrick and his Armagh heirs to 'over-swear whatever is sworn' never got further than Armagh's own records and was unknown to the Irish Law Tracts of the time. He underlined the fact that Irish men of law would have been only too willing to expound on this claim had it any legal basis. The same was true of Muirchu and Tirechan's bombastic claims for Tara as they were for Armagh.

Charles Doherty concurs with Deirdre Flanagan and Dr. Morhmann that the *'dominicati rhetorici'* (learned Churchmen) mentioned by Patrick in his Confessio were the aristocratic clergy of the 'Domnach' (*dominicatus*) churches, including those *'rhetorici'* mentioned in the now lost 'Leiden Glossary', a 12th century document based on 6th century Gaulish acounts of a migration of religious 'learned men' fled from France to Ireland during the invasion of Gaul by Germanic tribes at the beginning of the 5th century. "All the learned men on this

---

[710] 'Liber Angeli'; c.f. Charles Doherty, Op. Cit. p. 64.

side of the sea (Continental) took flight, and in Ireland brought about a very great increase of learning to the inhabitants of that region." Christianity was foremost in this body of learning. Walsh and Bradley noted that these Gallic 'literati' would still have had a presence there when Patrick began his mission. There are references to Gallic missionaries working in Ireland before and during Patrick's time in Irish records. Patrick's own emphatic mention of the presence of *'rhetorici'* (learned men) is a direct reference to these scholarly fugitives.[711] The early *domnach* churches were served by these learned 'dominicati' from the Continent who came long before Patrick and looked upon him as an 'unwelcome, unlearned, intruder', as his own words imply, when he ventured south to visit Cruthin enclaves. These 'domnach' churches were erected in places designated as 'magh', areas of concentrated population in the 5th century when the first dioceses were established. This applied especially to centres of royal power. "Despite the claims of Armagh, it is clear that most of the clergy associated with these churches were independent bishops of the early missionary period. Many were no doubt aristocratic clergy of Gaul (who apparently had come even before Palladius, not to mention Patrick)."[712]

Doherty concurred with Mohrmann's remark that this class of *rhetorici,* by whom Patrick was castigated, similarly despised St. Martin of Tours in France, and was decried by Gildas in Britain. Monasteries such as Clonmacnoise and Iona were engaged in building up their federation of churches by taking over these independent, nonaligned *'domnach'* churches. Armagh, itself formerly in the same category as the *'domnach'* churches, might have been swallowed up in a monastic 'paruchia' had it not decided to enter the lists and emulate them by engaging them in mortal combat for control of these *'domnach'* churches. In coming to this decision it aligned itself to the growing power of the S Ui Neill dynasty, persuading it to accept Patrick as its patron saint. Upon this base it founded a federation of churches, copying the 7th century rough-shod methods of the major monasteries to pressure the *'domnach'* churches to join their respective federation. Columcille's monastic federation had shown that neither distance nor sea was a deterrent to this expansion. The 7/8th century abbots of Irish monasteries were simultaneously abbots of monasteries on the Continent and equally involved in Continental politics as they were with Irish warlords. Columcille was an early prototype. Armagh was given a fabulous start by Muirchu, Tirechan, Ultan and Co., backed by the S Ui Neill dynasty.

PATRICK VIA A VIS PALLADIUS

Analyzing the growth of the Patrick Myth, Doherty noted that "while the cult of Patrick undoubtedly gathered the moss of primitive belief as it grew, yet it can hardly be compared with a cult whose patron (St Brigit) had a name not merely of a goddess, but which is found in place- and tribal- names worshipped throughout the Celtic world. The reason for the rapid spread of the cult of Patrick is much more embedded in the realities of late 6th and 7th century Irish politics than in assimilation to a pagan cult."[713] The rise of the parallel Tara Myth resulted from riding the same politic/ecclesiastical wave. It assimilated the pagan cults of Celtic gods and goddesses, but also the ancient regal traditions of the Fir Belg capitals in Western Ireland, namely, Turoe/Knocknadala and Rath Cruacha/Athenry, which it appropriated as its own 'from time immemorial'. The Patrick and Tara Myths merged. This potent cocktail went to Ireland's heart and head and took its soul by storm.

Patrick was an extraordinary saint as his writings reveal. Due to his writings he made an enormous impact on the minds of all the Irish. His association with the Cruthin of Ulster ensured an early pre-eminence for his cult initially in the NE of Ireland where he acted out

---

[711] St. Patrick, 'The Confessions of St. Patrick', 13.

[712] Charles Doherty, Op. Cit. p. 64-65.

[713] Op. Cit. p. 72-73

his missionary career. Apart from that he was unknown. The role of Palladius, sent by Pope Celestin as bishop to the Irish believing in Christ, was known. Yet, his cult, like that of the founders of the independent churches together with their status, had become insignificant or forgotten by the 7th century. That of Patrick might have been lost too had Armagh been taken over by another monastic federation, had not some Irish missionaries taken copies of his writings to the Continent and had not Muirchu and Tirechan invented the glorified Tara/Patrick Myth. **Significantly there is no mention of Patrick at all in early Irish literature, not even in the copious writings concerning early Irish saints, before the second half of the 7th century, apart from his own writings.** Little or nothing was known about Patrick as Muirchu admitted as he began Patrick's so-called biography late in the 7th century. Nevertheless his own writings, notably his 'Confessio', preserved the essence of his powerful personality. "Of the two 5th century missionaries it was this unique personality which gradually absorbed the 'acta' of the two men."[714] Were it not for his writings which project his humble and holy personality the real St Patrick would have been lost to history.

"We must turn to additional evidence, hitherto unpublished, because this new material provides crucial details which will help confirm" that the so-called 'Patrick's Easter Table' is in fact Palladius' Easter Table'. Its later ascription to Patrick was part and parcel of the attempt to link Patrick intimately to Rome and subvert Palladius."[715] In his 'New Light on Palladius', Ó Cróinín shows that "Palladius' Easter Table (and perhaps other books from his mission) passed into the southern (Irish) sphere of influence only to see its true origins obscured by the inexorable advance of the Patrician legend."[716] In a characteristic brilliant piece of detective work, Dáibhí Ó Cróinín shows, on Cummian's evidence,[717] that the known Irish (Paschal Table) usage was certainly not what Patrick could have introduced. "If we substitute Palladius for Patrick then all the pieces fall neatly into place."[718] The same can be said for so much else that was taken from Palladius and ascribed to Patrick, from Turoe of Galway to Tara of Meath and from Rath Cruacha of Athenry to Rathcroghan of Roscommon.

Independent bishoprics set up by Palladius and the Gallo-Roman missionaries were under threat by the 7th century. Tribes within whom these bishoprics were based were in political decline. New expanding dynasties favoured their own churches. Churches without powerful patrons were in danger of being absorbed by monastic federations. Armagh, in Patrick's name, posed as saviour of those under pressure or already absorbed by major monastic federations. She could not have done so without the backing of the most aggressive S Ui Neill dynasty. Thus Armagh was able to up the ante on other monastic federations. Old independent churches which retained the memory of a link with the Roman Christianity introduced by Palladius and the Gallo-Roman mission were conned into believing that Palladius and Patrick were two names of the same man. Armagh's ambassadors propagated this brand of propaganda, particularly Tirechan who emphatically asserted that Pope Celestin "first sent Bishop Palladius, who was called Patrick by another name."[719]

'Liber Angeli' claimed the Angel informed Patrick of the great responsibility the Lord placed upon him for all the tribes of the Irish. Patrick considered this overwhelming offer and asked himself whether there could be anything wrong in accepting the lands and offerings of so vast a Christian host freely offered.[720] Here is a not-too-pretty picture of greedy Armagh

---

[714] Op. Cit. p. 74.
[715] Dáibhí Ó Cróinín, 'New Light on Palladius', in 'Peritia' 5, (1986) p.276-283.
[716] Dáibhí Ó Cróinín, 'New Light on Palladius', in 'Peritia' 5, (1986) p.276-283.
[717] Cummian's Paschal Letter composed in 632-3.
[718] Dáibhí Ó Cróinín, 'New Light on Palladius', in 'Peritia' 5, (1986) p.276-283.
[719] Tirechan, 'Collectanea', 56, 2, p. 164-6.
[720] 'Liber Angeli', 12, p. 186.

caught in the act of placing herself in the shoes of the humble Patrick and deciding in his name to create under her authority a federation of all the churches it could grab by heaven's hook or Patrick's crook. Many independent churches were conned under severe pressure into accepting the claims of the exploding cult of Patrick. The 'paruchia' of Armagh expanded in tandem with the cult of Patrick as the old *domnach* churches of N Connacht, Ulster, the Midlands and Leinster turned to it for protection from the 7th century on. Tirechan was a walking *'Liber Angeli'*, an extension of the pompous claims put forward in that ignoble work in the name of God and Patrick. He had considerable success. In the 'Additamenta' appended to Tirechan's notes in the Book of Armagh are 'charters' of grants of churches to Armagh which he succeeded in winning over by the same formula. Several of these were later absorbed by other monasteries, such as Clonmacnoise as its Ui Briuin patrons conquered Rathcroghan district and N Connacht. It resulted in bitter bickering as the grapes of wrath bloomed on the *'Liber Angeli'*.

Just as Muirchu was inspired to concoct his 'Life of Patrick' by bishop Aed of Sletty, Tirechan was incited to compose his work by Ultan, bishop of Dal Conchobair, a division of the Deisi of Tara, an insignificant vassal people who had submitted their 'domnach' to Armagh to 'save' it. Tirechan mentioned the case of Domnach Sairigi, a church of the Corcu Sai, a sept near Duleek in Meath, so insignificant they failed to make an appearance in the genealogies. Their overlords, the Ciannachta were themselves and their vassals, in the process of losing lands S of the Boyne to the Ui Neill by the 2nd half of the 7th century. This points to the historic fact that the Ui Neill were only then for the first time in the process of making swordland of the territories of these earlier peoples who were the former proprietors of the Tara district until as late as the 2nd half of the 7th century. This gives the lie to the Ui Neill claim that their ancestors always ruled as High Kings of Ireland at Tara. They were not the original owners of the Tara district from time immemorial, or even from the time of Patrick, as the fabulous Annals would have one believe. The churches of these peoples round Tara were now being taken over by Armagh following the process seen in the case of Aed of Sletty. Examples could be multiplied.

A similar pattern was followed W of the Shannon from N Galway and S Roscommon up to Sligo. Just as Tirechan led Patrick to meet the alleged High King of Ireland at Tara, so too he led him to meet the rulers of Connacht at Magh Seolgha of Galway. Among the bishops said to be with Patrick on that occasion were Sachellus and Caeticus, two early Gallo-Roman bishops who accompanied Palladius. Their sphere of activity was Fir Belg Connacht. It did not include present-day NE Connacht which was firmly in the hands of the Cruthin whose power centre was Rathcroghan of Roscommon. The allegation by Tirechan and the *Tripartite* that both came before Patrick and operated independently of him until they submitted to him is most significant. It is a botched but subtle attempt to have pre-Patrician bishops who came with Palladius allegedly submit themselves to Patrick.

The meeting with the ruling elite of Connacht was made, not by Patrick who had no mandate to meet them, but by Palladius, accompanied by Sachellus whom he appointed as prelate over their territory to administer their province. This was precisely within the Papal-conferred portfolio of Palladius, not of Patrick. In Chapter 2, mention was made of Domhnach Shachell at the NW corner of the urban complex surrounding the inner ward of the Turoe/Knocknadala oppidum in Galway. In that area there were formerly 4 sites of special interest. Only one survives. The massive Caher Eochaidh fort was bulldozed away in living memory. Another fort was said to be the palace of Maine, son of Medb, who gave this townland and plain their names, Cloghar Ui Mhain and Maen Magh (Magh Main), respectively. This corroborates the *Dindsenchas Muigh Mhain*. A third site was known as Rahachell *(Rath Shachell)*, while closeby and obviously connected was a fourth site known as Downahachell *(Domnach Shachell,* the basilica of Sachell). Early records indicate a pre-sixth century monastery precisely there.

The Ui Briuin Seolgha descended from Briun, son of King Eochaid Moyvaun *(Muigh Mhain)*, ancestor of Connacht's medieval Kings. Eochaid Moyvaun reigned in this district, as his sobriquet asserts, before the invasion of Maine Mor in the 2nd half of the 5th century that up-rooted this Fir Belg centre of power. Eochaid's son Briun took refuge on Lough Seolgha (Hacket) near Lough Corrib. Caher Eochaid in Clogharevaun townland at the W end of Turoe/Knocknadala urban complex may have been his royal residence. The adjacent Domnach Shachell would seem to indicate Bishop Sachell[us] erected a basilica close to the royal residence at the heart of what was then the dominant secular power and chief Fir Belg oppidum in Ireland, like Patrick did beside Emain Macha. Palladius was commissioned by Pope Celestin to organize the Irish Church. It was missionary policy to choose a site for the principle church near the seat of secular power in order to exert maximum influence. Patrick chose Armagh, near the royal seat of the Cruthin of Ulster, Emain Macha, as Augustine chose Canterbury. The fact that it was Patrick who erected the first church beside Emain Macha is a clear sign that he was the first missionary among the Cruthin of Ulster and, hence, their apostle. Palladius's delegation may have requested the British Church to send missionaries to evangelize the Cruthin of Ulster. It was the Papal Prelate Palladius's portfolio to meet bishops and consolidate their efforts in christianizing the country and pay courtesy calls on dominant kings and princes. Hence he would have met not only Bishop Sachellus at Domnach Shachell but also have paid a courtesy call on Ireland's dominant Fir Belg King who reigned as *Rí Temhro*, not at Tara of Meath, but at Turoe *(Cnoc Temhro)*/Knocknadala oppidum in Galway. This was abandoned when Briun and his followers, with Sachellus in toe, fled NW to Lough Hacket district near Lough Corrib as a result of Maine Mor's invasion. Briun had expanded earlier into this area when driving a wedge through the growing kingdom of his brother Fiachra who opposed him. It became his permanent home. This scenario parallels that of Patrick who fled from Armagh after the saking of Emain Macha by the Airghialla. He followed his Cruthin converts who retreated E of Lough Neagh where he founded his new basilica, Domnach Padraig, at Downpatrick. Briun's retreat to Magh Seolgha forced the Ui Briuin Seolgha to expand N into the Cruthin kingdom of Croghan Ai. Sachellus led his foreign clergy to found churches along the new border with the Cruthin, a chief church being Basilica Sanctorum, now Baslic of Roscommon, where many of the foreign saints in his train died. He consecrated Bishop Felartus as chief bishop of the Ui Briuin Seolgha at their basilica of Domnach Mor Magh Seolgha. This was above the lake near King Briun Mac Eochaid Muigh Mhain's royal palace.

Unlike Palladius, Patrick carried no Roman portfolio apart from the fictitious one confered on him by Tirechan: "In 432 St. Patrick was sent to Ireland by Pope Celestin. In him all Ireland believed. He baptized almost the whole country." Bishop Tirechan copied this information "from the Book of his tutor, Bishop Ultan of Ardbraccan, who resigned AD 656."[721] He listed alleged sayings of Patrick in the Book of Armagh "showing that he traveled much in Italy and Gaul and there studied under Germanus, friend of Pope Celestin,"[722] who sent him to Rome to receive episcopal orders. This fictitious concoction by Tirechan parallels the dragging of Patrick all over Ireland to places he never visited. The purpose of bringing him to Rome was to have him receive his Roman Mission from Pope Celestin and replace Palladius whom Muirchu alleged had failed in his mission and left Ireland dejected within a year. This is clearly inconsistent with Patrick's own emphatic statements in his 'Confession' that he was uneducated and never set foot on the Continent,

---

[721] Quotation from 'The Book of Armagh'
[722] The Most Rev. Archbishop Healy, 'The Life and Writings of St. Patrick', p. 106-7, (1905)

much as he would have liked to (statements studiously excised from the censored 'Confession' in the Book of Armagh). Patrick made no reference to a visit to the Pope, to his Roman Mission nor to his alleged 14 years studies under Germanus. These are concoctions of Tirechan and Muirchu.

"The first to speak should have been Patrick himself, because the one object of the writer (of the 'Confession') was to defend himself from the charge of presumption in having undertaken such a work, rude and unlettered as he was. Had he received a commission from the See of Rome, that fact alone would have been an unanswerable reply."[723] Despite claiming Patrick had his Roman Mission from the Pope, Dr. Healy wrote: "We may accept that Patrick was not consecrated by Celestin at Rome, but by Amatorex at Euboria, an episcopal city impossible to identify."[724] The pseudo historians implied that Euboria was in Gaul so that the Gaulish missionary bishops, Auxilius, Isernnus and others who allegedly received lesser orders there the same day were led to Ireland by Patrick. Of the countless guesses to locate Eboria, not one linked the name to the British episcopal city of York whose Celtic name was Eborica (Eboria), the Briganten capital. Patrick never visited the Continent. He received his episcopal orders in Britain, possibly at York (Euboria). Tirechan and Muirchu were embarrassed that Roman records referred to Palladius and not Patrick. Muirchu alleged that Palladius having failed in his mision left Ireland within the year and died on his way home. Thus the way was readied for Patrick's alleged wildly successful mission. This fraud was perpetuated by Dr. Healy: "It is very doubtful if Prosper ever heard of the failure of the mission of Palladius or the subsequent mission of St. Patrick. It is said by some that Prosper died in 433 before he could have heard anything of the success of Patrick's mission."[725] Dr. Healy, like Tirechan and Muirchu, had never heard of Prosper's record of Palladius' success, written several years after his own and Palladius' alleged deaths. Dr. Healy's statement is inconsistent with the Roman record penned by Prosper a few years after the commencement of Palladius' commissioning. It tells that the organization of the Irish Church under Palladius was stamped with such great success that Pope Celestin was praised for having "made the pagan island (Ireland) Christian"[726] (through Palladius, not Patrick, be it noted). This record was written some 20 years before St. Patrick ever set foot in Ireland as a missionary on trustworthy evidence. Rome proclaimed Ireland to be Christian without any reference to Patrick and well before his time. This is the background to the scenario altered and manipulated by Tirechan who substituted Patrick for Palladius. His version of Patrick was 'Palladius by another name'.

Relics were used to bind over churches in Rathroghan district (in the course of the 7th century) which, like Tara of Meath, belonged to the Cruthin until the area was over-run by the Ui Briuin. Authors have put forward unassailable arguments to show Patrick was sent by the British Church to evangelize the Cruthin peoples, not those of the rest of Ireland.[727] As such it was within his sphere of work to visit the Cruthin royal centres of Tara and Rathcroghan, but not because Tara was seat of the High-Kingship of Ireland or Rathcroghan was the seat of the Kingship of Connacht at the time as pseudo-history proclaimed. They certainly were not. It was because they were important centres of the Cruthin people who ruled Ulster from their Capital, Emain Macha, beside which Patrick established his first primary church.

---

[723] J. H. Todd, 'St. Patrick.'

[724] Archbishop Healy, Op. cit. p. 114.

[725] Archbishop Healy, Op. cit. p. 111.

[726] Prosper of Aquitane writing in Rome of Pope Celestin in his 'Contra Collatorem' between 435-437 stated emphatically: "By ordaining a Bishop (Palladius) for the Scoti (Irish), while he (Pope Celestin) strove to keep the Roman island (Britain) Catholic, he made the pagan island (Ireland) Christian."

[727] John R. Walsh and Thomas Bradley, 'A History of the Irish Church 400 – 700 AD'.

Tirechan alleged certain clergy accompanying Patrick were showing signs of impatience, greedy to be given churches for themselves in fertile (royal) territories. Among these were "certain Franks who had accompanied Patrick from Gaul." Of these, 15 in number led by Sachellus, he named only Bernicius, Hernicius, and Sachellus' brother Cethecus. In alleging they came with Patrick from Gaul, a land he never visited, Tirechan blundered into admitting that they had founded their churches before Patrick's time. They had established themselves in several places, the names of which Tirechan claimed he did not know. Yet he named Sacellus as bishop of 'Basilica Sanctorum', so-called "because many of the foreign saints had lived and died there." "Patrick came after (later than) them and pointed out the places for them to set up their churches." Clearly they were already established in these places. This awkward hoax by Tirechan whitewashed the fact that they came long before Patrick. He alleged that although they had "gone ahead before Patrick to set up for themselves, they returned later to Patrick that he might sanction their choice of the places, unwilling to set up anywhere without his approval". His alleged circuit of Ireland was made to have them meet Patrick for that purpose. Patrick in his 'Confessio' stated that he never visited the Continent, a statement studiously excised from the censored version in the Book of Armagh. Hence "certain Franks" did not come from Gaul with him. Patrick was substituted for Palladius. The degrading of Continental missionaries by Tirechan was a botched bid to hide the fact that they had worked independently of Patrick before his day in order to glorify Patrick by claiming all the Continental missionary bishops were subject to his authority since it was his task to establish each in his proper place. This was a conspiracy to subject early churches and Continental clergy to Patrick and Armagh's authority despite the fact that many of the early missionaries may have died before he arrived.

An intriguing insight into Armagh's methods of binding churches over to itself is found hidden in the 'Calendar of Willibroad'. It concerns the church of Drumlease near Loch Gill in Sligo where an agreement was made with Armagh at the handing over of property by Bishop Fith Fio who had a family-right of inheritance to Drumlease. Armagh was utilizing a policy, analogous to that of Rome, of distributing relics she herself had allegedly received from Rome in order to bind churches to herself. The entry *"Dedicatio bassilicae Santi Pauli inrumleos* (i nDhrumlease)"[728] refers to the relics of St. Paul given by Armagh to bind over the basilica of Drumlease. If this gloss belongs to the underlying text of the 'Calendar of Willibroad' as Doherty noted, it is plump in the time and place in which Tirechan was active in the 680's. It underpins the reason for Tirechan's fascination for relics and his growing collection of alleged relics of Patrick culled from all corners of Ireland. Tirechan noted that Armagh had given some of the relics of Peter and Paul to Dun Sobairche in Antrim, no doubt for the same purpose. The Kilnasagart stone in south Armagh has an inscription indicating that the church and property had been given to Armagh by Ternoc (+ 714/716) when Muirchu and Tirechan were active. Such examples of acquisitions by Armagh sealed by the gift of relics are numerous,[729] the implications glaring. Far from Muirchu, Tirechan and *'Liber Angeli'*s' tendentious claims that all Ireland had been divinely delivered over to Patrick, one catches Armagh agents in the very act of acquiring these churches and their properties for the first time. They then claimed through the mouthpiece of the Angel that Armagh acquired all these as God's gift to Patrick in the 5th cent. *'Liber Angeli'* could not have been written before these charter deals had been negotiated. It was concocted to put a 5th century seal on a 7th century swindle of sorts.

The alleged baptism of the Ui Briuin princes of Connacht by Patrick is as fictitious as his alleged baptism of King Oengus of Cashel, ancestor of the Eoghanacht rulers of Munster.

---

[728] 'Calendar of Willibroad' under the date of May 29th.

[729] Charles Doherty, Op. Cit., p. 79.

Both were attempts to glorify Patrick and win over the Provincial dynasties and their churches in one fell swoop. The 5th century invasion of Connacht by Maine Mor forced the Fir Belg elite and their followers led by Briun, son of Eochaid Muigh Mhain, from their seat of power at Turoe/Knocknadala to Loch Seolgha near the NE of Loch Corrib. They overran lands of the Ciarraige, a Cruthin sept descended from Fergus Mac Riogh. They pushed them N into Roscommon where they became known as Ciarraige Ai, partly subjugated by the Ui Briuin. Sachellus was bishop and apostle of this Fir Belg dynasty when Briun and his people were driven to the Magh Seolgha district. He conesquently became bishop of that S segment of the Ciarraige overrun by the Ui Briuin. 'Baslic' of Roscommon had been in their possession until the Ui Briuin encroached, forcing them to encroach on the Cruthin of Croghan in the course of the 6th century. After Maine Mor's invasion, Sachellus followed his Ui Briuin flock and established the basilica of Domnach Mor Magh Seolgha for the Ui Briuin and Basilica Sanctorum for his band of elderly Continental missionaries at Baslic in the former lands of the Ciarraige. He was the apostle not only of the Ui Briuin, but of the Ciarraige and lesser tribes in the area.

From Tirechan's time in the mid 7th century, the Ciarraige and other vassal tribes such as the Corco Cuallu and Conmacne were succumbing to the Ui Briuin ominously expanding N from their Magh Seolgha stronghold in Galway towards Rathcroghan of Roscommon. Hostilities flared up frequently between them. In their NE advance the Ui Briuin lost a number of their kings in a violent manner at the hands of these tribes.[730] The Annals of Tigernach tell that in 649, Ragallach, the Ui Briuin King of Connacht, was slain by Mael Brigte of the Corco Cuallu, a subject people of the Ciarraige. Later they were a large population group in the Croghan Ai district until the Ui Briuin wrested it from them in the 8th century[731] and made Rathcroghan the seat of the Kingship of Connacht. The estrangement between the Ui Briuin and their vassal peoples led to an alienation of churches. The Ui Briuin patronized Clonmacnoise which now began to claim churches, such as Basilica Sanctorum in the former lands of the Ciarraige Ai, those of the Cruthin and other vassal groups. Conflict ensued. These looked for ways to disassociate themselves from Clonmacnoise's grasp and from Ui Briuin dominance. This tense situation brought Tirechan to their rescue. He became deeply entangled in the acrimonious alienation and transfer of these churches to Armagh's control claiming they were established by Patrick who, he alleged, placed them under Bishop Sachellus. Anger boiled over engendering the kind of bitterness that dripped from the sour grapes of *'Liber Angeli'*. The submission of these churches to Armagh took place towards the end of the 7th century with the astute political assistance of Tirechan. The handing over of "the relics of Peter, Paul, Stephen and Laurence which are in Armagh to these churches," admitted by Tirechan,[732] is the clue to this clever piece of chicanery. It shows that this is the stuff of greedy, relicmad, 7th century monastic empire building, and did not belong to the time of Patrick.

"Here again we have a paradigm which explains the justification for Armagh's control in the area. If we judge from a further piece of evidence in the 'Additamenta', there may have been some reluctance to submit to Armagh until pressure from all sides became too great. Holy Patrick united in concord his community in the region of the Ciarraige, that is Blessed Sacellus, Brocaid, Loarn, Medb and Ernascus, foreseeing through the Holy Spirit that (the community) was to be shaken on all sides, he united it in a union of eternal peace under the

---

[730] AU 746: slaughter of the Conmaicne; 766, Battle of Shrule (on Mayo/Galway border) between Ui
    Briuin and Conmaicne - many Conmaicne slaughtered; 796, Colla Mac Fergusa, King of Ui Briuin,
    and Duinechaidh, ruler of the Ciarraige, killed; 805, ' iugulatio Cormaic mic Muirgiussa abbatis
    Basilice et uastatio postea Ciaraighe la Muirgius (mac Tommaltaig, King of Connacht 786-815) etc.
[731] Francis John Byrne, 'Irish Kings and High Kings', p. 246-247.
[732] Tirechan, 'Collectanea', 30.

authority of the one heir of his apostolic 'cathedra' of Armagh."[733] The statement that the community "was to be shaken on all sides" relates to the consequences of the forcible entry of the Ui Briuin into the territory. "The heir of his apostolic 'cathedra' of Armagh" would surely not have been introduced into the text had it really belonged to the time of Patrick. This is just one of several clues to its concoction in Tirechan's day. To elaborate how gullible scholars have been in falling for this seething stew of Tirechan which become the boiling brew of *Liber Angeli,* another snippet from Dr. Healy's work is relevant. "The graphic language in which Tirechan tells how from the summit of Oran Patrick pointed out (to Sachellus) the site of the church of Baslic on high ground some 5 miles away due N, is a striking proof of the authenticity of the narrative, which he must have had directly or indirectly from eye-witnesses. Incidental touches of this kind, frequent both in Tirechan and the *Tripartite,* show that the original narrative was truthful and accurate."[734] Tirechan spent much time in the district allowing his imagination free reign to cunningly concoct his inebriating cocktail. His use of topographical features was sophisticated enough to dupe not only learned scholars, but even Archbishop Healy.

Not only did late 7th century Armagh's astute methods succeed in winning over the support of the vassal tribes and their churches, but amazingly conned their masters into accepting her claims as to Patrick's alleged role in the foundation of their churches. Doherty was duly impressed. "Here, as elsewhere, one has to gasp at the political skill of the 7th century politicians of Armagh who contrived to flatter, and ultimately gain the support, of the powerful dynasties who were subjecting the old tribal communities throughout the country, while at the same time bringing their old tribal churches under her wing."[735] Here was political brinkmanship at its most dangerous and dizzy heights. Armagh was not satisfied with backing the winning horse when she won the patronage of the Ui Neill dynasty, she determined to have as many thoroughbred dynasties as possible in her stables.

Catastrophic change took place in 6th and 7th century Ireland as on the Continent. Independent kingdoms and their churches were part of a social and political world that was rapidly collapsing, giving way to a brash new world. Political structures which supported Ireland's primary christianity in the 5th century were in the process of being replaced in the 7th century. Major monasteries that had their origins in the 6th and 7th centuries rose to greatness on the patronage of the new expanding dynasties.[736] This formed a background canvass to the Paschal Controversy of the same period. Armagh again backed the winner, Rome. Thus she attracted to herself all those who called themselves 'Romani', while those in opposition, like Iona, Colum Cille's great monastic federation, wilted and waned.

One piece of evidence vital to unravelling the Tara/Patrick Myth concerns the church of Trim in Meath. It is hidden in the first and longest entry of the *'Additamenta'* in the Book of Armagh. It was highly embarrassing for Armagh and her propagandists to admit that this church had been founded by the missionary Lomman long before Armagh itself and before Patrick's day. Armagh's familiar 7th century takeover pattern was in this case much more sophisticated than usual due to its far-reaching implications. Byrne has shown that the Ui Loeghuire around Trim and Tara were an independent pre-Ui Neill Cruthin sept fictitiously welded genealogically to the Ui Neill dynastic stem to justify its archaic claim on Tara. Only when Tara came into the possession of the Ui Neill could they begin to refer to themselves as Kings of Tara and Ulster. After the loss of Emain Macha in the time of Patrick, Tara became the seat of the Cruthin Overkings of Ulster and Scotland. The Cruthin

---

[733] Charles Doherty, Op. Cit., p. 80; 'Additamenta', 6, p.170-172.
[734] Most Rev. Dr. Healy, 'The Life and Writings of St. Patrick', p. 209.
[735] Charles Doherty, Op. Cit. p. 80.
[736] Ibid, p. 81.

Ui Loeghuire sept of Tara and Trim had no link with the Ui Neill until Muirchu fabricated a fraudulent genealogy for Loeghuire, ancestor of the Ui Loeghuire. He made him the son of Niall, ancestor of the Ui Neill dynasty, alleging he reigned at Tara as High King where Patrick accosted him. The Ui Neill and Ui Loeghuire fell for this hoax when Muirchu dangled it before their astonished eyes. After the fall of Tara to the Ui Neill, the Ui Loeghuire became their subjects in their reduced Trim territory. Their loss was partly compensated for by their genealogical royal insertion into the line of the powerful Ui Neill dynastic Kings and Loeghuire's alleged High Kingship.

Although scholars have shown there was no High King of Ireland in Patrick's day (High Kingship was an institution which came several centuries later), this hoax has hoodwinked all Ireland. Muirchu embedded this fraud in such an enthralling saga that it has etched itself on the soul of Ireland for all time. Nothing, not even the truth, can erase this luscious lie which burnt itself indelibly into the Irish psyche. Tara, like Croghan of Roscommon, was a power-centre of the pre-Celtic Cruthin in Patrick's day and for two centuries thereafter. Were there any truth in Tirechan's tantalizing tale of two daughters of Loeguire of Tara in fosterage at Rathcroghan when Patrick allegedly baptized them this would be another proof that Rathcroghan was not then the royal seat of the Fir Belg Province of Connacht. The Fir Belg and Cruthin were mortal enemies. The Ui Loeghuire of Tara were closely related to the Cruthin ruling families of Emain Macha and Rathcroghan, giving an extra dimension to Tirechan's embellished account.

The Ui Loeghuire sept descended from Fedelmid, son of Loeguire, which held the secular and ecclesiastical power in Trim was on the point of being excluded by the descendants of Endae, another son of Loeghuire, by the late 7th century. "In a desperate (but unsuccessful) bid to maintain their position the descendants of Fedelmid appealed to Armagh. This was her golden opportunity to take the church of Trim under her wing. In this manner Armagh gained not only Trim, but also her dependent churches in Meath, Westmeath, Longford, and, significantly, across the Shannon in the Croghan area of Roscommon."[737] Armagh felt it was well on the way to becoming a major monastic federation, maybe one of the largest in Ireland some day! It dreamt its metropolitan dream of dethroning Kildare. The works of Muirchu and Tirechan reflect the essence of this dream becoming reality. That several of these churches were later lost to Armagh is reflected in the frustration of Tirechan and of the '*Liber Angeli*'.

The pseudo-Patrician document, *Liber Angeli*, was a blatant attempt to buttress Armagh's claims to primacy over the Irish Church, a statement in hagiographical terms of the claims of Armagh, as to territorial and ecclesiastical supremacy. The actual document is framed by an account - later than the central text - that tells how Patrick was granted the honours due to him and his heirs in the See of Armagh by an Angel.[738] Hughes claims the document can hardly be earlier than the 8th century, for much of its ecclesiastical language belongs to a period later than that of the authors of the 'Life of Patrick' (Muirchu) and the 'Brief Account' (Tirechan).[739] The Angel declares to Patrick that God had granted privileges to his city, Armagh, including the extension of its '*termonn*' (area immediately subject to an abbot which he directly governed as distinct from the Paruchia over which he had only indirect control). Patrick demanded more privileges and honours, the right to tax all the free churches of Ireland and all monasteries of cenobites. These requests by the Patrick of the *Liber Angeli* are anathema to the humble Patrick of the 'Confession'. Monasteries of cenobites did not exist in his day - they belong to the 7th century. Armagh's Patrick wanted

[737] Charles Doherty, Op. Cit., p. 81.

[738] John R. Walsh and Thomas Bradley, 'A History of the Irish Church 400 - 700 A D', p. 46

[739] Kathleen Hughes, 'The Church in Early Irish Society' and 'Early Christian Ireland: Intro to Sources'

more and more. The 2nd part of the document details the privileges of Armagh and the heir of Patrick in a series of statements on her legal status as head of, and her precedence over, all churches and monasteries of all the Irish. These are based primarily on the alleged disclosure by the Angel to Patrick that God had established Armagh as His supreme church in Ireland, that it was especially hallowed because it possessed the relics of Peter, Paul, Stephen, Laurence and other saints, and 'a linen cloth steeped in the most holy blood of Jesus Christ,' 'the Shroud of Armagh'. These alleged relics reinforced Armagh's fictitious claims. It ended with a set of decrees establishing the ecclesiastical court of Armagh as the Supreme Court of Appeal in Ireland from which resort can be made only to Rome. It purports to have been signed by Patrick, Auxilius, Secundinus and Benignus. It is a pompous part of the padding in the very complex web of pseudo-Patrician material.

That Armagh resorted to such underhand methods in the name of God and His Angel, speaks volumes about her desperation to boost herself by any means, underpinning the fact that she had little to offer. Yet, it packed a punch in pressing Armagh's claims to metropolitan status. With *Liber Angeli's* use of the specific Latin word '*urbs*' to refer to Armagh as Patrick's 'city' she was deliberately describing herself as the 'Rome of Ireland', a title that meant much more at the end of the 7th century than it does now. Armagh unashamedly allied itself to the fictitious claims of the Ui Neill. The resultant Tara/Patrick Myth is the basis of Ireland's notorious pseudo-history still widely accepted. It gained credence as it was proclaimed so vociferously with such sophistication for so long. It found its way into the Annals and history books of every generation thereafter. Tirechan and Muirchu were interested, not in historical research, but in making out a case for Armagh's claims to an All Ireland 'Paruchia' confluent with the parallel Ui Neill dynastic designs for an All Ireland hegemony. Their object was to buttress Armagh's claims to supremacy over all monastic federations. Patrick's relationship with the alleged Tara monarchy and his foundation of Armagh are the 2 hinges of Muirchu's account. This juxtaposition has great significance in that the growth of the Patrick myth, on which Armagh's claim to primacy was based, is closely associated with the myth of the 'immemorial High-Kingship of Tara' on which the Ui Neill monarchs grounded their claim to hegemony.

Tirechan tells little about Tara, less about Armagh. He made Tara the point of departure and terminus of Patrick's circuits of Ireland. Muirchu minted much detail about Tara and its so-called High King. Both presented their newly-fabricated 'history' patronized by Armagh and the Ui Neill. They occasionally contradict one another. This did not matter since both were writing from a different perspective, for different motives and for different audiences. Both laid the foundations for the central thesis of the ostentatious *'Liber Angeli'* which could not have arisen without the support of Muirchu and Tirechan's work. Set in 7th/8th, not 5th, century ecclesiastical terminology and parlance, it was concocted ostensibly as a justificatory treatise in support of Armagh's grossly inflated claim to hegemony over all churches of Ireland, a claim similar to that put forward at the same time on behalf of the alleged Ui Neill King of Tara and High-King of Ireland, to suzerainty. "This is but one of the many indications that the ecclesiastical pretensions of Armagh, based on the Patrick legend, and the secular pretentions of Tara, based on the myth of the 'High-Kingship' advance hand in hand."[740]

The dual myths, that of Patrick and of Tara, conceived by Armagh are entwined so completely that any attempt to extricate them would cause terminal violence to both. The Tara Myth could not have come into existence prior to 637 because from the fall of the ancient Cruthin capital of Ulster, Emain Macha, right up to the massive defeat of the Cruthin at the Battle of Moira in 637, Tara was the royal seat, not of any king of the Ui

---

[740] D. A. Binchy, "Patrick and his Biographers: Ancient and Modern', in Studia Hibernica 2, 1962 p.61

Neill line, but of their bitter enemies, the pre-Celtic Cruthin Overkings of Scotland and Ireland. Prior to the fall of Emain Macha, the original Capital of the Cruthin, Tara was a satellite Cruthin outpost of the latter. The Battle of Moira brought the Cruthin reign at Tara to an end. The last Cruthin Overking who ruled from Tara, Congal Caech, was slain in that battle by Ui Neill warlords. Tara then for the first time ever became Ui Neill sword-land. In their fabricated records the Ui Neill chroniclers distorted the facts regarding Congal Caech, inventing their own version to support the Tara Myth. The Ui Neill, through the mouthpiece of Muirchu and Armagh agents, began to claim that Tara had been the royal seat of Loeghuire, alleged son of Niall, ancestor of the Ui Neill. Later it was alleged to be the royal seat of the ancestors of the Ui Neill from time immemorial. All contradicting evidence was suppressed. So they thought! The implications of the startling revelation hidden in an minor law tract on honeybees, *'Bech Bretha'*, is a time-bomb under the Tara Myth. This tiny tract miraculously escaped the attention and, consequently, suppressive hand of the Armagh/Ui Neill media shredders and interpolators. With the Moira watershed victory over the Cruthin, the Ui Neill were for the first time able to claim Overkingship, not of Ireland, but of Ulster. By the end of the 7th century, thanks to Muirchu riding a new notion launched by Adomnan, the Ui Neill political ambition blossomed brazenly nationwide. High-Kingship was a notion undreamt of before Adomnan plucked it from his magic hat and dangled it before the unbelieving eyes of his own Ui Neill dynastic kindred. Similarly, Armagh's astounding claim to hegemony over all the churches of Ireland arose suddenly and simultaneously with that of the Ui Neill Kings to a so-called All Ireland hegemony.

Tirechan was silent about Patrick's missionary work within the 'terminus' (*termonn*) of Patrick as defined in *Liber Angeli* which coincided roughly with the boundaries of the 8th century Airghiallan group of vassal states, although portions of the Dal nAraide kingdom are included. He sought to justify the high-flown claim to a paruchia conterminus with the whole of Ireland. Accordingly, he concentrated his entire attention on fabricating alleged activities of Patrick in territories outside his historical paruchia. In the absence of Tirechan's success the *Liber Angeli* would not have had a leg to stand on. Were the *Liber Angeli* the work of Tirechan, Muirchu or of their successors in Armagh, they could not have put their name to it without making it appear as an obvious forgery, which, anyhow, it was. No literary effort was made to dress *Liber Angeli* up in the appropriate archaic style, apart from Patrick's faked signature attached to it, despite the prime intention that it should be seen to date back to the time of Patrick.

What negates whatever semblance of veracity this so-called signature of Patrick might have had is that this pseudo-Patrician document also purports to have been co-signed by Auxilius and Secundinus, two Continental missionaries who came in the train of Palladius and never met Patrick. They may well have died before he set out on his mission. The so-called signature of Benignus appended to the document was the most fatal mistake of all by the anonymous compiler made in the hope of conferring on it the full weight of the early Irish Church. It backfired like a blunderbuss. Had the Tripartite record that Patrick baptized the infant Benignus in his mother's arms held any truth, Patrick was as many as six decades his senior, on the weight of Patrick's own words in his 'Confession' that he was already an old man when he set out on his Irish mission. The Tripartite's 'revelation' that the infant Benignus was consecrated bishop the day after his baptism by Patrick ends all credibility. That *Liber Angeli* made Benignus a signatory of this document shows it up for what it is. Its utterly dubious features drawn up to justify Armagh's claim to All Ireland Metropolitan hegemony shatter any semblance of credibility it might have had. It casts its ignominious shadow upon the parallel claim of the Tara Myth. Walsh and Bradley noted, "it should be obvious that this book *(Liber Angeli)* is an unapologetic attempt to justify the claims of Armagh. It is shameless propaganda."[741]

Before setting aside the *Liber Angeli,* a final issue and its implications show what lengths Armagh's pseudo-historians were prepared to go to hoodwink all Ireland. Binchy, an expert in the field of early Irish law, explained: "If the prohibitions formulated in the *Liber Angeli* had really applied in native Irish law, they would have effectively debarred the head of another monastic federation, or indeed of any Irish ecclesiastic of whatever rank, from bringing a suit against the abbot and community of Armagh. On the other hand the detailed rules of arbitral procedure laid down in the native law-tracts are expressly stated to apply in ecclesiastical as well as secular cases. But there is not a single word to suggest that the 'Heir of Patrick', who incidentally is not mentioned in the texts at all, had any right to 'overswear' the heads of other monastic federations or enjoyed any special privilege whatever. Had he really possessed superior status, he would inevitably have been invested with higher rank and increased honour-price which the jurists would have been only too eager to describe. But again there is not a word about this in the tracts; on the contrary, these state explicitly that the 'highest' honour-price payable to an ecclesiastic 'in Ireland' is due to a celibate bishop," not Armagh's abbot. Immediately prior to these remarks the law tract named 'the bishop of St. Peter's Church in Rome' as the highest ecclesiastical dignitary on earth. Was there even a shred of truth in Armagh's claim or had the primacy of Armagh been then in existence one would surely have expected the law tract to assign to the 'heir of Patrick' a corresponding position 'in Ireland'. The law-tract in question dates to the 1st half of the 8th century: The conclusion seems inescapable: like the alleged 'appellate jurisdiction' of Armagh, these further 'prerogatives' claimed for its abbot in disputes with other monastic corporations are **quite imaginary.** They are part of the propagandist literature associated with the Patrick legend and designed to provide a pseudo-juridical as well as a pseudo-historical basis for the claims of Armagh to the primacy. **Here again there is a striking parallel with the equally fictitious claim of the king of Tara to be king of Ireland: the fable of the immemorial 'High Kingship' is effectively disproved by the evidence of the law-tracts which state over and over that the highest grade of king is the king of a province.** So, everything Tirechan tells us about the rights and privileges of Armagh must be regarded as a statement of claim, **not a record of historical fact.**"[742] The same adjudgement applies to the "quite imaginary" claims of the S Ui Neill.

THE PATRICK MYTH vis-a-vis THE TARA MYTH

The 20th century produced a considerable quantity of scientific research to unravel the Tara Myth from the Patrick Myth, so inextricably linked as components in the composition of Irish Pseudo-History. The case put forward cogently by Binchy in his 'Patrick and his Biographers: Ancient and Modern' is an objective analysis of this work until then. He believed that most of the essential pieces of the Patrick 'puzzle' have been lost and are unlikely to be rediscovered. Yet, he shows how much can be learned from, as well as about, the highly suspect, politically motivated writing of early Irish 'history' and, particularly, the notoriously spurious Irish hagiography. He found it impossible to regard any of the highly conflicting theories of modern Patrician scholars historically justified. Much of it is riddled with contradictions and arbitrary assumptions. He grouped these scholars under 2 main headings: those who believe in a single historical Patrick, the 'national apostle,' namely, the 'traditional school', and those who held that the Patrick of the Book of Armagh is in reality a synthetic figure constructed from the 'acta' of 2 or more missionaries, which he called the 'orthodox school'. He recommended students in quest of the 'traditional' Patrick to have

---

[741] John R. Walsh & Thomas Bradley, 'A History of the Irish Church 400 - 700 AD.' p. 46.

[742] D.A. Binchy, 'Patrick and his Biographers: Ancient and Modern' in *Studia Hibernica* No. 2 1962.

recourse to 'The Life and Writings of St. Patrick' by Dr. Healy to taste "the pure, undiluted milk of tradition", albeit apocryphal.

This 'traditional' Patrick allegedly came to Ireland in 432 with a "direct commission from Pope Celestin and died at 2.34 p.m. on Wednesday, March 17th, 493AD aged 120 years, having completed the task of converting all Ireland". The answer which school children had to learn by rote as sober history, that the formal mission of Patrick was expressly authorized by Pope Celestin, has been diplomatically dropped from the Irish Catechism. No scholar of any school today would try to perpetuate that medieval hoax. Nor would any hold that this claim was "confirmed by the testimony of the St. Columbanus in 613." On the contrary, and conspicuously, despite the fact that he was the most prolific well-informed Irish writer of his day on Irish church affairs, Columbanus maintained a rigid silence about Ireland's 'national apostle', Patrick. So did the great St. Bede, copious church chronicler that he was. He never heard of Patrick. Amazingly, Patrick appears to have been unknown to all the principal Hiberno-Latin (Irish and foreign) writers of the 5th, 6th and early 7th century. There is not a word about him, apart from his own writings, until Armagh's Muirchu and Tirechan, minted their glorified Patrick. From then on the name of Patrick is the one which grew, becoming increaseingly more profuse throughout Irish literature and lore, a folk hero beyond compare. Binchy postulated the late resucitation of Patrick and the alleged 'Roman links' in the Patrick Myth as a "product of the controversies between the 'Roman' and Celtic' parties in the 7th century Irish Church." The political framework of 5th century Ireland as outlined by Tirechan and Muirchu stands or falls together with their claims for Patrick and his alleged All-Ireland paruchia. Both are presented by O Rahilly and Binchy as political propagandists, not only of an All-Ireland Patrician 'paruchia' controlled by Armagh, but also of the fabulous claims to a High Kingship based at Tara from time immemorial dominated by Ui Neill dynasts. Both are found at the root of Irish pseudo-history which claimed that Ireland achieved a national monarchy by the 5th century, something no other country had achieved. This is asking one to believe that Ireland alone had adopted such a national institution several centuries before any other people, not only among 'barbarian' peoples, but even among peoples who, unlike the Irish, had experienced the cohesive, unifying, discipline of Roman administration. As encountered so often in Irish pseudo-history, blatant anachronism rears its ugly head pinpointing the source of the fictional political framework pioneered by Tirechan and Muirchu. The claim that Loeghuire was High King of Ireland at Tara where St. Patrick visited him is but one of their many blatant fabrications.

With his epoch-making contribution to the controversy, 'The Two Patricks', O Rahilly mounted the most devastating criticism of the Armagh complex of documents originating from Muirchu, Tirechan and others working in the interests of the Ui Neill/Armagh alliance.[743] In his dramatic demolition of certain 'sacred cows' of the 'traditional school', O Rahilly exploded the claim that Patrick reached the age of Moses (120 years). K. Mc Cone exemplified just how the evolution of early Irish Law and 'history' was being deliberately represented along Biblical lines by monastic scribes from the 7th century on (Tirechan and Muirchu). The process became still more explicit in the full narrative account of Patrick's alleged 'review' of Irish law and institutions. "Tirechan represents Patrick as fasting for 40 days after the fashion of Moses, Elijah and Christ. Muirchu likens certain of the saint's actions explicitly to those of Christ or Moses, and implicitly to those of Elijah with whom he shares a penchant for self-fulfilling predictions about the demise of recalcitrant monarchs' dynasties.[744] Further similarities with Moses are alleged by the '*Supplementary Notes to*

---

[743] Binchy, 'Patrick and his biographers', p. 27:"O Rahilly's lecture, *The Two Patricks,* in 1942 had the
    effect of an atomic bomb dropped on the orthodox school...even today the 'fall-out' is still active."
[744] Biblical Book of Kings, 21:21.

Tirechan'. Patrick is thus made to merit comparison not only with the greatest lawgiver and prophet of the Old Testament but as instrument of the Irish people's salvation, with the Saviour Himself.[745] He is made Saviour and Judge of the Irish.

Typological emphasis through association with Moses was carried to the extent that Patrick's alleged 40 days and nights fasting and pleading with God for the Irish on Croagh Patrick's cone shaped peak is a carbon copy, duplicated by Armagh's 'venerable heroes', of Moses's Mount Sinai plea for the ancient Israelites. Patrick was dressed up as an Irish Moses or Elijah reproduced faithfully from the Old Testament. In Muirchu's account, the pagan nobility surrounding the alleged High King Loeguire of Tara is pointedly hostile to Patrick's mission. The reluctant conversion of the monarch and his followers was brought about only by a show of stunning displays of Moses/Elijah-style power by the saint, as McCone noted. "There are two notable exceptions to this pattern of resistance, Erc mac Dego and Dubthach maccu Lugair, each of whom on separate occasions, alone of a large company, rose as a mark of respect before Patrick to accept the faith and the saint's blessing." Typological emphasis is pushed even further in the scheme of Muirchu. The law is represented by Erc, and the prophets by Dubthach the poet, as the first witnesses to the new faith brought by Patrick. The implications are that Patrician law and poetry were related to the Christian dispensation in Ireland in much the same way as the law and the prophets of the Old Testament were to the New Testament. Patrick on Tara's Hill flanked by these representatives of the law and the prophets in the persons of Erc and Dubthach is yet another cryptic carbon-copy of the Transfiguration of Christ on the Mount flanked by Moses and Elijah, Old Testament representatives of the law and the prophets.[746]

This bit of politico-ecclesiastical propaganda did not come into being until Muirchu spun it to camouflage another piece of chicanery in conspiracy with the church of Sletty. "It is tolerably clear from Muirchu's prologue that his 'Life of Patrick' was written at bishop Aed of Sletty's behest in order to provide Armagh with a counter to the claims made by Cogitosus for Kildare. The expansionist aspirations of his Kildare neighbours alarmed Aed sufficiently for him to seek protection by submitting his monastery to Armagh during the abbacy of Segene, between 661 and 668 AD."[747] McCone noted that the record in the Book of Armagh's 'Additamenta' of Aed's submission of his Leinster church, linked to the Ui Chennselaig kings and founded by Fiach, to Armagh is directly preceded by a justificatory tale rather obviously produced for the circumstances of the mid 7th century despite being set in the 5th century. It individualises the new relationship between the 2 monasteries and projects it back to the so-called beginnings of Christianity in Leinster by telling of Fiach's alleged baptism and ordination as by Patrick. Patrick allegedly marked out and consecrated the Sletty site for him on land granted in gratitude for baptism at Patrick's hands by Crimthann, son of Enna Cennselach, eponymous ancestor of the Ui Cheinnselaig. Sletty was near the N limits of Ui Cheinnselaig territory, near the district to the N controlled by their powerful dynastic rivals, the Ui Dunlainge, and their church of Kildare. This was the peak period when Kildare was vigorously pressing primatial claims with Cogitosus as her mouthpiece. Sletty's submission to Armagh and incorporation into her paruchia was aimed at bolstering her position against pressure from her N neighbour Kildare.

In similar political circumstances the case of Sletty proved a boon to Armagh in many ways. Aed of Sletty was an accomplice with Muirchu and Tirechan. He was a powerful influence behind the scenes. The Sletty episode was seminal to the whole Tara/Patrick Syndrome. It boosted Armagh's ambitions at a time when she was seeking ways to address her problems.

---

[745] Kim McCone, "Pagan Past and Christian Present in Early Irish Literature'.
[746] Kim McCone, 'Pagan Past and Christian Present in Early Irish Literature.' p. 90ff.
[747] Ibid, p. 91.

The fact that Tirechan and Muirchu deliberately brought Sletty's founder, Fiach, into direct contact with Patrick indicates that they were currying Aed's submission to Armagh while working on the Tara Myth. Otherwise the appearance of the pagan poet, Dubthach, associated with the hostile Leinster people at the court of Loeghuire, the alleged Ui Neill King of Tara, would be anathema. It is an invention of Muirchu to give the newly allied monastery of Aed a powerful plug in the person of Dubthach's alleged pupil, Fiach, whose subsequent foundation of Sletty is duly emphasized by the hagiographer. Like Muirchu, Tirechan was already writing in the 670's. He made Loeghuire remain a pagan, unlike Muirchu's later dramatic version, which rapidly became the standard version, having Loeghuire baptized by Patrick under the developing impetus of Biblical typology being injected into Irish pseudo-history precisely from this time on. "The most probable explanation of the tradition of Loeguire's conversion not yet being in circulation when Tirechan wrote would be that the imaginative Muirchu invented it as part of a representation of the king that owed a good deal to those Biblical despots Nebuchadnezzar, Darius and Herod.[748] Liam Breatnach has shown that the High King's conflict with, and ultimate conversion by, Patrick presumably derived from Muirchu, are taken up almost immediately in a slightly later (680's AD) legal tract, Cain Fuithirbe'.[749]

On the discrepancy in the conversion or otherwise of the alleged High King Loeghuire in Tirechan and Muirchu, "Muirchu tells us that Loeghuire accepted Christianity, Tirechan that the King refused to be converted. Yet, if they were both dealing with a genuine historical event, it would have been the most important episode in the whole of Patrick's missionary career; how, then, are we to account for this disagreement? It can best be explained by regarding the whole Tara incident as a legendary outcrop of the Paschal controversy. The Tara monarchy did not become Christian for many years after Patrick's death. Hence the story that he began his missionary activities at its court, and having (Tirechan) failed in his main purpose, then proceeded to make it both the starting-point and terminus of his 'circuit' bears all the marks of later invention. The story of Patrick and the High King's confrontation had its origin in a much later period when the kings of Tara were vigorously asserting the claims of Armagh to ecclesiastical primacy together with their own claims to secular hegemony."[750]

Armagh employed the Sletty motif to incardinate churches into its federation of churches as it spread its influence further S in Ireland. This entailed the fabriccation of seemingly convincing, ingenious, tales surrounding alleged baptism of founders of local churches and of the defining ancestors of the newly burgeoning dynasties by Patrick. Thus they and their peoples were subordinated to him, although this involved gross anachronism. Tirechan closed his 'Memoir' with a prime example of this tactic alleging that Patrick "ordained Fiach of Sletty and baptized the sons of Dunlaing. He went via Belut Gabrain and founded a church in Roigne Martorthige. He baptized the sons of Nad Froech in Munster on Cothrige's (Patrick's) rock in Cashel."[751] Dunlaing was the eponymous ancestor of the Ui Dunlaing of N Leinster who dominated the Provincial Kingship of Leinster and the Abbey of Kildare from the early 7th century. Allied to the Provincial Kingship, Kildare had hoped to spread its influence over all the churches of Leinster. By the 670's/680's Armagh was taking over Kildare's role. Having dragged Patrick posthumously to Sletty, Tirechan felt it opportune to lug him all the way to Cashel and have him baptize Nad Froech, the defining ancestor of the central branches of the Eoghanacht of Aine, Airther Cliach, Glendamain and Cashel. Uninformed of the wider details of the history and politics of Munster, Tirechan had

---

[748] Kim McCone, Op. Cit., p. 91.

[749] L. Breatnach,'The Ecclesiastical Element in O-Irish Legal Tract 'Cain Fuirthirbe, 'Peritia', 5,36-52'

[750] D. A. Binchy, Op. Cit., in Studia Hibernica, No. 2, 1962. p. 104-5.

[751] Tirechan's 'Memoir'

to be satisfied with this swift Munster foray and leave the rest of Patrick's fictitious 'circuit' of the S of Ireland to others. McCone noted that "in both instances Armagh was apparently hoping to wean these important dynasties away from their major churches, Armagh's rival Kildare and Emly respectively."

A more elaborately structured encounter along these lines in Tirechan's work allegedly took place between Patrick and the 3 sons of Niall from whom significant Southern Ui Neill branches claimed descent. At Tailtiu, the site of the Ui Neill Oenach (Meeting Place), Patrick allegedly met Cairbre who proved to be "an incorrigibly hostile pagan." He earned Patrick's curse for trying to kill him: 'Your seed shall serve the seed of your brothers and there shall be no king from your seed forever.'" At Donaghpatrick W of Slane, on the Blackwater between Navan and Kells, (despite being enemy Cruthin territory until 637) Patrick allegedly met another son, Conall. He "received him with great joy, and he baptized him and established his throne for ever and said to him: "The seed of your brothers will serve your seed forever. You must render alms to my heirs after me forever, and your descendants must render to my sons in the faith (Armagh's Abbots) a perpetual due" - the bottom line. It was blatant commercial propaganda. Patrick shuddered in his grave. This lavish blessing was allegedly bestowed by Patrick on Conall Cremthainne, ancestor of the Sil nAedo Slaine, "who virtually monopolized the Tara kingship during the 2nd half of the 7th century. Since this dominance had an air of permanence when Tirechan wrote, Armagh had an obvious interest in establishing financially advantageous relations with this line while denigrating its main Southern rivals,"[752]

Loeghuire, alleged son of Niall, and King of Tara was next to be confronted by Patrick. "Muirchu's narrative centres upon a prolonged conflict between Patrick and Loeghuire who is hostile to the saint and tries to kill him but is forced rather against his will to accept the faith." Patrick said to Loeghuire: "since you have resisted my teaching and have been an obstacle to me, although the days of your reign shall be extended, yet shall there be no king of your seed forever." McCone noted: "Loeghuire's fate, then, is intermediate between that of Cairbre and Conall in line with his behaviour, whether as a friendly but reluctant pagan in Tirechan or a murderous adversary turned reluctant convert in Muirchu."[753] Since neither Niall nor any of his sons came anywhere near Tara in the time of Patrick, the so-called curse of Patrick upon Loeghuire can be taken to connote the later eclipse of Loeghuire's lineage, the pre-Ui Neill Cruthin sept of Ui Loeghuire centered on Trim E of Tara, by Sil nAedo Slaine. Far from being a son of Niall, the Loeghuire of Tara and Trim was the cousin of Conor Mac Nessa mentioned in the Tain, ancestor of the Ui Loeguire sept of Tara. Following the massive defeat of the Cruthin by the Ui Neill at Moira in 637 this Ui Neill branch subjected the pre-Ui Neill tribes around Slane E and N of Tara who were kinsmen of the Cruthin whose Overkings of Ulster and Scotland had ruled at Tara. Doherty noted the denouement of the devious descent of the Ui Loeghuire from Niall, seeing this pre-Ui Neill sept had no connection with the Ui Neill until its eponymous ancestor Loeghuire was artificially incardinated into the Ui Neill genealogy by Muirchu. Hence, in concocting this calculated curse of Patrick upon Loeghuire, he felt he could treat Loeguire with impunity without fear of ruffling Ui Neill/Armagh relations. Tirechan and Muirchu's essentially identical message, conveyed with somewhat different nuances by each, reflected the current 7th century political scenario, while fabricating 5th century fictionalized history as underlined by the above anomaly. Tirechan and Muirchu stand at the source of the muddling of early Irish history and political geography. This evolved round the main historical axis of Muirchu's 'Life of Patrick' based on the Patrick/Loeghuire episode at Tara. It was political and ecclesiastical propaganda united in a marriage of cunning

---

[752] Kim McCone, Op. Cit., p. 250.

[753] Ibid, Op. Cit., p. 250.

convenience. The origins of the synthetic historical approach in Irish history date from this time. The fraudulent concoctions of Tirechan and Muirchu evolved into the full bloom of Irish pseudo-history. New elements were added and adapted to fit changing political circumstances century after century. Among the mid 8th century Ui Neill dynasts the Clann Cholmain had effectively blocked off the Sil nAedo Slaine from the Tara kingship. This required urgent readjustment. It was suitably upgraded. The role of Dubthach, the Leinster poet who allegedly sat with Loeghuire at Tara, underwent major expansion in legal circles, as expounded by McCone.[754]

A newly concocted, updated, and detailed account of the activities of Patrick and his alleged associates appeared in the 8th century tract *'Corus Bescnai'* into which two new characters are introduced, for obvious political purposes. They render the tale anachronistic in the extreme. *"It is Dubthach who first paid respect to Patrick. It is Corc son of Lughaid who first bowed before him. He was in hostageship with Laoghaire (archaic Loeghuire, later Laoghaire). Laoghaire refused Patrick on account of the druid Mata mac Umhor who had prophesied to Laoghaire that Patrick would steal the living and the dead from him."* Corc mac Lughaid, founder of the Eoghanacht dynasty of Cashel, is one of the most conspicuous names in the early history of Munster. His inclusion here, as in the 'Committee of Nine' set up supposedly for the revision of the laws in the *'Senchus Mor'*, affords the clearest evidence that these statements were forgeries, since Corc died a century before Patrick commenced his Irish mission. His insertion was an offshoot of the 'Dail' at Terryglass in 737 between the Ui Neill King, Aed Allan, and Cathal mac Finguine, King of Cashel, and the proclamation of the *'Lex Patricii'* by Cathal throughout Munster as an outcome of the 'Dail'. Armagh's ambassadors in the train of Aed Allan gathered facts on the early history of Munster while at the Dail. They manipulated this material for ulterior motives. Corc had to be given a place somehow, anyhow.

Binchy pointed out that this "legend preserved in 'Senchus Mor' represents Corc as the first person in Laoghaire's court to bend the knee before Patrick. His presence in Tara is explained as being a 'hostage' – one of the most ludicrous blunders ever perpetrated by a mythmaker, for in his day (long before Laoghaire's) Corc was styled 'King of Ireland' by his subjects in Munster"[755] as an 8th century Munster text claimed. Munster's claim resulted from the ire roused by Armagh's blatant manipulation of their ancestral founder of Cashel, Corc. Munster retorted with its own 8th century counter-claims. Munster eyes were opened by Armagh's blatant shenanigans. Mata mac Umhor's name was inserted into the *'Corus Bescnai'* text for similar motives following the promulgation of the *Lex Patricii* throughout Connacht by its king in reward for favourable propaganda for his ruling dynasty and his new seat of power at Rathcroghan by Armagh's abbots and annalists. Here the anachronism which underpinned the blunders perpetrated by Armagh's mythmakers was utterly conspicuous. Mata mac Umhor lived more than 4 centuries before Patrick's time. Yet, Connacht was strangely silent!!!

Revision of Irish law "in a Christian spirit under the guidance of Patrick," titled *'Senchus Mor'*, is another hoax exposed by the law-tracts themselves. O Rahilly rejected as a late interpolation the entry in the Annals of Ulster under 438 AD, *"Senchas Mor do scribunn,"* which claimed *'Senchus Mor'* was written that year. Scholars have shown that the *'Senchus Mor'* was compiled in the 8th century describing a collection of tracts in one law-school. The introduction to this compilation of vernacular Irish Law, composed in the early 8th century, did not even mention Patrick's name. The 'Committee of Nine' allegedly set up to revise the code of law under Patrick's guidance made its appearance in a pseudo-

---

[754] Kim McCone, Op. Cit., p. 25, 44, 90-92, 96-98, 101, 165, 201, 227.
[755] Kim McCone, Op. Cit., p. 25, 44, 90-92, 96-98, 101, 165, 201, 227. A. D. Binchy, Op. Cit.

etymological gloss not earlier than the end of the 9th century. The alleged names of the 9 were given for the first time in an 11th century commentary, demonstrating how the Tara/Patrick Myth was still developing four centuries after its birth. "In this late 'Machwerk'" Binchy remarked, "we have one of the last outcrops of the Patrick legend, invented too late even for inclusion among the fables of the *'Vita Tripartite'*.

McCone analyzed various recensions of the pseudo-historical prologue to the *'Senchus Mor'*, offering a translation of what seems to be the prologue's original core with an analysis of its contents. He noted a number of salient features which flesh out the details of the passage from the 'Senchus Mor' tract *'Chorus Bescnai'* cited above. The narrative proper begins with Laoghaire urging the murder of one of Patrick's followers to test the saint's position on the Christian law of forgiveness. The King's brother Nuadu duly slays Patrick's charioteer, Odran. Terrified by an ominous earthquake and darkness resulting from the angry saint's invocation of his God, the men of Ireland offered Patrick arbitration and his choice of judge. This fell upon 'the chief poet of Ireland (falsely insinuating that Ireland was a united nation), Dubthach maccu Lugair, who was full of the Holy Spirit' (unique for a pagan poet!). Dubthach lamented the apparent unavoidability of offending either Patrick by recommending forgiveness, or God by opting for retribution in the teeth of the Gospel injunction to forgive one's neighbour. This fear was assuaged by a guarantee that God would speak through him after Patrick had blessed his mouth. Then Dubthach uttered a long *'roscad'* replete with arguments drawn from Scripture. As wise as Solomon under the Spirit's supernatural guidance, he advocated a compromise between the claims of retribution and mercy by sentencing Nuadu's body to death for his crime but granting God's mercy on his soul. Pseudo-historians were past masters in concocting spurious stories! "Patrick summoned the men of Ireland to an assembly, preached the Gospel, and dramatically demonstrated his miraculous powers so that all 'acknowledged the whole will of God and of Patrick.' Laoghaire called for 'the establishment and arrangement of every law amongst us.' Ireland's laws and institutions were allegedly Christianized by Patrick and Dubthach under the influence of the Holy Spirit as claimed by the fictitious prologue to the *'Senchus Mor'*. These medieval spin-doctors knew how to rewrite history for ulterior motives and impose 'the whole of their own will on all Ireland'. They forced Biblical-like interpretations on fictional scenarios to create Old Testament-like prophets and canonize pagan poets to propagate Armagh's agenda. Dazzled by their own brilliance they drugged themselves into believing their own propaganda. Despite all their sophistication they made 'ludicrous blunders'. Once again, outrageous anachronisms underpin the fraudulent nature of their politico-ecclesiastical propaganda war.

Another example of such anachronism which undermined the claims of Armagh was the fragment of what Binchy called 'an imaginary letter' allegedly written by Patrick to two bishops in Magh Ai in Roscommon who had ordained bishops and clerics 'without his sanction'. He marks it as a late attempt by Armagh to assert its authority over other churches by insinuating that all bishops were subject to Patrick. "The letter was never written," Binchy noted, "precisely on account of the alleged 'quotation from it that survives. That Patrick ever wrote such words is inconceivable, if only because the threat would have had no meaning in the episcopal Church which he (and earlier Gallo-Roman bishops) introduced into Ireland. It reflects the condition of a later age when the Irish Church had become a group of monastic federations, each with its own terminus and paruchia, in competition with others for 'manaig', ecclesiastical subjects (lay/clerical) who supplied the 'patronal' establishment with its main revenues. The use of a secular sanction is altogether out of keeping with what we know of Patrick's character from his own writings; on the other hand it is a commonplace in later Irish hagiography: clerics who have had the temerity to quarrel with a powerful saint are told that their churches will be poor and their subjects few."[756] 7th/8th century Armagh could not cast a crueler curse upon a cleric. Its mindset was firmly fixed on the bottom line. Binchy noted that "similar unedifying sanctions are put into Patrick's mouth by his 7th century biographers, but they belong just like the 'letter', to the Patrick of saga, not to the real St. Patrick."[757]

Armagh fathered on Patrick the so-called 'Canons of the First Synod of St. Patrick'. In the 9th/10th century manuscript of Worchester provenance in which the text is preserved, they purport to be decrees of a synod under the auspices of Patrick, Auxilius and Iserninus. They were unknown to Tirechan and Muirchu who would have noted such an event had it taken place. Nor is there a word about it in any Patrician documents in the Book of Armagh. On internal evidence, Binchy called it spurious. "My study of the sources has led me to the conclusion that the 'synod' and its 'decrees' are a product of the disputes which convulsed the Irish Church during the 7th century – unmistakable signs of lateness, such as the reference to a deacon who departs from a paruchia without permission of his abbot - a clear echo of the later monastic church. Similar canons were promulgated as late as the 6th century in Gaul and Spain. These provisions were taken over verbatim by the 'reform' party in the Irish Church, adopted at various synods between the 6th/mid 7th century, and fathered on Patrick for obvious reasons. For these reasons I submit that this record of Patrick's '1st synod' is no more worthy of credence than that of his '2nd synod' which is now admitted by all scholars to be a forgery."[758]

By the 9th centuries the monastic community of Armagh and the Ui Neill kings of the North and Central Midlands had been working in tandem in mutual conspiracy to boost each other's pretensions at the expense of all others. With Armagh as their mouthpiece, the Ui Neill and Airghialla manipulated both secular and ecclesiastical tradition for their own ulterior agenda. Since they dared to treat sacred ecclesiastical traditions relating to the early missionary work and development of the Irish Church with such impunity, then what were they not prepared to do with secular traditions? They suppressed early Irish history and political geography to make way for their newly-minted version. Their conspiracy accrued the traditions of the Turoe/Knocknadala and Athenry Fir Belg oppida of Galway to Tara and Rathcroghan respectively just as the activities of Palladius were accrued to Patrick within the same pseudo-historical Tara/Patrick Legend. They linked Patrick to Armagh's ecclesiastical dreams and Tara to the Ui Neill political ambitions. They were unanimous in projecting Patrick as the one and only 'National Apostle' of Ireland and Tara as the one and only Royal Seat of the High Kingship of All-Ireland from time immemorial. All Ireland fell for their sophisticated ruse.

O Rahilly rejected the single Patrick of the Book of Armagh. He saw Patrick as a composite figure constructed from the acts of 2 or more missionaries, one of whom, Palladius, 'was also known as 'Patricius'. Binchy regarded O Rahilly's lecture as "his most brilliant contribution to Irish scholarship."[759] O Rahilly identified 'Sen Phatric' of the 'early records' with Palladius, claiming he was also known as 'Patricius' following Tirechan. '*Patricius*' was an honorific Roman title in Continental circles precisely in Palladius' time. Considering his unique commissioning by Pope Celestin as 'first Bishop to the Irish believing in Christ' it would not have been amiss to confer on Palladius, not the name Patricius, but the honorary title '*patricius*'. The name Patricius was common at the time. St. Augustine's father was Patricius. Binchy noted that the "arguments in favour of the identity of Palladius with Sen-Phatric are far from conclusive." Dr. Mario Esposito, "a scholar with a long

---

[756] D. A. Binchy, Op. Cit., p. 44.

[757] Ibid, p. 44.

[758] D.A. Binchy, Op. Cit. p. 49.

[759] D. A. Binchy, Op. Cit. p. 28.

distinguished record in Hiberno-Latin studies," agreed much of the missionary activity claimed for Patrick in the Book of Armagh belongs to Palladius. Palladius' travels on the Continent and his long friendship with Germanus are accrued to Patrick. While the 7th century Lives of Patrick are a conflation of the 'acta' of 2 or more missionaries, in reality they tell much more about Palladius than about Patrick. Binchy noted that "so confused and unreliable are the traditions recorded by Tirechan and Muirchu that there may even have been a 3rd missionary whose 'acta' were pressed into service to complete the picture of the glorified Patrick painted by the 7th century 'Lives'.

The alleged record of Patrick's lengthy sojourn in Gaul as a disciple of the scholarly Bishop Germanus is a clear tradition plundered from Palladius. The strictly orthodox 'Mono-Patrician' school stubbornly upheld this spurious record, yet failed to account for the glaring discrepancy between Patrick's 'barbarous' Latin and his alleged 'education' at the feet of Gaul's best scholar over 14 years in one of the leading centres of Christian culture on the Continent, as Binchy noted. Patrick humbly, forcefully and deliberately acknowledged himself unschooled. This is obvious from the language of his 'Confession'. The linguistic expert, Professor Mohrmann, emphasized the enormous difficulties inherent in the task of wresting the true meaning from Patrick's uneducated and often eccentric Latin. She eliminates the "tradition of Lerins" in the Book of Armagh which made Patrick study under Germanus. "Linguistic evidence does not lie, as hagiographical documents sometimes do."[760] Patrick clarified in his 'Confession' in more ways than one, not only that he never studied under Germanus, but that he never even set foot on the Continent of Europe. Armagh's literati tried their utmost to whitewash these facts. In his *Memoir,* Tirechan railed against the "robbers of Ireland who have taken from Patrick what is rightfully his," his alleged All-Ireland 'paruchia'. Yet, Tirechan & Co. had no scruples in taking from Palladius and the early missionaries what was rightfully theirs and accruing them all to Patrick. Nor were they any less unprincipled in plundering the ancient traditions of the Turoe/Knocknadala and Athenry Fir Belg oppida in order to accrue them to the glory of Tara of Meath and Rathcroghan of Roscommon. The real robbers of Ireland's Iron Age history and early Christian traditions were these learned, looting 'venerable heroes of Armagh' themselves.

Binchy wrote "Of the life and labours of Patrick, apart from a few data furnished almost by accident in the 'Confessio' and 'Epistola', we know virtually nothing" about Patrick. Muirchu, opening his 'Life of Patrick', noted the difficulty of finding one's way in these dark, murky, waters. Muirchu & Co. felt it incumbent upon themselves to fill this gap. They invented minute details of the everyday life of Patrick and the 'Irish High-King', with episodes 'borrowed' from Biblical Prophets and Kings like Moses or Elijah, or traditions plundered from Palladius' life and of genuine Iron Age Fir Belg kings, notably those of Connacht. The Irish have shown themselves everlastingly grateful by accepting this pseudo-material as Gospel truth! "O men! how long will your hearts be closed! Will you love what is futile and seek what is false?"[761]

There is only one source of first-class evidence for Patrick, namely, the genuine writing of Patrick himself, consisting of the 'Letter to Coroticus' and his 'Confession' written in old age as a reply to charges leveled against him by British ecclesiastics. These two documents are the sole 5th century witness to Patrick. The remaining so-called 'contemporary' sources are for the most part 2 centuries, and some 3 or 4 centuries, later.[762] When one searches Patrick's own writings for historical facts one is confronted with a blank. This tempted 7th century Armagh heroes to 'streamline' Patrick to the measure of their own ambitions which

---

[760] Professor Christine Mohrmann, 'The Latin of St. Patrick', p. 82; D.A.Binchi, Op. Cit. p. 27.
[761] Psalm 4:2, "Why shut your hearts so long, loving delusions, chasing after lies?" Jerusalem Bible.
[762] D. A. Binchi, Op. Cit., p. 40.

were as limitless as the sky. They felt free to concoct Patrick's life and activities 'supported' by new writings and letters, elevating Patrick to an All Ireland supremacy, which they fathered on Patrick himself while drastically censuring the version of Patrick's own genuine 'Confession' as it was entered into the Book of Armagh. They suppressed his Letter to Coroticus altogether. This forged material in turn constituted a further temptation to scholars to fill in the numerous lacunae in Patrick's activities from 'faked' secondary sources, regardless of the vast abyss separating the fabricated glorified Patrick from the saint's own humble testimony, as Binchy noted.

THE ROLE OF FERDOMNACH: CENSORSHIP AND SUPPRESSION

The manuscript history of Patrick's two genuine writings has its own poignant story to tell. For the complete uncensored text of the 'Confession' and for the only copy of the 'Letter to Coroticus' Ireland is dependant on manuscripts preserved on the Continent. Binchy believes both works were in Armagh before the beginning of the 9th century when Ferdomnach, the scribe of the Book of Armagh, was at work, for he headed his transcript of Patrick's writings with the words "*Libri sancti Patricii*" (Books of St. Patrick). Despite the plural title, Ferdomnach suppressed the 'Letter to Coroticus' and copied only a drastically censored 'Confessio', the only version permitted to see the light of day in Ireland by Armagh which claimed it was the preserver of the writings of Patrick and of early Irish history. The deliberate omission of the 'Letter to Coroticus' and the crude censoring of the 'Confession' were part of the ongoing monumental fraud being perpetrated by Armagh. It was a blatant suppression of the humble, holy, often persecuted Patrick presented in the numerous uncensored sections of the 'Confession' and replaced him with Armagh's heroic, glorious, all-conquering Patrick. Ireland is profoundly indebted to its missionary *'peregrini'* who carried the uncensored copies of these 2 writings of Patrick to the Continent where they were preserved from Armagh's censors.

By comparing the uncensored copies of Patrick's 'Confession' from their Continental retreats with the highly censored version copied by Ferdomnach into the Book of Armagh one can analyze the rudely censored material and discover what Armagh was so crudely suppressing. Binchy noted, "if we examine the passages omitted from the *Confessio* (No. 26-29, 32-34, 36-37, 42-53, 55-61) we find that in virtually all of them Patrick appears in what to the peculiar mentality of an Irish (Armagh) hagiographer would have seemed a humiliating situation. His biographers present us with a 'Patrick Saga' modeled largely on the Irish heroic tales, in which the conquering hero marches from triumph to triumph without a single reversal. But how could this glorified Patrick of Tirechan and Muirchu be allowed to confess that he had been censured and rejected by his superiors (26-28), derided and despised as an ignoramus (45-46), betrayed by a friend who revealed his youthful sin (27, 32), accused of conduct bordering on simony (37, 50); or that he had encountered opposition and hostility during his mission (42), had been forced to purchase safe-conduct by making payments to tribal kings (51-52), and put in chains (52)." Though Patrick mentioned tribal kings, he never mentioned a High King of Ireland which he could not have avoided doing had there really been one in his day and had his Biblical-like encounter with him, as alleged by pseudo-historians, been true. Examination of these censured passages would convince the hardest sceptic that they were wilfully suppressed to uphold the glorified Patrick of the Book of Armagh. One has only to read sections 55 to 61 to realize why they too had to be excised. In section 55 Patrick described his daily expectation of meeting violent death or being reduced again to slavery. When he envisioned the likelihood of being slain and his body left lying unburied (59), one can see why Armagh was determined that these words of Patrick were suppressed. They were anathema to Armagh's conventional picture of its glorified Patrick triumphantly progressing like a conquering hero on his circuit of Ireland. "The total suppression of the 'Letter to Coroticus' would seem to clinch the argument."[763]

Patrick's 'Letter to Coroticus' was, in Dr. Ryan's words, "a sharp cry of anguish and indignation rung from the saint's heart by a savage outrage," a massacre and capture for slavery of his newly baptized Christians. This representation of a defeat for Patrick simply could not be allowed to find a place in Armagh's Patrick Saga for obvious reasons. That Patrick's suppressed letter was replaced by pseudo-Patrician material fathered on Patrick implicated Armagh's chroniclers all the more. The incriminating fact that Ferdomnach, the man responsible for recording and conserving Patrick's writings, still failed to transcribe the 'Letter to Coroticus' into the Book of Armagh after being queried on its absence, offering lame excuses that he had forgotten, underlines only too well the ongoing conspiracy. This created a chasm separating the saintly Patrick of the Letter to Coroticus from the fictitious Patrick of the Book of Armagh foisted on an unsuspecting medieval Ireland.

What has this to do with lost Belgic oppida, lost history and lost peoples of Iron Age Ireland? Everything! Patrick's biographers who suppressed Palladius and so much of Patrick's own writings to make way for their glorified, all-conquering Patrick were the same pseudo-historians who suppressed or stole the traditions of Iron Age Irish Fir Belg oppida in order to glorify Tara and its so-called High Kings of Ireland. These "heroes of Armagh" who hijacked early ecclesiastical history to glorify Patrick were, in O Rahilly's words, "very far indeed from being animated with a desire for historical truth; their object was to disguise the truth." They succeeded because of their sheer sophistication. Their "history of pre-christian Ireland imposed itself on our ancestors as historical truth, despite its spurious character." Thanks to Ptolemy's Record of Ireland preserved on the Continent beyond the reach of the Armagh/Ui Neill censors, thanks to the archaeological record preserved in vestiges of oppida linear embankments running across the face of the Celtic Irish landscape which escaped their attention, and thanks to scraps of genuine written legendary history and shreds of archaic oral history passed on faithfully, it is still not too late to resurrect something of what was so callously suppressed or cast aside.

Tara is as conspicuous by its absence from Ptolemy's 2nd century Geographical Record of Ireland as his Regia e Tera (Regia e Temhra =Turoe) is conspicuous by its presence at the centre of Co. Galway. The word *'Regia'* sets this West of Ireland Capital apart as one of the 2 Capitals of Ireland recorded by the celebrated cartographer. The other is the Capital of the Ulster Cruthin, Emain Macha. Armagh's literati suppressed the basic facts of Iron Age Irish history and geo-politics. Ptolemy's account is corroborated by numerous vestiges of archaeological evidence and by the Ulidian Tales which project the Fir Belg West of Ireland constantly at war with the Ulster Cruthin power of Emain Macha. He accurately recorded the very difficult O-Irish form of the name of Turoe Capital, *REGIA E TERA* (*Cnoc Temhro*, gen; *Regia e Te(mh)ra* dat.). Two centuries later when majuscule Greek lettering was officially transmuted to miniscule Greek, the copyist mistook this archaic Celtic name for a Greek adjective, and reduced it to *regia etera,* an illicit emendation which renders it altogether nondescript, 'just another capital'. Ptolemy recorded a renowned Celtic name, not some vague information. It should be emended to the original Regia e Te(mh)ra. Ptolemy, or his copyist, was all but accurate with his second conspicuous West of Ireland name, his city of Nag-na-ta(l). Were it not for his failure to catch the soft 'l' of 'Dál', or a transcriber misread the Greek Λ for 'A', he would have given a perfect rendition of the Old Irish *Cnoc na nDal* (Nag na nDal, Knocknadala today). 'T' and 'D' were interchangeable in his record. This Royal Assembly Place (Cnoc na Dal) with its urban complex surrounding the inner ward of the massive Western oppidum of Turoe is the Nag-na-Ta(l) of Ptolemy's record.

---

[763] D.A. Binchy, Op. Cit., p. 42.

His account is accurate: *"Nagnata, the most illustrious acropolis, (Nagnata[l] polis episemos), the most renowned and extensive population centre in all Britannia set in the Western part of Ireland."* There was no other extensive population centre in W Ireland, nor anywhere in Ireland or Britain for that matter, in name or amplitude, to accommodate the 'Nagnata' described by Ptolemy other than the Turoe/Knocknadala *oppidum-cum-polis* as reconstructed and delineated in Chapter 2. He based his record on information collected from sea traders. It was shown how the area of the final fortified limits of the outer ward of this vast Fir Belg oppidum far exceeded the extent of any other Celtic oppidum in Ireland or Britain. Its expansion was never suddenly cut short by Roman conquest as were those in Britain. The 5th century invasion of Maine Mor finally spelt the end for the illustrious Turoe/Knocknadala oppidum. Armagh's 7th-9th century pseudo-historians thus felt free to hijack its ancient traditions to glorify Tara of Meath from time immemorial.

Polis episemos (Πολισ επισεμοσ, illustrious city/population centre) was the term Ptolemy used for the Knocknadala/Turoe urban complex surrounding the core of the oppidum. He is corroborated in this claim of a dense population centre by Irish legendary history. The sole text referring to a great density of population any where in archaic Ireland refers precisely to this Turoe area, *"O Maen na treabh tuillte co rein na fairrigi"* (from densely populated Maen Magh to the sea). The core of the Turoe/Knocknadala Fir Belg oppidum stood at the heart of Maen Magh, the plain around Loughrea, E of Athenry, in Galway. It was named after Maen (Maine), son of Queen Medb who succeeded his mother as Regent of Connacht (Ól nÉgmacht). Knowledge of the suppressive nature of the spurious Tara/Patrick Myth helps one understand just how the history and traditions of such a massive Celtic oppidum in W Ireland could have become "lost". Scraps of genuine archaic history which miraculously escaped the shredders and censors point to the lost capitals and peoples or to the fraudulent ways in which these were suppressed. Before bidding a last farewell to the role of Armagh and its venerable heroes, such as Muirchu, Tirechan and Ferdomnach, in perpetrating the adulteration and suppression of genuine Irish Iron Age History and political geography, the external influences operative in their work should not be ignored. They were highly motivated by events taking place on the Continent to which they were closely attuned and kept well up to date. It may come as a revelation to learn that their propaganda war was very much on a par with the spirit of the age on a Continental scale.

EARLY MEDIEVAL IRELAND'S CONTINENTAL MODEL: *a la Francais*
Tirechan's censorious diatribe against the monastic federations of Columcille, Ardstraw, Clonmacnoise and Clonfert for 'unjustly detaining ecclesiastical properties' which 'should by right belong to Armagh' were in a few cases not far off the mark. For the vast majority of others, however, Tirechan was fabricating 'facts' to give substance to the illusory claims of Armagh which reached full bloom in the *'Liber Angeli'*. McCone explained that "the earliest Irish saint's Lives (7th century) owe much to continental models, but were subjected to increasing influence from secular tradition, particularly as regards a preoccupation with political status and connections expressed in geographical and genealogical terms. Irish monastic libraries boasted of access to the best models (of hagiography) available in Europe. Many themes and motives of Irish saint's Lives are borrowed from saint's Lives written by Athanasius, Jerome, Sulpicius Severus and Gregory the Great." Tirechan and Muirchu copied the worst examples in commencing an ongoing full-fledged Patrick Legend on a par with the 'Martin Legend' in France when they surreptitiously elongated the activities of Patrick throughout the length and breadth of Ireland. As Binchy emphasized, they and their successors emulated the fabricators of the Martin Legend which "subsequently spread St. Martin of Tours' activities throughout the length and breadth of France, bringing him to places he had never visited and among peoples to whom he had never preached." These fabricators had no scruples in forging wondrous miracles allegedly worked by Martin for their conversion, and so fictitiously named him the great 'Apostle of Gaul', a subtle ruse not

lost on Tirechan, Muirchu and Armagh's mentors. This particular Continental genre of politically motivated narrative itineraries was typified in Ireland by Tirechan's work on Patrick and the older Lives of Brigit by Ultan and Aileran.[764]

"It cannot be too strongly emphasized that we possess no Life of Patrick which can stand comparison with the 'Life of St. Martin' by Sulpicius Severus. For Patrick we have no such criterion apart from his own writings that were never intended to provide information for historians."[765] On the value of Sulpicius' 'Life of St. Martin' as a check on later fictions, Delehaye made a pertinent remark relevant to the Patrician problem, that without this check the subsequent fables would have duped the world into believing that Martin was the sole 'Apostle of Gaul'.[766] In the absence of any such check on the Patrick Legend against such forgeries, the world has been duped into believing Patrick was the sole 'Apostle of Ireland'. Authors of later Irish hagiography followed "the pattern set by Tirechan and Muirchu. Esposito gave cogent reasons for believing that those deplorable features which have given Irish hagiography such a bad reputation go back as far as their time."[767] It is the 7th century pan-Continental spirit of ecclesiastical politics and hagiography. The works of Muirchu, Tirechan and the *Liber Angeli*, were never intended to record the genuine traditions of Patrick. Their aim was to invent a glorified Patrick in the interests of Armagh's grossly inflated ambitions, a Patrick who had no relation to the humble saint of the 'Confession', but would be the sole 'Apostle of Ireland."

Continental influences affecting 7th century Irish 'historians' and 'hagiographers' resulted in the creation of the Tara/Patrick Myth. Kim Mc Cone illustrated how 7th century Irish monastic writers drew heavily not only on miracles of the canonical and apocryphal scriptures, but also on the "familiar continental hagiographical models."[768] Plummer underlies the fabrications perpetrated in the Lives of Sts. Martin and Patrick: "one very obvious way of expanding a saints life was to incorporate incidents relating to that saint from the lives of other saints." By accrediting to one missionary the activities of another, the life of the former could be inflated ad infinitum. Patrick was glorified at the expense of Palladius. Drawing on resources of continental-style hagiography of the worst genre and on native Irish saga to produce a well-constructed narrative, Muirchu's 'Life of Patrick' became a trendsetter in spurious hagiography. The most highly spurious models of continental hagiography, the fabulous Lives of St. Martin, were favoured by Muirchu and Tirechan. Armagh's newly-minted Patrick was elongated the length and breadth of Ireland for the purpose of claiming churches in his name all over Ireland in places the real Patrick never set foot, just as was done in the spurious "Lives" of St Martin.

Picard identified continental models for the native itinerary approach: "While the *Vita Martini* represents the main influence in early Irish hagiography, another trend was also in vogue. Its structure was akin to that of an 'itinerarium' in which the life of the holy man is presented against a background of travels. Jerome had made it famous in Latin hagiography with the *Vita Hilarionis* written in 391. It was known in Ireland in the 7th century, for Adomnan quotes from it in *Vita Columbae*."[769] This pattern was adapted in the 7th century Irish political environment in which it was pressed into service in the fictitious Lives of Patrick, first by Tirechan. It influenced his concoctions of Patrick's fictitious 'circuits' of Ireland. It came to play a major role in the Tara/Patrick Myth, insisting that virtually the

---

[764] Kim McCone, 'Pagan Past and Christian Present in Early Irish Literature', p. 180-181

[765] D.A. Binchy, Patrick, p. 56

[766] P. Delehaye, *'Cinq Lecons'*, p. 10; D. A. Binchy, Op Cit., p. 56.

[767] D. A. Binchy, Op. Cit., p. 56-57.

[768] Kim McCone, 'Pagan Past and Christian Present in Early Irish Literature', p. 180

[769] Kim McCone, Ibid, p. 181.

whole of Ireland had been converted by Patrick single-handedly and that Tara, controlled by Ui Neill dynasts, had been the royal seat of the High-Kingship of Ireland in Patrick's day. This claim was so sedulously propagated in so sophisticated a manner that it came to be universally believed as sober history. Binchy noted that paganism was still a powerful force in Ireland more than a century after Patrick's death. He gave cogent reasons to believe that the triumph of Christianity was achieved only after a long obstinate struggle. Similarly he showed that the High-Kingship of Ireland from Tara was an idea conspicuously absent from the Irish Law tracts before the 8th/9th century.

In Tirechan's 'Memoir', Armagh's newly-minted Patrick set off on a triumphant 'circuit of Ireland', marching from one territory to the next at the head of a large army of lay and clerical retainers, Continental and native missionaries, poets, lawyers, and church founders. This image and its accompanying terminology are strictly of 7th/8th century provenance. Patrick is portrayed as an invincible hero of Celtic folklore or Biblical leader, a conquering Cu Chulainn, a mighty Moses or Joshua taking possession of the promised land of Erin. This image delighted the Ui Neill dynasts and Armagh Abbots in their quest for such a 7th/8th century conquest of the 'promised' land of Erin. Not so, the "brutally suppressed humble servant of God who speaks so movingly in his own writings of his daily expectation of death, slavery and capture,[770] of persecutions and unmerited reproaches,[771] of massacres of his converts, and of money demanded by kings and brehons in return for his protection while preaching to the tribes.[772] These and similar passages were deleted from the Armagh recension of his 'Confession'. "They would have looked strangely out of place beside the picture of the conquering hero sketched by Tirechan and Muirchu." (Binchy)

Armagh's hagiographers knew no limits in their efforts to exalt their newly hewn hero, as Binchy noted: "This glorified Patrick is not merely the successor of the hero; he has inherited some of the more disagreeable characteristics of the very druids who were overthrown by him. He beats them at their own game, for he wins by 'bigger and better' magic; witness the ignoble competitions in thaumaturgy so industriously chronicled by Tirechan and Muirchu. Worse still, he shares to a remarkable extent their relish for malediction." What then is one to conclude on finding that the humble saint "whose own words about those who have injured him breathe the very spirit of charity and forgiveness has (at the hands of 'Armagh's venerable heroes') become a most liberal dispenser of venomous imprecations, not merely on his human adversaries, but even on inanimate things which have impeded his progress?" At least 3 Irish rivers were allegedly rendered barren of fish by Patrick's potent primatial curse. "The rewards and punishments meted out by him are nicely adjusted to the hopes and fears of a barbarian aristocracy rather than to the message of the Gospel. The local magnate who 'believes' is assured (not of reward in heaven) but that there will be kings of his seed forever; the recalcitrant chief, on the other hand, is told his line will either shortly become extinct or will survive only in poverty and subordination. These unedifying features are more prominent in the later Tripartite Life. Yet there are already sufficient examples of these in the works of Tirechan and Muirchu to justify Esposito's view that they go back to the beginning of Irish hagiography." So blatantly had his biographers debased the stature of the real Patrick in the interests of Ui Neill Armagh ambitions that, had his own writings perished, their glorified Patrick would have effectively obliterated his name from the Church's calender of saints.

Such chicanery in the name of monastic empire-building and the scramble for national kingship was not a eccentricity of the 'Island of Saints and Scholars'. This was the

---

[770] St. Patrick, 'Confessio', 55.

[771] Ibid, 46.

[772] Ibid, 52, 53.

atmosphere breathed by early medieval Europe. Distance was no barrier to Irishmen involved in this activity in other lands. Seventh century Ireland was quick to learn from Continental models. The period under review was a time of major upheaval in Ireland as on the Continent. It witnessed the emergence of national, ecclesiastical and social identities that shaped Europe. On both cultural and political levels, patterns were being created which were to mould its life and mentality for centuries to come. Old tribal identities were being replaced by new national names. Gaul became the land of the Franks. **For the first time in Europe from the mid 7th century, National Kingship was beginning to be established as a brand new institution, overruling tribal organizations and petty kingships. A similar trend is observable in the ecclesiastical realm. No High Kingship of Ireland could possibly have ever existed before then.** Note well!

Irishmen were playing no small part in these upheavals. They had a foot in every camp. Far from being isolated by its geographical position, Ireland was in close contact with its European neighbours. It played a startlingly significant role in major political and ecclesiastical continental changes. Abbots of Irish monasteries were simultaneously Abbots of major Continental monasteries and as much involved in Continental politics as they were at home. Columcille was no exception. A stream of inspiration flowed in from the Continent via Ultan and Aed of Sletty among others to Tirechan and Muirchu. This was honed to perfection in sharp contestation between them and the similarly inspired Adomnan.

BIRTH OF A BRAND NEW EUROPE VIS-a-VIS A BRAND NEW IRELAND
In the late 4th century Germanic tribes flooded the Roman Empire. The Franks ended Roman Gaul. Clovis' Merovingian kingdom lay between the Loire and Rhine covering Lower Holland, Belgium, N and SW France and part of Germany. Other Germanic peoples in Gaul were pagan or followers of Arius. Clovis and the Franks became half-hearted Christians. "Even the most cursory perusal of Gregory's *History of the Franks* leaves the reader in no doubt about the savagery, debauchery, and barbarity of Merovingian France. By the 7th century, it was made up of 3 rival kingdoms: Austrasia (NE Gaul), Neustria (NW Gaul) and Burgundy, a Germanic people assimilated by the Franks. In Neustria and Austrasia power was in the hands of the major dukes, Mayors of the Palace: Erchinoald in Neustria, Pepin II in Austrasia. In 687 Pepin II ruled Neustria and Burgundy."[773] France was thus united under the Carolingians.

One event in the rise of the Carolingians as rulers of the Franks underlines just how far Irish churchmen were prepared to go in the interests of the rising Frankish national monarchy. Irish Abbots on the Continent with links to Armagh were involved in the usurpation of the legitimately held Merovingian throne by a member of the powerful Pippinid family, the ancestors of the Carolingians. The episode of the enforced Irish exile of the infant King Dagobert II shows the sheer depth of the involvement of Irish Abbots in Frankish politics. *"Liber Historiae Francorum'* relates that when Pippin died, Sigibert, king of Austrasia, established Grimoald, Pipin's son, as mayor of the palace. Gerberding related the sequence of events: Early in 651, sensing the approaching death of the monarch, the two powerful magnates, Grimoald and Dido, Bishop of Potiers, met in the Abbey of Nivelles to discuss plans. When Sigibert died Grimoald tonsured the king's son, Dagobert. He sent him to Bishop Dido in order that he might be bundled off to Ireland out of harm's way. He then placed his own son, with the Merovingian name (C)Hildebert, on the throne. He ruled until 657 when the Neustrians invaded Austrasia and dragged Grimoald before their king, Clovis II, to be condemned to death. Some months after Grimoald's death Clovis died. He was succeeded as Overking of the united Franks by his son Clother III. In the abduction of the young Dagobert, as in the Ui Neill/Armagh alliance, the church was deeply involved. This

---

[773] J. R. Walsh & Thomas Bradley, 'A History of the Irish Church', p.96-98

was the Pippinids' 1st attempt at wearing the royal crown of united Frankish peoples. It was what Ui Neill dynasts were inspired to achieve for Ireland with Armagh's media support. What was at stake for the first time ever was not just a local power struggle, but national overkingship. Irishmen with Armagh connections who were on the scene were not mere spectators, they were involved to the hilt and played a vital role. Armagh's connections with this Frankish episode were seminal in the burgeoning ambitions of the Ui Neill for All-Ireland hegemony and of Armagh's ambitions for All-Ireland metropolitan status.

By 650 Grimoald, Peppin's son, had become ruler of Austrasia (Figure 66) and one of the wealthiest Franks. He controlled the administration of the kingdom and minted money in his own name. Sigibert retained the sacred Merovingian kingship, visible to all in the form of his long hair, a sign of royal blood.[774] When (C)Hildebert usurped the throne, Grimoald promptly ordered Dagobert to be tonsured to hide his royalty and render him unfit for the throne as he was sent to a monastery in Ireland with the connivance of Irish Abbots on the Continent and at home. Irish records are silent about this dangerous and highly political hijacking with the indispensable aid of at least one Irish Abbot and monastery at home and on the Continent. "The circumstances of Dagobert's abduction," Picard noted, "show that the coup was not the work of a single man. It required the support of other Austrasian aristocrats and Neustrian magnates and churchmen. The bishop of Potiers, Dido, was a member of the powerful Neustrian family close to the royal court."[775] Apart from his involvement in the abduction of Dagobert, his other wheeling and dealing earned him an unenviable reputation. In the 'Visio Baronti', written in 678 shortly after his death, Dido is seen in a vision by Barontus in the deepest dungeon in Hell. Dido engaged a leader and an armed escort to abduct Dagobert to a monastery in Ireland. He could not have done so without the full cooperation of an Irish Abbot and monastery.

One cannot refrain from asking which Irish Abbots and monasteries were involved in the murky affair of the forced exile of Dagobert. As it happens, the date of King Sigibert's death is linked to an important event in the history of the Irish mission in North France, namely the murder of St. Foillan (Faelan). Foillan traveled to the Continent after the death of his brother, St. Fursa, and was established at Peronne by Erchinoald, mayor of Clovis II's palace. Erchinoald's motives for granting a considerable investment in lands and buildings to Foilan's monastic community were more political than religious. To break the power of local magnates, secular and ecclesiastical, Erchinoald needed the help of outsiders who were dependant on him alone. It was a calculated political maneuver to secure better control of his peripheral territories by placing imported agents on the ground rather than relying on rebellious local independent-minded power-seekers, a common pattern observable elsewhere. In this case it backfired. Foillan and his community of Irish and Anglo-Saxon monks were expelled by a local despot who despised foreigners. Bercharius, a powerful local commander based in Laon challenged Grimoald at the time of St. Fursa's (Foillan's brother) death. When Erchinoald tried to recover Fursa's relics he had first to deal with Haymon, duke of Ponthieu, whose son Fursa miraculously restored to life, and then with Bercharius who challenged him with an army claiming he had been duke of the Peronne before anyone else. The expulsion of Foillan reflects the reaction of the local despot to tightening of controls in peripheral territories by Erchinoald, not hatred of Foillan.

St. Fursa was born beside Cruach Magh Seola near Lough Corrib in Galway, son of a Munster prince, Fintan son of Finlog, brother of St. Brendan. His mother was Gelgesia, daughter of Aedhfinn, a prince of the Ui Briuin Seolgha. He was baptized and educated by St. Brendan at his Inisquin monastery on Lough Corrib. Fursa joined the monastery of St.

---

[774] Jean-Michel Picard, "Irelande et France du Nord', p. 38
[775] Ibid, p. 38-39.

Enda (former fighting man of the Ciannachta of Louth) on the Aran Islands. He founded the monastery of Killursa at Rathmat on Lough Corrib near Annaghdown and was joined by his brothers Foillan and Ultan. Due to his association with Enda, Fursa was elected Abbot of Louth among Enda's people in 633. Later he become a 'pilgrim for Christ' and left his brother Ultan in charge of Louth monastery. He and his brother Foillan, whose monastery had been Cell Fhoillain (Killilan NW of Loughrea), crossed Britain to East Anglia where they were received by Anglo-Saxon King Sigebert. He bestowed Cnobhersburg fortress (Burg Castle of Great Yarmouth in Suffolk) on them with ample lands for a monastery. When war ravaged East Anglia, Fursa left for France in 644, having worked with the Frankish bishop, Felix, in the christianization of East Anglia. He was welcomed by Erchinoald and founded the monastery of Lagny near Paris. Visiting Italy, his visions of Hell and Heaven became the inspiration of Dante's illustrious poem. His miracles and visions made him famous in medieval literature, sung of by Dante, extolled by Bede. Fursa died in Mezerolles in 649. Foillan replaced him on the Continent.

Duke Haymon, whose son Fursa had restored to life, built a church in honour of Fursa, the miracle-worker, in which Fursa's incorrupt body would be enshrined. Erchinoald was even more determined to acquire Fursa's remains as a prized relic for his new Perronne church. The 'Life of Fursa' tells that in order to avoid a serious clash between Haymon and Erchinoald, Fursa's body be placed on a cart drawn by the 2 untamed oxen which were to be allowed to go whichever way they would. They bore Fursa's body from Mezerolles to Peronne. Fursa's tomb was erected there. War over Fursa's remains was averted. Not to be outdone, faithful to his promise, Haymon erected a shrine to Fursa at the site of the miracle of the raising of his son from the dead by Fursa. This gave its name to Forshem (*che Forsa*, house of Forsa) where his shrine stands today. The small town of Les Boeufs (Wild Oxen) is named after the place where the oxen were chosen (2 oxen are depicted on reliefs and paintings of Fursa).

Muirchu's narrative of Patrick's burial has all the ingredients of Fursa's burial down to details such as the number of oxen and the naming of the place where they were chosen, Findabhair, Co. Down. "Muirchu uses Biblical allusion to implant a congenial political message subversive of what, from Armagh's standpoint, must have been the rather unappealing surface implications of his account of Patrick's burial: 'when the angel came to Patrick he advised him concerning burial: *Let 2 untamed oxen be chosen. Let them proceed whither they will, bearing your body on a cart, and wherever they stop a church will be built there in honour of your body. Two bullocks were chosen (from Conall's cattle E of Findabair). They drew the cart with the holy body placed on their shoulders. From Clogher they went forth directed by God's will to Dun Lethglaisse (Down Patrick) where Patrick was buried*'" (McCone). Muirchu's account agrees with that of Fursa in that 2 cattle are chosen. The Biblical episode has cows, but was not due to a quarrel over the remains of a saint as was that over Patrick between the Airthir of Armagh and Cruthin of Downpatrick. It echoes its exemplar in the conflict over the body of Fursa claimed by 2 rivals, Haymon and Erchinoald. In Patrick's, as in Fursa's, case a battle for the remains was miraculously thwarted. Muirchu took the account of Fursa's burial from Ultan, Abbot of Peronne. 'Acutely alive to ecclesiastical politics', Muirchu moulded his material into a nuanced, justificatory treatise on Armagh's problematic lack of its founder's remains.

Muirchu told how 2 battles over Patrick's remains between the Airthir (Airghialla) who controlled the Armagh district and its church, and the Cruthin in whose territory Downpatrick lay, were miraculously thwarted. Two stormings of Downpatrick are recorded in the Annals of Ulster ascribed to the years 496 and 498 AD. This was deliberately placed shortly after the traditional date of Patrick's death in 493 AD. Even had the Airthir been in full control of Armagh at that early date, it is extremely unlikely that they would have gone to war over the remains of Patrick then. They might have gone to war for that purpose in the relic-mania 7th century. But such a late date would not satisfy the fraudulent intent of the Annals of Ulster in boosting its Patrick Syndicate. Muirchu was seeking to defuse more recent tensions over the control of Armagh which had become serious by the end of the 7th century. The lack of Patrick's remains was a keenly-felt defect for Armagh at a time when the importance of a founder's relics as a means of bolstering a monastery's status was considered sufficient excuse to go to war, as when Haymon and Bercharius' armies marched against Erchinoald for possession of Fursa's remains. Muirchu's narrative on Patrick's burial is a subtly nuanced justificatory treatise designed to allay Armagh's intense embarrassment. Muirchu consciously utilized Continental and Biblical parallels,[776] and drew some subtle allusions from the episode of the 'cart drawn by oxen' recounted therin. It is apparent from the circumstances, ideas and expressions used that the prime model manipulated by Muirchu here was none other than the events surrounding the burial of Fursa. His body was borne on an ox-drawn cart, and 2 conflicts were involved, one with Haymon and the 2nd with Bercharius, in Erchinoald's recovery of the remains of Fursa for his new monastery in which serious strife was miraculously avoided.

Doherty highlighted the association of Fursa and his brothers with Louth's monastery where the cult of St. Patrick had a special significance since its founder, the British missionary Mochtae, had been an associate and disciple of Patrick. This had important implications for the spread of the cult of Patrick to the Continent before it was manipulated by Muirchu and Tirechan who minted the glorified Patrick, motivated by Bishops Aed of Sletty and Ultan. St. Foillan first erected his monastic foundation at Cell Fhoillain (Killilan today) 4 miles NW of Loughrea in Galway at the SE of Dunsandle wood and Carrowbawn near the boundary between Hy Many and Hy Fiachrach. Surface traces of a circular enclosure, with traces of inner buildings, mark the site. St. Foillan's (Faelan's) Holy Well is closed in with stones from which protrudes the shaft of a bright standing stone and the upper portion of a Celtic cross. An intriguing local tale was current until 50 odd years ago, telling how every year on the feast of Foillan's martyrdom (Oct. 31st.) water flowing from the well turned into blood. This is confused with a similar, but conflicting, tale of a well which allegedly gave Elfin, Co. Roscommon, its name, as noted by the renowned 16th century Roderick O Flaherty in his 'Ogygia' who witnessed the prodigy.

As consecutive Abbots of Louth, Fursa and Ultan were in close contact with Armagh. Ultan was connected with her spurious activities in Patrick's name. Patrick was then being adopted and venerated in Armagh as its founder by the Airghialla as he had been by the Cruthin before they lost control of Emain Macha. This caused fresh enthusiasm for the Patrick cult in Louth monastery. As Fursa, Foillan and Ultan went to France, the cult of Patrick was imported by them to the Continental areas of Neustria and Austrasian areas, integral parts of the Frankish state. It was the cult of the real St. Patrick as practiced at Louth, not the cult of the glorified Patrick of Muirchu and Tirechan that they was instrumental in instigating. Irish associations with Peronne began after Foillan had been established as Abbot by Erchinoald over his new monastic foundation at Peronne and Fursa's incorrupt body had been transferred to a specially built shrine there in 654. Irish influence then became paramount in what are the Continental regions of Picardy and Flanders today.

In the chaos following the killing of King Sigebert by Penda of Mercia, Foillan was expelled from Cnobhersberg (Burg Castle) in East Anglia. He was welcomed by King Clovis II and Erchinoald and founded a new monastery on the tomb of Fursa in Peronne. Over the next two centuries it became known as 'Peronne of the Irish', the 'City of Fursa'. A local despot drove Foillan and his monks out of Peronne. They took refuge in Austrasia, called by St.

---

[776] 1 Samuel/Kings 5:7-9.

Gertrude, abbess of Nivelle in Brabant in Holland for learned Irishmen to instruct her nuns and preach in the surrounding countryside. They were welcomed by Itta, wife of Pippin I and mother of Grimoald I. Itta had founded a double monastery for monks and nuns at Nivelles for her daughter Gertrude. The presence of Foillan and Irish monks explains, as Dogherty noted, why the feast of St. Patrick is mentioned in the 'Life of Gertrude', a 7th century document. Foillan founded a monastery and hospital at Fosses in Maestricht on land bestowed by Gertrude. He was murdered by robbers at Serette around 656 while visiting Irish monasteries, including Peronne. Three centuries later Fosses was still known as 'The Irish Monastery'. Obscure in Ireland, famous abroad, the 3 brothers from Loch Corrib played a large role in the political and ecclesiastical affairs of Holland, France and Belgium where their cult is still alive. Up to 50,000 people took part in the procession of the relics of St. Foillan at Fosses in recent times.

On the death of Foillan, Ultan left Louth to become Abbot of Peronne and Fosses where he ruled for 20 years. He became embroiled in the political affairs of the Franks. His political activities on the Continent ran parallel to the myth-making activities of Tirechan and Muirchu for Armagh and her Ui Neill patrons which laid the foundations of Irish pseudo-history. Whether one looks for the Irish henchman of Dido and Grimoald in the affair of the enforced exile of Dagobert, or of Tirechan and Muirchu in the creation of Irish pseudo history, the finger points to Ultan. Dido found a kindred spirit in him. Ultan's Irish network carried Dido's coup to its successful outcome. Dido's meeting with Grimoald at Gertrude's monastery in Nivelles on the day Foillan's body was carried there, put him in contact with Ultan. When Dido sailed for Ireland in 656 with Dagobert, Ultan had succeeded his brother, Foillan, among the Franks. Come autumn of 675, Neustria was in a state of anarchy. The Pipinnids were again in a position to assume power in Austrasia. Pippin II needed a strong Merovingian king to take control of Austrasia and lend legitimacy to his own rule. Ultan reminded him where to find a thoroughbred erudite Merovingian prince in the prime of life ready to take hold of the reins of kingship. Pippin's uncle Grimoald had packed Dagobert off to exile in Ireland some 20 years earlier. As patron of Ultan's monasteries, Pippin II called on Ultan to organize the safe return of the new King, Dagobert, from Ireland. This was carried out in the Spring of 676[777] when Dagobert was crowned King. The Slane-Peronne connection would explain Dagobert's return through England where he spent the winter, as told in 'Vita Wilfridi'. Foillan and Ultan kept the link with England alive. Bishop Wilfrid of York had close links with them through Queen Aethendreda, wife of King Ecgfrith of Northumbria, Abbess of Ely. She was the daughter of Anna, King of the East Angles, who rescued Foillan following the Mercian raid on his Cnobhersburg monastery, and by whom it was lavishly endowed. Picard noted that in view of these connections the presence of Dagobert in England in the winter of 675-676 can be readily understood if the agent of Pippin II were Abbot Ultan of Peronne.[778]

Dagobert's presence in Ireland was covered in utmost secrecy in Irish records. The sole hint of his presence in a specific part of Ireland is preserved in an 18th century oral tradition recorded by Archdall, naming the place of residence of the Frankish prince as the monastery of Slane in Meath. He received an education fit for a king. Proof of this was demonstrated in the wisdom of his rule. Bishop Dido and Grimoald the money-minter would not have ensconced prince Dagobert in a monastery without having made ample provision for his protection, education and upkeep at a time when financial funding of monasteries by wealthy patrons in the form of real estate was considerable - 25,000 acres was the royal donation to the monastery of St-Amand at that time. 7th/8th century annalistic records showcase the monastery of Slane as in a state of extraordinary prosperity, one of the most wealthy

---

[777] Jean-Michel Picard, 'Irelande et France du Nord, VII - IX Siecles', p. 44 - 49.

[778] Jean-Michel Picard, Op. cit, p. 50.

monasteries in Ireland. It was so wealthy it attracted Armagh's utmost attention, efforts and supreme genius to win it over on the blatantly fictitious grounds that its founder and bishop, Erc mac Dego, had originally been a druid in the retinue of the alleged High King of Ireland. This fiction claimed that after his conversion by Patrick, Erc founded his monastery on a pagan burial site called Fert-Fer-Feig, now Slane. The death of Erc, bishop of Slane, is recorded in the Annals of Ulster under 512 AD. It did not occur to the 7th century mythmaker who implanted his coded, congenial message, making Erc a full-fleged elder druid in the retinue of the High King of Ireland when Patrick allegedly visited Tara in 432, was altogether incompatible with the trustworthy record of his obit in 512. Anachronism is the bane of the Tara/Patrick Myth and its far-fetched interpolators. It was subtly concocted as only an Ultan-inspired Tirechan or Armagh-inspired Muirchu-like manipulator could do, to link Bishop Erc, Slane and Tara to Patrick and thus to Armagh.

Most intriguing is the list of Abbots showing the close contact between Slane, Armagh, Ultan's monastery of Louth and his Peronne monastery. More revealing still is the list of sons of Abbot Cormac of Slane given in the Annals of Ulster which demonstrates just how close it was. His sons Muiredac (+758) was Abbot of Louth, Moinan (+779) Abbot of Fursa's Peronne in France, Fedach (+789) Abbot of Slane, Louth and Duleek, Ailill (+802) Abbot of Slane, and Colman son of Ailill (+825) Abbot of Slane and other monasteries in Ireland and France, including those of Fursa, Foillan and Ultan. Patrick and Mochta had established the original spiritual bond between Armagh and Louth in the 5th century. The connection between Peronne and Louth was created by Fursa, Foillan and Ultan. The inclusion of Slane in this monastic network lends credibility to the oral tradition of Dagobert's exile there as cited by Archdall. If, as Picard believed, Slane, like Louth, was connected to Ultan "this would explain some of the puzzling details of Dagobert's episode in Ireland and return to France in 676." The far-reaching political propaganda hatched in these closely allied monasteries leaves one flabbergasted.

Were Ultan the key man in this affair, it was not his sole involvement in politico-ecclesiastical hijacking. Hucbald, St-Amand's historian, noted that Theuderic III requested Ultan to detain Amatus, Bishop of Sens, to which Ultan consented. He incarcerated Amatus at Peronne until Ultan himself died. Despite his dubious reputation for holiness, Ultan was deeply involved in secular affairs of a questionable nature. He became a powerful 'churchman' roundly patronized by the Frankish aristocracy. He was Abbot of Peronne when Dagobert was spirited away to Ireland. He held the same position 20 years later when Dagobert was recalled to rule the Franks. It explains how Dagobert re-emerged in the nick of time when his countrymen needed him most. This perfectly planned operation with the indispensable collaboration of a powerful Irish Abbot playing a key role in the whole affair has Ultan written all over it. Picard concluded that the more one examines the case the more Ultan's name begins to loom larger.

Muirchu and Tirechan were deeply influenced by Continental trends, particularly Frankish affairs which had an affinity with what was afoot in Ireland. Prime models that affected them most were the Martin Legend, the burial of Fursa, and, above all, the new national over-kingship just then coming into existence on the Continent. To gauge the full extent of the influence of Frankish developments on the growth of the Tara/Patrick Mtyh would call for a much more detailed analysis. One thing is clear. A hot line existed between Ultan's Peronne and other Irish monasteries on the Continent on the one hand and Armagh's Muirchu, Tirechan and accomplices on the other. Just how extensive its influence on the growth of the Tara/Patrick Myth was would merit a full-fledged study, particularly since Ultan is named as Tirechan's mentor, informant and financier. Ultan of Louth and Peronne was Tirechan and Muirchu's source on Continental developments in the new arena of national ecclesiastical and political hegemony, and in fictional trends such as the Martin

Legend, whose repercussions thenceforth began to impinge on the Tara/Patrick Myth. There is no 'Life' of Ultan of Ardbraccan (Ard Breccain) of Meath to show what connection he had with Ultan of Louth and Peronne, or, indeed, if he were not one and the same man as the 'Martyrology of Aengus' would have one believe. Ultan of Ardbraccan was bishop of the Desi of the Tara district approximately until the time Ultan of Louth departed from Ireland to become Abbot of Peronne. A reference to Ultan of Ardbraccan in 'Felire Oengusa' states "This Ultan was elected into the abbacy of Mochtu in Louth and Fursa had been there before him"[779] thus identifying Ultan of Ardbraccan with Ultan of Louth and Peronne, brother of Fursa and Foillan. Were this authentic, the French connection with the birth and growth of the Tara/Patrick Myth is considerably enhanced. Were there two contemporary Ultans then both had a large hand in the conception of the Tara/Patrick Myth.

Cross-pollination took place between France and Ireland. Pippin II's national Overkingship of the Franks had a profound impact on the growth of the Tara/Patrick Myth in general and on the idea of the High Kingship of Ireland in particular. His creation of the Frankish national monarchy was played out before acutely observant Irish eyes. Seizure of power by Pippin II was a violent attempt by the Carolingians to reign as sovereign monarchs of the Franks. With Dagobert II and Theuderic III in their respective kingdoms, Pippin II emerged the most powerful man in the 3 kingdoms of the Franks. He became Overking of Frankia, creating a national monarchy for the first time ever. Ultan and pro-Armagh Irishmen who witnessed the birth of this institution saw similar prospects for Irish dynasts. National overkingship was an idea whose time had come. Armagh was raring to seize this raging bull by the horns to win over the powerful Ui Neill as prized patrons. Muirchu adapted this idea to the developing situation in Ireland.

Ui Neill dynasts were quick to take the bait and endeavour to emulate the Pippinids. If one is appalled at the violent methods of the Ui Neill warlords in their scramble for overkingship, one has only to look a little closer to find an exemplar in the atrocity of the contemporary Frankish society. It was an 'Era of Violence'. The murder of Foillan was noted. The murders of Clovis III in 675 and Dagobert II in 679 were part of the political game of winning overkingship. Queen Balthild who took over the reins of government after her consort's murder used cruder tactics in her campaign when the earlier policy of buying over loyalty no longer worked. She had nine bishops murdered. The same tactics were witnessed in Ireland where kings attacked monasteries that refused to submit. Monastery went to war against monastery with great slaughter for similar political and ecclesiastical reasons. The episode of the exile of Dagobert in Ireland and the forced detention of bishop Amatus by Ultan shows that the association of Irish churchmen with Frankish aristocracy went way beyond the bounds of spiritual ministration. The situation in Ireland was not at all that different from that on the Continent (Figure 67).

Frankish novelties which attracted Armagh's close attention were royal immunity for monasteries and the Martin Myth. Queen Balthild gave royal immunity to those monasteries which were major political and ecclesiastical centres of power. The immunity extended to the monastery of Tours responsible for bankrolling the snowballing Martin Myth, the fiction of a Circuit of France taking St. Martin of Tours to numerous distant parts of France where he never set foot in his life. This had an exorbitant attraction for Ultan's disciple Tirechan who modelled the alleged 'Circuits of Ireland' by Patrick on that of the Martin legend. Fursa, Foillan and especially Ultan were among the Franks when the Martin Legend bloomed. They played a vital role in exporting the cult of Patrick to the Continent with a

---

[779] *'Felire Oengusa'* (Martyrology of Aengus), Sept. 4: *"Ro togud Ultan i n-apdaine Mochta i l-Lug-baid 7 ro cuired Fursa remi esti'*; Jean-Michel Picard, 'Irelande et France du Nord VII - IXc' p. 34

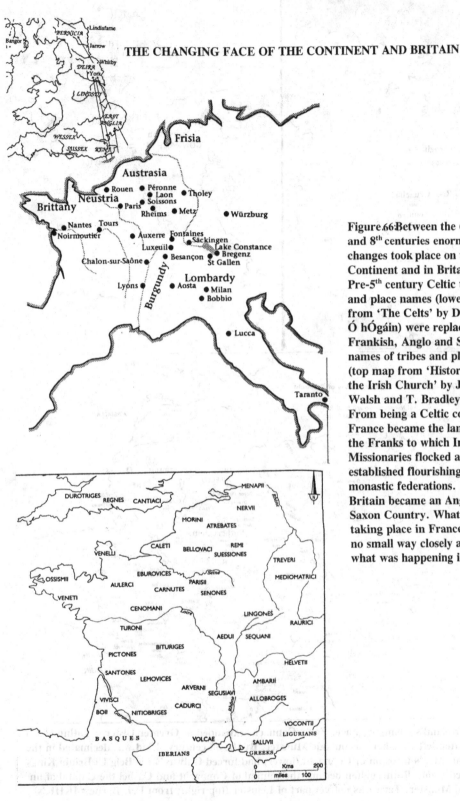

THE CHANGING FACE OF THE CONTINENT AND BRITAIN

Figure 66 Between the 6th and 8th centuries enormous changes took place on the Continent and in Britain. Pre-5th century Celtic tribal and place names (lower map from 'The Celts' by Dáithí Ó hÓgáin) were replaced by Frankish, Anglo and Saxon names of tribes and places (top map from 'History of the Irish Church' by J. R. Walsh and T. Bradley). From being a Celtic country France became the land of the Franks to which Irish Missionaries flocked and established flourishing monastic federations. And Britain became an Anglo Saxon Country. What was taking place in France in no small way closely affected what was happening in Ireland.

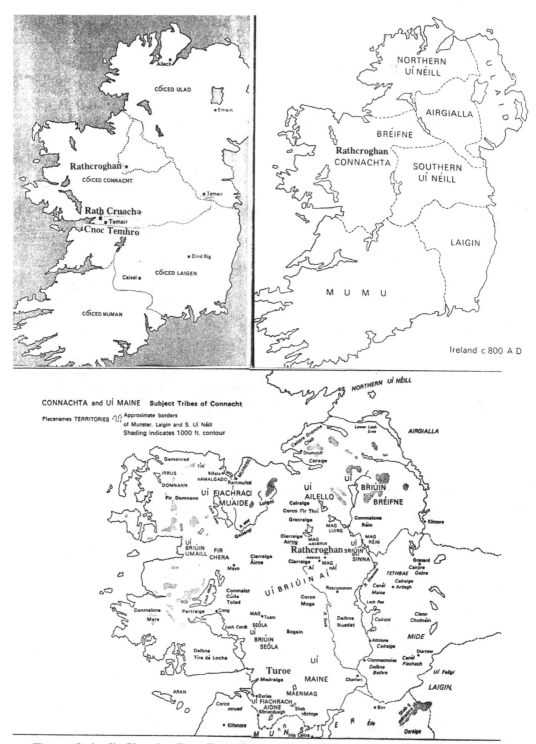

Figure 67 Ireland's Changing Face. Early Connacht expanded as Greater Ulster (Cruthin Ulad) declined (top left). Cashel was outside Munster. By the 8th century, Ulad was decimated in the NE. Maine Mor's invasion of Connacht (lower) had forced Galway's Fir Belg Ui Briuin Kings into Roscommon. Rathcroghan became the Capital of Connacht and Cashel the Capital of an expanded Munster. Tara was not yet part of Leinster (top right; from F.J. Byrne's IKHK's)

complete copy of his 'Confession' which saved the real Patrick from consignment to the dustbin of history by Armagh. They, particularly Ultan, played no less a role in importing the Martin Myth and news of the immunity of Tours and other Frankish monasteries to Armagh and its ambassadors, Tirechan and Muirchu. Armagh was alert and sensitive to such developments. Soon thereafter it began to make its thoroughly tendentious, though highly theoretical, claims to such immunity throughout Ireland as expressed literally in the 'Liber Angeli'. News of what was afoot in France filtered back to Ireland through Foillan and Ultan's former monastery of Louth to Armagh. It is especially significant that at least one of Louth's Abbots became Abbot of Armagh precisely at this challenging time, further strengthening its link to France through Ultan and his monastic family.

Relations between the Ui Neill and Armagh's monastic community were based on an exchange of favours not unlike that of Ultan among the Franks. In return for financial, political patronage, dynastic support for its claim to All-Ireland metropolitan status, and monastic immunity, Armagh provided media documentation, alleged historical background and logistic support, lending academic authority to the claims of Irish High Kingship for its Ui Neill patrons. The claims of the Armagh/Ui Neill alliance were played to a domestic audience. The wider medieval mindframe was ready to believe that if it were in writing then it was true. The sophisticated academic favours provided by Armagh bolstered the Ui Neill. The Patrick Myth mirrored the Martin Myth against this Hiberno/Frankish background. The type of manipulateion which went into the fabrication of the Martin Myth is a basic ingredient of the Patrick Myth. There is a parallel between the affairs of the Franks and the Irish. Secular and ecclesiastical manoeuvres in France influenced those in Ireland within the Armagh monastic milieu through the intermediary of Irish monks who were highly involved in all these affairs in France and Ireland.

The notion of national kingship making itself felt among the Franks exhilarated the hearts of Armagh's heroes. It exposed them to explosive possibilities when they were endeavouring to win over the patronage of Ui Neill dynasts who were emerging as the most aggressively powerful force in Ireland. Royal immunity for Armagh would only make sense were there a strong power like that in France to make it a reality. Having won over the patronage of the Ui Neill, it was in her interest to expedite the speedy rise of the S Ui Neill warlords to overkingship and outright national supremacy. News of the rise of the Carolingians to national overkingship in France, the first Continental land to attain such status, reached Muirchu and Tirechan through the intermediary of Ultan and others. Thus was set the scene for staging the Tara/Patrick Myth which suppressed genuine Irish Iron Age pre-and proto-history and the history of early Christian Ireland in favour of Armagh's newly fabricated 'official doctrine.' Ultan played a major role in the transmission of relevant material concerning the dynamics of national overkingship, monastic hegemony and immunity, and the mechanics of the Martin Legend to Armagh's venerable heroes, the framers of the Tara/Patrick Myth. French lessons helped it bloom and grow, bloom and GROW, and GROW and GROW and GROW and GROW!

SUPPRESSION OF IRISH IRON AGE HISTORY

What has this to do with the lost capitals of the Iron Age Belgic peoples of Ireland? Everything! For it was these same fabricators of the Tara/Patrick Myth who found it necessary to suppress the original context of Ireland's Iron Age political geography and genuine history to make way for their new 'official doctrine'. Just as Armagh's 'men of learning' deemed it expedient to suppress the facts about Palladius who was sent by Pope Celestin in 431 as Rome's Apostolic Delegate "to pastor the Irish believing in Christ" to make way for their glorified Patrick, so too they found it necessary to suppress the original context of the Fir Belg capitals of Turoe/Knocknadala and Rath Cruacha of Athenry in the W of Ireland to make way for their glorified Tara in the East. Traditions of the former capitals of the Irish

Belgae were transferred lock, stock and barrel to the newly minted 'Royal Capital of the High-Kingship of Ireland at Tara from time immemorial' just as the traditions of Palladius were transferred to Patrick. This boycott of western Belgic capitals in favour of Tara was perpetrated by the same 'heroes' who boycotted the traditions of Palladius in favour of Patrick. Having dealt with Palladius and Patrick as shown above, they felt bolder yet to do what they pleased with early Irish secular history and geo-politics, its peoples, their traditions, kings, and centres of power.

Fortunately a copy of Patrick's 'Letter to Coroticus' was preserved on the Continent. This sole survivor is found in the Brussels codex. Muirchu supplied the blatantly distorted Irish account preserved in the Book of Armagh. Binchy called it "an utter travesty of the facts." Muirchu claimed that because of the slaying of Patrick's newly baptized christians, Patrick "prayed to God to deprive the evildoer (Coroticus) both of this life and the next. In the presence of the whole court, the king (Coroticus) was changed into a fox. He fled and was never heard of again." This is a deliberate distortion of Patrick's own noble letter with its moving final plea for repentance and reconciliation. In answer to his own query, "Did Muirchu concoct this tawdry fable?" Binchy replied: "If so it sheds grim light on the technique and credibility of Patrick's early biographers," who also suppressed genuine Irish Iron Age history and laid the foundations for Irish pseudo-history by the concoction of the Tara/Patrick Myth. Binchy, inspired by Patrick's own example, preferred "the more charitable conclusion" of excusing Muirchu and Company while at the same time condemning their crime which "within a period of two centuries had so utterly distorted historical truth.[780] Pseudo-history waxed. History waned.

MUNSTER'S TEMPTATION AND FALL FOR ARMAGH'S ALLURING APPLE

Nowhere does Tirechan's work expose the Continental hagiographical influence, subtly adapted to the exigencies of the contemporary Irish political environment he was attemptting to manipulate, more than in the pattern he imposed on Patrick's alleged itinerary. Setting out from Tara he conducted Patrick on a 'circuit' of the Northern Half of Ireland. After traversing the territories of the Southern Ui Neill he proceeded through Connacht, the Northern Ui Neill along the NW seaboard, and back to Tara. 'Finito circuito' ('end of circuit') are his words. It is obvious, as Binchy noted, that he was about to conduct his all-conquering hero on an equally successful second 'circuit', this time of the Southern Half of Ireland. However, after a sketch of the opening stages of this so-called 'circuit' and a brief summary of the remainder, his narrative broke off inexplicably. It is obvious that Tirechan lacked similar precise knowledge of that Half's political and ecclesiastical traditions which manifested itself so meticulously in his 'Patrician circuit' of the Northern Half. Without this essential information on the South of Ireland, Tirechan was unable to manipulate its traditions to Armagh's advantage except on a very limited scale. He was a 'persona non grata' in the South of Ireland as he was in the South of Connacht. Perhaps death cut short his time-consuming investigations into the relevant data of that area preventing him from completing his task of manipulating it to Armagh's advantage. For the completion of a detailed account of Patrick's alleged 'circuit' of the South of Ireland one is entirely dependent on the compiler of the later 'Tripartite Life'.

After Tirechan's death, Armagh set about the task of collecting relevant data to complete the 'circuit' of the Southern Half by having its ambassadors invited as associates of the Ui Neill king to Munster where she knew the province's ecclesiastical and political traditions would be forthcoming under the right circumstances. Under the year 737 the Annals of Inishfallen refer to a *Dail*/Great Meeting between the Ui Neill King Aed Allan and Cathal mac Finguine, King of Cashel in Munster, at the monastery of Terryglass on the NE banks of

---

[780] Op. Cit., p. 66.

Lough Derg. Armagh's agents went along as annalists of the Ui Neill King and ambassadors of Armagh. They touted Armagh's 'vast library' of Annals of ecclesiastical and secular history, a commodity much sought after. They would talk shop and trade notes on the Northern Half for similar relevant data from the South, promising to record the traditions of Munster in the best light in Cashel's favour in Armagh's 'illustrious records'.

Nothing regarding the purpose of, or of what actually took place at, this 'Dail' is revealed in the Annals. However, the entry announcing the 'Dail' is immediately followed by another which can hardly have been pure coincidence. It resulted from this 'Dail'. The entry "*Lex Patricii tenuit Hiberniam*' proclaims that the Law of Patrick obtains throughout Ireland, in other words, that the Law of Patrick which the Southerners were duped into believing was a fact of life in the Northern Half was now proclaimed in the South too. The Law of Patrick (*'Cain Phatraic'*) was a tax allegedly due to St. Patrick and his successors at Armagh from the whole of Ireland because all Ireland, its peoples and churches had allegedly been given to him by God. This is the first time such a remarkable claim was made outside the area of Armagh's direct influence. If it were in fact proclaimed in the Northern Half, then it must have been to a very limited audience. That this entry made its appearance in an Annal of Munster provenance so soon after Tirechan's time is significant. Although there is no necessary textual connection between the 2 entries, it would indicate, as Keating assumed, that Cathal, King of Cashel, had been persuaded to formally accept the supremacy of the church of Armagh in Munster at the Terryglass 'Dail'. "This entry could have little meaning if Munster were not included, and would necessitate the formal proclamation of Patrick's Tax over Munster by Cashel's King."[781] What enticed King Cathal to make this astounding concession to a power with which until very recently he was at war, and to fill the coffers of Armagh at Munster's expense? What indeed!

The background to this meeting at Terryglass holds a clue to its real purpose. Cashel was not yet the Capital of Munster. Munster's capitals lay in W Munster. There was a practical division of early Munster into East and West quasi-provincial units. Three East branches of the Eoghanacht monopolized the Kingship of Cashel. West Munster was traditionally the stronghold of different Belgic/Erann peoples from those in the East. Cashel was a much later foundation of an offshoot of the former much as the Ui Neill dynasty was a later offshoot of the early Connacht Fir Belg. The overlordship of Cashel in West Munster was nominal at best. More often than not it experienced bitter hostility. The King of Cashel was looking for ways to make Cashel the Capital speaking for all Munster. He desired to unite Munster against the aggressions of the Ui Neill warlords who were beginning to strike further S into the N segments of Munster and Leinster. In 721, the year of his inauguration as King of Cashel, Cathal mac Finguine of the Glendomain branch of the Eoghanacht, in alliance with the King of Leinster, undertook the offensive against the Ui Neill dynasty at a moment when it was weakened by division. A manifestly partisan entry in the Annals of Inishfallen for the year 721 narrates that in the sequel to the latter offensive Cathal and the Ui Neill King made peace. However, in 733 Cathal took advantage of another spell of weakness and disunity among the Ui Neill to make yet another incursion into the heartland of the S Ui Neill. This time he was roundly defeated and a lesson driven home that the Ui Neill were as of now flexing a new-found determination, strength and unity of purpose. Without wider Munster support Cathal realized that his position had now become dangerously vulnerable. It was time for talking, peacemaking and much more!

The Ui Neill King, Aed Allan, showed off his growing prowess by defeating the Ulster Cruthin at the Battle of Fochairt in 735. He was serving notice that the Ui Neill were now united under a strong ambitious king who would tolerate no further raids on the Midlands.

---

[781] Francis John Byrne, 'Irish Kings and High-Kings', p.209-210.

He wished to leave Ireland in no doubt as to who was master of the North, but was not claiming to be High King of Ireland, be it noted, despite later claims by pseudo-historians. The high-flown claim to Ui Neill High-Kingship put forward by Adomnan, Muirchu and later pseudo-historians was purely for home consumption. The conclusion is inescapable. Byrne noted[782] that in the absence of any follow-up to Cathal's failed offensive by either side, efforts were being made to forestall further incursions which might be harmful to either party's interests. He views the Terryglass 'Dáil' of 737 as a secret deal hammered out by the Ui Neill King, aided by Armagh advisors, with Cathal, King of Cashel. The Ui Neill King and his Armagh mentors knew Cathal would not refuse outside help to cast his Cashel power-net over all Munster and gain overall Eoghanacht supremeacy and provincial hegemony in the South of Ireland. A negotiated transaction was greatly in the interests of both parties. So why not a 'Dáil' to seal the deal!

Cathal was lured by the offer of the Northern contingent to espouse his cause for Eoghanacht supremacy and provincial hegemony. Cashel was proclaimed Capital of Munster for the first time ever, and Cathal proclaimed King, not only of Munster, but of Southern Ireland, which as of now was officially designated *'Leth Mogha'*. This would be recorded as the 'official doctrine' in the Annals by Armagh's media moguls. The Ui Neill would lend logistic support to achieve this exalted aim. Cathal was beside himself with bewilderment beyond his wildest dreams. To seal the deal and make his impact felt throughout his 'suddenly expanded kingdom', Cathal was to proclaim Cashel as Capital of Munster, himself as Overking, not just of Munster, but of *'Leth Mogha'*, the Southern Half, and the Ui Neill King Aed Allan, not just as King of Tara, but Overking of *'Leth Cuinn'*, the Northern Half of Ireland, without consulting Leinster, West Munster, Connacht or the Cruthin of Ulster as to whether they acquiesced in this new-fangled claim. The Northern visitors kept mum as to its wider implications. Were Aed Allan to defeat Cathal after this Dail were proclaimed he could claim to be King of All Ireland in one fell swoop and Cathal could not gainsay him. High Kingship of All Ireland was not mentioned. It did not exist. It was almost too overwhelmming to speak of the new idea of the High-Kingship of the Northern or Southern Halves of Ireland, a necessary first step. Adomnan and Muirchu's hymns to Ui Neill High Kingship of Ireland were strictly for Ui Neill/Armagh ears only. Anyone else would have laughed this blatant claim to scorn. To test the efficacy of his deal, Cathal was to forcefully proclaim the Law of Patrick in Munster. This was the bottom line. If the Northern contingent succeeded in having the Law of Patrick enforced even in Cathal's portion of Munster this would have been a resounding success and a first step in having this important part of Munster become an accessory of the Tara/Patrick Syndrome.

Cathal was bamboozled by Armagh's subtle references to Patrick's so-called circuit of the Southern Half of Ireland and his blessing of the men of Munster from the rock of Cashel. These Northerners seemed to 'know' more about the history of Munster than did Munstermen themselves. How could this be? Proper Munster Annals were long overdue! This must be recorded! Cathal could not wait to hear more. It was only when Armagh's ambassador let slip at the appropriate moment in the presence of astonished merry Munstermen the never-before-heard account of how Cathal's ancestors, King Oengus and sons, were baptized by Patrick on the rock of Cashel that Cathal was wooed and won over, head over heels. He could not wait to proclaim Patrick's Law in Munster in memory of Patrick and his own glorious ancestors! Celebrations were called for. Munster's finest wines flowed freely. Night was as bright as day all round Terryglass' Lough Derg shores! Cashel abu!

---

[782] Francis John Byrne, Ibid. p.208-209.

Cathal proclaimed the Law of Patrick in Munster to the utter astonishment of 'less infomed' Munstermen. Similar surprise welcomed a new myth which became current precisely from this time as reflected in the later widely-held theory that although Ireland was originally united, it was later divided into *Leth Cuinn* (N Half) and *Leth Mogha* (S Half) under the Overlordship of Tara and Cashel respectively. It claimed Ireland was one nation under one High King until the time of Conn after whom *Leth Cuinn* was named. The Ui Neill King Aed Allan made no claim to the High Kingship of Ireland at the Dáil of Terryglass (still an idea strictly for Northern consumption only). This new concept promulgated following the Dáil prepared the ground for eventual acceptance of the claims put forward on behalf of Ui Neill High Kingship of Ireland. The memory of the old Iron Age Belgic Capitals which welded Munster and Connacht together was suppressed in the Annals, although well remembered in oral tradition. Iron Age history was overturned in the 'new history' projected by the Annals representing the Iron Age rulers of *Leth Cuinn* (named after Conn) and *Leth Mogha*, named after Mug Nuadat, as in a state of war. This was the Myth of the Partitioning of Ireland into these two Great Halves.

Early tradition and legendary history presented the families of Conn, King of Connacht, and Eoghan Mór, King of West Munster and ancestor of the ruling Eoghanacht before Cashel was founded, as intimately connected. Conn's daughter, Sadhbh, was consort of King Ailill Olom, son of Eoghan Mór. Conn's daughter, Sarait, was consort of King Conaire Mor, brother of Eoghan Mór. Conn aided Munster kings. Eoghan Mór aided Conn and brought his Oga Bethra fighting force from Cork and settled them around his stronghold at Rath Fidech just south of Athenry. In the invasion of Lughaid mac Con who ousted Art, son of Conn, and himself become Rí Temhro (King, not of Tara of Meath, but of Turoe of Galway), Ailill son of Eoghan Mór and his seven sons went to the aid of Art in the Battle of Magh Mucruime. They were assassinated together with Art near Clarenbridge, Co. Galway. Close friendship reigned between Munster and Connacht.

The pseudo-historical Myth which came into being following the Terryglass Dáil concocted "the partitioning of Ireland into 2 halves," following "the imaginary struggle for supremacy between Conn and Mug Nuadat (Eoghan Mór)" claiming that Tara was the Capital of *Leth Cuinn* (Northern Half) and Cashel the Capital of *Leth Mogha* (Southern Half), as O Rahilly noted. The intention was to project the idea that Ireland was allegedly always a united country under one High King until the time of Conn and explain how the division of Ireland came about in a manner amenable to all parties concerned but particularly ingratiating to the Ui Neill. "Eoghan Mór defeated Conn in ten battles and compelled him to yield the S half of Ireland. As Conn was ancestor of the kings of Ireland and was himself reckoned one of them, it was assumed that Mug Nuadat had compelled Conn by force of arms to yield him half the country. Conn's right to the kingship of Ireland was vindicated by making the division a temporary one which ended when he slew Mug Nuadat/Eoghan Mór at Mag Lena. This rivalry between Conn and Mug Nuadat is the theme of 'Cath Maige Lena.'"[783] As it was until Conn's time, so should it ever be! What now if the King of Leth Cuinn were to defeat the King of Leth Mogha? Hush!

Armagh ambassadors in the train of Aed Allan did not miss the opportunity to press the claims of Armagh as set out in the 'Liber Angeli' regarding the rights and dues of all the churches of Ireland to Patrick's heir at Armagh. They duped Cathal into believing his province alone had failed to pay its dues to Armagh and had better make good to save face. The Inishfallen text is significant: "The Law of Patrick obtained throughout Ireland." Armagh's men went back home pleased as punch armed with a mass of material, including the regnal list of Cathal's ancestors and of early kings, ecclesiastical founders and saints of

---

[783] F. T. O Rahilly, 'Early Irish History and Mythology', p. 191-192

Munster with other pertinent data. They were now ready to make up for Tirechan's shortcomings regarding the South of Ireland. Armagh's media moguls rose to the occasion and manipulated the material in Armagh's favour. This is amply demonstrated in the *Tripartite* Life of Patrick which exhibits their depth of knowledge of early Munster regnal lists. Armagh promptly proclaimed that all the early kings of Cashel dating from Oengus' time were each in turn consecrated Kings of Cashel by the heir of Patrick. And so it should continue forever! They could not be blamed for believing that this was an occasion to celebrate a significant step in the right direction for Cathal, moreso for Aed Allan, most of all for Armagh. The wine flowed freely. All danced to the music. Hurragh!

Cathal kept his part of the bargain which necessitated the formal proclaimation of Patrick's Tax. It was imposed on that part of Munster loyal to him, and paid to Armagh. Armagh's coffers overflowed. Business was booming. That is, until one dark day late in the same century Cashel discovered to its great shame that he had been conned by Armagh. Munster made a desperate attempt to reverse its embarrassment. In 784 the Law of Patrick was revoked and the Law of Ailbe was promulgated in its place. Byrne suggests the composition of the early Life of Ailbe should be associated with that promulgation.[784] To hide Munster's shame, "the pretence that Ailbe of Emly was a pre-Patrician saint was designed quite deliberately as ammunition against Armagh. It is not borne out by the meagre traditions concerning the saint who evidently lived in the early 6th century."[785] It was claimed that Ailbe "was baptized by Patrick's pre-cursor, Palladius. A clear attempt was being made to claim, if not superiority over Patrick, then at least precedence in time and equality in status"[786] Sharpe noted that although the author makes Patrick surrender **all** Munster to Ailbe, he had the motivation to present Ailbe as a fore-runner of Patrick. He saw it as "a response to the rise of Armagh and the cult of Patrick." The later Life of Ailbe assimilated all the pseudo-historic baggage of the developed Patrician Legend. 'Cain Patraic' was again promulgated in Munster in 823 by King Feidlimid mac Crimthann of Cashel which underlies the struggle taking place within Munster. Despite the above debacle and his defeat in the south of his province a year later, as a result of the joint agreement according him hegemony over Leth Mogha, the reign of Cathal mac Finguine was looked back upon in later times as a golden age. Kings of Cashel were claimed to have been High Kings of Ireland and Cashel to have been the Capital of Ireland by later Munstermen.

Despite the pseudo-historic claim that Aed Allan was High King of Ireland, what is conspicuous about this 8th century affair is that the Ui Neill King and his Armagh mentors were silent about the claim of the High Kingship of Ireland once outside their own stamping ground. Although the reputed High Kingship of Ireland had been alleged for Ui Neill dynasts by Adomnan and Muirchu, the Northern delegation at Terryglass did not dare mention this claim to their Munster hosts because there was no such institution as the High Kingship of Ireland even as late as the 8th century. The most expansive royal power at the time was that proclaimed at Terryglass Dail, Overkingship of either North or South of Ireland. Even that was highly tendentious. Far indeed from the High Kingship of Ireland being a reality at this late date, the Ui Neill were only then for the first time pressing their claim to the Overkingship of the Northern Half, albeit well out of the hearing of Connachtmen who would certainly not have acquiesced in this blatant claim. Nor would the Cruthin of Ulster. It is a shameful admission that the High Kingship of Ireland was still no more than a high-flown idea purely for home consumption, yet an idea whose time was in the offing. This bird's-eye view of 8th century secular and ecclesiastical politics is an eye-

---

[784] Francis John Byrne, 'Derrynavlan: The Historical Context', J Roy Soc. Antiq. Ire 110 (1980), 116-128; 118.

[785] Francis John Byrne, 'Irish Kings and High Kings', p. 210.

[786] Richard Sharpe, 'Quatuor Sanctissimi Episcopi: Irish Saints before St. Patrick' in 'Sages, Saints and Storytellers', ed. by D. Ó Corráin, L. Breatnach, and Kim McCone, p. 393.

opener on the real value of the pseudo-historic claims put forward on behalf of the Ui Neill/Armagh/Tara/Patrick Syndrome. The implications of the Terryglass Dail are shattering to the cause of the Tara/Patrick Myth. By the late 8th century the Ui Neill made their intentions known. When the Ui Neill King led two fiercely determined campaigns into Munster in 775 and 776 wreaking widespread devastation throughout the Province, the Eoghanacht dynasty of Cashel woke to the reality of Ui Neill ambitions. Cashel took time to recover from the shock. The ambitions of the Ui Neill dynasts and Armagh Abbots knew no bounds.

THE ULIDIAN TALES: IRELAND'S OLDEST TRADITION 'RECOVERED'

The Ulidian Tales were in touch with Ireland's primitive pagan tradition. They represent the Ulidians (Cruthin Ulstermen) holding sway over the whole Northern Half of Ireland. The rest of Ireland, led by Ól nÉgmacht (archaic Connacht), is represented as permanently in league against this greater archaic Ulster. Even as late as the 8th century, the Cruthin represented by the Dal nAraidi claimed to be the traditional representatives of the old Ulidian (aboriginal Ulster) race. "In time the Ulidian sagas, the hero-lore of the Ulstermen, were adopted as a chief part of the national hero-lore (due to the fact) (1) that the Ulidians had fallen from their ancient eminence; (2) that the Ulidian epic was early in the field of written hero-lore and thus acquired the prestige of a classic; (3) that it was actually a classic in the closeness of its touch with a primitive and irrecoverable past; (4) that the dominant dynastic families had no such body of hero-lore peculiar to themselves. The Ulidian sagas were armed with a prestige of nobility and antiquity that compelled respect even of the (new) masters of Ireland."[787] Mac Fir Bhisigh's account of the Fir Belg of Connacht and Ireland in his 'Book of Genealogies', leads up to the Ulidian tradition and down from it. MacNeill asked by what process did Ireland's 'men of learning' become the possessors of the 'Ulidian tradition'. The answer may shock you.

Medieval pseudo-historians showed themselves to be fully conversant with the original Ulidian tradition, yet they found it necessary to pretend the contents for the most part had been forgotten. They had no scruples in changing facts. There were many facts recorded in the Ulidian tradition that they were determined to alter. But how were they to present their manipulated 'facts' in a way that appeared they were passing on the original Ulidian tradition? They rose to the occasion by declaring that by the 7th century, through an unaccountable loss of memory, the literati had forgotten the story as a whole. They concocted a story to explain how this **unaccountable loss of memory by the learned classes** could be put right. It is a transparent lie to camouflage the concoction of a vastly altered version of the Uldian tradition. They did so in a way that gave them the authority to suppress the past and replace it with their own new version of events. They pronounced it a 'recovery' of the original epic, hoping their ruse was sophisticated enough to satisfy the gullible masses.

The 7th century King of Connacht, Guaire of Aidne, was a descendant of Fiachra, stepbrother of Niall of the Nine Hostages. He was celebrated for proverbial hospitality. The pseudo-historians declared that he entertained the men of learning and poets of Ireland. During their literary congress at Guaire's palace, Senchan Torpeist, so-called chief poet of Ireland, asked his fellow poets if any remembered the Táin Bó Cuailgne. They could remember only fragments of it. Senchan then inquired whether any copy of the original Táin existed. It transpired that one such copy existed but had conveniently been taken out of the country. Every possible effort was to be made to 'recover' the lost epic. The commission appointed for this set out to find it. When they came to the burial mound of the great Ulster hero, Fergus mac Roigh, one of the commission, the son of Senchan, delivered a poem in

---

[787] Eoin Mac Neill, 'Celtic Ireland', p. 13-14

praise of the memory of Fergus so potent that the spirit of Fergus arose from his tomb in the sight of all. There and then he dictated to them the whole of the Táin Bó Cuailgne. It was thus that the 'literati' (pseudo-historians) "regained" possession of the 'Ulidian Epic'. One can have little doubt that this new version of the Táin differed radically at many points from the original 'they so conveniently forgot.'

They had the audacity to make Guaire of the Fiachra Aidne instrumental in its 'recovery' and to father it on Fergus, King of the Cruthin of Ulster. These were the prime representatives of the two dynasties in Ireland that objected most fiercely and vociferously to the 'official doctrine' of the pseudo-historians, and whose original versions of archaic tradition, the *Lebor Balb* of Connacht and the original Ulidian Tales were silenced, suppressed, drowned out and destroyed forever. This hoax is analogous in character to the Tara/Patrick and Rathcroghan Myths. As these two dynasties were greatly reduced in size by the 8th/9th centuries, it was an easy task to claim that the memory of the original Irish tradition had dwindled to just a few scraps. Queen Medb, King Guaire and King Fergus must surely have turned in their graves. The time assigned to the 'recovery' is that in which pseudo-history began to be written.[788]

RATHCROGHAN and TARA MYTHS ARM IN ARM: Armagh presides over the nuptials

Tipraite's accession to the Connacht throne was marked by a portentous event, a visit by the Abbot of Armagh, Dub-da-Leithe, in 783 with the Southern Ui Neill dynasts in the wings. By then Armagh was less interested in small fry and their independent churches. It went for the big guns. King and Abbot established the Law of Patrick in Connacht. It was not a one-sided affair. Much much more lay behind this charade which of its nature had to be discreet. The Sil Muiredaig (Ui Briuin Ai) finally seated as kings of Connacht at Rathcroghan of Roscommon were hand in glove in conspiracy with Armagh and the Southern Ui Neill against the Northern Ui Neill and the Ui Fiachra. This was a conspiracy for ulterior motives involving the suppression of genuine history and the archaic Capitals of Connacht to ensure that pseudo-history would come to be accepted as the 'official dogma'. "The choice of site (of the meeting of Armagh's Abbot and Connacht's King) marked the mutual recognition of the claims of Armagh and of the (Síl Muiredaig branch of the) Ui Briuin. 'Cain Phatraic' was proclaimed" in Connacht.[789]

Armagh got what it wanted. The Ui Neill demanded that their ancestral kings be recognized as having ruled the North of Ireland from Tara of Meath from time immemorial. What did the Síl Muiredaig branch of the Ui Briuin demand from Armagh and the Ui Neill in return for the proclamation of their claims in Connacht? King Cathal of Cashel demanded the proclamation of Cashel as Capital of the Southern Half of Ireland and the suppression of W Munster's archaic Capitals in return for a similar proclamation throughout Munster of the Cain Phatraic and the hegemony of the Ui Neill kings of Tara over the Northern Half of Ireland. The Síl Muiredaig branch of the Ui Briuin of Rathcroghan of Roscommon demanded, and conspired in concert with Armagh's Abbot and the Southern Ui Neill, to have their newly-minted claims officially proclaimed in their great Annals, namely, that Rathcroghan of Roscommon had always been the Royal Capital of the Ui Briuin dynasty and of the Kings and Queens of Connacht, including Queen Medb, from time immemorial. They would promulgate the fictitious claims of both Armagh and the Ui Neill dynasts in return for this recognition and the heralding of their newly minted Rathcroghan Myth. This became the 'official dogma' proclaimed by the Annals of Ireland. Any Book which told the truth about the past was to be suppressed and silenced. The Book of Connacht which told a vastly different story from these new spurious Annals was 'drowned', as its disappearance was

---

[788] Eoin Mac Neill, 'Celtic Ireland', p. 15-16.
[789] Francis John Byrne, 'Irish Kings and High Kings', p. 250.

explained. It became known as the *Lebor Balb*, the Silenced Book. The Battle of the Books was being won by the new pseudo-historic versions.

The Connacht collateral Ui Fiachra dynasty fiercely resented these fraudulent pseudo historic claims, pointing to the well-known Capital of Fir Belg Connacht, Rath Cruacha of Athenry. That ancient oppidum with its Fir Belg defensive system intact stood within their own territory of Ui Fiachrach Aidne for all the world to see. The glaring ramifications of this disturbing truth led the Síl Muiredaig king of Rathcroghan to silence and suppress all archaic relics! This conspiracy continued and the Cain Phatraic was proclaimed in Connacht by several successive Abbots of Armagh at frequent intervals over the next few generations, as evidenced again in 799, 811, 818, 825 and 836 AD.[790] Thus the new 'official doctrine' came to be accepted as 'sober history.' Tipraite mac Taidg, King of Rathcroghan was so totally forgotten by later ages, due to lack of royal progeny, that his name is omitted from the regnal lists. Yet his 'actions' were ominous. His last will and testimony, the Rathcroghan Myth, has survived to this day side by side with the Tara/Patrick Myth. His reign was short (+786). Yet, it was marked by the acceptance, in 'official records' at the highest levels, of the Ui Briuin Ai and their ancestors as 'natural heirs' to the High Kingship of Connacht sited at the 'royal Capital of Rathcroghan of Roscommon from time immemorial,' in perpetuity. Despite fierce efforts by the Ui Fiachra to redress the pseudo-historic fictions fabricated by the Ui Briuin Ai with the aid of Armagh, the short reign of Tipraite was a watershed in the rise of the Sil Muiredaig branch of the Ui Briuin and in the final fate of the archaic Fir Belg Capitals of Turoe/Knocknadala and Rath Cruacha of Athenry. Pseudo-history reached its climax by consigning these to the dustbin of history.

From the late 8th century king Indrechtach mac Muiredaig, the Ui Briuin king, engaged in dogged war to occupy Rathcroghan of Roscommon. Connacht re-emerged once more as a powerful force on the Irish scene under Muirgius of the Sil Muiredaig branch of the Ui Briuin at *Croghan Ai* of Roscommon. His father, Tommaltach, (+774), first cousin of Tipraite, was the first Ui Briuin king to be given the title *Rex Ai,* king of *Croghan Ai,* impling that for the first time ever the Sil Muiredaig branch of the Ui Briuin had made the Rathcroghan district their own and could claim such a title and enjoy unchallenged possession of the ancient capital of the *Cruthintuatha Croghain*, Rathcroghan of Roscommon.

Tipraite's life was cut short before he had time to follow up his victories over the Ui Fiachra. Twice in the following year, 787, these defeated the Ui Briuin, first at Goula, and then by a massacre of the Ui Briuin of the Owles in Mayo in which all the latter's nobles were wiped out, including their king, Flaithgal. Then the Sil Muiredaig Ui Briuin began to assert themselves in a ruthless manner. In the following year Muirghius led them to victory at the Battle of Druim Goise where they delivered a crushing blow to the S Ui Briuin of Magh Seola and the sons of Cathail, then spreading E from Magh Seola into NE Galway and S Roscommon, to exclude them from the kingship of Connacht. The Luigne and other branches of former vassal allies had always supported the Southern Ui Briuin of Magh Seola and their cousins, the descendants of Cathail. Old king Ceallach of Magh Seola led his army to rescue them in a great victory at Corann in Sligo in 704 when their territory was invaded by Loingsech of Cenel Conaill. The Ui Ailello who supported the N Ui Briuin led by Muirghius were expanding their territory at the expense of the Luigne. They inflicted a slaughter on them at Achad Abla in Sligo and followed this up in 790 at the Battle of Agharois in the same county in which they decisively defeated the Luigne. Before the Ui Briuin Seola and Sil Cathail could go to the rescue of the Luigne, Muirghius fell upon them,

---

[790] Ibid, p. 250.

forcefully putting down dissension by defeating and slaying the grandson of Cathail, Cinaed mac Artgal, at the Battle of Cloonargid in Roscommon in 792.[791]

Annals date Muirghius' reign from this victory. He led a savage onslaught in all directions. At the Battle of Ard Maic Rime (Muc Dhruime) in 793 he effectively overthrew the Ui Ailello and the Luigne, his former allies. By taking their lands he greatly extended his kingdom. He eliminated a host of rivals, among them 2 grandsons of Cathal, Cathmug King of Cairpre and Cormac son of Dub Da Crioch, King of Breifne. Having suffered an embarrassing defeat in 796 at the Battle of Ath Feine on the N border of the Ciarraige of Croghan Ai, he ransacked their lands, sacred sites and capitals in reprisal. In 799 at Dun Gainiba he slew many Connacht princes. Muirghius stamped his authority and that of the Sil Muiredaig on the proliferating septs of the Ui Briuin, includeing the parent Ui Briuin branch of Magh Seola.[792] Enmity grew between the Sil Muiredaig branch of Ui Briuin of Croghan Ai and the parent tribe in Galway, the Ui Briuin Seola and Sil Cathail who were treated with savage contempt as rivals to be suppressed, as were the Ui Fiachra. Pseudo-historic tales were concocted to show up in the most unfavourable light the esteemed kings of the Ui Briuin Seola, Ragallach and Eoghan Bel, like that maliciously vilifying Guaire, king of the Ui Fiachra of SW Galway. The genealogical origin of some early Ui Briuin Seola kings were suddenly welded to the Ui Fiachra genealogy because their S Connacht origins clashed with the ambitions and newly minted claims of the Sil Muiredaig who vehemently proclaimed their royal seat of Rathcroghan of Roscommon was the Capital of Connacht from time immemorial. This claim was vigorously denied in South Connacht. Muirghius was determined to suppress all dissident voices. After his defeat at Ath Fene in 796 he swore to crush resistance and become Overking of all Connacht. He sought the support of the S Ui Neill and Airghialla factions connected with Armagh. As Mac Niocaill noted, "within 3 years (after the defeat of his opponents at Dunganiba in 799) he had asserted his overlordship over the subordinate kingdoms of Connacht by destroying the chief stronghold of the Ui Maine (at Loughrea in Galway). He was effectively master of Connacht until his death in 815."[793] He demolished the strongholds of his opponents, particularly in Magh Seola and Maen Magh, and wasted their lands. He desecrated their contemporary sites, and destroyed Queen Medb's archaic Capital of Rath Cruacha of Athenry and her royal crannog on Loughrea lake in the year 802 to suppress all memory of their ancient traditions and proclaim the Rathcroghan Myth more forcefully and convincingly.[794]

The Ui Maine never recovered from his raids into Maen Magh which forced them from their early centre of power. So badly was the area around Loughrea shattered that the Cruthin Sogain of Magh Sencheineoil (Tiaquin/Attymon district) of E Galway which had been loyally subject since their isolation in the prehistoric Fir Belg Belg invasion of Connacht, revolted in 803 against their Ui Maine overlords in that section of Maen Magh of which Loughrea was the centre. In 805 Muirghius imposed his son, Cormac, as Abbot on Baslick, the Basilica of the Ciarraige Ai.[795] He destroyed all old Annalistic records to make way for the 'official doctrine' of the Rathcroghan Myth propagated by Muirghius with Armagh's aid. After Armagh's Abbot, Nuadu, visited Muirghius at Rathcroghan in 811, the synchronization of the Rathcroghan Myth with the Tara/Patrick Myth was finalized to replace the ancient traditions of Turoe and Rath Cruacha of Athenry while a new version of *Táin Bó Cuailnge* was begun. Muirghius again devastated the S of Connacht in 812,

---

[791] Gearoid Mac Niocaill, 'Ireland before the Vikings',p. 137.
[792] F. J. Byrne, Op. Cit. p. 251.
[793] Gearoid Mac Niocaill, Op. Cit., p. 137
[794] Francis John Byrne, 'Irish Kings and High Kings', p. 251.
[795] Op. Cit. p. 251.

suppressing and destroying whatever records, traditions and traces of past history he could find, including the early *Lebor Balb* (Silenced Book).

Kings descended from Muirghius of the Sil Muiredaig Ui Briuin returned to this Fir Belg early settlement area of Galway and sited their castle residences in the Magh Seola and Maen Magh districts in Galway. Dynastic struggle for the Kingship of Connacht continued until the end of the 11th century between the three great houses of the Ui Briuin Ai (Sil Muiredaig) dominated by the O Connor, the Ui Briuin Breifne dominated by the O Rourke, and Ui Briuin Seola dominated by the O Flaherty. The O Connor (Ui Chonchobair) of Croghan Ai triumphed and drove the O Flaherty (Ui Flaithbertaig) from Magh Seola into Connemara. The last High King of Ireland, Rory O Connor, built his royal Romanesque Cathedral on St. Jarleth's 5th century monastic site at Tuam, in Magh Seola, close to his royal residence. It was over the Maen Magh branch of his Connacht dynasty in central Galway that his son, Connor Maen Magh, the last King of Connacht, presided. The tide had come full circle in the course of more than a millennium from the day the Fir Belg set up their primary settlement at the centre of Maen Magh to the return of this 'prodigal son', Connor Maen Magh, son of Rory O Connor, taking his epithet from this ancient district. Then suddenly the sky fell in with the coming of the Normans.

PSEUDO-HISTORY AND MEDIEVAL POLITICS SUPERIMPOSED ON THE TÁIN

The old hostility between the Ui Fiachra/N Ui Neill alliance and the Ui Briuin, dating back to the time of Briun and Fiachra, led the Ui Briuin to seek the support of, and close alliance with, the S Ui Neill in reprisal. It led the Ui Briuin into a sinister alliance with Armagh. Things came to a boil and bled into the Battle of the Books more than on the battlefield itself. A prime example is found in the new 9th century *Táin Bó Cuailgne,* the Cattle Raid of Cooley. Cattle raiding, the 'sport of kings', was so endemic at this time that *Cáin Da Í,* a heavy penalty for its perpetration, was promulgated 3 times in Connacht, Munster and Ui Neill territories respectively between the years 810 and 813 to eradicate this menace. In 826 it had to be reimposed on Connacht due to a resurgence of the problem there. Muirghius, its warlording King, was guilty of this crime at the turn of the century when he laid waste the lands of the Ui Maine of Maen Magh around Loughrea in Galway, slaughtering the innocents and carrying off vast booty and cattle. This angered segments of the Airghialla around Armagh who looked upon the Ui Maine as kinsmen of Airghiallan stock. These facts facilitated the depiction of Connachtmen as arrogant aggressors in the *Táin Bó Cuailnge* saga.[796] It was a highly topical subject. The blockbuster of the new *Táin Bó Cuailnge* was timed to a tick to cash in on this medieval market and satisfy a raging national hunger for such scandalously sweet cow-fodder. Holy cow!

Táin Bó Cuailnge is the centrepiece of Irish heroic saga. The 9th century version of the epic is fundamentally a highly politicized work of literature with strong pseudo-historic propagandist undercurrents. Scholars see it as a symbolic synopsis and genuine memory of the long drawn-out warfare between the Cruthin of Ulster and Fir Belg of Connacht, reworked and embellished for contemporary politically ulterior motives. Its plot began as pillow talk between Queen Medb and her consort Ailill at the royal palace of Rath Cruacha one sleepless night in archaic time. Each boasted that he/she brought more to their marriage in terms of wealth than the other. After passionate argument they found they were in all things equal save that Ailill owned a bull, the famous Findbennach, which had been a calf of one of Medb's cows, but rather than be owned by a woman had proudly gone over to to Ailill's herd, as her consort reminded her. Ailill was bullish, Medb bearish.

---

[796] Patricia Kelly, 'The Tain as Literature', in 'Aspects of the Tain', ed. P. J. Mallory, p. 89.

Words enough for this *mulier fortis*! Up! Summon her soothsayer! Was there a bull in Ireland to match mighty Findbennach? Informed that the sole match was the *Donn Cuailnge* of Daire in Ulster. Medb dispatched Mac Roth to seek a loan of Donn Cuailnge for a year. If Daire were reluctant, he must come himself with his bull to receive his reward that would include a choice portion of Connacht land. Pleased as punch with Medb's terms, Daire decided a little celebration was in order. The mead flowed freely while Medb's messengers sang of Daire's generosity. One lubricated Connachtman lost control of his tongue and boasted that were the bull not given freely it would be taken by force. Daire, enraged by this ribald remark, refused to loan the bull despite Mac Roth's efforts to dismiss the insult as inebriated blah-blah. The messengers returned to Rath Cruacha minus the bull. Mac Roth's apologies drew a sharp retort from Medb to refrain from further excuses since the bull would now have to be taken by force. Consternation! Connachtmen stood dumbfounded as the stubborn Medb declared war on Ulster. All for the sake of male/female equality! The Iron Age stock market turned suddenly bullish!

Medb mustered a mighty army drawn from the men of Munster, Leinster and Connacht. With early spring snows still on the ground she marched against Ulster, led by Fergus, taking Ulster completely by surprise with its frontiers undefended. Fergus, himself an Ulsterman who sought asylum in Connacht, led Medb's army astray to play for time for the Ulstermen to recover from their untimely debility. He sent a warning to Cu Culainn that Medb's army was advancing. Cu Culainn's long drawn-out single-handed defence of King Conor Mac Nessa's Province of Ulster against the assembled armies of Queen Medb is the centrepiece of Irish heroic epic. The war-goddess Morrigan appeared as a grey crow perched on a pillarstone in Temair Cuailnge. She warned the Black Bull (Donn Cuailnge) which then took himself off to Sliab Cuilinn. From Findabair Cuailnge Medb's army ravaged the land, rounding up cattle, women and children, but failed to capture the bull which had reached Glenn Gat. It attacked Medb's camp, killing 50 warriors and disemboweling Lothar, her cowherd, before racing off again. After slaughtering more of Medb's warriors, Cu Culainn played for time, awaiting the Ulstermen to come to his rescue. He took on a Connachtman a day in single-combat. Ailill agreed judging it better to lose one man a day than hundreds. After many were slain in single combat, Medb found no others willing to challenge Cu Culainn. She offered her lovely daughter, Finnabair, to any hero who would bring back the head of Cu Culainn. Fools dared, but lost their heads.

Medb conducted a cattle-raid north to Dunseverick on the NE coast. She brought back the bull, cattle and 50 women captives. She requested a truce with Cu Culainn. This was spurned. Finnabhair was offered to Cu Culainn to put an end to his attacks on Medb's army. Cu Culainn accepted. Ailill sent Finnabhair with his jester disguised as himself to fool Cu Culainn. Cu Culainn, recognizing the jester, dashed his brains out. He fastened Finnabhair's to a pillarstone. He impaled the jester. Thus ended the truce. The god Lug appeared to Cu Culainn and sung him into a three-day sleep. He awoke to discover that the young warriors of Emain Macha had been annihilated. He ordered his scythed chariot and battle-gear to be readied. He underwent his warrior's fury and attacked Medb's army. His victims were beyond numbering. Finally he was indisposed by severe wounds inflicted by his foster-brother Fer Diad, whom he slew. Conor mac Nessa summoned his forces from across Ulster. They converged on the Ulster Capital Emain Mhacha and marched S to Iraird Cuillenn, routing Medb's armies. The main force halted there to await Conor's sons who were bringing their forces from Tara (acknowledged as an Ulster stronghold under Conor's sons). Conor himself forged ahead. He attacked the rear guard of Medb's retreating forces at Airthir Mide, killing and decapitating as they went. Ailill and Medb had sent emissaries summoning the Ferchitred and mercenary triads of Ireland (the *Erainn*) to them. Mac Roth informed them that the Ulster army was bearing down on them like an ominous storm. By nightfall the two armies reached Slemhain Mide. A truce was made between Conor and Medb until sunrise. They established night-camps opposite each other.

All night the war-goddess Morrigan shrieked and chanted of the coming slaughter. Warriors shuddered from visions of massacres and gory nightmares. Sleep was murdered. Cu Culainn sent Laeg to rouse the Ulstermen before dawn. The triads were assigned to defend Ailill and Medb and assassinate Conor. Conor ordered his warriors to run naked into battle. The bloody battle of Gairech and Ilgairech was underway. Cu Culainn sprung from his sickbed and entered the fray, persuading Fergus and the Ulster exiles to withdraw from the battle on account of his pledge to him. These were followed out of battle by the men of Leinster and Munster, leaving Ailill and Medb and their Connachtmen to do battle. Medb charged 3 times until driven back by a wall of spears. Cu Culainn wreaked vengeance on her army. He caught up with Medb retreating from the battlefield, but spared her life as he did not kill women (a subtle dig at the Connachtmen). He thrice struck the flagstone at Athlone where Medb's army retreated west across the Shannon as a solemn warning.

BATTLE OF THE BULLS

This 9th century recension gathered the 2 armies to watch the battle between the bulls at Tarbga in Rathcroghan. The Rathcroghan Myth was toponomically enshrined in this Recension of the *Táin*. The Finnbennach impaled Donn Cuailnge and disemboweled its adversary, littering the landscape with choice morsels of its enemy's anatomy and a correspondingly expanded toponomy. Donn Cuialnge died of exhaustion on Druim Tairb. Futility reigned. The bulls represented the 2 warring powers, the S Fir Belg and the N Cruthin. Sarcasm dripped from the pen of the redactor as he placed the final insult to Queen Medb on the lips of Fergus: "What can one expect when a mare leads a herd of stallions!"

BATTLE OF THE BOOKS: LOCKED DYNASTIC HORNS

Táin Bó Cuailnge was part of a propaganda war that must be analyzed warily. An examination of the text in its own context of dynasty, time and place and in its pseudo-historic intent of heralding the Rathcroghan Myth shows that it drips with contemporary politics and localized affairs. Its main purpose, as an awesome weapon in the Ui Neill/Armagh arsenal, was to produce powerful propaganda for the political over-kingship of the Ui Neill and the ecclesiastical hegemony of Armagh. Linguistic analysis pinpoints a precise dating, namely, the early 9th century.[797] Patricia Kelly pointed out that "the most circumstantial anchoring of this *Táin* in time and place and politico-dynastic context is that of Kelleher who suggests tentatively that Recension 1 is a political allegory for the struggle between traditional and reforming clergy for control of Armagh in the 1st. quarter of the 9th century. According to this interpretation Emain Mhacha (Ulster Capital near Armagh) in the *Táin* is code for Armagh. The fight for power over Armagh had a local dimension in the dissensions between branches of the Airghialla who had displaced the historical Ulstermen from the territory around Armagh, and had long-standing claims to the prestigious ecclesiastical offices of the monastery, and a wider dimension in the rivalry between the N and S branches of the Ui Neill."[798] These festering scars bled profusely across the Shannon. A secondary strand of pernicious propaganda superimposed on this version of the *Táin* was concocted specifically on behalf of the Ui Briuin/S Ui Neill alliance as a ribald response to the earlier denigration of the Ui Briuin king, Ragallach and his S Ui Neill allies. A dip into contemporary history is necessary to light up the background canvass against which this drama was played out.

---

[797] Ibid, p. 88; Thurneysen's dating (1921) confirmed and refined by Manning (1985).

[798] Ibid, p. 88.

A turning point in the struggle between the Airghialla and Ui Neill was the battle of Leth Cam in 827 in which the Cruthin and Airghiallan Ui Cremthainn were defeated by the N Ui Neill king, Niall Caille.[799] Niall's father was Aed Oirdnide. His mother was hapless enough, in the light of contemporary developments, to be named Medb from the same Connacht Ui Fiachra district as the Iron Age Queen Medb, closely allied to the N Ui Neill. She was doubly so by her marriage to Aed Ornide, N Ui Neill (Cenel Eogan) king. Muirghius, the king of Connacht was allied to Conor mac Donnchad, the S Ui Neill rival of, and successor to, the N Ui Neill king of Tara, Aed Oirdnide. A struggle for supremacy raged among opposing factions. Would the rival names of Medb and Conor, and the contemporary struggles they represented, suggest the idea of superimposing this localized scenario onto the canvas of the Iron Age saga of Queen Medb of Connacht and Conor Mac Nessa of Ulster? They did, indeed, in the form of an extended *Táin Bó Cuailgne* after the style of a Greek Odyssey. King Muirghius was in the thick of it.

This 9th century Rathcroghan *Táin* was composed some years before the Battle of Leth Cam by Cu-anu, the reforming Abbot of Louth, who consciously identified himself with Cu Chulainn, hero of the *Táin,* on whose shoulders the burden of the defence fell. If the *Tain* is a *roman a clef,* "one is tempted to take the Ulster king (Conor Mac Nessa) as fictional code for his namesake Conor mac Donnchad. Intriguingly, the mother of Aed Oirnide's son, Niall Caille, who succeeded Conor as High King, was Medb, a Connacht woman" as Kelly noted. Her father was the Connacht King, Ailill Medraige (Maree +764) of the Ui Fiachra Aidni (SW Galway).[800] With this key one can interpret this version of the *Táin*. "Muirghius (+ 815) supported Conor mac Donnchad and opposed Aed Oirnide, Medb's consort."[801] Muirghius viciously opposed the Ui Fiachra and devastated their SW Galway territory from which Aed's queen, Medb, hailed. He and his sons in collusion with Armagh and the S Ui Neill concocted tales of a startlingly untoward nature insulting the Ui Fiachra in the person of Medb, and the N Ui Neill who supported the Ui Fiachra. Similarly they slandered King Guaire of the Ui Fiachra in another notorious tale. Muirghius abetted Cu-anu in the scurrilous treatment meted out to the contemporary Medb through the medium of his *Táin*. He supplied the Rathcroghan propaganda which made its appearance in this version of the *Táin*. He provided the salacious material accrued to Medb's name. The Rathcroghan Myth, which claimed Muirghius and his ancestors, dating back to the time of Queen Medb, ruled from Rathcroghan. It had its origin here. So too had this new *Táin* as a political propaganda waepon. Muirghius supported the S Ui Neill and the Louth/Armagh reforming party against Aed Oirnide. He won the favour of the church, giving sanctuary to prelates and kings such as Leinster king Finsnechta Cetharderc in 805 who was forced into exile by Aed Oirnide. In 808 he provided aid to another rebel against Aed Oirnide, Conor mac Donnchad, the S Ui Neill king. In that year Muirghius with a hosting of Connachtmen attended the S Ui Neill Assembly, Oenach Tailtiu Fair. It was lawlessly disrupted by Aed Ornide. Blatant outrage was traded for character assassination at the highest levels. Dynastic horns were locked. Skullduggery reigned. This Recension 1 of the *Táin* is its sophisticated literary expression.

Cu-anu, Abbot of Louth, the redactor of this Recension 1 of the *Táin,* sought asylum with Muirghius when fleeing from Aed Oirnide and Medb. His acid bitterness against them manifested in this *Táin* was not faked. It was livid. After Muirghius's death, Cu-anu fled to Munster. The Book of Dub-Da-lethe, Abbot of Armagh who visited Muirghius's uncle Tipraite at Rath Croghan, and the Book of Cu-anu (lost but much quoted) hosted this newly fabricated pseudo-historic Rathcroghan Myth. Louth and Armagh were coconspirators in the battle of the books. Twice during his reign (799, 811) Muirghius was visited by Armagh

---

[799] Ibid, p. 88.
[800] M. Dobbs, 'The Táin...' 1930, 310; 1931, 225. J. P. Mallory, 'The Táin', Notes on P. Kelly p.97
[801] Ibid, p. 88.

Abbots in collusion with Cu-anu, Abbot of Louth, in the concoction of the Rathcroghan Myth and its synchronization with its counterpart, the Tara/Patrick Myth.

Much more than an exhibition of Patrick's relics and the proclamation of the Law of Patrick took place during these visitations, particularly the last by Abbot Nuadu. The concoction of the Rathcroghan Myth, its integration into the *Táin* and synchroization with other tales connected to the Tara/Patrick Myth, reached its peak. Having traversed that section of the Slí Dála over Knocknadala and Cnoc Temhro in his warlording incursions against the Ui Maine of the Loughrea district of Maen Magh, Muirghius had seen for himself that the old Turoe/Knocknadala Fir Belg Capital where his ancestors reigned stood deserted and bereft of a future. On the other hand, his peregrinations across the Shannon to Meath taught him that the once and future title 'Rí Temhro' had better prospects of regaining glory by being transferred to Tara of Meath, the coming 'Capital' of those who dreamed of becoming High Kings of Ireland. With his Ui Briuin dynasty running with the bulls, stretching across the upper Shannon into Brefney, splitting the N Ui Neill kingdom in two and cutting it off from the S Ui Neill, he foresaw a distinct possibility that the High Kingship of Tara might one day soon not be beyond the grasp of his S Ui Briuin dynasty. What a vision! What a dream! In this bull market his dynasty was now in a position to trample the bears. He had no objection at all to Armagh pseudo-historians making his ancestors, who coincided with those of the Ui Neill, 'High Kings of Tara' provided they similarly gave publicity to his claims for his newly-minted Capital of Connacht, Rathcroghan of Roscommon. Pseudo-historians had his blessing. They were more than ready to have him indebted provided he promulgated the Law of Patrick in Connacht. Just as Cashel needed Armagh's advice and Annalistic clout to be finally proclaimed as the Capital of Munster, so too the 8th century Sil Muiredaig kings of Connacht needed Armagh's Annalistic alchemism to have Rathcroghan proclaimed as the eternal Capital of Connacht. Cu-anu rose to the occasion. It was good for the new Connacht to have this self-professed Cu Culainn on its side this time.

Commentators have unfairly judged the character of the Iron Age Queen Medb from Cu-anu's perniciously crafty *Táin,* influenced and heavily shaded by the alleged base character of the wily 9th century Medb and her vicious warlording consort, Aed Oirnide, so-called High King of Ireland reigning at Tara. This prepared the ground for the later Leinster Recension of the *Táin* where Medb was characterized as the goddess of Tara and consort of many Kings. Her character assassination was grossly unjust. Insult and rude indignity are heaped on Aed Oirnide's consort and son, Niall Caille (who carried on his father's detested policy), in the person of Medb, wife of the first and mother of the latter, cast in the role of the Iron Age Queen Medb in Cu-anu's *Táin.* Aed was fiercely determined to gain the honour of the High Kingship. Byrne noted that he twice crashed through the Midlands, devastating Leinster, deposing its king, and dividing the province between two imposters of his choice. He implemented a policy of divide and conquer as he did with Mide, Conor mac Donnchad's kingdom. Conor united it at the expense of his brother's life.

Such dire assertions of sovereignty against ecclesiastic and secular powers inaugurated an acutely unpopular regime. It elicited the utter disgust and vitriolic ire which drips from Recension 1 of the *Táin.* When Aed did seek to pose as a champion of the church it was only "when such piety coincided with his political ambition. In 809 he defeated the Ulaid and wasted their lands from the Bann to Strangford Lough for the violation of the shrine of Patrick. He suffered 2 humiliations by the clergy. In 811 the community of Tallagh imposed a boycott on the Highking's Assembly, the Oenach Tailten (not Tara, note well), which was so effective that neither horse nor chariot reached it. In 817 Columcille's community solemnly cursed 'Highking' Aed Oirnide. In 818 Cu-anu took the shrine of Louth's founder

St. Mochtae into exile in Munster, fleeing from Aed"[802] who was determined to destroy this sacred relic too. Nothing was sacred! Aed, Medb, and their son Niall Caille made a lot of bitterly disgruntled enemies in high places. Little wonder then that Medb (wife of Aed cast in the role of Queen Medb of Connacht) of Cu-anu's *Táin* is so shamefully denigrated, while Conor (mac Donchad cast in the role of Conor Mac Nessa) is exonerated. The character of Iron Age Queen Medb is blackened by the despicable nature of the warlording Aed Oirnide, his consort, Medb, and their warring son Niall Caille, as Patricia Kelly noted. Cu-anu's pacifist stance comes through clearly, representing a plea from the reformist clerics trying to gain control of Armagh for a cessation of hostilities in the long struggle between all parties. His Táin is a poignant *crie de coeur* from the soul of Ireland to stop the killing of innocents. "The victory of the Ulaid in the *Táin* is at best pyrrhic: Donn Cuailnge is lost to both sides. Before dying it turns on and kills the *innocentes* noncombatant women and children of its own tribe."[803] Killing of the innocents (Muirghius and Aed were guilty) was a widely condemned crime at that time.

Táin Bó Cuailnge is more a mirror of medieval political life than a window on the Iron Age. Apart from being the bearer of many coded, politically motivated, messages, it is a prime carrier of the Rathcroghan Myth, consort of the Tara/Patrick Myth. Its opening scene is set on a couch at Rathcroghan. Its closing scene is a bullfight near the alleged palace of Queen Medb at Rathcroghan, taking the bull of pseudo-history by the horns for ulterior motives. It still gores Ireland. The Battle of the Books waxed with the Middle Ages, waged with utmost vindictiveness on a par with cattle-raiding. This *Táin* is pseudo-history's *hors d'oeuvre*. Books and pseudo-historians, bulldozed history into oblivion. The pseudo-historic Rathcroghan Myth became a 'fact' of history just as did the Tara/Patrick Myth with which it was synchronised. It encountered disbelief and opposition at first but won eventual acceptance. The 12th century redactor who superimposed Leinster's pretentions on Cu-anu's 9th century *Táin* penned his disbelief in what he had written: "*But I who have written this story, or rather fable, give no credence to the incidents related therin. For some things in it are the deceptions of demons, others poetic figments, while still others are intended for the delectation of fools.*" It is precisely these demonic deceptions, figments and fools' delectations that have fooled all Ireland to this day. Hang down our heads in shame!

There was not just one version of the *Táin* as there was not one version of pseudo-history. There were several, one superimposed upon another, the later adapting the former for ulterior motives. Leinster redactors manipulated Cu-anu's *Táin* and related material to promote Tara's glory as seat of the High Kingship imposing a new Leinster layer of pseudo-history claiming Tara had belonged to Leinster from time immemorial. Eochaid Fedlech is not the ideal King of the Fir Belg, (*Rí Temhro*, King of Turoe) but King of Tara of Meath, placing his daughter Medb on Connacht's throne at Rathcroghan of Roscommon as a dependency of Tara. In line with this 'doctrine', the Book of Leinster *Táin* has Medb march her armies in an absurd semi-circular route from Croghan of Roscommon S to Athlone and E to Tara before advancing N against the province of Ulster. A Leinster king, Cairbre Nia Fer, is made king of Tara. "The Cairbre of pseudo-history is at once king of Lagin (Leinster)[804] and king of Tara,[805] but not king of Ireland. Once it had been decided to place the cattle-raid of Cualnge (*Táin*) in Cairbre's reign, it was no longer possible to regard him king of Ireland, for no 'king of Ireland' is known to the Ulidian tales. The Cairbre of the Ulidian tales is little more than a name. It is clear that his connection with them is artificial, and that the original Ulidian tales knew nothing of him. Leinstermen invented the idea that

[802] F.J. Byrne, Op. Cit. p.160-161.

[803] P. Kelly, Ibid, p. 89

[804] F.T. O Rahilly, EIHM, p.178, *"lan Rí Lagen* in a poem by Orthanach, ZCP xi, 109 # 9.

[805] Ibid, "Tara is in 'Cairbre's province',: *oc Temuir...hi coiciud Cairpri Nio Fer,* Eriu vi, 147.

Cairbre, Finn and Ailill (Medb's consort) were 3 brothers who ruled contemporaneously in Tara, Ailenn, and Croghan, respectively. This idea naturally proved very popular among Laginian writers.[806] It was taken up by the redactor of the Book of Leinster *Táin* and *Cath Rúis na Ríg*, and introduced by him into these tales." According to earlier tradition, Ailill, the husband of Medb, was of Fir Belg Leinster stock from Cruachan of Bri Eile (in Offaly), but was not a brother of Cairbre or Finn.[807]

An interpolation in *Serglige Conculainn* made Finn mac Rosa, not Cairbre, provincial king of Leinster, while Cairbre is consort of Connor mac Nesa's daughter, Feilm, Queen of Tara. He is not king of a province.[808] The silence of the Ulidian tales on the subject of Tara and absence of any allusion to a High Kingship of Ireland in the earliest stratum of legendary history presented pseudo-historians with the opportunity to concoct a list of alleged Kings of Ireland, interpolating an earlier fictional list, according to their political persuasion. It led to wholesale fabrication. In this chaos the counterfeit Medb was created, first through the work of Cu-anu and later through a Leinster layer of pseudo-history. Her character became muddled with that of the Leinster goddess, Medb Lethderg, who in Leinster tradition was made the sovereignty-goddess of Tara. O Rahilly was conned by this compounded concoction. "Medb, the goddess who typifies the sovereignty of Tara, is made to reign, not in Tara, but in Cruachain, together with her husband Ailill. And so in 'Táin Bó Cualnge' the narrator has first to bring Medb and her forces rapidly from Cruachain to the Tara district before they can march northward against the Ulaid (of Ulster)."[809] Thus the Tara/Rathcruachan Myth waxed while history waned.

Connacht's oldest Annals, *Lebor Balb*, was so called because it was willfully silenced by 'drowning',[810] since it told a diametrically different, true, story of Iron Age Connacht. Dissident records were sunk in a sea of silence. Skullduggery prevailed. Written records were blatantly distorted. Oral tradition could not be suppressed. It survived, carrying its diametrically different version of the past that flies in the face of pseudo-history. It is corroborated by archaeological remains and the classical record of Ptolemy of Alexandria.

THE NINTH CENTURY 'VITA TRIPARTITE' LIFE OF PATRICK

The Tara/Patrick Myth struck deep roots in Ireland. To explore the subsequent ramifications one must turn to the 9th century 'Tripartite Life of Patrick', the fullest expression of Armagh's ambitions and its elaboration of the Patrick Myth. Binchy declared this work "to have no value for the study of the historical Patrick, though brimful of interest for all who are concerned with the ecclesiastical, social and political condition of Ireland in the 9th century. Besides expanding and occasionally misunderstanding Tirechan's narrative, it purports to describe Patrick's second circuit. Patrick's 'circuit' of *Leth Mogha* (finally developed fully in this work) is a fable; in this as in other matters the *Tripartite* represents the final triumph of myth over history. By the time it was written Patrick had become part of what P Delehaye calls *'l'epopee nationale'* (a national epic) and all parts of Ireland were eager to claim a share in him. Their desires were amply catered for in this remarkable compilation."[811] It is therefore not surprising to find the *'Cain Patraic'* (church tax for Armagh's coffers) being promulgated again in Munster by Feidlimid mac Crimthann, King of Cashel in 823, having been revoked earlier. Binchy declared Patrick's 'circuit' of the Southern Half of Ireland to be 'fictitious from start to finish'. This applies to the *Vita*

---

[806] Ibid, Met. Dindsenchas i, 48 and R 118 b 4-6 (Laginian genealogies); AID i, pp. 17, 23.

[807] Ibid, p. 179, in the genealogy of the Fir Belg in LL 324 d.; Eriu ii, 174-176.

[808] Ibid, p. 179; IT i, 212.

[809] Ibid, p. 176.

[810] Connacht's other great Book, 'The Book of Hi Fiachrach' claims the Lebor Balb was 'drowned', destroyed.

[811] D.A. Binchy, 'Patrick & His Biographers: Ancient & Modern', in Studia Hibernica, No 2, 1962, p.69

Tripartite. As to Patrick's first 'circuit' of the Northern Half, Binchy noted that everything depends on our confidence in Tirechan's narrative. His own was nil. He sided with Mac Neill's verdict: "Nothing written by Tirechan becomes credible by reason of having been written by Tirechan, not a little can be shown to contain fictions of his own invention.[812]

'LEBHOR GABHALA' (BOOK OF INVASIONS) AND THE MILESIAN MYTH Just as the *Vita Tripartite* represents the triumph of fabricated legend over church history in relation to Patrick and Armagh, similarly the *'Lebhor Gabhala'* represents the triumph of pseudo-history and fiction over genuine Iron Age and Early Irish secular history. "The scheme of invasions of Ireland that was to burgeon into the tangle of later recensions of the *'Lebhor Gabhala'* grew up in response to a medieval problem - the vast blank separating Irish tradition from accepted world history - a problem it solved in a medieval way, allowing Christian universalism to multiply its patterns across the Irish stage."[813] Ó Corráin in his study of the growth of Irish nationality extended this insight: "Christianity both as an historical religion of the Book and as an origin-legend for all mankind naturally posed the question of the origin and identity of the Irish and their place among the nations."[814] One of Ireland's earliest secular poems, the *'Fursunnad'* of Laidchend mac Baircheda, concerns itself with this problem. Those portions of the poem which contain a detached list of the nations of the earth and trace the Leinster royal house back to Mil and thence to Noah and Adam, show the obvious Biblical influence. Archaic portions of the poem contain pagan elements at variance with the Biblical origins of the Irish and may be genuine. The material presents what Carney calls "the theory of the unity of Ireland through Mil and the world through Adam." Senchan Torpeist was the inventor of the politically useful idea of the common descent of the Irish from Mil of Spain.[815] This concept, though spurious and at odds with the true origin of the Irish, took root.

This alarming trend is next evidenced in a more extensive form in Nennius' *'Historia Brittonum'* at the start of the 9th century. It is developed in a poem of Mael Mura of Othain (+887)'. In his poem, *'Can a mbunadas na nGaedal?'* he set himself the scholarly question: "What is the origin of the Irish, where did they come from, why did they come to Ireland, and why are they called by various names such as Scuitt, Gaedil? "A scholarly question which was given a deceptively scholarly, but brazenly unscholarly answer which is having dire repercussions to this day. The answer of Mael Mura drew on the new Myth of Mil of Spain and on the alleged Biblical origin of the Irish. "For the early Middle Ages the Bible served as the primary source of ancient world history, the Chronicles of Eusebius and Orosius as its principle compendia, harmonizations and continuations, and Isidore's 'Etymologiae' as a general encyclopedia. These works inspired not only the historiographical context and framework for the *'Lebor Gabala'* but to a remarkable extent the content itself, which adapts even pagan theology and contemporary politics to Biblical myths of origin, migration, and population" wrote Scowcroft.[816] Suppression of the genuine origins of the Irish succeeded only too well. It has led to an utterly pathetic situation where one receives 100 varied fanatically-held replies, including those cooked up by pseudo-historians, when one sets 100 people of Irish origin the same scholarly questions: Who are the Irish? Where did they come from? They eagerly boast of their Milesian, Egyptian, Greek, Scythian, Spanish or SE European origin, or descendants of a Gaelic race of unknown origin, anything at all except full-blooded pre-Celtic Cruthin or Fir Belg Celts.

---

[812] Op. Cit., p. 65.

[813] R. M. Scowcroft, (1988): 'Leabhar Gabhala', part 2: the growth of thr tradition', Eriu, 39, 63.

[814] Donncha O Corráin (1978): 'Nationality and kingship in pre-Norman Ireland" in 'Nationality and the Pursuit of National Independence, Historical Studies 11' (T. W. Moody, ed.), p. 4.

[815] D. O Corráin, Op. Cit., p. 5.

[816] R. M. Scowcroft, Op. Cit.,63; noted in 'Pagan Past and Christian Present' by McCone, p.66.

McCone claimed early versions of the Lebor Gabala scheme went back to the 8th century on Nenius' evidence. The 10th century 'Sanas Cormaic', a compilation by Cormac mac Cuillenain, King-Bishop of Cashel (+908), advises "Read the Book of Invasions of Ireland if you wish to know more fully." He was drugged by this blatant balderdash. Versions of the early 9th century Latin work by Nennius recount only 3 invasions, i.e, of Partholon, Nemed, and the 3 sons of Mil, showing this scheme of invasions as elaborated in the '*Lebor Gabala*' was still in its early stages. The alleged wanderings of the Gael from Egypt to Ireland via Spain are outlined on the 'authority of the most learned of the Irish' thus: "When the sons of Israel came through the Red Sea the Egyptians pursued them and were drowned. There was a noble man from Scythia (Fenius Farsaid, grandfather of Goedel from whom the Irish derive their name). His consort was Scotta, daughter of Pharaoh, (from whom Scotia and the Scotti derive their name). He had a great family in Egypt. Expelled from his kingdom, he was there when the Egyptians were dronwned. Those who survived expelled him lest he occupy their kingdom since all their men had been drowned in the Red Sea. After his expulsion he wandered for 40 (Biblical) years through Africa till eventually he and his family reached the Pillars of Hercules, navigated the Tyrrhenian Sea and reached Spain. There they increased and multiplied. Later they came to Ireland." This became Irish 'tradition' by the 9th century. Thus the umbical Biblical cord link with the origin of the Irish was woven. In Ireland it was taught and believed as Biblical truth!

McCone notes this "pre-Milesian occupation of Ireland is reminiscent of recurrent themes of famine and journeying between Mesopotamia, Canaan and Egypt in the Old Testament Patriarch period. The Exodus story from Egypt and subsequent wanderings to Ireland via Spain represents a clear attempt to create suggestive parallels between Irish history and that of God's chosen people in the Bible. This made it possible to trace Goedel's role as eponymous ancestor of the Gaels and the names of key ancestors, linking him to Biblical genealogies, and explain the various names of the Irish. The role of Armagh/Ui Neill literati is evident in this 'Goedelic' Myth. McCone showed how the name of Goedel's father, Nel, provided the Ui Neill with an ancestor far more illustrious and immemorial than they had in Niall of the Nine Hostages. Through Nel's mother, Scotta, daughter of Pharaoh, the Ui Neill were thus given the incomparable glory of being directly linked to the Pharaohs of Egypt. McCone noted: "this had the advantage of supplying Goedel with a connection to Pharaoh's daughter even more impressive than that of Moses himself." Three key terms endowed the Irish with eponymous ancestors. In Mael Mura's poem "the Feni are named after Fenius, the Gael after Goedel, the Scots after Scotta."[817] The obvious trigger for the invention of the name of Goedel's father, Nel, meaning 'cloud' which led the ancestors of the Gael out of Egypt was Exodus 13:21-2 "the Lord went before them in a pillar of cloud to lead the way," an unabashed publicity plug for Ui Neill dynasts desiring to be recognized as High Kings. They rewarded Mael Mura with the prestigious title 'Royal Poet of Ireland', akin to an admission that credit for this latest glorification of the Ui Neill was to be laid at Mael Mura's door. This Pharaohnizing of the Ui Neill dynasty postdated the glory bestowed on it by Adomnan and Muirchu by 2 centuries. Later came the invention of Goedel's son Eber Scott, said to have taken possession of the Southern Half of Ireland as part of the so-called Gaelic invasion of Ireland. This name was inspired in that it was a reasonable eponym for Ireland's Latin name 'Hibernia', in addition to being identical with the name of the eponymous ancestor of the Hebrews in Isidore.[818]

There is repeated use of biblical material "in the formation and elaboration of this fundamental historical doctrine from the 7th century on. Short of anticipating Mormon heterodoxy by actually claiming descent from a lost tribe of God's chosen people, Ireland's men of

---

[817] LL., 16025-6.
[818] Isidore, 'Etymolog.,' IX ii 5: 'Heber a quo Hebraei', and 'Eber a quo...Hibernia', Corp Genealog 186

letters went as far as they could to equate their history with that of Biblical Israel by creating deliberate analogues between the two. An example of just how close they were capable of sailing to the wind is provided by Muirchu's account of the bargain struck by God's Angel Victor with Patrick before the latter's death: *'the 4ᵗʰ petition, that all the Irish on the day of judgement be judged by you - thus it is said to the apostles 'and you shall sit and judge the 12 tribes of Israel* (the Irish are all but the 13th) *so that you may judge those to whom you have been an apostle'*. One obvious implication was that God had selected Ireland as a Promised Land for her Gaelic conquerors, the sons of Mil."[819]

What has this to do with the lost Capitals, peoples and history of early Ireland? Everything! The men who distorted the writings of Patrick in favour of their own version and suppressed the origins of the Irish in favour of Biblical origins, were the same who suppressed the Belgic Capitals of Ireland in favour of Tara and Rathcroghan. Van Hamel dated the archtype of the recensions of 'Lebor Gabala as it exists today to the 2nd half of the 10th century. It continued to be transcribed and enlarged for centuries to come: "its influence proved all pervasive."[820] Ireland's main genealogical corpus is based on this fictitious origin-legend. Ó Corráin noted that "behind this self-conscious antiquarianism is the doctrine that all people of Ireland derive from one common source and form one nation. As the Franks, Saxons, Lombards, Goths and Greeks are *'nationes'*, so are the Irish."[821] He concluded that the Paschal Controversy of the 7th century in the course of which Irish practices were seen to differ from those of the rest of Europe, and, above all, the leveling effect of a Church which transcended local identities, must have deepened the Irish sense of 'otherness'. This growing sense of nationality spilled over into politics. It is implicit in the Ui Neill propagandists' claims of this later period. From the 10th to 12th century "the Irish were profoundly conscious of themselves as a larger community or *'natio'*, their learned classes were preoccupied with this very notion, and in the 11ᵗʰ/12th centuries the greater kings attempted to turn that consciousness to political advantage,"[822] to the High Kingship of a united Ireland. They did not openly dare make this claim until this late date.

Proponents of a Highkingship of Ireland from time immemorial based at Tara cite Muirchu who described Tara as "the *'caput'* (Capital) of the Irish." Adomnan dubbed Diarmait mac Cerbaill "ruler of Ireland, ordained by God." These claims are highly tendentious and testify to ambition rather than achievement. "They testify to an awareness of the Irish as a *'natio'*, rule over which was a laudable ambition for an Ui Neill overking. The expansive activities of these Ui Neill kings, the breakdown of localized petty kingdoms, contact with the Vikings and the emergence of more extensive power-blocks deepened that awareness. By the 11ᵗʰ/12th centuries poet-historians had elaborated in full the concept of a monarchy of All Ireland and projected it back into the pre-Christian past, so that the kingship of Ireland took on the character of an immemorial tradition."[823]

The apparently static picture of Irish society presented in pseudo-history deceived many. The most blatant example of this immutability is the idea of a 'Tara High Kingship of Ireland from time immemorial.' This has resulted in an insensitivity to shifts of emphasis and nuances of expression which indicate change in institutions and political and social innovations in society as a whole. *"This is particularly true of Ireland where the bulk of the early historical sources are literary and highly conventionalized products of specialist learned classes, retainers of the contemporary holders of power, who were at pains to*

---

[819] Kim McCone, Ibid, p. 68-69.

[820] A. G. van Hamel, 'Uber die Vorpatrizianischen Irischen Annalen', Zeitschr, f. Celt. Phil., 17, 241-60

[821] D. O Corráin, Op. Cit., p. 6.

[822] Ibid, p. 4.

[823] Ibid, p. 8.

legitimize all change by giving it the sanction of immemorial custom and who ruthlessly reshaped the past to justify the present. The unchanging Gaelic Ireland of modern historical scholars bears silent witness to the effectiveness of their medieval forebears in discharging their duty. "[824] This activity was not confined to Ireland. It finds a close parallel in British and Continental legend-building carried on at both lay and clerical levels, just as in Ireland, from the 10th to the 12th centuries. In the Dark Ages and through the Middle Ages there was a superabundance of literary activity restricted largely to a clergy closely related to those who wielded power. Many of the chronicles written by these men of learning were based on Eusebius and Biblical influence. They began with the Creation. The characteristic annalistic chronicle of the Middle Ages did not grow out of ancient biblical history. "It was invented, and on a completely new pattern" as shown by Denys Hay.

In introducing the 'first writers of history' Isidore named Dares Phrygius who "wrote a history of the Greeks and Trojans'. It survived in a 5th century Latin version. The work of an earlier author, Dictys of Crete, survived in Latin. These two authors provided material from which later writers wove into their national traditions the Trojan or Greek origin of their reputed first princes, much in the same way that the Egyptian/Scythian Goedel, Mil and Scotta were woven into the fictitious Irish origin-legend in 'Lebor Gabala'. France absorbed this spirit with Fredegar's chronicle. It was absorbed in later compilations and later still in its 'official history'. Out of this nonsense emerged Francus, the alleged eponymous founder of the Franks who was to debase French history until the 18th century just as Goedel, Mil and the Tara/Patrick Myth debases and confuses Irish history to this day. No European country was exempt from the bane of Troy, said Hay: "In Britain the Trojan was called Brutus, naturalized by Geoffrey of Monmouth who made him 'founder of Britain'. Brutus was absorbed into the medieval bestseller, 'The Brut'. Poets adjusted Arthurian myth to their audience, elaborating the heroic and chivalrous. *'Roman de Troie'* of Benoit de Sainte Maure (c.1150) enshrined the Trojan Saga in verse. The glow of heroic epic saga made these works best sellers. Ireland would not be outdone.

At this time a whole series of attempts were made to apply to various European peoples the theme of Virgil's *'Aenied'* of a noble group guided by God, or gods, towards a glorious destiny. The first essential step was to establish the descent of one's nation from the ancient Trojans, Greeks, Phoenicians, Scythians or Egyptians and then trace their subsequent 'history' through a series of wanderings and heroic conquests. This was done in Ireland in the person of the fictitious Fenius Farsaid, his son Goedel, grandson Mil and his Egyptian consort Scotta, daughter of the Pharaoh, in the concoction of the fictitious Milesian origin-legend elaborated in *'Lebor Gabala'*. Most ambitious of these works outside of Ireland was the *'Historia Regum Britanniae'* (History of the Kings of Britain) by Geoffrey of Monmouth (+ 1155) bishop of St. Asaph, which attempted to establish for the Celts a historical destiny greater than any other. It was intended as a counter-balance to Anglo-Saxon records which gave blatant pride of place to Anglo-Saxon dynasties over the Celts of Britain. Geoffrey was Bretonic. He claimed to have translated his work from an archaic book in the Breton Celtic tongue taken by Walter, Archbishop of Oxford, from Brittany. His 'History' was the most popular book of the Middle Ages, though its historical value was nil. It began with the settlement of Brutus, great-grand-son of the Greek Aneas, alleged eponymous founder of Britain, and the Trojan, Corineus, eponymous founder of Cornwall. Then came the reigns of British Kings down to the Roman conquest. It culminated with the account of Arthur's reconquest. Despite its huge popularity, contemporary writers were not deceived by Geoffrey's work. William of Newburg, best of the English 12th century historians, denounced the work as a 'tissue of absurdities'. Nonetheless it was accepted by almost all as authentic history, as Lebor Gabala was in Ireland. It had enormous influence on later chroniclers like

---

[824] Ibid, p. 12.

Ranulf Higden, Fabyn, Warner and Drayton who gave Geoffrey's claims wide currency and credibility. Ireland upped the ante in this affair.

As in Ireland, medieval British and Continental historians were monastic clerics under the patronage of local kings. They were considered, and considered themselves, court historians, royal propagandists, whose duty it was to glorify the royal patron and suppress whatever might be injurious to his royal status. 'Historians' of this period, like Matthew of Paris, abounded in blatant inaccuracies and anachronisms, a peculiar trait of historical writing between the 10th and 12th centuries. So in the Ireland of this period, fundamental political changes, such as the institution of a national Kingship of Ireland and altered circumstances of earlier and contemporary history, were frequently projected back into the remote past with all the suppression and rewriting of history this involved. John Gray noted how medieval revolutionary millenarians and anarchists from the 9th to 11th centuries were in thrall of a false apocalyptic myth which urged a policy of "creative destruction". A pioneering work by Norman Cohn[825] published 50 years ago underlined how the old wartorn world could be abolished and a new perfect world be brought into being, not by the hand of God, but by themselves according to their political agenda. If God would not alter the past, they would for the sake of a better world. Ireland's archaic past was creatively destroyed. Pseudo-historians minted a brash new Ireland according to their political agenda for ulterior motives. This took its place as the 'official doctrine'

It is borne out in the annals and genealogies that ordained clerics were dominant in the legal and learned circles, especially as court historians. What is significant is that all derived from one source, the junior politically unsuccessful segments of the ruling dynasties. This mandarin class, as McCone noted, provided the servitors of the great kings. It was this class that elaborated the idea of the High Kingship of Ireland. This 9th to 12th century mandarin class projected the High Kingship of Ireland from Tara back into the remote past creating what has been accepted for a whole millennium as the 'official history'. Their influence on the image which the Irish had of their past has been all-pervasive.

SUPPRESSION OF ARCHAIC HISTORY: INTERPOLATION: MANIPULATION

Among the more important of the Irish 'literati whom Mac Neill dubbed 'synthetic historians', and whom O Rahilly called 'pseudo-historians', are Mael Mura of Othain (+887), Cinead Ua hArtacain (+ 995), Cuan Ua Lothcain (+ 1024) and Flann Mainistreach (+ 1056). Mael Mura linked Irish origins to a fictitious Gaelic migration from SE Europe. He transferred ancestors of the Ui Neill who had been *Rí Temhro*, Overkings of Turoe of Galway to Tara of Meath and glorified their reputed archaic reign there. Most of Flann's work is concerned with the glorification of alleged High Kings of the Ui Neill line of Tara of Meath in the territory of the Southern Ui Neill, and of Ailech in the far N E, fortress and symbol of the Northern Ui Neill. A note in 'Lebor na hUidre' affords a glance at Flann's activity and scene of action. "Flann then gathered this material from the books of Eochaid Ua Flannachan in Armagh and from those of Monasterboice and other choice books besides, namely from the Yellow Book (of Lecan) which is now missing from the strong-room in Armagh." Flann was a bookworm who did the rounds of all the monastic libraries. Thus he acquired his sobriquet, 'Flann of the Monasteries'. Highly rated by Armagh and the Ui Neill dynasts for his high-handed manipulation of manuscript material in their best interests, he is repudiated as one who had his foot in every camp, his finger in every Annal and his censorial pen in every line he deemed anathema to the Tara/Patrick Myth. On pretext of gathering manuscript material he gained access to monastic libraries even in enemy camps. A dark cloud hangs over his activity while he had these great Books in his hands. It was the

---

[825] John Gray, Professor of European Thought at the London School of Economics, 'Politics of the Apocalypse' in 'The Tablet', 17th Jan, 2004; Norman Cohn, 'The Pursuit of the Millennium'

era of the 'great manuscript syncretisms'. On pretext of syncretizing material from Annals of early history, Flann had the opportunity to interpolate material in original manuscripts according to his own pseudo-historic bent in the interests of his Royal Ui Neill patrons. In the name of syncretism, multiple pages of prestigious Annals and whole Books of early history went missing, devoured by this bookworm.

Dating from this time an interpolator's hand, working in the interests of the Ui Neill, lies heavy on many Great Books of Annals. More than one disappeared and re-emerged in the strong room of Armagh's library. How Connacht's Yellow Book of Lecan, from which Flann lifted material as he made his rounds, as recounted in the 'Lebor na hUidre' note, disappeared and found its way into Armagh's strongroom is a mystery. Perhaps Flann could explain. Flann spent considerable time with the Books of his old friend, Eochaid Ua Flannachann (+ 1004) mentioned in the Lebor na hUidre note, as 'erenach' of Lis Oeiged in Armagh and Clonfeakle in N Armagh, and a 'collector' of such fine Books. His brother, Dub Da Leithe, was Abbot of Armagh and progenitor of 8 subsequent Abbots as noted by Cardinal Tomas O Fiach.[826] Armagh made herself **the** Media Mogul and Official Censor responsible for 'synchronizing' (censoring) all medieval media for its ulterior motives. It began with Ferdomnach in the 8th century. It continued to Flann's day. Nor was Flann alone! How Connacht's other great Book, the *Lebor Balb*, disappeared is an even greater mystery. King Muirghius and Abbots Cormac, Cu-anu and Nuadu, speak up! The reason for its disappearence is less enigmatic since this is spelt out by its nickname 'Balbh' (silenced). It was violently muffled simply because it contained material which flew in the face of the 'new official doctrine' of the pseudo-historians. Openly contradicting their fictitious concoctions, the Powers-that-be had no option but to have it 'done in'. The official version as told in the Book of Hi Fiachrach says it was 'drowned'. Its nickname spells out the naked truth: it was silenced, suppressed, assassinated.

DIARMAIT NA nGALL'S ROLE IN PERVERTING IRISH HISTORY

A nameless 12th century violent interpolator of Annalistic material, dubbed **H,** gained access to the Great Books of his day which he brazenly disfigured. Was not the infamous Diarmait Mac Murchada, King of Leinster in 1134, his patron? The Leinster legend of Labraid Loingsech influenced the bringing about of an event of cardinal importance.[827] The tale of Labraid's expulsion from his Leinster kingdom, triumphant return and his alleged crowning as King of Ireland with foreign aid from Gaul was all too familiar to 12th century Leinstermen, markedly Diarmait Mac Murchada and **H.** Ambitions of becoming High King of Ireland raged within Diarmait's heart and won him so many enemies that Irish kings insisted High King Rory O Connor banish him from Ireland.[828] In 1166 Diarmait fled to France to seek aid from Henry II. Following the footsteps of Labraid Loingsech incited his ambitions. Like Labraid, he would, with foreign aid, not just recover his kingdom but become High King of Ireland. His resolve was reckless. Returning with a Norman army, which earned him the inglorious title 'Diarmait na nGall', he engaged 'Historians' to invent a new Leinster 'official doctrine' and 'doctor' Ireland's Annals in a radical 'restructuring of history' in Leinster's favour, as evidenced by the violent interpolations in Lebor na hUidre and other Great Books. Byrne believes the Book of Leinster with its new recension of the Táin was commissioned by Diarmait. "Diarmait was by no means indifferent to his ancestral traditions, as the Book of Leinster, compiled by men devoted to him, if not under his actual patronage, amply testifies."[829]

---

[826] Cardinal Tomas O Fiach, 'The Church of Armagh under Law Control', v, pp. 111-124.

[827] F. T. O Rahilly, EIHM, p. 116-117; Francis John Byrne, 'Irish Kings and High Kings', p. 272-273.

[828] Francis John Byrne, 'Irish Kings and High Kings', p. 273.

[829] Ibid, p. 272.

The Book of Leinster glorified the origin-legend of Diarmait's Leinster dynasty noting that *"Labraid Loingsech suffered unjust exile and regained his kingdom with the help of allies from Gaul! He not only established the royal line of Leinster but won for himself the high-kingship of Ireland* (a fraudulent claim). *Diarmait had similar ambitions. Nothing short of a radical revolution could establish a national monarchy. Diarmait's readiness to overthrow Irish law to win Strongbow's* (Anglo-Norman) *support - thereby ignoring the claims of his sons and agnetic kinsmen - can only be explained on the hypothesis that he was aiming at total innovation."*[830] Diarmait's resolve to overthrow Irish law and order extended to the Great Books to make way for his planned revolutionary take-over of Ireland redated from time immemorial. If Diarmait did commission the Book of Leinster, its hand which closely resembles the violently interpolating hand of **H** throughout other 12th century Annals such as Lebor na hUidre (Book of Dun Cow), then **H** was Diarmait's right-hand man with his censoring hand in every Book to rewrite the record. "Diarmait was too old for such an enterprise and died before he could ride the tiger he had mounted. His success was inglorious, and his own descendants, like the rest of their countrymen, had reason to rue the day Diarmait na nGall brought the Anglo-Normans to Ireland."[831] History wilted and withered. Pseudo-history prospered violently under Diarmait na nGall. Though short his reign, like Connacht's Tipraite and Muirghius, his legacy was lasting.

Best and Bergin, editors of the *Lebor na hUidre* (Book of Dun Cow) drew attention to the crude hand of the highly motivated interpolator, **H,** throughout this 12th century work: "(In the 1920's) the true role of this '3rd hand' was made known. **H**'s intervention throughout is rude and violent. Not only single words and lines, but whole columns and pages have been erased by him, and leaves intercalated to make way for the particular recensions he favoured. He set to work with great determination and with no small interest in the texts. The membrane of many leaves have been rubbed down into holes, and is exceedingly fragile in places."[832] The hand of **H** "which has much in common with that of the Book of Leinster appears again as an interpolator in the so-called Annals of Tigernach."[833] **H**'s association with 2 Clonmacnoise manuscripts and his interpolations of material from Connacht's archaic history leaves one wondering what exactly he was so determined to suppress and in which 'he had no small interest'. If he were the author of the Book of Leinster with whose hand 'he had so much in common', this would give clues to what he wished to suppress. The Book of Leinster and Leinster manuscript material of this period produced substantially altered recensions of archaic history and saga such as *Táin Bó Cuailgne* redone in a Leinster context, making Tara the Capital of Leinster from time immemorial. It welded Connacht's Regents, Ailill and Medb, to the Leinster genealogy. It gave Leinster a role out of all proportion to what it had in Irish history. With Tara as its alleged immemorial Capital, it placed itself at centre stage throughout the course of Irish history. It pulled the pedestal from under the Ui Neill/Armagh 'official doctrine' and created a Leinster layer of fraud that has duped historians. Archaic traditions of Tara and of the early Fir Belg oppida were murdered. Yet the Book Of Leinster preserves not a few authentic, or only slightly altered, early texts relating especially to archaic Connacht.

THE SO-CALLED GAELIC INVASION AND MODERN-DAY PSEUDO-HISTORY
Some modern historians perpetuate the pseudo-history of their predecessors. "From the 8th century on a succession of learned Irishmen devoted themselves to the task of reconstructing the history of their country in pre-Christian times. The result of their labours is seen in

---

[830] Francis John Byrne, Op. Cit., p. 272-273
[831] F. T. O Rahilly, EIMH, p. 117.
[832] R. I. Best and Osborn Bergin , (ed.) introduction to 'Lebor na Huidre', p. xiv, xvi.
[833] Ibid, p. xvii.

Lebor Gabala.[834] While exposing *Lebor Gabala* as fiction, O Rahilly perpetuated belief in a Gaelic invasion: "While the *Lebor Gabala* in general may be described as a deliberate work of fiction, yet the compilers could not afford entirely to ignore the popular traditions current in their day. In the 8th century there was still a strong popular consciousness of the fact that the population of Ireland was composed of different ethnic strata, and that no small part of it was sprung from peoples who had been in Ireland before the dominant Goidels." His belief in a Gaelic invasion grew: "The task the literati set themselves was to endow all the septs which possessed any importance in their day with a common Goidelic origin. To affect this it was necessary to discountenance the popular view that the Goidels were, comparatively speaking, late comers to this country. So the authors of *Lebor Gabala* boldly and deliberately pushed back the Goidelic invasion into the remote past, somewhere in the 2nd millennium BC. A small number of tribal names (Fir Belg, Galioin, Domnainn) were retained as designations of the pre-Goidelic population of Ireland, whose invasions had naturally to be placed still further back than that of the Goidels."[835] Anachronism was its hallmark. The Gaelic invasion, named after the fictitious Greek/Scythian Goidel, is synonymous with the Milesian invasion, named after his son Mil.

O Rahilly regarded Conn and Eoghan as divine ancestors of the Goidels, but treated their respective grandfathers, Tuathal and Mug Nuadat, as historical personages. In the *Lebor Gabala* scheme of history the reigns of Conn, Eoghan, Tuathal and Mug Nuadat, fell within the first 3 centuries of the Christian era. *"It can hardly be without significance that these ancestors of the Connachta and the Eoganachta, the 2 branches of the Goidels, appear so late in pseudo-history. In popular belief the Goidelic invasion was a comparatively recent event which occurred not many centuries before the introduction of Christianity. It leaves us uncertain whether the Goidels arrived in the 1st century BC or 1st/2nd century AD. The Goidelic invasion is the latest of the Celtic invasions of Ireland. The Goidels on their arrival found Ireland occupied by the Fir Belg."*[836] O Rahilly erroneously postulated a 3rd/4th century BC date for the Fir Belg invasion. In fact, they began to arrive in the 2nd/1st century BC and continued to come throughout the 1st/2nd century AD, precisely the time bracket set by him for his Goidelic invasion. O Rahilly endeavoured to locate their earlier Continental homeland. The weight of his learning carried modern scholars in his train. "If anything is certain about them, it is that the Goidels reached Ireland direct from the Continent. Regarding the earlier home of the Goidels, several pieces of evidence unite in suggesting that the Goidels were connected with the southeast of Gaul. Before sailing to Ireland a body of Q-Celts first migrated from southeast Gaul to the West Coast. The Goidels must have left Gaul before 50 BC when the rest of the country was finally subjected to Roman rule. We are safe in placing it within the years 150-50 BC. The Irish evidence would favour the second half of this period rather than the first."[837]

O Rahilly's 'Irish evidence' is the pseudo-history he censured. The time frame for his Goidelic invasion is that of the Fir Belg invasion. The connection the Irish have with "the south of Gaul" is in the person of Commius/Gann who led the Fir Belg invasion to Ireland. Gann's invasion force came from the SE of England to the mouth of the Shannon. His descendants, the Gangani, appear precisely there in Ptolemy's 1st/2nd century record, corroborated by Irish legendary history. Connacht septs claimed descent from his sons, Sengann and Dela. Pseudo-history covered up the evidence of the Book of Lecan, Book of Ballymote and other Annals which told that the early Province of Connacht was known as *Coiced nÓl nÉcmacht, Coiced Medba & Ailella, Coiced Cruachna, Coiced nGaind, Coiced*

---

[834] F. T. O Rahilly, 'Early Irish History and Mythology', p. 193ff.
[835] Ibid, p. 194.
[836] Ibid, p. 204-5.
[837] Ibid, p. 207-8

Genaind, Coiced Sreing mac Sengainn mac Gainn, "stretching from Bealach Conglais in Limerick to Abha Dubh on the Mayo/Galway border, and later Drobhais."[838] It excluded Rathcroghan of Roscommon, the Cruthin Capital and Queen Medb's bitter enemies.

All versions of the so-called Goidelic invasion, including O Rahilly's, are as fictitious as the Milesian invasion which he so strongly castigated. O Rahilly's version resulted from erudite preconceptions. On the weight of his authority this segment of pseudo-history is perpetuated in an ongoing Irish obsession. The words 'Gael' and 'Gaelic' are forms of 'Goidelic' which have for long been used by the Irish to denote the Irish people as a whole and their language, without any tribal undertones. As Powell, among others, noted: "It was only when a situation developed that required a general name for all the people of Ireland, without discrimination, that one came into being. This was not the outcome of political unification." That name was 'Goidel' and first came into evidence in the 7th century. It was unknown earlier. Had there been a Gaelic (Goidelic) invasion of Ireland as O Rahilly insisted in concurrence with *Lebor Gabala,* and had these so-called Gaels become the dominant race in the land, then surely Ireland would not have had to wait until the 7th century to become aware of a 'Goidelic' racial group within its shores.

"The origin of 'Goidel' (Gael) *is that it is an adaptation of Gwyddel, the Welsh name for the Irish* (the Welsh word for 'foreigners'). *It was brought to Ireland under different circumstances, and taken over as Goidel. The reason is almost certainly the activity of Christian missionaries coming from North Wales in the 5th/6th centuries."[839]* It was taken up into *Lebor Gabala* and fictionalized into a separate people differing ethnically from those who occupied Ireland before the alleged Goidelic invasion. *"It was long before 'Goidel' developed any political or formal national significance; the onset of the Vikings at the end of the 8th century probably did most to bring this about."* The Irish needed a word to distinguish themselves from the Vikings. The term *'Goidel is Gall'* was widely used to serve this purpose. The Irish adopted *Goidel* to refer to themselves and *Gall* to refer to foreigners. "In the creation of a synthetic history of Ireland, a fictitious ancestral figure, Goidel Glas, was brought into being at this time. Irish Churchmen were anxious to provide an historical scheme for Ireland, equivalent to that set forth by Orosius for the Hebrews and other peoples. This movement started in the 7th century, and the name Goidel came in most usefully in the rearrangements and adaptions of traditional origin tales and genealogies that were extensively undertaken. The confusion has persisted until now, and has been aggravated by scholars (O Rahilly) who use *'Goidel'* in the same sentence as genuine traditional names such as *Ulad* and *Erainn*"[840] or in a philological sense of speakers of a form of Q-Celtic." Muirchu, Mael Mura and Flann Mainistreach all tried to make up for the conspicuous absence of Celts in the Bible. There never was a Milesian or Goidelic invasion. The name Goidelic (Gaelic) was a common Welsh name applied to all the peoples of Ireland in general, whether they belonged to the aboriginal Cruthin, or later Fir Belg who, except for the Cruthin, arrived in Ireland within the time-frame O Rahilly posited his Goidelic invasion. *Lebor Gabala* restricted the name Goidelic to the medieval dominant classes.

Brian Boru is said to be the first High King of Ireland. He accepted Armagh as the metropolitan seat of the Irish Church, but did not recognize Tara as the seat of the High Kingship of Ireland, nor did he reign from there nor from Cashel but from his royal seat near Limerick in the NW of Munster. He defeated the Danes at the Battle of Clontarf in 1014 reputedly with a united Irish army. *"As usual with Irish 'history' there is more*

---

[838] Bk of Ballymote, 4a, 16a, 17a; Bk of Lecan, 23, 553, 556; Ar. 32, 90, 242-3; Lebor na hUidhre, 41b; Annals of Tigernach, 33; Coir Anmann, 404; Bk of Buide Lecain, 899; Keating's History of Ireland, 121 a & b;

[839] T. G. E. Powell, 'The Celts', p. 204-5.

[840] Ibid, p. 205.

invention here than fact. Nationalistic historians confuse the extent of his power with their own ideas of what the high-kingship really was. We must begin to accept the fact that then, as now, there was no such thing as a united Ireland. The high kingship of Ireland fictionalized by the monks of Armagh, had become reality by the year 1000, at least as an idea. In practice its existence was a bit more shadowy. "[841] One gets a glimpse of its pitiable state even at this date in the life of Brian and his so-called united Irish army. The kingship of Cashel had been wrested from its traditional guardians, the Eoganacht, by the Dail Cais of Clare/Limerick region. The Dal Cais king, Brian Mac Cennetig, forced Leinster for a while to recognize the suzerainty of Munster by 984 thus making Brian temporarily supreme only in the South of Ireland but subject to no High King of Ireland.

The alleged High King was Maelsechnaill Mac Domnaill of the S Ui Neill, but his High Kingship did not extend over Southern Ireland where Brian ruled. In 999 Brian encamped at the gates of the Viking city of Dublin. The Viking chief Sigtrygg surrendered to him. "To cement their alliance Sigtrygg gave his mother to Brian in marriage, and he took as wife Brian's daughter from a previous union. With the Norse of Dublin behind him, Brian turned on Maelsechnaill and forced him to cede the title. In 1005 on a 'royal circuit of Ireland' Brian paid an official visit to Armagh and bolstered its claims to ecclesiastical primacy by offering twenty ounces of gold, placed on the high alter. In return, in the Book of Armagh, his title was ritualistically recorded - *imperatoris scotorum'*, Emperor of the Irish."[842] Armagh had its day of recognition from the South, while the Ui Neill did not. Brian's recognition of Armagh's alleged metropolitan status and the single full-page entry in the Book of Armagh did more for Armagh and the High Kingship of Ireland than any single act in history. Roy noted that Brian Boru "was not ruler of the entire country (nor was Maelsechnaill); he made no impact at all on the N Ui Neill and made no attempt to consolidate his power"[843] over Leinster when it renounced allegiance to him, nor over Connacht which never submitted to him. Even Sigtrygg, the Norse king of Dublin, was titled High King of Ireland in Icelandic Records despite having no influence outside Dublin. Roy pointed out the error of nationalistic historians who were "convinced Ireland was benevolently united" behind Brian Boru as High King of a united Ireland whom they believe led a united Irish army to defeat the Norsemen at Clontarf in 1014. Look closer!

Facts speak for themselves: "The opposing armies give some indication of the purely regional and private aspects of the fight. On Brian's side were levies from his Dal Cais and their allies, and Norwegians under Olaf Ospak, brother of Brodar (who assassinated Brian), King of the Isle of Man. Not included in Brian's army were the N Ui Neill or the men of Connacht who totally ignored the struggle. Opposing Brian were the Leinster King Maelmorda's contingent, the Norse Sigurd the Stout from the Orkneys and Brodar from the Isle of Man. Maelsechnaill, former High King, jockeyed back and forth with his army on the edge of the battlefield but never committed his forces; and on the other end of the field, viewing the fight from Dublin city walls, sat Sigtrygg with many of his Vikings. Maelsechnaill and Sigtrygg saw the battle for what it was, a fight for private prestige and profit, a feud"[844] (local event), and were sufficiently uncommitted as not to get involved. So much for Clontarf and Brian's High Kingship!

The situation after Brian death became explosive. *"Wars were prolonged and widespread because men had larger ambitions which broke the bonds of tribal and dynastic hierarchy; It was during the interregnum between 1022 and 1072 that the men of learning developed the*

---

[841] James Charles Roy, 'The Road Wet, The Wind Close - Celtic Ireland', p. 186-188.

[842] Ibid, p.188.

[843] Ibid, p. 188-189.

[844] James Charles Roy, 'The Road Wet, The Wind Close - Celtic Ireland', p. 189-191.

doctrine of an highkingship of Ireland centered at Tara and held from the coming of Christianity until the usurpation of Brian Boru by the descendants of Niall (of the Nine Hostages). The antiquarian fiction served as a spur to novel ambitions. It was in pursuit of this chimerical high-kingship that the provincial kings, Ua Briain (O Brians), Ua Conchobair (O Connors), Mac Lochlainn and Mac Murchada, marched and counter-marched until Ireland became a trembling sod. Some pedants explained laboriously that if the claimant were from Leth Cuinn (Northern Half) and held all Leth Cuinn together with one province of Leth Moga (Southern Half), he was entitled to be called king of Tara and of Ireland 'with opposition'. Yet the effective rule of earlier (so-called) high-kings had hardly been wider, and it was only in comparison with a pseudo-historical theory of their predecessor's powers that men like Muirchertach Ua Briain or Toirrdelbach Ua Conchobair (or Brian Boru) were (high-)'kings with opposition'. At no stage in Irish history did the high-kingship imply monarchy. Neither Brian Boru nor any other king exercised governmental authority over the whole island. Notions of national monarchy were foreign to them. Nothing short of a radical revolution could establish a national monarchy.[845]

FINAL JUDGEMENT ON ARMAGH AND ITS CLAIMS

Roy concluded *"The legends of (Brian's) kingship which developed the novel idea of a united country drove warlords into deadly campaigns for far-reaching authority. The phenomenon of High Kings 'with opposition' came into being. The Church played a prominent and conspiratorial role. (Monastic) Paruchiae took sides. The times became increasingly violent. Armagh emerged as the most flagrant example."* As to its ecclesiastical primacy' in the Irish Church, patronized by Brian, one might ask what it really amounted to. "Beginning in 966 and running through 8 individuals until 1105, 'bishops' of Armagh church were without exception married laymen with issue who passed on their positions in regular tribal fashion."[846] One holy monk remarking on this state of affairs sadly lamented: "Wickedness in the crook of the pastoral staff. Kings who barter the Church of God will be dumbfounded on the day of judgement." St. Bernard of Clairvaux, great friend of St. Malachy in his heroic efforts to reform the decadent Irish Church of the time, was still more emphatic: These 'bishops' of Armagh are "a damned race, an evil and adulterous generation."[847] So much for the 'ecclesiastical primacy'/metropolitan status' of Armagh and the alleged High Kingship of a so-called united Ireland associated with it!

EPILOGUE

The period from the mid 8th century on saw the consolidation of the major provincial dynasties in new provincial capitals. Monasteries became wealthy and secularized. This period saw the monastic compilation of the first great Annals, genealogies, and secular and ecclesiastical law codes, imbued with their own brand of pseudo-history. Kings patronized monasteries and became protagonists of the great monastic literary compositions which were not heroic saga but political propaganda and historical fiction. Kings and Abbots became media moguls. Political power was wielded as much by the pen as by the sword.

From this time Ui Neill kings and, later, other major dynasts fought war after war in an effort to make the concept of the High-Kingship of Ireland a reality. By the 11th century it finally become a fact, but always qualified by the quantitative term "with opposition." Ireland quaked under the feet of marching armies in quest of a prize to be won only by the sword. John Ryan remarked: "what the contestants fought so passionately to possess was a single prize, the title 'King of Ireland'." The issue in dispute was who possessed this title, whether a Mac Lochlainn prince descended from the Ui Neill, an O Connor prince

---

[845] Francis John Byrne, 'Irish Kings and High Kings', p. 269-274.
[846] Op. cit., p. 194.
[847] "generatio mala et adultera" in Vita Malachiae; cf. Francis John Byrne, 'Irish Kings and High-Kings', p. 125.

descended from the Ui Briuin of Connacht, or an O Brien prince from Munster, became chief ruler of the country. Their armies trampled Ireland bare in an increasingly gory quest for the title *'Rí Temhro'*. The titles 'Rí Temhro' and 'Rí Erainn' came to mean something vastly different in medieval times from what they had meant in Iron Age Ireland. Early legendary history claimed the Cruthin, whose overkings of Scotland and Ireland ruled from Tara of Meath, had their own pre-Celtic name for Tara, which was not *Temhair na Rí,* and Croghan of Roscommon, which was not *Rath Cruacha. Releg na Rí lamh le Cruacha* belonged exclusively to the Celtic Fir Belg, not to the pre-Celtic Cruthintuatha Croghain. The Iron Age *'Rí Erann'* and *'Rí Temhro'* were Celtic terms reserved for the institutions of overking of the Fir Belg or Erainn peoples who ruled from the Turoe/Knocknadala (*Cnoc Temhro/Cnoc na Dala)* oppidum of Galway in W Ireland. From the 8th century these titles were transferred to Tara of Meath and came to mean High King of Ireland. By the 11th century this had become an All-Ireland institution glorious enough to fight for. The title was old, a repository of archaic Celtic values and traditions. The site was new, embodying the corpus of Irish pseudo-history. Title, not site, mattered.

The core of the Tara/Patrick Myth was the fiction that Ireland was a united nation ruled over by High-Kings at Tara from time immemorial. This spawned a dangerous nationalism baying for blood until its demands are met. The Irish have been raised on this delirious brew. Many shed their blood and that of others to ensure the continuation of the chimera of an Ireland which must forever remain united "as it was in the beginning and ever shall be." This is the core of Ireland's perennial problem. She reaps the whirlwind seeded from the early middle ages. It continues to wreak havoc despite all efforts to bring peace. When one fails politicians try another in the belief that finally the right solution has been found to solve Ireland's 'burden of history'. Such 'peace' cannot last while falsehood reigns.

In the early 1990's Frank Byrne asked the pertinent question, "Are we so blinded by the myths and the half-myths that we can no longer recognize evil" and consequently reap the "'harvest of hate'...We must topple the old statues (and myths) that have lorded over us for too long...We must jettison the useless baggage of a nightmare journey that has led us into the dark tunnel of prejudice, bigitory and murder...Until that day dawns we will remain a petty (pitiful) people blinded by the dust of history and forever clutching at straws"[848]

These pages have underlined the fact that from time immemorial Ireland was a divided land. So too was England. Even in the 11th and 12th centuries when a number of kings were recognized as High Kings of Ireland, this was a title gained by force of arms and always qualified 'with opposition'. Not one of these ever ruled from Tara or resided there. The only time Ireland was 'united', if one dare say so, was under the pre-Celtic Cruthin in the millennia BC or under British rule. That may not say much for unity. The aboriginal Cruthin who gave the original name to the Britanic (Pritanic/Cruthin) Islands of Ireland and England, and were driven into the Northern parts of both islands by the Belgic invasion, always considered themselves as a separate people, a separate nation. In the North of Britain they withstood the Roman invasion. The Romans nicknamed them Picts (Picti) because of their tattooed bodies. They eventually merged with Irish Belgic invaders, forced into exile by the ongoing expansion of the Fir Belg from Connacht, to form the Scottish nation. Under British rule and even in their camouflaged status their ancient identity has been respected and treasured. Ireland should learn a lesson from history and the Book and "do likewise".

Numerous segments of the Cruthin peoples, kinsmen of the Picts of Scotland, were isolated by the expanding Fir Belg and merged with the latter to form the Irish people. They were kinsmen of the aboriginal Ulaid, the Cruthin of Ulster, whose lands were largely, but never

---

[848] Frank Byrne, 'Sunday Independent', July/August, 1991.

wholly, over-run by the Belgae, particularly by the Ui Neill and Airghialla. Even where their lands were conquered, both in Northern and Southern Ireland, large numbers of Cruthin remained. Those isolated intact had their own kings to rule over them well into medieval times. Late Bronze Age and early Iron Age burial and many other archaeological sites in Ireland belong to this ancient people. God alone knows how much Cruthin blood runs through the veins of the vast majority of Irish people both at home and throughout the world. It is rudimentary and of fundamental importance that the Irish respect and treasure whatever remnant and memory of these ancient ancestors has survived, particularly in Ulster, rather than attempt to crush or expel them. From the dawn of history the Cruthin endeavoured with utmost might to remain a separate nation. Their kings, and theirs alone, reigned from Tara of Meath and Rathcroghan of Roscommon until well into historic times. Iron Age Fir Belg Overkings and kings of Connacht who spearheaded the expansion northwards at the expense of the Cruthin reigned from Cnoc Temhro/Cnoc na Dala/Rath Cruacha of Athenry in central Galway. Silence pseudo-history, as it silenced history, once and for all! Let history tell the truth! Ireland, be true to yourself!

Ireland is so wrapped with multi-layers of pseudo-history that not even the most powerful politician on earth can solve her bloody perennial problems without first unbinding layers of falsehood. The fact that "false images of Ireland's past were undermining its present and mortgaging its future",[849] must be taken seriously. "An acute awareness of the nature of historical discourse"[850] made historiography itself an integral part of the study of Irish history. Truth should also be a part. Ireland needs a master of history, a glorious visionary, a slayer of the serpent of pseudo-history, a healer of preconceived ideas and wounds of the past, a bearer of the burdens of history and pseudo-history, a man of boundless patience, infinite optimism, a true peace-maker. The one person qualified was crucified 2000 years ago. This is not a cry of despair but an expression of the greatest, if not the only, hope for the future.

The historic perspective presented here is diametrically opposed to that put forward by pseudo-history. It is devoid of the dangerous nationalism inherent in the latter. This history should be in the hands of Irish people, young and old, North and South, of whatever persuasion; it should be essential reading for student and specialist alike in order to counteract all the untold harm and misunderstanding created by pseudo-history. Peace efforts without this historic insight will never succeed since these are approached with diametrically opposed expectations regarding the final outcome based on pseudo-historic misconceptions. Irish society, warped by naked bigoted sectarian hatred, has reaped the opprobrium of civilized society worldwide. Unless knowledge of the genuine pristine history of all Irish peoples, Celtic and Pre-Celtic alike, becomes wide-spread, as opposed to an enslaving pseudo-history which has brought only blood, death and destruction in its wake, Ireland will never experience true peace. That is, until the slippery slimy serpent of pseudo-history has done its wicked worst, until all Ireland can no longer endure the hurt, until Peace comes riding back on the clouds above. Until then, dare anyone say "Ireland is free."

O Ireland, if only....

"*Veritas liberabit*,"
"The truth will set us free!"

> **"Who has determined the course of history? I, the Lord, was there at the beginning and I will be there at the end."** (Isaiah 41:4)

---

[849] Ciaran Brady, 'Interpreting Irish History', *'The Irish Review'*, 4, (1988) p. 3.
[850] Ciaran Brady, 'Ibid, p. 24.

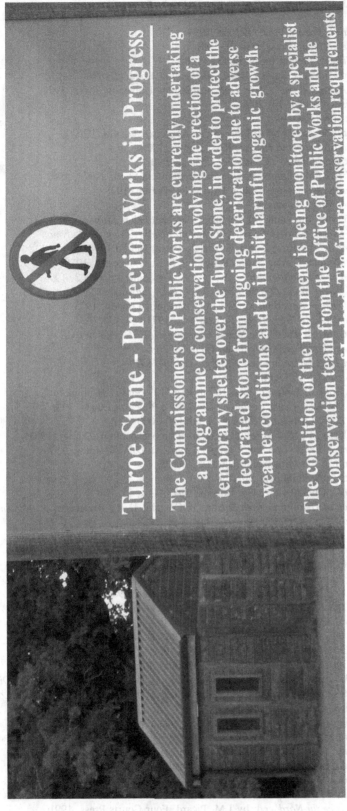

Turoe Stone - Protection Works in Progress

The Commissioners of Public Works are currently undertaking a programme of conservation involving the erection of a temporary shelter over the Turoe Stone, in order to protect the decorated stone from ongoing deterioration due to adverse weather conditions and to inhibit harmful organic growth.

The condition of the monument is being monitored by a specialist conservation team from the Office of Public Works and the

The-powers-that-be have boxed up the Turoe Stone (hut at left) under lock and key under the guise of protecting it (from the prying eyes of bus loads of tourists from all over the world who come to see this wonder of the ages) as they prepare to rob Turoe of its illustrious masterpiece and turn it into a high profile museum-piece to pique the pomposity of some university city bosses, hammering home the final nail in the coffin of Turoe's and Ireland's Iron Age history.

Select Bibliography

Adamson, Ian, *'The Cruthin'*, Pretani Press, Belfast, 1974.
    'The Ulster People', Pretani Press, Belfast, 1991.
    'The Identity of Ulster', Pretani Press, Belfast, 1982.
Allen,D, 'Celtic Coins', in Ordnance Survey, 1962; *'Britannia'*, London, 1976.
Andrews, Ian, *'Boudicea Against Rome'*, New York, Cambridge University Press, 1972.
Bagehot, in *'The Economist'*, October 14th 2000.
Best, R.I., editor of *'Cath Airtig'*, Dublin.
Best and Bergin, *Introduction to Lebor na hUidhre*, R. Ir Academy, Dublin, 1929.
    'Senchas na Relec' in *Lebor na Huidre*, RIA, Dublin, 1929
Berresford-Ellis, P. *'The Celtic Empire'*, Constable, London 1990.
Binchy, D.A. *'Patrick and His Biographers-Ancient and Modern"* in Studia Hiber, 1962
    'Corpus Iuris Hibernici', complete Brehon Law MS's, Dublin, 1978.
Bolandists, the, *'Acta Sanctorum'*, Tomus iv.
Book of Hi Fiachrach, refers to 'drowning' of Connacht's archaic *Lebor Balb*.
Book of Leinster, Book of Lecan, folio 169 in RIA, *Lebor na hUidhr, Book Of Ballymote* .
Brady, Ciaran, *'Interpreting Irish History'*, Irish Academic Press, Dublin 1994.
Branigan, Keith, *'The Catuvellauni'*, Alan Sutton Publishing Ltd., Gloucester, 1978.
Breathnach, Edel, *'Tara: A select bibliography'*, Discovery Programme Reports 3, 1995.
Breatnach, *'The Eccles. Element in the O-Irish Legal Tract, Cain Fuirthirbe'* in 'Peritia 5.
Byrne, Francis John, *'Irish Kings And High Kings'*, B.T. Batsford, London, 1973
    'Tribes and Tribalism in Early Ireland', Ériu xxii, 1971.
Caesar, Julius, *'De Bello Gallico'*, The Gallic Wars, *Commentaries*, 1st century BC.
Carette, Erneste, *'Les Assemblees Provinciale de La Gaule'*, Paris.
Carney, James, *'Studies in Irish Literature and History'*, Dublin, 1979.
    'The Problem of St. Patrick', Dublin.
'Cath Magh Mucrime', in Book of Leinster, folio 169 in RIA, 12th century, Dublin.
Chadwick, Nora & Dillon, Myles, *'Celtic Realms'*; *'The Celts'*, Phoenix, London, 1967
Charles-Edwards, T.M., *'Early Christian Ireland'*, Cambridge, 2000.
Charles-Edwards, T, and Kelly, F, *'Bech-Bretha'* (Law tract on beekeeping), Dublin, 1983.
Clifford, E.M., *'Bagendon, A Belgic Oppidum'*, London, 1961, in D.W. Harding, 1974.
Cohn, Normal, 'The Pursuit of the Millennium', London. 2003.
Confer, 'Zeitschrift fur Celtische Philologie', Berlin
Cunliffe, Barry, *'The Regni'*, Duckworth & Co. London, 1973.
Davies, Wendy, *'The Place of Healing in Irish Society'*, ÓCorráin, D, L. Breatnach, K. McCone in *'Celtic Studies, 'Sages, Saints and Storytellers'*, An Sagart, Maynooth, 1989.
Delehaye, 'Cinq Lecons', Paris, p275; Carey, in *'Eriu'* Dublin, 1999
De Paor, Liam, *'Aggrandisement of Armagh'*, Dublin
    'St. Patrick's World; the Christian culture of Ireland's apostolic age', Dublin, 1993.
    'Ireland and early Europe', Dublin, 1997.
Desticas, A, *'The Cantiaci'*, Alan Sutton Publishing Ltd., Gloucester, 1983.
De Vismas Kane, W.F., *'The Black Pigs Dyke: The Ancient Boundary Fortifications of Ulster'*,
in 'Proceedings of the Royal Irish Academy', Vol xxv and xxvi.
    'Additional Researches on the Black Pigs Dyke', RIA Proceedings, Op. 549. Dublin.
Dillon, Myles, *'Cycle of Crimthann'* in *'Cycles of the Kings'*, Four Courts Press, 1994.
Dindshenchas Material (History of the Famous Places), Metrical, Rennes.
Dindshenchas Ath Cliath Medrige, history of the Iron Age Seaport at Clarenbridge in Galway. *Dindshenchas Carn Conaill*, history notes of the Fir Belg Mac Morna tribes of Galway. *Dindshenchas Locha Riach*, history notes of the Loughrea area in Co. Galway.
Dindshenchas Medrige, Maree in Galway, occupied by descendants of Lughaid Mac Con.
Dindshenchas Mhaen Muighe, 'densely populated' Galway plain n. after Queen Medb's son, Maine.
Dindshenchas Cnoc na Dala, the core of the Turoe/Knocknadala oppidum in Galway.
Dindshenchas Sliab nEchtga, ed Whitley Stokes, Dublin. Relating to the Aughta Mt. area.
Dio Cassius, 1st century Roman Author, *'Letters'*, Rome.
Dobbs, M, *'The Táin'*, Dublin, 1930
Doherty, C, *'Irlande et France du Nord'*, ed. by J.M. Picard, Four Courts Press, 1991.
Driscoll/Nieke *'Power & politics in early medieval Britain and Ireland'*, Edinburgh, 1988.

Dumville, David (ed), '*St. Patrick, AD 493-1993*, Woodbridge, 1993.

Edel, D.R, '*Cultural identity/integ: Ireland & Europe - early middle ages*', Dublin, 1995.

Edwards, Nancy, '*The Archaeology of early medieval Ireland*', London 1990.

Edwards, Ruth Dudley, '*An Atlas of Irish History*', Methuen, 1973.

Evans, Estyn, '*The Personality of Ireland*'', Blackstaff Press, Belfast, 1981; Liliput, 1992.

Fanning, Ronan, '*The Meaning of Revisionism*', 'Irish Review', Dublin, 1998.

'*Felire Oengusa*', (Martyrology of Aengus), p282.

Ferguson, Samuel, '*The Battle of Moira*', ed. Ian Adamson, Pretani Press, Belfast, 1980.

Filip, Jan, '*Celtic Civilization and Its Heritage*', Acadamia, Prague, 1987.

Finnerty, Martin, '*Punan Arsa*' , The Connacht Tribune Press, in National Library, Dublin.

Foster, Roy, '*History and the Irish Question*', in '*Interpreting Irish History*', Irish Academic Press, ed. by Ciaran Brady, Dublin, 1994.

Frontinus, '*Stratagems*', in '*The Iron Age in Lowland Britain*' by D.W. Harding, 1974

Gray, John, '*Politics of the Apocalypse*', in *The Tablet*, London, 17th Jan. 2004.

Guiraud, M, '*Les Assemblees Provinciales*', iii, Paris.

Hall, Michael, 'Ulster, The Hidden History', Pretani Press, Belfast, 1986.

Hamlin, Anne, '*Historic Monuments of North. Ireland*', D.O.E. N. Ireland, Belfast, 1983.

Handford, S.A., '*Caesar and the Conquest of Gaul*', London, 1984.

Hanna, W. A., '*Celtic Migrations*', Pretani Press, Belfast, 1985.

Harding, D.W, '*The Iron Age in Lowland Britain*', Roulledge & Kagan Paul, London, 1974

Hawkes, C.F.C '*New Thoughts on the Belgae*', '*Antiquity*', 1968, in D.W. Harding ,1974.

Hawkes, CFC & Dunning, GC, '*The Belgae of Gaul and Britain*', Arch. Journal, 1930.

Hawkes, CFC & Hull, MR, '*Camulodunum*', Research Com. Soc. of Antiq, London, 1947

Hay, Denys, 'Annalists And Historians', Methuen & Co. Ltd. London, 1977.

Healy, Most Rev. Dr. John, '*The Life & Writings of St. Patrick*', Gill & Son, Dublin, 1905

Herrity, Michael, '*RATHCROGHAN and CARNFREE*', Colour Books, Dublin, 1991.

Hitchens, Peter, '*Abolition of Britain*', London, 2000.

Hirtius, the continuator of Caesar's '*De Bello Gallico*', 1st century.

Hogan, Edmund, SJ.,'*Onomasticon Gaedelicum*', Four Courts Press, Dublin, 1912,

'*Preface to Cath Ruis na Rí for Boinn*', Dublin, and '*Life of St. Grellan*', Brussels.

Hoskins, W.G., '*The Making of the English Landscape*', Constabl, London.

Hubert, Henry, '*The Rise of the Celts*', Constable, London, 1980.

'*The Greatness and Decline of the Celts*', Constable, London, 1987.

Hughes, Katleen, '*The Church in Early Irish Society*', London 1966.

'*Early Christian Ireland: Introduction to the Sources*', p261.

Hull, Vernam, 'Exile of Conall Corc', in PMLA,lvi, 1941.

Irish Manuscript at Stonyhurst College, England, 1700 AD.

Jackson, Kenneth, '*The Oldest Irish Tradition – A Window on the Iron Age*', London.

'*A Celtic Miscellany*', London 1951.

James, Simon, 'Exploring the World of the Celts', Thames and Hudson, London, 1993. Joynt, Maud, '*Echtra Mac Echdach Mugmedoin*' ÉRIU, Vol. IV p. 91-111 Dublin 1908-10

Keating,Geoffrey, '*History of Ireland*', Trinity College Press, Dublin, 1596.

Kelly, Eamon and Condit, Tom, '*Limerick's Tara*', in '*Archaeology Ireland*' Summer 1998

Kelly, Patricia, '*The Táin as Literature*' in '*Aspects of the Táin*', ed. P.J. Mallory,

Kinsella, Thomas, 'The *Táin*', The Dolmen Press, Dublin, 1969.

Knox, H.T., '*The Turoe Stone and the Rath of Feerwore, Co. Galway*' in GAHS.

Larkin, William, '*Map of Co. Galway*', published by Phoenix Maps, 1889.

'*Lebor Gabala Erenn*', ed. in 5 vols for Irish Texts Soc. by Macalister, London 1938-56.

Lett, Canon H.W, '*Researches on Black Pig's Dyke*', Ulster Journal of Arch, Vol 3, 1897.

'*The Great Wall of Ulidia*', Ulster Journal of Arch, Vol 3, No. 1, 1986; Vol 3. No 2, 1987.

Livi, Roman poet, quoted in S.A. Handford's '*Caesar and the Conquest of Gaul*'.

Lloyd, J.H., '*Formaoil na bhFiann*', in MRIA publication and the Journal of GAHS.

Lucas, A.T., '*Cattle in Ancient Ireland*', Boethius Press, Kilkenny, 1989.

Lyons, F.S.L, '*The Burden of Our History*' in '*Interpreting Irish History*', Dublin, 1994.

Mac Airt, Seán, (ed), '*The Annals of Ulster*', Dublin, 1983.

MacCana, Proinsias, '*Celtic Mythology*', Hamlyn, 1970.

Mackie, Mary, '*People of the Horse*', (the Iceni, Echni), Reuters, 2004.

Mac Carthaigh, Padraig, '*Naomh agus Laoch na Feoire* – A short History of Ossory, 1950.

Mac Cuillennain, King of Munster, in *'Sanas Cormaic'*, 900 AD.

MacCulloch, J.A., *'The Religion of the Ancient Celts'*, Constable, London, 1911.

Mac Fir Bhisigh, *'Lebor Buidhe Lecan'* and *'Book of Genealogies'*, Dublin,1650, in *Genealogical Tracts*, Dublin 1932

Mac Giolla Easpaig, Domnall, *'Early Ecclesiastical Settlement Names in Co. Derry'*, *'Early Ecclesiastical Settlement Names in Co. Galway.'*

Mac Neill, Eoin, *University Lecture*, Dublin, 1904. also *'Celtic Ireland'*, Dublin, 1921.
    'St. Patrick', Dublin; *'Phases of Irish History'*, Dublin, 1919,
    'Saorstat Eireann Official Handbook' Irish Free State Handbook, Talbot Press, 1932.
    'Three Poems in Middle Irish', in Proceedings of the Roy. Ir. Acad. 1894
    'Colonization under Early Kings of Tara', in Journal of GAHS xvi.

Mac Niocaill, Gearóid, *'Ireland Before The Vikings'*, Gill History of Ireland, Dublin, 1972.

Mallary, J.P., *'Aspects of the Táin'*, Notes on Patricia Kelly's *The Táin in Literature'*.

Mc Caffrey, Carmel, and Eaton, Leo, *'Ancient Ireland'*, Dublin, 2000.

McCone, K, *'Pagan Past & Christian Present in Early Irish Liter.'* Leinster Leader, 1990.

Metrical Dindshenchas, (History of the Famous Places), Prose Version.

Meyer, Kuno, *'Expulsion of the Deisi'* in *Y Cymmrodor*, xiv (1901) and *Ériu* iii, 1907,
    'Voyage of Bran', Vol 1, also in Ériu, iv. 1907.

Mohrmann, Christine, *'The Latin of St. Patrick'*, p271

Moody, T.W. *'Irish History and Irish Mythology'* in in *'Interpreting Irish History'*, 1994.

Moody, T.W., and Martin, F.X., *'The Course of Irish History'*, Cork, 1967.

Mongan, Norman, *'Menapia Quest'*, The Herodotus Press, Dublin, 1995

Muir, Richard, *'Reading the Celtic Landscape'*.

Muirchu Maccu Mochteine, *'Vata Patricii'*, Armagh, late 7th century.

Muller, *'Claudii Ptolemaei Geographia'*, Paris, 1883.

Newman, Conor, *Tara's 2500 BC Golden Age* in The Irish Examiner, Nov. 12, 2002.
    'Tara: an archaeological survey', Discovery Programme Monograph 2, Dublin 1997.

O Broin, in *'Celtica'* xxi, Dublin, 1990. Carey, in *'Eriu'* Dublin, 1999

O Cathasaigh, Tomas, *'Deisi and Deyfed'*, in Eigse xx. & *'The Heroic Biography of Cormac Mac Airt'*, The Dublin Institute for Advanced Studies, Dublin, 1977.

O Connell, Philip, *'Territory of the Luigni'*, Paper on Castle Kieran, Lis na gCon, Kells.

O Corráin, Donnchadh, Liam Breatnach and Kim McCone, editors of Celtic Studies *'Sages, Saints and Storytellers'*, An Sagart, Maynooth, 1989.

O Corráin, Donnchadh, *'Ireland Before The Normans'*, Gill History of Ireland, 1972, &
    'Prehistoric & Early Christian Ireland' in *'The Oxford History of Ireland*, Oxford, 1989.
    'Nationality and the Pursuit of National Independence', in *Historical Studies*, 11. Dublin.

O Corry, Eugene, *Manuscript Materials*, P 391. p.161, Dublin.

O Crónín, Dáibhi, *'New Light on Palladius'* in 'Peritia' 5, (1986) p.276-283.
    'Early Medieval Ireland', Longman Publishing, New York, 1995.
    Editor of *'A new history of Ireland, Prehistoric and early Irelad'*

O Cuiv, Brian, in *Eigse* II, Dublin, 1960.

O Daly, Máirín, ed. *'Cath Maige Mucrama'*, Irish Texts Society, Dublin, 1975.

O Donovan, Jh, *'Tribes and Customs of Hy Many'* & editor of the *'Book of Rights'*, Dublin.

O Fiach, Cardinal Thomas, *'The Church of Armagh under Law Control'*. P304.

O Grady, Standish. H., 'Silva Gadelica', London, 1892.

O Hanlon, O Leary, Lawlor, *'History of Queens County'*, Vol 1, Dublin.

O Looney, *'Táin Bó Cuailgne'* translastion in Journal of The Royal Irish Academy, Dublin.

O Malley, Padraig, *'The Uncivil Wars – Ireland Today'*, Blackstaff Press, Belfast, 1983.

O Neill, Joseph, ed. of *'Cath Boindi Andso'*, p.13

O hÓgáin, Dáithí, *'An Encyclop. of Irish Folk Tradition'*, Ryan Publishing, London, 1990.

O Rahilly, T.F. *'Early Irish History and Mythology'*, Dublin Inst. for Advd. Studies, 1946.

O Rahilly, Thomas Francis, *'The Two Patricks'*, Dublin, 1942.

O'Rahilly, Cecile, *'Táin Bó Cuailgne from the Book of Leinster'*, Dublin, 1967.

O Riordain, S.P. *'Antiquities of the Irish Countryside'*, Methuen & Co., New York, 1979.
    'Tara', Dundalgan Press, Dundalk, 1982.

Patsch, quoted Henry Hubert in *'The Greatness and Decline of the Celts'*, London, 1987.

Patterson, N.T, *'Cattle-lords & clansmen: social structure of early Ireland'*, London, 1991

Peacock, D.P.S.'*Roman Amphorae in pre-Roman Britain*', Jesson and Hill, London, 1971.
Picard, Jean Michel, '*Irlande et France du Nord*', Four Courts Press, Dublin, 1991.
Pope John Paul 11, '*Message for World Day of Peace*', Rome, 2001.
Powell, T.G.E., '*The Celts*', Thames & Hudson, London, 1958.
Prosper of Aquitane, in his '*Contra Collatum*', Rome, 437.
Ptolemy, Claudius, '*Geographica Hepigesis*', Irish Section, 100 AD.
Qualter, Aggie, '*Athenry –History and Folklore Recollections*', Galway, 1989.
Raftery, Barry, '*The La Tène in Ireland; its origins and chronology*', Marburg, 1984.
    '*Pagan Celtic Ireland*', London, 1994.
Rees, A & B, '*Celtic Heritage-Ancient Tradit. of Irel*', Thames & Hudson, London, 1961.
Richter, Michael, '*Ireland and her neighbours in the 7th century*', Dublin, 1999.
Rivet, A.L.F., '*Town and Country in Roman Britain*', Hutchinson, London, 1958.
Ross, Anne, '*Pagan Celtic Britain*', Sphere Books Ltd, London, 1974.
    '*The Everyday Life of the Pagan Celts*', Cardinal, London, 1970.
Roy, J.C, '*Celtic Ireland-The Road Wet, The Wind Close*', Gill & Macmillan, Dublin 1986
Ryan, Michael, (ed), '*The illustrated archaeology of Ireland*', Dublin, 1991.
Saint Patrick, '*Ego Patricius*', The Confessions of St. Patrick.
Salway, Peter, '*Roman Britain*', Oxford University Press, Oxford, 1984.
Sharpe, Richard, '*Adomán of Iona: Life of St. Columba*', London, 1995.
'*Quatuor Santissimi Episcopi: Irish Saints before St. Patrick*', O Corráin, D, L. Breatnach K. McCone (eds)
in Celtic Studies '*Sages, Saints and Storytellers*', Maynooth, 1989.
Simms, Katharine, '*From Kings to Warlords, the changing political structure of Gaelic
    Ireland in the later middle ages*', Woodbridge, 1987.
Sjoestedt, Marie-Louise, 'Gods and Heroes of the Celts', Turtle Island Foundat, CA, 1982
Smyth, Alfred P., '*Celtic Leinster*', Dublin, 1982; and '*Seanchas: studies in early and medieval
archaeology, history and literature in honour of Francis J. Byrne*', Dublin 2000.
Smith, C, '*State of the Co. Kerry*', Dublin, 1756.
Snowcroft, R.M., on the Lebor Gabala, in Ériu, 39.
Stokes, Whitley, in '*Revue Celtique*', 20, 21. Loth, '*L'Omphalos Chez les Celtes*', Paris.
Tacitus, Roman Historian, '*History*', Rome, 1st century AD.
Thurneysen, Rudolf, '*Die irische Helden-und Konigsage*', Halle, 1921.
Tirechan, Bishop, '*Memoir*', and his '*Collectanea*', 7th century.
Todd, '*St Patrick*', p256
Van Hamel, A.G., '*Uber die Vorpatrizianischen Irischen Annalen*', f. Celt. Philologie.
Vergeer, Ferdinand, English translation of Dutch '*Oude Geschiedenis*', 1998.
Virgil, '*Aeneid*' quoted in S.A. Handford's '*Caesar – The Conquest of Gaul*'.
'*Vita Tripartite*', 9th cent. Life of St Patrick ('*Bethu Phatraic*' K. Mulchrone, Dublin, 1939.
Waddell, John, '*The Prehistoric Archaeology of Ireland*', University Press, Galway, 1998.
Wakeman, '*Wakeman's Handbook of Irish Antiquities*', ed. J. Cook, London
Walsh, Paul, SJ, '*Connacht in the Book of Rights*' in JGHA', Vol 14;19, Galway, 1940.
    '*Tethbae and Ui Maine*', in Ériu xiii, Dublin.
    '*Early Kings of Connacht*', in JGAHS, xvii, Galway, 1939.
Walsh, J.R. & Bradley, T, '*A History of the Irish Church*', Columba Press, Dublin, 1991.
Webster, Graham, '*Rome Against Caratacus*',' *Cornovii*,'Alan Sutton, Lond. 1975 & 87
Wells, '*German Policy*', quoted in Peter Salway's '*Roman Britain*', Oxford, 1984.
Westropp, T.J. '*Ancient Forts of Ireland*', London.
    '*Notes on the Táin Bó Flidais*', in RSIA, 1912.
Wheeler & Richardson, '*Hillforts in Northern France*', London, 1957.
White, T.W., '*Celtic Conquest & Conflicting Identities in Ireland*', '*Celtic Cultural Studies*'
Wood, Dr. Juliette, Folklorist & Journalist, on Queen Boudicea, London.

ABBREVIATED REFERENCES FOR SOURCE TEXTS

Ac. = Annals of Clonmacnois, ed. D. Murphy.
Ai. = Annals of Inishfallen, in T.C.D. (Trinity College, Dublin).
Ar. = Life of Aed Ruadh Ua Domnaill.
BB = The Book of Ballymote.
Ca. = Coir Anmann, by Stokes in Irische Texte.
Corp. Gen. Hib = Corpus Genealogiarum Hiberniae, ed. M.A. O'Brien.
EIHM = Early Irish Hiostory and Mtyhology, T.F. O Rahilly
Fir = Mac FirBisigh's Book of Genealogies.
Fy. Tp. = Tribes of Ui Fiachrach, ed. O'Donovan.
GAHS = Journal of Galway Archaeological and Historical Society.
Gen. Tracts = Genealogical Tracts ed T Ó Raithbheartaigh.
H. = H, T.C.D.
Hc. = H.3.18, T.C.D.
Hz. = H.4.13, T.C.D.
IKHI = Irish Kings and High Kings, by Francis John Byrne.
Ir. Texts = Irish Texts, ed. Frazer, Grosjean and O'Keefe.
K. = Keating's History of Ireland.
La. = Laud 610 edited by Meyer.
Lbl. Col. Mac FirBhisigh = Lebor Buidhe Lecan ed. Mac FirBhisigh
Lec = The Book of Lecan.
LL. or Ll = the MS. of the Book of Leinster, in T.C.D
Lg = Leabhar Gabhála Érainn, The Book of Invasions.
Lr na gCeart = The Book of Rights, ed. O'Donovan.
Lu. = Lebor na hUidhre, in The Royal Irish Academy
Md. = Martyrology of Donegal, ed. O'Donovan.
Met. D. = The Metrical Dindshenchas, ed. Edward Gwynn.
Mis. Col = Miscellany of the Irish Archaeological and Celtic Society.
Ml. = Cath Magh Lena.
ML. = The Milan Glosses
MSS = MS materials ed. by O Curry.
Of. = O Flaherty's Ogygia.
Proc. R.I.A = Proceedings of The Royal Irish Academy.
R. or Rawl. B = Rawlinson B.
RC. or Rev. Celt. = Revue Celtique.
RSAI, = Proceedings of the Royal Irish Academy.
Sa. = D.2.2 of Stowe MSS, R.I.A.
Thf. or Three Frags. = Annals of Ireland, 3 Fragments.
Tig. an. = Annals of Tigernach.
ZCP. = Zeitschrift fur Celtische Philologie.

"I am enthralled with 'Hand of History'. I find the book and its website more than fascinating. It has answered many questions I've accumulated over the years in Celtic Studies on Ireland. It speaks volumns on early Irish history – a great gift to Celtic heritage."
(Eadhmonn Ua Cuinn, Spokesman for the Sequani Calendar Celtic Studies Group, Davis and Elkins College, West Virginia, USA)

"This book tells something really important about the Irish landscape, particularly around Athenry, and its relationship to the historical development of Connacht as a province in prehistoric and early medieval times."
(Professor Dáibhí Ó Cróinín, National University of Galway, Ireland).

Are you blest with Irish ancestors and think you know where the Irish originally came from? Well, think again! Are you a prisoner of a fictitious past? Hug the Touchstone of Truth. Let history ruffle your feathers and haunt you. The Ireland you thought you knew will never be the same again. Out-decoding 'Da Vinci Code' decoders, this work explodes pseudo historic myths.

Irish History in the making! On 8th May, 2007, in what was widely seen as a momentous occasion at Stormont, Belfast, Northern Ireland, "the swearing in of the new power-sharing Executive took place without controversy, without rancour and without incident. These events astonished political Correspondents everywhere." Mr. Paisley stated: "I believe that Northern Ireland has come to a time of peace, a time when hatred will no longer rule. How good it will be to be part of a wonderful healing in our province. Today we have begun to plant and we await the harvest."

Britain's King George V when opening Stormont in 1921 stated: "I appeal to all Irishmen to pause, to stretch out the hand of forbearance and conciliation, to forgive and forget and to join in making for the land which they love a new era of peace, contentment and goodwill."

"The first law of history is not to dare to utter falsehood, the second is not to fear to speak truth." (Pope Leo XIII).